ROMAN
CONSTRUCTION
IN ITALY

Memoirs of the

AMERICAN PHILOSOPHICAL SOCIETY

Held at Philadelphia

For Promoting Useful Knowledge

Volume 96

ROMAN CONSTRUCTION IN ITALY FROM NERVA THROUGH THE ANTONINES

MARION ELIZABETH BLAKE
Edited and Completed by
DORIS TAYLOR BISHOP

AMERICAN PHILOSOPHICAL SOCIETY
INDEPENDENCE SQUARE   PHILADELPHIA
1973

Copyright © 1973 by The American Philosophical Society

Library of Congress Catalog
Card Number 72-83463

ISBN 0-87169-096-9

FOREWORD

WHEN MARION ELIZABETH BLAKE died in her seventieth year on the first of September, 1961, she had been hard at work for many years on Roman construction during the empire, as the expected sequel to her first volume *Ancient Roman Construction in Italy from the Prehistoric Period to Augustus*, published by the Carnegie Institution of Washington in 1947. As early as October, 1952, she had already written chapters on the published monuments of the third and fourth centuries and needed only to compare her text with the monuments. Thus the work on the empire proceeded on several fronts at the same time. It soon became apparent that the first century could readily be treated as a separate unit, the second century likewise, especially because of the enormous amount of Trajanic, Hadrianic, and Antonine construction in Rome, Ostia, and the Villa Adriana, and that a fourth volume could contain the third and fourth centuries; otherwise a single all-embracing volume would indeed be very bulky. By the end of 1955 the text for Volume Two was complete. Early in 1957 the Carnegie Institution accepted it; and it was off the press in 1959. No sooner was the last section of page proof sent back to the United States from Rome than Miss Blake returned to the interrupted work on the third volume.

During the year 1959–1960 Doris Taylor (not yet Mrs. Bishop) was a Guggenheim Fellow in Rome. Since she had an automobile, she was able to take Miss Blake to various monuments she wished to examine. In return, Miss Blake imparted as much of her expertise as she could. The association was a happy and fortunate one. Thus when Miss Blake died, the natural choice to complete her manuscript of volume three was Miss Taylor. In the meantime all Miss Blake's papers had been gathered into a storage container, conspicuously marked, and placed in an empty storage room in the American Academy. It was soon decided that the Blake manuscript was substantially complete, that Mrs. Bishop (now no longer Miss Taylor) should put the finishing touches to it, prepare it for publication, and see it through the press.

The text which had been given to Mrs. Bishop at the end of 1962 was obviously not at all complete, not at all what Mrs. Bishop remembered from her Guggenheim year; further, contrary to Miss Blake's usual custom, there was only one copy of it, for she was in the habit of making multiple copies in case one became lost. Thus the task appeared to be quite large and to involve much rewriting and research into source material, for the text in hand was not well supplied with references to Miss Blake's sources. Hence when Mrs. Bishop went to Rome during her sabbatical leave in 1963–1964, her first purpose was to find all the notes and all copies of the text, including large blocks of text referred to in the copy in hand but not included in it. As luck would have it, the room in which that storage container had been placed was now full wall to wall. When it was emptied, there was no sign of the storage container. Three weeks later, if after seven years I remember her letters to me correctly, after emptying a successive series of storage chambers, that box of Blake material was finally found. Here were the multiple copies, the note cards, the bibliographies, the various versions of the text.

Mrs. Bishop's notations for this Preface begin with the phrase "Enormous task of checking references, identifying loose pages of text and footnotes." There was even the problem of creating a filing system for Miss Blake's notecards. Not only were the pages out of order, but frequently it was not easy to tell in which section a page belonged. Often there were several versions; not unusual, for Miss Blake would keep obsolete copies even though she had multiple copies of the current revision on hand. But to complicate matters, at least twice, if I remember correctly, Mrs. Bishop wrote of finding multiple versions which represented separate writings, not just revisions; and thus the task was more than just ascertaining which was the latest revision, for in such cases she had to collate differing texts. Other problems included certain portions of the text where Miss Blake had not yet completed descriptions, pending visits to certain sites. Still other problems were footnotes. Several sections, including two of the larger ones, had extensive lists of footnotes, but no numbers in the text; thus the problem was to find what part of the text the footnote belonged to. Other problems with footnotes included the "open" reference: a number in the text, but a footnote reading "Bull. Com." or "Not. sc." or "Lugli." The first two pose the problems of author, article, volume number, year, and pages; the third, the problem of which book and pages or which article. Problems with the Blake handwriting seem minor, compared to these; but from handwritten parts which I myself handled in accordance with Mrs. Bishop's marginal notes, I can testify that it was not easy to read Miss Blake's non-calligraphic hand on Roman tinted onionskin, especially since she wrote on both sides, used a No. 2 pencil, and the writing from the other side shows through. So much of this work and of the condition of the manuscript—its inconsistent alternation between typed and handwritten versions and the often rather marked disorganization—are so contrary to Miss Blake's habits of work that Mrs. Bishop was readily led to believe that Miss Blake felt she was working against time—as indeed she was— and that she was attempting to put down on paper as much as she could from what she knew and thought before it was too late and that knowledge was lost forever. No doubt her experience with Miss Van Deman's material, noted in the Preface to the first volume, led her to think that a text would be a better vehicle for transmitting to a successor the necessary knowledge than a mere set of notes no matter how complete they might be. Besides, there was the hope that she would live to see the work completed herself.

Mrs. Bishop thus spent her sabbatical year extracting a suitable text from Miss Blake's papers and in verifying references. When in the summer of 1964 I visited Rome for the first time, she had already "read back" the manuscript against the monuments in the vicinity of Rome, thus proving the descriptions on the site.

Since so many of Miss Blake's notes stated that she had not visited the site, Mrs. Bishop set out to visit every one to which she could gain admittance. Some monuments are on private property to which there is no admittance, for example S. Urbano, once the temple of Faustina-Ceres on the villa of Annia Regilla; obviously here one must rely on the published account. In the course of these on-site inspections many minor corrections in Miss Blake's sentences were made, all for the sake of clarity in finding one's way around the monument while reading the description, or to correct errors in the measurement of bricks and mortar, or other things similarly. For example, Mrs. Bishop supplied most of the compass directions in the section *Forum Traiani: Environs West*, and indeed also the description of the two stairways near each end of the hemicycle which lead to the upper levels of the Market. In addition, those monuments which Miss Blake had noted for inclusion but whose descriptions were sketchy or hesitant were more completely described by Mrs. Bishop.

Beyond the job of establishing a text, Mrs. Bishop had the problem of suitable photographs for the plates. Miss Blake left no indication at all concerning what construction she wanted illustrated. Thus the choice of photographs was made by Mrs. Bishop, as also of the plans. Her work with the photographs and plans was nearly complete when she laid aside this part of her task in order to resume classroom duties. Photographs had been assigned to specific plates; they had been marked for cropping; and the proper reduction in size noted.

Then as the school year began in 1968 she entered the hospital for the first of two operations. After the second, she underwent radiation therapy. Since she had planned a reduced teaching schedule in order to finish the manuscript, she was able to carry out her teaching duties as she regained strength. Indeed her last semester was one of her best. Nevertheless it was obvious that she was declining rapidly; and she died at the end of July, 1969. I reported to the authorities interested in the publication of the manuscript that I thought the work far enough along that I could finish the task; the American Philosophical Society and the American Academy in Rome agreed that this was an opportune and proper offer. After a year spent in reorganizing the department because of her death and because of the impact of curricular changes in the College, I took up the manuscript in the spring of 1970 in order to provide a clear copy for the printer.

I therefore read the text from beginning to end, paying attention first to marginal notes in which Mrs. Bishop indicated that either restudy or verification or rewriting seemed necessary. Mostly this consisted of adding new bibliography to the footnotes, such as Crema, Frova, Neuerburg, the new edition of the Forma Urbis Severiana, to those sections she would have finished except for her illness. There were several brick stamps to verify and evaluate. Professor Herbert Bloch with great kindness evaluated a broken stamp which Miss Blake had copied backwards; his clarity on this point removed the confusion which Mrs. Bishop's marginal note showed she felt about the text concerning the nymphaeum of the Domus del Ninfeo (III, 6, 4). A few other stamps which Mrs. Bishop had noted in the margin of the manuscript during her visits to Ostia I was able to handle with the help of Professor Bloch's works; accordingly they lie buried in the footnotes. One brick stamp in an Antonine building (III, 16, 3) was discovered by Mrs. Bishop where there was a doorway from the long hall into the back room of the northern wing. That doorway, however, was blocked up in antiquity. The stamp was readily identified as Bloch *Suppl.* no. 16 and thus too early for an Antonine structure. Mrs. Bishop's note did not say whether the brick was part of the original door jamb, or part of the ancient filling in of the doorway, or a modern placement of an ancient brick as part of conservation procedure. Professor Frank E. Brown, of the American Academy, persuaded Rufus Fears to brave the brambles; he reported that the brick was indeed part of the ancient blocking of the doorway; and thus the stamp was relegated to the footnote. Another problem arose from Miss Blake's statement that III, 1, 5 had an outside stairway to a second story, which was later blocked by the Basilica Cristiana. This stairway does not appear on the plan in *Sc. di O. I.* Rufus Fears reported that indeed the stairs are there; and

I have therefore drawn them in myself on the map of Ostia Antica. The high podium of a collegiate temple (V, 11, 1) contained two chambers. Miss Blake's text stated that a "depressed arch of *sesquipedales* led to an inner chamber." Mrs. Bishop's marginal query: "The smaller ones aren't they *bipedales*?" And once again Rufus Fears obtained the information which Professor Frank E. Brown transmitted to me: "Doris was right again; the arch is *bipedales*;" I corrected the text accordingly. Other corrections which I silently made consisted mostly of adding commas to clarify the flow of certain sentences, or rearranging the parts of the sentence for greater clarity; these things I did only where I myself felt a confusion. Probably the two major additions to the text which I am responsible for are the section on the Domus (Privata) Traiani under S. Prisca, as the note there explains, and the description of the interior of the temple to Faustina-Ceres in the villa of Annia Regilla. Since this building is on private property, neither Miss Blake nor Mrs. Bishop visited it; but instead Dr. Ernest Nash and Professor Frank E. Brown studied Lugli's description of it; and thus they were able to produce a description to replace the garbled version in Miss Blake's text which Mrs. Bishop had not yet corrected. Since I was intrigued by Miss Blake's mention of the inscription on the tomb of Veran(n)ius on the Appian Way, I tried to verify her note that Labacco had seen the inscription and reproduced it in his engraving. Mr. Edward N. MacConomy of the Library of Congress informed me that the Library's copy of Labacco showed no such thing. Since he is a reference librarian and not an art historian or an archaeologist, I felt a bit of uneasiness with this report; and so I wrote to Dott. Maria Marchetti, the Director of the Biblioteca dell' Istituto Nazionale d'Archeologia e Storia dell' Arte in the Piazza Venezia of Rome. Her gracious reply to my enquiry about Labacco and the inscription agrees with Mr. MacConomy's: "Nelle due edizione dell' opera (sc. of Labacco) possedute dalla nostra biblioteca non è contenuta l'incisione reproducente l'iscrizione che Le interessa." The matter is therefore referred to in a note at the appropriate place.

I am sorry to report that *I Supplemento* to Not. sc., vol. 24, 1970 (F. Zevi and I. Pohl, *Ostia: Saggi di*

Scavo) appeared (1972) when this book was in proof and thus too late for inclusion.

Aside from small reworkings of the text, I have written the Introduction, the Summary, compiled the Bibliography, verified and added missing identification numbers in the Ostia plans, and now this Foreword. Mrs. Bishop left some notes for each of these sections; but the writings, aside from the map numberings, are largely my own composition. The two main parts, the Introduction and the Summary, contain nothing from Miss Blake, except as I refer to the text or her notes, and little from Mrs. Bishop, except as I was guided by her outline. Whatever inaccuracies, omissions, infelicities one finds in these sections therefore are automatically superseded by the descriptions in the text itself.

Special thanks are due to Mr. Edmund N. Bacon and the Viking Press, Inc., for permission to reproduce his plan of Hadrian's Villa from his book *Design for Cities*, copyright 1967 by Mr. Bacon. Equally special thanks are due to Professor William L. MacDonald of Smith College and the Yale University Press for permission to reproduce plate 75 from his book *The Architecture of the Roman Empire*, vol. I, copyright 1965 Yale University Press; also to the Metropolitan Museum of Art for permission to reproduce the photograph of Piranesi's etching "Villa called The Sette Bassi near Frascati."

It is impossible for me to know what special debts Miss Blake would have acknowledged; but one who knows the field will know to whom she would have such indebtedness as well as how much is owed her in return. Nor do I know to whom Mrs. Bishop would have felt a similar special indebtedness, aside from those whom I list for myself. I have already named Professor Herbert Bloch; his courtesy and care for my questions I am sure reflect his knowledge of the high regard Mrs. Bishop had for him. Dr. Ernest Nash helped me not only with encouragement, as Professor Bloch did also, but with problems of identification of photographs; and I know that a special rapport arose between Dr. Nash and Mrs. Bishop because of the special and peculiar problems connected with the photographs in the plates; so many of them were taken specifically to illustrate certain important techniques of construction. Professor Frank E. Brown, who induced Mrs. Bishop to become an archaeologist by including her in the Cosa excavations, by persuading her to study the Cosa black glaze ware, and by continually keeping in contact with her in that way by which one fosters the career of a close friend and gifted colleague, is responsible for Mrs. Bishop's editing and completing of this book. To him, as to Dr. Nash, Professor Bloch, and many others, I owe the *will* to complete Mrs. Bishop's work. To Professor Brown and Dr. Nash I owe special thanks for their readiness and direct assistance just because they were in Rome. And to Professor Brown and to the American Philosophical Society, I owe the opportunity to indulge myself in performing this sacred duty: finishing the task Mrs. Bishop wanted so much herself to see to completion.

But most of all, to Doris Taylor Bishop I wish to offer whatever in this I can: to companion, to intellectual mate, to constant and intimate friend, to her who, though herself individualistic, did become one with me, did share my hopes and aspirations, did teach me new ideals, did show me new beauties and heights, did call forth out of me excellences I never dreamed of and the desire to strive for them—to this one woman of all, amidst *pietas* on the one hand but *lacrimae rerum* on the other, grieving that this is the one last great thing I can do for her yet glad that mine is the *summa manus*, I offer this, whatever it is that I have done.

J. David Bishop

Wheaton College
Massachusetts

CONTENTS

LIST OF ILLUSTRATIONS

PLANS

PLATES

ABBREVIATIONS AND BIBLIOGRAPHY

Anyone who has worked with Dr. Ernest Nash's *Pictorial Dictionary of Ancient Rome* is aware of the advantage he gained by rejecting normal bibliographical procedure—alphabetization by author as main entry—and substituting for it alphabetization by the method of reference within each article in his *Dictionary*. A further gain is that everything is filed under one alphabet, whereas Miss Blake used four separate filings in *RC II*. Mrs. Bishop therefore frequently declared her intention to follow Dr. Nash's example. This bibliography therefore consists of two columns: the first line contains the form of reference to a book or article used in the footnotes; the (subscribed) information gives the author and title and other bibliographical description as seemed necessary in each case. Utility, therefore, at the expense of formality. The bibliography is selective and does not include writings which have the normal bibliographical description at the time of citation in the footnotes. Whatever the system, there will always be something to test it. In this case they are the *Atti* of *Congressi* and *Convegni*; I have filed these references under *Cong.* and *Conv.* without regard to *Atti* nor to the numeral, on the basis that the numeral could be filed in two separate ways, *Atti* is not at all part of the abbreviation, but *cong.* and *conv.* are the first important words in the abbreviation.

Acc. It. Rend.
  Accademia d'Italia, Rendiconti della classe di scienze morali, e storiche. ser. 7: supplementi. Rome 1940.

Acc. L. Mem.
  Memorie della classe di scienze morali, e filologiche della Accademia dei Lincei. Rome, ser. 3, 1877–84; ser. 4, 1884–93; ser. 5, 1893–1924; ser. 6, 1925–38; ser. 7, 1940–43; ser. 8, 1948–.

Acc. L. Rend.
  Rendiconti della Accademia dei Lincei. Rome, ser. 4, 1884–91; ser. 5, 1892–1924; ser. 6, 1925–.

Acc. P. Diss.
  Dissertazioni della Pontificia Accademia Romana di Archeologia. Rome, ser. 1, vols. 1–25, 1821–80; ser. 2, vols. 1–15, 1881–1923.

Acc. P. Mem.
  Memorie della Pontificia Accademia Romana di Archeologia. Rome, ser. 3, 1924–.

Acc. P. Rend.
  Rendiconti della Pontificia Accademia di Archeologia. Rome, ser. 3, 1923–.

Acc. P. Sc.
  Atti della Pontificia Accademia della Scienza "Il Nuovi Lincei." Vols. 1–88 of Acta Pontificiae Academiae Scientiarum. Città del Vaticano 1847–.

AJA
  American journal of archaeology (Archaeological Institute of America). Concord, N. H., 1885–.

Anderson-Spiers-Ashby
  Anderson, W. J., R. P. Spiers, and T. Ashby, The architecture of ancient Rome: an account of the historic development. London and New York 1927.

Ann. d. Inst.
  Annali dell'Instituto di Corrispondenza Archeologia. Rome 1829–85.

Antike
  Die Antike: Zeitschrift für Kunst und Kultur des klassischen Altertums. Berlin and Leipzig 1925–.

Arch. Anz.
  Archaeologischer Anzeiger (Archaeologische Gesellschaft, Berlin), supplement to Jahrbuch des Deutschen Archaeologischen Instituts. Berlin 1889–.

Arch. cl.
  Archeologia classica, rivista dell'Istituto di Archeologia della Università di Roma. Rome 1949–.

Arti
  Le arti: rassegna bimenstrale dell'arte antica e moderna, a cura della Direzione Generale delle Arti. Florence, vols. 1–3, 1938/39–1943.

Arti fig.
  Arti figurative: rivista d'arte antica e moderna. Rome 1945–.

Ashby, Aqueducts
  Ashby, T., The aqueducts of ancient Rome. Oxford 1935.

Ashby, Campagna
  Ashby, T., The Roman Campagna in classical times. London and New York 1927.

Aurigemma, La Villa
  Aurigemma, S., La villa Adriana presso Tivoli; English trans.: Villa Adriana (Hadrian's Villa) near Tivoli. 3rd ed., Tivoli 1957.

Aurigemma, Villa Adriana
  Aurigemma, S., Villa Adriana. Rome 1961.

Ausonia
Ausonia: rivista della Società Italiana di Archeologia e Storia dell'Arte. Rome 1907–21.

BAC
Bulletino di archeologia cristiana. Rome 1863–94.

Bagnani, Campagna
Bagnani, G., The Roman Campagna and its treasures. London 1929; New York 1930.

Bastianelli, Centumcellae
Bastianelli, S., Centumcellae (Civitavecchia), Castrum Novum (Torre Chiaruccia). Regio VII, Etruria. Istituto di Studi Romani, [Rome] 1954.

Becatti, Case
Becatti, G., Case Ostiense del tardo impero. Rome 1949.

Beloch, Campanien
Beloch, J., Campanien. Geschichte und Topographie des antiken Neapel und seiner Umgebung. Breslau 1890.

Bernhart, Hb. z. Münzkunde
Bernhart, M., Handbuch zur Münzkunde der Römischen Kaiserzeit. Halle 1926.

Besnier, L'Ile Tibérine
Besnier, M., L'île Tibérine dans l'antiquité. Paris 1902.

Birt, Buchrolle
Birt, T., Die Buchrolle in der Kunst. Leipzig 1907.

Blake, RC I
Blake, M. E., Ancient Roman construction in Italy from the prehistoric period to Augustus. Washington 1947.

Blake, RC II
Blake, M. E., Roman construction in Italy from Tiberius through the Flavians. Washington 1959.

Bloch, Bolli
Bloch, H., I bolli laterizi e la storia edilizia romana (reprint of *Bull. Com.*, vol. 64, 1936, pp. 141–225; vol. 65, 1937, pp. 83–187; vol. 66, 1938, pp. 61–221). Comune di Roma, Rome 1947.

Bloch, Suppl.
Bloch, H., Supplement to vol. XV, 1 of the Corpus inscriptionum Latinarum (Harvard studies in classical philology, vols. 56–57 (1947) and 58–59 (1948)). Cambridge, Mass., 1947–48.

BMC, Emp
Coins of the Roman Empire in the British Museum, by Harold Mattingly. London, vol. 3, 1936.

BMIR
Bulletino del Museo dell'Impero Romano, supplement to Bulletino della Commissione Archeologica Comunale. Rome 1930–.

Boll. d'Arte
Bolletino d'arte; notizie delle gallerie dei musei e dei monumenti. Rome, ser. 1, 1907–20; ser. 2, 1921–.

Boll. dell'Assoc. Vel. di Archeol., St., ed Arte
Bolletino dell'Associazione Veliterna di archeologia, storia ed arte. Velletri 1926–34.

Boyd, Public libraries
Boyd, C. E., Public libraries and literary culture in ancient Rome. Chicago 1915.

Brissé and de Rotrou, Lac Fucino
Brissé, A., and L. de Rotrou, Desséchement du Lac Fucino execute par S.E. le Prince Alexandre Torlonia precis historique et technique. Rome 1876 (with English translation).

Brusin, Aquileia e Grado
Aquileia e Grado, guida storico-artistico. 4th ed. Padua 1956.

Brusin, Gli scavi di A.
Brusin, G., Gli scavi di Aquileia, un quadriennio di attività dell'Associazione Nazionale per Aquileia (1929–1932). Udine 1934.

Bryant, Antoninus Pius
Bryant, E., The reign of Antoninus Pius. Cambridge, England, 1895.

Bull. Com.
Bullettino della Commissione Archeologica Comunale di Roma. Rome 1872–.

Bull. Inst.
Bullettino dell'Instituto di Corrispondenza Archeologica. Rome 1829–85.

Calza, Guida
Calza, G., Ostia, 2d ed. Libreria del Stato, Rome 1949.

Calza, Necropoli
Calza, G., La necropoli del porto di Roma nell'Isola Sacra. Libreria del Stato, Rome 1940.

Calza, Nuovi scavi
Ostia (nuovi scavi). Libreria del Stato, Rome 1947.

Canina, Archit. rom.
Canina, L., L'architettura antica, sezione 3, Architettura Romana. Rome 1830–40.

Canina, Via Appia
Canina, L., La prima parte della Via Appia dalla Porta Capena a Boville. . . . 2 vols. Rome 1853.

Capitolium
Capitolium: rassegna mensile di attività del governatorato di Roma. Rome 1925–.

Castagnoli, Appia Antica
Castagnoli, F., Appia antica. Milan 1956.

CIL
Corpus inscriptionum Latinarum. 15 vols. Berlin 1863–.

Cohen
Cohen, H., Description historique des monnaies frappées sous l'Empire romain . . . 2d ed. 8 vols. Paris 1880–92.

Colini and Cozza, Ludus Magnus
Colini, A. M., and L. Cozza, Ludus magnus. Rome 1962.

I cong. st. archit.
Atti del 1° congresso nazionale di storia dell'architettura (Florence 1936). Florence 1938.

VII cong. st. archit.
Atti del 7° congresso nazionale di storia dell'architettura (Palermo 1950). Palermo 1950.

V cong. st. biz.
Atti del 5° congresso internazionale di studi bizanti . . . (Rome 1936). Tip. del Senato, Rome 1939–40.

I cong. st. rom.
Atti del 1° congresso nazionale di studi romani . . . (Rome 1928). Istituto di Studi Romani, Rome 1928.

II cong. st. rom.
Atti del 2° congresso nazionale di studi romani . . . (Rome 1930). Istituto di Studi Romani, Rome 1931.

III cong. st. rom.
Atti del 3° congresso nazionale di studi romani . . . (Rome 1933). Istituto di Studi Romani, Rome 1934–35.

IV cong. st. rom.
Atti del 4° congresso nazionale di studi romani . . . (Rome 1935). Istituto di Studi Romani, Rome 1938.

III conv. st. archit.
Atti del 3° convegno nazionale di storia dell'architettura (Rome, 1938). Rome 1940.

Cozzo, Corporazione
Cozzo, G., "La corporazione dei figuli ed i bolli doliari," (Acc. L. Mem., ser. 6, vol. 5) Rome 1936.

Cozzo, Ingegneria
Cozzo, G., Ingegneria romana. Rome 1928.

Crema
Crema, L., L'architettura romana (Enciclopedia classica 3. 12. 1). Turin 1959.

Cressedi, Velitrae
Cressedi, G., Velitrae (Velletri) Regio I, Latium et Campania. Istituto di Studi Romani, [Rome] 1953.

De Angelis d'Ossat, Le cupole
Angelis d'Ossat, Gu. de, Romanità delle cupole paleocristiane. Istituto di Studi Romani, [Rome] 1946.

De Angelis d'Ossat, Tecnica delle terme
Angelis d'Ossat, Gu. de, Tecnica costruttiva e pianti delle terme. Rome 1943.

Dedalo
Dedalo. Rassegna d'arte. Milan 1920–33.

De Franciscis and Pane, Mausolei
De Franciscis, A., and R. Pane, Mausolei Romani in Campania. Naples 1957.

Degrassi, Fasti cons.
Degrassi, A., I fasti consolari dell' Impero romano dal 30 avanti Cristo al 613 dopo Cristo. Rome 1952.

Degrassi, Fasti O.
Inscriptiones Italiae, vol. 13. Fasti et elogia, Fasti municipales, Fasti ostienses. A. Degrassi, ed. Libreria dello Stato, Rome 1947.

Dessau
Dessau, H., Inscriptiones Latinae selectae. 3 vols. Berlin 1892–1916.

Dioniso
Dioniso; bollettino dell'Istituto Nazionale del Dramma Antico. Syracuse 1937–.

Enc. it.
Enciclopedia italiana di scienze, lettere, ed arti. 36 vols. Milan and Rome 1929–39.

Eph. daco.
Ephemeris dacoromana (Sçoala Română din Roma). Rome 1923–45.

Frank, Ec. survey
Frank, T., An economic survey of ancient Rome. 6 vols. Baltimore 1933–40.

Fasti arch.
Fasti archaeologici: annual bulletin of the International Association for Classical Archaeology. Florence 1946–.

Frova
Frova, A., L'arte di Roma e del mondo Romano (Storia universale dell'arte, 2. 2). Turin 1961.

FUR
Carettoni, G., and A. M. Colini, L. Cozza, G. Gatti, La pianta marmorea di Roma antica; Forma Urbis Romae. 2 vols. Rome 1960.

Gazzola, Ponti
Gazzola, P., Ponti romani, vol. 2. Florence 1963.

Giovannoni, Tecnica
Giovannoni, G., La tecnica della costruzione presso i Romani. Rome 1925.

Gnecchi, Med. Rom.
Gnecchi, F., I medaglioni romani. Milan 1912.

Grossi-Gondi, Tuscolano
Grossi-Gondi, F., Il Tuscolano nell'età classica: escursioni archeologiche. Rome 1908.

Huelsen, Roman Forum
Huelsen, Ch., The Roman forum, trans. by J. B. Carter, 2d ed. Rome 1909.

IG
Inscriptiones Graecae ad res Romanas pertinentes auctoritate et impensis Academiae inscriptionum et literarum humaniorum collectae et editae. Vols. I, III, IV (all publ.). Paris 1906–28.

Jb. d. Inst.
Jahrbuch des Deutschen Archaeologischen Instituts. Berlin 1886–.

Jh. ö. arch. Inst.
Jahreshefte des oesterreichischen Archäologischen Institutes in Wien. Vienna 1898–.

Jordan-Huelsen

Jordan, H., Topographie der Stadt Rom im Altertum. 2 vols. Berlin 1871–85; vol. I, part 3 revised by Ch. Huelsen, Berlin 1907.

JRS

Journal of Roman studies (Society for the Promotion of Roman Studies, London). London 1911–.

Junyent, San Clemente

Junyent, E., Il titolo di San Clemente in Roma (Studi di antichità cristiana, no. 6). Rome 1932.

Kähler, Villa

Kähler, H., Hadrian und seine Villa bei Tivoli. Berlin 1950.

Klio

Klio: Beiträge zur alten Geschichte. Leipzig 1901–. ·

Krautheimer, Basilicae

Krautheimer, R., Corpus basilicarum christianarum Romae. Città del Vaticano. 2 vols. 1937–59.

Lanciani, Acque

Lanciani, R., Topografia di Roma antica. I commentarii di Frontino intorno le acque e gli aquedotti. Silloge epigrafica aquaria. Rome 1880. (Also published in Atti della R. Accademia dei Lincei, ser. 3, 1879–80, Memorie, vol. 4, pp. 215–616.)

Lanciani, Forma Urbis

Lanciani, R., Forma Urbis Romae, consilio et auctoritate Regiae Academiae Lyncaeorum . . . Milan (n.d.)

Lanciani, Pagan and Christian Rome

Lanciani, R., Pagan and Christian Rome. London 1895.

Lanciani, Ruins

Lanciani, R., The ruins and excavations of ancient Rome. Boston and New York 1897.

Lanciani, Wanderings

Lanciani, R., Wanderings in the Roman Campania. Boston and New York 1909.

Lehmann-Hartleben, Traianssäule

Lehmann-Hartleben, K., Die Traianssäule. Berlin and Leipzig 1926.

Libertini, Teatro

Libertini, G., Il teatro antico e la sua evoluzione. Catania 1933.

Lugli, Centro

Lugli, G., Roma antica, il centro monumentale. Rome 1946.

Lugli, Forma It.

Lugli, G., Forma Italiae, Regio I, Latium et Campania. Vol. I, Ager Pomptinus, part 1, Anxur-Tarracina; part 2, Circeii. Rome 1926–28.

Lugli, MAR and Suppl.

Lugli, G., I monumenti antichi di Roma e suburbio. 3 vols. Rome 1930–38; with supplementary volume 1940.

Lugli, Mon. min.

Lugli, G., Monumenti minori del Foro romano. Rome 1947.

Lugli, Tecnica

Lugli, G., La tecnica edilizia romana con particolare riguardo a Roma e Lazio. 2 vols. Rome 1957.

Lugli-Filibeck

Lugli, G., and G. Filibeck, Il porto di Roma imperiale a l'agro portuense. Rome 1935.

MAAR

Memoirs of the American Academy in Rome. New York 1917–.

MacDonald

MacDonald, W. L., The architecture of the Roman empire. Vol. I. New Haven 1965.

Magoffin, Praeneste

Magoffin, R. V. D., A study of the topography and municipal history of Praeneste. Baltimore 1908.

Maiuri, Campi Flegréi

Maiuri, A., I Campi Flegréi dal sepolcro di Virgilio all'antro di Cuma. Libreria dello Stato, Rome (1934).

Mancini, Adriana

Mancini, G., Villa Adriana e villa d'Este. 3rd ed. Rome 1950.

Martinori, Via Cassia

Martinori, E., Le vie maestre d'Italia: Via Cassia (antica e moderna) e sue derivazioni . . . Rome 1930.

Martinori, Via Flaminia

Martinori, E., Le vie maestre d'Italia: Via Flaminia; studio storico-topografico. Rome 1929.

Martinori, Via Nomentana

Martinori, E., Le vie maestre d'Italia: Via Nomentana, Via Patinaria, Via Tiburtina; studio storico-topografico. Rome 1932.

Marucchi, Palestrina

Marucchi, O., Guida archeologia della città di Palestrina. Rome 1932.

Meiggs, Ostia

Meiggs, R., Roman Ostia. Oxford 1960.

Mél.

Mélanges d'archéologie (Ecole Française de Rome). Paris 1881–.

Meomartini, Benevento

Meomartini, A., Benevento. Bergamo 1909.

Merckel, Ingenieurtechnik

Merckel, C., Die Ingenieurtechnik im Altertum. Berlin 1899.

Merlin, L'Aventin

Merlin, A., L'Aventin dans l'antiquité. Paris 1906.

Mesnard, Saint Chrysogone

Mesnard, M., La basilique de Saint Chrysogone à Rome. Paris 1935.

Mommsen, *Chron. min.*
> Chronica minora saec. IV, V, VI, VII, ed. Theodorus Mommsen. Berlin 1892–98.

Mon. ant.
> Monumenti antichi, pubblicati per cura della Accademia Nazionale dei Lincei. Milan 1890–.

Mon. ined.
> Monumenti antichi inediti, pubblicati dell' Instituto di Corrispondenza Archeologica. 12 vols. Rome 1829–85.

Monaco, *Forma It.*
> Monaco, G., Forma Italiae, Regio IX, vol. I, Libarna. Rome 1936.

Moretti, *Ancona*
> Moretti, M., Ancona (Ancona), Regio IV, Picenum. Istituto di Studi Romani, [Rome] 1945.

Mouseion
> Mouseion. Bulletin de l'Office international des Musées. Paris 1927–.

Müfid, *Stockwechbau*
> Müfid, A., Stockwechbau der Griechen und Römern. Berlin 1932.

Muñoz and Colini, *Campidoglio*
> Muñoz, A., and A. M. Colini, Campidoglio. Rome 1930.

N. bull. arch. crist.
> Nuovo bulletino di archaeologia cristiana. Rome 1895–1922.

Nash I, II
> Nash, E., Pictorial dictionary of ancient Rome. 2 vols. 2d ed. New York 1968.

Neppi Modona, *Edifici teatrali*
> Neppi Modona, A., Gli edifici teatrali greci e romani. Florence 1961.

Neuerburg, *Fontane*
> Neuerburg, N., L'architettura delle fontane e dei ninfei nell' Italia antica. Memorie dell'Accademia di Archeologia, Lettere, e Belle Arti di Napoli, vol. 5. Naples 1965.

Nibby, *Dintorni*
> Nibby, A., Analisi storico-topografico-antiquaria della carta de' dintorni di Roma. 3 vols. Rome 1837; 2d ed., 1848–49.

Nibby, *Roma 1838*
> Nibby, A., Roma nell' anno MDCCCXXXVIII, Antica, part 1, 1838, part 2, 1839. Rome 1838–39.

NNM
> Numismatic notes and monographs (American Numismatic Society). New York 1920–.

Nogara, *Mosaici*
> Nogara, B., I mosaici antichi conservati nei palazzi pontifici del Vaticano e del Laterano. Milan 1910.

Not. sc.
> Notizie degli scavi di antichità, pubblicate per cura della Accademia Nazionale dei Lincei. Rome 1876–.

Palladio
> Palladio; rivista di storia dell'architettura. Milan 1937–.

Pan
> Pan. Rassegna di lettere, arte, e musica. Milan 1933–35.

Paribeni, *La Villa*
> Paribeni, R., La villa dell' imperatore Adriano a Tivoli. Milan [1929].

Paribeni, *Optimus Princeps*
> Paribeni, R., Optimus princeps. 2 vols. Messina 1926–27.

Parker, *Prim. fort.*
> Parker, J. H., The archaeology of Rome, part 1: The primitive fortifications of the city of Rome. 2d ed. Oxford and London 1878.

Paschetto, *Ostia*
> Paschetto, L., Ostia, colonia Romana. Extr.: Acc. P. Diss., vol. 10, pt. 2. Rome 1912.

PBSR
> Papers of the British School in Rome. London 1902–.

Pietrangeli, *Mevania*
> Pietrangeli, C., Mevania (Bevagna), Regio VI, Umbria. Istituto di Studi Romani, [Rome] 1953.

Pietrangeli, *Ocriculum*
> Pietrangeli, C., Ocriculum (Otricoli). Istituto di Studi Romani, [Rome] 1943.

Pietrangeli, *Spoletium*
> Pietrangeli, C., Spoletium (Spoleto), Regio VI, Umbria. Istituto di Studi Romani, [Rome] 1939.

Platner-Ashby
> Platner, S. B., and T. Ashby, A topographical dictionary of ancient Rome. London 1929.

Prandi, *Basilica celimontana*
> Prandi, A., Il complesso monumentale della basilica celimontana del SS. Giovanni e Paolo, nuovamente restaurato per la munificenza del cardinale titolare Francesco Spellman, Archivescovo di New York. Città del Vaticano 1953.

Pullen
> Pullen, H. W., Handbook of ancient Roman marbles. London 1894.

RAC
> Rivista di archeologia cristiana (Pontificia Commissione di Archeologia Sacra). Rome 1924–.

Rassegna d'Arte
> Rassegna d'arte antica e moderna. Milan 1901–22.

RE
> Pauly-Wissowa, Realencyclopädie der classischen Altertumswissenschaft. Stuttgart 1894–.

Reynolds, *Vigiles*
> Reynolds, P. K. B., The vigiles of imperial Rome. Oxford 1926.

Rh. M.
> Rheinisches Museum für Philologie . . . Frankfurt am Main 1842–.

RIA

Istituto di Archeologia e Storia dell'Arte . . . ; rivista. Rome 1929–42; n.s., 1952/53–.

Ricci, Via dell'Impero

Ricci, C., dell'Impero. Libreria del Stato, Rome 1933.

Richmond, City wall

Richmond, I. A., The city wall of Imperial Rome, an account of its architectural development from Aurelian to Narses. Oxford 1930.

Ripostelli and Marucchi, Via Appia

Ripostelli, J., and H. Marucchi, La Via Appia, à l'époque romaine et de nos jours; histoire et description. Rome 1908.

Riv. fil. cl.

Rivista di filologia classica. Turin 1872–.

Riv. Roma

Roma: rivista di storia e di vita romana. Rome 1923–44.

Rivoira-Rushforth

Rivoira, G. T., Roman architecture and its principles of construction under the Empire, translated by G. McN. Rushforth. Oxford 1925.

Roccatelli, Brickwork

Roccatelli, C., Brickwork in Italy: a brief review from ancient to modern times. American Face Brick Association, Chicago 1925.

Röm. Mitt.

Mittheilungen des Deutschen Archaeologischen Instituts, Römische Abteilung. Rome 1886–.

Säflund, Le mura

Säflund, G., Le mura di Roma repubblicana. Uppsala 1932.

Sc. d. O.

Scavi di Ostia: I. Topografia generale, a cura di Guido Calza e di G. Becatti, I. Gismondi, G. De Angelis d'Ossat, H. Bloch. Rome 1953. II. I mitrei, a cura di G. Becatti. Rome 1954. IV. Mosaici e pavimenti marmorei, a cura di G. Becatti. Rome 1961.

Schanz-Hosius·

Geschichte der römischen Literatur bis zum Gesetzgebungswerk des Kaisers Justinian, von Martin Schanz. 4th neubearb. Auflage, von Carl Hosius. Munich 1927–35.

Scrinari, Tergeste

Scrinari, V., Tergeste (Trieste), Regio X, Venetia et Histria. Istituto di Studi Romani, [Rome] 1911.

Skrifter

Skrifter utgivna av Svenska Institutet i Rom. Lund 1932–.

Strack, Reichsprägung

Strack, P., Untersuchungen zur römischen Reichsprägung des zweiten Jahrhunderts . . . 3 vols. Stuttgart 1931–37.

Strong, AAR

Strong, E., Art in ancient Rome . . . 2 vols. New York 1928; London 1929.

Strong, Sc. rom.

Strong, E., La scultura romana da Augusto a Costantino; traduzione italiana di Giulio Gianelli dall'opera intieramente rifatta dall'Autrice. 2 vols. Florence 1923–25.

St. Rom.

Studi romani: rivista di archeologia e storia. Rome, vols. 1–3, 1913–22.

Studies DMR

Mylonas, G., and D. Raymond, edd., Studies presented to David M. Robinson. 2 vols. St. Louis 1951–53.

Thylander, Ins. du Port d'Ostie

Thylander, H., Inscriptions du Port d'Ostie (Skrifter, ser. 8, IV, 1 and 2). Lund 1952.

Toebelmann, Gebälke

Toebelmann, F., Römische Gebälke. Erster Teil. Heidelberg 1923.

Tomassetti, Campagna

Tomassetti, G., and F. Tomassetti, La campagna romana antica, medievale e moderna. 4 vols. Rome 1910–26.

Toynbee-Perkins

Toynbee, J. M. C., and J. Ward Perkins, The shrine of St. Peter and the Vatican excavations. London, New York, and Toronto (1956).

Urbe

L'urbe. Rivista romana. Rome 1936–.

Valentini-Zucchetti

Codice topografico della città di Roma, a cura di Roberto Valentini e Giuseppe Zucchetti. 4 vols. Rome 1940–53.

Van Deman, Aqueducts

Van Deman, E. B., The building of the Roman aqueducts. Washington 1934.

Van Deman, Atrium Vestae

Van Deman, E. B., The Atrium Vestae. Washington 1909.

Van Deman, "Methods"

Van Deman, E. B., "The methods of determining the date of ancient Roman concrete construction." AJA, vol. 16, 1912, pp. 230–41, 387–432.

Vatican report

Esplorazioni sotto la confessione di San Pietro in Vaticano eseguite negli anni 1940–49. Relazione a cura di B. M. Apollonij Ghetti, A. Ferrua, . . . , F. Josi, E. Kirschbaum . . . Prefazione di Mons. L. Klaas . . . appendice numismatica di C. Serafini . . . Città del Vaticano 1951.

Vermaseren, CIMRM

Vermaseren, M., Corpus inscriptionum et monumentorum religionis Mithriacae. The Hague, vol. I 1956, II 1960.

Vermaseren and van Essen
    Vermaseren, M., and C. C. van Essen, The excavations
    in the mithraeum of the church of Santa Prisca in
    Rome. Leiden 1965.

Vie d'Italia
    Le vie d'Italia: rivista mensile del Touring Club Italiano.
    Milan 1924–.

Vighi, Villa
    Vighi, R., Villa Hadriana. Rome 1958.

Werner, De incendiis
    Werner, P. C., De incendiis urbis Romae aetate impera-
    torum . . . Leipzig 1906.

Winnefeld
    Winnefeld, H., Die Villa des Hadrian bei Tivoli (Ergän-
    zungsheft III, Jh. d. Inst.). Berlin 1895.

ROMAN CONSTRUCTION IN ITALY
FROM NERVA
THROUGH THE ANTONINES

I. INTRODUCTION

THE broad survey of building materials given by Marion E. Blake in her first volume[1] is the necessary and valuable prelude to her survey of the first century A.D.[2] The present introduction to her third volume, covering approximately the second century A.D., must, considering the circumstances under which it was written, fall short of detailed notice of developments in construction which would be of great interest both to the serious archaeologist and the passing researcher. This loss is not irretrievable, even though the knowledge possessed by both Miss Blake and her successor, Doris Taylor Bishop, was detailed, sharply focussed, and marked by perspective in depth; for in the course of the text Miss Blake had already inserted appropriate comments on the special interest of particular examples of construction; and Mrs. Bishop carefully reconsidered these points. It seems to me then that my own part must be to make a series of general statements which will lead the reader into the text itself.

Notice of the types of evidence for methods of Roman construction and for dating must of course begin with the building materials. By the beginning of our period architects and construction men were ready to trust concrete as the superior building material. Stone was reserved for certain special effects. For example, peperino on a travertine base was used for fire walls in Trajan's Forum. A similar combination was used in the Basilica Argentaria. Whereas the podium of the Hadrianeum was faced with travertine under the columns, elsewhere it was faced with peperino; and the cella walls were peperino. These contrasts seemed to hold: the stone of preference where strength, sturdiness, and hard wear were expected was travertine, even to the insertion of travertine corbels into concrete walls. The great expansion of Roman trade made even more available a wide variety of rich marbles from abroad. Showpiece public buildings made extensive use of marble for columns, capitals, paving, facing, and various appointments. Granite, because of its hardness and strength, was used for columns.

The major building material was concrete. Various materials were used as *caementa*. Often there was an attempt by the builder to handle the *caementa* carefully by placing them in an orderly fashion as the cement was being poured. Obviously a strong aggregate contributes to the strength of the concrete, just as it also conserves the cement. But aggregate can

[1] RC I, pp. 1–69.

[2] RC II, pp. 3–9.

3

vary in weight. Hence, the podium in the wall separating the Forum Trai-ani from the Basilica Ulpia shows a gradation of *caementa* by weight, though its value here is not easy to see; but in the Pantheon, where the weight of the dome was an extremely important factor, the gradation of the aggregate was very carefully observed, culminating in the use for the last meters approaching the eye of alternate rows of lightweight yellow tufa and pumice. The Pantheon presents our earliest dated importation of pumice from Vesuvius to lighten vaulting. But at other times, when weight seems not to have mattered so much as speed of construction, cost factors including availability of rubble from a cleared site—even one's own site—the *caementa* become anything the builder found at hand.

Concrete by itself was not a very interesting material, a view not shared by modern builders. It was usually faced with brick; but again, brick could be viewed as a very ornamental way of extending the supply of cement. Other facings include block and reticulate of various types and also various combinations. It does not take the observant eye long to learn to distinguish between the brickwork of the various periods. The indicators include size (length, thickness, shape also where observable), color, texture, the actual laying up of the brickwork in the mortar bedding, use of bonding courses, arches, etc. Miss Blake's descriptions and running summaries provide the proper data at the important moment.

Concrete made possible the frequent use of vaulting. Generally, barrel vaulting was preferred, probably because the centering was easier to prepare; and so Trajanic vaulting seems to be only barrel. The Caseggiato delle Taberne Finestrate (IV, 5, 18) seems to preserve the only extant Trajanic vaulting in Ostia. The Terme delle Sei Colonne (IV, 5, 10–11) shows in one room the beginning of a cross vault; if this vaulting is original and not part of the many later alterations to the building, then it is an early example of a common later technique. Concrete also fostered the building of domes; but the technique was not a new invention.[3] What is new is Hadrian's experimentation with domes based on a preoccupation with curves.

Building space around Rome in many areas was quite circumscribed. It became increasingly so as the capital grew and imperial building occupied more and more space. At Ostia likewise; but both cities had areas into which mushrooming population could expand. In Ostia in particular it is often possible to chart the order of construction by observing the relationship of walls, even walls built approximately at the same time. Both cities had trouble with periodic flooding. Hence at Rome, control of the Tiber by embankments and raising of the level of the Campus Martius; at Ostia, the general raising of the level. These pieces of landscaping provide evidences which have certain valuable uses.

One of the most valuable tools in dating construction in the second century A.D. is brick stamps. One cannot study Roman construction of this age without ready access to the valuable works by Herbert Bloch. In the following pages there is indeed a certain wry amusement when one reads a Blakean sentence such as "brick stamps confirm the date suggested by the construction." But it is possible to move from the known to the unknown when two techniques work so well together; yet the principal

[3] *RC* II, pp. 163–164; Index, p. 194 s.v. "Vaults, concrete, domical;" "Vaults, cut-stone."

benefaction will probably be the closer dating of the construction through the brick stamp.

Further evidence for construction can be found in water pipes. Though no traces of construction may now be visible, an inscribed water pipe can show that there was once something. But the value of the pipe depends heavily on the circumstances of its finding. For example, that there are almost no imperial brick stamps at the villa known as Le Vignacce but instead private stamps and private water pipes are strong evidence that the villa was private, not imperial property. In Ostia, a water pipe in the Terme delle Sei Colonne with the name of Cornificia, sister of Marcus Aurelius, may give the date of the rebuilding of the room of the two pools; the brickwork is characteristic of the time of Commodus or Septimius Severus. And lastly, the restructuring of the warehouse area at Rome beside the Tiber was a prime commercial need in the second century. Part of the dating of the restructuring rests on the fact that a lead pipe of the Hadrianic period passed under the Horrea Seiana. But one must admit that not all the water pipes in this volume produce such results as this handful has; their value therefore is uneven.

Decoration, both architectural and interior, can be used as evidence for construction and dating. Mosaics, wall paintings, pavements, marble appointments, frescoed ceilings can under proper conditions yield much useful information to the trained eye. Brick bichromy, styles in architectural carving, the arrangement of façades, and similar architectural features can contribute to an approximate chronology. So far all the evidence listed could be classed as "direct," i.e., actually part of the construction itself.

Independent evidence is of various types. Numismatic evidence must be handled carefully. Trajanic coinage shows arches and temples of which little is known; but coins with the legend FORVM TRAIAN(i) help visualize the façade of the monumental gate and seem to show the Basilica Ulpia beyond. The Temple of Venus and Rome was dedicated A.D. 135; but the Antonine coins seem to show either that it was completed by Antoninus Pius, or that this is another affirmation of his *pietas*. Almost all our information concerning the Templum Matidiae and the Basilicae Matidiae et Marcianae comes from a badly struck coin of ca. A.D. 120 with the legend DIVAE MATIDIAE SOCRVI. On the other hand, the coin purporting to depict the Pons Aelius is of questionable authenticity. Coins of 172/3 showing Mercury in a peculiar shrine are referred to a restoration of that temple on the Aventine; but no remains have been found. One more example of the care required in using numismatics: a coin with the legend PORTVM TRAIANI was formerly thought to represent Civitavecchia, but is now ascribed to Porto.

Pictorial reliefs at times show buildings as background. Miss Blake had previously been able to point to certain instances in which such evidence was available, though as evidence such reliefs must be handled carefully.[4] In the current work, the same cautious handling would be in order; but in point of fact such reliefs have not been used as evidence. For example, Trajan's arch at Benevento on the side facing Rome does show a few background buildings, but their identification is hard to come by; nor did

[4] *RC* I, p. 4; *RC* II, pp. 7–8.

Miss Blake think they could contribute to her study, and Mrs. Bishop concurred. Of greater interest is the wall painting from the Villa dei Quintili, for it shows a villa countryside; but again, it does not constitute direct evidence; it has evocative value only.

The Forma Urbis Severiana, where it survives, is of great value, provided that its existing pieces and copies of pieces since lost can be assigned to their proper places. Though the principal value is topographical, still the buildings are shown by floor plans, a point of some importance for the study of construction. The great edition of the Marble Plan by Carettoni, Colini, Cozza, and Gatti came off the press the year before Miss Blake's death while she was hurrying to complete her text. Hence Mrs. Bishop made all the necessary adjustments before she in turn died, except one where I completed the marginal note left by her.

The great interest in classical antiquity engendered by the Renaissance led to drawings and engravings of the Roman ruins both then and in later centuries. When these works are correctly interpreted, much valuable information becomes available; but one must be able to sift fact from fancy when necessary, to see the difference between a representation and an evocation. In early 1964 Thomas J. McCormick, then of Vassar College but now Wright-Shippee Professor of Art and chairman of the Art Department at Wheaton College, wrote to Mrs. Bishop about a series of water colors and drawings by Clérisseau and a series of engravings after Clérisseau. Aside from problems connected with his own work and the fact that much of Clérisseau's work is based in fantasy, there was the very real question that at least those works in the Hermitage might be of value to the present study, since they were not available to Miss Van Deman or Miss Blake. For example, one of the Spalato drawings of a medieval church is important because the church is no longer standing; but the drawing confirms a scholar's reconstruction of it. Mrs. Bishop's correspondence file shows that she hoped to make on-site comparisons between existing remains in Italy and copies of photographs belonging to Mr. McCormick of the appropriate Clérisseau works. But the misfortune which seems to have pursued this study—absit omen!—interfered, and the copies were so bad as to be unusable. In the meantime Mrs. Bishop had left for Rome. It is my opinion that she thought the Clérisseau drawings would contribute little to a study of methods of construction but are of great potential interest to architectural historians; but it may be that her illness and death prevented her from resuming study of them as she prepared the final version of the text; but of all that she said nothing to me. Nevertheless one does await with eager interest Mr. McCormick's work on Clérisseau.[5] Old photographs, on the other hand, contain much more secure information; indeed Parker's photographs are the only record of much ancient construction uncovered when the old railroad station was built in Rome nearly a century ago.

While the Chronographer of A.D. 354 is important for the Flavians, his value for our period is negligible. Of greater importance are the Regionary Catalogues and the Notitia, for they locate specific structures in specific areas of the city; while primarily of topographical value, nevertheless they provide some help in specific identification of certain structures. Aside from the use of the Historia Augusta as a checklist of monuments constructed

[5] See already Thomas J. McCormick, "An Unknown Collection of Drawings by Charles-Louis Clérisseau," Jour. Soc. Architect. Historians vol. 22, 1963, pp. 119–126, especially fig. 7 ("So-called Temple of Venus, Baiae, by Clérisseau (reproduced by permission of the Syndics of the Fitzwilliam Museum, Cambridge)") and fig. 8 ("So-called Temple of Venus, Baiae, engraved by Cunego after Clérisseau (courtesy of the Royal Institute of British Architects, London)").

by our emperors, Pliny's ecstatic letter on the construction of Trajan's harbor at Civitavecchia, and Rutilius Namatianus's description of the same harbor in the fifth century, literature from the period and later contributes very little to this study.

Movable objects have limited value. Increasingly, archaeologists and specialist students have been developing criteria for a more careful assessment of such objects. But the presence of a find on a site is no guarantee that the object and the structure are coeval. Only under certain highly limiting conditions could such objects provide anything more than confirmation of a chronology based on other criteria. But archaeologists have become increasingly aware of the need for acute observation and increasingly skilled in interpretation. Nevertheless, the value will be greater for construction outside the confines of this book.

There may be times when a student of a piece of construction is unable to see it as documentation of human need, use, practice; but it would be hard to ignore the social, economic, and psychological factors when one compares what the second-century emperors built in Rome, Ostia, and elsewhere. One need think only of the differences between Hadrianic construction in Ostia and in the Villa Adriana, or compare the work of Trajan at Ostia and Rome with that of Commodus to realize that times, talents, personalities, needs differ from age to age even within our period.

The criteria which Miss Blake has so carefully detailed for Rome, Ostia, and the Villa Adriana "cannot be applied blindly to other parts of Italy," as she herself pointed out.[6] Construction is always subject to local conditions. If the local stone is too hard for easy dressing, then the reticulate will not have the geometric perfection of coeval reticulate at Rome. The construction may essentially be Roman, but local needs, materials, methods, workmen influence the final result. Of construction outside Italy nothing need be said; for its study is not part of this book.

—J. D. B.

[6] RC II, p. 9.

II. ROME

NERVA had little time in which to initiate important building operations even if he had been so inclined. His talents lay along different lines. He sought to return to the public as much as possible of the property confiscated by Domitian, to decrease public expenses, and to raise money by mortgages on property throughout Italy for the support of poor children.[1] He released Italian towns from the onus of supplying post horses[2] and encouraged philanthropy by permitting cities to receive legacies.[3] Inscriptional evidence points to some change or addition in the Colosseum[4] under his regime and to a Horrea Nervae[5] of which nothing further is known. Even the Forum which goes by his name was merely dedicated by him.[6] Of the extensive road-building program started by him, we shall speak in another connection.[7]

[1] Frank, *Ec. survey*, vol. 5 (Frank), pp. 65, 173.

[2] *Ibid.*, p. 102.

[3] *Ibid.*, p. 105.

[4] V. Spinazzola, *Anfiteatro Flavio* (Naples, 1907), pp. 27ff; Platner-Ashby, p. 6.

[5] *CIL*, vol. 6 (2), no. 8681 (33744); Platner-Ashby, p. 262.

[6] See RC II, pp. 105–106 under Forum Transitorium.

[7] See below, pp. 280 ff.

PUBLIC BUILDINGS

TRAJAN (A.D. 98–117)

When Trajan took up the reins of government in A.D. 98, the devastation of the fire of A.D. 64 had not yet been entirely remedied, to say nothing of the more recent conflagration of A.D. 80. There were also projects which Domitian had scarcely started; they had to be completed. A passage in Aurelius Victor[8] indicates that Trajan admired the splendor of fine architecture, but it is impossible to tell how much ability along that line he himself possessed. In any case, he was fortunate in being able to command the services of a great architect, Apollodorus, whose devotion to his art would brook no interference even from an emperor.[9] The result was a series of magnificent buildings which aroused the admiration of the ancients.[10] Two of the finest of these, the Baths and the Market behind his Forum,[11] are still impressive in their ruinous condition. In his interest in the embellishment of his Capital, he did not, however, neglect public utilities. He curbed the Tiber by a new embankment, repaired the old aqueducts and brought a new one, the Aqua Traiana, to the city. Away from Rome, he strengthened the Empire by improving the highways, constructing new harbors and bestowing benefactions on the colonies. In short, he became by proxy at any rate one of the great builders of antiquity.

ARCHES AND SACRED EDIFICES

Coins issued during the reign of Trajan give evidence of arches and temples of which little more is known. Besides the gateway to the Forum of Trajan,[12] two other triumphal arches appear on coins. The first, of A.D. 100,[13] depicts a monument having three archways of equal height framed within four columns, each with a simple base rather than a pedestal, but supporting a conventional entablature under a smooth attic. The only decoration is a team of ten horses drawing the triumphal car between two trophies. There has been a persistent attempt to identify this arch with the so-called Arch of Drusus[14] over the Via Appia, but this was almost surely built to carry the Aqua Antoniniana over the road[15] and was never designed as a triple archway. The side openings in stone merely served as the transition from the brick arches of the rest of the aqueduct to the ornamental gateway in the center. It is hard to imagine a greater contrast than that presented by the second coin type issued between A.D. 104 and 111,[16] in which every available surface is covered with carving. In the center, heavy columns on pedestals uphold a pediment over a single arch supported by pilasters. This central gateway stands out in bold relief. End pilasters, richly carved, seem to support merely a frieze of garlands on which rest reliefs of *bigae* facing inward. The pediment is built up into an attic topped by the inscription I O M (Jupiter Optimus Maximus) beneath a six-horse chariot between victories, flanked at a lower level by trophies and captives, with eagles at the corners, giving a pyramidal effect to the decoration on top. Sculptured panels adorn the pylons and Jupiter between giants (?) stands in the pediment. Not only the inscription but also the subject matter of the carvings make plausible the conjecture that this arch marked the entrance to the Precinct of Jupiter Capitolinus.[17]

[8] Sextus Aurelius Victor, *De Caesaribus*, 5. Cf. Paribeni, *Optimus Princeps*, vol. 2, pp. 23–24.

[9] Cassius Dio, 69, 4.

[10] Pausanias, 5, 12, 6; 10, 5, 11; Ammianus Marcellinus, 16, 10, 15.

[11] R. Paribeni, *Acc. It. Rend.*, vol. 4, 1942–1943, pp. 124–130 (see review of A. M. Colini in *Bull. Com.*, vol. 72, 1946–1948, p. 172).

[12] See below, p. 14.

[13] Mattingly, *BMC, Emp.*, vol. 3, p. xcvi; Strack, *Reichsprägung*, Part 1, pp. 92–95, pl. 4, fig. 331; Kähler, *RE, Triumphbogen*, no. 25, col. 387.

[14] Strack (*loc. cit.*) is the latest exponent on this theory.

[15] Van Deman, *Aqueducts*, p. 145; Ashby, *Aqueducts*, p. 158; G. Rosi, *Bull. Com.*, vol. 60, 1932, pp. 157–176.

[16] *BMC, Emp.*, vol. 3, Trajan, nos. 842–846, pl. 31, figs. 6–9; Strack *op. cit.*, pp. 114–116, pl. 6, fig. 387; Kähler, *op. cit.*, no. 26, cols. 387–388.

[17] Mattingly (*op. cit.*, p. ci) suggests with less plausibility Trajan's Forum as a second possibility.

Another arch was in the process of being erected in the Forum of Trajan in A.D. 116.[18]

Only two coin types were apparently struck to commemorate temples built by Trajan in Rome. One issued ca. A.D. 107[19] depicts an octastyle temple on a podium of two or three steps, with a cult statue, three figures in the pediment, and five along the roof. The cult statue varied in the different issues but in at least three seems to hold a scepter in one hand and a cornucopia in the other. It has been conjectured that it could be Divus Nerva. The pediment shows a seated figure between reclining ones. The cornucopia appears at least twice among the shields and spears which form the usual accessories of the figures along the roof. Nerva's predilection for Fortuna[20] on his own coins may have suggested the cornucopia motive in the decoration of his temple, if such it be. It seems strange that a temple of such pretension should have disappeared completely. The other coin type[21] (A.D. 104–107) is even more of an enigma. It resembles the first except that there is a higher podium; but the type shows a covered porticus on each side and, in one issue, an altar in front.[22] It may have been a temple dedicated to Divus Traianus Pater. Trajan's natural father was fully as outstanding as his adoptive father Nerva. A coin struck between 112 and 117 honored them both together,[23] and the emperor may have already caused to be erected two nearly identical temples in their honor. The dating of the coins as given above[24] makes it unlikely that a temple to Divus Traianus Pater stood at the head of the Forum where a temple was actually dedicated to Divus Traianus Filius, as Bernhart conjectured.[25] Possibly the temple was built in honor of Divus Traianus Pater and incorporated by Apollodorus in his plans for the Forum of Trajan; otherwise, we are left with a second pretentious temple of which no remains have been identified.[26]

Of a temple to Fortune mentioned by a fifth-century writer as dedicated by Trajan, nothing further is known.[27] The altar of Pudicitia erected in honor of Plotina is shown on another coin[28] to be a comparatively simple affair set on five steps. Nothing further is known of it.

IMPERIAL FORA

Trajan's interest was so centered in the new forum which he proposed to build that he did little or nothing to change the appearances of those already in existence. A statue in his honor was set up in the Forum Romanum in A.D. 101/2.[29] Possibly, the pedestal of the Equus Domitiani[30] became the tribunal represented in the "Anaglypha Traiani" after the *damnatio memoriae* of Domitian.[31] The "Anaglypha," now on exhibition in the Curia, belong to the field of decorative art. They may have been carved to refurbish an old edifice or to embellish a new one as yet not identified. There is no assurance that they are work of the Trajanic period.[32] A curved piece of marble bearing an inscription which can be dated A.D. 111/12 once belonged to an apse perhaps located in the Forum area.[33] Passing mention may be made of a brick-faced wall which may be Trajanic, east of the Temple of Antoninus and Faustina.[34] The building to which it belonged was apparently destroyed when a new edifice was erected in the time of Septimius Severus.

[18] See below, p. 17.

[19] *BMC, op. cit.*, nos. 354, 857–862, 915–916, 955, pls. 15, 5; 32, 5–7; 35, 3–4; 37, 7; Strack, *op. cit.*, pp. 147–149, pl. 2, fig. 152, pl. 6, fig. 392; D. Brown, *NNM*, no. 90, p. 42, pl. 4, 3.

[20] A temple of Fortuna is credited to Trajan in a late author (Lydus, *de Mens.* 4, 7).

[21] *BMC, op. cit.*, nos. 863–868, pl. 32, 8, 9; Bernhart, *Hb. z. Münzkunde*, pp. 129–130, pl. 93, 3, 4; Strack, *op. cit.*, pp. 149–154.

[22] Bernhart, *op. cit.*, pl. 93, no. 3; Strack, *op. cit.*, pl. 6, fig. 394.

[23] *BMC, op. cit.*, nos. 498–499, pl. 17, nos. 18 and 19.

[24] For the chronology, see Mattingly (*BMC, op. cit.*, pp. lviii-lx), where Strack's complicated presentation (*op. cit.*, pp. 25–35) is well summarized.

[25] Bernhart, *loc. cit.*

[26] Brown's conjecture (*NNM*, no. 90, p. 42) that it represents the Temple of Venus Genetrix in the Forum Iulium has little to recommend it.

[27] Platner-Ashby, p. 214 (Lydus, *de Mens.* 4, 7).

[28] Platner-Ashby, p. 433; *BMC, op. cit.*, no. 529, pl. 18, no. 15.

[29] Lugli, *Centro*, p. 167.

[30] For the monument, see Blake, *RC II*, pp. 112–113.

[31] Platner-Ashby, pp. 201–202; Lugli, *loc. cit.; idem, Mon. Min.,* pp. 107–109.

[32] Most critics now favor a Hadrianic date. See below, p. 40.

[33] A. Bartoli, *Not. sc.*, 1947, pp. 85–100.

[34] Lugli, *Mon. Min.*, p. 122.

[35] Degrassi, *Fasti O.*, no. 22, pp. 202, 203, 232.

[36] Blake, *RC II*, pp. 102–103. No construction can be definitely ascribed to Trajan. The only three brick stamps (*CIL*, vol. 15 (1), nos. 496, 597 (?), 1410) found in the south-east wall, which separated the temple from the forum, would seem to indicate a modification in the time of Hadrian. See Bloch, *Bolli*, pp. 62, 67.

[37] See below, pp. 18–19.

[38] See below, p. 18.

[39] Blake, *RC II*, p. 105.

[40] Cassius Dio, 69, 4, 1. Paribeni (*Acc. L. Rend.*, ser. 7, vol. 4, 1943, pp. 124–130) casts doubts on the credibility of this account.

[41] A paved street with a row of shops is practically all that Boni found in his investigations. See G. Boni, *Not. sc.*, 1907, pp. 389–394.

[42] Degrassi, *Fasti O.*, no. 22, pp. 200–203.

[43] Paribeni, *Optimus Princeps*, vol. 2, pp. 65–100; Platner-Ashby, pp. 237–245; I. Gismondi, *Bull. Com.*, vol. 61, 1933, Notizario, pl. A; Lugli, *Centro*, pp. 278–297; Crema, pp. 358–363; Frova, pp. 74–75; *FUR*, p. 89; Nash I, pp. 450–456; MacDonald *passim*.

[44] C. Ricci (*Via dell'Impero*, p. 126) expresses the belief that the temple was begun under Trajan.

[45] The east wall is clearly visible; part of the west wall was uncovered in 1931 (C. Ricci, *Bull. Com.*, vol. 59, 1931, p. 122).

The Temple of Venus Genetrix in the Forum Iulium, though not dedicated until A.D. 113,[35] was almost, if not entirely, the work of Domitian.[36] Since no credit could be given to Domitian after his *damnatio memoriae*, it is not strange that it should be inaugurated by a later emperor. There were some modifications in the offices along the southwest side of the Forum in connection with the erection of a comfort station at a higher level,[37] and the Basilica Argentaria was crowded into the space between the Domitianic retaining wall and the southwest side of the temple;[38] but these changes were clearly secondary to the grandiose scheme for constructing a new forum which should surpass all the others both in size and in magnificence. There is no Trajanic work, to my knowledge, in the other fora.

Forum Traiani

Domitian had evidently intended to make use of the valley between the Capitoline and the Quirinal for some grandiose building project. He seems to have progressed no farther than some terracing on the Capitoline and some rooms against the Quirinal, which were not utilized later.[39] The enormous booty from the Dacian campaigns was put at the disposal of Apollodorus[40] by Trajan for the construction of a forum which should not only be more splendid than any that had gone before but should serve as a memorial to the events which brought final victory over the Dacians by the triumph of Roman arms. The architect had to reckon with the Forum of Augustus and its northwestern hemicycle and the Forum Iulium with the Temple of Venus Genetrix which projected into the area, but the rest was free from buildings of any importance.[41] He must have planned first how he could employ the level space in the valley to best advantage and then how he could make use of what remained to remove from the Forum the business which would of necessity detract from its dignity and decorum. Although these supernumerary edifices were almost certainly finished first, it has seemed best to start with the analysis of the Forum and its dependencies. In any case much of the building must have been going on simultaneously. The Forum was dedicated in A.D. 112.[42] The groundplan of this central part (plan I) is certainly worthy of the genius of Apollodorus. The whole space was divided into three parts,[43] exclusive of the area which later contained the Temple and Precinct of Divus Trajanus,[44] but may have been intended for a different temple in the original scheme. First there was the spacious forum proper immediately to the northwest of the Forum Augusti, then the Basilica Ulpia with its axis at right angles to the main axis, and finally the Greek and Latin Libraries opening off from a central court in which the Column of Trajan rose like a mighty scroll recording the military exploits of the Emperor in Dacia. Forum and Basilica with their apses stood between fire walls of peperino.[45] These walls had a foundation of travertine blocks carefully grooved to receive the sectile floor of the porticus within. Both peperino and travertine blocks were fastened together by iron clamps, two to the long sides and one to the short. Brick-faced concrete was used for the walls of the libraries, possibly because the terra-cotta would absorb some of the moisture deleterious to books and scrolls. We turn now to separate parts.

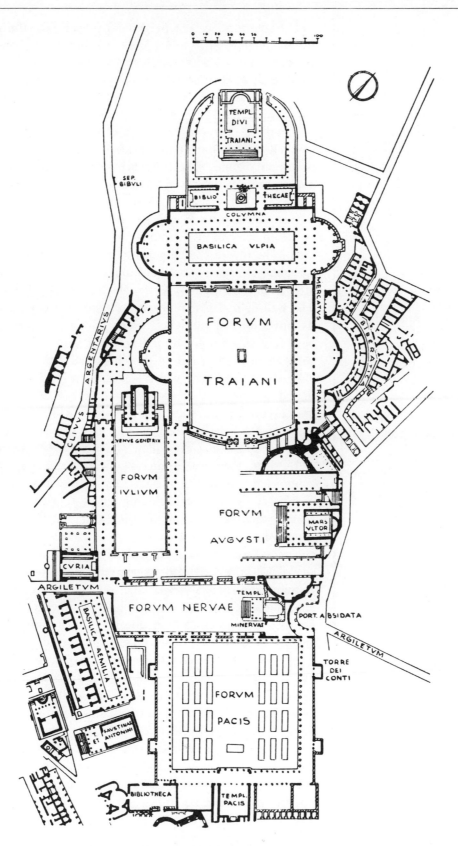

PLAN I. THE IMPERIAL FORA

Curtius-Nawrath, *Das Antike Rom,*
4th ed. 1963

46 A. Bartoli, *Acc. P. Mem.*, ser. 3, vol. 1 (2) 1924, col. 182–186.

47 There may have been shops flanking the gate. See Bartoli, *op. cit.*, col. 186. *Cf.* also Paribeni, *op. cit.*, p. 77.

48 *BMC, Emp.*, vol. 3, Trajan, nos. 509–510, 665, pls. 18, 3; 21, 15. See also Strack, *Reichsprägung*, Part 1, pp. 202–205; Kähler, *RE, Triumph-bogen*, no. 27, col. 388.

49 Bartoli, *op. cit.*, pl. 37.

50 Ammianus Marcellinus, 16, 10, 15.

51 *BMC, loc. cit.*, nos. 445–448, pls. 16, 18; Strack, *op. cit.*, pls. 3, fig. 196; 8, 432.

52 There are also fragments of both with deeper channeling.

53 Some, in all probability, now adorn the Arch of Constantine.

54 Lugli, *op. cit.*, p. 281.

55 M. Pallottino, *Bull. Com.*, vol. 66, 1938, pp. 35–39. See also Strong, *Sc. rom.*, vol. 1, pp. 142–150; R. Bianchi Bandinelli, *Arti*, vol. 1, 1938–1939, pp. 331–334; Frova, pp. 244–245.

56 *BMC, loc. cit.*, pls. 17, 15; 38, 8; Strack, *op. cit.*, pp. 204–205, pls. 3, fig. 202; 6, 411; 7, 424.

57 The basilica is about a meter higher than the Forum.

58 Remains of a smaller one were uncovered on the right.

The southeast wall of the Forum proper gave the impression of elasticity by curving outward. Only a part of its foundation remains, but there is slight evidence that it was of marble.[46] Doorways to the right and to the left of it led directly to the porticoes flanking the open space, but the curved wall was broken probably only by the monumental gate at its center.[47] Coins[48] labeled FORUM TRAIAN(i) depict the inside of this gate, and probably the exterior was similar. It was on the inside of the Forum, however, that the architect lavished the adornment that made it one of the most beautiful monuments in ancient Rome. The simplified coin picture of the arch shows a rather narrow central archway flanked by three columns on each side supporting the attic. Between the columns pedimented niches contained full-length statues, and above the niches were medallions for busts(?). Bronze statuary of the emperor in his triumphal car between soldiers and trophies topped the arch. The row of columns with composite capitals[49] in front of the gateway was almost certainly continued along each side to uphold projections of the attic, as in the Forum of Nerva, which probably served as pedestals for statues. The wall, if not of marble, was certainly faced with marble, but because of its curve none of the reliefs which have been ascribed to the Forum could have formed its decoration. The open area (118 m. × 89 m.) was paved with white marble and at its center had the statue in gilt bronze of the emperor on horseback which was so admired by Constantius.[50] It is represented on coins.[51] On the east and west sides, three steps of giallo antico led to covered porticoes, twelve meters wide, with a pavement mostly of giallo and pavonazzetto. Columns and corresponding pilasters of pavonazzetto were carved with shallow channels.[52] In the center of each porticus at the rear, there was a large hemicycle with a rectangular niche between columns of gray granite in the center of the curve. The columns at the front of it probably gave rise to the impression that the colonnades along the sides were double, before excavations revealed that they were single. The exedras had pavements of giallo, affricano, and pavonazzetto laid in a pattern of great circles and squares and were probably covered like the porticoes. Each porticus, as we have seen, had its own entrance from the southeast. Above the columns, the entablature served as pedestals for the statues of Dacian prisoners, some of which have come to light.[53] Shields or windows may have stood between the pedestals, and possibly the amorini panels unearthed in the vicinity were inserted under these hypothetical windows. A covered passage may have passed behind this attic,[54] but in any case there probably never was an upper porticus. No unbroken space remains here for the continuous frieze which was later dismembered and used in part to adorn the Arch of Constantine.[55] The northwest wall was given monumental treatment.[56] In the center, four columns on a sort of podium supported an attic having inscriptions and decorative reliefs on the side walls and a quadriga on top. Remains of this podium show a gradation of *caementa* according to weight—selce, travertine, peperino, and some refuse material—in a dark mortar. This was the façade for the triple gateway leading to the Basilica Ulpia which was at a higher level.[57] There were secondary gateways[58] in addition to those leading directly from the porticoes to the basilica. Traces of the steps in giallo antico have also been found. Three travertine bases with identical inscriptions ascribable to A.D. 112[59] are still *in situ*, and the place where the fourth stood is clear. They probably bore trophies of bronze. Through the doorways in the coin pictures, one sees vaguely the colonnade of the Basilica Ulpia and over it a row of ornaments which probably belonged to its roof.

The Basilica Ulpia (159 m. $\times$ 55 m.) consisted of a central hall enclosed in a double porticus with a large hemicycle opening out of it at each end. The columns of the central nave were of granito del foro from Mons Claudianus of wider diameter and greater height than those of the lateral aisles.[60] This indicates a roof sloping outward and perhaps a clerestory. The outer columns were of cipollino. It is not clear what variety of columns fronted the exedras. The entablature was of Pentelic marble, the walls lined with Luna, the central part paved with Luna, and the hemicycles with polychrome marbles. The roof was supported by rafters covered with gilded bronze.[61] A fragment of the Forma Urbis Severiana shows the word LIBERTATIS in almost complete form and belongs with another fragment containing the word ULPIA.[62] This probably indicates the presence of a shrine to Libertas rather than the Atrium Libertatis.[63] Probably a shrine to some other divinity was located in the other hemicycle. Travertine steps led down to the court between the two libraries. The Basilica was richly decorated with reliefs. One fragment of the entablature shows the architrave with fasciae outlined in the bead-and-reel motive and capped with a floral pattern below the frieze which depicts a victory slaying the sacrificial bull.

Brick stamps[64] prove what literary evidence implies: that the libraries were built about A.D. 110.[65] The exterior was plain, possibly with the brick facing exposed. Four columns *in antis* faced the central court on each side; and an inner colonnade of two orders supported, or at any rate, seemed to support the ceiling which was barrel vaulted with a pumice aggregate.[66] Three steps between the columns led to a platform in front of the rows of oblong niches prepared for the numbered cases[67] which held the books. A rectangular alcove at the rear was designed for the tutelary divinity. Bonding courses of *bipedales* appear in the brickwork, and lintel arches of the same almost certainly topped the niches. None of this brickwork showed in the interior of the finished libraries. Between the columns that stood at the entrance, the visitor to either library would have glimpsed the two-storied colonnade with columns of giallo antico and pavonazzetto and elaborately carved cornices and friezes, walls gleaming with a white marble revetment contrasting pleasantly with a pavement of polychrome marbles, and a sculptured architectural prospective in the alcove at the end to add to the impression of spaciousness, not to mention the many statues which were set up in the library.[68] Behind each hall a double stairway led respectively to the gallery within the library and perhaps to a passage along the vault on the roof from which a visitor could admire the carving of the great Column in the center of the court. Just how this was arranged is not clear. Beyond these stairwells, the Schola Fori Traiani may have been located.[69]

A colonnade architecturally integrated with the libraries and the Basilica Ulpia enclosed the court on three sides.[70] Because the concrete pavement was cut for the travertine plinth beneath the Column, some scholars[71] have

[59] *CIL*, vol. 6 (1), no. 959.

[60] The angle columns were still wider. See Ricci, *op. cit.*, p. 128. The identification of the marble has been made by Mr. J. B. Ward-Perkins.

[61] Anderson-Spiers-Ashby (p. 73) gives two other possible interpretations of the pertinent passages in Pausanias (5, 12, 6 and 10, 5, 11): covered with bronze plates instead of tiles; ceiling encased in bronze plates on the inside.

[62] *FUR*, p. 89 and pl. 28. Recent excavations have shown that any association with the Basilica Aemilia is untenable.

[63] Platner-Ashby, p. 56.

[64] Bloch, *Bolli*, pp. 57–61.

[65] Since they are not mentioned in the Fasti Ostienses in the record of the dedication of the Forum and the Basilica Ulpia in A.D. 112 or of the Column in A.D. 113, they were probably covered by the first entry. See Degrassi, *Fasti O.*, no. 22, pp. 200–203.

[66] G. Giovannoni, *Riv. Roma*, vol. 14, 1936, p. 40.

[67] At least Vopiscus, writing in the early fourth century, refers to *armarium sextum* (Tacitus, 8, 1). He has frequent allusions to *libri lintei*. See C. E. Boyd, *Public libraries*, pp. 37–39.

[68] Relatively small fragments found in the recent excavations make possible a general description. There has, to my knowledge, been no recent attempt at a detailed restoration.

[69] Platner-Ashby, p. 467.

[70] A wall with two doorways separated the court from the Basilica.

[71] See Paribeni, *loc. cit.*, pp. 87–88.

[72] *CIL*, vol. 6 (1), no. 960.

[73] Degrassi, *Fasti O.*, no. 22.

[74] Cassius Dio, 68, 16, 3.

[75] G. Boni, *Not. sc.*, 1907, pp. 361–427.

[76] Paribeni, *loc. cit.*, pp. 70–74; Platner-Ashby, p. 238; Lugli, *loc. cit.*, pp. 287–289.

[77] Birt, *Buchrolle*, pp. 269–315. This interpretation of the spiral is not accepted by everyone; see Lehmann-Hartleben, *Traianssäulle*, p. 3.

assumed that the Column was an afterthought, but since it was dedicated only a year after the Forum and Basilica, it is reasonable to suppose that all three were part of the same general scheme. The court may have been paved in concrete in preparation for the first dedication. The purpose of the Column has also led to long continued controversy. The inscription[72] leaves no doubt that it was voted by the Senate and the Roman people in honor of Trajan in A.D. 113. The Fasti Ostienses give the same year for its dedication.[73] The difficulty lies in the last two lines. Where one expects an allusion to the glorious victories in Dacia, which are portrayed in the reliefs of the shaft, one reads that it was a reminder of the amount of earth (*mons et locus*) that had to be removed for the Forum and its dependencies (*tant(is) oper(ibus)*). Cassius Dio[74] interpreted the statement literally, but disregarded the fact that it was the Senate and not the emperor that erected the monument. It is now known that, though there may have been a tongue of land between the Capitoline and the Quirinal, there was no massive hill to be cut away.[75] Of the many interpretations of the inscription[76] thus far proposed, none is entirely satisfactory. It seems clear, however, that the Column was erected to honor Trajan for providing a magnificent new civic center. If an equestrian statue of gilt bronze was to stand in the center of the Forum proper, the court of the libraries was the logical place for a monument commemorating the building of the whole complex. The treatment of the Column as a gigantic scroll,[77] if that was indeed in the mind of the architect, could have been inspired by the position. In any case, it offered another surface for recording the history of the Dacian campaigns, for which the whole monument was a memorial. There is no suggestion in the inscription of any intention to use the base as a depository for the ashes of Trajan and Plotina. This use of the Column, and not the Column itself, was the afterthought.

Our concern is, however, specifically with the construction. As we have seen above, the site had already been covered with a concrete pavement. This, which had an aggregate of selce, travertine, and marble, was cut for the substructure of the travertine platform on which the Column stood. The substructure, in selce concrete with a red pozzolana mortar, covered a somewhat larger area than the platform and was set within a wooden framework. The platform consisted of blocks (1.5 m. × 77 cm. × 30 cm.) laid in four rows so that the first and third were composed of lengthwise blocks and the others of crosswise ones. The blocks were fastened together with iron clamps leaded into place, two on each long side and one on the short. On this platform was set the first of the four courses of Luna marble which made up the pedestal. The lowest of these was cut to simulate a number of low courses and the base molding for the socle which was decorated with simple carving. The socle consisted of two courses with different heights, richly carved with the trophies of war. On the southeast side the upper one carried the inscription between winged victories over a doorway in a simple frame. The fourth course was cut into a plain capping molding, a concave molding for the sub-base of the Column adorned with swags of laurel fastened with sculptured ribbons at the corners, and the square base with eagles at the corners. The threshold of the doorway formed the second step from the concrete platform to an inner chamber, later adapted for use as a mausoleum. On the inside, great blocks on the northwest were cut into two ramps of steps leading to the spiral staircase within the shaft. A splayed window lighted the ramp. A short but thick transverse wall made a vestibule for the steps on the right and a short corridor on the left to what became the burial chamber. The blocks of the second course of the socle were hollowed out to make an oblong niche over a podium which was destined to be the depository for the urns containing the ashes of Trajan and Plotina. The splayed window giving light to this inner recess scarcely shows in the external carving.

The Column starts with a torus molding carved with laurel leaves. The shaft itself consists of seventeen drums of Luna marble[78] carved on the outside with the spiral relief depicting characteristic scenes in the two Dacian campaigns superbly brought together in a continuous whole, and carved on the inside into the steps of the spiral staircase, five to a block. The staircase is lighted by forty-three slit windows so inserted in the carving that they are scarcely noticeable on the outside. The shaft has the entasis appropriate for an Ionic column, but it terminates in a Doric capital with an ovolo molding, which is more suitable to its secondary purpose as the base of the bronze statue of Trajan on top.[79] All above the capital is not ancient, but belongs to the period of the substitution of the statue of St. Peter for that of Trajan. Any description of the reliefs is beyond the scope of a work of this sort.[80] One refinement may be mentioned with propriety: the band of the spiral was made wider toward the top to counteract what would otherwise be a distortion. The reliefs were almost certainly painted and details wrought in gold.[81] Because of the attention paid to minutiae, Colini[82] had conjectured that the drums were carved on the ground and that on account of the spiral form one already finished remained on the ground for all to see while the next was being carved. The joints would have to receive special attention after the blocks were in place. Fortunately the sculpture remains intact *in situ*, but it can best be studied in the casts, which, as the gift of the Vatican, now occupy a long corridor in the Museo della Civiltà Romana.[83] If, as Bianchi Bandinelli conjectures,[84] the Trajanic reliefs of the Arch of Constantine were designed by the sculptor who was responsible for the frieze on the Column in order to bring the tale of the Dacian campaigns to completion, a place for them should perhaps be found in this part of the Forum.

It is my conviction that Apollodorus planned a temple for the head of the Forum complex.[85] However that may be, the dedicatory inscription, of which fragments have been found, gives Hadrian the credit for the temple at the site, though only Aelius Spartianus declares that Hadrian actually built it.

Nothing further is known of the arch which was being erected by the Senate in the Forum in A.D. 116.[86] The decorative elements of the architecture of this Forum have been the subject of a recent monograph. This type of analysis is especially valuable for an understanding of the changing tastes in architectural ornament in Imperial Rome.[87] Lugli conjectures[88] that Apollodorus himself may have been responsible for the two great statues

[78] Not Parian marble. See L. Maddalena, *III cong. st. rom.*, 1935, vol. 5, p. 8.

[79] Lehmann-Hartleben (*op. cit.*, pp. 3–4), interpreting the figure on top in one coin issue (Strack, *op. cit.*, no. 386) as an eagle, suggests that the statue of Trajan was substituted for it when the Column became a grave monument. Strack (pp. 136–140), however, considers this and another coin (no. 388) issued at about the same time to exhibit an owl and by devious reasoning would connect it with Ludi Herculei. A later coin, issued in A.D. 115(?)–116 (*BMC, Emp.*, vol. 3, Trajan, no. 1025, pl. 41, 7) also bears a column surmounted by a bird. Coin pictures of Trajan's Column show many variations, but since we have the monument itself before us we can disregard them.

[80] The reader is referred to Nash I, p. 283.

[81] Lehmann-Hartleben, *op. cit.*, pp. 147–148.

[82] A. M. Colini, apud S. Ferri, *Capitolium*, vol. 15, 1940, p. 840.

[83] See also Ferri, *op. cit.*, p. 838–844 for a new approach.

[84] R. Bianchi Bandinelli, *Arti*, vol. 1, 1938–1939, pp. 331–334.

[85] See below, p. 41.

[86] Cassius Dio, 68, 29, 3. See also Kähler, *RE*, *Triumphbogen*, no. 28, col. 388.

[87] M. Bertoldi, *Ricerche sulla decorazione architettonica del Foro Traiano*, Rome, 1962.

[88] Lugli, *Centro*, p. 296.

of the emperor, the one on horseback in the center and the one standing on the Column.

Forum Traiani: Environs West

A retaining wall of Domitian[89] made available a terrace about a meter and a half higher than the Forum Iulium immediately west of the Temple of Venus Genetrix, which Apollodorus or some other architect used for the *Basilica Argentaria*.[90] This consisted of a double porticus, which continued the line of the columns on the west side of the Forum Iulium and then, when the retaining wall made an obtuse angle, turned twice at right angles to utilize to advantage part of the space behind the west hemicycle of the Forum Traiani. Piers (pl. 1, fig. 1) were employed rather than columns for the Basilica. Those of the outer row on the west were composed of rusticated blocks of travertine in the lower courses and of similar blocks of peperino above; those on the north were entirely of rusticated peperino, two to a course laid as headers and stretchers in alternate rows. The rustication resembles that in the precinct wall of the Forum Traiani, and the difference in material was concealed by stucco, traces of which remain. Those of the inner row to the west were made of brick-faced concrete; the inner row of the north rusticated peperino is similar to the outer row. The brickwork is entirely different from that of the Domitianic retaining wall. The pinkish cast is lacking, and the general effect is yellowish red. The bricks are thinner (3.6–4.3 cm.) and of finer texture; the bonding courses, of lighter red and yellow *bipedales*, are also thinner (4–4.5 cm.); the joints are closer (1 cm. or less), exhibit a finer mortar, and are raked. The piers terminate in an impost molding of tiles similar to those in the Mercati; those on the north, in a molding of peperino.[91] The cross vaulting is still preserved over the inner passage. Brick stamps link all this construction with the Mercato.[92] Meanwhile with the cutting away of a tongue of land between the Capitoline and Quirinal the Clivus Argentarius had become an important thoroughfare between the Via Lata and the Via Sacra.[93] A nymphaeum and a row of shops were built against the Domitianic wall mentioned above, which was here raised above the level of the ground. The bricks of the facing are wide and very red without any trace of the pinkish cast observed below. The partition walls display a different type of brickwork. The semicircular nymphaeum has an oblong niche with a lintel arch of upright tiles at its head for a fountain and a curved one with a full arch on each side for a statue. Brick stamps[94] prove that all this construction belongs either late in the first century or early in the second. The building has been plausibly identified with the Insula Argentaria mentioned in the Regionary Catalogues.

Connected with these changes no doubt was the construction of an elaborate semicircular *forica* or latrine (pl. 1, fig. 2) at an upper level above the offices on the southwest side of the Forum Iulium.[95] Travertine stairways were inserted in the third and ninth chambers to give access to this as well as the Clivus Argentarius.[96] The walls of the intervening offices were strengthened somewhat by brick-faced concrete, and new vaults were made to carry the additional weight. The impression of *besales* at regular intervals in the concrete marks a new development in vault construction. The vaults were

[89] Blake, *RC* II, p. 105.

[90] C. Ricci, *Capitolium*, vol. 6, 1932, pp. 383–389; *idem*, *Via dell'Impero*, pp. 43–45 (where he revises the dating from Hadrian to Trajan); A. M. Colini, *Bull. Com.*, vol. 61, 1933, p. 264; O. Grossi, *MAAR*, vol. 13, 1936, p. 219; Lugli, *MAR, Suppl.*, vol. 1, pp. 21–23; *idem*, *Centro*, pp. 251, 257; Nash I, "Forum Iulium," p. 424, 430–431.

[91] For the Mercati, see below.

[92] Bloch, *Bolli*, pp. 61–67.

[93] Ricci, *Capitolium*, loc. cit., p. 381; *idem*, *Via dell'Impero*, p. 45; Colini, *loc. cit.*

[94] Bloch, *loc. cit.*

[95] Ricci, *Capitolium*, loc. cit., pp. 369–378; *idem*, *Via del Impero*, pp. 40–42; Colini, *loc. cit.*

[96] Lugli, *MAR, Suppl.*, vol. 1, p. 33; *idem*, *Centro*, p. 257.

further reinforced by frequent arches of *bipedales*. Above the vaulting a double floor, like the hypocaust of a Bath, was clearly intended as a protection against the infiltration of water. There was the usual drain following the curved back wall of brick-faced concrete and in front of it a colonnade defining a semicircular space between it and the façade toward the Forum Iulium,[97] which remained unchanged except for the closing of the oblong apertures of the mezzanine floor. Travertine corbels supported the marble bench which was essential to this type of edifice. The walls were lined with *opus signinum*. The brickwork resembles closely that of the more utilitarian parts of the Mercati Traiani, with which brick stamps prove it to have been contemporaneous.[98] Here also the builder inserted relieving arches wherever he considered them structurally necessary. The space between the *forica* and the Clivus was reorganized at the same time. Partition walls of the same type of brickwork[99] made odd-shaped rooms, but they presented a straight façade to the Clivus. There is no reason why these rooms should not have served as shops. Shops on the other side of the street were probably part of the same systematization. More fundamental than these contributions to the Forum Iulium was the reorganization of the slopes of the Capitoline above them into three terraces.[100] The first and third were lined with shops, the partition walls of which would be buttressing agents for the retaining wall at the rear. The middle wall was very thick. It also served to hold back the earth but was decorated on the outside with niches between buttresses. It was eight meters high and more than twenty meters long. Most of this construction was destroyed when the Museo del Risorgimento was built, but the truncated parts of two niches of the intermediate terrace were incorporated in the façade of the museum. Another utilitarian piece of work was the repair of the main sewer serving the Capitoline.[101] Traces of it were found near the Temple of Saturn. It was large (67 cm. × 1.5 m.) and covered with tiles "a cappuccina." The tiles bear Trajanic stamps.

Forum Traiani: Environs East: Mercato

The slopes of the Quirinal offered a greater challenge to the genius of Apollodorus than those of the Capitoline. He utilized the space for a great market,[102] depending on the fire wall of the Forum to obviate the noise and confusion of the mercantile establishment. The builder of the Augustan Forum had already cut into the hill to gain space, and Domitian's contractor had made further inroads for a three-story edifice,[103] which was abandoned almost as soon as it was built; but Apollodorus worked out a masterly system of terraces to provide room for his market (plan II). Probably the nature of the terrain suggested the great hemicycle of the Forum which became the focal point for the market. Brick-faced concrete was chosen for its construction. At each cutback, the partition walls between the shops became the buttresses for the back wall, which also served as the sustaining wall for the hill behind. The device was not new, though it had never before been carried out on such a grand scale. The clever fashion in which so many elements were welded into a harmonious whole will become clear in the description of the separate parts.

A paved road skirting the peperino wall stood in front of a hemicycle of

[97] Lugli, *MAR, loc. cit.*, p. 18; *idem, Centro*, p. 247.

[98] Bloch, *loc. cit.*

[99] A similar use of a relieving arch appears in one wall.

[100] Lugli, *MAR, loc. cit.*, pp. 12–13, 31; *idem, Centro*, p. 53.

[101] A. M. Colini, (apud A. Muñoz) *Capitolium*, vol. 17, 1942, p. 272.

[102] Thanks to the excavation of 1928–1931, if the word excavation can be used for the liberation from the accumulation of later structures, one can roam at will through this important monument. The carrying out of the project illustrates both the advantages and the disadvantages of the dictatorial form of government. Without such concentration of both power and means, the plan might well still be in the paper stages. The task was entrusted to a genial and enthusiastic scholar, Corrado Ricci, and was carried out as well as was possible under the condition imposed. No time was allowed for studying the changes due to the vicissitudes of rooms in constant use for eighteen centuries. Instead, orders were given to restore the edifice as nearly as possible to its original state so that it could again be used, if not for the actual sale of goods, at least for commercial fairs. The first was an enormous book fair which caught the popular imagination. It is doubtful whether those in charge always had at their disposal the necessary evidence for a completely trustworthy restoration of more than a hundred and fifty shops. Since there has been no official publication, the modern investigator must rely almost entirely on the evidence of his own eyes. The following pages are largely the result of personal observation, but the writer makes no claim to have tested the accuracy of each bit of restoration. Bibliography: C. Ricci, *Il Mercato di Traiano*, Rome, 1929 (the same article, somewhat abbreviated and illustrated by different photographs, appears in *Capitolium*, vol. 5, 1929, pp. 541–555); *idem, Via dell'Impero*, Rome 1933, pp. 115–121; G. Lugli, *Dedalo*, vol. 10, 1929–1930, pp. 527–551; *idem, MAR*, vol. 1, pp. 69–85; *idem, Centro*, pp. 299–309; A. Pernier, *III conv. st. architet.*, 1938 (pub. 1940), pp. 103–113; Crema, pp. 363–364; Frova, pp. 75–

PLAN II. TRAJAN'S MARKETS, ISOMETRIC DRAWING

W. L. MacDonald, *The Architecture of the Roman Empire* I, Yale Univ. Press.

small chambers between flights of travertine steps. This grand hemicycle (pl. 1, fig. 3) was two stories high. A course of travertine blocks following the curve of the travertine sidewalk was cut to furnish thresholds between the travertine jambs of the doorways. Between the doorways themselves the blocks doubtless served as benches along the wall. The door frames were carved with appropriate moldings. At a suitable height great arches of *bipedales* now mark the line of the barrel vaults of the rooms but in antiquity they were concealed by a series of projections resting on travertine lintels. There are faint traces of pediments surmounting these projections. A small window with a lintel arch of "upright" tiles in the face of each gave light when the shutters of the doorway were closed.[104] The eleven offices, perhaps the stations of the *arcarii*[105] were each provided with a coarse black-and-white mosaic of simple geometric design[106] and adorned with equally simple wall paintings. Two stairs, one near each end of the hemicycle, lead to the upper levels. The openings for these are narrower than those for the offices, and the arches of *bipedales* extend higher. Both of these openings apparently had travertine frames at the same level as the offices. A travertine cornice marks the transition from one story to the next and indicates the position of an *ambulacrum* resting on the vaults of the chambers below.

A windowed wall formed the façade for the *ambulacrum*. Slight projections carried upward the line of the travertine door jambs below and supported pilasters, which in their turn upheld a continuous entablature. The brick-faced pilasters had travertine bases and capitals. The entablature, entirely of tile, was composed of an architrave with fasciae and capping molding, a frieze, and a capping cornice. The frieze consisted of a series of lintel arches of "upright" *besales*, and one member of the capping cornice was dentilated. Pilasters and entablature framed a series of twenty-five arched windows[107] diversified by having a square niche with a lintel arch and a curved niche with a full arch at each extremity. A prominent tile impost supported the voussoir arches of *bipedales* which had an equally prominent capping molding of tile. The same capping molding outlined the pediments which added the final decorative element to the façade. Five arched openings, the central one under its own lunette, grouped under a broken pediment, were alternated with three of which the one in the middle was pedimented. The scheme could not be fitted exactly into the available number of openings; and the necessary adjustments were made at the east end. The chances are that this irregularity has not been noticed by one in a hundred observers. The impression remains of three broken pediments symmetrically arranged. A travertine course and a brick-faced "attic," actually the parapet for the terrace above, completed the façade for this part of the edifice. A mere trace of the parapet is original. On the inside, the outer wall terminated in an impost molding for the barrel vaulting of the *ambulacrum* and was matched by a similar one at the same height on the opposite side. The semicircular corridor came to an end on each side with a wide doorway having a small window over it. The arrangement of corridors, stairways, and shops opening off from the *ambulacrum* was purely functional.[108] Most of the doorways had travertine frames with small windows over them.[109] Over each window a relieving arch supported a lunette breaking into the barrel vault of the

77, Nash II, pp. 49–58; MacDonald, *passim*, esp. 75–93. The recent study by W. MacDonald is especially valuable for its analysis of the markets as a new form of urban architecture.

[103] Blake, *RC* II, p. 105.

[104] Marks in the travertine jambs attest the use of shutters.

[105] Lugli suggests this possibility.

[106] M. E. Blake, *MAAR*, vol. 13, 1936, pp. 78–79.

[107] An old photograph (reproduced in *Boll. d'Arte*, vol. 5, 1911, fig. 15) shows clearly that the arched curtain was added after the frame was built. Every fourth or fifth *bipedalis* in the arch was whole to furnish bond.

[108] From north to south, arched opening to a passage, arched opening to an ascending staircase, ten doorways with windows over them, two adjacent doorways with covering windows under a single barrel vault for a stairwell with two descending ramps, a higher doorway for an ascending staircase, and finally a wider doorway with the usual window to give additional light to the space containing the barrel vault supporting the stairs.

[109] Two had full arches and one a lintel arch.

[110] The procedure seems to have been to set the travertine doorway and topping window frame in place, then to lay the brick curtain up to the relieving arch of *bipedales*. The structure would then be ready for the centering of the lunetted barrel vault.

[111] The relieving arches supporting the vaulting bear no relation to the barrel vaults in the shops.

[112] All arches unless otherwise specified are of *bipedales*, probably always with only an occasional voussoir or whole tile for bonding.

[113] The lintel arches are always of this form unless otherwise specified.

[114] A sustaining wall is particularly vulnerable to injury from the pressure behind.

corridor.[110] The concrete vaulting contained small *caementa* of seemingly miscellaneous material set in the mortar in irregular rows. As below, these chambers took the place of a sustaining wall with buttresses and must have been built before the façade. The shops were barrel-vaulted at right angles to the ambulatory,[111] and the barrel vaults were set increasingly higher in accommodation to the ascent of the Via Biberatica at the next level. The ambulatory was paved with brick in the herringbone pattern.

On each side of the grand hemicycle, a straight wall orientated with the Forum conceals a lesser hemicycle. At the northwest, this curtain wall exhibits five great windows in the lower row and three flanked by a relieving arch[112] on each side within a huge lunette in the upper tier. The windows have slightly curved lintel arches of "upright" tiles,[113] which once rested on the architrave of the window frame. The lunette is outlined in a brick molding of five or six courses. An arched doorway at the east led into a lofty vaulted semi-circular reception room, for such it must have been. At the right of the door, a relieving arch protects a small triangular sewer. The back wall once had a bench following the curve and above it three large relieving arches symmetrically placed. A second door, also arched, stood at the opposite corner. Beneath the five large windows mentioned above are five large niches—three rectangular with lintel arches, two curved with full arches. A tile impost at the top of the back wall supported the semispherical dome, in which small *caementa* were laid in rough rows before the mortar was poured over them. The extrados was stepped, and the steps faced with brick. Nothing remains of the pavement, which was probably of marble since holes in the brick facing of the wall attest the presence of a marble dado below the plastering, of which traces remain. At the southeast, the façade of a somewhat smaller hemicycle was topped by a narrower lunette outlined in similar fashion. The extrados of the semidome bears the impressions of *bipedales* (pl. 2, fig. 1). The rest of the façade was treated differently. An arched doorway in the center gave access to the chamber. A window with a low segmental arch stood over the doorway, and two similar ones flanked it on each side, but at a slightly lower level. At the extreme left, a small window with a travertine frame lighted a stairway; at the extreme right, the beginning of a double relieving arch appears and is continued around the corner (pl. 2, fig. 2). The curved wall inside shows a curious series of narrow brick piers with concrete between them, two of which seem to extend upward as "ribs" for the dome. Whether this work is original or not, it is difficult to tell.[114] At this southwest end an open flight of travertine steps led to a street at a higher level. Originally, an alcove with the double voussoir arch stood at the turn, but the lower part was soon masked by the same kind of masonry. At the top of this wall, three shops were accommodated to the ascending staircase. The inner walls show a curious arrangement as though for a series of drains. Possibly they were intended to make these shops dry enough for perishable goods. The base molding of the lunette was continued over the double arch of the alcove at the corner and then in a straight line across the façade over the arched doorways of the three shops. Over these openings travertine corbels supported the concrete vaulting of a balcony. There was a second story with four windows[115] under huge relieving arches, the doors of which opened out on to the south branch of the Via Biberatica above. Over the windows a straight line of travertine consoles once upheld a capping cornice of tile over this section of the edifice.

To the north of the ambulatory and about a meter below it, an arched opening gave admittance to another group of somewhat humbler shops. A short passage led into a corridor skirting a second apse,[116] from which a narrow corridor flanked by shops turned northward. One large shop, with the usual door and window framed in travertine, opened on to the passage; and probably the three along the curve were similarly treated. On the opposite side of the curve, low windows under relieving arches admitted ample light (pl. 3, fig. 2). Beyond the apse, shops stood on both sides of the narrow corridor leading northward, but those on the west are still blocked.[117] Three on the east exhibit doorways with lintel arches of tile and small covering windows. The rooms themselves are deep; and since they were obviously excavated out of the hillside, they were damp and particularly adapted for the storage of oil and wine. Each is supplied with a hole in the floor through which any liquid spilled could drip into a jar provided for the purpose. Relieving arches appear only where there was apparently some weakness in the foundation. There was the usual tile impost molding to carry the centering for the barrel vaults and some use of *besales* in the intrados. Beyond these shops, there was an ascending staircase and a shop with a back room fitted into the awkward space left by a change of orientation.

Between the parapet of the main hemicycle and the rear wall of a row of shops facing in the opposite direction,[118] there was a semicircular passage three meters wide, which was paved with selce mosaic. At the northwest end a doorway gave access to a flight of descending travertine stairs.[119] The head was clearly marked by travertine blocks. A window of practically the same size adjoined the doorway on the right and gave light to the first landing. Both door and window have identical segmental arches. At the opposite end, an elaborate stairwell originally presented toward the Forum a large door with a travertine frame and a pediment of brickwork. A small slit window high up above the door and another low down on the left lighted two of the ramps of the stairwell. They have sills and lintels of travertine. A row of travertine consoles, such as we have already encountered, upheld the crowning member of this wall also. An irregularly shaped court is paved with selce mosaic having a substructure of concrete resting on a subpavement of herringbone brick; this court forms the transition from the passage to the section at the south.

Probably Apollodorus found a street part way up the hill which he utilized as the center of the next building terrace. The medieval Via Biberatica, which theoretically follows its course, has roughly the shape of a pulled-out W with the central part curved. The northern branch gives the best impression to be found in Rome of an ancient street of the early second century of the Empire (pl. 2, fig. 3). At the ground level on the east side, there were six shops with lintel arches of *bipedales* under segmental relieving arches of the same having small windows between the two series.[120] Travertine corbels firmly set in the piers carried a concrete balcony on arches of the same form

[115] These probably originally had travertine frames.

[116] Since this secondary apse merely complicated the architectural scheme, reason for it should probably be sought in the configuration of the hill at this point.

[117] Consequently both the corridor and the shops on the east side are very dark.

[118] These shops will be described below.

[119] These steps mark the beginning of an elaborate system of stairways connecting all parts of the edifice.

[120] The segmental arches were so low and the windows so small that they probably were never framed in travertine.

[121] It was too narrow to have formed a public passage to the ancient street at the north.

[122] Such care in reinforcing the walls confirms the conjecture expressed above that there was some weakness in the terrain at this point.

[123] This would be the fourth from the level of the Forum.

as the relieving arches.[121] The shops were barrel-vaulted. Rows of *besales* were apparently laid across the centering, the *caementa* set between them, and mortar poured over them as the initial process in making the vault. At the first floor level, a door with a covering window under a relieving arch gave admittance to the balcony from a sort of vestibule, and five windows with lintel arches under large relieving arches supplied light to the rooms opening out of the "basilica" to the north of the street. Higher yet a row of identical windows lighted the gallery. The termination of the wall is not preserved in this higher section. On the opposite side there are five shops with travertine doorframes and small windows, also framed in travertine, under somewhat higher relieving arches. Travertine corbels attest the presence of a balcony here also. The shops are shallow with barrel vaults rising from tile imposts. The second, third, and fourth from the south display two large relieving arches in the back wall—a segmental arch with a full arch over it.[122] Near the turn, a wide doorway led to a vestibule from which one could pass by means of corridors and stairs to any part of the edifice on the west side of the street. Traces of seven windows with lintel arches remain of an upper story. We pass now to what remains behind those decorous shops. The architect had to deal with a space made irregular by the two semicircular vaults. An open corridor paved with selce mosaic skirted the first and led to an irregular court bounded on one side by the chord of the second apse, from which one can see the semicircular wall with four arched windows and a smaller one at the end. A corridor paved with herringbone brick passed behind this windowed wall with extensions to both the right and left. Doorways with windows above them, both framed in travertine, gave admittance to shops of strange shape. In the back wall of three, one recognizes the large segmental and full relieving arches seen on the other side. The next floor[123] shows very little original work. Travertine steps led up from a landing to a semicircular corridor with extensions like the one below. Doorways framed in travertine faced the corridor but had no windows over them since the rooms were amply lighted by the windows facing the Via Biberatica. There were lintel arches of *bipedales* over the travertine lintels and a lunetted barrel vault over the corridor. All the shops had barrel vaults somewhat distorted in places in accommodation to the shape of the room.

At the change in orientation to the curved part of the W on the west side of the street, a window framed in travertine, now walled up, once gave light to an odd-shaped space approached from the landing of the descending staircase mentioned above. The road shows a steady rise which was accompanied by an occasional step of travertine in the sidewalk accommodated to the different levels of the nine shops on this side of the street. The first shop retains much of its original state. It has a doorframe of travertine with a lintel arch of tiles over it, a window under a similar lintel, and finally a balcony overshadowing all. An impost molding in the wall opposite the door and two large corbels at the same level on each side of the travertine architrave of the door once supported a mezzanine floor lighted not only by the window over the door but also by a slit window in the back wall. What remains of the second shop is like the first except that it was lower. Little is left of the others. The line of shops ends in the stairwell mentioned above, which presents on this side a large doorway framed in travertine, a flanking window at the left and one above. The capping cornice supported by travertine consoles already noted on the other face of the north wing was continued on this side also.

On the opposite side of the street, one encounters at the north first the end of the edifice facing the north branch, then a low brick-faced substructure masking somewhat the change in orientation. The end of the building had a door on to a small triangular space on the top of this podium and above it travertine corbels to support a balcony at the end of the west gallery of the "basilica." The podium had an opening framed in travertine for an oblique flight of steps leading to the "basilica" and three other openings wide enough to have had travertine frames to shallow shops. In spite of the rise of the street in front, the same height is maintained for the slightly curved lintel arches over the doorways. The first, being higher than the others, had a small window between two of these segmental arches. Two units had this substructure in common. The first was a transitional element of two stories behind the "basilica." The wall was pierced by two windows, one skewed inward to light the stairs, the other, in a bay at the end of the great hall above.[124] Between the hall and the next unit there was a roughly triangular open space masked by this wall. The three-story unit was a purely functional edifice with large windows above the first opening in the basement and three smaller ones in a line for each story in the rest. Windows were added wherever they were needed to light the interior.[125] All were probably framed in travertine. Travertine consoles supported the capping cornice. The unit presented an oblique face to the triangular court mentioned above. On this side, the second story shows an arched doorway, an arched window, and a large square window with a travertine frame;[126] for the floor above it, two large windows[127] each with a smaller window above it[128] for an upper floor. A string cornice of tile separated the two main floors and the same capping cornice terminated this face also.[129]

A common balcony supported on corbels of travertine brought together two other units. The first presents to the Via Biberatica four doorways framed in travertine with four windows, not identical in size, at the upper level (pl. 2, fig. 4).[130] The windows were topped with lintel arches of tile. The thresholds are progressively higher as the street ascends. None of the façade is preserved above the balcony, but much remains of a second façade facing an upper street. It presents no peculiarities not noted in the rest of the structure. The next change in orientation is marked by a flight of travertine steps to this upper level with two ramps at right angles to each other. The oblique lintel arch of *bipedales* carrying the second ramp is clearly visible within the first of four great arches on spur walls supporting an open paved area above. A great arched passage between this and the edifice at the south end of the whole complex, which has already been described,[131] makes the transition to the south branch of the W. It has been largely restored in modern times. Some of the voussoirs in the first and second arches over the passage are original. The damaged condition of the arches shows clearly that the face was of broken *bipedales* with every fifth one whole

[124] This has a travertine lintel with a tile lintel over it.

[125] There was an extra one at the extreme right in the second story and two at the mezzanine level between the second and third stories.

[126] This has been restored with a straight lintel of tiles over the travertine architrave.

[127] Low segmental arches were used in the modern restoration. They probably contained travertine frames.

[128] Straight lintel arches of tile appear in the restoration.

[129] See *Capitolium* (vol. 5, 1929, p. 549) for a photograph. There were two rooms with travertine doorframes along this façade, and a corner room of irregular shape with a blocked doorway obviously leading to rooms on the front face.

[130] Whether they had travertine frames is incapable of proof.

[131] See above, pp. 22–23.

[132] These shops were probably beyond the limit of the state-controlled Mercato.

[133] The outer wall also terminated in a segmental arch under the vaulting.

[134] There was an open court between the great hall and the next unit.

[135] G. Giovannoni, *II cong. st. rom.*, vol. 1, 1931, pp. 283-285.

[136] The doors between the rooms reveal the slightly curved lintel arches of *bipedales* which presuppose in this case a wooden doorframe.

to make a bond. The capping cornice on travertine consoles was the same as that used on the two sides of the southern building.

Beyond this arched passage, the Via Biberatica descended to a street (Salita del Grillo) crossing the Quirinal farther to the east. The shops fronting this branch on the right rest on the vaults of the shops at the lower level which we have already described. The relieving arches of *bipedales* which crown the openings maintain a constant level so that the doorways are increasingly higher as the road descends. These shops are extremely well lighted by large windows opening on the street below. The doorframes have disappeared in three, but the fourth has a travertine frame with a lintel arch of tile above it and higher still a window framed in travertine under its own segmental arch beneath a relieving arch similar to those over the other three doorways. It is not now apparent why this particular opening needed so much protection. The line of travertine consoles which once supported the capping cornice appears on this side also. The merest trace of shops appears on the left side of the Via Biberatica; and such remains as there are of the shops which once faced the street below the Salita del Grillo are concealed for the most part under later masonry.[132]

We have already mentioned an oblique flight of steps which led up from the Via Biberatica to the great hall, now known as the Basilica Traiana (pl. 3, fig. 3). The main entrance to it was, however, under the great arch facing Via Quattro Novembre. An arched window on each side at a higher level completed this façade. At the other end, segmental arches[133] helped to support the quadripartite vaulting of two bays under the transverse gallery mentioned above. The stairs came up into the right bay; a door with a travertine frame and a covering window, also framed in travertine, stood in the bay to the left. It opened into a corridor to the next unit.[134] The space above the gallery was probably left open. Stout brick-faced piers terminating in huge travertine corbels formed the visible support for the six bays of the cross vaulting.[135] Between the piers, there were identical shop fronts on both sides. The six rooms on the west were intercommunicating[136] and very light not only from the wide doorways and covering windows framed in travertine, but also from the windows facing the north branch of the Via Biberatica. The first five on the east were independent and very deep and dark. Between them and the retaining wall of the hill, a space was left, perhaps for storage, which would, however, have obviated some of the dampness from the earth behind. In place of the sixth shop two adjacent doorways gave admittance respectively to an ascending stairway and the storage space behind it. It is possible here to see the oblique lintel arch of *bipedales* with the curved end which helped to carry the stairs. Beyond the stairs, there was another shop. All these chambers were barrel-vaulted. The face of the vault appears as a relieving arch at the top of the curtain between the piers. Some of the shops show arches of tile embedded in the concrete to help support a recessed wall above. All were laid on a lining of *bipedales*. Segmental arches stretched from the continuation of the great piers to the pilasters in the wall of the upper tier of shops over the open gallery on each side. These arches are the forerunners of the ramping buttress. The shops of the upper tier were shallower by the width of the gallery, but the shop fronts were the same as those below. On the east side, there was yet another story marked by small windows under a concrete balcony supported by travertine corbels. The spaces between the piers were left open so that light poured down on the great hall below.

The stairs from the "basilica" led up to a group of rooms well adapted to serve as offices for the Administration. An apsed room[137] with three windows facing the Via Biberatica[138] would have made a pleasant office for the director himself. One wall was given a narrow doorway under a straight lintel arch of tiles at one end and a wide one with a low segmental arch at the other; both were included under an enormous relieving arch. The barrel vault consisted of rough rows of small pieces of tufa set in a light mortar. A trapezoidal room led into a little court, which exhibits one wall decorated with a semicircular niche between rectangular ones beneath a projecting molding of tiles (pl. 3, fig. 4). Great arches[139] opened into a single room on each side, also fitted with the same arrangement of niches. It has been suggested that the central niche in each case was intended for a statue, the others for cases containing the archives. This group of rooms could be approached also from the east through an ornate entrance at the upper level.[140] It is quite possible that these rooms were added by Hadrian.[141] Even so, they may have been included in the original plan.

A roadway, probably earlier than the Mercati,[142] took a tortuous course across the Quirinal higher than the Via Biberatica. It rose rapidly from the front of the "basilica," turned abruptly to skirt its east side, swerved eastward, and after a short flight of steps made another south turn to the paved area approached by the steps from the Via Biberatica of which we have already made mention.[143] The wall at this level at the east side of the "basilica" was unbroken except for an elaborate pedimented doorway (pl. 3, fig. 1) framed in peperino,[144] which formed the official entrance for our hypothetical directors, and two windows. It terminated in the capping molding upheld by travertine consoles that marked the top of various units in the whole complex. An analysis of what remains of the other façades facing this crooked street on the west adds nothing to our knowledge of Trajanic practices. The doorways led to odd-shaped rooms resulting from frequent changes in orientation. There are signs of many modifications. For our purpose it is not necessary to attempt to resolve the tangle of wall on the other side of the street.[145] A cistern is clearly traceable. The water, a necessity in this kind of market, was supplied by the Marcia.[146]

The Market of Trajan gives a fine opportunity to see how Trajan's builder adapted brick-faced concrete to an unusual site.[147] No foundations have been revealed. The concrete core for the walls, at least in the lower part, contains a brick aggregate with an admixture of dark tufa in small pieces laid in rough rows. The brick fragments are the crushed remains of the triangles of the Neronian and Flavian period. The mortar is composed of medium coarse, predominately red pozzolana and moderately clean lime. The bricks in the facing are yellowish red, very hard with sharp edges where they have not been chipped off. Disregarding for the moment the finer bricks used in the upper story of the main hemicycle, we can establish for the rest a range in thickness from 3.4 cm. to 3.9 cm. The mortar joints are close, averaging

[137] The wall with the apse is faced with brick to a higher level than the side walls so that the half-dome is lower than it otherwise would be.

[138] The facing arch rests on tile imposts but the voussoirs are carelessly shaped.

[139] The archways were lined with marble or travertine. Above them was a tile cornice and the holes by which some decorative member was fastened to the wall.

[140] See below.

[141] Ricci, op. cit., p. 18.

[142] Traces of earlier reticulate work appear in its upper reaches.

[143] See above, p. 25.

[144] Possibly this doorway was salvaged from some building destroyed to make rooms for the Mercato at this level.

[145] An arch made of a double curve of *bipedales* may be mentioned in passing. This area may also have been the limits of the Mercato itself.

[146] Van Deman, *Aqueducts*, p. 143.

[147] Technical details are from Dr. Van Deman's notes combined with personal observation.

a little over a centimeter, and the mortar is the same as that employed in the core except for being a little finer. Bonding courses appear throughout the structure, but are used with more regularity in the lower parts. The *bipedales* used for them are either a lighter yellowish red or a clear yellow and are somewhat thicker than the bricks (4–4.5 cm.). Relieving arches in the body of the structure occur only when considered necessary to give stability and are sometimes of great size. The same kind of tiles were employed in them as in bonding courses. Lintel arches of "upright" tiles, segmental, and full arches are found over openings (pl. 3, fig. 2). Tile relieving arches are regularly used over travertine lintels, but, though found, are less common over tile lintels. Oblique lintel arches of *bipedales* were used in at least two instances to support staircases on one side. It is probable that the practice of making every fourth or fifth voussoir deeper to form a bond was common.[148] Except for the rooms devoted to the Direction there was no use of ornamental niches. It is, however, the ornamental brickwork of the upper floor of the great hemicycle which makes the deepest impression on the visitor. Although such a decorative use of brickwork was not entirely new, the succession of pediments and lunettes combined with broken pediments certainly was new and without doubt had its influence on the architects of the Renaissance. The bricks here are thinner (3.1 cm. to 3.5 cm.) and finer grained. They were cut with a projection of the face at the top to make possible an almost invisible joint. Cornices were hacked and not molded.[149] One was dentilated. It is possible that the lower story was stuccoed over, but the upper one certainly was not. Travertine was used freely for steps, door and window frames, corbels, and consoles.[150] Most of the chambers were barrel-vaulted. In places *besales* and, in one case at least, *bipedales* were laid on the wooden centering before the aggregate was set in place and a light mortar poured over it. Rudimentary "ribbing" is also found. The semicircular corridors have lunetted barrel vaults, and a magnificent series of cross vaults covered the great hall. The lack of an official publication of this vast complex has made necessary a disproportionately long analysis of its structural elements. There are, however, few places where one feels nearer to the ancient Romans than when lingering over these dim corridors and shops.

There can be no question, I think, that the Mercato was state-controlled and to be connected logically with the Forum.[151] Brick stamps[152] indicate that it was finished for the most part[153] before the Forum, though both must have been a-building at the same time. Its function was primarily to provide the wine, oil, and wheat which were distributed to the people at a reduced rate or in the case of grain sometimes gratuitously. It was under the control of the Praefectus Urbi and would have required a great many offices in addition to the rooms given over to the sale and storage of commodities. The great hall suggests all the noise and confusion of an exchange as well as the subdued murmur of the *congiaria*, or free distribution,[154] which took place in the presence of the emperor himself. We have located the private quarters of the administration and seen where the *arcarii* or some other lesser officers carried on their business. I am not entirely convinced that some of

[148] The double voussoir "ring" occurs twice.

[149] A tentative use of ornamental string cornices of tile in the ordinary brickwork may be mentioned in passing.

[150] The use of peperino in one of the doorframes is disconcerting.

[151] Lugli, *Centro*, pp. 306–309.
[152] Bloch, *Bolli*, pp. 49–57.

[153] It is conceivable that it was enlarged at the top by Hadrian.

[154] Boethius, *Riv. Roma*, vol. 9, 1931, pp. 447–454.

the shops in the periphery were not let out by contract to other merchants not otherwise under the control of the State.

BATHS

Thermae Traiani

The great Baths of Trajan on the Oppian[155] were built at a somewhat earlier period than the Mercato and may or may not have been designed by Apollodorus.[156] The fire of A.D. 104 which seriously damaged the Domus Aurea prepared a place for them.[157] They were dedicated A.D. 109,[158] and the Aqua Traiana[159] which was dedicated two days later was constructed probably partly to supply an additional source of water for them. Brick-faced concrete was chosen for their masonry. Brick stamps[160] confirm what is obvious to the eye that all the parts belonged to the same building period. Conversely, the Baths are invaluable for supplying a list of stamps that can be dated within narrow limits.

When the architect decided to give the Baths a northeast-southwest exposure[161] so as to capture the maximum amount of sunshine, he needed a large area on which to build. Although advantage was taken of some rooms and corridors at the lower level of the Domus Aurea to service the Baths above, the major part of that level was reduced to a mere substructure. Doors and windows were stopped up with concrete either unfaced or faced with brick; new foundation walls were built where necessary; and vaults were pierced so that the rooms could be filled with debris to make a more solid bed for the superstructure. The Trajanic brickwork can easily be distinguished from the Neronian by the quality of the bricks, which are more homogeneous, of finer texture, narrower, and, for the most part, made of broken tiles rather than having the triangular shape of the earlier bricks. The color is not essentially different. The new foundation walls under the great exedra display neat insets of reticulate work in a brick frame[162] like that in the Trajanic work at Porto.[163] This type of masonry is not found in Rome in any other important work of the period of Trajan, except possibly in an addition to the Domus Tiberiana along the Nova Via.[164]

This is not the place to enter into a minute description of the rooms in the Baths themselves. Suffice it to say that the architect here established the norm for all the great Baths that followed by placing the rooms devoted to bathing ·in the center, flanking them with gymnasia, encircling all this central part by a garden with rooms in the periphery for the milder forms of recreation, and placing a large exedra opposite the entrance which could serve as a theater for sports and other kinds of entertainment (plan III). Little of all this remains today,[165] but that little is important for its revelation of Trajanic methods of building between A.D. 104 and 109. The entrance faced the Colosseum. For a knowledge of the central unit, we are dependent, for the most part, on Renaissance drawings. Enough brick stamps have come from the region to prove that it was coeval with the rest. The so-called *tepidarium* at the center is said to have been the first instance of a cross vaulting carried on columns.

The plan called for a number of apses in addition to the great exedra. Fortunately for our purpose, three are preserved, though in a somewhat

[155] Platner-Ashby, pp. 534-535; Lugli, *MAR, Suppl.*, pp. 103–104; *idem, Centro*, pp. 369–372; Crema, pp. 403–404; Frova, pp. 73–74; *FUR*, p. 69; Nash II, pp. 472–477.

[156] Pausanias, 5, 12, 6. For the ascription of them to Domitian by the chronographers, see Blake, *RC* II, p. 98. Paribeni (*Acc. L. Rend.*, ser. 7, vol. 4, 1943, p. 128) considers them more in the style of Rabirius, the architect of Domitian.

[157] Werner, *De incendiis*, p. 34. The lower floor of the Domus Aurea shows no signs of fire (*Bull. Com.*, vol. 67, 1939, p. 192).

[158] Degrassi, *Fasti O.*, no. 22, pp. 198–199, 229.

[159] See below, pp. 274–275.

[160] Bloch, *Bolli*, pp. 36–49.

[161] See H. Sedlmayr, *Palladio*, vol. 1, 1937, p. 153, fig. 5. The same plan occurs in Gu. de Angelis d'Ossat, *Tecnica delle Terme*, p. 16.

[162] Anderson-Spiers-Ashby, pl. 16 [1]; Platner-Ashby, fig. 16.

[163] See below, pp. 286 ff.

[164] See below, p. 39.

[165] Lugli (*MAR, Suppl.*, pp. 103–104; *Centro*, p. 369) attributes the disappearance of the rest largely to ignorance of how to counteract the stresses of mighty vaults.

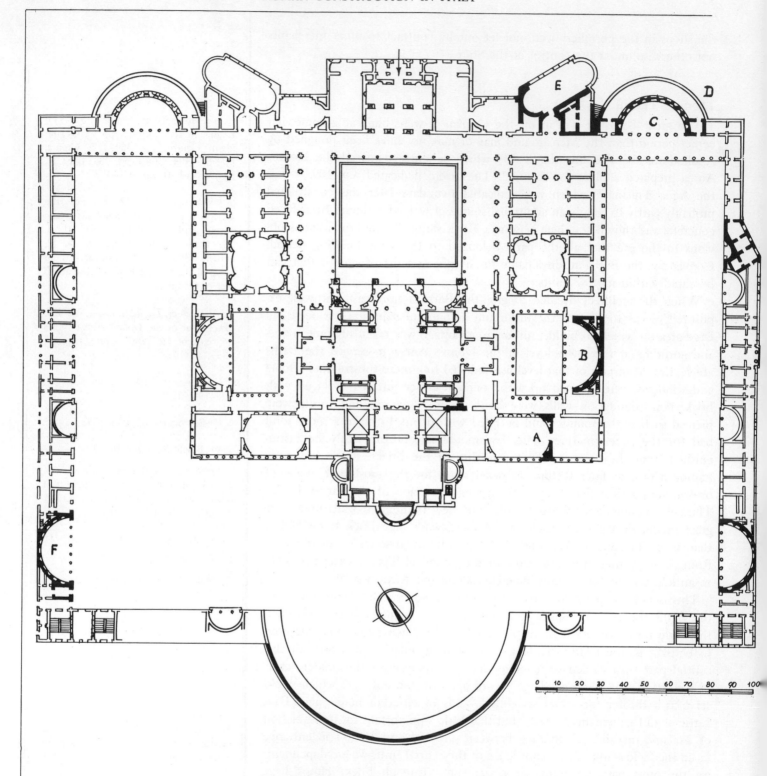

PLAN III. TRAJAN'S BATHS

I. Gismondi

ruinous state. In C, (pl. 4, fig. 2), on the northeast side near the east angle, an alternation of curved and rectangular niches stood a meter or more above the floor of the apse.[166] The curved niches were topped with half domes, each faced with an arch of *bipedales*; the rectangular ones, with the usual lintel arch of "upright" *bipedales*[167] under a relieving arch of the same somewhat higher up in the curtain. This inner wall exhibits light reddish yellow bricks[168] and terminates in an impost of tile. Enough of the vault remains to show a hexagonal coffering of tiles, three layers thick, which was plastered and painted. The thick wall was broken on the outside also by niches. What remains of the facing shows bricks, somewhat redder than those used on the inside, which were certainly made, for the most part, from broken tiles. The arches over the niches in their present state reveal that every fourth or fifth tile was a whole *bipedalis* to form a bond, whereas the rest were broken pieces that did not display their fragmentary condition on the outside. A stringcourse of tile divided the wall into two parts. A second wall, following the curve at a discreet distance, indicates the presence of an ambulatory on the outside, which was doubtless covered with a barrel vault. This would add somewhat to the stability of the half dome within. Apse B connected with the palestra on the northeast side exhibited seven broad niches rather widely spaced, but otherwise similar to those just described.[169] The semidome was treated in the same fashion except that the coffers are square instead of hexagonal. This apse was included in straight walls. The wall at the back was part of the perimetric wall of the central unit and was unbroken except for two small windows. Bonding courses of yellow *bipedales* are conspicuous here.

The most interesting of the extant parts is the apsed library (F) near the west corner (pl. 4, fig. 1).[170] It was not an isolated structure, but was included in a group of rooms within a rectangle jutting out from the perimetric wall, which ended in a tower at the corner. On the inside it exhibits two tiers of niches. The central niche of the lower tier, intended no doubt for a statue of the tutelary divinity, is wider and higher and has a low segmental arch at the top. The five on each side for the bookcases are identical, each with a lintel arch of "upright" tiles[171] protected by its own relieving arch.[172] Between the relieving arches, there are square depressions, each topped by a small lintel arch of "upright" tiles, intended to hold the corbels for a balcony to give access to the niches in the second tier.[173] The central niche of this upper tier has a higher sill in accommodation to the niche below, and is wider than the other ten in the same row. They have the same lintel arches, but the relieving arches over them extend beyond the lintels until they meet in the space between the niches. There are similar depressions between these arches, those flanking the central niche being double, which may have anchored the entablature over columns supported by the corbels below. The brickwork terminates in a capping molding of tile, above which the beginning of a large semidome is still preserved. The walls are faced, for the most part, with triangles made from slightly reddish yellow tiles similar to the tiles used for the various arches, but brick stamps prove that they were the output of different brickyards.[174] In spite of its neat appearance all of this brickwork was undoubtedly concealed from view.

[166] It probably contained a pool.

[167] Brick stamps from arches, see Bloch, *op. cit.*, pp. 40–41, nos. 84–86.

[168] Brick stamps from walls, *ibid.*, nos. 87–89.

[169] Brick stamps from walls, *ibid.*, nos. 99–108; in arches, *ibid.*, nos., 92–98.

[170] There was undoubtedly a corresponding library near the south corner.

[171] All the arches are composed of *bipedales*.

[172] All relieving arches are skew arches.

[173] Other square depressions cutting into the relieving arches must belong to later modifications.

[174] Bloch, *op. cit.*, p. 39.

[175] See below, p. 290.

[176] Whole *bipedales* serve as bonding members in arches made of broken pieces.

[177] A floor with a layer of *opus signinum* beneath a coarse mosaic pavement sloped to assure drainage still remains at the upper level.

[178] *Arch. cl.,* vol. 8, 1956, pp. 53–55.

[179] Recent excavations (*The New York Times,* October 16, 1966) confirm that these chambers are 40 yards long, 7 wide, and 9 high. This same article reports that brick stamps enabled the excavators to date the construction to A.D. 103 and identify the builder as one Herennio Pollione (*sic*). The microfilmed edition of the *Times* omits almost all the important details.

[180] The measurements are Dr. Van Deman's.

[181] Nash I, pp. 52–54.

[182] Platner-Ashby, p. 433.

These Baths show Trajanic work before it had become entirely standardized. Insets of reticulate work appear in the foundation walls, a type of construction not often seen in Trajanic masonry in Rome. The core of the walls regularly contains an aggregate of broken tile. The majority of the bricks employed in the facing were made by sawing faces in broken reddish yellow tiles, most of which were 3.5 cm. in thickness though specimens occur up to 4 cm., but triangles are to be found among them. Furthermore, yellow triangles like those in use at Porto[175] form the entire inner facing of the extant library. The bricks and tiles are mostly fine-grained, though some contain coarser inclusions. The mortar is rather coarse showing red pozzolana with a slight admixture of black. It varies from red to gray. The joints range from 1.2 to 1.5 cm. The use of *bipedales* for bonding courses is not general,[176] though they appear regularly in impost moldings for vaults. Lintel arches of "upright" tiles over niches are always protected by relieving arches which may start at, above, or below the lintel arch. Relieving arches are not common elsewhere. Small pieces of yellow tufa form the aggregate of the vaults. Coffered ceilings had already appeared in the Domitianic "Stadium" on the Palatine, but not in the large hexagons and squares which appear here. Apparently the use of columns to support a cross vault was a new development.

Every great Bath needed a reserve of water. Because the enormous cistern known as Sette Sale or Le Capocce, though somewhat apart, was orientated with the Domus Aurea, it has long been held that it was Neronian and merely appropriated by the builder of the Thermae Traiani.[177] This view seemed reasonable to me until I visited the site. I was immediately convinced that the vaulting with the imprints of the *besales* once clinging to its soffit was Trajanic, built perhaps to sustain an upper terrace which was not there before. It was so dark that I was ready to reserve judgment on the wall construction. Since then Dr. Castagnoli has discovered Trajanic stamps[178] in essential parts of the walls. The great reservoir actually consisted of nine parallel chambers[179] terminating at a curved wall at one end to facilitate the circulation of the water. The partition walls were each pierced with four openings so arranged that the water had to flow diagonally from one to another. Thus the force of the current was broken somewhat and the water forced to deposit its impurities. Pavement and walls were lined with *opus signinum*; and the ceiling was a series of barrel vaults. The curved end wall and the adjacent side walls were reinforced externally by niched buttresses; the fourth wall, with pilasters at the end of the partitions. The walls are of brick-faced concrete. The bricks range from 3.7 cm. to 4.3 cm. in thickness with the majority 4–4.2 cm., in length from 21 cm. to 28 cm.; the mortar joints, from 1 cm. to 1.6 cm.[180] A branch of the Aqua Traiana[181] was probably the main source of water. It is quite possible that this took the place of an earlier Neronian cistern.

Thermae Suranae

Trajan himself before his adoption lived on the Aventine in what is named the Privata Traiani in the Notitia.[182] Topographers have usually located it under Sant' Anselmo where some Trajanic stamps have been found;[183] but van Essen has marshalled the evidence that it was under Santa Prisca. A wealthy friend of his, L. Licinius Sura by name, dwelt on the Aventine near the Temple of Aventine Diana, whence he could view the games in the Circus Maximus,[184] and constructed a gymnasium probably nearby, for the use of the Roman people.[185] Aurelius Victor[186] credits Trajan with founding Baths in honor of Sura. Paribeni suggests that Sura at his death may have left his house to Trajan, who made it the nucleus of the Baths named after him.[187] Four fragments of the Forma Urbis Severiana[188] have been fitted together to show a street having a line of shops with an arcade in front as well as a colonnaded court marked BAL(nea) SVRAE. To the north, separated from the rest by a wall, was a relatively small colonnaded court behind another row of shops opening on to the same arcade, which could have served as a gymnasium if half of it was not taken up with a square edifice of some sort. This may have been a later addition. The street with the shops could have run between the ancient equivalents of Via di Santa Prisca and Via di Santa Sabina. Remains of a Bath came to light in 1930 or thereabouts when the Castello dei Cesari was demolished just north of Santa Prisca.[189] Its walls were of brick-faced concrete.[190] Remains of the aqueduct which supplied it, a branch of the Marcia rebuilt by Trajan, were discovered near the Casa della Gioventù Italiana del Littorio at about the same time. This site accords well with the position given to these Baths in the Regionary Catalogues as well as with the allusion in Martial. Part of an architrave inscription[191] recording a restoration of these Baths almost certainly by Gordianus III[192] was discovered in a fifth-century doorway at Santa Sabina, which may, however, have been brought from anywhere in the vicinity; but remains of a Bath of the second or third century were found under the monastery of Santa Sabina, that Colini[193] is inclined to identify with the establishment built by Trajan in memory of Sura. The conjecture has little to recommend it. The date is not surely Trajanic, and they are too far removed from the dwelling of Sura if credence is to be placed in Martial's remarks.

Places of Amusement

Literary, numismatic, and epigraphical evidence shows that Trajan was interested in seeing that the people had adequate buildings in good repair for all forms of entertainment in which they delighted. By one of the many ironies of fate very little remains of this contribution of Trajan to the enjoyment of his people.

Circus Maximus, Restoration

The renovation of the Circus Maximus was one of the earliest of Trajan's building exploits. Cassius Dio[194] gives him the credit for enlarging and embellishing it and by inference repairing it where its walls had crumbled away. This sounds like a much more far-reaching restoration than the rebuilding of the long sides burned, according to Suetonius,[195] in the time of Domitian. Pausanias[196] lists it among the buildings of Trajan. An inscription[197] gives the date of the enlargement, A.D. 103, and coins commemorating it are ascribable to that date or a little later.[198] Stone from the Naumachia of Domitian went into its repair.[199] Unfortunately, most of the walls brought to light in

[183] G. Gatti, *Not. sc.*, 1892, p. 478; *idem, Not. sc.*, 1893, p. 32. For Privata Traiani under Santa Prisca, see below, pp. 75–77.

[184] Martial, 6, 64, 12–13.

[185] Cassius Dio, 68, 15, 3.

[186] Sextus Aurelius Victor, *De Caesaribus*, 13, 8; *Epit.*, 13, 6.

[187] R. Paribeni, *Not. sc.*, 1920, p. 142.

[188] *FUR*, p. 79, pl. xxiii. For a slightly different location for these baths see Nash II, p. 467, and Vermaseren and van Essen, p. 10, fig. 2, and p. 11.

[189] Platner-Ashby, pp. 532–533; Lugli, *loc. cit.*

[190] Photographs from the Comune are my only source of information regarding it.

[191] Paribeni, *op. cit.*, pp. 141–142.

[192] Julius Capitolinus, *SHA, Gordiani Tres*, 32, 5.

[193] A. M. Colini, *Bull. Com.*, vol. 66, 1938, p. 286; Lugli, *MAR*, vol. 3, pp. 54 55. Parker's identification (*Prim. fort.*, pl. 10) is surely erroneous.

[194] Cassius Dio, 68, 7, 2.

[195] Suetonius, *Domitianus*, 5.

[196] Pausanias, 5, 12, 6. At least his building for horse races probably means the Circus Maximus.

[197] *CIL*, vol. 6 (1), no. 955.

[198] Strack, *Reichsprägung*, vol. 1, pp. 145–147, pl. 6, fig. 391; *BMC, Emp.*, vol. 3, pl. 32, nos. 2, 3, 4.

[199] Suetonius, *loc. cit.*

200 A. M. Colini, *Bull. Com.*, vol. 62, 1934, pp. 175–177.

201 Lugli, *Centro*, pp. 605–606.

202 C. Pietrangeli, *Bull. Com.*, vol. 68, 1940, p. 234.

203 *CIL*, vol. 6 (4, 2), no. 32255. See also, Platner-Ashby, p. 6; Lugli, *Centro*, p. 324.

204 E. Gatti, *Not. sc.*, 1916, p. 228; Platner-Ashby, pp. 502–503.

205 Colini and Cozza, *Ludus Magnus*; Nash II, pp. 24–26.

206 Blake, *RC II*, p. 110.

207 Colini and Cozza, *op. cit.*, pp. 145–146.

208 Suetonius, *Domitianus*, 5.

209 Paribeni (*op. cit.*, pp. 30–31) suggests with less plausibility that Trajan merely diverted material intended for the naumachia and then later completed it. Still, it was already in working order for seafights to take place in it before Domitian.

210 *Vatican Report*, pp. 13–14; Toynbee-Perkins, p. 6. The walls are faced with reticulate.

211 Ch. Huelsen, *Acc. P. Diss.*, ser. 2, vol. 8, 1903, pp. 360–374; Jordan-Huelsen, pp. 660–661. He is followed by Ashby (Platner-Ashby, p. 358) and Lugli (*MAR*, vol. 3, pp. 688–690); *idem, Tecnica*, p. 523.

212 G. Gatti, *Not. sc.*, 1899, p. 436; *idem, Bull. Com.*, vol. 39, 1911, pp. 204–205.

213 *Vatican Report*, p. 13; Toynbee-Perkins, pp. 5–6.

214 Degrassi, *Fasti O.*, no. 22, pp. 200, 201, 229.

215 Aelius Spartianus, *SHA, Hadrianus*, 9, 1.

216 Paribeni, *op. cit.*, pp. 32–35.

fairly recent excavations had to be covered over again before they could be adequately studied. Colini[200] reports red bricks, 3.5 to 4.1 cm. thick, made from broken tiles and mortar joints about 1 cm., which he apparently considered Domitianic. The description sounds more like the bricks of the Trajanic period. Lugli,[201] on the other hand, describes the Trajanic brickwork as yellow and reinforced with travertine. Pietrangeli[202] contents himself with noting the excellence of the brickwork.

Amphitheatrum Flavium, Modification

Inscriptional evidence[203] indicates that Trajan made some improvement in the cavea of the Colosseum, but nothing further is known of it. Passing mention may be made of the Summum Choragium,[204] although it cannot be dated more precisely than prior to Hadrian. Slight remains of it came to light in 1912 on the south side of Via Labicana between the Ludus Magnus and San Clemente. They consisted of concrete foundations, brick-faced piers, and a marble floor.

Ludus Magnus

Excavations started in 1937 and resumed in 1959–1960[205] have shown that Trajan was responsible for extensive rebuilding of the Ludus Magnus (plan IV) on the design initiated by Domitian.[206] Brick stamps[207] indicate that the Trajanic work was carried out about A.D. 112 and that Hadrian completed the structure that was built on Domitian's plan. Later rebuilding and modern reinforcements make it difficult to identify the nature of the Trajanic construction. Near the bottom and the top of the back walls of the cavea broad relieving arches of *bipedales* (pl. 5, fig. 2) are visible. The core of the mass which supported the seats consisted of broken tiles packed tightly and laid almost in layers. Triangles were used in the facings (pl. 5, fig. 1).

Naumachia

We shall probably never know what prompted Trajan to take stone from the Naumachia of Domitian to repair the Circus Maximus[208] and then apparently turn about and build a naumachia of his own.[209] The destruction of the Domitianic building would, of course, have been welcomed with enthusiasm by the people provided that they lost nothing in its suppression. Trajan may have had in mind a site across the Tiber, where remains of a naumachia(?) came to light in 1949.[210] They were west rather than northwest of the Castel Sant' Angelo, where Huelsen[211] identified some remains[212] with the Naumachia Vaticana. These are now thought to have belonged to the Gaianum.[213] The Naumachia Traiani was completed and dedicated in A.D. 109.[214]

Theater

Spartianus[215] reports that a theater of Trajan was deliberately destroyed by Hadrian. Paribeni[216] suggests that Hadrian ordered the work suspended and such material as could be adapted to other uses be removed. He would connect with the salvage operation nine pieces of Luna marble, much of it already carved for a specific place in an edifice of mixtilinear form, and some

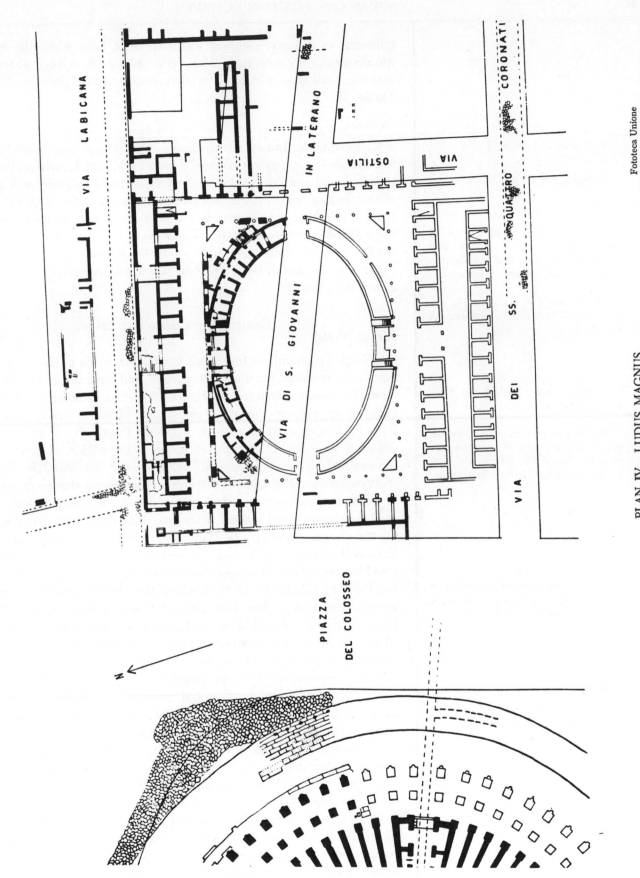

PLAN IV. LUDUS MAGNUS

fragments of alabaster columns which came to light when the *ustrina* of Montecitorio were excavated. The pieces seem to have been abandoned in antiquity, and it is possible that they were intended for the Theater of Trajan.

Odeum

[217] Cassius Dio, 69, 4, 1.

[218] Blake, *RC II*, pp. 108–109.

[219] Ashby (Platner-Ashby, p. 371) and Paribeni (*op. cit.*, p. 31) interpret the passage to mean that Apollodorus completed the Odeum of Domitian.

[220] Degrassi, *Fasti O.*, no. 32, pp. 208, 209, 239; Valentini-Zucchetti, p. 123, n. 4.

Xiphilinus, the epitomizer of Cassius Dio,[217] mentions incidentally that the odeum was a creation of Apollodorus. The article used indicates that there was only one odeum. Since the Odeum of Domitian[218] was an edifice of outstanding beauty, it may have come to be associated with the name of the great architect of Trajan after it had become a nameless monument through the *memoriae damnatio* of its founder.[219] Xiphilinus may even have interpolated the information from another less authentic source. Unfortunately the fragment of the Fasti Ostienses which may refer to its dedication cannot be dated.[220]

EDIFICES FOR COMMUNAL LIVING

Atrium Vestae

[221] Bloch, *Bolli*, pp. 67–85; Nash I, pp. 154–159.

[222] Cf. Van Deman, *Atrium Vestae*, pp. 29–42. Although the brick stamps have invalidated her dating, her work is still fundamental for construction.

Though Trajan did not find much left for him to do in the Forum proper, he was responsible for the enlargement and renovation of the Atrium Vestae[221] usually attributed to Hadrian.[222] This building more than any other as yet analyzed shows the importance of the evidence to be derived from brick stamps when properly applied. Practically all the stamps not definitely ascribable to some other phase of the edifice are found in other demonstrably Trajanic structures. The majority discovered *in situ* in the walls comes from the kilns of Rutilius Lupus, whose stamps do not appear in Hadrianic construction. Most of the others are reported from *bipedales* used in pavements and arches. A few may have come from bonding courses. Of the stamps which may be Hadrianic, only two have not been found in Trajanic buildings. Some appear in pavements, doorjambs, and steps which could be renovated without essential change, or in slight modifications clearly

[223] These occur in the mezzanine at the northeast corner and near the main stairway to the Nova Via.

ascribable to Hadrian,[223] or loose where they have a reduced value as evidence. Brick stamps show that Trajan's transformation began at the stairs behind the partition wall between shops six and seven on the north side; it added the entire extension to the east and with the help of old walls was continued along the south side to the steps leading up to the Nova Via at the northwest corner. The part added contained a group of rooms about a meter higher than the great central court.[224] It consisted of three large halls separated each from the other by three small rooms, with additional rooms at the north and south ends. The three rooms, having doorways from the central hall and wide windows toward the lateral ones, may well have

[224] This part has been largely rebuilt in modern times, but enough remains to show the construction.

served as offices for the six Vestal Virgins. The central hall or court had a transverse barrel vault at front and back, but was apparently open to the sky in the center. There were rudimentary hypocausts under the floors of at least the halls at the side. These were doubtless covered with lengthwise barrel vaults. Thus the Vestal Virgins were provided with halls suitable for receptions or state banquets both summer and winter. To Trajan they were indebted for this contribution to the amenities commensurate with the increasing luxury of life under the Empire. One unit of three rooms opening into a narrow corridor along the south side, which took the place of the old *tablinum*, may have been used for more intimate conferences. The rest of the Trajanic work is important only for the light that it sheds on methods of building. The construction is simple. A selce aggregate was employed exclusively in the foundations, and probably the usual brick aggregate in the walls. The bricks (3.3–3.7 cm. thick) were made in part from roof tiles. They are normally magenta red and of fine texture, though not properly fired. Bonding courses of yellow *bipedales* occur every twenty-one to twenty-eight courses. The openings were covered with camber arches of *bipedales* protected by relieving arches of the same. The mortar joints are regularly 1.5 to 1.75 cm. wide. Wherever it is possible to judge, only barrel vaults were used, and in them lighter tufas served as aggregate. The mortar employed was the same throughout. The pozzolana in its composition—usually red, occasionally reddish brown or gray—had been washed and sifted. Such a combination of clean pozzolana and fresh lime makes a firm mortar.

Castra Priora Equitum Singularium

Trajan instituted the Equites Singulares early in his reign[225] and, in all probability, was responsible for the barracks which housed them.[226] Numerous votive altars and inscriptions indicate its site near the Campus Caelimontanus to the northwest of the Scala Santa. One ascribable to A.D. 118[227] proves that it was in use at the beginning of the reign of Hadrian. In 1885 some remains of it were unearthed bordering an ancient street under Via Tasso. There was a niched wall with a row of pedestals and votive altars in front of it, not to mention traces of other rooms, one of which contained stairs.

Statio Cohortis V Vigilum

A series of rooms facing a court with a pavement of herringbone brick seems to belong to a Trajanic reconstruction of the Statio Cohortis V Vigilum on the Caelian.[228] The foundations were of concrete; the walls of brick and reticulate work. The bricks, made of broken tile, 3.5 to 4 cm., are the proper thickness for the Trajanic period though the joints (3 cm.) are rather wide. Travertine blocks mark where columns once stood. Inscriptions of A.D. 111 and 113,[229] marking the dedication of an altar and a shrine respectively, to a certain extent confirm the date suggested by the construction.

TIBER EMBANKMENT AND RIVER PORT

Eighteen cippi[230] have come to light in a more or less complete state to show that Trajan was responsible for a far-reaching regulation of the banks of the Tiber between A.D. 101 and 103. Their distribution proves that both sides of the river were included for practically the whole length of the ancient city. Attention has been called to the fact that none have been found in the Marmorata district at the foot of the Aventine,[231] which was certainly the most important part of the bank from the standpoint of shipping. A wall faced with quasi-reticulate work of the late Republican period runs along this entire strip.[232] Possibly, it seemed to give adequate protec-

[225] Paribeni, *Optimus Princeps*, vol. 1, pp. 187–190; vol. 2, pp. 184–185.

[226] Platner-Ashby, p. 105; A. M. Colini, *Acc. P. Mem.*, ser. 3, vol. 7, 1944, pp. 314–317.

[227] *CIL*, vol. 6 (4, 2), 31138.

[228] A. M. Colini, *Capitolium*, vol. 7, 1931, pp. 159–161; idem, *Acc. P. Mem.*, ser. 3, vol. 7, 1944, pp. 228–231.

[229] *CIL*, vol. 6 (1), 221–222.

[230] *CIL*, vol. 6 (4, 2), nos. 31549 (12 exs.), 31550 (4), 31551 (1); P. C. Sestieri, *Bull. Com.*, vol. 59, 1931, p. 213.

[231] G. Cressedi, *Not. sc.*, 1956, p. 51.

[232] *Ibid.*, pp. 45–51, *passim*.

tion so that work here was postponed until a new river port could be consolidated to care for the increased shipping made possible by the new canal from the Tiber to Trajan's port near Ostia.[233] It is unthinkable that Trajan should not eventually have had this whole region systematized. It is my conviction, based largely on a study of the old photographs,[234] that the substantial remains uncovered in 1868 belonged to that systematization. Bruzza apparently intended to publish the results of this excavation, but abandoned the attempt because of seemingly contradictory evidence. His manuscript has recently been published by Guglielmo Gatti with pertinent comment. Fortunately there are good photographs (pl. 5, fig. 3) to supplement this information.[235] The actual embankment (3.5 m. high) was inclined and faced with reticulate broken by a band of five rows of brick. In front of this, at least two triangular sections of wall blunted at the top, having the same inclination and the same type of masonry, supported ramps leading to a short flight of steps. Along the foot of the wall, there was a platform five meters wide of beaten earth and stone with a travertine curb a meter wide at the side toward the water. Three mooring blocks of travertine were placed at intervals in the top of the embankment farther downstream; one was also inserted at the top of each triangular projection. None of this construction has been seen since 1868 and so it is not possible to get further information regarding the actual method of construction. Several brick stamps were found which occur in Trajanic buildings.[236] They point to the last ten years of the reign of Trajan as the period when the river port was systematized. Farther downstream, spurs projecting from the quasi-reticulate wall make seven vaulted chambers.[237] The first and last had vaults lower than the others. These walls are faced with an entirely different type of masonry—either brick or a combination of reticulate and tufa blocks which has been found occasionally in Hadrianic but never in Trajanic work. Four Hadrianic cippi[238] have been found in this general region. Cressedi is inclined, therefore, to ascribe this whole section of the embankment, including the part described by Bruzza, to Hadrian. It would seem more likely to me that Hadrian merely added this part.[239]

Connected with this river port, there were great warehouses of every period. Whereas some may have been the result of private enterprise, most were probably constructed or at any rate controlled by the state. Remains of one such have come to light in the area south of the Porticus Aemilia on the bank of the Tiber.[240] Only two of the rooms[241] along the river were uncovered. The partition walls alone appear to be original. They have concrete foundations and an excellent facing of reticulate (tesserae 7.5 cm. × 7.5 cm.) reinforced by brick. There are three bands of brick—one at the bottom, one at the top, and one halfway between. The last-named is cut by an enormous relieving arch of *bipedales*, which stretches the entire length of the wall. The middle band and, to judge from the photographs, the bottom band as well are composed of bricks made from the same type of yellow *bipedales* as form the relieving arch. The upper band which served as the impost for the vault was made of a different kind. As a further refinement, tesserae outlined both sides of the relieving arch. These walls were entirely independent of the back wall, which was apparently built when a

[233] See below, p. 286.

[234] One of Verzaschi is reproduced by Gu. Gatti, *Bull. Com.*, vol. 62, 1934, pl. 5; *idem, Bull. Com.*, vol. 64, 1936, p. 55; Lugli, *MAR*, vol. 3, p. 598; one of Parker, by Castagnoli, *Bull. Com.*, vol. 73, 1949–1950, p. 174, fig. 36.

[235] Gu. Gatti, *Bull. Com.*, vol. 64, 1936, pp. 55–82; Nash I, pp. 380–386.

[236] Bloch, *Bolli*, p. 346.

[237] Cressedi, *op. cit.*, pp. 46–52.

[238] *CIL*, vol. 6 (4, 2), no. 31552 (3 exs.); Cressedi, *loc. cit.*, p. 50. One of the four found near Ponte Rotto gives some support to Cressedi's theory.

[239] Another section of the embankment, faced with reticulate reinforced by bands of brick, was uncovered on the right bank in the region known as Pietra Papa. A flight of travertine steps took the place of the ramps. See G. Jacopi, *Bull. Com.*, vol. 68, 1940, pp. 97–98.

[240] Cressedi, *Not. sc.*, 1956, pp. 19–22.

[241] These are M, N in the above account.

new warehouse was erected at a higher level. The fallen vaults show a tufa aggregate. These rooms were at too low a level to avoid floods and were gradually filled in antiquity in a vain attempt to make them safe from inundation. Farther back, two other chambers[242] seem to belong to the same building period and perhaps to the same edifice. A connecting door was covered with a voussoir arch of *bipedales*. These rooms were also filled with earth. Many triangular bricks in the filling bear witness to an earlier structure demolished in the vicinity.[243] The type of construction is certainly Trajanic.[244] Another warehouse north of this seems to have been modified in the early years of the second century.[245]

At the opposite end of the City, just east of the Porta Septimiana on the right bank, the Aurelianic wall[246] passed over a great Trajanic warehouse for the storing and distributing wine wholesale. Remains were found and destroyed when the banks of the Tiber were reorganized in the eighteen-seventies.[247] An inscription furnishes the identification and the date A.D. 102.[248] There was a series of vaulted chambers at the level of the river which were probably used for storage and above it a long double porticus facing in both directions. The columns were of travertine covered with stucco to simulate fluting. Dolia were found in the court at the rear and pieces of dolia everywhere in the excavations. To the north of this at a different orientation, there was a large warehouse of a type familiar at Ostia.[249] It apparently had at least two rows of long narrow chambers for storage on the side nearest to the river, with central courts flanked by somewhat smaller rooms behind them. A row of shops faced a street on the north. How far it extended inland is unknown. The walls were faced with reticulate reinforced by bands of brick. Possibly these were the Cellae Arruntianiae and the other the Cellae Vinariae Novae. In any case, the privately owned cellars of the Arruntii were apparently appropriated and enlarged by Trajan.

IMPERIAL RESIDENCES

Domus Tiberiana

Certainly Trajan did not need to add to the luxurious palace erected by Domitian on the Palatine.[250] He did, however, apparently try to regulate the façade on the Domus Tiberiana along the Clivus Victoriae.[251] Partition walls converted the space between the Flavian construction and the street into a series of rooms. The brickwork is identical with that in the Trajanic parts of the Atrium Vestae, and the same type of yellow *bipedales* is employed for bonding courses. Doorways are covered with camber arches, but instead of individual relieving arches they display enormous relieving arches stretching the entire length of the wall. These are also of yellow *bipedales*. This construction became part of the Hadrianic enlargement which brought the façade down to the Nova Via.

Water pipes[252] indicate that Trajan had a suburban villa just outside the City on the Via Nomentana. Lanciani gives a plan of the colonnade and the rooms opening out of it which were uncovered in 1869.[253] Nothing further is known of its construction.

The villas at Arcinazzo and Centumcellae are presented elsewhere.[254]

[242] These are P, Q (*ibid.*, pp. 28–30).

[243] Cressedi (*Amor di Roma*, Rome, 1956, p. 119) speaks of traces of walls with triangular bricks, yellowish red, 4 cm. thick with mortar joints 2.5 cm.

[244] Cressedi (*Not. sc.*, 1956, pp. 31–32) would broaden the range somewhat.

[245] E. Gatti, *Bull. Com.*, vol. 53, 1925, pp. 279–280. For others possibly Trajanic, see G. Cressedi, *Bull. Com.*, vol. 73, 1949–1950, pp. 94–95.

[246] I. A. Richmond, *Bull. Com.*, vol. 55, 1927, p. 46; idem, *City wall*, pp. 13, 16–17; Nash I, pp. 225–226.

[247] R. Lanciani, *Not. sc.*, 1879, pp. 15, 40, 68; 1880, pp. 128–129, 140–141; 1884, p. 238; Platner-Ashby, p. 109; Ricci, *Via dell'Impero*, p. 116; Lugli, *MAR*, vol. 3, pp. 653–654.

[248] Lanciani, *Not. sc.*, 1878, p. 66; *CIL*, vol. 6 (2), no. 8826.

[249] Lanciani, *Not. sc.*, 1880, p. 140, FGHI.

[250] See Blake, RC II, p. 115–122.

[251] Lugli, *Centro*, p. 482.

[252] *CIL*, vol. 15 (2), nos. 7263, 7304.

[253] Lanciani, *Forma Urbis*, pl. 4; cf. T. Ashby, *PBSR*, vol. 3, 1906, p. 32.

[254] See below, pp. 236–237.

[1] O. Richter, *Jb. d. Inst.*, vol. 13, 1898 with n. 28.

[2] Huelsen (*Roman Forum*, p. 161) wavers to the extent of suggesting Trajan as an alternative.

[3] Toebelmann, *Gebälke*, p. 51. The controversy has not ceased. See the recent arguments for an Augustan date (D. E. Strong and J. B. Ward-Perkins, *PBSR*, vol. 30, 1962, pp. 1–30) vs. a Trajanic or even Antonine one (A. von Gerkan, *Röm. Mitt.*, vol. 60–61, 1953–1954, pp. 200–206 and *Arch. Anz.*, vol. 79, 1965, cols. 648–656).

[4] Mrs. Strong (*AAR*, vol. 1, p. 134) considers columns and entablature Augustan but re-used in a Hadrianic restoration.

[5] Platner-Ashby, p. 287.

[6] *BMC, Emp.*, vol. 3, Hadrian, pl. 81, no. 10; Brown, *NNM*, no. 90, pl. 5, no. 1; Strack, *Reichsprägung*, vol. 2, pl. 9, no. 599.

[7] Strack, *op. cit.*, p. 115.

[8] For the extensive bibliography on these reliefs consult Nash II, p. 176 "Plutei Traiani"; add Frova, pp. 241–242.

[9] Bloch, *Bolli*, pp. 84–85.

[10] Dr. Van Deman's Hadrianic phase of the Atrium Vestae has been proved to be Trajanic (see pp. 36–37 above). For slight Hadrianic modifications, see Bloch, *op. cit.*

[11] Blake, *RC II*, p. 47.

[12] Muñoz, *La Sistemazione del Tempio di Venere e Roma*, Rome, 1935; *idem, Capitolium*, vol. 11, 1935, pp. 215–234; A. M. Colini, *Vie d'Italia*, vol. 41, 1935, pp. 513–519; *idem, Bull. Com.*, vol. 63, 1935, pp. 180–182; G. Lugli, *Pan*, vol. 5, 1935, pp. 364–375; *idem, MAR, Suppl.*, pp. 83–94; *idem, Centro*, pp. 234–240. For a fuller bibliography of this temple consult Nash II, p. 496; add Frova, pp. 82–83.

[13] Aelius Spartianus (*SHA, Hadrianus*, 19, 12) states that this was accomplished with the help of twenty-four elephants.

[14] A. M. Colini, *Bull. Com.*, vol. 66, 1938, p. 247; Nash I, p. 268.

[15] A wall faced with rather wide triangular bricks along the north side is Neronian.

[16] Van Deman, "Methods," p. 418.

HADRIAN (A.D. 117–138)
ROMAN FORUM; TEMPLE OF VENUS AND ROME

There was no longer room in the Forum Romanum for the grandiose edifices so dear to the heart of Hadrian. Nor was there any major disaster which necessitated the restoration of any edifices already in existence. A conjecture of Richter[1] endorsed by Huelsen[2] that the Temple of Castor was repaired by Hadrian was rejected by most scholars, after Fiechter[3] pointed out the similarity of its construction to that of the Tiberian Temple of Concord.[4] Numismatic evidence has been used as proof that Hadrian restored the Temple of Divus Iulius.[5] The coin was more likely struck to commemorate the scene which was taking place in front of it.[6] Strack interprets this as the *laudatio funebris* of Hadrian for Plotina.[7] In any case, there is no construction extant which can be referred to the Hadrianic period. The "Anaglypha Traiani"[8] may be evidence of another construction of the time of Hadrian for the embellishment of the Forum, but neither their original location or purpose is known.

With the exception of the addition of the Aedicula[9] at the entrance of the Atrium Vestae,[10] Hadrian made no changes in the appearance of the Sacra Via from the Forum to what had been the vestibule of the Domus Aurea.[11] This his builders destroyed in A.D. 121 to make room for the great platform upon which the Temple of Venus and Roma[12] was to be erected. The Sacra Via at that point was moved somewhat to enlarge the area available for the temple. In the course of preparing the site, the Colossus of Nero, now a statue of Helios, was moved to an open space to the northwest of the Colosseum,[13] where the remains of its base stood until modern times (1936).[14] It was brick-faced with a marble revetment. The great concrete platform was 145 m. $\times$ 100 m. Incorporated in it were some remains of earlier structures.[15] In places, the aggregate consisted of a mixed lot of tufa, travertine, selce, and brick, partly at any rate the refuse of buildings destroyed. In general, however, small pieces of selce and travertine closely packed in regular rows appear in the concrete where a firm foundation was obligatory; elsewhere an aggregate of tufa[16] was more loosely laid. The lofty side of the platform on the north and east[17] was faced with squared blocks of peperino and travertine. A flight of steps made a facing on the west unnecessary. On the south, however, some brickwork of unusually light-colored bricks was used.[18] Brick stamps of A.D. 123 and 134 have been found from time to time.[19] Tiles covering drains also yielded Hadrianic stamps. Besides the western steps, a two-ramp staircase, probably of marble steps, at the ends of the eastern face gave access to the precinct from the area in front of the Colosseum. On the north side, the facing of the platform was concealed by marble where it was exposed to view. On it in all probability rested a marble wall to shut out the irregularity of the escarpment of the Velia. Such a wall would also have served as the back wall of the north porticus of the precinct, where there was room for only a single row of columns facing the temple area. The wall was probably of marble. At the south, a wider space made possible a double row of columns for what was probably an open colonnade. Because the presence of earlier buildings would have obscured a full view of the Forum on the west, it seems likely that the north and south porticoes would have continued around the corner for at least a part of the distance, but the evidence is not clear. There is every reason for believing that there was no porticus on the east to obstruct the view of the Colosseum. All these columns were of unchanneled gray granite with bases and capitals of white marble. The fragments of cipollino columns which came to light in the course of excavation probably belonged to a monumental entrance in the center of each of the long sides, of which the foundations were found. It jutted inward to break the monotony of the long row of columns. Although what remains of the superstructure belongs to a restoration made by Maxentius, foundations show that he was following the plan of Hadrian, though he was using a different medium. The story of his cavalier way of treating Apollodorus when he ventured to criticize the "blueprints" is too well known to need repetition.[20] Except for its immense size (10 columns[21] across the front, 20 along the sides) the exterior was entirely traditional, but the juxtaposition of two cellas back to back with apses touching was something new under the sun. Each had its own pronaos with four columns *in antis*. Traces of the large pedestals for seated figures of Roma Aeterna in the west and Venus Felix[22] in the east were seen in the Hadrianic pavement.[23] In the walls of peperino enclosing the concrete podium, travertine appears under the places where the columns would have stood. A wooden roof of the time of Hadrian probably contributed to the fire which made necessary the complete rebuilding of the superstructure of Maxentius.[24] The temple was dedicated in A.D. 135.[25] The Antonine coins suggest, however, that it was completed by Antoninus Pius.

During the reign of Hadrian, the Atrium Vestae underwent only minor modifications:[26] an aedicula at the entrance, a hypocaust in the second room behind the shops on the north, and a bit of masonry inserted at the mezzanine level in a wall near the northeast corner. The walls present no peculiarities. The dating is based on the brick stamps.[27]

IMPERIAL FORA

There was little for Hadrian to add to the imperial fora. Brick stamps[28] found in the southeast wall which separates the Temple of Venus Genetrix from the Forum of Caesar place it early in his reign. The construction offers no peculiarities. A temple formed the focal point of the fora preceding the one built by Trajan. Consequently, it seems quite possible, as we have seen,[29] that Apollodorus had one in mind or used one already in existence as the culmination of a complex serving so many different purposes. However that may be, a Hadrianic inscription[30] proves that the temple at the head of the Forum was dedicated to Divus Traianus and Diva Plotina, and, according to Spartianus,[31] it was built by Hadrian. Furthermore, Lugli had produced a Hadrianic (?) coin[32] which is almost a duplicate of the Trajanic coins referred to this temple. Although none of it is visible above ground today, enough remains have come to light from time to time to prove that the edifice, whether Trajanic or Hadrianic, stood on a high podium, had eight columns across the front, and was flanked by colonnades.[33] Fragments of

[17] The irregular chambers in the east face were hollowed out later.

[18] Rivoira-Rushforth, p. 214, fig. 261.

[19] Bloch, *Bolli*, pp. 250–253.

[20] Cassius Dio, 69, 4, 3–4.

[21] *BMC, Emp.*, vol. 3, Hadrian, nos. 1490, 1554, pls. 87, no. 6; 89, nos. 5 and 7; *ibid.*, vol. 4, Antoninus Pius, nos. 1279–1285, pls. 29, nos. 10–13; 30, nos. 1–3; Strack, *Reichsprägung*, part 2, pp. 174–177.

[22] The identification is through coins.

[23] Lugli, *Centro*, p. 238.

[24] Platner-Ashby, p. 553. For the Hadrianic architectural ornament of this temple see D. Strong, *PBSR*, vol. 21, 1953, pp. 127–129.

[25] Strack's attempt (*op. cit.*, part 3, p. 89) to explain these coins as a declaration of the religious policy of the new emperor seems farfetched to me and forces him to ascribe a later date to the dedication.

[26] The phase attributed to Hadrian by Dr. Van Deman is Trajanic. See above, pp. 36–37.

[27] Bloch, *Bolli*, pp. 84–85.

[28] Bloch, *Bolli*, p. 67.

[29] See above, p. 17.

[30] *CIL*, vol. 6 (1), no. 966 with vol. 6 (4, 2), no. 31215.

[31] Aelius Spartianus, *SHA*, Hadrianus, 19, 9.

[32] Lugli, *Centro*, p. 295, fig. 87.

[33] Lanciani, *Forma Urbis*, pl. 22; Platner-Ashby, p. 244; Lugli, *op. cit.*, pp. 295–296.

[34] I. Gismondi, *Bull. Com.*, vol. 61, 1933, pl. A.

[35] See above, p. 27.

[36] Aelius Spartianus, *SHA*, *Hadrianus*, 19, 10–11.

[37] Platner-Ashby, p. 85.

[38] Lugli, *MAR*, vol. 3, pp. 589–590; G. Calza, *Not. sc.*, 1942, pp. 156–157.

[39] The extensive bibliography of these discussions is everywhere available; see especially Nash II, pp. 170–171; add Frova, pp. 80–82, and K. de Fine Licht, *The Rotunda in Rome. A Study of Hadrian's Pantheon* (Copenhagen 1968). The recent study by W. L. MacDonald in his book, *The Architecture of the Roman Empire* (vol. 1), deserves special mention.

[40] G. Cozzo, *Corporazione* (Acc. L. Mem., ser. 6, vol. 5), Rome, 1936, pp. 327–343 (whose conclusions are vitiated in my opinion by an erroneous conception of the purpose of the stamps); J. Guey, *Mél*, vol. 53, 1936, pp. 198–249; Bloch, *Bolli*, pp. 102–117

[41] *CIL*, vol. 6 (1), no. 896. New bronze letters have been inserted in the grooves.

[42] Aelius Spartianus, *SHA*, *Hadrianus*, 19, 9.

[43] L. Beltrami, *Il Pantheon*, Milan, 1898, pp. 17–75; A. M. Colini, *Bull. Com.*, vol. 54, 1926, pp. 67–87; I. Gismondi, *ibid.*, pp. 87–92; Cozzo, *Ingegneria*, pp. 257–297; idem, *Boll. d'Arte*, vol. 8, 1928–1929, pp. 291-309; Platner-Ashby, pp. 382–386; A. Terenzio, *Mouseion*, vol. 20, 1932, pp. 52–57; idem, *Enc. It.*, vol. 26, pp. 212–214; Lugli, *MAR*, vol. 3, pp. 123–150.

[44] Lugli, *op. cit.*, p. 139.

[45] Beltrami (*loc. cit.*, p. 64) reports brick reticulate, Terenzio (*Enc. It.*, *loc. cit.*, p. 212) *semilateres*, i.e., triangles.

two sizes of granite columns and of Corinthian columns were found in the residue. In any case, it has nothing to contribute to a knowledge of construction. Gismondi's restoration with curved porticoes is aesthetically satisfying.[34] The director's suite in the market connected with the Forum of Trajan, as we have seen,[35] may not have been built until the time of Hadrian.

No evidence points to the erection of any commemorative arch in Rome during the reign of Hadrian. Four great temples have been attributed to him. The Temples of Divus Trajanus and Venus and Roma have already been described in their proper setting; the Pantheon and the Temple of Matidia form part of a large building complex in the Campus Martius which will be described below. Besides the Pantheon, he is credited by Spartianus[36] with restoring many temples, but little evidence of this is left. Spartianus implies that the Temple of Bona Dea was a new construction, but that is not in accord with known facts.[37] It is generally located by topographers on the Aventine below Santa Balbina, but no remains of it have been identified.[38]

PANTHEON AND ENVIRONS

Few monuments have given rise to so much controversy as the Pantheon.[39] Investigations made possible when the edifice was thoroughly overhauled in 1930–1931 have somewhat reduced the number of unsolved problems. Brick stamps[40] found in every part of the rotunda and vestibule prove that they were built from the very foundations by Hadrian's contractors in the first ten years of his reign. The dedicatory inscription[41] on the architrave was a tribute to Marcus Agrippa, who was responsible for the first Pantheon, in accordance with the expressed policy of the emperor to retain the names of the original builders on edifices restored by him.[42] There is every reason for believing, as we shall see, that the portico belonged to the same building period as the rest. The monument as re-erected was a mammoth undertaking. Its construction has been reported with an exactness vouchsafed to few ancient monuments.[43] Without the ingenuity of the engineers, the carefully made plans of the architects might well have come to naught. The complete rebuilding of the temple was a part of an attempt to raise all this part of the Campus Martius above the flood level of the Tiber. The engineers covered the area with a layer of bluish clay before constructing the foundations. There are abundant traces of earlier edifices which do not concern us here. Because of the long controversy over the relative chronology of rotunda, vestibule, and portico, it has seemed advisable to present each part separately. By so doing we can perhaps come nearer to an understanding of the problems which confronted those who had the construction in hand.

The rotunda is obviously the focal part of the whole design. The foundation is an enormous ring of concrete over forty meters in diameter, four and a half meters high, and more than seven meters wide (plan V). Even so, it was found to be too narrow for stability and was reinforced with an inner ring.[44] The concrete was composed of horizontal rows of travertine *caementa* in a firm pozzolana mortar. Encircling this concrete foundation, traces have been found of a wall, 60 cm. wide, rounded at the top and faced on the exposed surface with brick.[45] Cozzo explains it plausibly as a method of

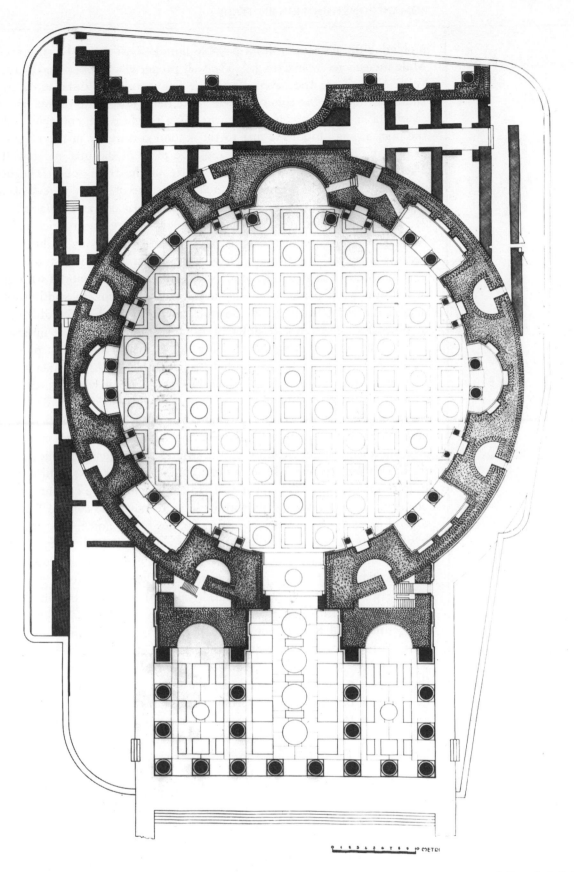

PLAN V. PANTHEON, FLOOR PLAN

A. Terenzio, in R. Vighi, *Il Pantheon*, Rome 1959, p. 6.

[46] Cozzo, *Ingegneria*, pp. 268–269.

[47] Lugli (*op. cit.*, p. 135) calls them marble.

[48] Cozzo (*op. cit.*, p. 276) conjectures that these were intended to facilitate the drying of the great mass of concrete.

protecting the foundation from possible inundations of the Tiber, especially while the concrete was setting.[46] The wall proper was of brick-faced concrete (plan VI). From the pavement to the first cornice, a distance of twelve and a half meters, the core consisted of alternate rows of travertine and tufa *caementa* in a firm mortar with apparently a roughcast 60 cm. thick behind the brick facing. From the first to the second cornice (9 m.), an aggregate of tufa and brick in alternate rows took the place of the tufa and travertine. There is no specific report on the concrete of the third zone. The bricks were made from close-grained well-fired tiles, some of which were broken to triangular shape. They vary in width from 2.8 to 4.3 cm. and in length from 21.5 to 30 cm. There is a wide range in color from yellow to brick red. Dr. Van Deman in her notes describes the majority as having a dusty white texture, whatever that means. These were higher up in the structure and may have been triangles. The joints show the usual white mortar with grains of red and black pozzolana. They average about 1 cm. in width with no notable difference between the horizontal and vertical ones. Bonding courses of *bipedales* not essentially different from the bricks occur at intervals of 1.2 m. The great relieving arches (pl. 6, fig. 2) which are such a prominent feature of the exterior are, as we shall see, an integral part of inner architecture. They must, therefore, be whole *bipedales*. Small windows, each with its own slightly curved lintel arch of *bipedales*, introduced in order to light the passageway at the second external cornice, curiously enough have not been placed with reference to the relieving arches. The string cornices, an even more conspicuous feature of the exterior, are equally implicated with the interior architecture. The lowest one, composed of six rows of tiles chipped to form moldings, corresponds roughly to the height of the columns in front of the niches inside; the second with its series of travertine consoles[47] between rows of *bipedales*, to the impost of the intrados of the dome; the third which is similar to the second but slightly more elaborate, to the impost of the extrados of the dome and serves as a coping. These three cornices may be an indication that the original intention was to leave the brickwork exposed.

The thickness of the great circular wall is broken on the inside by a series of eight alcoves alternately semicircular and rectangular, the entrance being substituted for the one in the north. Pedimented niches later converted into altars cut slightly into the spaces between the alcoves. In the second zone a series of empty chambers is concealed by paneling; and in the third zone a narrow corridor occupies the space between the outer wall and the soffit of the dome. Small semicircular voids facing outwards were left in the concrete between the alcoves for some reason not now apparent.[48] So many empty spaces required a bewildering number of relieving arches. On the inside at the ground-floor level each alcove, fronted by two columns of either giallo antico or pavonazzetto *in antis*, had three rectangular niches in the rear wall, the central one being taller than the other two. Each niche had the usual slightly curved lintel arch of *bipedales* and individual relieving arch beneath the great relieving arch which covered all three. It is double and continues through the masonry until it is visible on the outside. In the second zone behind the rich marble façade of panels separating pedimented windows, there is a wealth of unexpected structural detail. Above

PANTHEON
SEZIONE =

PLAN VI. PANTHEON, SECTION OF THE WALL

A. Terenzio, in R. Vighi, *Il Pantheon*, Rome 1959, p. 50.

the entablature that encircles the edifice, marble impost blocks support slightly curved segmental arches of *bipedales* to place the weight on the columns and pilasters. Low relieving arches over the segmental arches serve to make assurance doubly sure. Cross walls resting on marble foundations start at the imposts. Each cross wall has an arched opening covered by a double curve of *bipedales*. In front, great triple relieving arches of *bipedales* over the alcoves concentrated the weight of what came above on the pilasters. Beneath them a segmental arch followed the curve as an added protection of the central part. Between them and resting on them were lower relieving arches composed of a double arc of *bipedales* intended to protect the pedimented niches between the alcoves. Both varieties of large relieving arches extend through the masonry to the outside. This framework, somewhat modified, was carried straight up into the third zone behind the first and part of the second row of coffers of the finished dome (pl. 6, fig. 1). Great double relieving arches over three small relieving arches support secondary relieving arches which are also double. The extrados of the dome may be said to rest on the top of this series of great relieving arches, which are carried through to the outside. It cannot be emphasized too strongly that this framework of arches in the third zone was part of wall construction and did not follow the curve of the dome. It was these relieving arches that led to so many fantastic but utterly erroneous theories of dome construction.

For the construction of the dome, a complete wooden framework must have been erected upon which to lay the coffering,[49] intended for decoration rather than for whatever value it may have had in lightening the weight. There are no structural ribs penetrating the mass of the concrete. The meridial lines of the coffering in the majority of cases show Hadrianic stamps,[50] but two are reported to have yielded those of Septimius Severus.[51] These would seem to have constituted a repair rather than a complete rebuilding of the dome as some have thought. The space between the centering and the inner corridor within the third zone was filled with concrete. The true impost came at the coping of the circuit wall. The *caementa* were apparently thrown in up to a certain point and then laid in thin layers by hand. They show a discrimination in the choice of material throughout.[52] For the first eleven and three-quarters meters the aggregate is of small pieces of brick with rather frequent bonding courses of *bipedales*; for the next two and a quarter meters, of tufa and brick in alternate rows with two bonding courses near together; and for the rest, lightweight yellow tufa and pumice, also in alternate rows. This is the earliest dated example of the importation of pumice from the region around Vesuvius[53] to lighten vaulting. Not only did the *caementa* become lighter in weight as the dome approached its apex but the concrete became narrower. The cupola when completed was a great monolithic structure rising to an "eye," nine meters in diameter outlined in horizontal rows of *bipedales* set into the concrete for greater stability. The inner surface was gilded. The height from the pavement to the "eye" equals roughly the diameter of the circle and is equally divided between the circuit wall and the apparent impost of the dome. The pavement of pavonazzetto, giallo antico, porta santa, porfido, and granito dips toward the center to facilitate the draining off through small apertures of rain water coming in

[49] Terenzio, *Enc. It.*, *loc. cit.*, p. 213; G. Giovannoni, *Riv. Roma*, vol. 14, 1936, pp. 37–42 (repeated V *cong. st. biz.*, vol. 6, 1940, pp. 134–136.

[50] Bloch, *Bolli*, p. 106, with explanation, pp. 112–113.

[51] *Ibid.*, p. 116.

[52] G. de Angelis d'Ossat, *III conv. st. archit.*, 1938, Rome, 1940, pp. 244–245. Brick would absorb moisture and yellow tufa and pumice would lighten weight.

[53] *Idem*, *Acc. P. Sc.*, 1930, pp. 211–215. For the use of pumice in building, see Blake, *RC I*, p. 41.

through the "eye." To return to the dome, it is stepped on the outside for roughly half of its height, or up to the top of the fourth row of coffers inside; and the steps are faced with brick. Above the steps "*semilateres*" are laid scale-fashion. The whole was then covered with *opus signinum* to make it impermeable and provided with a roof of bronze tiles.[54] Traces remain of a bronze cornice at the "eye."

The vestibule[55] represents a change of plan while the Pantheon was in the process of construction. Its foundations,[56] though of identical concrete, rest against those of the rotunda in such a way as to prove that they were later though of the same building period.[57] The core of the walls where it could be examined was of alternate rows of brick and tufa *caementa*. The brickwork is practically the same as that in the circular wall and yields brick stamps which are contemporaneous.[58] The lower cornice of the drum was in place when the vestibule was added;[59] the middle and upper cornices were duplicated in the new construction. The raking cornice of the brick pediment was also supported by travertine consoles. There is the same dependence on relieving arches to strengthen the walls as in the main structure. A great arched doorway, protected by a segmental relieving arch fitted in under the peak of the pediment, cuts the front wall. A semicircular arched niche on each side of the door has above it a relieving arch with practically the same curve in each of the upper zones. All these relieving arches are of *bipedales*. The presence of the great relieving arches in the drum complicated the problem of the addition of the vestibule, but the awkwardness of the junction was eventually concealed by stucco. There is a slight setback at the height of the epistyle of the porticus and a wider one at the horizontal cornice of the pediment. Such a refinement was probably intended to lighten the effect of the massive superstructure. The central part of the pediment was destroyed in Bernini's attempt to improve the appearance of the monument in accordance with the taste of his age. What shows today was inserted when his excrescences were removed. Converging lines of *bipedales* cut into the pediment and mark the position of the roof of the portico. Perforated pieces of travertine set into the face were probably used to hold some of the scaffolding in the process of building.

Cozzo, Colini, and Gismondi have proved that portico and vestibule arose together,[60] and surely such an elaborate plan goes far beyond the mere need of buttressing the dome. The foundations of the portico, resting in part on earlier structures, were, to be sure, more heterogeneous than those in the rest of the edifice; and there was some reuse of travertine blocks; but the conjecture that the portico was a residue of the Agrippan Pantheon is untenable. Where the walls were independent, as under the cross walls bearing the rear columns, the concrete was identical with that in the rest of the monument. All parts are definitely earlier than the substructure of the platea outside. The portico originally had a row of eight gray granite columns across the front and two rows of four columns each of rose granite behind it.[61] The capitals were of marble and supported a conventional entablature (*cornice epistilio*). A white marble revetment between decorative pilasters covered all the brickwork of the front of the vestibule at the rear of the portico, and brought it into harmony with the marble in front. Capitals

[54] The lead covering belongs to the time of Gregory XI.

[55] A. M. Colini, *Bull. Com.*, vol. 54, 1926, pp. 67–87, is fundamental for a study of the vestibule.

[56] I. Gismondi, *ibid.*, pp. 87–92.

[57] Cozzo (*Boll. d'Arte*, vol. 8, 1928–1929, p. 296) remarks that sufficient time had elapsed between the building of the two for the mortar in the earlier to harden.

[58] Bloch, *Bolli*, pp. 107, 116–117.

[59] Cozzo, *op. cit.*, pl. 117, fig. 213.

[60] *Opera citata.*

[61] The column at the east corner was replaced by one of rose granite by Urban VIII and two others at the east end by gray columns from the Thermae Alexandrinae by Alexander VII. For identification of the granites and marbles in the portico see C. H. O. Scaife, *JRS*, 43, 1953, p. 37, and MacDonald, pp. 97–98.

62 Traces of stucco were found here and there. See Colini, op. cit., p. 79.

63 Pullen, p. 186.

64 Beltrami (op. cit., pp. 31–32) conjectures that bronze beams, stretching from the architrave of the alcoves inside to marble corbels which are still extant on the rear wall, secured a coffered ceiling of bronze. There is nothing, so far as I know to either prove or disprove the theory.

65 The present roof was erected by Urban VIII.

66 These have been replaced in modern times.

67 Only the holes for affixing it are preserved. See Colini, Bull. Com., vol. 51, 1923, p. 331 with n. 1.

68 Ibid., p. 325.

69 The capitals of the portico are identical with those in the rotunda. See Rivoira-Rushforth, p. 122.

70 Platner-Ashby, p. 384; Lugli, op. cit., p. 150.

71 G. Gatti, III conv. st. archit., 1938, Rome, 1940, pp. 70–72. For additional bibliography consult Nash I, p. 196.

72 Aelius Spartianus, SHA, Hadrianus, 19, 10.

73 A drawing of Alò Giovannoli (reproduced by Gatti, op. cit., fig. 5) shows the south side.

of pilasters, travertine blocks supporting the epistyle, and the epistyle itself penetrated the wall in such a way as to prove contemporaneity. Furthermore, the bottom cornice of the brick pediment of the vestibule was apparently tapered off in anticipation of the position of the roof of the portico. Even more conclusive evidence lies in the opposing rows of bipedales marking the line of the roof, since they were set in when the wall was built. Colini conjectures that they may have projected to protect the junction, but the wall has been worked over so many times that there is no proof. The cornices with their rows of small consoles are practically identical with the string cornices in the rest of the monument.[62] The latter, stuccoed over in the general stuccoing of the exterior, would increase the harmonious effect. The portico was paved with a suitable pattern of granite and colored marbles. The threshold is of affricano. The pilasters at the doorway are said to be of Thasian marble,[63] though the doorframe is of Luna. Some slabs carved with festoons have been recovered and restored to place at either side of the doorway. Hadrian's architect did not, however, rely wholly on marble to give richness to the entrance. The great bronze door with its bronze pilasters and the covering window with its bronze grating are original though they were repaired in the sixteenth century. Bronze girders,[64] removed in 1625, originally supported the roof,[65] which was covered with gilded bronze tiles. The architrave was inscribed with bronze letters;[66] bronze figures adorned the pediment; and a metal cornice probably of bronze topped the cornice of the pediment.[67] The corners of the tympanum were interlocked with the cornice blocks at the ends[68] to give greater protection from earthquake shocks. It is possible that a pedimented portico was part of the original plan,[69] though it was not built until after the vestibule was interposed for strategic reasons.

Rotunda, vestibule, and portico, though exhibiting a radical change in the process of construction, belong to the same general building period. A paved area in front was enclosed in a colonnade facing the monument.[70] The travertine foundations which served as the start of the side colonnades appear at the head of the cross walls extending east and west from the portico of the temple a little behind the line of the marble steps. An ornamental arch may have graced each of these extremities. From this colonnade, the visitor would have an unrestricted view of the monument, probably glistening like marble from its stuccoed exterior; but from every other angle it would have been hidden by structures erected in part at least for strategic reasons.

Gatti[71] by a careful examination of all the evidence has established beyond reasonable doubt that the great hall south of the Pantheon (plan VII) was the Basilica of Neptune mentioned by Spartianus[72] among the buildings restored by Hadrian. It was a large rectangular structure (45 m. × 19 m.) of brick-faced concrete. Its long walls, of which only the northern one is extant (pl. 6, fig. 4),[73] were provided with three niches—one semicircular between two rectangular—on each side of a large apse containing a brick-faced base for a large piece of statuary. The rectangular niches were covered with slightly curved lintel arches of bipedales protected by relieving arches of the same in true Hadrianic fashion. The walls were unusually thick (1.75 m.).

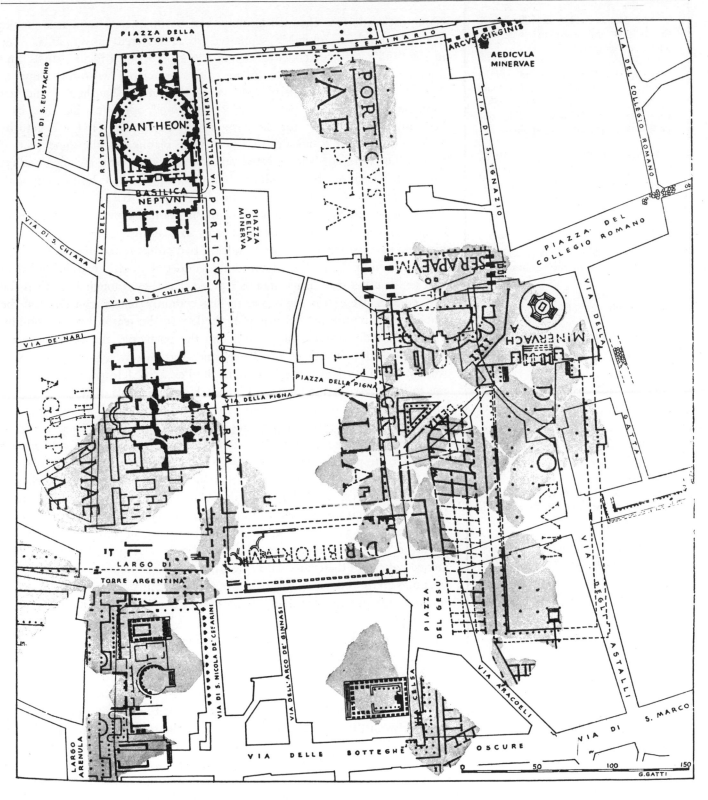

PLAN VII. ZONE OF THE PANTHEON AND BASILICA NEPTUNI,
SHOWING FRAGMENTS OF THE MARBLE PLAN

G. Gatti, in *La Pianta Marmorea
di Roma Antica* I, 1960, p. 98.

[74] So Platner-Ashby, p. 520 (where the hall is still associated with the Thermae Agrippae).

[75] One has been identified in the Vatican (L. Respighi, *Acc. P. Rend.* (vol. 7, fasc. 2, 1929–1930, 1930–1931) 1932, pp. 109–117). The one *in situ* is a modern restoration.

[76] Cozzo (*Boll. d'Arte*, vol. 8, 1928–1929, pp. 300–302) believes that a door was originally planned for this position, a conjecture rejected categorically by Lugli (*MAR*, vol. 3, p. 139).

[77] Platner-Ashby (*op. cit.*) connects them statically with the basilica alone.

[78] The resultant rooms could be used for shops or offices.

[79] Bloch, *Bolli*, pp. 108–109.

[80] G. Gatti, *Urbe*, vol. 2 (9), 1937, pp. 18–19; *idem, Bull. Com.*, vol. 67, 1939, pp. 203–205; *idem, III conv. st. archit.*, pp. 68–70; *idem, FUR*, pp. 97–101.

[81] Spartianus, *op. cit.*

[82] G. Gatti, *Urbe*, vol. 7 (1), 1942, pp. 2–14; *idem, Acc. P. Rend.*, vol. 20, 1943–1944, pp. 137–150.

[83] The date is confirmed by brick stamps found in the course of demolition.

[84] Cozzo, *Boll. d'Arte*, vol. 8, 1928–1929, pp. 291–309.

[85] Van Deman, "Methods," p. 426.

Along each side four channeled columns of pavonazzetto[74] and rose granite having Corinthian capitals[75] supported three coffered cross vaults. The marble wall revetment ended in a fine frieze depicting tridents, shells, and dolphins—symbols appropriate to an edifice associated with the name of Neptune. The brickwork is very similar to that of the Pantheon. The fact that the drum was built out into a straight line[76] opposite what may have been intended originally for the entrance to the basilica (but was actually filled with the apse) indicates that both were planned at the same time, if indeed they were not being erected simultaneously. At first, an open passage existed between the two buildings, but soon eight heavy buttressing walls were thrown between the two, intended perhaps to balance the weight of the dome against the heavy vaulting of the basilica.[77] Openings covered with arches of *bipedales* were left in these walls so that the public should not be deprived of its passageway. Barrel vaults in two orders rested upon the walls.[78] The junction of the walls of the rotunda seems to be better coordinated than that at the other end. Brick stamps[79] prove that they, though later than the two edifices, were still Hadrianic. They certainly reflect concern for the stability of the vaulting and may give the key to the reason for the addition of the vestibule between the rotunda and the portico at the north.

The niched wall east of the Pantheon[80] was merely a part of the long west wall of a porticus corresponding to the Porticus Meleagri, which, according to the latest interpretation of the Marble Plan, flanked the Saepta Iulia on the east side. It has been plausibly identified as the Porticus Argonautarum, or Porticus Neptuni, forming an integral part of the Saepta, which, according to Spartianus,[81] was restored by Hadrian. The niches stood between pilasters corresponding to the columns of the porticus. They were covered with lintel arches of *bipedales* protected by relieving arches. The brickwork resembles closely that of the Pantheon. Gatti[82] has shown that the restored Porticus Meleagri was embellished in the time of Hadrian[83] with an elaborate central archway, which undoubtedly took the place of a simple passageway from the Saepta to the precinct of Isis and Serapis. It apparently had a long arched passage in the center with side passages low enough to admit identical openings above them as a species of upper story. Since none of the construction remains *in situ*, the chief value of the information lies in the field of topography.

The three monuments mentioned together by Spartianus as restored by Hadrian were, therefore, part of a well-integrated plan. Rotunda, Basilica Neptuni, and Saepta Iulia were apparently all started at approximately the same time. Cozzo[84] believed that cracks in the dome when the centering was removed led to the interposition of the vestibule and the buttressing walls between the rotunda and the basilica at the south. The main difficulty with his conjecture is the impossibility of dating the cracks which he undoubtedly saw. There would seem to be no reason why concern for the stability of the dome may not have led to both measures. But if the part of the back wall of the Pantheon (Porticus Neptuni) was intended as a buttressing agent, it should have been duplicated by a similar wall on the west side. There is trace of a wall there, but it is Severan not Hadrianic.[85] We have here an example of the city planning in which Hadrian delighted.

It was coupled in this instance with the raising of the level of the area in an attempt to bring it above the danger of inundation from the Tiber. Bloch[86] conjectures that the plans may even have been initiated by Apollodorus before he fell from favor. Other monuments in the neighborhood may belong to the same scheme, but we have less information concerning them.

One other monument, "Il Tempio di Siepe,"[87] which has disappeared from this same general region without leaving any trace, must be mentioned in passing because of its importance to the study of architecture. Engravings show it to have been the type of building in which Hadrian delighted. It was fundamentally a square edifice with curvilinear niches in the angles, a shallow vestibule with a small curvilinear niche on each side, a rectangular projection opposite the main entrance furnished with similar curved niches at the sides and an apse at the head, and a doorway in each of the two remaining sides. Two columns preceded each of the three entrances, and eight interior columns supported a heavy architrave under an eight-sided pavilion cupola with curved sections of the kind aptly named "ad ombrello" by the Italians. The architect was apparently experimenting with the cantilever principle for giving support to the heavy dome. There was an "eye" at the top and a round window in every other section. The engraving of Alò Giovannoli shows the shell protected by a low-pitched roof, whereas a Windsor drawing gives it an extrados resembling the Pantheon though on a smaller scale. The building was probably a nymphaeum.

Directly east of the porticus in front of the Pantheon and north of the Saepta, if we accept Gatti's interpretation of Spartianus, Hadrian apparently had a space cleared of whatever structures, if any, it may have held for a temple in honor of his deified mother-in-law, Matidia,[88] who died in A.D. 117. At any rate, five great columns of cipollino[89] were found not far from a lead pipe bearing the inscription TEMPLO MATIDIAE.[90] These columns suggest a large and imposing edifice. In the seventeenth century, three massive walls with an aggregate of selce were encountered in laying a sewer under Via dei Pastini. They may have been part of the foundation of the temple. In the middle of the nineteenth century remains of a pavement of giallo antico were still extant which probably belonged to the cella. Huelsen's conjecture that the temple faced north has been generally accepted.[91] We should have no more information concerning it, if it were not for a badly struck coin of 120/21,[92] which shows a small temple[93] facing a square flanked by what appear to be porticoes (pl. 10, fig. 1). It carries the legend DIVAE MATIDIAE SOCRVI. The porticoes have been identified, whether rightly or wrongly, as the Basilicae Matidiae et Marcianae mentioned in The Regionary Catalogues (plan VIII).[94] Travertine blocks which may have served as the steps of the basilicas and the pavement of the square were uncovered in 1745. Every detail in the above account is open to question, but this is not the place to enter into a discussion of minutiae since there are no further data of importance to this study. Huelsen would place the "Tempio di Siepe" to the north but on the axis of the east basilica and would conjecture a similar one in a corresponding position on the west.

The great porticus along the west side of the ancient Via Lata (Via del Corso), which has been plausibly identified with the Porticus Minucia Fru-

[86] Bloch, *Bolli*, p. 116.

[87] Rivoira-Rushforth, pp. 134, 136 with fig. 154; G. de Angelis d'Ossat, *Riv. Roma*, vol. 14, 1936, p. 338; idem, *BMIR*, vol. 12, 1941, p. 125 n. 8; idem, *Le cupole*, p. 18; idem, *III conv. st. archit.*, p. 234; Lugli, *MAR*, vol. 3, pp. 231–233. Crema, p. 571, fig. 757; Neuerburg, *Fontane*, p. 71. Lugli differs from the others in ascribing it to the third century.

[88] Ch. Huelsen, *Jh. ö. arch. Inst.*, vol. 15, 1912, pp. 135–142; Platner-Ashby, p. 331; Lugli, *MAR*, vol. 3, pp. 229–231; Nash II, pp. 36–37.

[89] Cipollino columns had a short period of popularity in the second century.

[90] *CIL*, vol. 15 (2), no. 7248.

[91] Lugli in his Forma Urbis Romae still clings to Lanciani's east-west orientation.

[92] Gnecchi, *Med. Rom.*, vol. 2, no. 25, pl. 39, no. 5; D. Brown, *NNM*, no. 90, pl. 5, no. 3.

[93] The small size of the temple is disconcerting, but it may be due to inept drawing.

[94] R. Lanciani, *Bull. Com.*, vol. 11, 1883, pp. 5–16; Platner-Ashby, p. 81.

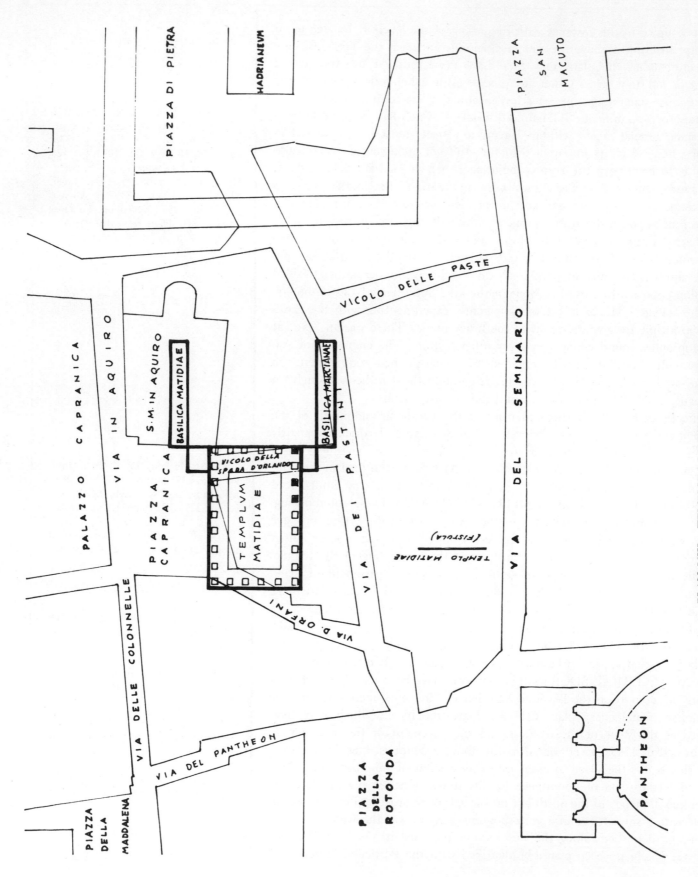

PLAN VIII. TEMPLUM MATIDIAE, BASILICA MATIDIAE,
AND BASILICA MARCIANAE

Fototeca Unione

mentaria,[95] was apparently gravely injured by fire and rebuilt rather early in the second century.[96] It was no longer an open porticus, but became a warehouse enclosed in brick walls. The remains of this second phase, though scanty, attest a complete rebuilding. The bricks were carefully shaped from red tiles and joined with a minimum of fine mortar. The one Hadrianic stamp reported of A.D. 123 is not sufficient evidence for the date. The bricks are thinner (2.5–3.2 cm.) than those used until the end of the reign of Hadrian. They cannot belong to a later date because of the relation of the walls to later phases. We have, therefore, in all probability another monument included in the general reorganization of this part of the Campus Martius in the time of Hadrian.

Along the east side of the Via Lata three porticoed complexes comparable to Hadrianic projects at Ostia indicate an expansion of the city in this area. As a result of discoveries in 1955 in the excavations for the underpass at Largo Chigi, Gu. Gatti[97] was able to identify a vast span of porticoes and shops extending from the modern Via delle Muratte to Via di S. Claudio (plan IX). Brick stamps found on *bipedales* of an arch and in a wall are evidence for a date near A.D. 123. Gatti's important study has greater significance for topography than for construction. The types of brickwork and the use of travertine shown in the photographs of his report are consistent with Hadrianic practices elsewhere.

Precinct Wall around the Ara Pacis

The discovery in 1930 of a Hadrianic pomerial cippus at the corner of Via della Torretta and Via di Campo Marzio nearly three meters above a Vespasianic[98] one attests a general raising of the northern part of the Campus Martius; this left the Ara Pacis[99] in a sunken area which needed protection. When the residue of the monument was gathered up (1937–1938) and restored at a new site near the Mausoleum of Augustus, a brick-faced precinct wall was found. It was distant from the marble enclosure 2.8 m. on the north, east, and south but only 55 cm. on the west. The core contained a heterogeneous aggregate of tufa, tile, and the debris of buildings demolished when the level was raised. It was left rough on the outside since it was obviously a retaining wall for a fill, but it was faced on the inside with fine brickwork. The bricks were triangles rather than those from broken tiles more usual in the period, but they yielded stamps of A.D. 123. Pieces of a convex travertine coping undoubtedly capped the wall and showed the marks for a grille presumably of bronze. The two cippi mentioned above have an added interest in that they bear the same number[100] proving thereby what is stated in the inscription[101] that Hadrian renewed terminal stones rather than extended the pomerium itself. The reason for the renewal is obviously the elevation of the Campus Martius.

Pons Aelius

When Hadrian chose a site on the right bank of the Tiber for his Mausoleum, he had to build a new bridge over the Tiber to make a worthy approach for it from the city. This became the Pons Aelius mentioned by Cassius Dio[102] and Spartianus.[103] Curtailed and somewhat modified, it is the Ponte

[95] For this phase, see Blake, RC II, p. 28.

[96] E. Sjöqvist, *Skrifter*, vol. 12, pp. 52–88 with conclusions in pp. 82–83, 88.

[97] Gu. Gatti, "Caratteristiche edilizie di un quartiere di Roma del II secolo d. Cr." *Saggi di storia dell'architettura in onore del Professor Vincenzo Fasolo* (Rome, 1961) pp. 49–66.

[98] P. Romanelli, *Not. sc.*, 1933, pp. 240–244.

[99] G. Moretti, *Ara Pacis Augustae*, Rome, 1948, pp. 94–98. For the monument, see Blake, RC I, pp. 177–178.

[100] The CLIIX in the report of the Hadrianic stone must be an unusual rendering of CLVIII, which is given on the other.

[101] *CIL*, vol. 6 (4), no. 31539. The date is A.D. 121. See also Platner-Ashby, p. 396; Lugli, MAR, vol. 2, pp. 97–98; M. Labrousse, *Mél.*, vol. 54, 1937, pp. 166–167.

[102] Cassius Dio, 69, 23, 1.

[103] Aelius Spartianus, SHA, *Hadrianus*, 19, 11.

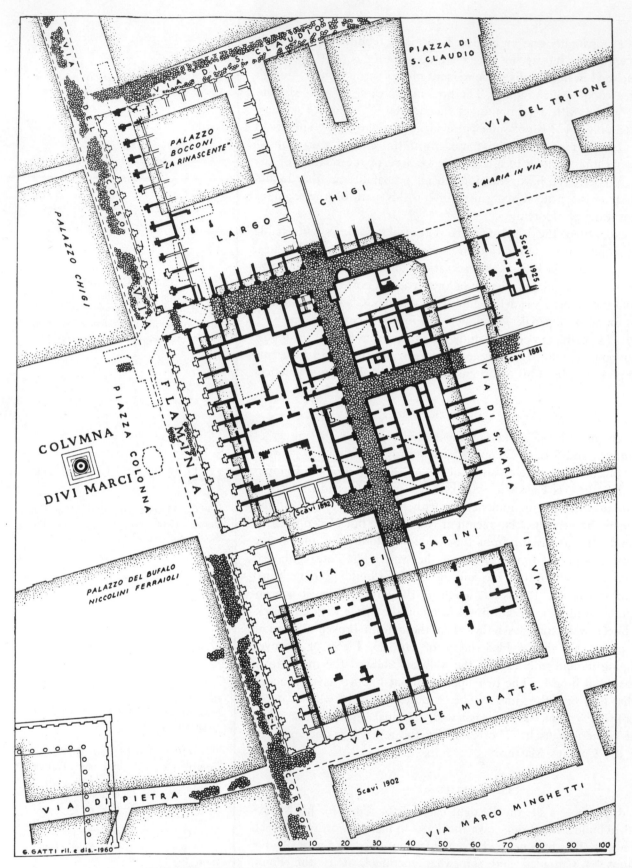

Within the plan, the following labels appear:

VIA DI S. CLAUDIO

PIAZZA DI S. CLAUDIO

VIA DEL TRITONE

PALAZZO BOCCONI "LA RINASCENTE"

S. MARIA IN VIA

CHIGI

LARGO

Scavi 1925

PALAZZO CHIGI

VIA DEL CORSO

VIA FLAMINIA

Scavi 1881

COLVMNA DIVI MARCI

PIAZZA COLONNA

Scavi 1892

VIA DI S. MARIA IN VIA

PALAZZO DEL BUFALO NICCOLINI FERRAIOLI

VIA DEI SABINI

VIA DE-L

VIA DI PIETRA

Scavi 1902

VIA DELLE MURATTE

VIA MARCO MINGHETTI

G. GATTI ril. e dis. -1960

0 10 20 30 40 50 60 70 80 90 100

PLAN IX. HADRIANIC SHOP AND PORTICO COMPLEXES
OPPOSITE THE COLUMN OF MARCUS AURELIUS

G. Gatti, in *Saggi di Storia dell'Architettura
in Onore di Vincenzo Fasolo*,
Rome 1961, p. 59.

Sant'Angelo today.[104] Before the bridge was built the engineers regulated the banks of the river in the vicinity by a stepped embankment[105] so that there should be provision for the Tiber when it was low, high, and in spate respectively. On the right side and presumably on the left side as well, the embankment, faced with a tufa reticulate,[106] sloped down to a landing, then dropped perpendicularly to a second landing, whence it sloped down to the river bed. At the right bank, a series of vaulted chambers made entirely of concrete with a tufa aggregate joined the embankment to the foundations of the Mausoleum.[107] The tiles covering a sewer connected with these chambers yielded brick stamps of the period, one of which is datable in A.D. 130.[108] The construction of the bridge was clearly revealed in the excavations of 1892–1893 and carefully reported by the archaeologists of the period, who were, however, unable to preserve it in its entirety (pl. 7, fig. 1).[109] Two piers of concrete with a tufa aggregate were erected in the stream up to the height of the lower landing platform. They terminated in imposts which, with the help of a low pier on the land side, supported the three arches that carried the bridge over the central channel. The arches rose between buttresses which were stepped from the level of the second landing for about half of the remaining height. The central part of the passage rested upon the tops of the four piers and the crowns of the arches. A ramp leading up to the central part from each side was supported by a smaller lower arch at the lower landing and a still smaller one resting on the upper landing. These openings would serve as extra passages for the water in time of flood. The ramp on the left (pl. 7, fig. 2) required one more arch in its descent to the level of the Campus Martius. All the side arches were heavily buttressed on both faces. Thus there were eight arches for a causeway about a hundred and thirty-five meters long.[110] All this masonry was of concrete faced first with Gabine stone,[111] which appears only in the foundations and in the intrados of the arches. The rest was covered with travertine fastened together with iron bar clamps leaded into place (pl. 8). The travertine blocks forming the sidewalks on each side projected beyond the facing about 30 cm. to make a plain coping.[112] The blocks were irregular in size and fastened together with clamps. A parapet of piers and sculptured panels was added for the protection of the pedestrians.[113] An inscription copied by Giovanni Dondi dall'Orologio in 1375[114] before it fell into the river probably formed the central panel[115] and was duplicated on the other side. This proves that the bridge was dedicated in A.D. 134. Pedestals for statues were found on the side toward the Mausoleum. A coin displaying four pedestals over the main piers, supporting columns surmounted by statues,[116] cannot be accepted as evidence for the appearance of the bridge until its authenticity is established.

MAUSOLEUM HADRIANI

It is not known precisely when Hadrian's contractors started work on the Mausoleum itself,[117] which was not dedicated until A.D. 139,[118] a year after the death of Hadrian. A firm foundation was prepared by laying an enormous platform of concrete about two meters thick. The main entrance to the precinct was at the head of the Pons Aelius across a street which followed

[104] Only the three central arches remain in their original form. The other two have been raised to equal them in height.

[105] R. Lanciani, *Bull. Com.*, vol. 21, 1893, pp. 14–26.

[106] For the Hadrianic modification of the embankment near the Marmorata, see p. 38 above.

[107] L. Borsari, *Not. sc.*, 1892, pp. 420–421.

[108] *CIL*, vol. 15 (1), no. 1212a, found also in the Mausoleum (Bloch, *Bolli*, p. 254).

[109] R. Lanciani, *Bull. Com.*, vol. 16, 1888, pp. 129–130; idem, *Bull. Com.*, vol. 21, 1893, pp. 14–26; idem, *Ruins*, pp. 22–24; C. L. Visconti, *Bull. Com.*, vol. 20, 1892, pp. 263–265; L. Borsari, *Not. sc.*, 1892, pp. 231–233, 412–428; Ch. Huelsen, *Röm. Mitt.*, vol. 8, 1893, pp. 321–323. See also S. R. Pierce, *JRS*, vol. 15, 1925, pp. 95–98; Platner-Ashby, pp. 396–397; Lugli, *MAR*, vol. 2, pp. 310–315; Nash II, pp. 178–181; Gazzola, *Ponti*, pp. 131–132.

[110] These measured 3, 3.5, 7.59, 18.39, 18.39, 18.39, 7.59, 3.75 meters or thereabouts from left to right. Lugli gives the central ones as 18.2.

[111] Lugli, *op. cit.*, p. 312.

[112] Lugli's figures: sidewalks ca. 2.2 m., roadbed 4.5 m. for a total width of 10.89, or, without the parapet, of 8.85 m. The road was relaid at the height of the sidewalks in the Middle Ages.

[113] They proved inadequate for the pilgrims of 1450 who were precipitated into the river.

[114] *CIL*, vol. 6 (1), no. 973.

[115] Lugli (*op. cit.*, p. 314) would place it at the bridgehead.

[116] T. L. Donaldson, *Architectura Numismatica*, London, 1859, pp. 246–247; Cohen, vol. 2, p. 234, no. 1508; Gnecchi, *Med. Rom.*, vol. 2, p. 8, no. 51, pl. 42, no. 4.

[117] Platner-Ashby, pp. 336–338; M. Borgatti, *Castel Sant' Angelo in Roma*, Rome, 1931, pp. 11–71; Lugli, *MAR*, vol. 3, pp. 693–708; Nash II, pp. 44–48; Crema, p. 484; Frova, p. 83; H. Windfeld-Hansen, "Les couloirs annulaires dans l'architecture funéraire antique," *Acta Instituti Romani Norvegiae*, vol. 2, 1965, pp. 35–63. S. R.

Pierce, *JRS*, vol. 15, 1925, pp. 75–103, is particularly valuable for details of construction. In the following pages, no attempt is made to enter into controversial questions.

[118] The dedicatory inscription (*CIL*, vol. 6 (1), no. 984) gives the date.

[119] L. Borsari, *Not. sc.*, 1892, pp. 422–423.

[120] The spans are 2.1 m., 2.4 m., 2.1 m. respectively.

[121] One is pictured in Borgatti, *op. cit.*, p. 60, fig. 38.

[122] The exact measurement is 115 m.

[123] The evidence for the bronze work goes back ultimately to the Mirabilia (twelfth century).

[124] See especially the study by D. Strong in *PBSR*, vol. 21, 1953, pp. 129, 142–147.

[125] This is almost certain though the reference in Petrus Mallius for *cancellis (aeneis)* concerns the doors in the outer enclosure wall.

[126] *CIL*, vol. 6 (1), nos. 985–995.

[127] Such an extensive use of Parian marble (Procopius, *B.G.* 5, 22, 13) seems strange at this time when Luna marble was being used almost exclusively. Possibly microscopic analysis would prove this to be Luna. Strong, *op. cit.*, writes that the marble seems to be Luna.

[128] A fragment of a horse's tail in Parian marble gives confirmation to the conjecture.

[129] Pierce, *op. cit.*, p. 82 n. 2.

[130] *Ibid.*, p. 101, II (a).

[131] Borgatti, *op. cit.*, p. 16.

[132] *CIL*, vol. 15 (1), no. 319. On the brick stamps in general, see Bloch, *Bolli*, pp. 253–256.

the line of the Tiber embankment.[119] A great travertine threshold, when uncovered in 1892, still retained traces of four piers of travertine blocks which defined three passageways.[120] They were covered with fluted marble pilasters which ended in Corinthian capitals.[121] Bronze doors, perhaps in the form of grilles, protected the openings. Similar piers occurred at regular intervals along the low wall of peperino blocks which enclosed an area of over a hundred square meters.[122] Both travertine and peperino were doubtless concealed by a marble revetment. There may have been a gate with bronze doors at the center of each of the other three sides, but there were certainly bronze grilles[123] between the piers surrounding the whole area through which passers-by could view the splendor within. Peacocks of bronze completed the decoration. It is not known how many there were, but two may still be admired in the Cortile della Pigna of the Vatican.

The square basement of the tomb itself stands about fifteen and a half meters behind the present wall. It did not apparently, as we shall see, figure in the original specifications, but represents a change of plan in the course of construction. The basement was over eighty meters long and slightly over eight meters high. The wall, ca. 1.2 m. thick, rests on a low socle which supported angle pilasters with beautifully carved capitals that appeared to carry a frieze depicting swags of poppy seeds and oak leaves depended from bucrania. The curtain was composed of blocks of travertine probably covered by a marble revetment. Its appearance from the Pons Aelius can be reconstructed with a reasonable accuracy from various Renaissance drawings.[124] A bronze door[125] stood in the center within a marble frame. The dedicatory inscription may have been placed over it. The lower part of the wall was reserved for the funerary inscriptions[126] of those buried within; the upper part, with a revetment of Parian marble[127] cut to simulate rusticated blocks. Statuary of marble[128] rather than of bronze as popularly supposed, representing horses and men, stood at the angles between the square basement and the circular drum. It is probable that the other sides were the same though without the central door or the honorary inscriptions. Inside this wall but half a meter distant there was a wall of brick-faced concrete from which radiated walls of the same type of masonry, making sixty-seven chambers. These were manifestly constructed after the drum was finished. It has been suggested that at some stage of the construction the outer wall of brick-faced concrete was intended as the outer wall of the basement.[129] The core of the walls shows a tufa aggregate; the facing, a good brickwork though not quite up to the usual standard for the time of Hadrian (pl. 9). The bricks were triangles, but made from roof tiles.[130] In any case, the surface would have been concealed by plaster, were it intended for some purpose other than buttressing the part above, as the traces of travertine corbels to support a flat wooden ceiling and the matrix for a pavement of some kind would seem to indicate. There were communicating doors with lintel arches of *bipedales* in the partition walls between the barrel-vaulted chambers. The vaults sloped outwards a bit, so that the adjustment had to be made in the brick-facing in accommodation to the *bipedales* that served as imposts.[131] The Hadrianic stamps of A.D. 123[132] on these cannot be taken as evidence for a precise dating. At the corners square masses of concrete were inserted as foundations for the statuary on top.

The Mausoleum was originally intended, as we have seen, to be a circular monument. At the ground-floor level, a lofty corridor, starting from the vestibule giving access to the radial chambers, led through the circular mass of concrete to an apsed chamber in the center. All the fundamental masonry, including the vaults, was in a squared-stoned masonry of travertine blocks carefully shaped and laid without mortar. Those of the barrel-vaulted corridor had been made wedge-shape for precise joining. Beneath the impost, a projecting cornice shows grooves for the insertion of bronze ornaments, perhaps oak leaves. The actual pavement, laid over the substruction of irregular pieces of inferior stone visible today, was certainly marble and probably polychrome; the walls were covered with a revetment of giallo antico;[133] the ceiling was doubtless stuccoed. The apsed chamber must have been decorated in the same fashion. The apse undoubtedly contained a more than life-sized statue of Hadrian standing on a pedestal, which would seem to greet visitors at the entrance. On the left there was a rectangular niche; but on the right, the entrance to the spiral ramp within the core leading to the upper story. The arch over the opening shows clearly the careful fitting of the wedge-shaped blocks of travertine. This spiral ramp, which is nearly three meters wide, led to the actual burial chamber placed directly over the apsed chamber. The concrete walls are faced with a brickwork which is somewhat different from that in the radial walls below. The bricks are magenta red (3.5 cm. $\times$ 3.3–3.35 cm.), laid with a whitish mortar speckled with black pozzolana in close joints (0.65–0.9 cm.).[134] Bonding courses of yellow *bipedales* are a characteristic feature. The walls were apparently covered with a marble revetment treated architecturally with base molding, pilasters, and cornice. Grooves in the wall three meters up mark the position of the cornice. Above this there was undoubtedly painted stucco to harmonize with the ceiling, which was definitely prepared for stuccoing. Upon the wooden centering of the barrel vault, tiles were laid between more or less upright *bipedales* designed to penetrate the mass of concrete. The underside of the tiles was then covered with the appropriate stucco work. Halfway up, the ramp became lower,[135] and there is no longer any trace of preparations for stucco work, which would not in any case have been visible in the dim light. The pavement was made with great care, having a substruction in four levels—travertine, concrete, tile, *opus signinum*—for a simple black-and-white mosaic. Four splayed openings in the vault gave light and air to the ramp and also facilitated the passage of rain water from a drain beneath the floor to sewers below. The stepped interior of these shafts was covered with *opus signinum*.

The spiral ramp ended in a square vestibule from which a corridor, 3.2 m. wide, led to the actual burial chamber. The lower part of the walls of the corridor displays a fine brick facing similar to, though not identical with, that of the spiral ramp. The bricks are reddish yellow rather than magenta red, show a somewhat wider range in thickness, and are laid with coarser joints but with the same yellow *bipedales* as bonding courses. Apparently Lugli took his measures from this room,[136] though they differ slightly from

[133] The marks of the clamps by which it was held are clearly visible.

[134] The measures are Pierce's (op. cit., p. 100, I (a)).

[135] Borgatti (op. cit., p. 20) sees in this evidence of the resumption of work after the death of Hadrian.

[136] Lugli, *Tecnica*, pp. 605–606. *Cf.* Pierce, op. cit., p. 100 I (b).

[137] Borgatti (op. cit., p. 22) thinks that they were without decoration.

[138] Pierce (op. cit., p. 87) calls it tufa.

[139] See Lugli, Tecnica, pp. 214–218.

[140] Pierce (ibid.) interprets what is apparently the remains of this pavement as a sort of bench against the wall.

[141] Pierce's conjecture (ibid., pp. 88–89) that there was a spiral stepped ramp is not accepted by Borgatti (op. cit., pp. 53–54).

Pierce's. He gives the added information that they were triangles made from *sesquipedales*. The black pozzolana is lacking in the mortar. The coarser brickwork in the upper part of the wall may indicate a resumption of work after a temporary suspension. The pavement of peperino from Viterbo was no doubt covered with marble in antiquity; and probably the walls were also.[137] At any rate there was the same sort of decorative cornice to suggest a treatment similar to that in the entrance corridor below. No trace of the stuccoing which doubtless decorated the concrete barrel vault has survived the various vicissitudes of the monument. A shaft at the south end seems to have supplied a little light to the corridor.

The burial chamber proper was a square (8 m. per side) of cut-stone masonry of travertine[138] similar to that in the apsed chamber below. The voussoirs in the arch at the entrance were cut in accommodation to a rectangular doorway. Piranesi is the authority for ascribing to them the mysterious "bozzi" which have occasioned a good deal of speculation.[139] A niche with a curved head opposite the entrance and one with a rectangular top in each side wall converted the lower part into a Greek cross, but the chamber was covered with a barrel vault of travertine. There are traces of the travertine pavement[140] which rested on the peperino floor preserved today. The travertine of both pavement and walls up to the springing of the arch was doubtless concealed by marble. The one piece of the wall revetment preserved is giallo antico. The vault and the "lunette" at the top of the end walls were almost certainly decorated with stucco work. The chamber was only dimly lighted from the corridor except when it was illuminated with torches. The windows there now are not ancient.

Above the burial chamber, there was a second one similar to it but lower and without the niches. Openings in the east and west walls are probably what remain of original doorways. Only the end walls are of squared-stone masonry of tufa; the side walls are of brick-faced concrete, an indication that the barrel vault was also of concrete. In the tufa masonry, wherever found, mortar was used in between the joints. The brickwork is the same as that in the corridor leading to the burial chamber. Brickwork and stonework were carefully bonded at the corners. There is no indication of how this room was decorated, and its purpose is unknown. How access to it was managed has led to much speculation.[141] The top of this chamber was at the apex of the drum. Above this was the central tower which was certainly circular on the inside and probably on the outside as well. It was divided horizontally into two parts and finished with a hemispherical vault under the probably hollow pedestal of the statuary on top. Its walls were of brick-faced concrete similar to that in the radial walls, which confirms the dating of the latter. It was apparently approached from the garden on top of the drum by a short flight of steps leading to an encircling staircase of the same masonry as the walls.

We return now to the exterior. The drum (pl. 9) emerging from the square basement is 64 m. in diameter and 21 m. high. It is defined by a concrete wall faced on the outside with squared-stone masonry preponderately of tufa but with some courses of travertine and lined on the inside with *opus signinum* where the mound of earth which topped the drum came against it. Rubble filled the lower part. Pierce has carefully analyzed the concrete.[142] The whitish gray mortar is essentially the same throughout the wall, and the *caementa* are laid in the same sort of irregular rows. Up to the lowest travertine course, the heterogeneous aggregate probably came from buildings destroyed in the vicinity. Above this, the *caementa* seem to be roughly graded by weight—selce first, then travertine, finally tufa—though there is a certain amount of intermingling. Where the main axes of the basement cut the drum there are four relieving arches of brick (*bipedales?*) which have no apparent structural value. Pierce suggests that they may have been intended as the heads of ornamental niches before the change of plan involving the addition of the basement hid them from view.[143] The blocks of the outer facing were laid in an abundance of mortar and the surface faced with Parian (?) marble. There is still not much unanimity among scholars as to how the facing was treated architecturally.[144] The most satisfactory, on the whole, presents a series of pilasters supporting the pedestals for the many statues brought by Hadrian from Greece to adorn his monument.[145] Pieces of pilasters of the proper size have been found. There may have been a repetition of the frieze of bucrania and garlands, but the curved piece used for confirmation has the wrong arc and probably belonged higher up. Pierce places an ambulatory behind the parapet with the statues. Be that as it may, the space between the periphery and the central tower was covered with a concrete cap, 18 to 21 cm. thick, sloping outward for drainage to the airshafts and then on to the wall of the drum. On this rested the mound of earth. There were holes suitable for the planting of cypresses. Traces of earth were found in the pockets where there is every reason for thinking that it was placed by the ancients. The pockets were five or more meters deep. According to some of the old drawings, the central tower which arose among the cypresses was decorated to look like a mighty rectangular altar, but the majority of modern scholars visualize it as circular, which is certainly more satisfactory aesthetically than the square tower posited by Borgatti.[146] Above it was a platform, probably hollow, to support the pedestal of the statuary on top. Among the many restorations, that of a quadriga with Helios or Hadrian himself is the most acceptable. The entire monument reached a height of about fifty-four meters.

IMPERIAL RESIDENCES

Domus August(i)ana

Hadrian did not feel the urge to erect a new palace for himself in Rome;[147] but, unlike Trajan who was content to dwell in the Domus August(i)ana as it was with practically no alteration,[148] he discovered much that needed to be done to add to its comfort or impressiveness and to bolster up the overbold experiments in vaulting of Domitian's architect.[149]

His first change,[150] namely the insertion of a hypocaust in the state dining room, was actuated by a consideration for the comfort of the guests to be entertained there and had no connection with the general restoration. His contractors took such advantage as they could of the walls of the rooms buried below to construct an *L*-shaped gallery across the hall by means of

[142] Pierce, *op. cit.*, p. 102.

[143] *Ibid.*, p. 84.

[144] Borgatti, *op. cit.*, pp. 37–46.

[145] These were the statues broken up and used as missiles in the Gothic War. See Procopius, *B. G.* 1, 22, 22.

[146] Borgatti, *op. cit.*, pp. 44–48.

[147] Before his adoption by Trajan, Hadrian dwelt in a house on the Aventine near San Saba in all probability which he in turn gave over to Antoninus Pius (*SHA, Marcus Antoninus*, 5, 3).

[148] For a possible Trajanic change along the Clivus Victoriae, see p. 39 above.

[149] Blake, *RC* II, pp. 115–124; Frova, p. 70.

[150] G. Carettoni, *Not. sc.*, 1949, pp. 73–76.

which heat from an outside furnace could be introduced and through an opening near the center allowed to spread in the space between the two floors and be dispersed through four wall vents. The hypocaust was of the usual form with a double floor of *bipedales* separated by piers of *besales* 60 cm. high, but there were no wall tubes. Brick stamps as well as the nature of the construction bespeak a Hadrianic date.[151]

By the time of Hadrian it had become increasingly apparent that Rabirius had not paid sufficient heed to the great weight of the bold vaulting of the public rooms of the Domus Flavia.[152] The makeshift strengthening attempted perhaps before the end of the reign of Domitian apparently was not enough. Hadrian himself was particularly interested in the problems posed by intricate vaulting and no doubt gave this matter his personal attention. The approved scheme provided for the closing of a southern doorway in the west wall of the Basilica and for the construction of spur walls with doorways from the columns[153] of the West Porticus to the west wall of the Basilica. The wall, extending outward to the fifth column, was left solid to support a stairway. Similar spur walls were constructed in the southern part of the porticus where there was no strategic necessity. Brick stamps found in every part of this construction leave no doubt as to its date. Most are of A.D. 123, but there is a smattering of those of A.D. 126 and 127, and of 129 which furnishes the *terminus ante quem non*.[154] The core consists of refuse material thrown in without order—yellow and brown tufa, bits of marble and travertine—in a light mortar with a fine aggregate of red, red brown, and dark gray pozzolana. The pozzolana was apparently washed but not sifted. The facing was of triangular bricks in the walls to the west of the Basilica and of broken tile for the rest of the way. They vary in color from yellow red to magenta red with a little streaking of red and yellow at times and in width from 3.3 cm. to 3.7 cm. Bonding courses appear at regular intervals made of *bipedales* similar in color and texture to the bricks. Both are close knit and well fired. The mortar between the bricks varies from 0.8 to 1.7 cm. in width and shows the same unsifted pozzolana in clean lime.

In the throne room itself apparently no restoration was needed. In the "*lararium*" five[155] piers were inserted on the inside of each of the long walls obviously to support a barrel vault. It is possible that a flat roof of the time of Domitian was replaced by a vault at this time. The *caementa* used in the concrete—brick, travertine, marble—seem to be refuse material from some fire. They are laid in orderly rows in mortar similar to that used in spur walls of the Porticus. Triangular bricks face the core with bonding courses of magenta tiles at regular intervals.

The Palatine Stadium, as we have seen,[156] was the last addition made by Domitian to the Domus August(i)ana. It is possible that work upon it continued up to the time of Hadrian,[157] though on the whole that would seem to me unlikely. Sufficient brick stamps of the Hadrianic period have been found in the excavations of past years[158] to point to some minor alteration, but the construction which remains seems homogeneous throughout, except for the Severan restoration which is easily discernible. The exedra in particular has been and still is attributed to Hadrian by many scholars[159] purely on the evidence of brick stamps found there.[160] The brickwork of

---

151 Bloch, *Bolli*, p. 211.

152 H. Finsen, *Domus Flavia sur le Palatin: Aula Regia-Basilica* (Copenhagen, 1962; = *Analecta romana instituti danici II supplementum*).

153 The corner piers of the Basilica.

154 Bloch, *Bolli*, pp. 211–217.

155 Two on the west side are joined together. The corner ones were intended to be 3.25 m. long though the one at the northeast has been curtailed to accommodate a doorway; the others are 2.2 m.

156 See *RC* II, p. 122–123.

157 V. Massaccesi, *Bull. Com.*, vol. 67, 1939, p. 122 n. 8.

158 Three (*CIL*, vol. 15 (1), nos. 847, 1035, 1115a) were found in fallen vaults; one hundred and thirty-four loose stamps came to light in the course of the excavation. It is quite possible that the majority if not all of these came from other buildings in the neighborhood. See G. Gatti, *Not. sc.*, 1893, p. 118; idem, *Mon. ant.*, vol. 5, 1895, cols. 67–69.

159 P. Romanelli, *The Palatine*, Rome, 1950.

160 R. Lanciani, *Not. sc.*, 1877, p. 203. Only six (*CIL*, vol. 15 (1) nos. 122b, 593, 565, 580, 1073, 1075) out of fifteen are Hadrianic.

the curving rear wall seems, however, to be of the same quality as in the rest of the Domitianic part. This monument more than any other shows the importance of noting the exact provenience of each stamp found. When Hadrianic stamps are discovered in essential parts of the monument, we shall be justified in claiming that Hadrian had a part in its construction.

A large area at the northeast corner of the Palatine, though rather recently excavated, remains unpublished. Since brick stamps of the time of Hadrian (varieties not specified),[161] were discovered in the two-story substruction along the Nova Via, it is probable that its monumental gate[162] was also Hadrianic. If Lugli's analysis[163] is correct, this was the site of the *templum (vetus) divi Augusti* which was burned in A.D. 68. We have already noted some Domitianic work;[164] and now we must apparently credit Hadrian with preparing the site[165] for the later *Aedes Caesarum*.

Domus Tiberiana

The great reception hall behind the Temple of Castor was apparently adopted for the use of some of the palace retinue.[166] A hypocaust was installed for the comfort of the men; and the west wall on the inside and perhaps the east wall as well were lined with rooms probably to a height of at least three stories. Most of the west wall has collapsed but there are substantial remains of partition walls on the outside, which may be all that is left of another block of eight rooms possibly also three stories high.[167] If, on the other hand, the original vault ran parallel to the Vicus Tuscus, as Lugli believes,[168] or if such were substituted for an earlier one running in the opposite direction, these "partition" walls may have been primarily buttresses to strengthen a wall inadequate to bear the weight of the vault. These walls have been dated from their similarity to walls in other parts of the edifice which have yielded stamps belonging to about the middle of the reign of Hadrian.[169] The core of the walls had an aggregate of broken brick and the facing was of dark red bricks made for the most part from broken roof-tiles. Pavements were of herringbone brick and the barrel vaults rested on tile imposts. Delbrueck lists an alteration in the vaulting at the entrance to the atrium to bring it into alignment with a superstructure of arches in the center and a stairwell with the usual latrine in the southeast corner. There were minor changes also in the rooms behind and in the ramp leading to the Palatine.

Horti Sallustiani

The Hadrianic façade of the imperial palace in the Horti Sallustiani[170] must next claim our attention. Near the head of the narrow valley between the Pincian and the Quirinal, a rather shallow vestibule between two wings led to a lofty circular hall (pl. 10, fig. 3). Preoccupation for the stability of the great cupola controlled all the planning for this monumental Hadrianic façade (plan X). The substruction of exceptionally firm concrete consisted of entirely straight walls. The perimetric walls were strengthened by ponderous cross walls.[171] Arches were thrown from wall to wall where the transition from the vestibule to the rotunda caused a potential weakness. Environmental conditions led to inaccessible basement rooms with a low barrel vault under the antechamber to a hall opposite to the entrance, under the prolonga-

[161] Nibby, *Roma 1838*, part 2, p. 473.

[162] Lugli, *Bull. Com.*, vol. 69, 1941, pp. 52–53.

[163] *Ibid.*, pp. 37–53.

[164] See *RC II*, p. 124.

[165] See also P. Bigot, *Bull. Com.*, vol. 39, 1911, p. 84. Walls in reticulate and brick mentioned on p. 82 must be earlier than the systematization.

[166] R. Delbrueck, *Jb. d. Inst.*, vol. 36, 1921, pp. 23–27.

[167] Delbrueck conjectures that these opened on to a roofed area. If so, the Vicus Tuscus must have passed through it.

[168] Lugli, *Bull. Com.*, vol. 69, 1941, pp. 30–31; *idem, Centro*, pp. 187–190.

[169] Bloch, *Bolli*, pp. 33, 34 n. 37.

[170] K. Lehmann-Hartleben and J. Lindros, *Skrifter*, vol. 4, 1935, pp. 196–227. For the general bibliography see Nash I, p. 491; add Crema, pp. 473–477, figs. 620–621; Neuerburg, *Fontane*, pp. 66–67.

[171] Lugli (*MAR*, vol. 3, p. 329) still considers them remains of an earlier building.

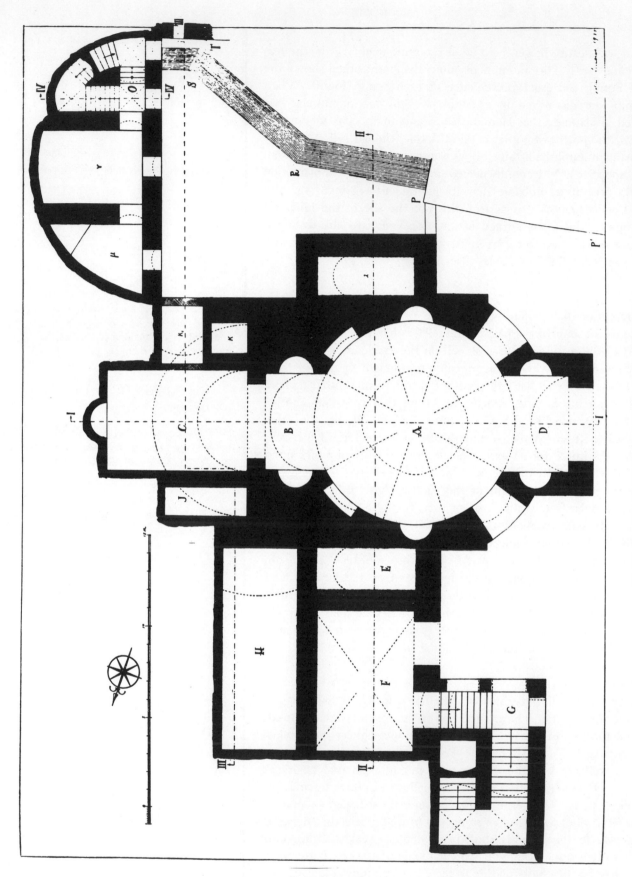

PLAN X.   PLAN OF THE HORTI SALLUSTIANI

J. Lindros, in *Acta Inst. Sueciae*,
vol. 4, 1953, pl. 2.

tion of the hall at the east, and under a mezzanine apartment in the north wing. Even the substruction of the pavement was particularly heavy. The rotunda itself was encompassed by chambers, which, whatever their ostensible purpose,[172] served as buttressing agents. The vestibule was apparently considered adequate to give stability to the front part of the dome, since the narrow side chambers start only at the line of a superstructure at the upper level. We have already mentioned the vaulting under the antechamber to the hall at the east. Narrow rooms flanking this hall up to the line of the prolongation were included with it under a large barrel[173] vault above the individual barrel vault of the hall itself. The hall is said to have been partly open to the sky originally. A single curvilinear niche decorated each side wall of vestibule and antechamber; a curvilinear niche between two rectangular ones was planned for each side of the rotunda; but a window took the place of the one on each side of the entrance, and doors were substituted for those at the east. They seem to have been more widely spaced in the upper register. Segmental relieving arches at strategic points along the floor level were inserted to strengthen the wall; and a continuous line of arches over niches and relieving arches between them served almost as an impost for the mighty dome, which was of the pavilion type with every other section concave. Pilasters prove that there was an ornamental doorway at the main entrance of the type familiar at Ostia; and holes for travertine corbels show that some of the niches at any rate were converted into small shrines. The side rooms on the south contained fountains.

A narrow façade slightly recessed stood between the entrance unit and a monumental stairwell on the north. An overhanging balcony, supported on concrete vaulting resting on huge travertine corbels, drew these two units together architecturally. The façade presented to the west merely a window and a door at the ground-floor level and two corresponding windows above. The windows had the usual slightly curved lintel arches of *bipedales*, whereas the door had a rampant arch apparently because there was a steep outside ramp leading indirectly to the terrace above. The window belonged to the narrow room flanking the rotunda; the doorway, to a large hall connected indirectly with the rotunda and giving access to the tower within which the stairs ascended around three sides of an air shaft.[174] The stairs were carried in part on rampant lintels of *bipedales* and the landings were supported on cross vaults,[175] but the most remarkable feature was the ample provision for light. A window stood over the entrance to the stairs, two faced the south, and one the west at each story. Originally, there was no communication between these front rooms and the space behind them which served merely as a substructure for the mezzanine apartment. This must have been reached originally from the grand staircase, though later it had an inner staircase leading to the terrace, which as we have seen could be approached by an outside staircase. Not much of this mezzanine is preserved.

The south wing[176] was set somewhat higher up the slope well back from the front line of the entrance unit. Three stories of this façade (pl. 6, fig. 3) with a high mezzanine brought this wing up to the level of the terrace above the central unit. This purely functional façade was terminated by a row of rather small corbels of travertine supporting brick arches under an over-

[172] They formed secondary entrances to the rotunda.

[173] Lugli (*op. cit.*) calls a depressed vault what is really part of a full arch.

[174] This innovation was an inspiration to Renaissance architects.

[175] The steps were covered with marble, the landings with mosaic, and the vaults were painted.

[176] This façade resembles those of the apartment houses of Ostia.

[177] Oliver (*MAAR*, vol. 10, 1932, p. 160) considered it Trajanic, but brick stamps confirm the Hadrianic date.

[178] Marks of the temporary wooden boxing are plainly visible.

[179] Oliver, *op. cit.*

[180] The bricks are almost all triangles according to Lehmann-Hartleben (*op. cit.*, p. 209); from broken tiles, according to Oliver (*op. cit.*).

[181] This is one of the earliest examples of the cupola "a conchiglia," "a spicchi," or "ad ombrello." See G. de Angelis d'Ossat, *III conv. st. archit.*, pp. 226–227.

[182] See below, pp. 249–251.

[183] Lehmann-Hartleben, *op. cit.*, pp. 214–217; Bloch, *Bolli*, pp. 184–185. Stamps found in the Canopus of Hadrian's Villa (*ibid.*, pp. 141–144) prove that the two structures were being erected at practically the same time.

[184] Lehmann-Hartleben, *op. cit.*, pp. 216–217.

[185] For the bibliography see Nash I, p. 163.

[186] *CIL*, vol. 15 (1), no. 812. See G. Schneider-Graziosi, *Acc. P. Diss.*, ser. 2, vol. 12, 1915, pp. 171–172.

hanging balcony. It stretched from the central unit to another monumental staircase deftly fitted within a curved outer wall. Probably the curve here and behind the two adjacent rooms at each story was due to the configuration of the hill. There were in all fourteen ramps serving six stories of this mammoth staircase. It comes as a surprise that so imposing a façade concealed so few rooms. The two on the ground floor had travertine sills and were not intercommunicating. Doors and windows, as elsewhere, were covered with slightly curved lintels of *bipedales*, and the mezzanine windows rested directly on the lintels of the doors. A superstructure over the central unit extended over the northern part of the wing. In contrast to the lower part it exhibited reticulate insets in brick frames. The bricks used in both parts are identical. Little of the upper part remains.

The actual construction is in accord with Hadrianic practices.[177] An aggregate of travertine was used in a tenacious white mortar in the heavy foundations, of terra cotta in the core of the walls,[178] and of tufa in the vaults. The lower part both inside and out was faced with bricks[179] about 3 cm. thick.[180] Practically no whole *bipedales* appear in the wall itself but they were employed for all arches. As usual, however, only every fifth or sixth tile voussoir was whole to make a bond; the rest were broken pieces used as facing. The barrel vault of both vestibule and antechamber contained a tile reinforcing arch at the end toward the dome, and the lower part of the straight sections of the dome were faced with brick. Brick and reticulate combined appear at the upper level, and one hall at any rate had brick-faced columns. The vaulting exhibits great variety. The barrel vaults over vestibule and antechamber were to be expected. The oblong rooms flanking the rotunda were also barrel-vaulted as was the hall opposite the entrance. Its barrel vault was protected by a higher one encompassing the three rooms. Cross vaults appear only in the hall in front of the northern staircase and under the landings in both wings. The pavilion cupola[181] of the circular room dominated them all. Thus did the architect strive to distribute the stresses. The vaulting belongs to the same period of experimentation as the Canopus of Villa Adriana.[182] Minor changes, primarily blocking niches and filling holes intended to support ornamental members, exhibit practically the same type of masonry and seem connected with a change of taste in which the richness of marble paneling was substituted for the variety of line furnished by the alternation of semicircular and rectangular niches. A hundred or so brick stamps of A.D. 123[183] suggest a date of A.D. 125 or thereabouts for the original brickwork; a score variously dated from A.D. 124 to 134 indicate that the renovation was also Hadrianic.[184] There was a small nymphaeum farther down the slope to the southeast of the rotunda.

SACRED EDIFICES
Imperial Residences

Between the "Domus Liviae" and the Temple of the Magna Mater, there are the remains of a small edifice, perhaps a temple which is possibly of the Hadrianic period.[185] A brick stamp of approximately A.D. 123 in the aggregate of the foundation gives the *terminus ante quem non*.[186] Fragments of tufa, peperino, travertine, selce, and white marble are laid in roughly alternate rows with rather large pieces of tile. The mortar varies somewhat in color in the various parts but contains the usual unsifted red, brown, and black pozzolana. One to three rows of roughly laid tiles were used to prepare the bed for a row of thin (2.8–3.5 cm.) *bipedales*, all with one exception of the red-brown which we think of as brick color. This foundation course undoubtedly supported a wall of brick-faced concrete. What remains seems to have been relaid in modern times. The facing of the earlier wall at the north shows a slightly different technique. The bricks are light yellowish red and speckled and the tiles are yellow. These bricks are triangles. The exact orientation of this little edifice suggests that it replaced a primitive structure of some sort, but whether the Auguratorium mentioned as restored by Hadrian in an inscription[187] discovered in the Lateran is still open to question.[188] The earlier wall at the north has a slightly different orientation.

LUDUS MAGNUS

Brick stamps found in the excavations of the Ludus Magnus prove that Hadrian continued construction on the plan initiated by Domitian.[189] It is not possible now, however, to differentiate the Hadrianic work from the additions made by Trajan.

THE ANTONINES

ANTONINUS PIUS (A.D. 138–161)

During his long reign Antoninus Pius more than justified his sobriquet by the construction of monuments motivated by filial piety. He completed a certain amount of work started by Hadrian and made necessary repairs, but the greater number of buildings for which he was responsible at Rome were monuments commemorating the imperial family. We are fortunate in having a list of public works in Julius Capitolinus as a guide. Of buildings in Rome he writes, "Of the public works that were constructed by him the following remain today: the temple of Hadrian at Rome, so-called in honor of his father, the Graecostadium, restored by him after its burning, the Amphitheatre, repaired by him, the tomb of Hadrian, the temple of Agrippa, and the Pons Sublicius."[1]

MAUSOLEUM HADRIANI

The Mausoleum of Hadrian was dedicated by Antoninus Pius to Hadrian and the Deified Sabina before the deification of the latter in A.D. 139. This information is given in the dedicatory inscription.[2] Whether any of the actual construction was left for Antoninus to finish is an open question,[3] but in any case Julius Capitolinus was not justified in attributing the erection of the monument to him.

USTRINUM ANTONINORUM

With the completion of the Mausoleum, a new *ustrinum* for the members of the imperial family would seem almost obligatory. Consequently, when a

[187] *CIL*, vol. 6 (1), 976. See G. Schneider-Graziosi, *op. cit.*, pp. 153–178.

[188] A. Bartoli, *Acc. P. Mem*, vol. 6, 1943/47, p. 238. Most of the evidence adduced to prove that this was the Auguratorium has been vitiated by subsequent discoveries. The building is mentioned in the Mirabilia as located where San Caesarius stood in the twelfth century. San Caesarius has been discovered in another part of the Palatine. A sixteenth-century manuscript places it between Templum Jovis Victoris and Siciliae locus. What used to be considered Juppiter Victor is now generally identified with Apollo Palatinus. The site of Juppiter Victor is unknown and of the Sicilia problematical.

[189] See above, p. 34.

[1] Julius Capitolinus, *SHA*, *Antoninus Pius* 8, 2–3 (Loeb Classical Library).

[2] *CIL*, vol. 6 (1), no. 984.

[3] See above, p. 55.

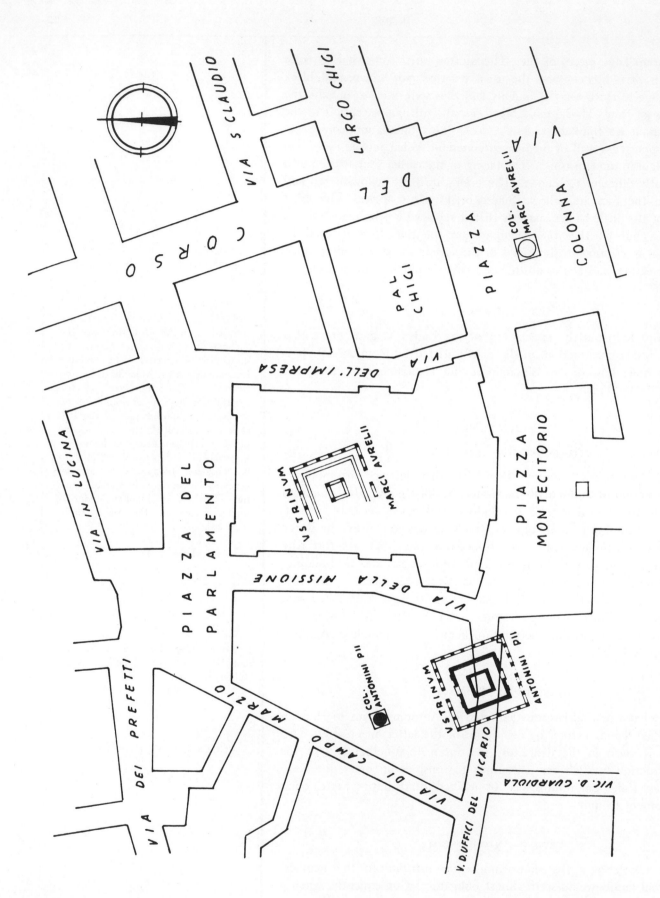

PLAN XI. USTRINA ANTONINI PII ET MARCI AURELII

suitable enclosure was uncovered in 1703 northwest of the Piazza de Monte Citorio (plan XI), it was immediately called the Ustrinum Antoninorum.[4] It is reasonable to suppose that Antoninus caused it to be constructed, but there is no proof. There were three enclosures, one within the other,[5] 3.2 m. apart. The outer one with an entrance from the south consisted of a travertine curb, travertine posts fastened to it by iron clamps, and an iron barrier of some sort. The middle one was a solid wall of travertine about a meter thick with an ornamental doorway in the north face flanked by two niches. The doorway was covered by a pediment supported by richly decorated consoles within the entablature with which the entire wall was finished; the niches had separate pediments upheld by small Doric columns. The inner wall, also of travertine, faced the platform upon which the pyre was erected.[6] The travertine blocks were re-used, and so there is little hope of more information with regard to the technique employed. Much of the travertine was probably covered by a marble revetment.

TEMPLE OF VENUS AND ROMA

A number of coins issued between A.D. 140 and 143 depict the Temple of Venus and Roma.[7] Mattingly[8] interprets the choice of subject as a commemoration of the fact that Antoninus completed the temple which must then have been dedicated unfinished by Hadrian. Strack,[9] on the contrary, sees in the coins a reaffirmation on the part of Antoninus Pius of the religious policy of his predecessor. If so, the numismatic evidence furnishes another instance of filial piety. Too little remains of the Hadrianic phase of the temple[10] to permit a solution on archaeological grounds.

TEMPLE OF ANTONINUS AND FAUSTINA

Faustina died in A.D. 141, and the Senate decreed a temple in her honor.[11] Coins were issued with the legend DEDICATIO AEDIS to commemorate the vote[12] and with PIETAS AVG[13] to call to mind the loving care with which the emperor sought to assuage his grief.[14] A place was found for the temple east of the Basilica Aemilia on the Sacra Via where it still stands as one of the most conspicuous monuments visible from the Forum (pl. 11, fig. 1).[15] It was raised up on a lofty podium and approached by a fine flight of steps in the middle of which are the remains of an altar. It was hexastyle prostyle with a porch showing three intercolumniations at the sides, but uncluttered by interior columns. The columns are of unchanneled cipollino with bases and Corinthian capitals of white marble and a white marble entablature. The frieze probably encircled the whole building at the top of the cella walls, which like the podium were covered with a white marble revetment. Much of the delicate frieze of griffins, garlands, and sacrificial instruments remains *in situ*. An inscription on the architrave records the original dedication to Faustina and a second on the frieze bears witness to a later dedication to Antoninus himself.[16] Not enough remains, or at any rate has come to light, to make feasible any restoration of the interior. Beneath the glistening white marble there was a substantial masonry of squared-stone construction of peperino which lies exposed today. This rested on a founda-

---

[4] Ch. Huelsen, *Röm. Mitt.*, vol. 4, 1889, pp. 48–64; Platner-Ashby, p. 545; Lugli, MAR, vol. 3, pp. 249–251; Crema, p. 505; Nash II, pp. 487–488.

[5] The dimensions are 30 m., 23 m., 13 m. per side respectively.

[6] It is possible that the central square was a mighty altar rather than the platform for the funeral pyre. The pyre of Faustina is depicted on a coin (*BMC, Emp.*, vol. 4, pl. 34, 10).

[7] *BMC, Emp.*, vol. 4, Antoninus Pius, pls. 29, nos. 10–13; 30, 1–3; 31, 3, 8, 9; 32, 8; Brown, *NNM*, no. 90, pl. 5, 2; Strack, *Reichsprägung*, vol. 3, pl. 10, nos. 849, 864.

[8] Mattingly, *BMC, op. cit.*, p. lxxxii.

[9] Strack, *op. cit.*, p. 69.

[10] See above, pp. 40–41.

[11] Julius Capitolinus, SHA, *Antoninus Pius*, 6, 7.

[12] *BMC, Emp.*, vol. 4, Antoninus Pius, nos. 306 and 479 with pl. 10, 13.

[13] *Ibid.*, nos. 319–323 with pls. 8, 2 and 7, 17; 1454–1457 with pl. 35, 3 and 4.

[14] Others bear the legend AETERNITAS (nos. 383 with pl. 9, 6; 1506–1508 with pl. 36, 2 and 3; 1562–1564 with pl. 37, 12; 1605 with pl. 38, 10).

[15] A. Bartoli, *Mon. ant.*, vol. 23 (2), 1916, cols. 949–974; Platner-Ashby, pp. 13–14; Lugli, *Centro*, pp. 220–221; Nash I, pp. 26–27; Frova, p. 90.

[16] *CIL*, vol. 6 (1), no. 1005.

tion course of travertine. Since quarry marks had apparently gone out of use years before, the few blocks of peperino showing them may represent a re-use of old material.[17] Headers and stretchers were employed for the podium, stretchers alone for the cella walls. A thin layer of red earth mixed with water was spread over the blocks to assist in the process of sliding them into place,[18] but clamps were used instead of mortar to hold them together. The surface is still marred with the holes made by the seekers after the lead that held the clamps in place. The rough face of the blocks was smoothed after they were in place[19] and the ugly stone concealed by the marble revetment.

HADRIANEUM

Antoninus Pius had no sooner completed the temple to his deified wife than he must have turned his attention to a temple in honor of his deified adoptive parents.[20] According to Julius Capitolinus,[21] he dedicated the temple, presumably finished, on the day that Verus assumed the *toga virilis*, which should have been in A.D. 145. There is, however, a coin of A.D. 150–151[22] depicting two seated figures at the center between the columns of an octastyle temple with the legend PIETAS which seems more appropriate for the Temple of Divus Hadrianus et Diva Sabina[23] than that of Divus Augustus et Diva Livia which he erected eight years later. Whatever the date of the dedication, there are substantial remains of the temple itself where the Regionary Catalogues indicate that the Hadrianeum should be (pl. 11, fig. 2). The site chosen was east of the Temple of Matidia, Hadrian's deified mother-in-law. Modern scholarship[24] has demolished many conjectural restorations and placed the remains in their proper setting. A broad flight of steps supported by a barrel vault gave access to the top of a high podium, the walls of which were faced with travertine under the columns and with peperino elsewhere. The cella was enclosed on all four sides by a pycnostyle colonnade of eight by thirteen Corinthian columns of white marble. Four intercolumniations at the sides correspond to the depth of the porch, which was apparently without inner columns. If so, the supports for the roof must have been of wood. The floor of the cella was four steps higher than the porch. Its walls were of peperino and, with the colonnade, supported a narrow outer barrel vault and a broad inner one over the cella. The soffit of the latter was deeply coffered. The pedestals of the engaged columns along the inner walls of the cella gave a place for the well-known statues of the provinces;[25] the spaces between them were decorated with reliefs of trophies and garlands. As in the Temple of Antoninus and Faustina, a marble revetment concealed all the peperino, both inside and out. The temple stood in a paved court surrounded by porticoes, the back wall of which was also of peperino covered with marble within but rusticated on the outside. The columns at the entrance at any rate were of giallo antico. Castagnoli[26] has brought together a considerable body of evidence in support of a conjecture that a commemorative arch with three openings led from the ancient Via Lata into the precinct of the Hadrianeum. Since nothing remains of it today except a sculptural relief in the Palazzo dei Conservatori, it falls without the province of this study. The temple in times past has been called erroneously the temple of Neptune. It now serves as the Bourse.

[17] Lugli, *Tecnica*, pp. 200, 204 n. 3.

[18] *Ibid.*, pp. 242–243.

[19] *Ibid.*, p. 235.

[20] Julius Capitolinus, SHA, *Antoninus Pius*, 8, 2.

[21] *Idem*, *Verus*, 3, 1.

[22] *BMC, Emp.*, vol. 4, Antoninus Pius, no. 1869, pl. 45, 17.

[23] Strack, *Reichsprägung*, part 3, pp. 144–145; Mattingly, *BMC, op. cit.*, pp. lxv, lxix, lxxxix.

[24] V. Passarelli, *III conv. st. archit.*, pp. 123–130; Lugli, *MAR*, vol. 3, pp. 164–168. For additional bibliography and photographs consult Nash I, pp. 457–461; Crema, p. 382, figs. 451–452; Frova, p. 90.

[25] They did not decorate the podium as was assumed earlier. A restoration of some may be seen in the Museo Nazionale delle Terme; see also Frova, pp. 268–270.

[26] F. Castagnoli, *Bull. Com.*, vol. 70, 1942, pp. 74–82.

Temple of Divus Augustus

Although coins of A.D. 158–159[27] prove that Antoninus Pius restored the Temple of Divus Augustus,[28] by a strange oversight Julius Capitolinus fails to mention it, unless he inadvertently called it the Temple of Agrippa.[29] The coins depict an octastyle façade of Corinthian columns with a view between them of two figures, presumably statues of the Deified Augustus and his wife. A lost fragment of the Marble Plan,[30] shows the inscription (g)RECOST(asis)[31] at the side of what would appear to be an octastyle temple on a high podium. Lugli[32] identifies this with the Temple of Augustus; Nash, however, has shown that this is the entrance hall to the Domus Tiberiana, built by Domitian.[33] The fire to which Julius Capitolinus ascribes the destruction of the Graecostasis may have consumed the Temple of Augustus as well. Topographers still tend to locate both the Graecostasis and the Temple of Divus Augustus in the area south of the Basilica Julia which has never been systematically excavated. Until some remains have come to light, neither monument has anything to contribute to this study.[34]

Sanctuaries

In addition to the great monuments of state, three small sanctuaries can be attributed to Antoninus Pius for one reason or another. They have little or no importance to a study of construction, but they serve to complete the story of the building activity of the period. By the middle of the second century, there was little room in the space enclosing the Forum Romanum for a shrine of any sort, but one was crowded against the steps of the Porticus of Gaius and Lucius where, no matter how beautiful it may have been in itself, it would certainly detract from the impressiveness of the building behind it. Most of what remains belongs to a restoration in the fourth or fifth century, but the walls behind the later marble revetment were faced with brickwork which Lugli[35] adjudged to be Antonine. None of it is visible today. The divinity to which it was dedicated is unknown. A piece of a curved epistyle (3.9 m. in diameter when complete), found in 1899, now lies along the Sacra Via opposite the Basilica of Maxentius.[36] The fragmentary inscription[37] proves that it once belonged to an edifice restored by Antoninus Pius; and the relief upon it of a dancing Maenad suggests that the edifice was a temple of Bacchus. Martial[38] alludes to a temple of Bacchus in the vicinity. A coin of Antoninus Pius[39] (pl. 10, fig. 2) depicts a small round shrine containing a statue of Bacchus to which worshipers are bringing offerings. Behind the shrine, there is a semi-circular colonnade. Du Jardin[40] identified the sanctuary with a podium in the form of a half circle near where the piece of peristyle now lies. Such of the brick facing as remains may well be Antonine. Furthermore, it is entirely possible that Antoninus Pius restored a Temple of Aesculapius on the Tiber Island,[41] but it is questionable whether a single coin of A.D. 140–141 depicting the arrival of the serpent at the island should be taken as absolute proof. The coin could be one of a series representing historic traditions.[42] No remains of the temple have been discovered.

[27] BMC, Emp., vol. 4, Antoninus Pius, nos. 938–943 with pl. 20, 5–7; 2051 with pl. 49, 20; 2052; 2063 (there are others which cannot be dated precisely); Strack, Reichsprägung, part 3, pl. 4, nos. 336, 347, pl. 15, nos. 1162, 1167, 1194; Brown, NNM, no. 90, pl. 6, no. 5; Nash I, p. 164; Frova, p. 71.

[28] For the older temple, see Blake, RC II, p. 13.

[29] Two brick stamps (Bloch, Bolli, p. 116) indicate that some work was done on the Pantheon but scarcely enough to justify the claim that Antoninus Pius restored the Temple of Agrippa.

[30] FUR, pp. 75–76, Frag. 18e.

[31] Platner-Ashby, pp. 248–249; Lugli, Centro, pp. 93–94. Lugli (Bull. Com., vol. 70, 1941, pp. 55, 57–58) points out that it could not be the Graecostasis, of which no mention is made after the time of Augustus.

[32] Lugli, Bull. Com., vol. 70, 1941, pp. 53–58.

[33] Nash I, p. 164 and especially p. 365 where the pertinent articles are cited.

[34] On the Vicus Tuscus just beyond the Basilica, two pilasters of a commemorative arch are still extant which may have served as the entrance. Lugli (Centro, p. 179) attributes the brickwork to the end of the century.

[35] Lugli, Mon. min., pp. 118–120.

[36] G. Gatti, Not. sc., 1899, p. 223; idem, Bull. Com., vol. 27, 1899, p. 147; D. Vaglieri, Bull. Com., vol. 31, 1903, pp. 27–29; Ch. Huelsen, Röm. Mitt., vol. 17, 1902, pp. 95–96; Platner-Ashby, p. 321; Lugli, Centro, pp. 219–220; Nash I, pp. 165–168.

[37] CIL, vol. 6 (4, 3), no. 36920.

[38] Martial, 1, 70.

[39] Cohen, Antonin, no. 1187; Gnecchi, Med. Rom., vol. 2, pl. 55, 9; Brown, NNM, no. 90, pl. 6, 1.

[40] L. du Jardin, III cong. st. rom., vol. 1, pp. 77–80.

[41] Besnier, L'Ile Tibérine, pp. 191–192, 317; Platner-Ashby, pp. 2–3; Lugli, MAR, vol. 3, pp. 623–625.

[42] Besnier, op. cit., pp. 175–183. Even the interpretation of the coin has led to controversy. See A. W. Van Buren, JRS, vol. 1, 1911, pp. 187–195.

Secular Buildings: Repairs and Restorations

In a reign as long as that of Antoninus Pius, it was inevitable that a number of secular buildings should need to be repaired or restored. We have already mentioned the Graecostasis[43] as being in that category. After a serious collapse causing the death of over a thousand persons at some time during these years,[44] the Circus Maximus must have been repaired almost immediately, but no trace of this restoration has been identified up to the present time. Julius Capitolinus[45] also attributes to him a repair of the Colosseum. Dr. Van Deman[46] detected traces of his work in the four walls to the left and the three to the right of the Forum entrance on the ground floor only. The concrete core shows an aggregate of brick (one Flavian triangle was noted) and yellow tufa in a red and white mortar made of medium fine pozzolana and lime; the facing exhibits bricks made from magenta tiles (3.5–3.9 cm. $\times$ 27–33 cm.), of the same quality as those used in the arches, for which they were rendered slightly wedge-shaped. The horizontal joints are finer than the vertical ones but are not raked. No vaulting remains of this restoration. Dr. Van Deman also suspected that the work over the travertine piers of the imperial entrance on the north was Antonine.

Four Antonine stamps[47] discovered in the west wing of the Atrium Vestae point to some minor change in that part of the edifice, but there is no essentially Antonine phase. Brick stamps of M. Rutilius Lupus found in practically all the walls adjudged Antonine by Dr. Van Deman[48] seem never to occur after the time of Trajan.[49]

There is inscriptional evidence[50] that in A.D. 143 Antoninus Pius granted headquarters to a guild of athletes which came to be called the Curia Athletorum and that it was located near the Baths of Trajan. The conjecture of Ricci[51] that he gave over to them an apsed hall of the Domus Aurea which remained contiguous to though independent of the Baths is attractive. In any case no Antonine work has been reported from the vicinity which can be ascribed to it.

Bridges and Tiber Embankment

The connection between a record inundation of the Tiber and a restoration and dedication of the Pons Agrippae in A.D. 147 reported in the Fasti Ostienses[52] is obvious. It is possible that the same flood made necessary a restoration of the old Pons Cestius in A.D. 152, which is also recorded in the Fasti.[53] Until the discovery of the Fasti we had no knowledge of these two restorations. Unfortunately, nothing remains of either one. Julius Capitolinus[54] credits him with a restoration of the Pons Sublicius. Even its site is a matter of controversy. A coin of Antoninus Pius[55] depicting a bridge in the background of a representation of Horatius belongs to a series representing episodes in the legendary history of Rome and does not in my opinion commemorate the restoration of a bridge. In A.D. 161, a renovation of the boundary stones along the Tiber was started by Antoninus Pius[56] and continued under the same curator riparum under Marcus Aurelius and Lucius Verus.[57] This was probably accompanied by any necessary repairs to the embankment, but no trace of any such has been reported.

[43] See above, pp. 65, 69.

[44] Jordan-Huelsen, p. 131; Platner-Ashby, p. 117 where the text of Chron. Min., 146, is given.

[45] Julius Capitolinus, SHA, Antoninus Pius, 8, 2.

[46] Unpublished notes.

[47] Bloch, Bolli, p. 85.

[48] Van Deman, Atrium Vestae, pp. 35–42.

[49] Bloch, op. cit., p. 77.

[50] IG, xiv, nos. 1054, 1055, 1102–1110; CIL, 6 (2), nos. 10153, 10154; Jordan-Huelsen, p. 314; Platner-Ashby, p. 142.

[51] C. Ricci, Bull. Com., vol. 19, 1891, pp. 185–209.

[52] Degrassi, Fasti O., pp. 206, 207, 236.

[53] Ibid., pp. 206, 207, 238.

[54] Julius Capitolinus, SHA, Antoninus Pius, 8, 3.

[55] Cohen, Antonin, no. 127.

[56] CIL, vol. 6 (4, 2), no. 31553.

[57] Ibid., no. 31554; C. Caprino, Not. sc., 1948, pp. 139–140.

MARCUS AURELIUS (A.D. 161–180)

Marcus Aurelius was not a builder. His talents lay in other directions. He performed his duty by the memory of Antoninus Pius and was himself honored during his lifetime by commemorative monuments. A couple of minor temples are accredited to him.

COMMEMORATIVE MONUMENTS AND TEMPLES

Columna Antonini Pii

Since it seemed appropriate to dedicate the temple of the Deified Faustina anew to Antoninus Pius after his deification,[58] Marcus Aurelius did not consider it necessary to build another in his honor, but he and his brother by adoption, Lucius Verus, erected a memorial column to him in the Campus Martius[59] twenty-five meters north of the "ustrinum." It consisted of a richly sculptured base, a monolith of red granite nearly fifteen meters high, terminating in a Corinthian capital and supporting a colossal statue of the late emperor. It was protected by a grating. None of it remains *in situ*. The base may now be seen in the Giardino della Pigna in the Vatican, and the general appearance may be seen from coins.[60]

Columna M. Aurelii Antonini

To the southeast of these structures, on the ancient Via Lata (modern Via del Corso), the Roman people erected a column to celebrate the victories of Marcus Aurelius over the Marcomanni and Sarmatii in A.D. 172–175.[61] Although it was probably begun almost immediately, it was not finished apparently until long after his death. It is a distinct imitation of the Column of Trajan, though carried out in Luna rather than in Pentelic marble, and preserves the same proportions and architectural features. There was no burial chamber in its pedestal, but a special stairway cut in the blocks and lighted by slit windows led to the great statue of Marcus Aurelius on top. Since the reliefs on the pedestal were in damaged condition and the dedicatory inscription gone, the Renaissance restorer, Fontana, encased it in marble which he took in part from the Septizodium. The historic reliefs on the spiral are not so well executed as those of Trajan's Column, and yet the Column of Marcus Aurelius, still standing in the Piazza Colonna, is an impressive monument, though it now bears a statue of Saint Paul. It is probable that the Temple of Divus Marcus mentioned by Julius Capitolinus,[62] stood just to the west of it, but no remains have ever been found which could be identified with it. Ashby[63] supposes that both column and temple were enclosed in a porticus.

Ustrinum M. Aurelii Antonini

About seventy meters to the northeast of the Column with the same orientation, a second structure (plan XI; above, p. 66) similar to the "Ustrinum Antonini Pii" came to light when the new parliament building was in process of construction.[64] Its central podium was over ten meters square. It was surrounded by an ambulatory six meters wide paved in travertine and by two precinct barriers, respectively twenty-five and thirty meters square,

[58] Platner-Ashby, p. 13.

[59] *Ibid.*, p. 131.

[60] Nash I, pp. 270-275; coins: *BMC, Emp.*, vol. 4, Marcus Aurelius, pls. 54, 17; 71, 9; 72, 1 & 11; Frova, pp. 90, 272–274.

[61] Platner-Ashby, pp. 132–133; Lugli, *MAR*, vol. 3, pp. 240–248. For the extensive bibliography pertaining to this column consult Nash I, p. 276; add Crema, p. 505, figs. 649–650; Frova, pp. 90, 276–287.

[62] Julius Capitolinus, *SHA, Marcus Antoninus*, 18, 8. See Platner-Ashby, p. 327; Lugli, *op. cit.*, pp. 248–249.

[63] Platner-Ashby, p. 133.

[64] D. Vaglieri, *Not. sc.*, 1907, pp. 525–528, 681; A. Pasqui, *ibid.*, 1909, pp. 10–11; G. Gatti, *Bull. Com.*, vol. 35, 1907, pp. 326–327; vol. 36, 1908, p. 86; vol. 37, 1909, p. 113; G. Mancini, *St. rom.*, vol. 1, 1913, pp. 3–13; R. Delbrueck, *Arch. Anz.*, 1913, cols. 140–143.

to speak in round numbers. The space between them was two and a half meters except at the back where it was narrowed to 1.8 m. and was paved in *opus signinum (intonaco testaceo)*. The barriers consisted of travertine posts with iron grilles. Blocks of Luna marble belonging to the facing of the central podium, pieces of cornices, and acroteria, found in the course of the excavation, give some idea of the elegance of the structure, which was apparently two stories high. Because of the elaborateness of this decoration, Delbrueck believed that the monument was an altar rather than the Ustrinum of Marcus Aurelius. In any case, it would seem to be later than the "Ustrinum" and Column of Antoninus Pius. No remains are available for study *in situ*, and so this brief description must suffice.

Arches

Three or four commemorative arches have been ascribed to Marcus Aurelius, but since no one of them is preserved, they need not delay us long. The so-called Arco di Portogallo, spanning the Via Lata near San Lorenzo in Lucina until its destruction in 1662, has been attributed to him by most modern topographers,[65] but a recent analysis[66] seeks to prove that its level belonged to a later period and that its construction—a nucleus of travertine faced with marble—was probably not earlier than the fifth century of the Christian era. Old engravings show it as a conventional one-span archway with reliefs borrowed from some Hadrianic period. The Regionary Catalogues list an arch erected in honor of Divus Lucius Verus in Region I[67] which must have been built after A.D. 169. An inscription[68] found on the Capitoline bears witness to another voted to Marcus Aurelius by the Senate in A.D. 176.[69] Three reliefs found at the foot of the Capitoline have been ascribed to it.[70] They differ widely in style from the eight panels on the Arch of Constantine which record events terminating in A.D. 174. These latter were undoubtedly taken from some structure of the time of Marcus Aurelius and may give evidence for a fourth commemorative arch.[71]

Temple of Mercury

Coins of A.D. 172/3[72] depict a statue of Mercury in a strange looking shrine with herms for columns and various attributes in a semi-circular pediment. Presumably, this is a restoration of the Temple of Mercury on the Aventine.[73] No remains of it have ever come to light.

COMMODUS (A.D. 180–193)

Commodus was even less of a builder than his father; and his interests were entirely frivolous and ephemeral. He left no monument in Rome which can be ascribed with assurance to his personal influence, and few elsewhere. Such public buildings as belong, in all probability, to his time are listed below for convenience.

TEMPLE OF DIVUS MARCUS

So great was the affection of all for Marcus that a temple was decreed to him at his death by both the Senate and the people.[74] As we have seen,[75]

[65] Platner-Ashby, p. 33; Lugli, MAR, vol. 3, pp. 267–270; Kähler, RE, Triumphbogen, no. 30, cols. 388–390; Crema, p. 602.

[66] S. Stucchi, *Bull. Com.*, vol. 73, 1952, pp. 101–122.

[67] Platner-Ashby, p. 47; Kähler, *op. cit.*, no. 31, col. 390; Frova, p. 90.

[68] *CIL*, vol. 6 (1), no. 1014.

[69] Kähler, *op. cit.*, no. 33, cols. 391–392; Frova, p. 90.

[70] Platner-Ashby, p. 37; Kähler, *op. cit.*, no. 32, cols. 390–391.

[71] On the complicated topographical and chronological problems of the Column and arches of Marcus Aurelius see the recent discussions of M. Dobias (*Charisteria Francisco Novotny octogenario oblata*, Prague, 1962, pp. 161–174), J. Ruysschaert (*Acc. P. Rend.*, vol. 35, 1962–1963, pp. 101–121), and G. Lugli and P. Mingazzini (*Arch. cl.*, vol. 17, 1965, pp. 147–153).

[72] *BMC, Emp.*, vol. 4, Marcus Aurelius, pl. 83, no. 7; and a contorniate of Faustina *senior*, dated A.D. 356–395—see Maria Panvini Rosati Cotellessa, *Bull. Com.*, vol. 75, 1953–1955 (1956), pp. 99–107.

[73] Blake, RC I, p. 120.

[74] Sextus Aurelius Victor, *De Caesaribus*, 16, 15: *denique, qui seiuncti in aliis, patres ac vulgus soli omnia decrevere, templa columna sacerdotes.* See Frova, p. 90.

[75] See above, p. 71.

it probably faced his column but, to the best of my knowledge, no remains of it have ever come to light.

TEMPLE OF JUPITER HELIOPOLITANUS: SECOND PHASE

On the evidence of certain dedicatory inscriptions, the Temple of Jupiter Heliopolitanus has been ascribed to A.D. 176.[76] Since, however, there was a sacred enclosure here from the second half of the first century of the Christian era, it is possible that these dedications preceded the actual building of the temple. In any case, Commodus was particularly interested in Oriental cults and undoubtedly encouraged the erection of the sanctuary, probably by the M. Antonius Gaionas mentioned in the inscriptions. Only a part of the square court and two small rooms with mosaic floors have thus far been excavated. Like the precinct wall of the earlier sanctuary they were orientated with the points of the compass. Like it, the court showed rows of upright ollae arranged at right angles to each other. They undoubtedly had ritualistic significance of some kind. With the exception of the northern boundary of the court, which was a wall three meters high of jars laid horizontally, what little construction remains offers little of interest. The eastern wall of the court, based on the wall of the earlier precinct, was of rough blocks of tufa laid on a stratum of *opus signinum (ciment de tuileaux)* 12 cm. wide. The other walls are relatively solid though faced with rough pieces of stone and brick. The threshold of one of the small rooms had a stamp[77] usually ascribed to Septimius Severus but by Bloch listed among those of Caracalla (A.D. 212–217). A threshold could be restored. It is possible that further excavation will give precision to the chronology of this second phase of the sanctuary. The wall of jars appears to be unique.

THERMAE COMMODIANAE

Even the Baths to which his name was given were built by his favorite, Cleander. They are generally thought to have been south or southeast of the Baths of Caracalla,[78] but no trace of them has come to light to my knowledge.

PRIVATE CONSTRUCTION

The increasing use of brick stamps with consular dates in the second century has made it possible to reduce the private building of the period to a fairly close chronology. Although comparatively few such stamps were used before the reorganization of the brick industry in A.D. 123, a long list of those in use under Trajan can be compiled from his public monuments.[1] The reorganization would seem to have led to an overproduction so that bricks of A.D. 123 were being used in Antonine buildings, even though bricks were still being manufactured and stamped with consular dates practically every year from A.D. 124 to 164.[2] The reader must not, therefore, exaggerate the extent of Hadrianic building activity beyond its due proportions on the evidence of brick stamps alone. Where there is no admixture of later stamps the attribution is fairly conclusive. Unfortunately, the reports mentioning the stamps frequently do not give the information necessary for an analysis

[76] G. Nicole and G. Darier, *Le Sanctuaire des Dieux orientaux au Janicule*, Rome 1909, pp. 28–31; P. Gauckler, *Le sanctuaire syrian du Janicule*, Paris 1912, pp. 227–249; G. Darier, *Les fouilles du Janicule à Rome*, Geneva 1920, gives a complete bibliography up to 1917. To that should be added Platner-Ashby, pp. 294–295, and the bibliography cited by Nash I, p. 525.

[77] *CIL*, vol. 15 (1), no. 762b; Bloch, *Bolli*, pp. 300 and 302.

[78] Platner-Ashby, p. 525.

[1] Bloch, *Bolli*, pp. 36–85.

[2] *Idem, Suppl.*, pp. 84–87.

of the construction. Where stamps are not present it is not always possible to distinguish between late Domitianic and early Trajanic masonry, nor between late Trajanic and early Hadrianic. After the time of Hadrian there is much less help from stamps. In general, the construction offers a few aids to chronology. Triangular bricks continued to be used in private building after the use of them had been virtually discontinued in public monuments. Although seldom used in the Trajanic period, they are not uncommon in the Hadrianic. Where roof tiles were broken to make bricks, the construction is more likely to be Trajanic or Hadrianic than Domitianic. A mixture of the two types of brick is always possible. The use of neat insets of reticulate in brick frames for secondary walls reached its highest perfection under Trajan and Hadrian. After the wealth of construction which can be ascribed with confidence to the reign of Hadrian, the Antonine material seems meagre. There is little to distinguish it from the less careful work of the contractors of the preceding years; and there are fewer brick stamps to confirm the ascriptions. The use of narrow bricks certainly began as early as Commodus, but it is impossible in a private edifice to differentiate masonry of his time from that of his successor. Although these contractors followed the general methods employed in public monuments, there was plenty of scope for individual experimentation. Sometimes the quality of the work fell way below the standard required for public edifices. Generalizations are always difficult. The presentation of the private construction by categories makes possible the insertion of some material which is not strictly datable.

Private construction within the city falls into two main classes—dwellings and mercantile establishments. To these must be added the tombs which were outside the city limits and the country estates near enough to the city to have been entrusted to city contractors. As in modern cities, shops on the ground floor of apartment houses with an occasional market catered to the fundamental needs of the residential areas. Private baths[3] must have depended largely on the dwellers in the neighborhood for their clientele. It is difficult to tell to what extent the great granaries and storehouses filling in the entire quarter between the Aventine and the Tiber were constructed by the State rather than by individuals; but since they cannot be attributed to specific emperors, it has seemed best to link them all together. Though the masonry in these two categories must be presented for completeness, the remains are seldom extensive enough to yield anything new to information derived from other sources. Tombs and country estates, on the other hand, being better preserved, have more to offer.

DWELLINGS

When the Regionary Catalogues were compiled in the fourth century, it was possible to divide the habitations into *domus et insulae*. It seems unlikely that by the second century space could have been found in the thickly settled residential areas for many new houses (*domus*) consisting for the most part of one story and belonging to a single proprietor. Many no doubt were handed down from one generation to another. In the outskirts more often than not, the dwelling was a villa built on terraces with various supernumerary structures. Neither of these two types presented any new structural

[3] If Sextus Petronius Mamertinus, who was praetorian prefect in A.D. 139–143 and suffect consul in A.D. 150, built the Balneum Mamertini mentioned in the Regionary Catalogues as being in Region I, it falls within our period. No remains so far as I know have ever been associated with it, nor is its location known. See Platner-Ashby, p. 70, and M. Hammond, *The Antonine Monarchy* (Rome 1959, Papers and Monographs of the American Academy in Rome, vol. XIX), pp. 247, 271 n. 24.

problems. The well-integrated apartment house (*insulae*) had come into being only slightly, if at all, earlier than the time of Trajan. His contractors had shown such resourcefulness in the erection of public monuments that it is incredible that they should not have contributed much to this development, which reached its peak in the reign of Hadrian. Experimentation in non-essentials continued, but the fundamentals of construction were fixed. Ostia, as we shall see, is the place to familiarize oneself with the Hadrianic and Antonine apartment houses, but traces of similar ones have come to light in Rome itself. It is possible that many more remain to be discovered. Today, too little is preserved in the majority of cases to make the distinction between *domus* and *insulae* in the remains, but from the standpoint of methods of construction it does not greatly matter. A rapid survey follows of only such masonry as seems to belong to new edifices in the three categories without regard to minor modifications in existing structures. Although it does not add greatly to a knowledge of methods employed, the picture of structural activity in the second century would be incomplete without it. For convenience in reference, the residential areas are presented in alphabetical order. Except where brick stamps are present, it is seldom possible to reduce this type of building to a more precise category with assurance.

Aventine

The mention of a Privata Domus Traiani in the Notitia indicates that Trajan dwelt on the Aventine as a private citizen.[4] Topographers generally have located his residence near Sant'Anselmo; van Essen, however, locates it under Santa Prisca.[5] After he became emperor he restored to the region the branch of the Aqua Marcia[6] which had been destroyed by Nero. An ample water supply must have increased the desirability of the quarter as a dwelling place for the aristocracy;[7] and all over the greater Aventine traces of edifices have come to light which apparently belonged to the second century. Not enough has come down to modern times to give a clear picture of what the hill looked like at this period of its history. It was always primarily a residential area dotted with a plethora of ancient temples.[8] There is little evidence of importance to a study of methods of construction. Consequently, a brief resumé must suffice. Not far from the Privata Traiani, to judge from the position of the entry in the Notitia, there was a Dolocenum. This was uncovered in 1935[9] where it had been inserted in an earlier building. The masonry of reticulate reinforced by brick bands was homogeneous throughout and could be Trajanic.[10] Tiles prove that a new roof was built perhaps when the edifice was adapted to the worship of Jupiter Dolichenus. The earliest of these was A.D. 159. Trajan or his friend L. Licinius Sura was responsible for a large private or semipublic Bath in the same general locality. Of this and another Bath under Santa Sabina sometimes identified with it, we have already treated.[11] Some walls of brick-faced concrete near the apse of Santa Sabina belong to an edifice of the second century superimposed on one of the first.[12] Passing mention may be made of three rooms forming part of a dwelling which was destroyed when the Thermae Decianae were erected in the third century.[13] The brickwork was ascribed to the second half of the second century. Two rooms showed signs of cross vaults. Wall

[4] Platner-Ashby, p. 433.

[5] See below, pp. 76–77.

[6] Van Deman, *Aqueducts*, pp. 16, 68, 143.

[7] Merlin, *L'Aventin*, pp. 342–347.

[8] Lugli, MAR, vol. 3, pp. 572–594.

[9] A. M. Colini, *Bull. Com.*, vol. 63, 1935, pp. 157–158; Lugli, *op. cit.*, pp. 590–594. This is not far from either Sant'Anselmo or Santa Prisca.

[10] Loose brick stamps ranging from A.D. 116 to 138 may have come from other buildings in the neighborhood.

[11] See above, p. 33.

[12] Lugli, MAR, vol. 3, p. 55.

[13] *Ibid.*, pp. 51–52.

[14] Platner-Ashby, p. 177. The pipe is *CIL*, vol. 15 (2), no. 7439.

[15] *CIL*, vol. 15 (2), no. 7507.

[16] M. E. Blake, *MAAR*, vol. 13, 1936, p. 160.

[17] G. Gatti, *Not. sc.*, 1892, p. 314.
[18] The account here is that written by Marion E. Blake, based on the bibliography available at the end of 1959, for which see Nash II, p. 79, revised in accordance with marginal notes inserted by Doris Taylor Bishop in 1966. These notes were based on the major publication by Vermaseren and van Essen, which she reviewed (*AJA*, vol. 71, 1967, pp. 108–109). –JDB.

[19] Vermaseren and van Essen present a thorough survey of the excavations, season by season, pp. 1–106. Their chapter 12 (pp. 107–116) summarizes the architectural history of these ancient buildings.

[20] Neuerburg, *Fontane*, pp. 228–229, no. 184.

[21] Vermaseren and van Essen, p. 110. Stamps for House I are listed on p. 109. A complete set of tabulations of all stamps listed in the reports of the seasons' excavations can be found on pp. 241–337.

paintings resembling the fourth Pompeian style and pavements of marble and mosaic prove that it was a dwelling of some pretension. These rooms are not accessible today. A water pipe[14] revealed the presence of a house of Sextus Cornelius Repentinus who was praetorian prefect under Antoninus Pius. Another pipe[15] from the site of Sant'Anselmo names a Postumeia Lucilia. Two silhouette mosaics from it—a contest between centaurs and wild beasts, and Orpheus among the animals—appear to be Antonine.[16] The lower part of the walls was faced with polychrome marbles.[17]

Considerable remains of a suburban villa or palace have been uncovered under Santa Prisca and its dependencies.[18] It faced the Clivus Publicius (Via di Santa Prisca). Van Essen, who, with Vermaseren, has made an exhaustive study of the remains, would identify it with the Privata (Domus) Traiani.[19] He has found two main phases within the Trajanic period. Of the original construction, dated to ca. A.D. 95, enough remains to show that there was a house of the type with central court, frequently found in Ostia, which he calls House I. There was an east garden, surrounded by travertine pillars which supported barrel vaults. The east wall of the house had a series of rooms with small windows looking out over the garden. Another garden seems to have existed at the same time on the south side of the house. A little later, perhaps shortly after A.D. 98, the west wing of the porticus around the east garden was altered into a series of chambers to form a substructure for a terrace overlooking the east garden. The windows of the east wall of the house now opened into these rooms. Perhaps at the same time, after water was restored to the Aventine, a semicircular nymphaeum was added part way down the slope of the south garden.[20] Where its curved back wall penetrated the south wall of the house, relieving arches were inserted to carry the weight. Later, perhaps about A.D. 110, to judge from the stamps,[21] the villa was modified by the addition of House II for which the entire east garden was sacrificed. Within the perimetric wall of what was left of the earlier quadriporticus, a rectangular room (the excavators' Room Y) was built as a substructure. It was partly underground, with its floor about 60 cm. lower than that of the rooms to the west. Its one outside wall had neither door nor window; light and air came from a court above it through two splayed windows in the vault. The other rooms in this basement complex of House II had no such opening to the outside. The brickwork of this room (Room Y) was quite different from the earlier structure. Not only were the bricks thinner (3.8–4.3 cm. as opposed to 4.5 cm.), but they were laid up with a mortar so deficient in lime as to have little adhesive power. All the parts were barrel-vaulted. A row of rooms was then added to the south to support a larger terrace replacing the east terrace; this gained considerable space for the palace itself. One of the new partition walls cut through the curved back wall of the nymphaeum so that its vault had to be rebuilt and its relieving arches renewed. This terrace was about a meter higher than the one on the east had been. Brick stamps attest a slight modification in the time of Hadrian; the insertion of a relieving arch against the back wall of the central basement room seems to be the only survival of the Hadrianic work. The Trajanic masonry did not make use of relieving arches. One can only speculate on the grandeur of the palace for which such complicated substructures were built. At the very end of the second century, after our period, Severan additions were made. Shortly thereafter portions of the substructures were converted into the most important Mithraeum discovered in Rome. Some time after that the Christians got a firm foothold in the western part of the building. By A.D. 306 the Christians were able to raid the Mithraeum. The struggle between the two bodies came to an end when in A.D. 400 the Christians invaded the Mithraeum, destroyed it, and filled it with earth and rubble. As fascinating as this story of the Privata Traiani is, it is beyond our period; yet it reminds us that structures had human occupants, human uses, and human occasions of which we know all too little.

On the Lesser Aventine, remains of Roman walls of indeterminate date were found under San Saba.[22] Inscriptions prove that the Statio Cohortis IV of the Vigiles was located here,[23] but the evidence is not sufficiently clear to give the slightest indication of how they appeared in the second century. The Privata (Domus) Hadriani[24] was southwest of them, but no remains can be definitely associated with it; and, in any case, ownership does not necessarily imply that they were built by Hadrian before he became emperor. The Regionary Catalogues place a Domus Cornificiae[25] between the Statio and the Privata. It was probably the palace of Annia Cornificia Faustina, the younger sister of Marcus Aurelius, who married M. Ummidius Quadratus. But the origin of two water pipes which could have confirmed the evidence of the Catalogues is unknown;[26] on the other hand, the fragment of the Marble Plan with the legend CORNIFICIA does not fit this site and probably had another connotation. Five large rooms apparently belonging to the Domus were uncovered in 1887, some of which at least were heated. Stamps found in a hypocaust bearing the name of Faustina Augusta definitely belong to the person under consideration. But no technical details are given of the construction, which is reported as excellent brickwork. Some mosaic pavements indicate that there was a dwelling of the second century to the east of San Saba.[27] To the period of Hadrian must be ascribed the villa built up against the Servian Wall which later came into the possession of L. Fabius Cilo as a gift from Septimius Severus.[28] A retaining wall with niches as well as various other walls under Santa Balbina, all faced with reticulate between bands of brick, certainly belonged to it. Brick stamps of the period were found in the excavation. Others of A.D. 161 to 169, discovered on the *bipedales* of the pavement of the hall later incorporated in the church, indicate that it was an addition of Marcus Aurelius rather than of Septimius Severus as formerly supposed. Unfortunately, it is not possible to determine the nature of the walls that went with the pavement.

Beyond the Aventine where the Baths of Caracalla stood at a later time, a house apparently built for one proprietor[29] had an outside staircase to accommodate one or more tenants in upper floors. Stamps of A.D. 134 indicate a date late in the Hadrianic or early in the Antonine era.[30] The house was not entirely excavated, and the ground plan is not clear. There was some reticulate work; but the main body of the masonry was faced with good brickwork. Apertures were arched or topped with slightly curved or flat lintel arches of tile; and in one case at least a square window appeared above a lintel arch. No report is given of the type of brick used. Bigio and

[22] M. E. Cannizzaro, *Not. sc.*, 1901, pp. 10–14; *idem* with U. C. Gavini, *Not. sc.*, 1902, pp. 270–273, 465–466.

[23] G. Gatti, *Bull. Com.*, vol. 30, 1902, pp. 204–206; Merlin, *L'Aventin*, p. 324; Reynolds, *Vigiles*, pp. 51–52.

[24] Platner-Ashby, p. 433. The site is deduced from the Regionary Catalogues.

[25] R. Lanciani, *Bull. Com.*, vol. 19, 1891, pp. 210–216; Ch. Huelsen, *Röm. Mitt.*, vol. 7, 1892, p. 296; Merlin, *op. cit.*, pp. 325–326. Platner-Ashby, p. 178; Lugli, *MAR*, vol. 3, pp. 569–570.

[26] *CIL*, vol. 15 (2), nos. 7442, 7567. *FUR*, pp. 79–80.

[27] E. Gatti, *Not. sc.*, 1925, pp. 383–384; M. E. Blake, *MAAR*, vol. 13, 1936, p. 190.

[28] Platner-Ashby, p. 176; T. Ashby, *JRS*, vol. 23, 1933, p. 5; Lugli, *MAR*, vol. 1, pp. 412–413; Krautheimer, *Basilicae*, vol. 1, pp. 84–93; Nash I, p. 352.

[29] A. Pellegrini, *Bull. Inst.*, 1867, pp. 109–119; Lanciani, *Ruins*, pp. 101, fig. 39, 533–534; P. Harsh, *MAAR*, vol. 12, 1935, p. 52.

[30] The disproportionately large number of stamps of A.D. 123 belong to the overproduction of that year.

[31] See below, p. 194.

[32] F. Castagnoli, *Bull. Com.*, vol. 73, 1949–1950, pp. 167–173. Cf. M. E. Blake, *MAAR*, vol. 13, 1936, pp. 94, 143.

[33] L. Cozza apud F. Castagnoli, *Bull. Com.*, vol. 73, 1949–1950, pp. 125–127.

[34] A. M. Colini, *Acc. P. Mem.*, ser. 3, vol. 7, 1944. First century construction has been gathered together in Blake, *RC II*, pp. 54–55, 126–127.

[35] Colini, *op. cit.*, p. 214 with n. 49.

[36] *Ibid.*, pp. 239–240.

[37] *Ibid.*, p. 258.

[38] *Ibid.*, pp. 258–263.

pavonazzetto were employed in the revetment of the fountain in the cortile, which stood against a wall mosaic; bianco, rosso, verde, and giallo, in the one marble floor. An impressive mosaic of sea monsters in black and white follows the style made familiar by the Neptune Baths at Ostia,[31] which were built at approximately the same time. After a reappraisal of the other mosaics, I am inclined to agree with Castagnoli[32] that most were laid at a later period. The detailed description given by Pellegrini brings regret that such a fine dwelling could not have been preserved in the state in which it was found. Whatever upper floors it had were removed when the Baths of Caracalla were built.

With the actual Thermae Severianae et Commodianae we are not concerned at present, but we must deal with the somewhat contradictory chronological evidence presented by the so-called Terme di Severo e Commodo.[33] The remains, buried up to the springing of the vaults, are still extant in a locality known as Monte d'Oro south of the Baths of Caracalla. A Trajanic stamp on the cover of a drain furnishes a *terminus post quem*. Such brickwork as could be studied yielded red and yellow triangles said to have come from *besales*. The majority were 3 cm. thick, but many were under the norm. The chambers showed a variety in vaulting. The largest was covered with two cross vaults, two almost equally large with barrel vaults strengthened by brick arches projecting from the soffit, and one over a corridor with a ribbed barrel vault (*nervatura a cassetta*). Although such construction can conceivably be as early as the reign of Hadrian, I am inclined to date it rather late in the Antonine period. The monument was probably the platform for a suburban villa with a cistern of many chambers enclosed in it.

Caelian

Colini has brought together data concerning private building on the Caelian.[34] Enough fragmentary walls have come to light from time to time to show that it was still in the second century essentially a region of suburban villas which had begun to be invaded by apartment houses. Practically none of the edifices can be identified. Much of the masonry appeared in modifications of existing structures. Most of the walls have been destroyed or are inaccessible. Little, if any, of this adds to a knowledge of construction gained from other parts of the city. In order to round out the picture of the Rome of the second century, a brief summary follows of the material given by Colini in the order of his presentation. The edifice in the garden of the Istituti di San Gregorio on the west slope of the hill exhibits a substantial renovation in the substitution of brickwork[35] for reticulate in the upper part of the wall, in which bricks 3.5 cm. × 20–26 cm. were joined by mortar 2.1–2.2 cm. wide, and travertine corbels were inserted to support vaulting. In the medley of walls uncovered along the south side of Piazza della Navicella, some walls faced with a combination of brick and reticulate, others with brick alone apparently belonged to the period under discussion.[36] That an earlier edifice of Hadrianic times preceded the Domus Valeriorum is proved by the discovery of six brick stamps.[37] Remains of a villa adjudged by its brickwork to belong to about the middle of the century was uncovered under Villa Fonseca where the Ospizio dell'Addolorata now stands.[38] It supplanted an earlier one at a lower level. Little remains of it today except a horseshoe-shaped crypto-porticus having a vault decorated with a floral pattern in mosaic; but description by Nolli of what he saw in the eighteenth century gives the impression of a succession of cryptoportici and nymphaea decorated with "pumice" and mosaic, revealing something of the magnificence of a suburban villa of the middle of the second century. This later became the property of L. Marius Maximus Perpetuus. The one barrel-vaulted room of a series forming the substructure of a villa along the line of Via della Navicella[39] was ascribed to the second century on the basis of its brickwork. When the great military hospital was built in 1885–1889 on the site of Villa Casali, remains of pretentious villas came to light[40] belonging, to judge from the stamps, in part at least to[41] the middle of the century. One room, later modified, displayed Ionic columns in combination with walls of brick-faced concrete. Two silhouette mosaics,[42] not in my judgment contemporaneous, may be mentioned in passing, though one is probably later than our period. Sometime in the first half of the second century, a semicircular porticus of the time of Nero behind Santi Quattro Coronati was destroyed; an ancient street (Vicus Statae Matris?) was cut through at a higher level; and apartment houses were erected on each side of it.[43] A modification of another dwelling along Via Merulana in the Trajanic or early Hadrianic period can be deduced from a wall having an aggregate of terra cotta and a facing of red bricks.[44] Under the fourth-century hall below the Ospedale Lateranense, a deep stratum of broken brick bore witness to the collapse of a building of several stories.[45] Brick stamps of A.D. 125–135 suggest the approximate date of the original building and that of a modification at about A.D. 150, but a layer of loose bricks tells nothing of the methods of construction. Brick stamps attest various modifications of the first-century palace under the nave and apse of San Giovanni in Laterano in the course of the century.[46] Colini ascribes the remains of a palace and two villas in this region to the early years of the second century.[47]

The remains under the Church of Sts. John and Paul (Santi Giovanni e Paolo) can be visited.[48] They consist of two and perhaps three apartment houses of the second century after Christ, not to mention one better preserved of the Severan epoch. A preponderance of stamps of the Hadrianic period found in various excavations suggests the dating with which the type of construction is entirely in accord. Not much is left of the house bordering the Clivus Scauri because it stood, for the most part, to the west of the area occupied by the church. Only the lateral wall on the east and the merest beginning of the south wall connected with it are visible today. It was three stories high, and the lateral wall was constructed of concrete faced by rather light, yellowish red bricks with insets of tufa reticulate. Light colored bipedales furnished bonding courses, one of which marks a slight setback at the beginning of the second floor. A relieving arch appears in the center of the first floor, and there are traces of three windows. It is probable that the façade facing the Clivus was faced with brick. Another house having its main façade on Via del Tempio di Claudio seems to have been fitted into a space previously occupied by a dwelling of the Flavian era. Its main orientation was the points of the compass, but there were other walls, appar-

[39] Ibid., p. 268.

[40] Ibid., pp. 272–276.

[41] Some were probably earlier.

[42] In one, the sea-monsters look to me Hadrianic, but the athletes which I once published as Antonine (MAAR, vol. 13, 1936, p. 166) now appear to me much later.

[43] Colini, op. cit., pp. 290–295 (Remains DD' and UU' in pl. 16).

[44] Ibid, p. 310. In RC II, p. 127, I described an edifice uncovered between Via Merulana and Via Tasso which may be either Flavian or Trajanic.

[45] Ibid., pp. 324–327.

[46] Ibid., pp. 347, 351–352. The mosaics under the apse were ascribed by me (MAAR, vol. 17, 1940, p. 83) to the Severan epoch.

[47] Colini, op. cit., p. 375.

[48] There is an enormous bibliography for this house, little of which is pertinent to a study of construction. P. Germano, La Casa Celimontana, Rome 1894, is fundamental. V. E. Gasdìa, La Casa Pagano-Cristiana del Celio, Rome 1937, is excellent as an exhaustive guide, though difficult to follow for chronology. A. M. Colini, Acc. P. Mem., vol. 7, 1944, pp. 164–168, presents the evidence for each house with archaeological perspicacity. Prandi, Basilica celimontana, describes elements revealed when the church was restored. See Nash I, pp. 357–361 for a plan, photographs of the remains now visible, and additional bibliography; also Frova, pp. 92–93, 102, 117.

[49] Junyent apparently considers it a separate house. See *San Clemente*, p. 106, fig. 30. A reproduction of it is given on p. 108, fig. 31.

[50] A. Pasqui, *Not. sc.*, 1911, pp. 338–339; A. M. Colini, *Acc. P. Mem.*, ser. 3, vol. 7, 1944–1945, pp. 381–382.

[51] R. Paribeni, *Boll. d'Arte*, vol. 7, 1913, pp. 162–165; M. E. Blake, *MAAR*, vol. 13, 1936, pp. 82f.

[52] M. E. Blake, *MAAR*, vol. 13, 1936, pp. 158–159.

[53] D. Marchetti, *Not. sc.*, 1890, p. 80; R. Lanciani, *Not. sc.*, 1890, p. 113.

[54] Colini, *op. cit.*, pp. 48, 59, 278–280, 442 n. 279.

[55] Bibliography, map, plan of excavation, and mosaic in Nash I, pp. 183–185.

[56] Gu. Gatti, *Bull. Com.*, vol. 62, 1934, pp. 125–126, with references to brief reports from the time of excavation.

[57] They are *CIL*, vol. 15 (1), nos. 1410 (1st); 633 (Vespasianic); 1007 (A.D. 93/4–108); 276 (115–120); 115 (120); 103, 121, 563, 1021, 1029 (123); 1436 (130); 515, 1073 (134); 1056 (Hadrianic); 1563 (late).

ently coeval, which did not fit into this scheme. The walls, in so far as they can be separated from those of earlier and later epochs, are normal for the period. Some are faced with reticulate reinforced by brick bands; others with brick alone, having the customary relieving arches of *bipedales*. To this period apparently belongs the wall which was later decorated with the famous painting of Thetis or Proserpina. The bricks in this wall vary from 3.5 to 4 cm. with a scattering above and below. This house had a secondary façade[49] on the Clivus Scauri, which can just be distinguished from later reorganizations at the southeast corner of the church. It shows a curious adaptation to environment. Three doorways, topped by slightly curved lintel arches of *bipedales*, increase in width as well as height with the rise of the street. The first-story windows decrease in width and height under identical relieving arches placed at the same level. In the second story, smaller windows, all in alignment, seem to have established the line of the third-century house to the west. This façade has been altered by later building operations so that it cannot be used as an example of second-century methods of building; but two piers came to light in fairly recent excavation which show the characteristic construction. They rested on blocks of travertine and were faced with fine brickwork, having bonding courses of *bipedales*. It may be noted that a travertine keystone and impost mark the lintel over the largest of the three doorways. Traces of fine stucco work, wall paintings, and mosaic floors have been found in rooms behind this façade. One room had a herringbone pavement.

A room excavated on Via Emanuele Filiberto,[50] probably belonging to a villa, is of more than ordinary interest for its mosaic floors.[51] A pavement of swimming sea-monsters cannot antedate the Hadrianic period much if at all. It was, however, divided and repaved with new mosaic floors, which appear to be Hadrianic also. The walls were of the usual combination of reticulate and brick.

The Basilica Hilariana is practically the only building which can be identified. Its date is controversial. In an earlier study I came to the conclusion that it was probably Hadrianic;[52] and on a reexamination of the evidence I see no reason to change my opinion. Of the brick stamps found,[53] two are Hadrianic, one is of the time of Marcus Aurelius, and one[54] is Severan. Colini ascribes the building to the time of the latter, but since the stamps were not *in situ*, they cannot be accepted as evidence against other criteria, namely the date of the mosaic floor with the *malocchio*, the orthography of the inscription, and the style of the portrait head.[55] The walls which were preserved to the height of three meters are described as good brickwork by one scholar and as mediocre by another. The hall was either a place of worship or a schola of the Dendrofori, an important guild of the period.

Campus Martius

The preparation for Trajan's Forum apparently left a space available for building at the northwest; and in 1902 to 1904,[56] when the Istituto delle Assicurazioni Generali di Venezia was built, walls came to light at two different orientations. The brick stamps found were so preponderantly Hadrianic[57] as to leave no doubt about the date of the main structure. Triangular bricks were used in the facing. The number of columns of different kinds of marble and the remains of architectural decoration attest to the elegance of the edifice. Signs were not lacking, however, that there had been a later reconstruction to which must be attributed the part encroaching on the street that followed the curve of the Temple of the Deified Trajan. The southern part had been clearly adjusted to the curve, and a semicircular exedra masked the triangle caused by the two orientations. In 1933 more walls comprising among other things a porticus and a small exedra were uncovered,[58] which followed a third orientation in conformity with the turn in the Via Lata. These were also adjudged Hadrianic.

Farther north on the Via Lata (now Via del Corso), parts of no less than seven apartment houses were unearthed in 1914–1917 in the excavation for the Società Anonima "Roma" and the Banca Commerciale Italiana.[59] The block most completely uncovered presented a row of shops to each of the four streets enclosing it.[60] Wherever brought to light, they showed brickfaced pilasters with travertine bases. One shop, or possibly office, had a semicircular room at its rear perhaps to support the wall of an apsed hall above. Stairs on the west side gave access to upper floors, but were probably not the only ones, though the position of others is not clear. The plan of the interior arrangements is also somewhat vague, but seems to have yielded halls of some pretention. Two adjoining rooms had heavy piers for supporting cross vaulting. This could have been a later modification. These and one other room had splayed windows toward a narrow entrance corridor. Brick stamps[61] prove that this edifice was also Hadrianic. There were some relieving arches in the masonry. About the middle of the century the openings of the shops were closed and the building devoted to another purpose.[62] At this time, a staircase was inserted in the northeast corner. On the other side of Via del Tritone, travertine piers[63] were used as wall ends for a series of partition walls to convert an earlier porticus into a row of eight or nine shops. The brickwork seemed to the excavator to be identical with that of the building just described. No more of this block was excavated except the side walls of the stairs to the street parallel with Via Lata. The building to the south of the one first described presented an unbroken wall toward it with pilasters corresponding with those on the opposite side, a blank wall with at least two similar pilasters at the north end of the east wall and three groups of splayed windows in the part excavated to the south, and a row of shops to the Via Lata. The south side did not fall within the area excavated. This edifice almost certainly also belonged to the Hadrianic building period. The three or possibly four blocks to the east were probably built at about the same time,[64] but they were too thoroughly modified in later times to show their original form.

Capitoline

The isolation of the Capitoline in the late 1920's uncovered the remains of edifices which were erected during the reigns of Trajan and Hadrian[65] on the strip of land secularized when Vespasian moved the Pomerium.[66] With the multiple dwellings of Ostia in mind, it is possible to gain an idea of what these buildings were like from the rather inadequate remains. The

[58] A. M. Colini, *Bull. Com.*, vol. 61, 1933, pp. 257–258.

[59] E. Gatti, *Not. sc.*, 1917, pp. 18–20; Lugli, *MAR*, vol. 3, pp. 272–273. Perhaps the excavation for a pedestrian underpass has uncovered more.

[60] Via del Tritone, Via del Corso, and two streets parallel to them for which there are no modern counterparts. (In the margin of the manuscript Mrs. Bishop had written "try to find a copy of *Via del Corso*." The book does not exist in the U.S. Dr. Ernest Nash of Fototeca Unione writes that it was a gift edition sponsored by a Roman bank, the exact title being "Via del Corso a cura della Cassa di Risparmio di Roma nel 125° Anniversario dell'Fondazione. Roma 1961;" further, that the copies given to the American Academy, the German Archaeological Institute, and the Biblioteca Hertziana have disappeared. Dr. Maria Marchetti, Director of the Biblioteca dell' Istituto Nazionale d'Archeologia e Storia dell'Arte, confirms Dr. Nash's report and adds that the chapter "Il Corso nell' antichità" (pp. 13–54) is given in condensed form on p. 25 of Lugli's *Il Tratto Urbano della Via Flaminia*. Nothing of importance for construction here; hence this bibliography need be pursued no further.—JDB).

[61] *CIL*, vol. 15 (1), nos. 957, 1466.

[62] *Bipedales* at the landing (nos. 90, 226) give the date.

[63] These undoubtedly belonged to the Porticus Vipsania.

[64] Very many Hadrianic stamps were found: L. Cantarelli, *Bull. Com.*, vol. 42, 1914, p. 211; idem, *op. cit.*, vol. 43, 1915, p. 58.

[65] Muñoz and Colini, *Campidoglio*, J. Oliver, *MAAR*, vol. 10, 1932, pp. 153–157.

[66] Blake, *RC II*, pp. 96, 128.

67 Colini apud Muñoz and Colini, pp. 30, 45–52; Oliver, *op. cit.*, pp. 155–156; A. Boëthius, *Antike*, vol. 11, 1935, p. 130; *Palladio*, vol. 1, 1937, p. 240 (Gismondi's reconstruction); Lugli, *MAR, Suppl.*, pp. 10–12; *idem, Centro*, pp. 47–48; Crema, p. 453, figs. 579, 580; Frova, p. 92; Nash I, pp. 506–507.

68 Bloch (*Bolli*, p. 29 n. 33) ascribes the house to the Flavian period on the evidence of the stamps. Both Colini (Muñoz and Colini, *op. cit., errata-corrige*) and Lugli (*Centro, loc. cit.*) have been won over to the later date in spite of the stamps.

69 This device is found in the Mercato.

70 Via Biberatica displays a similar balcony. The porticus in front, with the slender piers supporting arches facing vaulting with amphorae, belongs to the third century.

71 Colini (*op. cit.*), contrary to the usual continental practice, counts the lofty mezzanine as a separate story.

72 This façade is at the present street level. Much that was visible when excavated has been covered over again.

73 A similar intercalary space occurred in the Domus Aurea. See Blake, *RC II*, p. 50.

house at the foot of the stairs leading to Ara Coeli, known as "La Casa di Via Giulio Romano,"[67] is nearly as well preserved as any in Ostia. It will be recalled that terracing was a part of the preparation for the Forum of Trajan on the side toward the Capitoline as well as the Quirinal. The adaptation of this six-story apartment house to the slope just around the corner from the formal terracing calls to mind the use made of the Quirinal for the Market of Trajan. The construction could be from either the end of the first or the beginning of the second century of the Christian era.[68] The retaining wall was faced with reticulate until it became free-standing at the fifth story and was faced with brick. The façade which is preserved formed the eastern boundary of a court paved with selce. Traces of the inner façades on the north and west sides came to light; the south side may have been enclosed merely with a row of shops. The ground floor of the eastern part consisted of six shops with wide openings and one with a narrow opening toward the court but a wide one at the side. Wooden frames were fitted into these openings under a straight lintel arch of *bipedales* on which rested the sill of large windows for the mezzanine floor. These had curved tops which were part of large relieving arches to divert pressure from the voids caused by the wide openings below. A continuous stringcourse of tile outlined the series of curves produced by the relieving arches.[69] Limestone corbels supported a narrow balcony of concrete faced with segmental arches of *besales*.[70] The wooden pavement of the mezzanine floor was supported by beams resting on a tile cornice. Barrel vaults undoubtedly supported the floor of the next story, the first by European reckoning, the second by Colini's,[71] the third by ours. The façade[72] displays windows in groups of two or three to give the maximum light to the rooms within. The room at the southeast corner not only had two windows facing the court and three on the south side, but also a small window above them on the west face apparently to supply some light when the shutters were closed. The same small window appears over the three windows in the next room. All these windows had straight lintel arches of *bipedales*. A horizontal stringcourse marks the transition from this floor to the next (the fourth story). There is some indication that the barrel-vaulted rooms within were subdivided by wooden partitions. The next floor (fourth) had a similar façade, but the space was treated differently. A barrel-vaulted corridor stood between the rooms and the hill.[73] Three cross corridors subdivided the space into five parts. A large well-lighted room, possibly subdivided by wooden partitions, occupied the southeast corner. Three chambers, barrel-vaulted lengthwise, were subdivided by cross walls into three small rooms. Those at the front would have been amply lighted by the windows on to the court, but the others would receive light only from the corridors. In some a splayed window in the back wall was provided, perhaps for cross ventilation rather than light. The rear passage must have been very dark. Barely enough remains of the next floor (the fifth) to show that its rear wall rose above the level of the ground and that it had a rear corridor. As soon as the masonry was free from the rock, it was possible to have another façade along the Capitoline at right angles to the one below. Remains of it came to light many years ago, but all traces of it have disappeared. It is open to question whether it belonged to the same or a later building period. Brick stamps were reported of A.D. 133. Barely enough remained to show that there was a sixth floor.

A house under the Piazza del Campidoglio[74] probably belonged to this same building complex. The small part uncovered in the recent systematization of the hill showed a wide doorway with a lintel arch of *bipedales* having a large window above it under an all-embracing relieving arch. Tile cornices supported the beams of the mezzanine floor. Piers of Gabine stone upheld corbels for a balcony across the front. Passing mention may be made of remains uncovered many years ago between the Arx and the Capitoline which Lanciani considered belonged to a private residence, rather than an apartment house, of the second half of the second century.[75]

Farther south along the foot of the hill between the Casa di Via Giulio Romano and the Casa dei Mulini, remains of other walls were uncovered.[76] One was faced with triangular bricks, others with bricks 4 cm. thick having mortar joints 2–2.5 cm. wide. They are not significant for our purpose. The Casa dei Mulini[77] was only partially excavated but even so revealed clear traces of two different periods, the first being certainly of the second century. No information is given of the nature of the brickwork, but great arches outlined in brick cornices, lintel arches of *bipedales* (both straight and slightly curved), and splayed windows which are reported accord well with Trajanic and Hadrianic practices. There was evidence of a second floor, one room of which had a mosaic floor, an indication perhaps that there were apartments over an edifice given over to the manufacture of olive oil. A structure to the south of it would appear to be slightly earlier and was apparently in place when the Isola Grande was built. Little of it came to light.

Brick stamps[78] indicate that Isola Grande[79] was an early Hadrianic structure. Not enough was uncovered to show the entire ground plan, which by the way had to be adapted to the rock at the northeast corner. Although a little reticulate appears, the main construction was of brick-faced concrete. Unfortunately no technical details of the brickwork were reported. Photographs do not give clear evidence of bonding courses. The most characteristic feature of its construction was the use of enormous relieving arches in the masonry, over windows, and flanking stairs (pl. 12, fig. 2). On the inner façade of the west side segmental arches were inserted over windows facing the court at the upper level with each touching the other in haphazard fashion. Neither here nor elsewhere did any opening have its own lintel arch under a relieving arch. Where space allowed, full arches were used in this way in place of segmental ones; and once at any rate a full arch was curtailed because of lack of room. Straight lintel arches were employed alone over small windows, and a segmental arch over one doorway. The use of arches over apertures had obviously not yet been standardized. Travertine stairs ascended in two ramps with doors at the landing to mezzanine floors. Only barrel vaults were used in the original construction, though one room was furnished with piers for cross vaulting at a slightly later period. There were important restorations at the end of the third or the beginning of the fourth century.

Between Isola Grande and a Hadrianic *balneum*[80] at the southwest angle of the Capitoline, there was a triangular space caused by the change in

---

[74] A. M. Colini, *Bull. Com.*, vol. 67, 1939, p. 200.

[75] R. Lanciani, *Bull. Com.*, vol. 1, 1873, pp. 143–146; Muñoz and Colini, *op. cit.*, pp. 43–44.

[76] *Ibid.*, pp. 52–53.

[77] *Ibid.*, pp. 52–54.

[78] A revised chronology of the stamps follows: *CIL*, vol. 15 (1), nos. 1007 (A.D. 93/94 to 108), 917 (early second), 115 (possibly Trajanic; see Bloch, *Bolli*, p. 101), 1410 (early Hadrianic; see Bloch, *op. cit.*, p. 67).

[79] Muñoz and Colini, *op. cit.*, pp. 54–60.

[80] To be described next, below.

[81] Muñoz and Colini, *op. cit.*, pp. 64–68.

[82] One stamp (*CIL*, vol. 15 (1), no. 1347), datable between A.D. 120 and 129, is a slight confirmation of the Hadrianic date of the edifice.

[83] Muñoz and Colini, *op. cit.*, pp. 68–76; Lugli, *Centro*, 50–51.

[84] Lugli (*op. cit.*) mentions hypocausts as well as cisterns.

[85] They may be triangles.

[86] M. E. Blake, *MAAR*, vol. 13, 1936, pp. 79, 200.

[87] Notably a lintel arch of travertine with a relieving arch of tile, in which two Neronian stamps of L. Ru(—) Sosias were found. For the date of the stamp, see Bloch, *Bolli*, p. 45.

orientation, into which an edifice was inserted[81] probably early in the Hadrianic period.[82] Its outer wall on the southeast, against which the wall of the *balneum* was erected at a slightly later period, was faced with triangular bricks (3.5–4 cm. $\times$ 16–24 cm.) united by mortar joints a little over 2 cm. wide. Other walls were faced with insets of reticulate in brick frames. One segmental arch appears imbedded in the masonry, in a drawing made at the time of excavation; and a long camber arch, in one of the photographs. Brick cornices served to support the beams for wooden mezzanine pavements. One room at any rate was vaulted. A flight of stairs apparently led directly from a paved alley way to a group of rooms in front. Although there must have been other stairways, no trace of them came to light. One plain black-and-white mosaic and two herringbone brick pavements were uncovered, and remains of superimposed paintings give an added interest to this dwelling. Fragments of the wall paintings from upper floors appeared in the debris. This house also showed signs of repairs in the fourth century. It could be excavated only in part.

At the southwest corner there was an edifice[83] appropriate for public use, perhaps a *balneum*[84] which can be ascribed to the time of Hadrian on the evidence of its stamps. Not enough was left to establish the ground plan, but there were sufficient remains to add to our knowledge of Hadrianic methods of building. The foundations were of concrete with a tufa aggregate which had been poured into a wooden form prepared for it. The core of the walls had a brick aggregate, in which an unusual number of pieces of small paving bricks appeared. The bricks in the wall facing were 3.4–4.5 cm. $\times$ 18–21 cm.;[85] the joints 1.5–2 cm. wide. There were some bonding courses. One long narrow room at the north could be reasonably reconstructed. The north wall was not pierced with any apertures, but its austerity was broken by a projecting cornice made of tiles. The south wall had a framework of stout piers supporting great arches of *bipedales*. There was a curtain between them broken by large doors under lintel arches of *bipedales* with large arched openings above them, which probably faced a terrace. These arches were also made of *bipedales*. At the east end of the long hall a small rectangular niche had its own lintel arch under a second one spanning the entire wall space. A black-and-white pavement with a pattern of undulating lines[86] covered the floor; and a marble bench seems to have run around the three inner walls of the room. There are traces of wall paintings and sure signs of the cross vaults which once formed the ceiling. A door at the east end led to a hall with three large niches—a rectangular between two curvilinear. The first had an arched window over a door with a lintel arch opening out onto a terrace; the second, an arched opening reaching down to the ground; the third probably a duplication of the second. A change in orientation in the southern part was due to the configuration of the hill, but it seems to have been accomplished with less finesse than usual perhaps because of the presence of an early building of which there are some traces.[87] At about the center, a wall with two large alcoves exhibiting the same great arches as in the rest of the edifice seems to have been built against the wall of a hall covered with two cross vaults. The first was furnished with a pool lined with *opus signinum*; the second with a cistern supported by a barrel vault. There were signs of restorations in both the third and fourth centuries.

At the foot of the east slope backed against the rock but extending under the church of Santa Maria della Consolazione, Colini reports an apartment house with walls of brick-faced concrete and travertine piers,[88] which he adjudged to belong to the early years of the second century. High up above the Vico Jugario, opposite the headquarters of a unit of the city police, a little brickwork combined with reticulate looks as if some Hadrianic builder had taken advantage of the spot to erect a narrow apartment house.[89]

We have already called attention to the Insula Argentaria along the Clivus of the same name.[90]

Esquiline

After the fire of A.D. 64, Nero had appropriated most of the western branch of the Esquiline, the Oppian, for his Domus Aurea, which was in due course superseded by the Baths of Trajan.[91] Brick stamps show that there was considerable building activity in the area behind the Baths in the second century but casual finds contribute nothing to a study of this kind.

The Cispian, built over in the late Republic and early Empire,[92] became a popular residential area in the late Empire.[93] Brick stamps prove, however, that there was plenty of building activity in the second century.[94] One such edifice was uncovered several years ago between Via Olmata and Via Paolina.[95] It yielded four rooms faced with good reticulate work combined with lintel arches and archivolts composed of carefully shaped tiles. The rooms were barrel-vaulted. Above the vaults a sub-pavement of herringbone brick was laid for a black-and-white mosaic. However, no technical details were reported.

More recently, a palatial villa of the time of Hadrian, incorporating remains of an earlier villa of fine reticulate work, was unearthed on the slope of the Cispian facing the Viminal,[96] the extent of which cannot be determined with the means at our disposal. Rooms richly decorated with marble floors and to a certain extent with marble wall revetments[97] served as the approach to a fountain area consisting of an oblong pool between square stepped fountains of pyramidal form. Pedestals of brick-faced concrete covered with marble for statues were strategically placed to enhance the vista. The importance of the excavation rests on the recovery of these four statues in unusually good condition rather than on any contribution to a knowledge of Hadrianic construction. Brick stamps found *in situ* give the date.[98] Hypocausts were inserted in two neighboring rooms in the early Antonine era,[99] to judge from the stamps.

The rest of the Esquiline was as thickly settled as today. It had been a sepulchral area until it was reclaimed for habitation in the Augustan era, when much of it was given up to villas and parks. The terminal reservoirs for all the aqueducts which entered the city by the Porta Maggiore made possible a disproportionate number of private baths, nymphaea, and fountains. Several lead pipes bear witness to the distribution of water to private individuals who presumably had dwellings not too far distant. Seven or eight of these have been ascribed to the second century. Of these only two[100]

[88] A. M. Colini, *Bull. Com.*, vol. 68, 1940, p. 228.

[89] Personal observation.

[90] See above, p. 18.

[91] See above, p. 29.

[92] R. Lanciani, *Not. sc.*, 1890, p. 213.

[93] Lugli, MAR, vol. 3, p. 394.

[94] Lanciani, op. cit.

[95] Ibid.

[96] A. M. Colini, *Capitolium*, vol. 15, 1940, pp. 861–876.

[97] Verde antico appears among the marbles.

[98] *CIL*, vol. 15 (1), no. 811.

[99] Ibid., nos. 617, 1070.

[100] *CIL*, vol. 15 (2), no. 7379, L. Aemilius Iuncus, consul suffectus in A.D. 127; no. 7438, Cornelius Fronto, tutor of Marcus Aurelius and Lucius Verus (?).

101 G. Gatti and L. Borsari, *Not. sc.*, 1887, pp. 70, 108.

102 *CIL*, vol. 15 (1), no. 755.

103 *CIL*, vol. 6 (1), no. 1517.

104 *CIL*, vol. 15 (1), no. 811 f (Trajan), no. 495 (Hadrian), no. 860 (A.D. 141), no. 1189 (*ca.* Antoninus Pius), no. 236 (mid second century). See Lanciani, *Bull. Com.*, vol. 2, 1874, p. 213.

105 B. M. Felletti Maj, *Not. sc.*, 1948, pp. 308–319.

106 Lugli, *MAR, Suppl.*, p. 105; *idem, Centro*, pp. 450–451.

107 Personal observation.

108 P. B. Whitehead, *AJA*, vol. 31, 1927, p. 408; Lugli, *MAR*, vol. 1, p. 399; *idem, Centro*, p. 612; E. Junyent, *RAC*, vol. 7, 1930, pp. 95–96.

bear the names of celebrities, and with only one[101] could remains be associated which yielded one stamp[102] in confirmation of a date early in the second century. No details of its construction were given, other than that it was brickwork. An inscription[103] names M. Servilius Fabianus who was consul suffectus in A.D. 158. Everywhere columns of precious marbles, pieces of marble pavements and marble wall revetments, traces of mosaics and frescoes have come to light to attest the elegance of the quarter. Everywhere brick stamps of the second century have been picked up to show that much of the building belonged to the century with which we are now concerned, but in few cases has the nature of the construction been reported. It is significant that few if any of the remains belonged to apartment houses. Brick stamps[104] prove that the Macellum Liviae was restored or modified at various times in the second century for the convenience of those who dwelt in this vast region.

A difficult excavation under the cloister of the Scuola di Ingegneria near San Pietro in Vincoli has been reported with great care by Bianca Maria Felletti Maj.[105] The east wall of the more northern of the two edifices uncovered in part was faced with red triangles, 4 cm. thick, joined by mortar of the same width reinforced by bonding courses and relieving arches of yellow *bipedales*. Because of the width of the mortar the excavator ascribes the wall to the second half of the second century; because of the thickness of the bricks I should ascribe it to the time of Hadrian, the date given by the brick stamps found. A different brick was used in the edifice to the south. The triangles were reddish yellow to yellow and 3 cm. thick. Here again the mortar is wide (3 cm.) for the Hadrianic period suggested by the stamps. If it was roughly contemporaneous with the other, it was certainly built by a different contractor. Both edifices supplanted those of an earlier date and showed later modifications. The more southern one was richly redecorated in the third century. These rooms have now been integrated with an extensive investigation beneath the church itself.

Palatine

Private edifices of the apartment house type were erected in the second century on the slopes of the Palatine toward the Velabrum.[106] Construction which appears Hadrianic is clearly visible in front of Domitianic work. It shows walls of reticulate work neatly set into brick frames. Near the foot of the slope there is a series of barrel-vaulted chambers with travertine corbels for supporting a mezzanine floor. The bricks of the facing are 3–4 cm. thick and the mortar joints, about 2 cm. wide. *Besales* appear in the soffit of the barrel vaults, which show an aggregate of tufa and tile mixed. "Ladders" can be seen reinforcing the vaulting. These chambers served as the foundation for upper rooms of good light-red brickwork strengthened by bonding courses. The orientation appears to be that of the rooms above, but the construction seems a little later and may be Antonine.[107]

No stairs have come to light to show whether the edifice under Santa Anastasia[108] in its second-century phase had upper floors. If it was a warehouse, it may not have. On the other hand, the row of rooms looks very much like the typical ground floor of an apartment house. At this time, the peperino piers of the earlier porticus[109] were incorporated in the end walls of six rooms. Each shop presented to the street in front a wide opening covered by a slightly curved lintel arch of upright *bipedales* under a relieving arch of the same, which was integrated with the width of the aperture rather than the lintel. Between the two arches there was a window without sill or lintel of its own to light a mezzanine floor. At the back, smaller doors with straight lintels gave access to a row of smaller rooms, for which others were substituted at a later date. Above the doors were windows of the same width. In this back wall *bipedales* were used for the lintels, but *sesquipedales* for the relieving arches. Holes in the side walls show where the mezzanine floor stood. Later it was removed, and the sill of the rear window was lowered. The chambers were barrel-vaulted. Brick stamps found *in situ* range in date from the late first to the early Hadrianic period. Because the brick work falls far below the standard of Hadrianic work, those who have dealt with the edifice have been inclined to ascribe it to a later period and have fallen back on the theory of re-used brick. After examining as thoroughly as possible in the dim light, I should classify it as poor Hadrianic work. To the west of this edifice, there are walls of a similar structure contemporary with it.[110] These shops faced the Circus Maximus, but the rear walls show arches and a tile cornice resting on a row of corbels which would seem to indicate that the shops originally faced the street behind.

The southeastern slope, like the southwestern, has never been completely excavated. Such structures as have been uncovered have never been adequately published and are difficult of access today. Some of them, at any rate, have been ascribed to the second century and may have belonged to privately owned apartment houses.[111]

Pincian

The part of the Pincian bounding the valley of the Via Flaminia on the northeast was given over entirely to gardens, all of which were laid out before the period with which we are now concerned. Although there were undoubtedly modifications and additions to the structures within them, none has been reported in sufficient detail to be of interest to this study. When new quarters were laid out on the rest of the hill toward the end of the last century and at the beginning of this, enough walls were found to show that the entire territory with the exception of that contained in the Horti Sallustiani was built over, and occasional brick stamps prove that some of the construction belonged to the second century, but little can be added to the fact that it was manifestly a residential area.

More recently the preparation of the ground for the Banco del Lavoro between Via Veneto and Via di San Basilio (1935–1938) exposed a welter of walls belonging to a century of building activity before systematization of the site in the second century.[112] The first addition was apparently a turret-like structure.[113] Its perimetric wall showed an obtuse angle before continuing in a curved front. An open staircase following the curve and supported by a concentric wall, led either to upper stories or a terrace. Walls and steps were of brick-faced concrete. They rested on a concrete foundation having an aggregate of broken tufa and tile in a mortar made with red

[109] Blake, *RC* II, p. 29.

[110] Lugli, *Centro*, pp. 609, 613.

[111] Lugli, *MAR*, vol. 1, p. 324.

[112] Blake, *RC* II, pp. 129–130.

[113] A. L. Pietrograndе, *Not. sc.*, vol. 16, 1933, pp. 356–359, 419.

[114] The range is, however, 14 to 28 cm.

[115] *CIL*, vol. 15 (1), 646; Bloch, *Bolli*, pp. 178–179.

[116] Pietrogrande, *op. cit.*, pp. 360–368.

[117] One pier abutted the wall of an edifice at the southeast.

[118] The bricks were 10 cm. long.

[119] Pietrogrande, *op. cit.*, pp. 413–419.

[120] *Ibid.*, pp. 410–414. For a general discussion of the chronology, see *ibid.*, pp. 419–422.

pozzolana. The core of the walls, on the other hand, had an aggregate predominately of terra cotta with a slight mixture of tufa, pebbles, and marble. The bricks were well fired, red, 3.5–4 cm. thick, and mostly 22–24 cm. long.[114] The joints of the same red mortar varied from 1 to 2 cm. There were traces of one door and one window. In the lintel arch of the former a stamp[115] confirms the Hadrianic date suggested by the type of construction.

Confronted with the tower-shaped structure on the north, a wide sustaining wall on the east, and a wall adjoining it at the southeast, the contractor[116] first reinforced the sustaining wall with stout piers[117] supporting arches of *sesquipedales* carefully laid at the ends but more carelessly on top. He next chose the lines for his north and south wall and joined them with a straight façade facing westward, behind which were six rooms and an entrance corridor. Each room had a window in the west wall equipped with a low sill such as ordinarily opened onto a court or private passageway. These openings were probably framed in wood. There was no communication from room to room, but each opened onto a corridor at the east. Adaptation to the change in orientation made two of the chambers to the south irregular in shape. The pavements were all of yellow bricks[118] laid in the herringbone pattern. The rooms were covered with barrel vaults set so low that special half lunettes had to be provided to allow for the opening of the doors which were at the side rather than in the center as usual. Hadrianic contractors were ready to attempt any type of vaulting for which they could construct the centering. Above the vaulting were vestiges of a black mosaic belonging to an upper floor. The corridor was barrel-vaulted. In preparation for the vaulting a series of segmental relieving arches with a different curve was inserted in the masonry between the larger relieving arches stretching from pier to pier. Little of this construction remained. The space between these rooms and the turret-like structure was utilized for two irregularly vaulted rooms which served as a passageway to it and the stairs encircling it. The walls of the ground floor were thick enough to have supported more than one story, but the height was limited by environmental conditions at the north, although it may have extended out over a terrace to the east. The whole suggests that it was a part, albeit a humble one, of one of the great villa complexes of the Pincian.[119] Since the ancient edifice had to be sacrificed to modern needs, no check is possible nor indeed necessary after the detailed report of the construction. The walls were faced either with brick or more generally with brick surrounding insets of reticulate. The tesserae of tufa (variety not specified) were accurately cut to surface dimensions of 7–7.5 cm. and united with a lean mortar in joints 1–1.5 cm. wide. The bricks were broken to shape (3–5.3 cm. $\times$ 15–30 cm., but with the majority 3.5 cm. $\times$ 22–25 cm.). They were made from well-baked, mostly reddish but partly yellowish tiles. The mortar joints varied for the most part from 1.5 to 2 cm. within a range from 1 to 2.2 cm. The core of the walls consisted of an aggregate of tufa pieces about the size of a fist or smaller in a red pozzolana mortar. The foundations and the vaulting exhibited the same kind of concrete except that the latter showed practically no brick fragments. The necessity of destroying the edifice made possible the discovery of enough brick stamps *in situ* to date the building in the time of Hadrian.[120] An overwhelming number were ascribable to A.D. 123 and 124. One found loose of A.D. 127 may furnish the *ante quem non*. Many of the same stamps were found at Villa Adriana near Tivoli and in other Hadrianic structures. In front of the south end of the façade, but at a level low enough not to have interfered with the outlook, there were scanty remains of what appeared to be a *fullonica*.[121] Could it have been a private one connected with the villa? Insignificant remains of masonry along the south side[122] and an independent structure with a different orientation to the southwest[123] are also ascribable to the second century. The latter, faced in brickwork with reticulate insets, showed a slightly different technique. The tesserae in the reticulate were of the same size, but the bricks, though equally well fired and broken to shape, were a different color (rosso corallino) and distinctly wider (4–4.5 cm.). The mortar joints (2 cm.) are also wider. Not enough was uncovered to determine the purpose of the structure or even an approximate date.

An inclined cryptoporticus,[124] uncovered along Via Lucullo in the garden of the Villa Ludovisi (now the property of the American Embassy), is of more interest for its frescoes than for its construction. It was barrel-vaulted with the usual splayed windows to give light and air. A tufa aggregate was used for the concrete and red bricks for the facing of the walls. The bricks varied greatly in the visible dimensions. Such brickwork can be as early as the Antonine era; the frescoes have been adjudged Antonine-Severan. This cryptoporticus was located in the Horti Sallustiani.

Brick stamps and coins indicate that a rather extensive habitation, of which scanty remains were uncovered in 1913 between Via Sicilia and Via Toscana,[125] was built toward the middle of the second century. Remains of wall paintings and mosaics[126] attest its importance, but the nature of its brickwork was not reported.

It is not my intention to enter into the field of early Christian archaeology; and I should gladly pass over the Catacombs of Santa Priscilla along the Via Salaria,[127] were it not for the fact that the "Capella Greca" contains two of the rather rare *volte a vela*. This sacred retreat was constructed in subterranean passages and drained reservoirs[128] belonging to the Villa of Acilius Glabrio. Its masonry of courses of tufa blocks alternated with three rows of bricks accords well with the year A.D. 140, the date ascribed to it on other grounds by Profumo. Most commentators, on the other hand, consider the wall paintings somewhat earlier.

Though the Pincian was fundamentally a region of villas, out beyond the Piazza Fiume to the southeast of the junction of the Via Tevere with the Via Isonzo, the remains of a small pottery manufactory were uncovered in 1925 in rather ruinous condition.[129] The kiln was a rectangular structure divided into two chambers one above the other. The entrance to the lower one was by means of a doorway made by placing the half of a rim of a large dolium on blocks of tufa and travertine. It led to a small semicircular space for the man who operated the kiln. The lower chamber where the fire was built had walls of unfaced concrete gently sloping toward a low vault. This was constructed with upright tiles between cylinders lined with an infusible material to assure a proper diffusion of heat. Irregular spaces were filled with broken pieces of brick, some of which bore the stamps of A.D. 123 and

[121] *Ibid.*, pp. 364–367.

[122] *Ibid.*, pp. 385–387.

[123] *Ibid.*, pp. 396–399.

[124] D. Faccenna, *Not. sc.*, 1951, pp. 107–114; Nash I, pp. 491, 497–499.

[125] G. Mancini, *Not. sc.*, 1912, pp. 14, 33; G. Gatti, *Bull. Com.*, vol. 10, 1912, p. 162; E. Katterfeld, *Röm. Mitt.*, vol. 28, 1913, pp. 92–112.

[126] One mosaic at any rate would seem to me to be Severan. See M. E. Blake, *MAAR*, vol. 17, 1940, p. 84.

[127] A. Profumo, *St. Rom.*, vol. 1, 1913, pp. 71–160; O. Marucchi, *N. bull. arch. crist.*, vol. 20, 1914, pp. 95–123.

[128] Profumo (*St. Rom.*, vol. 2, 1914, pp. 150–151) repudiates the idea of cisterns completely.

[129] E. Gatti, *Bull. Com.*, vol. 53, 1925, pp. 282–288.

130 The stamps furnish merely an *ante quem non*, but there is no evidence to indicate that the establishment was much later.

124.[130] The upper chamber was somewhat smaller. Its walls were faced with square tiles (21 cm. per side) embedded in thick layers of clay intended to prevent an escape of as much heat as possible. It was broken off below the springing of the vault, which must have had a vent at the top. No mention is made of any external facing. Connected with the kiln there were mortars of brick-faced concrete lined with *opus signinum* for working the clay, which had to be brought from a distance.

The Horti Sallustiani, which became imperial property early in the first century of the Christian era, occupied most of the eastern part of both the Pincian and the Quirinal. Little has come to light of the structures erected there by Julius Caesar and Sallust; and few of the scattered remains of cisterns, nymphaea, and various appurtenances of a large suburban villa of the imperial age can be dated with enough precision for our purpose. But there are extant at the head of the depression between the Pincian and the Quirinal, impressive remains of a western façade of several stories, which brick stamps prove was Hadrianic. Like many structures of this kind it consisted of terraces against the hill, but unlike many of them it shows a carefully integrated plan from bottom to top, to reverse the usual phrase, which is clearly the work of Hadrian's architect if not indeed of the emperor himself. It has seemed best, therefore, to describe its structural peculiarities in another section.[131]

131 See above, pp. 61–64.

Quirinal

With the exception of a number of temples, most of them very old, the Quirinal was almost exclusively a residential area. Even the structures given over to commerce were confined to the Latiaris, the summit above Trajan's Market, and seem to have been provided with apartments in the upper stories.[132] Private houses of the second, third, and even fourth centuries had to be destroyed to make room for the Baths of Constantine.[133]

132 See below.

133 Platner-Ashby, p. 525.

When Via Nazionale was put through in 1876, three rows of shops, each separated from the other by a paved passageway, were uncovered under the Villa Aldobrandini.[134] Each unit seems to have had a flight of steps to apartments above, and most of the shops went straight through from one passage to another, though they may have been divided by a wooden partition. The western unit had a single communicating door from one shop to the next; the others, two. The broad openings leading to the shops and the narrow doorways giving access to the type of stairway which served at least two upper floors had lintel arches of tiles under relieving arches of the same, whereas the doorways in the partitions had merely the lintel arch. One shop at any rate had a window between the lintel and the relieving arch for a mezzanine floor. Brick stamps range from the first century to A.D. 134.[135] The excavator ascribed the whole complex to the date of the latest stamp. Perhaps a more logical explanation would be that construction was started in the first century possibly on land laid bare by the fire of A.D. 64 and the establishment gradually enlarged. If one knew exactly where the stamps were found, he would know the answer. No record was kept of the kind of brickwork. More recently walls were uncovered along Via Mazzarino which would seem to be a part of the same complex. They are still visible. The

134 V. Vespignani, *Bull. Com.*, vol. 4, 1876, pp. 102–106; Harsh, *MAAR*, vol. 12, 1935, pp. 60–61; M. Santangelo, *Acc. P. Mem.*, ser. 3, vol. 5, 1941, p. 145.

135 Vespignani, *op. cit.*, pp. 115–120.

brickwork would appear to me either Trajanic or early Hadrianic, a date with which the excessive use of relieving arches of *bipedales* is certainly in accord. They appear in several instances supporting cross vaulting. One wall shows the end of a segmental arch over an opening which was apparently too wide for stability. In any case, the opening was narrowed a little, and an enormous full arch substituted for the other in a similar masonry. The arch end was outlined in a tile molding after a fashion popular at the time.

Traces of two large houses have been discovered under Santa Susanna which undoubtedly gave the name "ad duas domos" to the titulus.[136] A brick stamp of the middle years of the second century from an arch confirms the date suggested by the nature of the brickwork. Two walls with large irregular tufa tesserae (8.5–9.5) may belong to the same period. They are clearly later than walls and mosaic pavements of a structure which can be assigned to the middle of the first century. The meagre reports of the excavations made for the three great ministries along the Via Venti Settembre[137] yield nothing to the study of Roman construction, but the welter of walls of every period brought briefly to light gives an impression of a bustling city in which the old was constantly yielding to the new. Brick stamps prove that the second century contributed its share to a gradual transformation of the city. Excavations for a Methodist-Episcopal Church on Via delle Quattro Fontane[138] unearthed several stamps of the second century although most of the remains seemed later. The majority of the walls of the period were undoubtedly of brick-faced concrete, but when a wall with a reticulate facing contains two arches of yellow *bipedales*, semicircular niches, and occasional travertine corbels, such as was uncovered along the same street,[139] it probably belongs to the Trajan-Hadrian period, even though there is no proof.[140] A library with walls of block-and-brick work was inserted in an earlier edifice of brick-faced concrete.[141] Two stamps of the period may indicate the date of the earlier walls. The block-and-brick work is probably not earlier than the Antonine period. The arrangement of niches suggests a private library, for which amphorae were placed under the floor as a protection against dampness. Amphorae were also used in the vaulting. The earliest instance of that practice known to me in the vicinity of Rome is Hadrianic. Both walls and floor were sumptuously decorated with polychrome marbles. It is unfortunate that the evidence for dating this interesting room is so meagre.

Hadrian brought the Aqua Marcia to the Quirinal,[142] but inscriptions on water pipes leading from its distributing basin cannot be taken as incontrovertible evidence that the persons named[143] owned houses in the neighborhood.[144] Even though they may have, the mere names tell us nothing of the type of house in which they dwelt.

Excavations for buildings along the relatively modern Via Nazionale tell the same story. One of the largest was for the Banca d'Italia on the southwest side. Inscriptions have served to identify some ruins on the property of the bank along Via dei Serpenti as the dwelling of Virius Lupus Iulianus, who was legate to Lycia and Pamphilia in the second century.[145] Brick stamps of A.D. 123 indicate the date; columns, capitals, and pilasters attest its elegance; but no report mentions the nature of its construction. A part of an inscription bearing the name of T. Iulius Frugi, a legate to the

[136] A. M. Colini, *Bull. Com.*, vol. 66, 1938, p. 251; R. Krautheimer and W. Frankl, *AJA*, vol. 43, 1939, pp. 398–400.

[137] For the Ministerio della Guerra, R. Lanciani, *Not. sc.*, 1881, pp. 137–138; *idem*, *Not. sc.*, 1883, p. 339; for the Ministero dell' Agricoltura, D. Vaglieri, *Not. sc.*, 1907, pp. 439, 504–525, 651, 679–680; *idem*, *Not. sc.*, 1908, pp. 19, 46, 438; A. Pasqui, *Not. sc.*, 1909, pp. 222–223; G. Gatti, *Bull. Com.*, vol. 37, 1909, p. 294; for the Ministero delle Finanze, R. Lanciani, *Not. sc.*, 1879, p. 140; *idem*, *Not. sc.*, 1881, p. 89; D. Marchetti, *Not. sc.*, 1891, pp. 250–251.

[138] G. Gatti, *Not. sc.*, 1893, p. 358.

[139] R. Lanciani, *Not. sc.*, 1883, p. 340; D. Vaglieri, *Not. sc.*, 1913, p. 347.

[140] For another example, this one between Via delle Finanze and Via d. Santa Susanna, see G. Boni, *Not. sc.*, 1910, p. 509; J. Oliver, *MAAR*, vol. 10, 1932, p. 159.

[141] E. Gatti, *Not. sc.*, 1920, pp. 277–279; J. Oliver, *op. cit.*

[142] Van Deman, *Aqueducts*, p. 153.

[143] M. Santangelo, *op. cit.*, p. 146. The list is as follows: Aemilia Paulina Asiatica (*CIL*, vol. 15 (2), no. 7380), Appius Claudius Martialis (no. 7427), T. Flavius Claudius Claudianus (no. 7450) and Claudia Vera (no. 7434), L. Fabius Gallus (no. 7449), T. Flavius Salinator (no. 7452), Iulius Pompeius Rusonianus (no. 7475). For further information see Platner-Ashby, *Domus* with the name of the individual in the nominative.

[144] See Blake, *RC II*, p. 5.
[145] A. Pasqui, *Not. sc.*, 1910, pp. 162, 419–420; G. Mancini, *Not. sc.*, 1911, pp. 316; G. Gatti, *Bull. Com.*, vol. 39, 1911, pp. 201–202.

[146] R. Lanciani, *Bull. Com.*, 1886, pp. 184–186; idem, *Bull. Com.*, 1922, p. 7.

[147] R. Lanciani, *Not. sc.*, 1878, pp. 233, 340; idem, *Not. sc.*, 1886, p. 158; L. Borsari, *Not. sc.*, 1892, p. 343; G. Gatti, *ibid.*, p. 406.

[148] R. Lanciani, *Not. sc.*, 1880, pp. 465–466; idem, *Not. sc.*, 1881, pp. 56–57; G. Gatti, *Not. sc.*, 1887, p. 447; idem, *Not. sc.*, 1888, pp. 225, 275; idem, *Not. sc.*, 1893, pp. 262–263, 419, 430, 517; idem, *Not. sc.*, 1901, p. 511; Gu. Gatti, *Bull. Com.*, vol. 59, 1931, p. 223.

[149] Lugli, MAR, vol. 3, 648.

[150] Because of its interest to Christian archaeology, much has been written about the structures under this church. For the bibliography, plan, and photographs, see Nash I, pp. 295–296, 349–351.

[151] Van Deman, *Aqueducts*, pp. 16–17, 331.

[152] Lugli, *op. cit.*, pp. 649–650; Mesnard, *Saint Chrysogone*, p. 25; Krautheimer, *Basilicae*, vol. 1, p. 145. For an earlier house in the neighborhood, see Gu. Gatti, *Capitolium*, vol. 18, 1943, pp. 91–92.

[153] G. Mancini, *Acc. P. Rend.*, ser. 3, vol. 2, 1923–1924, pp. 154–155.

[154] A. Pellegrini, *Bull. Inst.*, 1867, pp. 8–12; Lanciani, *Ruins*, pp. 544–546; Lugli, *op. cit.*, pp. 645–648; Reynolds, *Vigiles*, p. 59 with a ground-plan at the end.

[155] G. Lugli apud R. Battaglia, *Il Palazzo di Nerone e la Villa Barberini al Gianicolo*, Istituto di Studi Romani (Rome), 1943, pp. 3–6.

[156] Blake, RC II, p. 129.

east in the time of Marcus Aurelius,[146] came to light, but since it had been re-used in a drain near the shop of some mediaeval marble workers, it may have been brought from elsewhere. Many stamps of the early years of the second century were, however, found in the course of the excavation.[147] On the other side of Via Nazionale the preparation of the site for the Palazzo dell'Esposizione yielded plenty of evidence of sumptuous dwellings of the rich in marble columns, traces of wall paintings, and mosaic pavements.[148] A sufficient number of brick stamps were found loose to ascribe some of them to the century under consideration, but once again no detailed report of the type of construction used was ever made.

Transtiberim

With the exception of the land included in the well-known gardens of the late Republic and the early Empire, the region across the Tiber was given over for the most part to the abodes of the poor and to buildings connected directly or indirectly with shipping. The house under Santa Cecilia[149] shows that there were some more pretentious dwellings before the period with which we are now concerned. Santa Cecilia herself probably dwelt in the house of brick-faced concrete erected on the site in the first half of the second century. Brick stamps of 116 and 123–134 were found in the course of excavation. Walls uncovered in the cortile in front, which may or may not have belonged to the house, were faced with triangular bricks. Too little is preserved to have any real value for a study of this sort.[150] With the building of the Aqua Traiana[151] the section was provided with good water for the first time. Still, few remains of houses have come to light to show that this did much to change the character of the quarter. A second-century house under San Crisogono[152] illustrates the difficulty of dating an edifice from the character of the construction alone. Mesnard ascribes it to the first half of the century, whereas Lugli places it about the middle. But bricks as thin as those reported (2.5 cm.) are seldom found before the time of Commodus. Narrow joints (0.8–1.2 cm.) contribute much to the fine appearance. The remains consist of an atrium with rooms opening out of it. Earlier Mancini[153] had announced traces of houses of the late second century. A porticus supported by pilasters on blocks of travertine seems to have formed a part of its plan. Substantial remains of a private house of the time of Hadrian were discovered in 1866 opposite San Crisogono.[154] The brickwork is described as mediocre. Its chief interest lies in its conversion into the Excubitorium of the Seventh Cohort of the Vigiles at a later period.

Janiculum

In the Antonine period, according to Lugli,[155] a large cistern was added to the villa on the northern slope of the Janiculum.[156] It consisted of three chambers 12 m. × 3.75 m. with three arched doorways in each partition wall. The whole was lined with opus signinum with quarter-columns at the corner. The form was a common one. The only unusual feature is the use of reticulate and brick for Antonine construction within the city limits. It is not, however, unknown in villas of the period, further removed from the Capital.

As in modern cities, a shift of the population to more salubrious quarters led to the adaptation of residences to commercial enterprises. An example of this trend was found in the region known as Pietra Papa on the right bank of the Tiber below Porta Portuensis.[157] Unfortunately, it had to be destroyed in the systematization of the embankment of the Tiber in 1939–1940. An elaborate nymphaeum had been added to an earlier house, in my opinion as late as the reign of Nero,[158] but by the time of Hadrian a circular edifice probably connected with it became part of a business establishment. It was given a concentric inner wall faced with yellow bricks broken to triangular shape (dimensions 16 cm. × 8 cm. × 4 cm.) united by a mortar joint 2 cm. wide. This wall was pierced at regular intervals by arched passages, 60 cm. high, to the space between the walls, which was 37 cm. wide. The room was furnished with a hypocaust having piers of *besales* resting on an under-pavement of *bipedales* and *sesquipedales*. A concrete conduit with a depressed vault under the floor led to a vaulted gallery parallel to the embankment, which seems to have been designed to bring hot air to the hypocaust. A cement pavement (*coccio pesto*) 12 cm. thick was laid above this conduit. On the pavement there were remains of deposits of yellow and blue coloring matter, indicating that this room at any rate was used for dyeing. There was also a drain leading toward the Tiber. A stamp of A.D. 123 was found in a hypocaust pier. Three passages sloped up from the center of a second unit to the west to the impost of the vaulted gallery on the south side.[159] They were barrel-vaulted also. The south wall was two meters thick; and within its thickness there were rectangular voids connected with the interior by low arched passages. Walls projecting inward seem to have furnished alcoves along the south side of the chamber. On the north side, a small rectangular room was walled off in the northeast corner. It contained amphorae placed horizontally along its walls. The rest of it showed voids similar to those in the south wall, though of varying lengths in a somewhat thinner wall, which were connected with the interior by similar passages. Behind the longest one at the east end there was an additional void with no outlet in a semicircular projection. Low walls made seven compartments of different widths along this side of the hall. Such an arrangement is a familiar feature in an ancient cleaning establishment.[160] The west wall was apsed, and a drain led outward from its center straight through a number of rooms, of which too little was preserved to reveal their purpose. All this unit was faced with triangular bricks.

Above the cleaning and dyeing establishment, a villa of the late Republican or early Augustan age was made over into Baths in the time of Hadrian.[161] The date is clear from the *besales* in a hypocaust[162] and the *bipedales* used behind the paintings in another room.[163] Modification walls showed a coarser reticulate with the tesserae joined by a richer mortar, which was reinforced by brick bands. The core of the walls had terra-cotta *caementa* mixed with the tufa. The piers of the hypocaust were made of *besales* chipped to a circular form to facilitate the circulation of the hot air. A barrel vault was preserved in one room, whereas possible traces of a cross vault appeared in another. The vaulting over a stairway gave evidence of the use of *bipedales* on the centering beneath a layer of *besales*. Two rooms at a lower level are particularly noteworthy for their fine decoration. One had a black-and-white

[157] G. Jacopi, *Mon. ant.*, vol. 39, 1943, cols. 1–166.

[158] Blake, *RC II*, p. 58. See the comments of Neuerburg, *Fontane*, p. 49.

[159] This was probably connected somehow with the circulation of hot air.

[160] Two superb examples have recently been uncovered in Ostia.

[161] G. Jacopi, *Bull. Com.*, vol. 68, 1940, pp. 97–107; *idem, Mon. ant.*, vol. 39, 1943, cols. 4–15.

[162] Gu. Gatti, *Mon. ant.*, vol. 39, 1943, cols. 171–174, nos. 8–15, 27–29.

[163] *Ibid.*, no. 24.

mosaic with the familiar pattern of stars of lozenges and squares, the other a rich polychrome mosaic of hexagons, squares, lozenges, and triangles, all of which was outlined in a two-strand *guilloche*. Vegetable motives appeared in all the larger spaces. The walls showed the preparation for a marble dado as well as the traces of the lining of *bipedales* to protect the frescoes from dampness. In one room, the artist depicted richly decorated boats of various kinds in a sea full of fish.[164] The paintings belong stylistically to the same school as the large painting in the house under Saints John and Paul.[165]

Nearer to the Tiber at a slightly different orientation, what was probably another thermal establishment was also built into an edifice of an earlier period.[166] The walls of this modification were faced with either brick or reticulate reinforced by brick. In one case, the inner facing was of brick whereas the outer one was of brick and reticulate. The bricks seem to have been largely triangular. A circular room was cut by a heavy buttressing wall toward the Tiber which contained a semicircular niche; and it was further strengthened by a curved, stepped buttress in the angle between it and the adjacent wall of a corridor with a sloping vault. The outside of the rotunda was stuccoed. An elegant latrine of the usual type had a black-and-white mosaic floor in which the picture of a crocodile was still preserved. One room at any rate was supplied with the suspended floor and the wall tubes indispensable to a Roman Bath. The level was the same as that of the other establishment, but the tiles in a drain indicate that it was built a little later.[167]

Viminal

No public building was ever erected on the Viminal proper, with the possible exception of the Lavacrum Agrippinae.[168] A fifteenth-century copy of a water pipe[169] with a note added that it was restored by Hadrian and a sixteenth-century plan of Bufalini (1551) are the only sources of information with regard to it. Possible confusion with the Lavacrum Agrippae[170] makes any association of it with Hadrian open to suspicion. In any case, no remains are left for study. For many years casual excavation has revealed the presence of private building activity of many periods, but technical details of the construction have not been reported with sufficient exactitude for a chronological study. Water pipes[171] give the names of a few notables who dwelt on the hill in the second century but give no indication whether they had built new dwellings for themselves or had merely modified and renewed the plumbing in the old ones. We are dependent, therefore, for such little knowledge as we have of the masonry of the second century on the hasty notes made by Dr. Esther Van Deman in 1907, when the excavation was made for the Ministero dell'Interno, on rather recent research under Santa Pudenziana for the Viminal proper, and on the careful analysis of the pomerial strip made by James Oliver in 1932.[172] As elsewhere, this construction must be sorted out from a medley of walls belonging to many periods.

When the Ministero dell'Interno was built (in 1913), remains of private edifices ranging in date from the Republic to the late Empire came to light only to be destroyed before they could be adequately studied. Only brief notices have ever been published.[173] Our indebtedness to Dr. Esther Boise Van Deman (noted just above) for the additional knowledge supplied by

[164] See also G. Jacopi, *Arti*, vol. 1, 1938–1939, pp. 513–516.

[165] See pp. 79–80 above.

[166] Jacopi, *Mon. ant.*, vol. 39, 1943, cols. 16–26.

[167] *Ibid.*, col. 18, n. 1.

[168] R. Lanciani, *Storia degli Scavi di Roma . . .*, Rome 1902–12, vol. 1, pp. 230–231; Jordan-Huelsen, p. 375 with n. 8; M. Marchetti, *Bull. Com.*, vol. 42, 1914, pp. 368–369; Lugli, *MAR*, vol. 3, p. 349.

[169] *CIL*, vol. 15 (2), no. 7247.

[170] See Platner-Ashby, p. 316 for the difference between *Agrippinae* and *Agrippae*. For the structure, see Blake, *RC* I, pp. 250, 270 (called "Agrippinae," its earlier name; see now Nash II, pp. 66–68, for bibliography and corrected identification). The site of the Lavacrum is still unknown.

[171] *CIL*, vol. 15 (2), nos. 7445, 7456, 7467.

[172] J. Oliver, *MAAR*, vol. 10, 1932, pp. 161–168.

[173] G. Mancini, *Not. sc.*, 1913, pp. 170–171 (republished also in *Bull. Com.*, vol. 41, 1913, pp. 257–259); Lugli, *MAR*, vol. 3, pp. 352–353.

her hasty notes and photographs taken during the process of demolition does not stop with the report of Claudian and Neronian construction.[174] These were engulfed in four massive substructures which brought the level of the slope up to the top of the hill (51 meters above sea level). Toward the west the second row was sunk into virgin soil to a depth of seven meters or more and was then built up in a wooden casing for almost two meters in addition. Along the southwest slope, the foundations were laid in trenches two meters deep cut in the tufa of the hill and raised two or three meters in wooden frames. These foundation walls were a meter or more in width. In general, the *caementa* were almost wholly of medium-sized pieces of travertine laid in rough rows usually with the flat side at the bottom in the trench, thereby showing that the concrete was not pre-mixed. Furthermore, it was not free enough from interstices to have been rammed down into place. An aggregate of red-brown tufa was found in one pier. An insufficient tile aggregate in a friable reddish gray mortar formed the core of the walls. The facing commenced with six or eight rows of rather thick bricks some of which bore Hadrianic stamps.[175] Above this semi-foundation, there was a facing of thinner yellow triangles made by sawing tiles. One wall near the top showed coarser bricks on one side and thinner yellow ones on the other. One tile came from a bonding course. Lintel arches of *bipedales* and at least one voussoir arch of the same show faintly in the background of some of Dr. Van Deman's photographs. The question arises immediately whether this yellow-tile house was of the same date as the foundations. Narrow yellow bricks are not unknown in the Hadrianic period. Of ten measured by Dr. Van Deman only three fall below a thickness of 3 cm., which was not at all uncommon at the time. Triangles also continued to be used, especially in private buildings. I see no reason why these may not have been part of a Hadrianic palace.[176]

Important construction has been uncovered under Santa Pudenziana.[177] A second-century house was built on the site of a late Republican dwelling. Brick stamps of A.D. 128, 129, 134 found *in situ* fix the date of the house rather late in the reign of Hadrian. Remains of three ground-floor rooms and of three identical rooms above them are all that are left of what was probably an extensive habitation. The walls were of good brickwork. The north façade facing the hill had two doors and three windows symmetrically arranged on the ground floor and five windows on the first floor. All apertures were covered with slightly curved lintel arches of *bipedales*. All six rooms were cross-vaulted. Soon, however, the owner apparently began making plans for a more extensive edifice on top of the hill. First he had at least five barrel-vaulted galleries built from the north side of the house to the hill, bringing the level up two stories to the height of the elevation behind the house, which incidentally may have been leveled off to give a flat surface. The walls were of brick-faced concrete like those of the house, which now became part of a mighty substructure. Apparently the space proved to be too small for what the owner had in mind. Consequently four more parallel galleries were added to those already built at the west to increase the available surface. These are slightly later and may have been built by a different contractor. The wall facing is unique in consisting of herringbone panels be-

[174] See Blake, RC II, pp. 55–56.

[175] Of seventeen stamps seen, fourteen (*CIL*, vol. 15 (1), 454 (2 exs.), 482 (2 exs.), 482 or 484 (2 exs.), 484, 801 (4 exs.), 1187, and two others unidentifiable, were dated by the names of the consuls of A.D. 123. The other three though illegible were Hadrianic in type.

[176] Dr. Van Deman in one of her plans labeled the walls "Aurelianic yellow."

[177] A. Terenzio, *Bull. Com.*, vol. 59, 1931, p. 222–223; *idem*, *Boll. d'Arte*, vol. 25, 1931–1932, pp. 188–191; A. Petrignani, *La Basilica di S. Pudenziana in Roma*, Città del Vaticano 1934, pp. 25–44 (reviewed by A. M. Colini, *Bull. Com.*, vol. 63, 1935, pp. 183–186); Lugli, *Tecnica*, p. 610. See Nash II, pp. 465–466, and additional bibliography cited there.

[178] The presence of water prevented me from visiting the galleries. Could that have been the reason why the Hadrianic house was abandoned so soon after it was built? (Neither Miss Blake nor Mrs. Bishop left any further note on this water.—JDB)

[179] The pools were later covered with the fish mosaic, of which traces remain.

[180] Petrignani (op. cit., p. 33) interprets some doubtful evidence as proof that cross arcades divided the hall into three parts.

[181] Mr. Spencer Corbett pointed out to me the proof that the columns were original and immured in smaller piers in the border of the mosaic mentioned above.

[182] I received help from Mr. Corbett here also.

[183] These were removed in the modern adaptation of the space to a passageway.

tween brick bands. The pattern is composed of alternate rows of bricks and small blocks of tufa. The bricks used in this strange wall are 2.8 to 2.9 cm. thick with mortar joints ca. 2 cm. wide. These galleries are cross-vaulted.[178] There seems to have been another series of chambers at right angles to these farther to the west which have not been excavated. So much for the substructures of the edifice to which we have not yet given a name.

A long, narrow, basilica-type hall above the first series of galleries is commensurate with the church built over it in the fourth century. The center of the space was filled with a remarkable set of pools outlined in the same bizarre fashion as the later galleries (pl. 12, fig. 1). The bricks and the little blocks are slightly wider (3 cm.) and the mortar joints correspondingly narrower (1.9 cm.). The focal point of the design was a deep pool roughly resembling a Latin cross with curved extremities. A little later, shallow pools were added at the north and south with curved sides and straight ends. These were lined with marble.[179] A quadriporticus with curved ends enclosed this elaborate arrangement of pools.[180] Columns partly immured in piers supported arches of bipedales,[181] each outlined with a tile molding. Above the arches, there was more of the same strange masonry pierced by seven high windows, presumably on both sides. The curved south wall was destroyed when the edifice was converted into a church. On the north, a heavy sustaining wall supported a wall following the curve of the pool with semi-circular niches near each end. It had high windows like those at the sides. It was faced outside and probably inside as well with the same opus spicatum. Not long afterward, however, the windows were made smaller in the same type of masonry and a wall was added following the line of the north wall but 1.8 m. distant.[182] It was faced on the inside with the same opus spicatum but on the outside with fine brickwork. The piers were reinforced with travertine blocks set in, three to a side apparently merely for decoration. The openings were topped with segmental arches of bipedales,[183] and above them large arches of the same were outlined in a tile molding. The bricks are 3 cm. thick with mortar joints little more than 0.5 cm. wide. Such a fine brick façade was certainly not intended to be covered by stucco, but the side walls were probably stuccoed over to conceal the opus spicatum. The arches of bipedales which topped the windows had a tile molding on the outside also. In antiquity, the entire windows would have been visible above the vaulted porticoes flanking the hall with the pools. The arched tops of the first and last two windows penetrated the barrel vault which extended over the hall from north to south. Above the three middle windows, on the other hand, a transverse barrel vault pierced the main barrel vault in such a way as to form a cross vault with north and south extensions. A small window with a segmental arch stood under the crown of a relieving arch which protected the central group of windows. It is generally assumed that the room with the pools was part of a Bath, which it may well have been. Although what we have described does not fit into any conventional plan for bathing establishments, there is no reason why a private individual should not have introduced novelties to attract clients to his Baths. The substructures indicate that it was part of a large complex, and traces of walls faced with opus spicatum appear in the walls of the Capella Gaetani on the west side. Peruzzi[184] has left a sketch of a circular room inscribed in a square with a cluster of niches in each angle separated by rectangular alcoves or passages of a type popular in Baths with vague indications of other rooms at the sides. It was discovered in the neighborhood in 1613 and may have belonged to the complex. Whatever its purpose, the construction would appear to be Antonine with two phases close together.

Tradition ascribes the site to the house of Pudens associated with the ministry of St. Peter in Rome. If so, it was the late Republican house that sheltered the Apostle. The prevalence of stamps[185] from the kilns of Servilius Pudens indicates that the property was still in the hands of the same family in the time of Hadrian, and tradition would ascribe its transformation into Baths to Novatus, a brother of Pudentiana, the daughter of the Pudens who befriended St. Peter, and possibly a second brother, Timotheus. Far be it from me to try to untangle the web of early tradition woven about the site. I see no reason why it may not be true.

Oliver's careful analysis[186] of the walls abutting the substruction of the agger to the south of the Viminal gate on the outside was scrutinized and approved by Dr. Van Deman. It reveals clearly the difficulty of applying a fixed canon to private construction. A-B, G-G′, G-H, H-H′ and J-M[187] in his diagram are Hadrianic, but they show considerable variety in technique. The aggregate in the G-H′ group is entirely of tufa, in A-B mostly of tufa with some tile, in J-M of both tufa and tile; the mortar is brown, whitish, and red respectively. The facing of the C H′ group is entirely of brick, whereas that of the others is a combination of brick and reticulate. The bricks for the G-H′ group were made from light red and yellow tiles (3–3.5 cm. × 22–30 cm.) and tended to be triangular, whereas the bricks of A-B and J-M were of broken roof tiles, those of the latter at any rate being red and compact. Those of A-B are ca. 3 cm. whereas those of J-M are 3–4 cm. in thickness. Mortar joints are close in both G-H′ and A-B, but not so specified in J-M. Bonding courses appear only in walls wholly of brick. Farther south in the Piazza Manfredo Fanti a small niche can be seen exhibiting in its arch the hard red tiles which were popular in the time of Trajan or the early years of the reign of Hadrian. East of this, a little brickwork probably Hadrianic occurs in an older building. Here yellow and light red bricks, ca. 3 cm. thick, partly triangles and partly broken tiles, face a concrete with a mixed aggregate of tufa and tile.

On the inside, considerable construction in brick or brick with insets of reticulate ascribable to the late first, or more often to the early second, century, came to light when the old railroad station was erected in the seventies and eighties of the last century,[188] but little if any of it has survived to modern times. Parker's photographs are the only record of much of it.[189] An old drawing depicts a shop characteristic of the period which was later incorporated in a Christian oratory.[190] A house of the same construction was reported in 1876.[191] A second edifice of at least three stories with an elaborate nymphaeum exhibited walls faced entirely with brick.[192] Brick stamps would seem to indicate that it belonged to the late Hadrianic period rather than to the Antonine era as reported.[193] It is quite possible that traces of other apartment houses went unrecognized when the land was cleared for the

[184] Lanciani, *Ruins*, p. 390.

[185] Bloch, *Bolli*, p. 244 n. 182.

[186] J. Oliver, *MAAR*, vol. 10, 1932, pp. 163–169.

[187] G-H′ and J-M are represented in Säflund, *Le mura*, pl. 24, 4.

[188] See F. Castagnoli, *Bull. Com.*, vol. 73, 1949–1950, pp. 130–134.

[189] Oliver, *op. cit.*, pp. 163–164, pls. 55–56.

[190] *Ibid.*, p. 168; G. B. de Rossi, *BAC*, 1876, pp. 48–49, pls. 6–7.

[191] Oliver, *loc. cit.*; *Not. sc.*, 1876, p. 42.

[192] C. L. Visconti, *Bull. Inst.*, 1869, pp. 212–213; R. Lanciani, *Ann. d. Inst.*, 1871, pp. 61–63.

[193] *CIL*, vol. 15 (1), nos. 507, 1212. No. 780 probably belongs to the same period.

[194] S. Aurigemma, *Fasti arch.*, vol. 3, 1948, no. 3202; A. W. Van Buren, *AJA*, vol. 52, 1948, p. 504.

[195] V. Massimo, *Notizie Istoriche della Villa Massimo alle Terme Diocleziane*, Rome 1836, pp. 213–216 (quoted by Lanciani in *Mon. ant.*, vol. 16, 1906, cols. 266–268); P. Harsh, *MAAR*, vol. 12, 1935, p. 51 which includes a floor plan; Crema, pp. 151, 228, fig. 241.

[196] These eventually went into the collection of the Duke of Bristol.

[197] G. Calza, *Mon. ant.*, vol. 23 (2), 1916, cols. 575–576 with pl. 5c; Richmond, *City wall*, p. 13 with fig. 5.

[1] See below, pp. 139ff.

old station. However that may be, the excavation for the new station revealed three.[194] The one best preserved had a lofty porticus in front, surrounding shops, and outside stairs to upper apartments. The two were adjudged to belong to the time of Antoninus Pius or Marcus Aurelius. An adjoining block contained "*un palazzo signorile*" and a thermal establishment. Both are noteworthy for their wall paintings and mosaics. No estimate is given of the time when this block was built but it may well have been contemporaneous with the other two. This brief notice must suffice until there is a more detailed report.

A small house of at least two stories, uncovered in 1777 between the Esquiline and the Viminal,[195] had an attractive arrangement of rooms with a colonnaded court in the center. A series of wall paintings found in it so aroused the admiration of Anton Raphael Mengs that he made copies of as many of them as he could before his death.[196] No record was made of the construction. One brick stamp of A.D. 134 gives the only hint of the date.

Although it is not possible to date with precision the rear façade of an apartment house still visible in the Aurelianic wall south of Porta Tiburtina,[197] it has the earmarks of a fairly early date in the second century. The whole face was doubtless brick-faced, though the ground floor is concealed below the modern street level. Only the top of a small window probably lighting a stairway and of three rather large windows belonging to the mezzanine floor are now visible. Travertine corbels once supported a balcony across the whole façade at the first floor level. Four round-headed windows symmetrically arranged gave light to the interior of this floor. The two central ones near together were flanked on each side and topped by small windows. At the left, a row of small holes once held corbels or beams for a balcony at a door of the second-story level. This floor was lighted by small slit windows. The apertures showed a variety of coverings—slightly curved lintels of upright tiles at the mezzanine level and over the small windows of the first floor, arches of *bipedales* over the large windows of the same floor, a wooden lintel under a slightly curved relieving arch over the doorway, and travertine sills and lintels under similar relieving arches for the slit windows of the second story. These windows call to mind some of those in the market of Trajan. The absence of relieving arches over the windows of the mezzanine floor may be an indication that wooden ceilings were used instead of vaults.

MERCANTILE ESTABLISHMENTS

A clear distinction cannot always be drawn between markets, bazaars, and warehouses. The Latin word *horrea*, which should be confined to the last named, has come to be used indiscriminately for all three. From the standpoint of construction it does not make a great deal of difference. The great warehouses were certainly the most important for the life of the time. Ostia is undoubtedly the better place to study them,[1] but Rome also had her full quota. We know the names of some from the Regionary Catalogues and their general location but not their date. The following can be ascribed to the second century, but no remains have been identified with them. A broken inscription found under San Saba,[2] as restored by Gatti, proves conclusively that the Ummidii had built a private storehouse probably on land belonging to the younger sister of Marcus Aurelius, Cornificia, who married M. Ummidius Quadratus. A similar inscription reused in the pavement of San Martino ai Monti on the Esquiline[3] mentions the private *horrea* of Q. Tineus Sacerdos. The Horrea Peduceiana[4] may have been located near the Horti of the same name outside Rome on the Via Latina, but the name has not been associated with any ruins. A Marcus Peduceius Stloga Priscianus was consul in A.D. 141. Most edifices of this sort were, however, erected near the Tiber.

By the second century, the huge Republican Porticus Aemilia,[5] the Horrea Sulpicia as restored by the Emperor Galba,[6] the almost equally large warehouse to the south of the Emporium commonly identified with the Horrea Seiana,[7] and a large brick building to the west of the Porticus Aemilia were all[8] in place in the great commercial area between the Aventine and the Tiber. Probably all four were modified to satisfy the demands of the ever-increasing commerce. Brick stamps[9] prove that that was the case for the Porticus; the great warehouse near the Tiber gave evidence of the narrowing of doorways and the subdivision of overly large rooms; a lead pipe[10] of the Hadrian period passed under the Horrea Seiana. For the region farther downstream we have the evidence of the Marble Plan for at least four more *horrea*.[11] Some, if indeed not all, of these may have been made possible by the Trajanic embankment.[12] East of the "Horrea Seiana" along Via Galvani, a brick wall above walls of reticulate work, a brick stamp of A.D. 123, and a water pipe with the name of Antoninus Pius[13] give slight evidence of structural activity in the Antonine period. Again farther to the east more brick-faced walls on top of those faced with reticulate uncovered in 1935 revealed an imperial substitution for an earlier building and showed that this mercantile area extended at least as far as the Pyramid of Cestius.[14] It consisted of rooms on two sides of an open square. On the west side the foundation walls were faced with brick only on the inside since the outside was banked with earth. Other walls, also brick-faced, were backed against the brick wall for about half its height. I can see no reason for these except as a protection from dampness. The brickwork was ascribed to the second-third century without the analysis which might have led to a more precise ascription. More recently *horrea* having walls faced with reticulate insets in brick frames have been uncovered inside Porta Ostiensis.[15] Such construction belongs to the first century or the first half of the second. The modern Via Marmorata, which bounds the area on the northeast has a different alignment from the ancient street which preceded it. Consequently, the site of the modern street has yielded fragmentary remains, some of which certainly belong to the second century,[16] but only where brick stamps have been found can one be sure of the approximate date.[17] Only one is significant from the point of view of construction because it showed pieces of broken vaults with amphorae in the vaulting.[18] This device for lightening the load did not appear in Rome, to the best of my knowledge, before the time of Hadrian. Near Santa Maria in Cosmedin, remains of a large brick porticus were uncovered in 1891,[19] which may have been a new edifice of the second

[2] A. Pasqui, *Not. sc.*, 1910, p. 90; G. Gatti, *Bull. Com.*, vol. 39, 1911, pp. 120–128.

[3] *CIL*, vol. 6 (4, 2), no. 33860.

[4] Platner-Ashby, p. 262.

[5] Blake, *RC I*, p. 249.

[6] *Idem, RC II*, p. 87.

[7] *Ibid.*, pp. 15–16.

[8] E. Gatti, *Bull. Com.*, vol. 53, 1925, pp. 279–280.

[9] Jordan-Huelsen, pp. 173–174, n. 54. For the remains of brick walls brought to light, see Gu. Gatti, *Bull. Com.*, vol. 62, 1934, pp. 137, 139, 140.

[10] G. Mancini, *Not. sc.*, 1911, p. 446.

[11] *FUR*, pp. 83–84, 95, pls. 25 and 62b.

[12] See above, pp. 38–39.

[13] C. Gatti, *Not. sc.*, 1906, pp. 181, 206; G. Mancini, *Not. sc.*, 1914, p. 223.

[14] Gu. Gatti, *Bull. Com.*, vol. 63, 1935, pp. 191–192.

[15] C. Pietrangeli, *Bull. Com.*, vol. 72, 1946–1948, p. 216.

[16] Blake, *RC II*, p. 125.

[17] G. Gatti, *Not. sc.*, 1907, pp. 83–86.

[18] R. Lanciani, *Not. sc.*, 1881, p. 90.

[19] G. Gatti, *Not. sc.*, 1891, p. 336.

[20] Lugli, MAR, Suppl., pp. 154–155. Lugli's, "Forma Urbis Romae" does not follow this description.

[21] Lanciani, Ruins, pp. 529–530; Platner-Ashby, p. 512.

[22] G. Mancini, Not. sc., 1913, p. 117.

[23] Cf. Platner-Ashby, p. 262.

[24] I. A. Richmond, Bull. Com., vol. 55, 1927, p. 46; idem, City wall, pp. 10, 16–17.

[25] R. Lanciani, Not. sc., 1879, pp. 15, 40, 68; idem, Not. sc., 1880, pp. 127–141; idem, Not. sc., 1884, p. 238; Platner-Ashby, p. 109; Lugli, MAR, vol. 3, pp. 653–654.

[26] Lanciani, Not. sc., 1878, p. 66.

[27] Idem, Not. sc., 1880, p. 140.

[28] Blake, RC I, p. 272.

century, but no brick stamps were reported and no record made of the nature of the brickwork. This commercial quarter extended northward to include the street leading from the Forum Boarium to the Forum Holitorium.[20] On the east side, there was a cross-vaulted porticus of travertine piers in front of five shops having brick-faced walls and an apartment house, the ground floor of which was given over to shops. On the west side, there were three great provision markets, in which two lines of shops facing in opposite directions shared a common back wall. The row toward the Tiber was at a lower level. They were built in the second century and showed the usual later modifications. They have not been published officially and are not visible today. All this utilitarian construction has little to contribute to a study of methods of building. Monte Testaccio[21] stands as a monument to the intense activity which took place in the area. We do not know when the site was set aside as a dumping ground for the broken jars which brought grain, oil, wine, and other commodities to Rome. Since many of the inscriptions which have been reported belong to the second century, it seems appropriate to make mention of it here.

There may have been another mercantile quarter across the Tiber. The right bank would have been equally convenient for the deposit of commodities though less so for their distribution. Traces of one in brick-faced concrete have been reported without any indication of its date.[22] This has been thought by some to be the Horrea Lolliana.[23] When the Aurelianic Wall was built, an area to the north of it on the right bank was apparently abandoned and gradually covered,[24] thereby preserving the remains of an important mercantile establishment, which unfortunately had to be sacrificed to a modern (1880) reorganization of the banks of the stream.[25] In fact, the wall cut across a great warehouse for storing and distributing wine wholesale just east of Porta Septimiana. An inscription dated A.D. 102[26] found in the course of the excavation proves that they were in part at least the Cellae Vinariae Novae et Arruntianae. All stamps found belonged to the second century;[27] and most of them came from imperial kilns. Above the vaulted wine cellars at the level of the Tiber, two separate units were made up of courts more or less enclosed in porticoes. The columns were of travertine covered with stucco to simulate marble fluting. The walls were faced with the combination of brick and reticulate characteristic of the time of Trajan and Hadrian. Dolia were found in the courts and fragments of them throughout the excavation. Of the ten dolia stamps picked up, six bear names which occur on brick stamps to be dated between A.D. 75 and 125. The elegance of this warehouse suggests that its architecture was influenced by the proximity of the Farnesina.[28]

VILLAS NEAR ROME

Behind the tombs along the main highways from Rome the line of villas was practically continuous. They also dotted all the hillsides in the Roman Campagna. Villa sites in the country are exposed to damage from agricultural operations and all the disintegrating forces of time; but they have seldom been covered or destroyed by later buildings. These country estates often show three or four phases which are difficult to date with precision. At times they reveal experimentation with building methods and a divergence from the normal procedure which is refreshing. Of the hundreds which once dotted the Campagna only three are presented which have something definite to contribute to an understanding of Roman construction in the second century of the Christian era; but notice is taken of a few others. Imperial villas are not included in this exposition of private building.

Villa di Annia Regilla

Between the Via Appia and the Via Latina and now cut by the Vicolo della Caffarella, there was once an enormous villa[1] (2 km. × 1 km.) belonging to Annia Regilla, the wife of Ti. Claudius Herodes Atticus, who died in A.D. 161. An inscription locates the property at the third milestone, but its remains are spread from the second to the third mile. There are a few structures, mostly cisterns in selce concrete[2] which belong to an earlier period and some notes of later construction,[3] but the most important edifices seem to belong to about the middle of the second century of the Christian era. Unfortunately, the main building occupying the top of the hill at the southeastern end of the property has been reduced to little more than debris.

There is a corner of a substruction in selce concrete lined with fine stucco. Irregular reticulate tesserae and triangular bricks indicate the nature of the wall construction; pieces of affricano, cipollino, and pavonazzetto attest the richness of marble floors; and pieces of red and blue stucco show the garishness of the painted walls. Near it was a reservoir with a wall of concrete unfaced on the outside because it was banked with earth, but lined with brick. The core consisted of a rather small aggregate of yellow tufa in the usual mortar. The bricks, mostly yellow, are either triangles (3.5–4.2 cm. × 18–20 cm.) or pieces of tile (2.6–3.4 cm. × 25–29 cm.). Such brickwork accords well with the practice of the middle of the second century. Brick-faced walls of the same period appear in another structure of uncertain use a little to the southwest near Sant'Urbano.

There is inscriptional evidence[4] that the lands of Annia Regilla contained a temple to Faustina the Younger as a new Ceres. Consequently it is natural to assume that the temple which was converted into the church of Sant' Urbano[5] should be identified with it. In antiquity it presented to the front a podium of seven steps (no longer visible) and a colonnade of four Corinthian columns and simple entablature of Pentelic marble.[6] A rather elaborate cornice of molded tiles—dentello, astragolo, ovolo, astragolo, dentello, listello —formed the transition to a lofty brick-faced attic, which terminated in a similar cornice under an ornate capping cornice supported by consoles made of three vertical tiles properly shaped. Upon the attic rested the pediment with raking cornices similar to the horizontal cornice except for the absence of consoles. The pediment had a round frame of besales in the tympanum for a marble protime. The tiles used for the cornice were new; the bricks used for the walls were made from broken tiles. The mason who built them still relied upon bonding courses 1.78 m. apart. A rather unusual feature was three windows in each of the short sides to give light to the interior.[7] The interior, a single room, was given a less flamboyant treatment. The walls

[1] G. Lugli, *Bull. Com.*, vol. 52, 1924, pp. 94–120.

[2] *Ibid.*, p. 119; Lugli considers that at this period the estate was dedicated to agriculture alone.

[3] *Ibid.*, pp. 117–119, 120. These are easily differentiated from the rest by block-and-brick work of re-used bricks and badly squared blocks which bespeak the fourth century.

[4] Lanciani, *Pagan and Christian Rome*, pp. 287–291; Tomassetti, *Campagna*, vol. 2, pp. 71–73, who considered the temple a tomb.

[5] Castagnoli, *Appia Antica*, fig. 13; Frova, p. 93, also considers this monument a tomb.

[6] The space between the columns was filled in after an earthquake in the late antique period.

[7] Only two of those in the rear wall still remain open.

were divided into three parts. The lowest was smooth and may have been painted. A projecting cornice of tile was upheld by flat arches of *pedales* between trapezoidal springers of travertine and tufa or peperino alternated; this cornice supported pilasters, one for each two arches below, with Corinthian capitals in peperino. These, in turn, supported a second cornice, like the first, made up of flat arches with a single keystone in each bay. A similar cornice formed the transition to the third part which was a narrower band. The barrel-vaulted ceiling was decorated with fine stucco work. At the impost there were two pictures with trophies. The field was divided into octagonal coffers connected by squares with rich cornices, whereas in the center there seems to have been a sacrificial scene. This temple was probably erected after the death of Annia Regilla at about the same time as her tomb. Her grief-stricken husband chose for her tomb approximately the central point of her estate when he decided upon a monument of the type most popular at that time. He apparently gave orders that it should be richer in decoration than any known up to that time. The tomb's moldings and cornice resemble closely those of the temple described above, but there are many other decorative features which will be described below under Tombs.[8]

A suburban villa of this sort would be incomplete without at least one elaborate nymphaeum; and the villa of Annia Regilla has one,[9] part way down the hill, which is very picturesque in its dilapidation. It consists of a vestibule with two lateral chambers provided with niches and a rectangular chamber with an alcove and niche opposite the entrance and three niches along each side. The vestibule was open to the sky and may have been preceded by a porticus. The niches were all semicircular with arched tops. The facing of the interior shows the type of mixture of reticulate and brick that is sometimes found in the time of Hadrian but is more apt to be early Antonine. Reticulate faces the podium and the space above the niches; brick, the spaces containing the niches, which terminate in arches of *besales*. The reticulate tesserae are small and regular; the bricks (3.2 cm. $\times$ 25–29 cm.) are reddish. The mortar joints approximate 1.5 cm. A barrel vault covered the structure. There was serpentine in the floor decoration and verde antico in the walls, both chosen no doubt to add to the impression of coolness; and the niches were adorned with glass mosaic and shells. Traces of water pipes leave no doubt as to the purpose of the structure.

Le Vignacce

The villa known as "*Le Vignacce*"[10] on a crossroad from Via Tuscolana to the Via Appia Nuova is of especial interest because it was privately built in the time of Hadrian and almost certainly the property of Q. Servilius Pudens, the brickmaker.[11] That it was private is indicated by the almost complete absence of bricks from any of the imperial kilns and the presence of water pipes bearing the names of private individuals. All the brick stamps bearing the names of consuls with one exception fall between A.D. 123 and 127. The name of Q. Servilius Pudens occurs on more stamps than that of any other brickmaker and twice on one of the water pipes. It may seem strange that Servilius did not use exclusively the products of his own kilns, but we cannot know the business transactions which may have brought other

[8] See below, pp. 129–130.

[9] Castagnoli, *Appia Antica*, figs. 14, 15; Crema, pp. 464–465; Neuerburg, *Fontane*, pp. 34, 47, 86, 94, 98, 161–162.

[10] T. Ashby, *PBSR*, vol. 4, 1907, pp. 74–78; Ashby & Lugli, *Acc. P. Mem.*, ser. 3, vol. 2, 1928, pp. 183–192; Bloch, *Bolli*, pp. 185–191; Lugli, *Tecnica, passim*; Neureberg, *Fontane*, p. 166.

[11] A lead pipe indicates that he became the owner of a sumptuous villa just off Via Nomentana between the fifth and sixth kilometer from Rome. This villa he apparently acquired from L. Funisulanus Vettonianus, who succeeded Frontinus as curator aquarum in A.D. 106. See T. Ashby, *PBSR*, vol. 3, 1906, pp. 54–55.

supplies into his possession. Although the villa extended over considerable territory, relatively little of it remains for study; and unless something is done to protect it before it is too late, even that little will disappear. The walls were of concrete faced with reticulate reinforced by bands of brick. The angles ordinarily show alternate rows of tufa blocks and bricks, though the alternation is not always carried out with precision. The same alternation was extended to the voussoirs of the arches. It seems unlikely that these minor divergences are significant. The spur walls along the garden terrace are manifestly later than the sustaining wall, but even they may belong to the same general period of construction. They are faced with bricks unusually thin for the time (barely 3 cm.), but they supply a stamp similar to *CIL*, vol. 15 (1), 1430 ascribable to A.D. 127, of which several specimens were found at the site. The builder was no longer interested in the facing as such, since he intended to conceal it; and he had perfect confidence in the tenacity of the concrete core. He was, on the other hand, evidently preoccupied with the stability of the vaulting and the proper distribution of the thrusts. He practically always alternated cross vaults; he placed small niches in the corners from which he started apses; he gave his one circular room a depressed vault[12] and encircled it with small vaulted chambers; he placed niches along the outside of three of the five sides of the long two-story reservoir[13] for which he used cross vaulting for the three lower chambers and barrel vaulting for the four upper ones. He also revived the use of amphorae[14] to lighten the weight of the walls in the upper story. More significant, however, was the use of two rows of thirty-two ollae each set at equal intervals in the dome of the circular chamber, where they served not only to reduce the weight but have an integral part in the construction as partial supports. This builder did not set for himself the complicated problems of vaulting which taxed the ingenuity of the architect who planned the contemporary Villa Adriana near Tivoli. The villa was richly decorated with precious marbles and fine statuary.

Villa dei Quintili

Conspicuous remains of a vast estate[15] are visible both from the Via Appia and the Via Appia Nuova about five miles from Rome. Water pipes[16] prove that it was owned at some time by the Quintilii brothers, Condianus and Maximus, who were consuls together in A.D. 151 and perished together about A.D. 183 at the command of Commodus, who took possession of their villa. Such a vast estate would be long in taking final form and subject to constant changes perhaps even within a short space of time. Only by an analysis of construction can one reach an approximation of its chronology. In the northwest corner, there are fragmentary walls of several edifices more or less isolated by the configuration of the land. Only two were well enough preserved to show that they were cisterns. A great circular one (29 m. in diameter),[17] divided into six intercommunicating chambers, had walls of selce concrete. The other at the extreme northwest was rectangular and divided into two parts by a cross wall, and each part was subdivided by a cross partition with a doorway. This cistern was heavily buttressed at the corners and had three buttresses along each side corresponding to the cross walls within.

[12] De Angelis d'Ossat, *III conv. st. archit.*, p. 226.

[13] For a detailed description of the reservoir, see Van Deman, *Aqueducts*, p. 109–110. Some of the walls show blocks alone.

[14] De Angelis d'Ossat, *Palladio*, vol. 5, 1941, p. 243 with figs. 1 and 2; idem, *Le cupole*, p. 22; idem, *III conv. st. archit.*, p. 246.

[15] T. Ashby, *Ausonia*, vol. 4, 1909 (pub. 1910), pp. 48–88; Crema, p. 464, figs. 599–600; Frova, pp. 406–407; Neuerburg, *Fontane*, pp. 56, 82, 96, 160–161.

[16] *CIL*, vol. 15 (2), no. 7518.

[17] No. 9 in plate 1 of Ashby's publication.

18 Mean *thickness* is not so illuminating as the range.

19 Ashby, *Aqueducts*, pp. 223–224.

20 Ashby's term *opus mixtum e quadrelli di tufa* is ambiguous. Lugli (*Tecnica*, p. 652) lists it as *opus vittatum misto di pietra e laterizio.*

21 A. Muñoz, *Bull. Com.*, vol. 41, 1913, pp. 14–21.

22 The specus on top of the wall was cut in this operation.

23 Nos. 14 and 16 in Ashby's publication, plates 3 and 4 (see note 15 above).

24 Lugli, *Tecnica*, p. 608.

There were apparently rooms over the southwest end. The walls were faced with irregular bricks having a mean thickness[18] of 3.6 cm. well laid with mortar joints 1.8 cm. wide. There were bonding courses at regular intervals. Slightly thicker bricks (3.9 cm. in no. 2; 4 cm. in no. 8) were united with correspondingly narrower mortar joints. One partition wall (no. 6) exhibited reticulate work with brick bands. It had squared-stone masonry along the Via Appia with the blocks fastened together by swallow-tailed clamps. This may well have been left from some earlier period.

At this same period a narrow "hippodrome" garden with a curved end toward the Via Appia was laid out to the southeast. The walls were composed of selce concrete like that in the round cistern, and they presented rectangular niches to the inside. To the southeast of this a rectangular cistern was faced with the same kind of brick (4 cm. thick) as was used in the edifices just described. It was divided by piers into two barrel-vaulted chambers. A square room at the east end was apparently designed for the control of the flow of water into an arched aqueduct with piers of selce concrete. A specus carried the water on top of the "hippodrome" wall toward the living quarters of the villa further east. Above it, a second specus seems to have been connected with the Aqua Claudia.[19] Later the "hippodrome" was widened into a broad rectangular garden which was bounded by a narrower wall with a curved casino at least in the south and east corners. This wall was faced with block-and-brick work,[20] and the space between it and the great hemicycle was converted into a nymphaeum[21] with the same type of masonry. A wide entrance was cut through the center of the curve[22] and finished with pilasters of fine brickwork having two columns of bigio between them. A pavement of peperino blocks led to a large apse, whereas coarse mosaic paved the space in front of rectangular wings marked by cipollino columns. A curved niche between rectangular ones diversified the lower register of the apse; and a double order of niches did the same for the wings. There was a pool in the apse and reservoirs behind the wings. The whole façade was covered with a marble revetment.

Separated from the Via Appia by the "hippodrome" garden, the residential unit must always have been placed on a slight elevation to the northeast. Two halls,[23] sufficiently preserved to make a picturesque ruin, appear as isolated edifices but were actually part of the living quarters. Hypocausts and wall tubes reported in old excavations indicate that the northwestern part was a private Bath. One of the halls mentioned above contained a large pool; the purpose of the other is unknown. It is of interest architecturally for the lower rooms at each of the four corners and the large arched windows high up on three of its four sides. Only the thin side walls of this hall, a mysterious round building, and a ponderous substructure are faced with the same type of block-and-brick work as the walls of the "hippodrome" and the nymphaeum with which they were presumably contemporaneous. The substructure is entirely bereft of its superstructure. The rotunda was probably open to the sky inasmuch as it was thirty-six meters in diameter. The circumference was pierced with doorways at frequent intervals. What it was used for is a matter for speculation. The hall was reinforced with brick corners on the inside to carry the cross vaulting. The bricks[24] were mostly from tiles broken to trapezoidal shape, but there are some triangles. The bricks were dark (*brucciato*) and homogeneous, though there were bonding courses of thicker and yellower ones. In general, they measured 19–27 cm. $\times$ 3.3–3.8 cm. in the visible faces. The mortar was gray and firm with a fine aggregate of rounded particles. It will be noted that the bricks were slightly thinner than those used in the first phase. They represent a third building period. All the other edifices were entirely of brick-faced concrete and sometimes showed modifications in a brickwork of similar technique. Cross vaulting was employed over square or nearly square chambers, barrel vaulting over long narrow corridors, and an occasional example of mixed vaulting appears, such as is found at Sette Bassi. *Besales* were laid on the wooden centering in horizontal and vertical rows with an occasional one laid on end to form a bond.[25] So little of the palace remains above the foundations that it is impossible to say more than that there were apparently three building periods, probably close together, identified by the use of brick, block-and-brick, and brick. One room was heated.

It is possible that a long, comparatively narrow strip of ground to the south at right angles to the earlier "hippodrome" garden served as a new one after the latter had been widened. Near the center of the southeast side, a building is preserved in part which could have been used as a vantage point for watching any spectacles that might have taken place in the area. Its masonry was the block-and-brick work used to enlarge the earlier "hippodrome." This garden was also well supplied with water from an open channel which encompassed the area and filled three reservoirs widely separated. Selce concrete formed the walls of the underground cistern at the east corner. The use of selce here has no chronological significance since weight was essential to withstand the pressure of the water. The walls decreased in thickness as the pressure became gradually less intense. The other two were of brick-faced concrete. Traces of heavily buttressed substructures and of three or four buildings of indeterminate uses are all that remain of this part of the villa. Scanty traces of a ramp from a cross road and of three cisterns are visible at the north corner of the estate.[26]

Brick stamps are not so helpful for dating the various building periods as they would be if we knew that those reported from old excavations came from the .villa site and not from nearby tombs. Even if they were found in the villa, they have little value unless the exact provenience is known. Over-production of stamped tiles in A.D. 123 detracts from the importance of the one stamp picked up by Ashby in the northwestern unit. If the stamp of A.D. 138 reported by Fabretti[27] as coming from an aqueduct was found in that one which connects cistern no. 12 with the wall of the "hippodrome," it gives a slight indication that the first phase belongs to the early Antonine period. A stamp of Marcus Aurelius from the second phase of the "hippodrome" suggests a reasonable date for the block-and-brick work, but a single stamp is weak evidence. Later stamps attest modifications later than the three phases with which we are now concerned. Where small round stamps without lettering appear on small square tiles,[28] they may indicate changes in the last of the three phases.

[25] *Ibid.*, p. 681.

[26] These same two brothers gained possession of a villa near Tusculum where Mondragone now stands. Water pipes attest its existence, but practically nothing of it is visible today. See Ashby, *op. cit.*, p. 88. It is not known whether Commodus took possession of that also.

[27] Fabretti apud Ashby, *op. cit.*, p. 88.

[28] Ashby, *op. cit.*, pp. 79, 83, 84.

[29] T. Ashby, *Röm. Mitt.*, vol. 22, 1907, pp. 311–323; Lugli, *Tecnica*, pp. 577–578, pl. 180; Crema, p. 472, fig. 605.

[30] J. Ward-Perkins, *PBSR*, vol. 23, 1955, p. 66 (new series, vol. 10).

[31] T. Ashby, *PBSR*, vol. 4, 1907, pp. 97–112; N. Lupu, *Eph. daco.*, vol. 7, 1937, pp. 117–188; Crema, pp. 461, 464, fig. 598; Frova, p. 93. The name Sette Bassi may be a corruption of Septimius Bassus, a later owner.

[32] G. Lugli (*Palladio*, n.s., vol. 2, 1952, pp. 176–177; and *Tecnica*, pl. 195, fig. 1) publishes photographs taken before the collapse.

[33] Block, *Bolli*, pp. 256–268; *idem*, *HSCP*, vol. 63, 1958, pp. 401–414.

Anguillara Sabazia

A substantial residue of a strange building stands alone[29] on the Via Cassia in a small locality known as Crocicchie near Lago Bracciano as a monument to a villa, of which only slight traces remain. The ruin is known as Muracci di San Stefano from the dedication of the Chapel within it in the Middle Ages. It is a square edifice (15 m. per side) of three stories with a double stairway at the south of brick-faced concrete. The bricks employed on the inside were slightly thinner than those on the outside, but compensation was made by the use of wider mortar joints with the latter. All the bricks were probably broken from flanged tiles. At any rate, there were no triangles. The exterior showed the polychromy popular in the tombs of the Antonine period. Pilasters on the outside of each story were faced with red bricks, whereas the curtain between them was yellow. There was a door between two windows on the north side and three windows in each of the side walls, and windows alone held corresponding positions in the two upper stories. The windows were slightly splayed. A row of marble corbels stood above the entablature of the ground floor. Pilasters on the inside were clearly designed to support the vaulting, which was quadripartite over the ground floor and received additional support from four pillars near the center. According to the plan of Ligorio, the middle floor was divided into nine compartments of which the one in the center was a light well and the others crossvaulted. The niches on the inside, of which Ashby writes, were functional rather than decorative. Tile arches faced their vaults. Lugli follows Ashby in accepting a conjecture of Egger that the building was a storehouse for the provisions necessary for a large country estate, similar to one found in the Villa Adriana. Ward-Perkins,[30] however, cited evidence of elaborate decorative elements found in excavation within the structure to suggest that it may have been "the central block of the residential wing of a wealthy *villa rustica*."

Sette Bassi

Between the Via Tuscolana and the Via Latina at about the sixth mile from Rome, there was a grandiose villa known as Sette Bassi,[31] of which important remains are still extant in spite of the collapse of 1951.[32] It displays at least five different periods, but three Antonine phases attested by brick stamps[33] established its characteristic form. Three blocks of rooms constitute the main part of the villa. All the brick stamps found in the first unit are ascribable to A.D. 139 or thereabouts. The majority were made by Arabus, Hedys, and Abascantus in the employ of Q. Servilius Pudens, but Q. Aburnius Caedicianus supplied some to this and some to the next unit. The stamps in the second unit range from A.D. 138 to 140, thereby proving that a part at any rate of this small independent block was erected a year or two later, whereas a decade passed before the third unit was added to the complex. The collapse of the windowed wall gave a rare opportunity for a reappraisal of the stamps of this unit, which brought a greater precision to the dating without changing fundamentally the accepted chronology. Barring one loose stamp of A.D. 123, all those which can be dated exactly fall between A.D. 134 and 150. A span of sixteen years in a single building period calls for speculation. Bloch explains the phenomenon as either the sale of a deposit at the death or retirement of the owner or as the use of a large deposit made in anticipation of a future building program. The first alternative seems the more plausible.[34] The third unit must therefore be dated somewhat later than the date of the latest stamp (A.D. 150). The stamps occurring on *besales* from the vaults or broken in half longitudinally from the walls all came from the Figlinae Sulpicianae. The majority (35 out of 57) on *bipedales* from the lintel arches over the windows came from the brick-yards of Domitia Lucilla (Domitianae, Fulvianae, Terentianae), whereas an additional eighteen bear the name of Lucius Verus. By this time the imperial family was well established in the brick industry.

In its earliest phase,[35] the villa occupied the south and west sides of a peristyle, which was enclosed on the north, east, and south by a colonnade elevated on a parapet. Holes for the insertion of roof beams for this can still be seen on the north façade of the southern unit. On the west, an ambulatory with a windowed wall toward the peristyle gave access to a single row of rooms, each having one or two windows opening out toward the open country. The walls were of brick-faced concrete with some of the bricks showing evidence of flanges. The southernmost chamber, on the other hand, was a cistern having a hollow wall on the east side up to a certain point, in order to protect the ambulatory from dampness. Its barrel vault was at right angles to those in the other rooms. A narrow service stairway at the south of it descended to cellars; stairs at the opposite side probably gave access to a terrace. The plain western façade was terminated by a simple tile molding. The southern unit consisted of a number of apartments more or less systematically arranged to provide the maximum of comfort for different seasons. One heated room in a southeast apartment was not only given a hypocaust and the necessary furnace room but had a double vault as well. A corridor on the opposite side had the same type of insulation in its ceiling. Four rooms and a furnace in the southwest corner comprised a small private Bath. A detailed analysis of the ground plan is beyond the scope of this study. The core of the walls in both units was composed of small pieces of peperino laid in regular rows in a fair mortar; the facing of the southern unit was of brick alone or of brick combined with reticulate. The bricks were made from flanged tiles averaging 3.1 cm. in thickness; the mortar joints were about 1.7 cm.[36] There were ample windows in the outside walls especially those facing east and west. Four square rooms and one or two narrow corridors were cross-vaulted; but the rest of the chambers were covered with barrel vaults.

The second phase[37] consisted merely of the addition of a series of rooms to the row along the west side of the northeast peristyle. Possibly the austere western façade of the original building repelled a new owner; or more likely the small chambers seemed devoid of comfort to one inured to the greater luxury of the age. The ground had to be lowered, a sustaining wall built to hold back the earth, and a substructure erected to support the platform for the new apartments. Doors with lintel arches gave access to a service corridor lighted by splayed windows. Before the builders could proceed further, they had to close all apertures—except two saved for intercommuni-

[34] The same combination is found elsewhere (Bloch, *Bolli*, p. 267).

[35] Ashby, *op. cit.*, pp. 98–100; Lupu, *op. cit.*, pp. 136–145.

[36] These are Ashby's figures. Lugli's (*Tecnica*, p. 609) are 20–26 cm. × 3–3.5 cm. with mortar joints 1.5–1.8 cm. The bricks are described as generally red and compact with an occasional light-colored one among them; the mortar as gray, granular, and rather friable. Lugli publishes a photograph (*ibid.*, pl. 162, fig. 3) showing two different thicknesses of bricks irregularly shaped from *besales* and *sesquipedales* respectively in the same wall with traces of some flanged tiles.

[37] Ashby, *op. cit.*, pp. 101–102; Lupu, *op. cit.*, pp. 145–150.

cation—in the west wall of the original edifice and reface the outside with brick and reticulate. This second phase took place too soon after the first to show any marked change in building methods. The core of the walls contained a little dark limestone among the predominately peperino *caementa.* The bricks average 3.2 cm. in thickness and are somewhat less red in color. Brick and reticulate are more neatly interlocked in the facing. A few walls display brick alone. The most unusual feature was the large semicircular bay projecting westward with a large hall, probably divided into three parts with piers and quadripartite vaulting, facing it. A fountain niche in the center of the back wall was supplied with water from the cistern in the corner of the original building.[38] A large room with an alcove for a bed facing westward was also cross-vaulted. Barrel vaults probably covered the rest of the rooms. One room may have been heated. When the west façade was finished, it bore no resemblance to its predecessor. According to Lupu, an ambulatory probably followed the curve of the projection at the lower level. Traces of travertine corbels above the splayed windows of the substructure are an indication that a narrow decorative balcony ran along the whole face. Next to the semicircular projection a vestibule with one curved wall marked the transition to the straight part of the façade. The *cubiculum* with the cross vault had a high window; the room at the northwest corner had an enormous window in each outside wall, the one in the north opening onto an ambulatory. Travertine consoles supported a tile capping cornice.

The main block[39] stood at the northern end of a sunken garden of the kind to which the ancients applied the name "hippodrome," more than five meters below the level of the two earlier sections. The great substructure is of special interest for its vaulting, which shows a further development of the tendency discernible in the Villa Adriana to balance cross vaults against barrel vaults. The cryptoporticus which bounded the substructure on the south was covered with a long barrel vault reinforced at intervals by transverse arches of tile which were entirely concealed in the masonry except at the key. Buttresses on the outside helped to carry the weight of these arches, and between the arches there were windows. A similar corridor on the north, on the other hand, seems to have been covered by a series of cross vaults. It is terminated on the east in a commodious projection having three chambers— a large barrel-vaulted one flanked on the east by two smaller ones, of which one is barrel-vaulted, the other cross-vaulted—and on the west end with three barrel-vaulted chambers facing north. Windows between buttresses presumably lighted this corridor also. Between the cryptoportici the space was divided roughly into three parts. A large square room at the east end had four rows of cruciform piers, possibly planned for quadripartite vaulting alone, but actually displaying cross vaults only in the periphery. Three barrel vaults occupy the center. The next section, a group of rooms comprising about the same area, had barrel vaults over the narrower chambers and cross vaults over those which were approximately square. The largest one has quadripartite vaulting with definite structural ribs, 65 cm. wide. These are composed of double rows of *semilateres* bonded together by *bipedales*, 4 cm. thick, 40 cm. apart.[40] This is one of the earliest uses of laddered ribbing in cross vaulting. In the next space, two long narrow barrel-vaulted chambers

[38] Neuerburg, *Fontane,* pp. 47, 165–166.

[39] Ashby, *op. cit.,* pp. 104–105; Lupu, *op. cit.,* pp. 153–155.

[40] Lugli, *Tecnica,* pl. 205, fig. 4.

alternated with one covered by three cross vaults. The barrel vaults show ribbing like that in the cross vault mentioned above. The cross vaults were laid on a double layer of square tiles (20 cm. to 40 cm. per side) with an occasional tile at right angles for bonding. The walls at the east show a brick facing, those at the west a mixture of everything—reticulate, brick, block in various combinations. Traces of travertine corbels suggest that there was a balcony at the northwest corner. Above this substructure there was an elaborate Bath. Small service stairways, some perhaps in wood, furnished the only communication between the two floors.

The superstructure[41] was lofty enough to have two stories over some parts. A balustraded balcony supported on low arches resting on travertine corbels probably marked the transition from substructure to superstructure on the south side. Two pilasters perhaps carrying a pediment were apparently the focal point for a colonnade across the front at this height, but there is no trace of any such remains. The north façade was much more austere with merely a recession over the northern cryptoporticus. Lupu identifies the rooms beginning at the east as a *frigidarium* with pools at the east end where they would be slightly warmed by the morning sunlight and with a summer *triclinium*, *cubicula*, latrine, and stairs in the projection opening out of it; a *tepidarium* and *calidarium* equipped with the necessary hollow tiles[42] and having various supplementary rooms; an *occus* facing in both directions between two through passages; a large hall and a small apartment at the extreme west. Interest in the layout of the rooms must not, however, divert attention from our main preoccupation, which is, of course, the masonry. The core of the walls consisted of an aggregate of peperino and tufa with a slight admixture of terra cotta in a poor light gray mortar. The facing was regularly of eight to thirteen or more rows of blocks of peperino or tufa to five, six, or seven of brick (pl. 13, fig. 2).[43] The bricks, for the most part made from *besales ca.* 3.6 cm. thick[44] cut into rectangles, were red and compact. Some were from flanged tiles broken to roughly trapezoidal shape. The blocks of local materials—tufa, peperino, or selce in foundations—were 18–26 cm. × 6–7 cm.[45] The joints of a clear gray mortar with small dark grains were *ca.* 1.5 cm. wide. The north wall before its collapse showed the three great doorways of the *oecus* with lintel arches between travertine springers protected by relieving arches. Above these doorways were three large windows with slightly curved lintels having segmental relieving arches at an appreciable distance above them (pl. 12, fig. 3). All these arches were composed of yellow *sesquipedales ca.* 4 cm. thick. A somewhat lower and wider doorway on each side was given the same treatment as the other doorways except that the relieving arches were segmental. The marks by which a marble revetment was fastened to the inside up to the very top are clearly visible in the photographs. The rooms devoted to the Bath, the *frigidarium* excluded, show traces of cross vaults over square spaces. In one room two barrel vaults at right angles to each other supplemented two cross vaults. Once the centering was in place, one form was as easy to lay as another; and the monolithic quality of the concrete defied collapse. The rest of the ceilings were probably wooden.

The "hippodrome"[46] belongs to the same period as the main block, which

[41] Ashby, *op. cit.*, pp. 102–106; Lupu, *op. cit.*, pp. 151–165.

[42] Lugli (*Tecnica*, p. 581) calls attention to some *tegulae mammatae* of the form used at Sette Bassi, for which the protuberances were part of a flange made by striking out the part between them. I do not know whether this ingenious device was employed in this villa.

[43] This is what Lugli calls *opus vittatum*. See *Tecnica*, pp. 633–655.

[44] Lugli's figures (*Tecnica*, p. 645) are 24.5–27.5 cm. × 3.4–3.8 cm.

[45] *Ibid.*

[46] Lupu, *op. cit.*, pp. 165–173.

[47] Sloping buttresses along the south face were a later reinforcement. The buttresses along the pavilions are claimed by Rivoira-Rushforth (p. 147) as the earliest to be found on an apse. The use of buttresses made possible a less massive wall.

[48] These walls had to be strongly buttressed to counteract a steep slope at this point.

[49] Reproduced by Lupu, *op. cit.*, p. 123, fig. 5. Lugli (*Tecnica*, p. 578) assumes that it was an entrance from the Via Latina.

[50] Ashby, *op. cit.*, p. 107; Lupu, *op. cit.*, pp. 179–183.

[51] Lugli, *Tecnica*, pl. 62, fig. 3. On p. 609, he gives 3.6 cm. as the thickness.

[52] Bloch, *Bolli*, pp. 261–262, 266, 274, 282, where he shows that the stamps (1019a, b) considered by Ashby to be a product of A.D. 120 are found in three or four Antonine periods.

[53] Ashby, *op. cit.*, pp. 108–109; Lupu, *op. cit.*, pp. 173–176.

[54] Bloch, *op. cit.*, p. 262.

stands at its head, though local conditions have given it a slightly different orientation. On the east, it is bounded by a simple retaining wall with buttresses on the inside; on the south and west, by a cryptoporticus with a rounded pavilion at each extremity. Both presented a plain well-buttressed[47] wall to the outside except perhaps for an occasional window. There is a slight indication that a summer triclinium facing the garden jutted outwards beyond the center of the west wall and that a series of small rooms opened off from it toward the north end.[48] The inner wall on the west may have been diversified by niches alternating with windows in the spaces between the decorative pilasters; in the inner wall on the south, high arched windows brought light and air to the cryptoporticus. The lower part of the walls was faced with brick and reticulate, the upper part in the combination of bricks and blocks characteristic of the third phase of the villa complex. The southern cryptoporticus was barrel-vaulted, whereas a wooden roof covered with tiles was considered sufficient for the western branch. No paving has ever come to light. Piranesi[49] (pl. 13, fig. 1) shows an elaborate pedimented doorway of fine brickwork which probably graced a state entrance at the southeast corner.

Isolated structures to the northeast need not concern us long. Most of them from their construction would seem to belong to the third building period, or a little later. One, a temple-like structure[50] with a porch in front and a barrel-vaulted niche for the presiding deity at the back, is unusual only for the five slit windows in each side wall in the lower register and the three over the center ones above, which penetrated into the mass of the barrel vault of the hall itself. In accordance with the general practice observed in the villa proper, the porch was covered with a series of three cross vaults, of which the merest trace remains. The walls were faced with bricks made from broken tiles, some of them flanged,[51] which are slightly wider (4.1 cm.) than the norm for the villa. The mortar was earthy but compact. The brickwork was concealed on the inside by a marble revetment up to the springing of the vault. The *bipedales* at the top and bottom of the windows yielded Antonine stamps.[52] It can be dated between A.D. 150 and 160.

Far to the south on the Via Latina, an isolated *villino*[53] probably belonged to the same estate. Its walls were faced almost entirely with brickwork. Brick stamps[54] indicate that it was built somewhat later than the third phase of the main villa, but before all the bricks from the deposit had been used up, though apparently no flanged tiles remained to be broken into bricks. In spite of its ruinous condition, a fairly complete ground plan has been worked out. The most unusual feature was a great hall shaped like a Greek cross, one of the arms of which ended in a semicircular wall. Barrel vaults covered the arms and probably a cross vault the center. In general, cross vaults were preferred to barrel vaults in this villino. Windows over doorways augmented the lighting of some of the inner rooms; splayed windows appear in one room on the east side toward a secondary street.

Sette Bassi seems to have been less lavishly supplied with cisterns than most of the great Roman villas. Possibly the reason is to be found in the proximity of the aqueducts, which assured a constant supply of water. On the highest ground to the east, traces of one cistern[55] remain more or less imbedded in a modern farm house. It displays masonry identical with that in the third phase of the villa. The walls were reinforced by buttressing spurs. Later, perhaps toward the end of the century, a second cistern[56] was constructed near the first. Semicircular niches—eight in the long sides and two in the ends—were hollowed out of the upper part of unusually thick walls. This arrangement was substituted for the more common buttressing found in the first cistern. A cross wall divided the reservoir in two parts with a flight of stairs built against it to facilitate cleaning. The walls were all faced with good brickwork, and the cistern was covered with a barrel vault. Later still, according to Lanciani,[57] a branch aqueduct brought water from the Anio Novus, not the Claudia as he believed, to the second cistern. It had a miscellaneous facing of blocks separated by bands of block-and-brick.

Velitrae (San Cesareo)

The site of the modest villa near Velitrae where Augustus probably spent much of his childhood[58] had passed out of the hands of the imperial family before Suetonius published his "Lives" (ca. 120). The new owner had a sumptuous country villa[59] built where the great cistern of the earlier villa had stood. The ground plan is not entirely clear, but at least, in the bewildering number of courts and chambers, there was not so much as a single apse to break the austerity of the straight lines. It is refreshing to find an individual who did not share Hadrian's penchant for curved lines. Foundation walls everywhere showed irregular but flat pieces of selce[60] laid in relatively regular rows with a minimum amount of mortar. The core of the walls was apparently the same; the facing was an irregular reticulate of selce reinforced by selce quoins and bonding courses of brick. The tesserae were roughly 9 cm. per side; the bricks, broken to roughly trapezoidal shape from dark yellow tiles about 3.5 cm. thick, laid in a mortar about 1.5 cm. wide. The bricks have yielded a number of stamps of A.D. 123. Several walls wider than the rest, especially in the western half, were probably designed to support upper floors.

At a somewhat later date, perhaps in the reign of Antoninus Pius, although the living quarters were kept as they were, the lower level was brought more into conformity with the prevailing mode. A small semicircular niche for a fountain was placed at the foot of the stairs; another larger one with a fine black-and-white mosaic pavement was inserted at about the middle of the south retaining wall of the upper terrace; and a rectangular room was hollowed out toward the east end of the same wall. A small apse[61] formed the transition to the straight west wall, which was also broken somewhat north of the center by a semicircular nymphaeum lined with small niches and reinforced with disproportionately heavy buttresses. An addition to some earlier rooms at the southeast provided space for the octagonal pool of what was doubtless a private Bath.[62] Traces of the piers of a colonnade came to light along the north side of the area, but not enough of them to show how much territory was enclosed in this way. Lugli believes that a cryptoporticus stood behind the south retaining wall of this terrace. Scattered remains may indicate that there was yet a lower terrace. Although the same

[55] Lupu, op. cit., p. 177.

[56] Ibid., pp. 178–179.

[57] Lanciani, Mél., vol. 11, 1891, pp. 172–173; Ashby, op. cit., pp. 109–110; idem, Aqueducts, p. 228; Van Deman, Aqueducts, p. 322; Lupu, op. cit., p. 179 n. 1. The date is far from sure.

[58] Suetonius, Augustus, 6.

[59] A. Pelzer Wagener, AJA, vol. 17, 1913, pp. 413–418; Lugli, Bull. Com., vol. 58, 1930, pp. 5–28 (republished with slight changes by O. Nardini in Boll. dell' Asso. Vel. di Archeol., St., ed Arte, vol. 9, 1934, pp. 7–17); R. Vighi, BMIR, vol. 12, 1941, pp. 17–33; Cressedi, Velitrae, pp. 81–84.

[60] The irregularity is due in part to the intractability of the stone.

[61] Apses in this position occur at Sette Bassi and in the Villa of the Quintilii on the Via Appia. For the nymphaea, see Neuerburg, Fontane, pp. 152–153, fig. 69.

[62] The bricks used in the Bath were red and thicker (3.8 cm.).

63 Passing mention may be made of a villa near the railroad station for its irregular use of reticulate work, blocks, and brickwork. There is no way of ascribing a definite date to it. See Wagener, *op. cit.*, pp. 406–412.

64 Ashby, *PBSR*, vol. 1, 1902, p. 156.

65 *Ibid.*, p. 170.

66 *Ibid.*, p. 210. See also *Not. sc.*, 1887, p. 121. The stamps are *CIL*, vol. 15 (1), nos. 366, 367, 370.

67 Lugli, *Bull. Com.*, vol. 43, 1915, pp. 139–141, 150–154, 158–160; *idem, Tecnica*, pp. 440, 523.

68 Lanciani, *Mon. ant.*, vol. 16, 1906, cols. 241–268; *idem, Wanderings*, pp. 316–324, plus hasty observations from a brief visit in September, 1952 (Miss Blake), and again in early summer of 1964 (Mrs. Bishop).

general type of construction was used for this transformation as in the earlier phase, the reticulate tesserae were smaller (ca. 7 cm. per side); and bricks were used along with the blocks in the quoining. Similar bands of brick were used in both. The one cross vault for which there is evidence belongs to this phase.[63]

Via Praenestina—Villas

Isolated villas along the Via Praenestina reveal an experimentation with the uses of tufa blocks in various combinations. A villa wall[64] on the south side of the road about 3 km. from Rome exhibits a facing of blocks with quoins of block and brick in alternation. Such quoining has no structural meaning. If this masonry is a reflection of "opus mixtum," that is, reticulate units in a brick frame, it probably was not employed too long after "opus mixtum" went out of style, say toward the end of the second century. At about the 11th km. on the north side, a reservoir[65] was contained within walls faced on the outside with tufa blocks between bands of five bricks 1.3 m. apart which ran straight through the concrete. This is also an imitation of brick technique. It was reinforced by buttresses at the corners and at the center of each wall. It undoubtedly served some villa. At Le Colonnelle some eight kilometers farther on, walls of several periods were found.[66] One showed bonding courses of tile in brickwork. Brick stamps belonging to the period of Commodus were found loose.

Via Praenestina—Cisterns

Two remarkable cisterns of an earlier period[67] apparently still served the Villa dei Gordiani on the Via Praenestina. The one on the right hand side of the road replaced a yet earlier one in reticulate work with tufa quoins and bricks; this later one shows tufa quoins for a construction primarily of reticulate work with brick bands. A characteristic feature of this and a reservoir on the opposite side of the street was the use of a curved wall converting the space between the great buttresses into apsed niches. The second cistern had two stories of which only the upper one was lined with *opus signinum* to make it impermeable. The lower story was divided into two parts with two arched openings in the partition wall. Splayed windows, three on each side and one at each end, lighted the two chambers. The masonry with insets of reticulate extended even to the buttresses. It is impossible to date such construction exactly, but it certainly belongs to the first half of the second century and probably to the earlier part of it.

Of the same type of masonry and probably contemporaneous was a room apparently of the Bath which they supplied with water, of which only the apsed end is preserved. The apse was fitted into a rectangular chamber in such a way that curved niches filled the angles and a shallow rectangular niche stood between them.

Via Severiana

Below *Tor Paterno* on the left-hand side of the modern Via Severiana enough survives of a charming seaside villa of the early Antonine period for a practically complete restoration.[68] It presented to the ancient street a porticus *in antis* of eight columns.[69] Toward the garden facing the sea six spur walls, ending in pedestals for statues or urns, flanked three stairways leading up respectively to a bedchamber with a dressing room beyond, to a sitting room with a detached curved wall, and to a second bedchamber and dressing room. Remains of hollow tiles in the walls prove that at least one room was heated.[70] Since there is no sign of any kitchen or servants' quarters, there must have been a service unit nearby. There was no stairway to an upper story. Brick stamps[71] from kilns apparently situated near the mouth of the Tiber prove that the villa was constructed soon after A.D. 142, partially on the site of an earlier one of which there are considerable remains in reticulate with tufa quoins. The brickwork of the villa follows the norm established in the Hadrianic period. The bricks are for the most part yellowish in color and about 3.5 cm. thick. The mortar joints are narrow. The majority of the bricks are, however, triangles. Slight Severan alterations in narrow red bricks are discernible. The mosaic pavements in simple geometric designs in black and white are also Hadrianic in spirit. It was here that the Discobulus, now in the National Museum at Rome, came to light.

Via Appia

The church of San Cesareo on the Via Appia[72] has preserved two rooms of a sumptuous private edifice, perhaps part of the Baths of a villa. The walls were faced with bricks, 3 cm. thick, accurately laid with joints 1.8 cm. wide. A bit of vaulting adhering to a brick cornice proves that one room was covered; the other may have been open to the sky. Both rooms had black-and-white mosaics depicting lively scenes in a fantastic sea full of imaginary sea creatures. The tesserae in the original parts were small (0.7–0.8 cm.) for this type of mosaic.[73] The mosaics would seem to belong to about the same period as in the nearby house under the Baths of Caracalla,[74] that is to say late Hadrianic or early Antonine. There are traces of a cippolino revetment in one of the rooms and of doors to other rooms no longer extant.

A curious heated room, probably not part of a Bath but certainly belonging to a villa, once faced the Via Appia near Le Frattocchie. It had already suffered severely between its discovery in 1931 and its publication in 1934.[75] The entrance led to a chamber of mixtilinear form with a marble pavement of oblongs of bigio separated by guidelines of rosso antico. Four brick-faced columns, one-quarter buried in the concrete of the walls, supported cross vaulting on a square plan. The elongation opposite the entrance ended in a semicircular niche and had a rectangular niche on each side. At the sides, three steps of upright tiles led to a rectangular niche with a lintel arch of upright tiles, which in its turn was framed in pilasters probably upholding a pediment or lunette. Voussoir arches of *bipedales* appear elsewhere. The concrete core of the walls[76] was faced with brickwork of clear red or yellow bricks, often triangles (3.5–4 cm. × 21–30 cm.), held together by joints 1.5–2 cm. wide. The walls had a socle of Luna marble nearly a meter and a half high fastened on with bronze clamps. Above the socle there was stucco work in an architectural design. The columns were also stuccoed. The vaults were adorned with glass mosaic.[77] Under the floor, piers of *besales*, 50 cm. high, made the necessary space for the circulation of hot air, which

[69] In ancient times the street passed on the other side of the villa.

[70] Lanciani states that all the floors were suspended and that there was an unusually wide layer of concrete (50 cm.) as substructure to the floor of the porch. These would be precautions against dampness.

[71] *CIL*, vol. 15 (1), nos. 716, 1065. The one Hadrianic stamp (no. 377a) is the same as that reported in Antonine work at Sette Bassi.

[72] G. Matthiae, *S. Cesareo "de Appia,"* Rome 1955, pp. 14–18.

[73] There was a considerable amount of ancient patching.

[74] See above, p. 78.

[75] A. L. Pietrogrande, *Not. sc.,* 1934, pp. 221–228.

[76] These had a rather coarse aggregate of peperino.

[77] None of the vaulting was preserved.

ascended through the flues made of a double row of roof tiles with flanges turned in so that each tile made two flues. Two Trajanic stamps[78] found in the debris serve to confirm the date suggested by the type of brickwork. The rectangular niches approached by steps would have furnished a suitable place for bookcases. Possibly we have here the heated library of some bibliophile of the early years of the second century. The room was inserted in a circle. It was later used as a tomb.

Via Nomentana

Along the Via Nomentana to the northwest of Torre Mancini about 16 kilometers from there is a second-century villa; only a small but elegant bath was excavated, and that many years ago.[79] The part excavated showed a large room with a small semicircular pool opening out of a large hall having a stepped pool at the end and a small exedra at the side. A tank lined with *opus signinum* at the corner supplied both pools with water. A large hall on the opposite side of the hall from the semicircular pool was equipped with a hypocaust supported by rectangular piers. There is no indication how the draft necessary for the circulation of the warm air was managed. Between the furnace room at the corner and the large apsed room there was an irregular dressing room furnished with benches. Except for one wall of reticulate work, the walls were faced with brick. Brick stamps (only three, to be sure), ranging in date from Trajan (?)[80] to Marcus Aurelius suggest a date in the second half of the second century for the Bath at any rate. It was lavishly decorated with marble, some of which belonged to fourth-century renovation. A reservoir on the hill probably supplied the water for its functioning.

Not all heated rooms belonged to Baths. Nine rooms of a vast edifice were uncovered many years ago at Roma Vecchia.[81] One large hall was heated, but the part excavated does not suggest a Bath.[82] The suspended floor was supported on hollow cylinders of terra cotta with holes in the sides to allow a freer circulation of air.[83] The walls were faced with a combination of reticulate insets in brick frames which was adjudged Hadrianic. The rooms were beautifully adorned with pavements of polychrome marble and mosaic, columns of bigio and breccia corallina, and fine wall paintings. Nothing remains of that elegance today.

Faccenna[84] has given a detailed description of a part of a Bath belonging to a villa probably of the Antonine period built on a series of terraces, partly artificial, along the slope of the mountain at Ciciliana near Tivoli. The wall construction showed the same use of reticulate and brick, of brick alone, and even of brick with rough blocks of stone as is often found in the villas of the period. The reticulate tesserae (7 cm. × 7 cm. in the surface dimensions) were of local limestone; the bricks, triangles of clear yellow or pale rose (3.5–4.5 cm. × 23–25 cm.), were probably of local manufacture. At any rate there were no Roman stamps to attest a Roman provenience. Two rooms were paved with black-and-white silhouette mosaics depicting sea creatures and athletes respectively. These were taken up and deposited in the Villa d'Este at Tivoli. A piece of concrete from a cross vault was found; and there were traces of stucco work which resembled that of the Tomb of

[78] *CIL*, vol. 15 (1), no. 440 (A.D. 103–117); Bloch, *Suppl.*, no. 125 (Cornelius Severus was suffect consul A.D. 112).

[79] Lanciani, *Not. sc.*, 1888, pp. 285-288; Ashby, *PBSR*, vol. 3, 1906, pp. 66–67.

[80] *CIL*, vol. 15 (1), no. 710 is or may be Trajanic. See Bloch, *Bolli*, p. 38.

[81] Lanciani, *Not. sc.*, 1883, pp. 210–212; Ashby, *PBSR*, vol. 4, 1907, pp. 89–90.

[82] Two halls terminated in apses back to back as in the Temple of Venus and Rome.

[83] Similar cylinders were used in Baths added to the Villa of Voconius Pollio (Lanciani, *Bull. Com.*, vol. 12, 1884, p. 161). This villa, on the road to Marino at Il Sassone, was built or purchased by a member of the Voconian family in the Augustan Age and rebuilt and doubled in extent in the time of Hadrian by Q. Voconius Pollio (Lanciani, *Wanderings*, p. 55).

[84] D. Faccenna, *Not. sc.*, 1948 (pub. 1950), pp. 294–307. The remains are in the vicinity of the Ospedale di S. Giovanni.

the Valerii on the Via Latina, and also traces of marble wall revetments. No heated rooms were uncovered.

With the increase in luxurious living in the second century, private Baths were considered essential in country estates. The ones described above are typical of those within easy access to Rome. No useful purpose can be served by merely listing insignificant remains which may or may not belong to the period. A few oddities prove that builders were still experimenting. Not enough attention has been paid to the heating arrangements, and the position of the furnace or furnaces has seldom been noted in the reports. Probably in private as in public Baths, as many furnaces as were required were placed at strategic points on the outside. Ashby describes a furnace which was apparently situated in the center of the Bath belonging to an extensive Hadrianic villa beyond the Osteria delle Colonne on the Via Labicana.[85] It was round and released heat through four apertures into a square room, whence it was distributed through two pipes in each corner to various parts of the Bath. He does not tell how the furnace was serviced. A semicircular pool belonging perhaps to the Bath of a second-century villa situated along the Via Latina northwest of Casale Ciampino[86] was also heated by a furnace directly under the pavement. Hypocausts are usually reported. The piers upholding the pavement, here as elsewhere, were normally composed of *besales* set two Roman feet apart from center to center to support the *bipedales* of the upper pavement. Occasionally they were round to allow a freer circulation of air. Terra-cotta cylinders were alternated with the usual tile piers in a villa uncovered many years ago about eight miles from Rome on the Via Nomentana.[87] We have already mentioned the use of hollow cylinders found under a suspended floor at Roma Vecchia and in the Baths added to the Villa of Voconius Pollio in the time of Hadrian.[88] Socket-pipes instead of plain cylinders were employed for the purpose in a villa of the second half of the second century brought to light just beyond the eighth milestone of the Via Praenestina, known as Muraccio dell'Vomo.[89] Two marble-lined pools equipped with suspended floors and wall tubes were discovered on the south slope of Monte Cavo a number of years ago.[90] Brick stamps indicate that they were built in the early years of the reign of Antoninus Pius as an adjunct to a suburban villa. Hadrian's Villa near Tivoli shows that sometimes there are no remains where wall tubes or some other type of vent must have existed to insure the proper functioning of the hypocausts.

Roman ingenuity discovered a novel way of insulating a floor in an edifice of uncertain purpose which could not have been a Bath. It was uncovered just outside the Aurelianic Wall between Via Appia Nuova and Via Latina.[91] The upper pavement rested on the apexes of triangles made of *bipedales* set *a cappuccio* and filled with mortar. The empty triangles between them formed a succession of air spaces under the floor. Small concrete walls between the first and second and the second and third gave additional support.[92] A brick stamp from the kilns of Faustina Minor, found both in this hollow floor arrangement and in the beginning of the walls, dates this experiment in the middle years of the second century. The walls resting on a course of *bipedales* were faced with bricks 3 cm. thick.

The countryside about Rome is dotted with reservoirs used to store water

[85] Ashby, *PBSR*, vol. 1, 1902, p. 236. The date is indicated by the stamps.

[86] *Idem, PBSR*, vol. 4, 1907, p. 129.

[87] Ashby, *PBSR*, vol. 3, 1906, p. 64. The villa has not been dated.

[88] See above, p. 114 and n. 83.

[89] Ashby, *PBSR*, vol. 1, 1902, pp. 164–165. The villa is dated by a stamp found under the floor of the hypocaust.

[90] M. Salustri, *Not. sc.*, 1894, p. 405.

[91] A. L. Pietrogrande, *Not. sc.*, 1937, pp. 45–48.

[92] There was no provision for the circulation of hot air.

not only for Baths but also for the numerous fountains and nymphaea which embellished the country estates. Some were supplied by the great aqueducts bringing water to Rome. Hydraulic arrangements were as important as heating arrangements. An understanding of the water facilities is necessary for a complete understanding of the functioning of Roman Baths of all kinds. I commend the subject to some enterprising young archaeologist. Only a small number of these reservoirs, however, have anything to contribute to a chronological study of construction.

A square structure connected with a villa in the territory of Marino[93] was included in such thick walls that it must have supported a cistern. The walls were faced with reticulate reinforced by brick quoins. The vaulting consisted of two barrel vaults terminating in a transverse barrel vault. Some of the *besales*, used to cover the meeting point of four *bipedales* placed directly on the wooden centering, still adhere to the soffit of the vault. In the villa walls the concrete is strengthened with quoins of peperino and bands of brick. Two rooms show cross vaulting resting on angle piers. The one brick stamp found was Antonine.[94]

One two-story cistern in the area of Marino,[95] doubtless supplying a nearby villa, merits more than a passing mention. The lower chamber, obviously not intended for water, had three openings in the north wall and one in each end covered with lintel arches of *bipedales* and *besales* in walls of brick-faced concrete. The south wall was faced with reticulate (tesserae 8 cm. × 8 cm.). Three cross vaults supported the upper chamber which was entirely of brickwork. It was lined with *opus signinum* as befits a cistern. None of its vaulting was preserved. The concrete showed an aggregate of peperino, larger pieces being used in the vaulting than in the core of the walls. The bricks were red and yellow triangles (3.5–3.8 cm. thick) joined by mortar 2 cm. wide. Brick stamps of A.D. 123 give the date.

Peperino blocks (7.8 cm. × 15.25 cm.) face the exterior of a hexagonal structure near Marino,[96] which must have been a reservoir, to judge from its thick walls (1.2 m.) and heavy buttresses at the corners and the center of each side wall, not to mention its being of *opus signinum*. Blocks of peperino were in use throughout the second century in this territory, so that it is quite possible that this cistern was constructed within this period.

Important as these examples of villas are to a knowledge of methods of building in the second century, they do not give the whole picture. Unfortunately, for a facile tabulation, the various types of masonry cannot be confined within narrow chronological limits, especially in the country. Reticulate work with or without block quoins predominates. Although most specimens belong to the Republic or early Empire, it would be unreasonable to maintain that none belonged to a later date, since some reticulate work with stone quoins and brick bands can be ascribed with confidence to the second century. The Villa of Matidia in Tusculum, identified by inscribed water pipes, shows a selce reticulate with selce quoins and brick bands.[97] Traces of a house in Tivoli on Via del Collegio, adjudged Hadrianic, exhibited tufa quoins with reticulate (tesserae 7–7.5 cm. per side) and brick bands (bricks 3–3.5 cm. thick).[98] Although the villa on the Via Ferentina about 4 km. from Marino[99] having this same combination cannot be dated cate-

[93] C. Daicovici, *Eph. daco.*, vol. 4, 1930, pp. 56–59.

[94] *CIL*, vol. 15 (1), no. 754b.

[95] Daicovici, *op. cit.*, vol. 4, 1930, no. 6, pp. 48–50.

[96] Daicovici, *op. cit.*, vol. 4, 1930, pp. 51–52.

[97] Ashby, *PBSR*, vol. 5, 1910, p. 375.

[98] D. Faccenna, *Not. sc.*, 1948, pp. 283–284.

[99] Daicovici, *Eph. daco.*, vol. 4, 1930, pp. 51–52.

gorically, the triangular bricks 4 cm. thick suggest a date fairly early in the second century. Triangular bricks (3.5–4 cm. thick) were also found in another villa in the same general region[100] in which a niched wall showed a favoring of reticulate, blocks, and bricks combined. "Le Vignacce" proves that tufa blocks were already occasionally employed with bricks as quoins as early as the time of Hadrian and warns against too facile an ascription to a much later date of the walls in which the combination is found. It is quite possible for example that the villa east of Villa Bernabei in the Marino region,[101] where they are found used in this way, was built in the second century. In a villa between Monte Porzio and Rocca Priora,[102] a mason departed from the norm to lay some of the reticulate tesserae in horizontal rows. Whereas it is possible that this wall in which this anomaly was found was later, the villa at any rate is proved by brick stamps to be Hadrianic. The three Hadrianic villas described above were faced with a combination of brick and reticulate ("opus mixtum"), which is a common type of masonry but can seldom be dated exactly. Brick stamps prove that a villa near Colle Santo Stefano was Hadrianic. It has sometimes been regarded as a part of Villa Adriana, but it probably belonged to the Vibii Vari. The construction was largely of reticulate with bands of brick. A villa near San Marino,[103] possibly to be dated by a fragmentary stamp in the Hadrianic period, had walls faced with reticulate and brick. The bricks were 4 cm. thick.

TOMBS NEAR ROME

No other type of monument brings us so close to the hearts of the men of old as the tombs which they provided as the final resting places for their dead. One is tempted to linger over the pathetic inscriptions in which not only the years, months, and days but sometimes even the hours of life of the loved one were considered worthy of mention. With the passing of the great columbaria of the burial guilds, the record becomes more personal until we seem to be dealing with the living persons of long ago and sharing the poignancy of their grief. Our concern, however, is with the construction of these tombs. Since we are dealing with men and women instead of categories, we must expect to find every type of masonry known to the ancient Romans.

Sepulcreta

Tombs continued to be built along the great arterial highways as long as the Roman Empire remained strong enough to protect them; but not everyone could aspire to so exalted a final resting place. Until cremation gave way to inhumation, there was little incentive for using the soft rock surrounding the city for rock-cut burial places. In any case, the miles and miles of catacombs dug out by the early Christians and Jews for the disposal of their dead have only a rare contribution to make to a study of construction. Few great columbaria were built by burial guilds in the second century; but to the sepulcreta engirdling the city were added smaller family tombs. In the early years of the century, these were built to accommodate burial urns for ashes. Gradually they come to reflect the transition from cremation to

[100] Ibid., pp. 56–59.

[101] Ashby, op. cit., p. 261.

[102] Ibid., p. 406.

[103] Daicovici, Eph. daco., vol. 4, 1930, no. 5, pp. 47–48.

inhumation. The *sepulcreta* are invaluable for giving an epitome of methods of building where definite limits have been imposed by raises in level of the whole area. Within these limits a relative chronology can often be established by the relation of one tomb to another. Stucco work, frescoes, and mosaics, besides revealing the loving care expended on relatively simple tombs, sometimes help to date the individual burial chamber. Inscriptions almost never give a name known from other sources. In general, *sepulcreta* have a greater value for chronology, whereas separate tombs are of more interest for architectural details. Theoretically, one should start with the *sepulcreta* encircling Rome, but actually one is too dependent on isolated finds to recreate a unified picture. Isola Sacra, the necropolis for Porto, may not give a quite accurate impression of the cemeteries of Rome but it is an entity within definite chronological limits near enough to Rome to reflect definite tendencies and to be of inestimable value in presenting the individual tombs of middle-class people.

Isola Sacra

Isola Sacra, the necropolis for the ancient port of Rome, will always appeal to the imagination for the insight that it brings into the life of the ordinary men and women of old. But over and above the sentimental value, it has more or less crystallized the vague chronology developed from the parts of the vast *sepulcreta* unearthed in the immediate vicinity of Rome. Only the accumulation of sand augmented by the usual debris of a neglected site had to be removed to reveal a hundred and fifty tombs of a cemetery laid out along the road which preceded the Via Severiana in facilitating communication between Porto and Ostia. About a hundred have been left exposed in a sort of park, and the region has been carefully drained for their protection. These tombs have been reduced to an exact chronology by the excavator, Guido Calza.[1] No tomb in the excavated part is earlier than the establishment of the Trajanic port,[2] and although old tombs continued to be adapted to new burials, no new tomb was apparently built after A.D. 250. The raising of the level for the Via Severiana furnished the *ante quem* for the tombs of the second century. Although few brick stamps have come to light,[3] the chronology was worked out from the structural environment of each tomb, and this shows a steady development in tomb architecture and decoration. Methods of construction follow the same trends as can be observed in other types of building. The tombs were practically all erected for what we should call the lower middle class; but in the sand among them were buried jars containing the ashes of the poor who clung to cremation, and on the sand were reverently laid and covered with tile and masonry the bodies of those who preferred inhumation. These humble graves have nothing to contribute to a study of construction.

Apparently the type of sepulchre that has come to be associated with Isola Sacra did not really begin to emerge until late in the Trajanic epoch. Only one tomb of any pretention (No. 46) can be ascribed to a date earlier in his reign. It has the usual type of travertine doorframe, but all four sides are faced with a tufa reticulate neatly interlocked at the corners with brick from magenta tiles. The inside is lined with an inferior reticulate. The

[1] Calza, *Necropoli* (reviewed by G. Becatti, in *Riv. fil. cl.*, 1941, pp. 70–75; by H. Bloch, *AJA*, vol. 48, 1944, pp. 213–218). See also Meiggs, *Ostia*, pp. 455–470; Crema, pp. 486, 491–493, figs. 628–629, 631–635; Frova, pp. 94, 411–412.

[2] For the Port, see below, pp. 286–290. Of the bricks found not *in situ* in 1930 and listed by Thylander (*Ins. du Port d'Ostie*), only one (*CIL*, vol. 15 (1), no. 1094; Bloch, *Suppl.*, no. 285; *Bolli*, p. 225) is definitely earlier than Trajan; of the bricks found in 1911, none need be earlier than Trajan.

[3] Trajanic stamps were found in nos. 64 and 78; Hadrianic, in Nos. 56, 75, 77, 79, 81, 83. See Calza, *Necropoli*, pp. 278–279.

chamber was barrel-vaulted, and a lunetted pediment indicates a curved extrados. The other three early examples (Nos. 49, 63, 64) are small and low. Tomb No. 64 yielded three stamps which are Trajanic.

Throughout the second century, the majority of tombs here were single chambers, isolated or erected in groups. Only a few consisted of a precinct and chamber of the same building period, and all of these belong in the Hadrianic period. Tomb No. 97 (pl. 14, fig. 1) was all precinct for a funeral altar on a high pedestal. The altar, according to Calza, was Trajanic. Tomb No. 75 in its original form was unique in having its burial chamber flanked on each side by a barrel-vaulted hall within a huge precinct later subdivided. Of the twin tombs Nos. 88 and 90 facing west, each had its own precinct, as did Tomb No. 87 crowded in between Nos. 88 and 86. Though scarcely larger than a single chamber, No. 92 consisted of two parts, one of which was open to the sky. In general, precincts were added in front when the need for more burial space became acute. Where there was no precinct (pl. 15, fig. 1: Tomb 15) and in one case where there was (No. 89), inclined couches (*biclinia*) for funeral feasts occasionally flanked the entrance. Examples are about equally divided between the Hadrianic and Antonine periods.[4]

Few tombs reveal remains of a second story. Only one (No. 86), consisting of a hypogeum under an upper chamber, belongs to the Trajan-Hadrian group;[5] two others (Nos. 42 and 29) are Antonine[6] (pl. 15, fig. 2: Tombs 41 and 42); a third of indeterminate date was excavated near Sant'Hippolyte (O).[7] Here the upper floor was supported by a cross vault. No. 42 shows one chamber superimposed upon another. The upper one has the more elaborate façade with the travertine doorframe flanked by brick columns on marble bases, whereas the lower one has merely the travertine frame surmounted by the inscription. A cross vault covered the lower chamber; the ceiling of the upper one is not preserved. The fact that the tomb was given over almost entirely to inhumation burials, coupled with the quality of the mosaic floor, suggests an Antonine date. A precinct with a separate tomb at the second story level was added to a conventional square tomb (No. 29) giving it a new façade toward the street and a vestibule paved with mosaic. The lower floor of the precinct was divided into two rooms for inhumation burials and vaulted over. Four splayed windows furnished light and air. Steps led from the vestibule to an upper terrace (*solarium*) and the upper burial chamber, of which mere traces remain. Where every trace of vaulting is lacking, Calza suggests the possibility of a terrace instead of a gable roof. He ascribes one to No. 19 even though no stairs are preserved. The fact remains that only No. 29 furnishes a sure example within the period.

The use of reticulate in façades was not entirely abandoned in the Hadrianic era. Although the precinct of Tomb No. 87 presented a façade of fine brickwork to the street, the tomb itself was faced with reticulate like that in the rear, and like it was originally stuccoed over. Thylander considers the practically identical inscriptions on precinct and tomb to be Hadrianic.[8] In the Hadrianic Tomb No. 56, the façade of reticulate work was topped with a brick entablature; and in one of the tombs (*I*) near Sant'Hippolyte,[9] reticulate insets appear in rather poor brickwork. An inscription proves that this

[4] Hadrian: Nos. 15, 79, 81, 87; Antonine: Nos. 13, 14, 30, 80.

[5] Calza, *op. cit.*, p. 343, assigns this tomb to the period of Trajan.

[6] Calza, *op. cit.*, p. 75, assigns No. 42 to the period of Hadrian.

[7] G. Calza, *Not. sc.*, 1928, p. 149.

[8] Thylander, *op. cit.*, nos. A 268, 269.

[9] G. Calza, *Not. sc.*, 1928, p. 147.

[10] Thylander, *op. cit.*, no. A 5.

[11] In one tomb (No. 85) the "I" was built up in masonry.

[12] Calza, *Necropoli*, pp. 88–89.

[13] Calza, *op. cit.*, pp. 85–87.

[14] Tomb No. 80 (Calza, *op. cit.*, fig. 16) is a case in point. A Ligorio drawing shows a rounded tympanum from Via Latina. See Ashby, *PBSR*, vol. 4, 1907, p. 58.

[15] Calza, *op. cit.*, p. 66.

tomb is Hadrianic.[10] No specimen is preserved of any reticulate in Antonine façades.

Throughout the second century, façades were usually faced with special fine-grained red bricks. Those in Trajanic tombs are slightly thicker as a rule (3–3.5 cm.) than those in the Hadrianic tombs (3 cm.).Whereas bricks as thin as 2.5 cm. are included with wider ones in some earlier masonry, the era of thin bricks (2.2–2.5 cm.) was initiated in the Antonine period. Occasionally a tomb was faced entirely with ordinary bricks as in Tomb No. 57. All these façades will be treated in more detail below.

Normally the façade was pierced by a doorway. These show little variation throughout the second century (pl. 15, fig. 4: Tomb 16). Unadorned travertine jambs were firmly set on travertine sills, and the architrave, also of travertine, was usually carved into a molding with an overhang to protect the entrance. Sometimes the architrave was covered with a terra-cotta molding or with *opus signinum* for added protection; and sometimes it extended beyond the jambs. In either case, architrave and jambs were practically always outlined in a single row of red tile. Traces of one door (Tomb No. 87) came to light to show what all were like, in all probability. It consisted of two parts swinging on pivots and fastened in the center with iron hasps. The wood of the blades was covered with lead held in place with iron studs. The scanty remains have been removed from the doorway and deposited in the Antiquarium Ostiense.

The marble inscription was usually placed above the architrave (pl. 16, fig. 2: Tombs 80, 79, 78, 76). In the earlier tombs, it was regularly flanked by a splayed window on each side which was masked by a tile or marble screen with an opening. The slit appears in a number of shapes, of which the capital *I* was the most usual.[11] Calza calls it a double *T* or Russian cross. Occasionally, the windows were topped by miniature pediments or lunettes outlined in tile. Inscription and windows were framed in moldings.[12] These did not become ornate until the time of Hadrian. Not until late in the Hadrianic period were the openings for the slit windows cut in the same marble slab as the inscription. This was the usual practice in the Antonine period (pl. 15, fig. 3: Tomb 11).

Façades were often decorated with entirely non-functional pilasters.[13] These have Attic bases and usually terra-cotta capitals (composite or Corinthian) (pl. 14, fig. 3: Tombs 29, 30). Marble half-capitals appear in No. 21–22, which is Antonine. In two Trajanic tombs (Nos. 86 and 95; pl. 14, fig. 2) a square plaque decorated with a rosette in an "*intarsio*" of brick and pumice took the place of the capital (pl. 14, fig. 2: Tomb 95). When the pilasters stood at the corners they seemed to uphold a simple entablature of conventional form. The same "entablature" was used when there were no pilasters. Where façades are preserved high enough to show how they were terminated, they practically always present triangular pediments outlined in rather simple tile moldings (pl. 16, fig. 2: Tombs 80, 79, 78, 76). Occasionally, the moldings were supported by consoles composed of two or three bricks cut to shape. There is slight indication that some of the pediments were lunetted.[14] Ornamental shrines decorated the exterior of the twin tombs Nos. 88 and 90.[15]

Framed terra-cotta plaques calling to mind the occupation of the man by whom the tomb was built supply an added interest to four or five tombs, but have no chronological significance.[16] The earliest (No. 78),[17] which is probably late Trajanic, displays two—one with a ship, the other with a mill—to mark the final resting place of a dealer in grain. The others were probably either late Hadrianic or Antonine. Tomb No. 29[18] (pl. 14, fig. 3: Tombs 29, 30) has no less than three to depict the various phases in the ironmonger's trade; and the very nearly contemporaneous tomb (No. 30) proves that even the humble water carrier could provide a dignified tomb for himself (pl. 14, fig. 3: Tombs 29, 30). Most interesting of all are the two in No. 100[19] depicting a physician at work—in one assisting a woman in childbirth, in the other performing some kind of operation on the leg of a man. Two reliefs not *in situ* show shops with amphorae and other containers for water. One of the tombs near Sant'Hippolyte (H) yielded a plaque depicting two men, of which the significance is not clear. One seems to be carrying a sack. Another represented the occupation of the owner more simply by the relief of a hammer set into the brickwork above the architrave at the left of the door. Such plaques were not confined to tombs but were used in Ostia occasionally in edifices connected with the everyday life of the city.[20] They were modeled in clay before firing. A more or less elaborate *intarsio* of two shades of brick or brick and pumice, found sporadically in the first century,[21] was employed occasionally here to give further embellishment to a façade.[22] We have seen how rosettes of this sort took the place of capitals in one or two instances.[23] In one tomb (No. 16) rather large tufa dolphins were inserted on each side of the door by way of variety.

It is not without interest that Tomb No. 19, which displays the earliest use of fine yellow brickwork in a side wall, retained the red brick in its façade. Red and yellow were neatly interlocked at the corner; and the fine yellow masonry was as neatly joined with the coarser yellow at the rear. The fourth side was not exposed, except for a little which showed the same red facing as the front. Provision was made for both cremation and inhumation burials inside (pl. 14, fig. 4: Tomb 19). The yellow façade of No. 18 is definitely later than the tomb next to it (No. 16) which has been ascribed to A.D. 140 (pl. 15, fig. 4: Tomb 16), but earlier than No. 17 which belongs to the third century. Its yellow bricks are slightly wider than some (2.5–3 cm.); and the same or coarser were employed for the side and rear walls. The inside of the west wall was also faced with brick, though the others were of block-work. This tomb was prepared for inhumation alone. Nos. 29 and 30 were of practically identical masonry originally having red façades but rear walls of coarse yellow brickwork. They were provided with niches for urns and arcosolia for sarcophagi. A little later No. 29 was enlarged, as we have seen, by a precinct on two sides. The new façade (pl. 14, fig. 3: Tomb 29 with 30) was of yellow brickwork diversified by three pilasters faced with rather ordinary red bricks, having composite capitals of buff-colored terra cotta. Red tile outlined the door and base molding, and one brick row appears in the capping cornice. The slit windows in the precinct wall were also outlined in red tile.

The side and rear walls connected with these fine façades were faced with

[16] Calza, *Necropoli*, pp. 247–256.

[17] *Ibid.*, p. 45, fig. 9.

[18] *Ibid.*, p. 252, figs. 150, 151; p. 253, fig. 152.

[19] *Ibid.*, p. 249, fig. 148, and p. 251, fig. 149.

[20] M. F. Squarciapino, *Bull. Com.*, vol. 76, 1958, pp. 183–204.

[21] See Blake, *RC II*, p. 68.

[22] Calza, *Necropoli*, p. 89.

[23] See p. 120 above; Calza, *op. cit.*, p. 44, fig. 8.

[24] Reticulate with block reinforcements are found in Nos. 85 and 86; reticulate alone in Nos. 87, 94, 77.

[25] Calza, Necropoli, p. 63.

[26] The date is assumed from the beautifully lettered inscription. See Thylander, op. cit., no. A 80.

[27] Calza, op. cit., p. 90–96.

[28] Calza, Not. sc., 1928, p. 145, fig. 6.

[29] Thylander, op. cit., pp. 65–66, A 63.

[30] See above, p. 119.

[31] Calza, Necropoli, pp. 97–160.

[32] Ibid., pp. 161–186.

inferior masonry. Where exposed, foundations show an aggregate of large pieces of tufa. Reticulate alone or more often with brick reinforcements was normal in the Trajan-Hadrian period;[24] coarser brickwork, often of yellow bricks, was almost universal under the Antonines. Occasionally an exposed side wall shows the same fine masonry as the façade. The fine brickwork of the façade was regularly interlocked neatly with whatever type of masonry was used for the side walls. Inferior masonry was plastered over and painted red. Calza reports[25] that even when brick was used it was treated in the same fashion. Since the coarser brickwork of the sides is sometimes neatly interlocked with yet coarser in the rear, it is possible that brickwork was not covered with plaster anywhere. Precinct walls have the same fine façades as the tomb proper when they belong to the same building period. One early enclosure for an altar (No. 97) had a façade of reasonably fine brickwork but other walls faced on the outside with reticulate reinforced by brick bands and brick quoins (pl. 14, fig. 1). A Hadrianic precinct to a Trajanic tomb (No. 86), on the other hand, had tufa quoins for its reticulate facing.[26] Usually, however, precincts were additions which cannot be dated with precision. The normal facing for both sides was reticulate work.

The ancient builder apparently had no interest in what he used for facing the inside of the walls of the tomb, but concentrated on the pattern of niches given to him to make. Subconsciously, though, he followed the trends of his time; for reticulate work combined with blocks and whatever else was handy prevails in the earlier part of the period and blockwork with a little brick later. Occasionally, especially when slit windows were lacking in the façade, he added splayed windows elsewhere. The earlier tombs together with such precincts as were added to them contained only small niches for urns and sometimes a larger one for a bust or a statue. The builder achieved infinite variety in the arrangement of rectangular and curvilinear niches, which he sometimes covered with pediments or lunettes outlined in brick.[27] In the transition period between cremation and inhumation, he provided arcosolia for sarcophagi below and niches for urns above (pl. 14, fig. 4). Comparatively few tombs even in the Antonine period show only arcosolia for the type of burial which became almost universal in the third century.[28] Even the arcosolia present considerable variety in form. Except for the cross vaults to support an upper chamber, they employed only the barrel vault. The aggregate, consisting of rather small pieces of tufa, was laid by hand in horizontal rows. In the majority of cases the extrados formed the rounded roof of the tomb, but occasionally it was protected by a gable roof. One of the tombs near Sant'Hippolyte (E) showed many of the roof tiles still in place. It has been ascribed to the Hadrianic period on the evidence of its inscription.[29] There may have been terraces in more instances than are apparent today.[30]

The interior decoration of mosaic floors, frescoes, and stucco work on walls and ceilings, which amply repays the visitor for the effort involved in visiting the site, is beyond the scope of this study. Calza has brought to his treatment of the pictorial decoration a unique background of knowledge and a sensitive appreciation.[31] He has also dealt with the mosaics with his usual thoroughness.[32]

Ostia

Isola Sacra was the necropolis for Portus, but parts of two *sepulcreta* belonging to Ostia have been uncovered.[33] The one outside the Porta Romana was the older, though probably none of its tombs were older than the second century before Christ. Older burials have either left no trace or were concentrated in some other area. Here tomb succeeded tomb without a definite raising of the level at a given period. It is possible to find meager remains of tombs ascribable to the second century, but with one exception they are too meager to add anything to a knowledge gained from the other cemeteries. They will be presented in the second volume of the official publication of the tombs. More substantial remains of one tomb are left on the right side just as one enters the excavations on the Via Ostiensis. It will be remembered primarily for the inartistic black-and-white mosaic in front of it depicting Oedipus confronting the Sphinx, but it displayed an ornamental façade of the finest of fine masonry, of which only the lower part is preserved. It had almost full columns, faced with the same fine-grained red bricks as the rest of the façade, resting on elaborate bases of molded buff-colored tiles which extended across the base of the wall as well. The bricks used in the façade were not particularly thin (ca. 3 cm.), but the joints are very narrow and uniform. Ordinary brickwork faced the back of the wall.

Like Isola Sacra, the level of the Laurentine necropolis[34] was raised in the time of Septimius Severus, thus establishing a definite *terminus ante quem* for all the earlier tombs, but only after the cemetery, in the part excavated at least, had witnessed no new structure for more than a generation. A few tombs were renovated with fresh wall paintings ascribable to the first half of the second century.[35] Calza saw a facing of reticulate between brick pilasters in Tomb No. 31 which appeared to him Hadrianic.[36] The façade of this tomb is under the Lido road.

Rome

The tombs uncovered along the Via Ostiensis near the Basilica of San Paolo in 1918 or thereabouts[37] and still visible were only a part of a vast necropolis. At about the beginning of the second century a new level began to be established at approximately a meter and a half above the early Augustan one[38] and was itself superseded when the level of the Via Ostiensis was raised at about the beginning of the third century. We have therefore rather definite chronological limits for many of the tombs. The small rectangular tombs of the first half of the century were faced with good brickwork but not, I think, with the special fine-grained bricks found elsewhere. Façades followed the style common in the period with travertine doorframes topped by marble inscriptions enclosed in simple terra-cotta frames, with or without slits on each side marking the presence of splayed windows. Blocks were coming into use occasionally to face exterior walls at about the middle of the century[39] without in any way affecting the general plan. Block-and-brick work is found only once among the tombs published.[40] A few tombs can be ascribed to the second half of the century from the nature of the brickwork.[41] Reticulate work normally faced the inside.[42] Most of the tombs were planned for urns, though some ascribable to a date near the end of the

[33] For the early history of the cemetery, see M. F. Squarciapino, *Sc. di O.* III (1), pp. 11–60. For the cemeteries in general, see Meiggs, *Ostia*, pp. 455–470.

[34] G. Calza, *Not. sc.*, 1938, pp. 26–74; M. F. Squarciapino, *Sc. di O.* III (1), pp. 63–127; *idem, Not. sc.*, 1961, pp. 145–177. For those of the Claudian period (?) see Blake, *RC* II, pp. 69–70.

[35] Notably Tombs No. 9 (Calza, *op. cit.*, p. 51) and No. 22 (Calza, *op. cit.*, pp. 60–62).

[36] Calza, *op. cit.*, p. 69.

[37] G. Lugli, *Not. sc.*, 1919, pp. 285–354. The following analysis is based on the thirty-three tombs analyzed by him. The following can be ascribed to the second century for one reason or another: Nos. 3–14, 19, 21, 22, 24, 25A and B, 27(?), 28(?), 29, 33.

[38] See Blake, *RC* II, p. 131.

[39] Tombs Nos. 6, 9, 22. A small shrine in No. 4 is of blockwork.

[40] No. 29.

[41] No. 8 had reticulate reinforced by brick.

[42] No. 3, p. 295 (Lugli, *op. cit.*).

43 *Ibid.*

44 *Ibid.*

45 B. M. Felletti-Maj, *Not. sc.*, 1957, pp. 336–358; Frova, pp. 415–418, fig. 386.

46 E. Gatti, *Bull. Com.*, vol. 54, 1926, pp. 235–257; M. Pallottino, *Riv. Roma*, 1941, pp. 432–433. A more detailed account promised for *Notizie degli Scavi* has never been forthcoming.

47 Lanciani, *Pagan and Christian Rome*, pp. 269–270; Frova, p. 398.

48 P. S. Bartoli, *Gli antichi sepolcri*, Rome 1727 (first ed. 1697).

49 R. T. O'Callaghan, *The Biblical Archaeologist*, vol. 12, 1949, pp. 1–23; *Vatican Report*, pp. 23–117; Toynbee-Perkins, pp. 3–124; E. Kirschbaum, *The Tombs of St. Peter and St. Paul* (Eng. ed.), London 1959, pp. 19–50; Crema, p. 492, fig. 630. For bibliography, see J. Ruysschaert, *Triplice omaggio a Sua Santità Pio XII*, Città del Vaticano 1958, vol. 2, pp. 33–47, and A. De Marco, *The Tomb of Saint Peter*, Leiden 1964.

50 P. Romanelli, *Bull. Com.*, vol. 59, 1931, p. 240; E. Josi (reported by A. M. Colini), *Bull. Com.*, vol. 61, 1933, p. 285; *Vatican Report*, pp. 17–20; F. Magi, *Triplice omaggio a Sua Santità Pio XII*, Città del Vaticano 1958, vol. 2, pp. 87–99.

51 Toynbee-Perkins, p. 67.

period show provision for both types of burial. We are not concerned here with the rather dainty frescoes decorating some of the walls. One tomb had columns made of hollow tubes in front of its inner shrine.[43] All were probably barrel-vaulted. Only one had steps,[44] which may have led to an upper chamber, terrace, or merely to an upper level. The steps were supported in part at least by a rampant arch of tile.

A landslide has preserved in excellent condition the interior decoration of two tombs of a *sepulcretum* near Porta Portuensis.[45] Both the stucco work and the wall paintings belong to the Hadrian-Antonine period, but since the tombs were rock-cut they do not concern us here. The tomb between them had a façade of fine brickwork (bricks 2.5–3 cm. thick with narrow joints) which is more likely to have been Antonine than Hadrianic. Two others stand free. The outer facing of one is of reticulate work with corners of block-and-brick work, the other of blockwork alone. Both had an inner facing primarily of blockwork, though details were added in brick; and one arcosolium at any rate was lined with reticulate. Such heterogeneous masonry was intended to be concealed by wall paintings. These five sepulchres belong to the period of transition from cremation to inhumation. One brick stamp of A.D. 134 was found.

Brick stamps prove that another *sepulcretum* was started at about the middle of the second century near the Circonvallazione Gianicolense[46] not far from the Trastevere station. Unfortunately, the tombs had been plundered long ago, but enough remained of mosaics, frescoes, and stucco work to reveal the same aspiration toward elegance that appears at Isola Sacra. These were also built by freedmen or their immediate descendants. Much of the masonry was ascribable to the second half of the century. One tomb at any rate had exactly the kind of façade common in Isola Sacra—a doorframe of travertine with a projecting molded architrave outlined in tile, a marble inscription between slit windows enclosed in a simple terra-cotta frame, an entablature without angle pilasters, and a low pediment. The barrel vault yielded another example of coffered stucco work.

Remains of another very elegant cemetery have come to light from time to time in the Villa Doria Pamphili merely to be destroyed.[47] Of many hundreds only one is now visible. Engravings of thirty-four made by Pietro Santi Bartoli[48] add poignancy to the regret that such fine examples of polychrome brickwork could not have been preserved. Some were reported to have had marble doors.

The street of the tombs brought to light under St. Peter's[49] was merely a part of a vast sepulchral area.[50] Burials were started there at least as early as the time of Augustus and continued into the third and fourth centuries. The majority of the tombs thus far uncovered are ascribable to the first century, but an occasional tomb in other sections was later. This particular street, however, was definitely a development of the second century. Even here, humble burials, including the reputed grave of St. Peter, had been made sporadically before it acquired its present aspect of little houses of the dead along a secondary passageway.

The earliest tomb (O) can be dated in the Hadrianic period from a brick stamp found in an essential part of its masonry,[51] the latest (Φ) is ascribable

to the early years of the third century. After that time no new tombs seem
to have been built, though old ones were adapted to new burials and in some
cases redecorated. Although the occupants here as at Isola Sacra were freedmen or their descendants, they were apparently secretaries, scribes, and the
like[52] rather than merchants and shopkeepers. There was no longer space for
the precincts which are characteristic of the earlier tombs at Ostia and
fairly common in Isola Sacra. Only one true precinct (O) remains. Three
others (B,D,H) had two rooms of which the first one was open to the sky.
In B, the two parts were separated merely by pilasters terminating in tile
moldings supporting an enormous arch of *bipedales* outlined in a tile
cornice.[53] A cemetery laid out on sloping ground presented obvious problems. The back wall of the tombs on the north side of the street was laid
up against the hill; and in some cases the evidence shows that platforms
were dug out for them. The stairs found in E, F, G, H, and O were probably built to give access from an upper level rather than to terraces on top.
Walls were covered with *opus signinum* where they would be exposed to
surface drainage from the higher ground above.[54]

Tomb architecture remained essentially the same throughout the second
century. Façades were faced for the most part with fine-grained red bricks
(2.8–3.2 cm.) laid with very narrow joints. The surface was washed with a
thin coat of red and the joints marked by a mere thread of white stucco.
Yellow bricks occur in only two of the façades preserved (H and L); and
both of these show the thin bricks which do not appear until late in the
Hadrianic period. In general, the tombs do not display the polychrome
effects of some of the isolated tombs of approximately the same period. As
at Isola Sacra, doorframes were of travertine outlined in a simple terra-cotta
molding; the marble inscription, framed in a more elaborate cornice of terra
cotta, stood over the architrave; and splayed windows, represented on the
exterior by slits either in the slab bearing the inscription or in a tile also
framed in terra cotta and sometimes topped by a pediment, flanked the
inscription. The molding outlining the doorframe was often continued as
a base molding across the front. The façade was completed by a terra-cotta
entablature seldom well enough preserved to show its character. One decorative frieze displays an "*intarsio*" of terra cotta and pumice, another a maean-
der of terra cotta, and yet a third row of terra-cotta rosettes; one or two
capping moldings are supported by consoles of terra cotta. In the majority
of cases, the entablature was doubtless topped by a pediment, though G
alone shows a mere trace of it. One tomb (H) had four pilasters across the
front to reproduce in low relief the façade of a temple. Others had pilasters
at the corners to seem to support the entablature. Only one capital is
preserved (Φ); and that is of terra cotta. Terra-cotta decoration is carried a
step further in the graceful pediment of a scroll and palmette pattern produced in low relief in the first tomb of the Caetennii (F).[55] Far to the right
an inlay of terra cotta simulated a shrine with a lunetted pediment; and in
the corresponding position on the left a tile set in a simple frame depicts a
quail. The second tomb of the Caetennii (L) has terra-cotta amphorae in
relief flanking the central inscription and a relief of a hammer in the center

[52] *Ibid.*, pp. 105–124.

[53] Kirschbaum, *op. cit.*, p. 26, pl. 4.

[54] Toynbee-Perkins, p. 65.

[55] *Ibid.*, pp. 44–51.

[56] *Ibid.*, pp. 51–57.

[57] *Ibid.*, pp. 74–75. See also A. Ferrua, *Acc. P. Rend.*, ser. 3, vol. 24, 1949, pp. 226–228.

[58] Toynbee-Perkins, pp. 75–80.

[59] *Ibid.*, pp. 80–88.

[60] E. Gatti, *Bull. Com.*, vol. 33, 1905, pp. 186–188; *idem*, *Not. sc.*, 1923, pp. 364–379; G. Lugli, *Not. sc.*, 1917, pp. 288–304.

[61] Lugli, *op. cit.*, p. 300.

[62] *Ibid.*, p. 294 with fig. 3.

[63] Via Taranto is in the region east of Via Tuscolana. The Tombs are no longer available for study. See Crema, pp. 264, 491; Frova, pp. 399, 406.

[64] See Blake, *RC II*, p. 60.

[65] M. Pallottino, *Bull. Com.*, vol. 62, 1934, pp. 41–42, 52–60.

of the plain frieze. It apparently once had a decorative plaque at the right of the door. Two tombs had mosaic pictures in their façades. Where foundations and secondary walls faced streets or passageways, they exhibit reasonably good brickwork though not ordinarily the fine masonry of the façades. Fine and coarse brickwork are often interlocked at the start of the lateral wall. Φ shows the same kind of brickwork on all four sides; and V exhibits thin bricks (2.7–2.8 cm.) on the back and west walls.

Interior facings were of rougher masonry than those on the exterior, but they were much more carefully faced than those in the tombs of the Isola Sacra. It is not without interest that two of the earliest (O and D) are the only ones that show reticulate panels in the coarse brickwork of the interior. Coarse brickwork and block-and-brick work are employed about equally in the rest without chronological significance except for a tendency to use a single course of bricks in the earlier ones. All this work was, of course, concealed by stucco. Only one of the earlier tombs (D) was provided with niches alone for cinerary urns; only the latest (Z)[56] had arcosolia alone for sarcophagi; the others clearly belong to the transition period when both burial customs were in vogue. With the exception of the barrel vault over the inner chamber of D and a shallow domical vault over Z, cross vaults appear wherever the type of ceiling can be determined. There is no evidence of flat ceilings under terraces; and it is probable that the vaulting was protected by pitch roofs, though no trace of any such remains.

The interior decoration of the individual tombs is beyond the scope of the present study. Only two floor mosaics[57] of any interest have come to light. Both are black-and-white—one depicting the Rape of Proserpina, the other a large vase with tendrils. I recall one marble pavement of simple pattern. Frescoes[58] and stucco decoration,[59] though similar in character, are richer and more varied than what are found in the tombs of Isola Sacra. Any chronological study of the decorative art must take into consideration the fact that such interior decoration was sometimes renewed even in tombs.

A few columbaria were apparently erected in the early years of the second century in the vast necropolis of the Via Salaria[60] but yield little or nothing to a knowledge of construction. One adds a fine stuccoed vault[61] to the lengthening list belonging to the century; another, a black-and-white mosaic with a Hadrianic pattern.[62]

Two tombs uncovered in building new apartment houses along Via Taranto[63] were probably part of another *sepulcretum*. One belonged to the first century.[64] On the basis of the wall paintings, a second tomb was ascribed by Pallottino[65] to the Trajan-Hadrian period. The walls were faced on the outside with blocks and left unfaced inside, but were covered with plaster three centimeters thick both inside and out. Blockwork was rare at this time, but the façade on one of the short sides took the familiar form: having a travertine doorframe topped by a marble inscription, now gone, in a terra-cotta frame flanked on each side by a marble screen for a slit window also in a terra-cotta frame. The wall at the entrance at any rate was stuccoed and painted red. The floor of beaten earth may have had a marble pavement resting on it. A semicircular niche with a shell top stood opposite the entrance; and rectangular niches filled every other available space. The wall paintings were simple but the more effective for the simplicity. They were completely independent of the architectural framework. Columns at the corners helped to support a barrel vault which was apparently laid on tiles lying flat on the centering. It was left curved on the outside. The use of blocks as a complete facing does not, to my knowledge, appear in dated edifices before the time of Hadrian.[66] Its architecture belongs to the period before this type of tomb had become standardized.

The necropolis of Porta Capena[67] was inside the pomerial restriction established by the Aurelianic Wall. In the preparation for Rome's first subway it was laid bare briefly in too great haste for a detailed analysis, but wall paintings, stucco work, and mosaic floors[68] showed that the majority of the tombs in this restricted area belonged to the Hadrian-Antonine period. The walls were faced with reticulate, brick, or a combination of the two. At about the middle of the century, two rooms[69] were built against a row of first-century tombs[70] under San Sebastiano probably to be used in the cult of the dead. The walls were faced with reticulate work having bonding courses of four rows of brick. Toward the end of the century two more rooms were added in the same type of masonry but with two rather than four courses of brick. These rooms yielded wall paintings of no particular interest.

Though part of a *sepulcretum*, three chamber tombs clustered against the rock under the church of San Sebastiano on the Via Appia are an entity inviting individual treatment since they furnish early examples in the vicinity of Rome of brick-faced tombs which became popular in the second century. The façades are very nearly contiguous though the tombs themselves follow the configuration of the rock and are for the most part rock-cut. The tomb of M. Clodius Hermes (X),[71] named from its last (?) occupant, is best known for its dainty frescoes and black-and-white mosaic floor.[72] Brick stamps found in essential parts prove that the edifice was erected in the time of Hadrian. It presents in simple form a type of façade which does not reveal the presence of a hypogeum inside. A travertine doorframe having a projecting architrave with a white marble slab above it, containing the inscription between slit windows, makes a contrast to the façade of good brickwork washed with red but having the narrow joints marked with white stucco. Brick pilasters seem to support a low pediment outlined in a simple cornice composed of five rows of projecting tiles. Originally there was apparently an emblem of some sort in the center of the tympanum. The lower chamber, approached by an inner staircase, was originally a columbarium. It is cross-vaulted, whereas the upper chamber has a depressed barrel vault. The other two tombs (Y[73] and Z[74]) have similar façades without the corner pilasters and with the capping cornices broken in accommodation to the marble inscription over the travertine doorframe. The brickwork of Z is a little finer than that of the other two; and the marble screen for the splayed windows at the sides of the inscription is framed in terra cotta. In Y, terracotta masks flank the inscription, and a marble pine cone decorates the tympanum, whereas a relief in stucco of a pickaxe between whorls made of three lunette-shaped openings gives individual character to the pediment of Z. The left side of Z was exposed and provided with a splayed window. Y and Z differ from X in masking a stairway leading down immediately into the hypo-

[66] The use of Hadrianic stamps on an inhumation tomb within the columbarium is not significant since old tiles were frequently used for the purpose.

[67] P. E. Arias, *Arch. Anz.*, 1940, cols. 451–452; M. Pallottino, *Riv. Roma*, vol. 19, 1941, p. 365.

[68] Scores of these were removed and deposited in the Museo Nazionale delle Terme.

[69] P. Styger, *Acc. P. Diss.*, ser. 2, vol. 13, 1918, pp. 105–110 (who considers it part of a villa); G. Mancini, *Not. sc.*, 1923, pp. 35–36; T. Ashby, *JRS*, vol. 23, 1933, p. 5.

[70] Blake, *RC II*, pp. 131–132.

[71] G. Mancini, *Not. sc.*, 1923, pp. 51–61; Frova, pp. 412–414, 423–425, 428. For convenience I have used the traditional lettering X, Y, Z for the three tombs.

[72] R. Paribeni, *Rassegna d'Arte*, 1920 (1), pp. 6–8. The pavement is probably original; the frescoes belong to the transformation from cremation to inhumation.

[73] Mancini, op. cit., pp. 61–71.

[74] *Ibid.*, 71–75.

geum, which in its present form shows only inhumation burials, though it was probably prepared originally for urns. In two steps of each stairway an opening gave light to the space below.[75] The stucco work in each is outstanding.[76]

INDIVIDUAL TOMBS ALONG THE HIGHWAYS

The practice of constructing tombs along the highways was not restricted to the arterial road system, but we must confine ourselves to it in the search for tombs characteristic of the century under consideration. Some of the innumerable concrete cores along the roads, robbed of their facing with the possible exception of headers too firmly imbedded to be removed by searchers after building material, may belong to the second century. No canon is applicable to them since each builder used whatever material was readily available for both mortar and aggregate. For convenience, the roads are presented in alphabetical order.

Via Appia and Its Derivatives

The quality of the brickwork in a tomb uncovered in 1940 just outside Porta San Sebastiano[77] confirmed the date at the end of the second century suggested by the nature of the frescoes and the polychrome mosaic pavement. Paintings and mosaic were removed before the tomb was destroyed to make room for the Via Ardeatina.

Near the entrance to the Jewish Catacombs just beyond the junction of the Via Appia Pignatelli with the Via Appia, there are substantial remains of a tomb with the same fine yellow brickwork.[78] It is no longer possible to tell how the front was treated. In the interior there are traces of niches upon which pediments alternate with lunettes. As usual in monuments of this class the inside facing was of more ordinary brickwork.[79] Unfortunately, external evidence for dating is lacking.[80]

A two-story tomb of brick-faced concrete on the right side of the Via Appia at about the fourth milestone has been plausibly identified with the tomb which Santa Marmenia erected for Sant'Urbano,[81] who suffered martyrdom in the persecution of A.D. 177. If this identification is correct, we have an example of tomb architecture ascribable to the later years of the second century. The hypogeum consisted of a vestibule with a door at each end and a square chamber with a curved alcove jutting out of the back wall and rectangular ones from the side walls. It was faced with ordinary brickwork. Four splayed windows in the side walls gave light and air, and four angle piers and a pier in the center supported the cross vaulting. The upper chamber was originally approached by steps probably within an antechamber of some sort which was apparently destroyed in the time of Diocletian and rebuilt later as a tetrastyle pronaos with a broad stairway in front. Two granite columns with Corinthian capitals which may have belonged to it have been found in the neighborhood. The façade is gone. Corinthian angle pilasters supported an entablature with a capping cornice resting on consoles. Windows with decorative frames, two on each side, pierce the side walls.

Not far from the eighth milestone of the Via Appia, there are remains of

[75] For a brief history of the site, see Toynbee-Perkins, pp. 172–175. 172–175.

[76] E. Wadsworth (Mrs. H. F. Cleland), *MAAR*, vol. 4, 1924, pp. 64–65.

[77] C. Pietrangeli, *Bull. Com.*, vol. 68, 1940, pp. 216–217; *idem, Capitolium*, vol. 15, 1940, pp. 911–915; author (?), *Urbe*, vol. 5, 1940 (9), p. 14 with a water color by L. Cartocci.

[78] Personal observation.

[79] Some of the bricks are a fine reddish yellow.

[80] J. H. Parker (*The Archaeology of Rome*, part xii, "The Catacombs," Oxford, England, 1877, p. 120) ascribes it to the first century without evidence.

[81] G. B. Lugari, *Intorno ad alcuni monumenti antichi esistenti al IV miglio dell'Appia*, Rome 1882, pp. 5–30; Ripostelli and Marucchi, *Via Appia*, pp. 196–199; Tomassetti, *Campagna*, vol. 2, p. 81; Ashby, *Campagna*, p. 184; Castagnoli, *Via Appia*, pls. 33 and 34.

two tombs which are certainly contemporaneous.[82] An old engraving of Labacco showed the name of Q. Veran(n)ius on one of them (pl. 17, fig. 2), but this was certainly not the famous individual of the name who died in Britain in A.D. 62.[83] It has seemed better, therefore, to regard them as products of the second century when tombs of this type became common. Each had a lower story with a simple base molding, a plain surface except perhaps with provision for an inscription in a terra-cotta frame, and its own entablature on which rested the upper story. The façade of each had a niche flanked by recessed columns and angle pilasters supporting an entablature. The terra-cotta capitals were Corinthian. In one, polychromy was achieved by a careful selection of tiles, in the other through coloring. Only the façades as restored by Canina remain of the upper story. The exterior brickwork is fine, and the bricks were tapered to make extremely fine joints. Many of them are speckled with grains of pozzolana, and some are mottled. The dentil molding found in the entablature lacks the finesse of the best examples. The interiors, lined with ordinary brickwork, had low cross vaults and large shallow niches not adapted to burial urns. The entrance to the burial chamber was at the back; and in one at least the doorframe was of peperino. The tombs have been so restored that a more detailed analysis would not simplify the matter of chronology. The brick interior facing and the lack of provision for cremation burials suggest a date not earlier than the middle of the century.

The Crypta Quadrata of St. Januarius, though located in the Catacomb of St. Praetestatus on Via Appia Pignatelli,[84] differs in no way from the pagan monuments of the period. It was not hollowed out of the rock like most catacomb chapels, but was built up in a fine masonry of yellow brick variegated by pilasters faced with red brick. It had a rich capping cornice made up of the usual decorative moldings. St. Januarius died in A.D. 162.

The most elaborate of the tombs of this type is the so-called Tempio Redicolo[85] on the Vicolo della Caffarella, which branches off from the Via Appia shortly after the church of Domine Quo Vadis. There would seem to be no reason why it should not have been the Tomb of Annia Regilla, the wife of Herodes Atticus, the wealthiest man of his day; she died in A.D. 161 under mysterious circumstances while giving birth to his fifth child. It stands in the center of her estate and was obviously prepared for a single occupancy. The two-story monument (pl. 16, fig. 1) depended on the judicious use of red and yellow bricks for polychrome effects as well as ornate moldings for added sumptuousness. The doorway to the lower chamber was placed in the center of the south side. This story was faced with fine red brickwork.[86] Slight pilaster-like projections are the only breaks in the smooth facing. They correspond to pilasters above[87] except on the north side where the space between the end pilasters is divided equally so that the projection stands in the center. The capping cornice supports the red base molding of the upper story. On the east side, the concrete core of a pronaos[88] concealed the front wall of the lower chamber. Traces of the same fine brickwork appear on the north side of this core. From the pronaos, entrance to the upper chamber was through a lofty doorway with an architrave of tufa, which seems to have been stuccoed over; it was covered with a terra-

[82] Nibby, *Dintorni*, vol. 3, pp. 552–554; Canina, *Via Appia*, pp. 170–171, pl. 41, fig. 3; p. 182, pl. 44; Tomassetti, *Campagna*, vol. 2, pp. 109–111; Bagnani, *Campagna*, pp. 42–43. For the so-called Tomb of the Poet Persius, see also Roccatelli, *Brickwork*, pp. 32, 35; *Enc. it.*, vol. 25, pl. 72 (foll. p. 472); Castagnoli, *Via Appia*, pl. 60; Crema, p. 503, fig. 642. (Mr. Edward N. MacConomy, Reference Department of the Library of Congress, informs me that he is not able to find the Veran(n)ius inscription in that Library's copy of Labacco. Since I did not fully trust the report of a general reference librarian, I wrote to Dr. Maria Marchetti, Director of the Biblioteca dell'Istituto Nazionale d'Archeologia e Storia dell'Arte, who states that "nelle due edizione dell'opera (*sc.* of Labacco) possedute dalla nostra biblioteca non è contenuta l'incisione riproducente l'iscrizione che Le interessa." Miss Blake's source then is Nibby, who is responsible for the spelling Q. VERANNIO; I do not know Nibby's source.—JDB)

[83] See *RC II*, p. 62.

[84] G. B. de Rossi, *BAC*, 1863, pp. 17–21.

[85] G. Lugli, *Bull. Com.*, vol. 52, 1924, pp. 109–115; Roccatelli, *Brickwork*, pp. 40–42, figs. 30–32, pl. 37, colored pl. 38; Rivoira-Rushforth, pp. 151–152 with fig. 182; Castagnoli, *op. cit.*, nos. 7, 8, 9; Crema, pp. 493, 496, fig. 641; Frova, pp. 92–93.

[86] Richmond's measures for Dr. Van Deman: length varying from 2.7–26.7 cm., height 2.5–2.7 cm.; mortar, horizontal joints 0.2–0.3 cm., vertical 0.1–0.2 cm.

[87] There are none under the recessed half columns on the south side.

[88] A restoration with a four-columned porch is presented tentatively in *Palladio*, vol. 1, 1937, p. 227.

[89] The facing arch is made of *semi-pedales*.

cotta cornice. Above the doorway a curved niche[89] was lined with alternate rows of tufa and brick which were also doubtless concealed by stucco. It was covered with a pediment of rather ugly shape under which two small columns once apparently upheld a simulated entablature with architrave and frieze adorned with ornamental moldings under a capping cornice. A console-supported architrave also of decorative terra cotta covered a window on each side of the niche. At the line of the top of the doorway a band of buff-colored terra cotta with a meander pattern framed on each side by a three-layer band of red brick divided the yellow curtain in two uneven parts. End pilasters faced with red bricks supplied a further contrast. On the south and north sides, the yellow façades are divided vertically into three parts by recessed octagonal half columns in red brick. On the west, two pilasters, also in red brick, have the same effect. The band with the Greek fret was carried over from the east side all around the edifice to divide the curtain horizontally. Composite capitals of buff-colored terra cotta topped all the red pilasters and columns and supported a conventional entablature of yellow brick with a crowning member resting on consoles. Red bricks were used over the pilasters on the south and west and neatly interlocked with the plain yellow frieze. On the south side a richly decorated window like the ones in front pierced the curtain above the meander in the center and was flanked on each side by a framed space for an inscription; on the west side three similar windows occupied the same relative positions between pilasters. The north side corresponded to the south except that it had no provision for framed inscriptions. The inside was faced with a more ordinary brick-work. A curved niche between rectangular ones stood in the north wall of the upper chamber. Slightly curved lintel arches protected all architraves. Both chambers were covered with cross vaults supported on pendentives. There are faint traces of ceiling decoration in stucco and color.

It is manifestly impossible to analyze all the tombs of the period through-out the length of the whole Via Appia, but it is instructive to note that the influence of Rome was not paramount in the vicinity of Naples. There is, to my knowledge, no tomb faced with *opus incertum* near Rome definitely ascribable to the second century; but a sepulchral monument, known as La Conocchia,[90] near Santa Maria Capua Vetere (pl. 17, fig. 3) proves that this type of masonry could be used with brick in sophisticated fashion at the time or perhaps even a little later. Blocks strengthened the corners of the square basement, but bricks were employed sparingly elsewhere. The actual masonry was concealed by stucco, but it is not possible to tell whether any of the brick cornices were left to give color to the white façades. It is not only the wall construction that differs from that used near Rome. There were, to be sure, lofty mausoleums of three stories, but none with so baroque effect of constant contrast between straight and curved lines. The first story was a plain square, the third story, a circular foundation for a structure having round-headed niches between semi-columns supporting a low entablature under a low cupola, but the intermediate story had four identical façades, each having a central aedicula consisting entirely of straight lines from its rectangular base to its pedimented top, built out into an attic, projecting from a concave wall with a round-headed window on each side

[90] Giovannoni, *Tecnica*, p. 55; L. Crema, *IV cong. st. rom.*, vol. 1, p. 446 with pl. 12, fig. 3; U. Ciotti, *Arti fig.*, vol. 1, 1945, pp. 65–68 with pl. 35; de Franciscis, *Mausolei*, pp. 34–35, figs. 65–73; Pane, *ibid.*, pp. 76–87; Crema, p. 327, figs. 379–380; Frova, p. 94.

between cylindrical masses at the corners. Each niche was embellished with a round false window.

Not far from this, a huge circular mausoleum, known as Carceri Vecchie,[91] also shows too great a mixture of elements to be readily classified (pl. 17, fig. 1). The masonry was, however, concealed by stucco. The anular wall with alternate rectangular and curved niches displays semi-columns of block-and-brick work. In the rectangular niches, the side walls were mostly of blocks with a very few bricks interspersed, whereas the back wall was of *opus incertum* or *quasi-reticulatum* with two rows of brick between sections; in the curved niches, block quoins with occasional tiles were used with *opus reticulatum*. The semi-columns supported an architrave of continuous lintel arches of tile and the frieze of tiles resting on it (pl. 18, fig. 4). The encompassing wall of concrete was wide enough to support a second story set back on it, which was low and consisted of short pilasters of brickwork (?) and panels of reticulate. The entrance corridor led to a relatively small burial chamber in the form of a Greek cross inside a circle of concrete. Concrete walls connected this with the outer circle, but the space between the two was filled with earth. The whole was undoubtedly covered with a mound of earth. The inner rooms had barrel vaults over the arms meeting in the center to form a cross vault. There seems to have been part of an anular corridor with a barrel vault within the outer circle of concrete, which did not, however, have any connection with the burial chamber.

The Mausoleum of Marano[92] near Naples shows how two media could be used together for decorative effect. The square basement had façades with a brick framework of pilasters and contiguous lintel arches. The end pilasters were deep enough to contain a narrow arched recess. The intervening spaces were filled with reticulate work having purely decorative pediments and half pediments outlined in tile. A reticulate frieze under a tile cornice supported by consoles completed the facing of the first story. The drum was faced with a bichrome reticulate having string courses of tufa blocks. The lower chamber had a barrel vault; the upper one, a cupola preserved in part. Such masonry is certainly not earlier than the second century and may be later.

Via Labicana

Between the fifth and sixth milestone of the Via Labicana, now Casilina, there is a tomb of ornamental brickwork[93] which may belong to the period under discussion. It is conspicuous for loophole windows and a fine cornice of cut terra cotta.

At about the ninth kilometer of the Via Labicana, four large pieces of architectural members led to the discovery of the foundations of one of the great circular tombs of squared-stone masonry,[94] such as began to be erected about the middle of the first century before Christ as dynastic monuments.[95] Stefani, who excavated it, judged it to be a product of the early years of the second century. A marble drum stood on a square foundation, which was faced with small blocks of tufa probably concealed by stucco or a marble revetment. Within the base substantial walls of concrete crossed in the center to help bear the weight of the mound of earth which once rose behind a row of "altars of crenelation"[96] and connecting slabs that formed

[91] De Franciscis, *op. cit.*, pp. 36–38, pls. 74–84; Pane, *ibid.*, pp. 87–94; Crema, p. 326, figs. 371–373.

[92] De Franciscis, *op. cit.*, pp. 28–29, pls. 57–64, Pane, *ibid.*, pp. 72–76; Crema, p. 426, fig. 624.

[93] T. Ashby, *PBSR*, vol. 1, 1902, pp. 231–232.

[94] E. Stefani, *Not. sc.*, 1931, pp. 506–509; B. Götze, *Ein römisches Rundgrab in Falerii; Baugeschichte des römischen Adels- und Kaisergrabes; Grabbau und Bauplanung des Augustus*, Stuttgart 1939, p. 13; Crema, p. 248.

[95] Blake, *RC I*, pp. 169–170. Aurigemma (*BMIR*, vol. 12, 1941, pp. 83–84) gives another example of upright slabs decorated with armor and horizontal slabs with palmettes which he ascribes to the first century.

[96] This is a theory developed by Götze, *op. cit.*

97 The Mausoleum of Hadrian in Rome forms a fitting conclusion to the series though no hint of "altars of crenelation" remains.

98 Nibby, *Dintorni*, vol. 3, p. 588; T. Ashby, *PBSR*, vol. 4, 1907, p. 23; Tomassetti, *Campagna*, vol. 4, p. 35. Its present municipal number is 51 since it now serves as a dwelling.

99 Nibby and Tomassetti ascribe it to the first century.

100 Tomassetti, *op. cit.*, p. 36; Ashby, *op. cit.*, p. 27.

101 Nibby, *op. cit.*, pp. 589–590; Ashby, *op. cit.*, p. 60; Tomassetti, *op. cit.*, p. 62; Roccatelli, *Brickwork*, pp. 35–36, figs. 26–28, pl. 31, color plate 32, supplemented by personal observation; Crema, p. 496.

102 Roccatelli, *op. cit.*, p. 35, note by G. Mass.

the crowning member of the drum. Here there was no difference in height between the so-called altars and the slabs. The "altars" may have been merely pedestals for statues.[97]

Via Latina

The Via Latina is particularly rich in tombs of fine brickwork. The first appears on the left side just before the crossing for the railroad to Civitavecchia.[98] It consists of two stories above ground. The lower one was faced with very red bricks made from tiles carefully arranged to breakjoint in orderly fashion and displays two Doric pilasters supporting a frieze of yellow brick under a capping cornice in which there was a dentil molding; the upper one, of somewhat coarser brickwork in lighter shades, was framed by Doric half columns supporting a pedimented entablature over a slightly curved lintel arch. The same dentil molding appeared in this entablature also. The lower chamber (3.55 m. $\times$ 3.39 m.), which served as a columbarium, was decorated with painted stucco and covered with a barrel vault. The upper chamber was approached by an outside staircase. It contained nothing of note. The tomb was almost certainly a product of the second century,[99] though two brick stamps found loose are scarcely sufficient evidence for a precise dating. A little farther along on the same side of the street, a tomb of fine brickwork was reported in the Vigna Santambrogio,[100] but I have no further information regarding it.

Shortly after the military road crosses the Via Latina on the right, a tomb of fine brickwork still stands which is known as "Sepolcro Barberini."[101] The two-story tomb (pl. 16, fig. 4) rests on a platform paved with black-and-white mosaic, beneath which is a subterranean chamber lighted by slit windows with travertine lintels and sills, two for each side. The tomb proper was faced with fine-grained red bricks (2.5 cm. $\times$ 26 cm.)[102] diversified by decorative members in buff-colored terra cotta. Broken edges prove that some of the fine joints at any rate widened behind the surface in accommodation to a purposeful tapering of the bricks. Angle pilasters with ornate carved capitals of light terra cotta (pl. 18, fig. 3) supported the entablature at the top of each story. The capitals of the lower story (Corinthian) were twice as high as those above (composite). In the entablature a plain frieze of red contrasted pleasingly with the architrave decorated with simple moldings and the elaborate capping cornice with its crowning member supported by consoles, each made of three tiles carved to a graceful shape with a scale pattern between them. A raking cornice of the same ornamental moldings formed the pediment. The door stood at the back. It had a peperino frame which was doubtless stuccoed over to contrast with the façade which shows traces of red coloring matter. Above it was a space for an inscription between two windows now walled up. On the front face, an aedicula for a statue stood between two windows in the second-story façade. These windows were also walled up, but the breaks in the brickwork are an indication that they were also framed in rich moldings. Block-and-brick work lined the interior. The lower chamber was covered with a cross vault. If the builder followed the usual practice, the upper chamber was barrel-vaulted. Nibby ascribes the tomb to the first century; Tomassetti to the time of Hadrian. Its decorative members resemble so closely those of the Tomb of Annia Regilla as to have been the work of the same artisan. In my judgment, the tomb is Antonine.[103]

The "Tomb of the Valerii"[104] seems to be an integral part of a rather extensive structure with walls of reticulate-faced concrete. The lower part of its walls exhibits the same type of facing as the rest. Traces of brickwork remain above the reticulate, but unfortunately practically all the upper part is a modern restoration. The plan is strange for a tomb. It presented to the street an entrance flanked by a wall on each side. The entrance itself had two brick-faced columns in antis with marble bases and capitals. Behind this was a porticus in front of a vestibule with a flight of steps on each side leading down to an antechamber and an inner room where sarcophagi were found. Toward the rear of the antechamber a light well furnished sufficient illumination for the two rooms. Remains of marble pavements and wall revetments came to light in the excavation. The inner chamber had a particularly fine stucco work on its barrel vault;[105] the room between the stairs, also barrel-vaulted, probably had a frescoed intrados. The facing arches for all the vaults were of bipedales. A brick stamp with the consular date of A.D. 159[106] found in the vaulting would seem to be sufficient evidence for ascribing the edifice to the early years of the reign of Marcus Aurelius. The entrance to the vestibule was marked by two columns in antis, and a similar arrangement led to a hall in the rear which was three steps higher than the rest. The bricks used in the monument were made from good flanged tiles or magenta bipedales varying in thickness from 3–3.8 cm. (majority 3.5 cm.); mortar joints averaged 1.5 cm., though they were often as wide as 2 cm. The bricks in the staircase were slightly thinner, but there is no sign of the very fine brickwork usually found in the tombs of the period. My responsibility ends with the analysis of the masonry, but the feeling persists that the structure was planned as a sanctuary of some sort and was later converted into a place of burial.

Opposite the tomb just described there is the Tomb of the Pancratii,[107] of which only the subterranean part is preserved, approached by a single stairway with two ramps. Well known for the fine polychrome stucco work[108] on the cross vault of the inner of the two chambers,[109] it is of interest to this study only for the fact that the walls were faced with reticulate instead of the brick more usual in the tombs of the Antonines, to which it owes its origin. It was prepared for sarcophagi rather than urns. A black-and-white mosaic depicting sea monsters formed the pavement of the upper chamber.

On the same side of the road beyond the "Tomb of the Valerii," another two-story tomb[110] above a subterranean chamber resembles the tomb just described closely enough to have been the work of the same builder. Two slit windows on each side gave light to the underground room in the same way. Only the west façade is preserved. It was red with yellow pilasters at the corners; they had Doric(?) capitals. Like the other tomb, it had a buff-colored base molding and entablature of elaborate moldings with a plain red frieze. The crowning member of the capping cornice was supported by

[103] See pp. 129–130 above.

[104] L. Fortunati, Relazione generale degli scavi e scoperte fatte lungo la Via Latina, Roma 1859, pp. 41–42; E. Petersen, Ann. d. Inst., vol. 32, 1860, pp. 348–415; T. Ashby, PBSR, vol. 4, 1907, p. 61, carefully checked by personal observation.

[105] E. Wadsworth (Mrs. H. J. Cleland), MAAR, vol. 4, 1924, pp. 69–72, pls. 20–24; Frova, pp. 414–415, 423.

[106] CIL, vol. 15 (1), no. 1368.

[107] Petersen, Ann. d. Inst., vol. 33, 1861, pp. 190–242; Ashby, op. cit., pp. 62–63.

[108] Wadsworth, op. cit., pp. 73–78, pls. 25–35; Crema, p. 347, fig. 397; Frova, pp. 290, 414–415.

[109] The outer chamber was later.

[110] Personal observation. This is E on the plan of Fortunati. See also Ashby, op. cit., p. 62; Crema, pp. 496–497, fig. 643.

111 Ashby, op. cit., p. 67.

112 Ibid., p. 67.

113 Ibid., p. 71.

114 Ibid., p. 80.

115 Ashby, op. cit., p. 147; Rivoira-Rushforth, p. 151. The description is entirely from personal observation. It seems probable that this tomb is depicted in an engraving of Rossini in Enc. it., vol. 3, p. 757 labeled "presso il Tavolata," and is the so-called Temple of Health in an engraving by Piranesi reproduced by Roccatelli, Brickwork, pl. 39.

consoles which here were made of four tiles instead of three, separated by the scale pattern in terra cotta. It also had a doorframe of peperino doubtless concealed by stucco and a façade washed with red. A shrine (?) once flanked by splayed windows decorated the front of the upper chamber. The one window still preserved retains its light-colored moldings and shows clearly where a rich architrave was supported by carved consoles doubtless also of buff-colored terra cotta. This is certainly another Antonine tomb.

A few other tombs may be mentioned in passing, though there is no specific evidence for dating them. On the left side of the road near Santo Stefano, a two-story tomb of brick-faced concrete exhibits brick columns at the corners standing on square pedestals.[111] Both chambers are cross-vaulted. Little of it remains. A little farther along, a large brick tomb (9.95 m. × 8 m.)[112] was covered with a coffered barrel vault. Traces of fine stucco work remain. In a group of seven tombs northwest of Tor Fiscale, one rectangular sepulchre of fine brickwork[113] with two ornamental windows has an unusual interior of semicircular shape with a half dome. There are three niches in the curved wall, the central one lunetted, the other two pedimented. A single brick stamp of A.D. 123 is the indication of the date of a columbarium of ornamental brickwork,[114] the foundation of which was laid bare in 1902 shortly before the railway crossed the line of the Via Latina.

On the left of the Via Appia Nuova at about the eleventh kilometer (fifth mile), there is an impressive funerary monument in rather ruinous condition,[115] which doubtless faced the Via Latina. The usual two-storied tomb appears faced with narrow yellow brick separated by almost invisible joints, but diversified by red pilasters and an occasional red course in the rather elaborate cornices. The door was at the back of the lower story, and there are traces of the pilasters which flanked it. The rest of the curtain was plain up to the capping cornice. Four slit windows, two each in the north and west walls lighted the interior. Four pilasters to a side gave a tripartite division to the walls of the upper story. Narrow bands of ornamental terra cotta under decorative moldings were inserted in the panels at the side toward Rome about two-thirds of the way up. The side ones were decorated with rosettes, the central one with an acanthus scroll. The Corinthian capitals of the pilasters upheld the usual entablature with ornamental moldings marking the fasciae, and corbels supported the capping cornice. Two (?) windows with ornate moldings, of which the merest trace of one remains, stood high up in the side panels of the façade toward the Via Appia. There may have been others in the part that is gone. The interior was faced with more ordinary brickwork. There was provision for inhumation in the lower chamber; a row of small niches at the bottom of the upper chamber could have been intended for burial urns. Higher up there was a curved niche for a statue and above it a small slit window. Both chambers were cross-vaulted. An Antonine date is reasonable for this tomb also.

Via Nomentana

The Via Nomentana, though an old road, was not a thoroughfare and was, therefore, less popular for the tombs of the well-to-do. It has, however, three or four tombs which are especially noteworthy for their vaulting. The two most important have the picturesque names of "Sedia del Diavolo" and "Torraccio della Cecchina"[116] and are probably very nearly contemporaneous though there is unfortunately no external evidence by which they may be dated. It would seem unlikely that such experiments in vaulting were made before the time of Hadrian. The conventional dating at about the middle of the second century would appear to be substantially correct.

About three kilometers from the city in the valley to the left, the "Sedia del Diavolo,"[117] a two-story tomb with an antechamber, though in ruinous condition can still be visited (pl. 16, fig. 3). Only the core remains of the pronaos. The lower story, faced both inside and out with courses alternately of brick and reticulate, serves merely as the podium, so to speak, of the chamber of fine brickwork above. On the inside, the walls exhibited a symmetrical arrangement of five niches rising to a peak and descending again with low arched recesses at the ends, intermediate ones with a lintel arch of tile, and a lofty arched one in the center. The base line is constant. Above the intermediate niches are windows of very nearly the same proportions. The chamber was covered with one of the few examples of the *volta a vela*.[118] The aggregate consisted of lumps of tufa laid by hand on the wooden frame. The upper chamber was faced on the outside with the fine brickwork usual in tombs of this kind. The façade displays four brick-faced pilasters with Corinthian capitals supporting a simple entablature, above which the low dome is visible. High up between the pilasters there are two small windows. The inside facing was more ordinary brickwork. On the walls there are traces of pilasters of stucco and one fine shell of stucco work. The ceiling was a low dome resting on spherical pendentives.

The "Torraccio della Cecchina" or "Spuntapiede" is nearly three and a half kilometers farther along the Via Nomentana beyond Casale dei Pazzi on the right.[119] It is somewhat smaller, but it also had two stories. The lower chamber, of which merely the top of a large arch on each side is now visible, is said to have been crowned by a depressed barrel vault. The upper chamber was faced on the outside with fine red bricks from tiles on the main façade, and this red brickwork was interlocked with yellow on the sides. There were no end pilasters but the façade is terminated by simple tile moldings similar to those used in entablatures. There was evidently a tall sepulchral cippus just off center and above it an oval aperture which was reduced to a circle before it pierced the dome. Beneath the opening a festoon was carved in the brickwork. A little lower down on each side of the cippus, there was a splayed window which became a mere slit inside. The windows are not identical. The smaller one at the left has corbels supporting columns for a pedimented entablature, whereas the larger on the right has a plain frame beneath a pedimented top. A simple slit window appears in at least one side wall. The entrance was apparently in the opposite side and has a square window above its stone architrave. Tall semicircular niches covered with segmental arches of tile stood in the other three side walls. The interior was lined with ordinary brickwork. The vault was a true cupola supported in part by spherical pendentives.[120] For both pendentives and

[116] L. Crema, "Due monumenti sepolcrale sulla Via Nomentana," in *Serta Hoffelleriana*, Zagreb 1940, pp. 263–283 (not available to me), reviewed by C. Pietrangeli, *Bull. Com.*, vol. 72, 1951, p. 235.

[117] T. Ashby, *PBSR*, vol. 3, 1906, p. 45; Bagnani, *Campagna*, p. 261; Martinori, *Via Nomentana*, pp. 29–30; Crema, art. cited in note 116; Crema, pp. 340, 493, fig. 394; Frova, pp. 93–94.

[118] For *volta a vela*, see below, p. 302. Giovannoni, Crema, Schiavo, de Angelis d'Ossat consider this a *volta a vela*; Rivoira, a depressed vault on flat pendentives; Ashby and Bagnani, erroneously, a quadripartite vaulting.

[119] T. Ashby, *PBSR*, vol. 3, 1906, p. 53; Martinori, *Via Nomentana*, pp. 42–43; Rivoira-Rushforth, p. 155, figs. 185–187; Crema, art. cited in note 116; Crema, pp. 340, 496; Frova, p. 94.

[120] G. de Angelis d'Ossat, *III conv. st. archit.*, p. 228; Giovannoni, *Tecnica*, p. 35.

dome, pieces of tufa were laid in almost horizontal courses on the wooden framework, and the mortar was poured over them and allowed to set before the centering was removed. Artificial triangular voids[121] in the concrete reduced the weight to a certain degree. This device seems to appear in the neighborhood of Rome first during the reign of Hadrian. Traces of painted stucco were found on the walls, and the cupola was probably stuccoed.

The Tomb of P. Aelius Agathemer,[122] in the ex-villa-Patrizi along the Via Nomentana, furnishes an early example of the use of block-and-brick work in the vicinity of Rome. The outer facing was standardized to one row of blocks between two of bricks. A shallow shrine was hollowed out of the concrete above the doorway, in which half-columns supported a projecting architrave over an arched niche. The wall opposite the entrance was faced with a bichrome reticulate of tufa and tile. The walls were thin, as often in tombs (35 cm. and 40 cm.), but supported a barrel vault over each chamber. The name is that of a freedman of Hadrian or one of the Antonines.

The tomb near the start of the Via Nomentana, uncovered in the ex-villa-Patrizi when the ground was prepared for the Palazzo della Direzione Generale delle Ferrovie dello Stato,[123] was neither polychrome nor probably of particularly fine brickwork; but it also had a *volta a vela*.[124] Its pitch roof was unusual in having scale-shaped tiles. Its floor had a black-and-white mosaic with a pattern divided into three parts;[125] its walls and ceilings were richly decorated with painting and stucco work. Above the door with its travertine frames was an inscription which enables one to date the tomb within narrow limits. A freedman of Marcus Aurelius and a veteran of service under the joint rule of Marcus Aurelius and Lucius Verus (A.D. 161–169) together with two freedmen erected the tomb.

Another tomb of ornamental brickwork,[126] in which the front was yellow[127] and the side walls red, stood on the Via della Buffalotta, which debouches from the Patinaria, itself a branch of the Via Nomentana. It is known as the Chiesuola Buffalotta. As usual there is no external aid for even an approximate dating.

Via Praenestina

Impressive remains of a tomb of fine brickwork without polychromy, I think, may be seen near the sulphur spring known as Acqua Bollicante on the right side of Via Praenestina at about the second mile from Rome. It is unique among Roman tombs in having small arches of tile supported by corbels to uphold the capping cornice. Rivoira ascribes the tomb to the Antonines.[128]

Via Tiburtina

The Via Tiburtina yields three tombs near Santa Bibiana[129] which from the evidence of the brick stamps can be ascribed to the Hadrianic period. The walls of the best preserved were faced with good brickwork belonging to the same period as the *bipedales* covering the benches inside, which have

121 De Angelis d'Ossat, *op. cit.*, p. 246. The voids are usually made by inserting amphorae.

122 A. Pasqui, *Not. sc.*, 1911, pp. 41–42.

123 G. Mancini, *Not. sc.*, 1911, pp. 133–138.

124 See below, p. 302, for *volta a vela*.

125 M. E. Blake, *MAAR*, vol. 13, 1936, p. 159.

126 Ashby, *PBSR*, vol. 3, 1906, pp. 47–48.

127 Lugli (*Bull. Com.*, vol. 52, 1924, p. 116) considers yellow bricks a sign of the mid-second century, but the tombs of Isola Sacra prove that they can be Severan.

128 Rivoira-Rushforth, p. 151 with fig. 181; Ashby, *Campagna*, pp. 129–130; Bagnani, *Campagna*, p. 180.

129 G. Annibaldi, *Bull. Com.*, vol. 66, 1938, p. 249; *idem*, *Not. sc.*, 1948, pp. 129–135; Lugli, *MAR*, vol. 3, pp. 46–47.

stamps of A.D. 123.[130] It had the usual travertine doorframe with over-hanging architrave entirely outlined in a single row of tiles, marble inscription —now gone—in a terra-cotta frame, and a splayed window on each side having a marble screen in a yet more elaborate frame. The interior was fitted with arcosolia below and niches for urns above and was adorned with a polychrome mosaic floor and the usual combination of frescoes and stucco work on the walls. The vaulting had fallen in, but pieces of coffered stucco remained. The second tomb at a different orientation apparently had an underground chamber lighted by slit windows with marble screens on each side of the steps of the upper chamber, which had a travertine doorframe, a pleasing terra-cotta base molding for corner pilasters. The upper part had been entirely destroyed. Not enough remained of the third tomb to make possible a description. Brick stamps found in demolishing these last two tombs bear the consular date A.D. 123.[131] A precinct wall, also in good brick-work with a travertine doorframe, enclosed an area paved with herringbone brick.

Halfway between Rome and Tivoli in undulating territory beyond Sette-camini known as Monte Incastro, in the estate named Inviolata, a hypo-geum[132] was discovered many years ago and finally excavated in 1927–1929. It was a domed circular chamber six meters in diameter approached by a long somewhat curved corridor. All this was underground. A vestibule paved in herringbone brick led to the corridor which was lined with reticulate and supplied with a barrel vault. The chamber, which had two and possibly three niches, was lined with very fine brickwork of the type often used for the exterior of tombs, but it showed none of the fancy molding associated with the type. A projection of two courses served as the impost for the vault over each niche; one outlined the curve of the arch of *sesquipedales* belong-ing to the same, and the other was used to terminate the wall. The chamber had a marble floor and a mighty concrete dome with an eye,[133] which was lined with a rough white mosaic. The miniature half-domes over the niches were decorated with a finer mosaic bearing a scroll pattern in blue and green glass on a white ground. The chamber has been considered a tomb, a nymphaeum, and more recently a sanctuary of Hercules.[134] The Hadrianic date proposed by Mr. Hallam seems reasonable.

Via Traiana

Remains of a two-story tomb faced with fine brickwork on the Via Traiana at Bagnoli (Canosa)[135] prove that this type of tomb masonry was not con-fined to the vicinity of Rome. The tomb was rectangular rather than square. The bricks were for the most part yellowish red triangles, those inside being slightly coarser than those on the exterior. There was no use of polychromy, but there was a fine decorative cornice. It is obvious that no pretentious tomb along the line of the Via Traiana is likely to be earlier than Trajan.

Although these types of tombs can be found in the second century, the *sepulcreta* prove conclusively that brick-faced concrete was the usual method employed at the time in Rome and her vicinity. Façades of fine brickwork

[130] *CIL*, vol. 15 (1), nos. 272, 421.

[131] *Ibid.*, nos. 71, 267, 454, 485, 1113, 1303.

[132] T. Ashby, *PBSR*, vol. 3, 1906, pp. 104–105; Bagnani, *Campagna*, p. 208; G. Hallam, *JRS*, vol. 21, 1931, pp. 276–282, fig. 29.

[133] The window through which Ashby crawled to view the chamber was a later modification.

[134] An enormous relief of Hercules partially obstructed the passage. See Neuerburg, *Fontane*, p. 66.

[135] T. Ashby and R. Gardner, *PBSR*, vol. 8, 1916, p. 154 with fig. 23.

with exceedingly thin joints are more characteristic, but the use of ordinary bricks continued. Unless there are stamps these can seldom be dated precisely. *Sepulcreta* are of more service to chronology than are individual tombs. As the great burial areas became overcrowded, a complete reorganization from time to time furnishes general limits for the construction below and above the new level. By studying the relation of each tomb to its neighbor, it is possible to establish a relative chronology within these limits. After that, one can sometimes arrive at an approximate date by the use of other well-known aids.

III. OSTIA

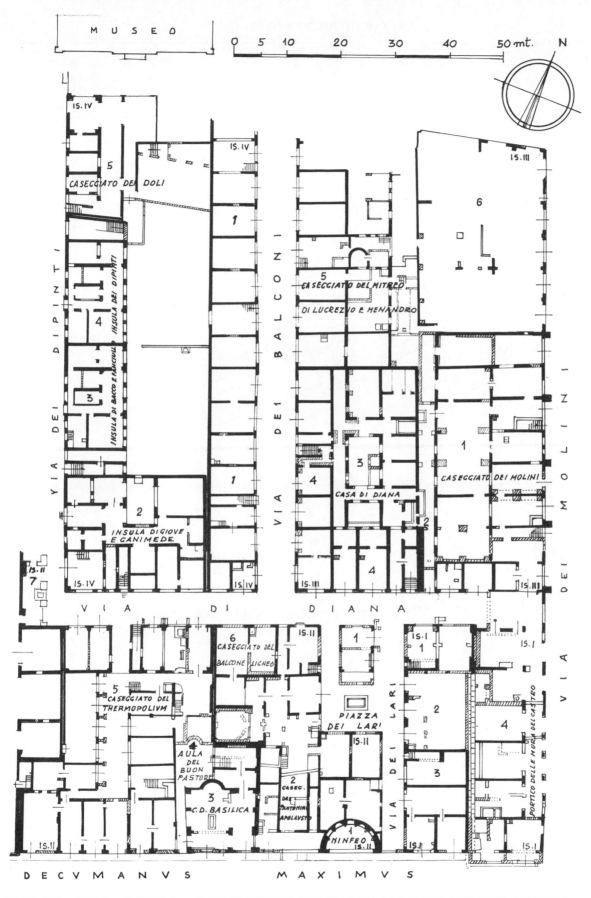

MUSEO

0 5 10 20 30 40 50 mt.

N

IS. IV

5
CASEGGIATO DEI DOLI

IS. IV

1

IS. III

6

VIA DEI DIPINTI

INSULA DEI DIPINTI

INSULA DI BACCO E FANCIULLO

4

3

5
CASEGGIATO DEL MITREO
DI LUCREZIO E MENANDRO

VIA DEI BALCONI

1

VIA DEI BALCONI

1

VIA DEI MOLINI

3

4

CASA DI DIANA

1

CASEGGIATO DEI MOLINI

2
INSULA DI GIOVE
E GANIMEDE

4

2

IS. II

7

IS. IV

IS. IV

IS. III

4

IS. III

VIA   DI   DIANA

6
CASEGGIATO DEL
BALCONE LIGNEO

IS. II

1

IS. I

1

IS. I

5
CASEGGIATO DEL
THERMOPOLIVM

2

2

4

VIA DEI LARI

PIAZZA
DEI LARI

PORTICO DELLE MURA DEL CASTRO

VIA DEI MURA DEL CASTRO

AVLA
DEL
BVON
PASTORE

IS. II

3

3

CASEG.
DEI
ANTONINI
APOLAVSTO

3
C. D. BASILICA

2

1
NINFEO
IS. II

IS. I

IS. I

IS. II

DECVMANVS   MAXIMVS

PLAN XII. OSTIA. REGIO I: AREA BETWEEN DECUMANUS MAXIMUS AND THE MUSEUM

I. Gismondi

I. Gismondi

PLAN XIII. OSTIA. REGIO III: AREA BETWEEN VIA DELLE FOCE AND CARDO DEGLI AURIGHI

PLAN XIV. OSTIA. REGIO V: AREA BETWEEN DECUMANUS MAXIMUS AND SEMITÀ DEI CIPPI   I. Gismondi

TRAJAN (A.D. 98–117)

TRAJAN did not confine his energies to the port which he was having constructed on the other side of the Tiber, but left his mark on every part of Ostia as well. Many dedicatory inscriptions and portrait busts attest the affection in which he was held in the older site at the mouth of the Tiber.[1] It was probably during his reign that the Senate and People of Ostia had the civic pride to encase the Sullan Porta Romana in marble. Public monuments, Baths, and warehouses were the more spectacular contributions to his time, but markets, business establishments, and habitations came in for their full share of attention. Becatti suggests that he may have been responsible for the aqueduct bringing water to the city.[2] Some of the work started by Trajan had to be finished by Hadrian, and it is obviously impossible to distinguish late Trajanic masonry from early Hadrianic.

Among the monuments, a temple-like public building (I, 9, 4) was constructed in place of an edifice in *opus reticulatum* at the west of the smaller of the two tufa temples opposite the Temple of Roma and Augustus.[3] Scholars have assumed that it was the Curia largely because no other structure seems to qualify as well.[4] It was manifestly erected before the early Hadrianic buildings which fill the rest of the block and is certainly not later than the time of Trajan; it may possibly be Flavian. It consisted originally of a square hall (11.7 m. × 11.7 m.) with an open passage on each side and a pronaos on a high podium with six granite columns between pilasters with semi-columns at the ends. The walls were faced with triangular bricks (26–28 cm. × 3.7–4 cm.) made from reddish yellow to brick-red *besales* which were often speckled with pozzolana. Three rectangular niches stood in each wall. The official report mentions windows above them, but no trace of any such remains today. Five pilasters decorating the outside of the wall bore no structural relation to the niches within. The outer west wall belongs to the next building period. The floor was paved with oblongs of bigio outlined in giallo antico. Enough remains to show that the walls had a revetment or at any rate a dado of polychrome marble. Podium, pavement, and walls of the pronaos were all covered with white marble.

The Basilica (I, 11, 5)[5] on the opposite side of the Decumanus obviously belongs to the same building period. It was a colonnaded hall differing from others of its class in being open on two sides. To the Decumanus it presented an outer colonnade with a tetrastyle porch between lateral stairways, and to the Forum, two colonnades. The outer columns supported arches; the inner columns of bigio with white Corinthian capitals probably upheld a second order. The brickwork of the south and west walls, unbroken by bonding courses or relieving arches, resembles closely that in the Curia (?). The floor was paved with the same marbles, though the pattern was large squares of bigio outlined in giallo on a gray field. Traces of a marble wall revetment appear here also. There was a brick-faced tribunal near the south end of the hall. The architectural decoration led to the ascription of the monument to the time of the Antonines, but there would seem to be no reason why the carving should not have been somewhat later than the building it adorned. Five doorways in the west wall gave access to a piazza paved in

[1] Becatti, *Sc. di O.* I, p. 123.

[2] *CIL*, vol. 14, Suppl., no. 4326; Becatti, *loc. cit.*

[3] Becatti, *op. cit.*, pp. 123–124. For the complete layout of Ostia, see Plan XVI at the back of this book.

[4] G. Calza, *Not. sc.*, 1923, pp. 185–187. The form is not typical. Meiggs, *Ostia*, pp. 219–220, concludes that it was the headquarters of the *seviri Augustales* and of Domitianic date.

[5] Becatti, *loc. cit.*; idem, *Bull. Com.*, vol. 71, 1943–1945, pp. 38–46; Crema, p. 371, fig. 685. Meiggs, *Ostia*, p. 66, implies that it is Domitianic, since it is clearly contemporary with the "Curia."

marble and enclosed in a marble colonnade which was probably contemporaneous with the Basilica. Although it was destroyed when the Tempio Rotondo was built, significant remains were uncovered at a lower level in recent excavations. A row of shops (I, 10, 3) on the inner pomerial strip faced this open square on the west. The walls were placed with reference to the travertine piers on an earlier double colonnade possibly left from the Tiberian systematization of the area. The walls were faced with rather wide (4–5 cm.) triangular bricks, light in color, such as are occasionally found in Trajanic work in Ostia. Bonding courses and relieving arches were not necessary since there was to be no upper story to cause additional weight. Passing mention may be made at this point of a row of shops (I, 8, 5) facing a porticus erected on the outer pomerial strip farther to the north fronting Via Epagathiana, since brick stamps show that it had a Trajanic phase. Tufa bases of piers and at wall ends, along with some reticulate at a low level, prove that it was not the first structure at the site. The brick-faced back wall was apparently substituted for the Castrum wall when the other side was built up at a later date fronting Via del Larario. Consequently, the only Trajanic masonry preserved is the brick and reticulate work of some of the partition walls.

Another example of a growing feeling that the port of Rome should have a beauty commensurate with the city which it served may be seen at the southwest of the Temple of Roma and Augustus. An awkward change in orientation at that point, caused by the acute angle between the Cardo Maximus and the pomerial street, Via del Tempio Rotondo, was cleverly masked by a nymphaeum with niches (IV, 4, 5),[6] which took the orientation of neither. Its walls were of brick-faced concrete concealed by a revetment of white marble. The fountain has been rebuilt almost completely in modern times, but what little remains of the original brickwork resembles Trajanic work in the vicinity. The two halls at the east of the temple may also be Trajanic. The workmanship is, however, mediocre. Two lots of triangular bricks were used, one a bright brick-red, the other a light buff. Both kinds were approximately 4 cm. thick, and the mortar joints were about 2 cm. wide. The mortar was black and white, but the pozzolana in its composition was obviously unsifted as there are large inclusions. The mediocre work would have been concealed by marble or plaster in the finished edifice.

The restoration of the Sacred Area of the Republican Temples begun by Domitian[7] was continued by Trajan.[8] At the west, the low level was raised to the height of the podium of the Temple of Hercules (I, 15, 5). The cella walls were rebuilt[9] in brick-faced concrete with large insets of reticulate and stuccoed over to look like ashlar masonry in marble. They are not preserved high enough to show conclusively whether the brick and reticulate were interlocked in the usual manner. A public building of some sort (I, 15, 1) which had been fitted into the irregular space between the Tempio d'Ercole and the passage area from Via del Tempio d'Ercole and Via Epagathiana, had to be adapted to the new level. The construction changes from reticulate with tufa blocks to brick with reticulate insets at the east wall of the second of the four chambers. Whereas the higher level was maintained along the northern passage way, two rooms were constructed at

[6] Becatti, *op. cit.*, p. 124; Neuerburg, *Fontane*, pp. 55, 83, 85, 191 (no. 129), fig. 89; Crema, p. 433.

[7] Blake, RC II, p. 133.

[8] See Bloch, *Sc. di O.* I, pp. 218–219.

[9] Becatti, *Sc. di O.* I, p. 126.

[10] Becatti, *op. cit.*, p. 234.

[11] Gismondi, *Sc. di O.* I, p. 208, n. 6.

[12] Further excavations might cast more light on this subject.

the lower level which were accessible from the Area Sacra at the north of the pronaos. The walls of these were faced with reticulate insets in a brick frame. The bricks were broken tiles, 4–4.5 cm. thick, and the mortar joints were about 1.5 cm. wide. The Aula delle Are Repubblicane (I, 15, 3)[10] at the east of the Area seems also to have been raised to the same level. The original part of the new walls shows a facing of brick and reticulate similar to that in the Temple of Hercules. Brick stamps confirm the date of the first two edifices; and the third was apparently earlier than the Trajanic Terme di Buticosus which it adjoins.

By the beginning of the second century, bathing facilities proved to be quite inadequate for the growing population. During the reign of Trajan no less than five Baths were added or at any rate begun. As those already in existence served the eastern part, the new ones were distributed in the western part of the city. Since, with one exception, the builders had to reckon with earlier construction at the site, the Baths do not follow any standard plan.

In a block where Trajanic construction is omnipresent, the Terme della Basilica (III, 1, 3) alone exhibit brickwork similar to that of the Curia (?).[11] As a Bath it was a makeshift affair. There are underground passages, but the heating arrangements are not clear. Apparently one furnace at any rate was under the floor of the *calidarium*, but no hypocaust piers remain,[12] and a single specimen of hollow wall tubes seems to have served as a drain. Possibly it was stripped in antiquity when some of the late Baths were being erected. In the space to the east, which may have served for a gymnasium, only one isolated structure of uncertain purpose could have been Trajanic originally. This has a door at one end and a pair of slit windows in each of the other walls. It has been more or less rebuilt; and minor alterations appear throughout the entire Bath to further complicate the picture. The façade along the Decumanus is a later addition. The bricks in the original masonry are thick yellow triangles laid with a friable mortar, though the joints were pointed with a finer quality.

The walls defining the area appear to be earlier than the Terme delle Sei Colonne (IV, 5, 10–11) which were installed within them. The first two shops from the west with the narrow corridor between them belong to the same period as the west wall of the area. Rooms behind them were obviously diverted from their original purpose to the service of the Bath. The shops in front of the eastern unit show practically the same type of masonry as those to the west and may be contemporaneous. They are deeper than the others and have intermediate pilasters in the lateral walls. The partition walls were faced with reticulate framed in rather thick (4 cm.) bricks—some, fine-grained red ones from broken tiles, others, light-colored triangles from *besales*. The bricks facing the pilasters, on the other hand, are a rich brick-red and coarse-grained of a different quality from the others. Stairs rose between the two units to apartments above the shops. An entrance corridor led to the court with six columns from which the Baths take their modern name. From this the bathers could pass to the various rooms devoted to the relaxation afforded by the ancient Baths. For our purpose, it is necessary to differentiate the Trajanic masonry from later modifications of which there were several. Brick stamps are about equally divided between the end of the first century and the Antonine period. Service corridors in the western part yield stamps of the time of Hadrian.[13] There were other changes in the thin bricks of the Severan epoch, and later still windows and doors were closed in preparation for the installation of a new system of hollow tubes for heating. Trajanic masonry appears in most of the essential walls, though often it gives way to the similar brickwork of the Antonine period. The facing is composed of light-colored bricks (3.5–4 cm. thick), triangles and broken tiles mixed,[14] with mortar joints 1.5–2.5 cm. wide, strengthened by an occasional bonding course. Huge relieving arches of *bipedales* are frequent in the body of the wall.[15] A nearly square room toward the rear had hollow tubes with thicker walls than those employed in later modifications. This room shows the beginning of a cross vault in which *bipedales* were placed on the wooden centering and covered with *besales* before the concrete of the vaulting was laid. If this vaulting is original, it is an early example of a method which became common later. Other traces of vaulting are later, as is evidenced by the small circles stamped on the *besales*.

A small edifice of the time of Julius Caesar or a little later[16] was incorporated in a much larger structure, possibly a Bath (IV, 2, 1), in the Trajanic period.[17] One stamp (*CIL*, vol. 15 (1), 910), still visible in an arch, is ascribable to the early years of the second century.[18] The walls of this phase were faced with triangular bricks[19] varying in color from yellow to brick-red and in thickness from 3.8 to 4.2 cm. Many of them were speckled with pozzolana. One relieving arch was made of thick *bipedales* such as are occasionally found in Trajanic masonry. There were no bonding courses, and relieving arches were employed only where they were absolutely necessary.

East of the Area Sacra dei Templi Repubblicani, the first Baths in the region, Terme di Buticosus (I, 14, 8), were erected in the time of Trajan.[20] Brick stamps give the date of their building as A.D. 112–115.[21] Though the place for them was found in the middle of the block, they could be approached originally from Via della Foce, Via Epagathiana, and a passageway leading through from Via del Tempio d'Ercole. Here the presence of the Tempio Tetrastilo and the Aula delle Are Repubblicane left an *L*-shaped space for the Baths, which originally consisted of six rooms. A raise in level supplied space for the furnaces. Evidently, the contractors had difficulty with the heating arrangements. Hypocausts were remade about the middle of the second century with a liberal re-use of Trajanic tiles. Doorways were blocked and covered with wall tubes. The entrance from the south was walled up apparently so that another furnace could be placed in front of it. Reticulate combined with brick faced most of the outer walls. The rest exhibits a brickwork composed of fine-grained bricks, partly triangles and partly broken tiles,[22] normally about 4 cm. thick. There are occasional bonding courses.[23] Enormous segmental relieving arches of *bipedales* are conspicuous in the caldarium with the two heated pools of a later modification.[24] One arch of *bipedales* protects a full arch of *sesquipedales* (pl. 18, fig. 1). The thickness of the walls suggests that there was a cistern over this room. Such openings as are preserved are covered with lintel arches under relieving arches of *sesquipedales*. The mosaic floors featuring sea monsters belong to the period of

[13] Seven examples of *CIL*, vol. 15 (1), no. 1143, and two later ones on which *Caesaris Aug. N.* seems to be legible (Bloch, *Bolli*, p. 226).

[14] Gismondi, *loc. cit.*, n. 7.

[15] Gismondi, *op. cit.*, p. 201 with fig. 48.

[16] Becatti, *Sc. di O.* I, pp. 108, 127, and Gismondi's plans opposite pp. 114, 122; *cf.* Meiggs, *Ostia*, p. 419.

[17] Becatti, *Sc. di O.* I, p. 217.

[18] Bloch, *Bolli*, p. 79.

[19] Gismondi, *Sc. di O.* I, p. 208, n. 6.

[20] Becatti, *op. cit.*, p. 127.

[21] Bloch, *Sc. di O.* I, p. 218.

[22] Gismondi, *Sc. di O.* I, p. 208, n. 7.

[23] Gismondi, *op. cit.*, p. 198.

[24] Gismondi, *op. cit.*, p. 201.

reorganization at the middle of the second century. A crude mosaic portrait inscribed with the name Epictetus Buticosus, which was inserted in these mosaics at a later time, gives the Baths their modern designation.

The Baths were merely one unit of a larger complex.[25] A porticus extended fronting Via Epagathiana which can be divided into two sections. The first displays piers resting on travertine foundations, which have rather elaborate base moldings of tiles and shafts faced with yellowish red bricks made from fine-grained tiles (3.5–4 cm. thick) united by narrow joints (0.5 cm.); the second which is contiguous has the same base moldings, but they are discontinued at the back as though there had been a masonry barrier. In the first, travertine insets held metal grilles. The brickwork is essentially the same in the two. All these piers probably supported full arches. An ornamental doorway, featuring travertine bases and brick-faced half-columns having base moldings identical with those in the piers, marked the main entrance to the Baths through the southern section. A passageway led to a broad transverse corridor separating the Baths proper from a unit given over to shops and other rooms devoted to the service of the bathers. The inner façade was decorated with niches.[26] Two flights of travertine steps led from the passage and corridor respectively to a common landing resting on a barrel vault faced with *sesquipedales*. The walls were of a more ordinary brickwork than the piers, but the bricks were fairly fine-grained and about 4 cm. thick. Both broken tiles and triangles were used. Bonding courses occur, and apertures were covered in one case with a full arch of *bipedales*; in another, with a lintel arch of *sesquipedales*. Thresholds and corbels to support mezzanine floors were of travertine. Remains of an earlier edifice with walls faced in reticulate exist beneath the floor.

A common wall separated I, 14, 8 from I, 14, 7 to the north of it. The porticus fronting Via Epagathiana was continued in a slightly different form, but a *bipedalis* specially cut to accommodate a drain between the contiguous piers proves that the two were contemporaneous. In the northern porticus the piers rested on re-used (?) travertine blocks, each carved with a frame as for an inscription. Otherwise, the piers were practically identical with those of the units to the south. The porticus probably extended along the north side as well. It had the usual row of shops opening onto the porticus and a single flight of steps on the east side leading directly to apartments above. The interior has not been wholly excavated, but yellow and orange-red bricks, mostly triangles 3.5 cm. thick, faced the outside walls; brick neatly interlocked with reticulate faced the partitions. There are some bonding courses in the brickwork; and lintel arches, both straight and slightly arched, covered apertures. A more detailed analysis must await the complete excavation of the site. Brick stamps indicate that it was, in general, a little later though still within the period.[27] In any case, the block is definitely a forerunner of the type of apartment houses which became common under Hadrian.

The unit to the north of the Baths containing an obviously later pool has been built over until it is difficult to deduce the original form. What remains looks as if the ground floor was given over almost entirely to shops. A flight of steps at its northern extremity led directly from the porticus to

[25] Bloch, *Sc. di O.* I, p. 218.

[26] These were later concealed by piers.

[27] Bloch, *loc. cit.*

rooms above. These steps are supported by an oblique lintel arch of *sesqui-pedales*. The construction is analogous to that of the southern section.

West of this and directly north of the Baths there was a nearly square hall (I, 14, 4) amply supplied with doors and windows. Only its north wall has the same orientation as the rest of the complex. It was probably an independent structure, but the original brickwork would seem to me Trajanic. It was large enough to house a four-room dwelling at a later period.

Two brick stamps found in the area, though not *in situ*,[28] first suggested that Trajan was responsible for founding the Terme di Porta Marina (IV, 10, 1). They have not been entirely excavated and are sufficiently full of loose stones, thistles, and brambles to make investigation uncomfortable if not indeed hazardous. Even a cursory examination shows that most of the essential walls were faced with a variety of light yellow brick often found in Trajanic masonry at Ostia. The Baths were considerably modified under the Severans. A more detailed analysis must await complete excavation.

More storage space for grain was needed at Ostia than was afforded by the Claudian *horrea*, and a number were built in the time of Trajan. Since no two exhibit the same type of construction, each was probably entrusted to a different contractor. In any case, a standard procedure had not yet been established. Space for at least three new ones was found near the mouth of the Tiber. Others may lie in the unexcavated sections between them. Some walls of one of these near Tor Boacciana have yielded stamps of the period. Of another, only the heavily buttressed east wall with an inner row of storage chambers and a part of the south wall are visible behind the Serapeum. Stamps[29] indicate that these *horrea* belong in the years ca. A.D. 112–117. The partition walls were faced with a combination of brick and reticulate.

The third warehouse (I, 19, 4) and its dependencies on the other side of Via della Foce can all be presented in more detail. A little temple (I, 19, 2) standing at the southwest corner of the area was rebuilt at a higher level to serve as the collegiate temple of the grain-measurers. Its orientation with the points of the compass was not brought into conformity with the adjacent *horrea* which were aligned with the Tiber. The reticulate facing of the lower part of the podium is certainly earlier than the time of Trajan; the brick facing above it rests on a bonding course of yellow tiles which is identical with that which marks the beginning of the cella wall. The brick facing in the upper part of the podium is less careful than that of the cella, which resembles that of the *horrea* and shows one Trajanic stamp[30] at the top of the extant part of the west wall. This second phase of the temple presents no peculiarities. It consisted of a nearly square cella with a deep tetrastyle porch approached by a flight of five travertine steps. The irregular space caused by the two different orientations was utilized for a station of the grain-measurers.[31] The brick-faced outer wall showed the same type of masonry as the *horrea* and produced a number of the same stamps.[32] In its earliest state, the station probably consisted merely of piers and angle piers against the outer walls to support a roof over the measures. The inner part was entirely remade in the Severan age when it was paved with the black-and-white mosaic depicting the grain-measurers at work. An insignifi-

[28] Bloch, *op. cit.*, p. 227. See also Meiggs, *Ostia*, pp. 407–409.

[29] Bloch, *AJA*, vol. 63, 1959, p. 227.

[30] Bloch, *Suppl.*, no. 335.

[31] Calza, *Nuovi Scavi*, p. 11; Becatti, *Sc. di O.* I, p. 125.

[32] Bloch, *Sc. di O.* I, p. 219.

cant little edifice of two or three rooms (I, 19, 1) on the other side of the tempietto was probably also Trajanic. Brick and reticulate faced its walls.

The Horrea dei Mensores (I, 19, 4) were well planned. One or two courses of re-used (?) tufa blocks form the foundation of the perimetric walls. The façade fronting Via della Foce exhibits a fine masonry of brick-red broken tiles. It was pierced near each extremity by an ornamental doorway having pilasters faced with the same type of brick united by narrower joints. There are remains of one base molding in cut tiles. On three sides, a passageway paved with herringbone brick separated the outer walls from the *horrea* proper. The perimetric wall was well supplied with secondary entrances. One at the northwest corner is preserved up to the impost and displays a rounded stringcourse near the top as in many Hadrianic doorways. The merest traces are left of the arcades flanking the central area. Barely enough is preserved of the single row of chambers on the east to show that, although there were secondary entrances from the alley at the side to two wide chambers, all the rooms were served by broad openings from the court. In the western unit, a continuous wall originally divided the storage rooms on the west from those facing the court. The wider chambers had transverse walls presumably to help support the upper floor. A wide ramp[33] at the southeast corner gave access to storage space above. At the north, the central court ended in a wall in which there are two openings. Unfortunately, this northern end has not been excavated except for a flight of steps and two rooms at the northwest corner which are entirely cut off from the rest. It would have been a suitable place for apartments facing the Tiber. The *horrea* present a homogeneous construction of brick alone or brick with insets of reticulate. The bricks are light reddish brown, 3.5–4 cm. thick, and of the fine texture that bespeaks the use of broken tile.[34] *Bipedales* appear at the base of the walls, but there are no bonding courses or relieving arches. The walls are not preserved high enough to show how the apertures were covered.

Another large warehouse (V, 11, 8), on which the name Horrea dell' Artemide was imposed because of a statue found in the area, was erected to the west of the Claudian Horrea di Hortensius. Brick stamps establish the date of these *horrea*,[35] the construction of which might appear somewhat earlier. In general, it was orientated with the Decumanus, but its east wall follows the irregular line of the earlier warehouse, from which it is separated by an intercalary space. This narrow corridor furnishes a secondary entrance. Remains of an earlier edifice are visible beneath the central court,[36] and the arcade in front is definitely a later modification of the *horrea*. Although insets of reticulate in a frame of brickwork face the walls toward the court, reticulate work alone resting on a base of brickwork accounts for the rest of the walls. Only occasionally is the expanse of reticulate broken by a band of brick or a vertical inset. Pilasters seem to serve as buttresses in the center of the rear wall of the five wider chambers at the south end of the east side, but there is no indication that there was ever an upper floor. The bricks used throughout are the thick triangles occasionally found in the Trajanic work in Ostia.

Each of these *horrea* had a large central court suitable for the heavy traffic in grain. A smaller warehouse on the Cardo degli Aurighi (III, 2, 6) with

[33] The few steps preserved belong to a later modification.

[34] Gismondi, *Sc. di O.* I, p. 208, n. 5.

[35] Gismondi (*op. cit.*, p. 199) gives Bloch, *Suppl.*, no. 252, as authority.

[36] Becatti, *Sc. di O.* I, p. 125.

a smaller court may have been used for the storage and possibly the sale of a commodity more costly than grain. Both the environment and the single brick stamp[37] leave no room for doubt that they were also Trajanic, though the construction resembles that of an earlier epoch.[38] The façade exhibits a conglomeration of types of masonry which shows clearly that methods of building were still far from standardized in the time of Trajan, at least in Ostia. An ornamental doorway (pl. 18, fig. 2) of medium-fine workmanship stood in the center. It consisted of a pediment supported by three-quarter columns framing the actual entrance, which had a sill of travertine, side walls of brick dovetailed into the reticulate of the wall facing, and a lintel of "upright" *bipedales*. The general effect is rather heavy and clumsy. The bricks used here are about 3 cm. thick as opposed to those employed in the rest of the edifice which vary from 3 to 4 cm. Brickwork forms a band at the bottom of the wall and above the mezzanine level. There is, however, no indication that there was a mezzanine floor. The one side doorway has a slightly curved lintel arch of tufa quoins which breaks into the brick dovetailing in awkward fashion. Both bricks and tufa blocks were used in framing the slit windows near the top of the wall. Adjacent buildings imposed a certain irregularity of plan, but the warehouse consisted in general of two wings with three chambers on each side of the corridor. An alcove opposite the door masked somewhat the irregularity. Except for the brick courses on the inside of the façade, the perimetric walls were lined with reticulate reinforced by tufa quoins at every partition wall. The inner façades display reticulate insets in a frame of tufa blocks. Projections of the walls safeguard the doorways. Beams were inserted in the masonry to hold fastenings, and beams served as lintels with small windows above them. The partitions were faced with shapeless angular pieces of tufa. There is no indication how the rooms were covered. The alcove shows some reorganization in brick. A semicircular niche in the center exhibits a simple base molding between travertine corbels presumably to support columns for a miniature pediment. The court was paved with herringbone brick. An inner stairway gave access to an upper story over the front part of the edifice. A door, later blocked, permitted entrance from the west. Other slight modifications in brick are easily discernible on the inside.

The same mixed masonry appears in a business establishment in an entirely different part of the city (V, 3, 2), which is clearly earlier than the Hadrianic structures on each side. It consisted of a passageway out from Via della Casa del Pozzo to via delle Ermette with two rooms opening out of it on each side. Wide openings toward the streets prove that three of these were shops; a small door and window beside it may indicate that the fourth room served a different purpose. There were no stairs to an upper story. The essential masonry was of reticulate work combined with blockwork, but bricks mark the transition from the smaller reticulate work of an earlier structure at a lower level, appear with the blocks in some of the quoining, and form an ornamental doorway of rather ordinary workmanship toward the road on the west. The masonry is not preserved high enough to show how the entablature was treated. Presumably, the entrance on the opposite façade was similar, but the present gateway is almost entirely modern. The

[37] Bloch, *Sc. di O.* I, p. 222.

[38] Becatti, *op. cit.*, p. 125.

south wall displays brick dovetailing into the reticulate at the partition and at the ends; the north wall shows considerable patching at different periods. Doorways in the lateral walls were apparently covered with wooden lintels.

A small edifice of no particular importance (III, 16, 1) presented a corner shop and one other room to the Cardo degli Aurighi; a shop and a long narrow room faced Via di Annio. There may have been wooden stairs to a terrace where masonry steps were inserted later, but there is no positive indication of an upper story in the original structure. It was earlier than the late Trajanic or early Hadrianic market which adjoins it on the northwest. Its walls were faced with a mediocre reticulate carelessly interlocked with brick, but there was one buttress in blockwork to link it with the mixed masonry found in a few other Trajanic buildings. The edifice shows considerable remodeling.

Besides the great central market (IV, 5, 2), there was from early times a market (III, 1, 7) opposite the entrance to the Area Sacra dei Templi Repubblicani. This was completely reorganized under Trajan. It consisted of a row of shops on each side of a broad passage. The northwestern row was entirely rebuilt; the southwestern row was lengthened with a space taken from an earlier edifice; rooms were added at the southwest facing a street which was closed when the Christian Basilica was built. The Trajanic masonry shows various combinations of brick and reticulate. For example, partition walls are faced, sometimes with reticulate alone, sometimes with reticulate reinforced by bands of brick, and sometimes with reticulate insets in brick frames. Fine-grained red bricks from broken tiles predominate, most of which fall within the range 3.5–4 cm. in thickness. There were neither bonding courses nor relieving arches. Since there was no upper story, the walls did not need special reinforcement. The central area was paved with herringbone brick. One shop has a pavement of *bipedales*, which may or may not be original. Beam holes at the pavement level in another probably indicate that there was a wooden floor with an air space under it. Slits lined with *besales* in the back wall of two shops may have been either air shafts or chutes. The walls are not preserved high enough to show how the openings were topped or what type of ceiling was employed. There were minor alterations later.

A long row of shops (III, 9, 26), little more than half excavated, differs from the others in being the ground floor of an apartment house which could conceivably have had three or four stories. Only one staircase of the original construction remains but there may have been another not as yet uncovered. There was a porticus in front along the Cardo degli Aurighi. Enough Trajanic stamps were found *in situ* to date the edifice.[39] The masonry is typically late Trajanic. Piers and wall ends facing the porticus show fine-grained red bricks, 3.5–4 cm. thick, made from broken tiles, though some were triangular in shape. The mortar joints were 1.5–2 cm. wide and contained a little red pozzolana in addition to the black of its composition. Bricks also lined the staircase, though the outer facing of each wall was of the same type of reticulate work interlocked with brick as the other partition walls. In these walls dovetailing occurred only at the ends. The rear wall on the outside shows a series of neat reticulate insets with the brick inter-

[39] Bloch, *Sc. di O.* I, p. 223.

locking, showing the position of the partition walls. Each shop had a back door, but the walls are not preserved high enough to show how the openings were covered. The next unit to the southeast (III, 9, 25) was a similar type of edifice fitted into a space made irregular by a bend in the Cardo. Although travertine columns from an earlier porticus were utilized at the southeast end, there were brick-faced piers like those in the unit to the northwest in proximity to it. The brickwork at this end was identical with that in III, 9, 26; and some similar masonry appears at the other end where the wall is manifestly earlier than that of the Hadrianic structure which adjoins it. All the rest is rather mediocre brickwork. There were no bonding courses. Each shop had a rear door, and one of these still shows a slightly curved lintel arch of *bipedales*. Brick stamps confirm the date of this structure also.[40]

The edifices thus far described fulfilled obvious needs of the growing city and are comparatively easy to identify and date. The more or less ambitious attempts of private contractors to supply mercantile establishments, business blocks, and living quarters are equally important for a study of ancient methods of construction. Individual initiative had free reign before the standardization marking the systematization of large areas of the city under Hadrian. Except where brick stamps are present, the chronology of this private construction depends largely on the structural environment and a careful analysis of the masonry. In general, the official dating has been found reasonable, even when unproven.

The area bounded by the Via della Foce, the Decumanus, the Cardo degli Aurighi, and the Tiber is full of the remains of this kind of Trajanic enterprise. The structures fronting Via della Foce are the most outstanding. A narrow strip (III, 1, 8), later filled with Hadrianic construction,[41] separated the market (III, 1, 7) already described from an important Trajanic development.[42] A long row of Hadrianic shops (III, 1, 14)[43] completed the Trajanic systematization of a large area (III, 1, 9) into a hollow square. The dating depends largely on the relation to other structures in the vicinity. The formal entrance was between two chambers (shops ?) at the west corner. A large latrine at the south angle proves that many men must have been employed in whatever activity was carried on in the long narrow halls on each of the three sides. The one on the southeast side was the most symmetrical. A wide entrance in the center, later buried under a shrine of some sort,[44] and a threefold entrance in the center of each half gave access from the court. The walls are not sufficiently preserved to show whether there were windows to light the interior or how the doorways were covered. Its north wall abutted a business establishment of five rooms (III, 1, 15) at the east corner of the area. The other two halls were similar but modified to suit local conditions. The one at the northwest abutted a spacious hall (III, 1, 10). The doorway between the two belongs to a later modification. The hall was amply lighted by windows toward the court. Piers down the center helped to support the roof which may well have been wooden. An apartment house toward the northeast end of the square (III, 1, 12 and 13) was divided into two halves by a blank wall. Three doorways in each of the long outer walls indicate that the rooms could be apportioned in different ways, though four rooms and a latrine were apparently the normal plan. There never was an upper

[40] Bloch, *loc. cit.*

[41] See below, p. 180.

[42] Becatti, *op. cit.*, p. 126.

[43] See below, p. 180.

[44] The masonry is clearly an addition, but the neat dovetailing of brick and reticulate could even be Trajanic. It is probably Hadrianic, however.

story. The apartment house in front of this (III, 1, 11) was a later addition. The perimetric walls of the development were faced with reticulate strengthened by bands of red and yellow bricks; the walls toward the court, with the same combination reinforced by quoins of block as well as brick; the partition walls, with poor *opus incertum*.[45] The business establishment and the apartment house in the center show the same combination of blocks and bricks with reticulate, whereas the hall shows a more regular use of block-and-brick quoins dovetailed into the reticulate work (pl. 19, fig. 4: III, 1, 10).[46] Only two relieving arches appear in the whole complex and these protect obviously some weakness in the foundation. Slightly curved lintel arches of *bipedales* capped such apertures as are preserved. Once again we are dealing with structures having no upper story.

Via della Calcara separated this development from an imposing structure which was partly incorporated in the Hadrianic Caseggiato del Serapide (III, 10, 3) and the Terme dei Sette Sapienti (III, 10, 2).[47] It contained the tavern with the paintings that gave the Baths their modern name. Remains of its brick and reticulate work are visible within these structures, among which a relieving arch of thick (6 cm.) *bipedales* along the later stairs is worthy of note, but the remains of the façade along Via della Calcara (pl. 19, fig. 2) have more interest for a study of ancient construction.[48] Two doorways, one much wider than the other, are covered with lintel arches of *bipedales*. At the right, reticulate insets in a brick frame have been substituted for the brickwork of the rest of the extant part of the façade. Four or five rows of brick form a continuous band over the lintel arches. The relieving arch over the wider opening was placed to divert the weight to the center of each side wall with the result that the window over the door is not in the center. The window has its own lintel under the relieving arch and the usual jambs of brick interlocking with the reticulate of the rest of the curtain filling the space under the arch. Only a complete lack of plan or some radical change at the last minute can account for the irregularities over the narrower doorway. Space was lacking to bring the relieving arch down to the brick band over the lintel. Consequently, it rests directly on the reticulate curtain extending up to a smaller and higher window, the lintel of which reaches the relieving arch. The sides show the same interlocking of brick and reticulate as over the other doorway, but there is no band of brick beneath the sill. To add to the irregularity, an awkward bit of interlocking appears on the left-hand side under the foot of the relieving arch. Traces of a façade fronting Via della Foce also came to light; and there is evidence that there was an Augustan building at the site before this. The Trajanic date of the edifice under consideration is attested by brick stamps.[49]

A great housing development arose to the west of the edifice just described, consisting of four or possibly five units.[50] In these days of world-wide housing shortage, ancient attempts to solve the same problem have an interest transcending their structural importance. Two units (III, 11 and 15)[51] faced Via della Foce. The first one (No. 11) contained three large shops with a small apartment of three rooms behind them and a flight of steps (of which only the threshold is preserved) leading to either an upper story or a terrace.

[45] Russell Meiggs aptly dubs this *opus informe*.

[46] The combination is apt to be Antonine elsewhere.

[47] Becatti, *Sc. di O.* I, p. 126; Crema, pp. 458, 482, fig. 590.

[48] Gismondi, *Sc. di O.* I, p. 197, fig. 47.

[49] Bloch, *Sc. di O.* I, p. 223; *idem*, *Bolli*, p. 202.

[50] Becatti, *op. cit.*, pp. 125–126; Crema, p. 453.

[51] These are the numbers of the official map.

The second (No. 15) consisted merely of four shops—two facing the main street, two the street parallel to it. The main façades of these two were of brickwork; the rest of the masonry, including the outer faces of the side walls, show insets of reticulate in a brick frame. In No. 11, the reticulate was framed by brick without interlocking; in the other it is neatly dovetailed into the brick frame. The bricks came from broken tiles (mostly 4 cm. thick). The two units (III, 12 and 13) behind 11 are by far the most interesting: the Casette-Tipo.[52] A paved street separated them, and each unit held two apartments with a space for stairs between them. Each apartment had a fair-sized corner room, a short corridor parallel to the outside wall leading through a narrow passage to a small kitchen and latrine, and three small rooms opening off from the corridor. Not enough remains to show how the windows were treated. Since the walls are too narrow to have supported an upper story, the staircases probably housed wooden steps to a mezzanine floor or more likely a terrace. The outer walls (pl. 19, fig. 3) show panels of careless reticulate framed in brick without dovetailing, with occasional bands of brick to serve as a bonding member. The inside of the walls and the partitions were faced with small stone work too crude to be called opus incertum. Across Via Sud delle Casette Tipo there exists a row of shops (III, 10, 4) which belonged to the same development. Little more than the rear wall, thresholds, and the beginning of partition walls is preserved today, but that little is sufficient to show the type of masonry. Such were the Casette-Tipo.

The next house to the west (III, 16, 5) also shows the same type of construction and may have been built at the same time. It was fitted into an awkward space left over by a change in direction of Via della Foce. The ground floor was given over to shops, three facing on Via della Foce and one on an alley at the east, but a narrow entrance from the alley led to a small apartment of little more than a single room, though it may have been somewhat larger before the next to the west was constructed. Outside stairs from Via della Foce led to upper apartments.

The construction along the Decumanus has less of interest to offer. Beyond a corner edifice of a later epoch, four shops (III, 1, 2)[53] show some brickwork which is apparently Trajanic. They have, however, been renovated too many times to have much importance for a study of this kind. The façade of the Terme della Basilica, as we have seen, was later. West of this, two units, one behind the other (III, 1, 5), presented two shops to the Decumanus and a number to a street at right angles to it which was later abandoned. The farther end was entirely rebuilt so that one cannot be sure of the original plan. The ground floor of the first unit was made up entirely of shops except for a stairway which rose from an alley between the two units. The shops along the Decumanus belong to a later restoration. What little remains of the original masonry of the edifice is an ordinary brick-faced concrete without bonding courses or relieving arches. A gateway topped with a fine arch of bipedales led from the alley to the area at the southwest. Outside stairs for the next unit rose from the side street, and a narrow entrance corridor led to what may have been a small apartment for a caretaker.[54] Shops filled the rest of the ground floor. The walls were faced with the usual combination

[52] Meiggs, Ostia, pp. 134, 242, 257, plan 245; Crema, p. 453.

[53] There are Augustan shops underneath.

[54] These stairs do not show on the maps and plans in Sc. di O. I, dated 1950 (publ. 1953). The Pianta Generale of 1949 (Arch. I. Gismondi, Dis. O. Visca) "aggiornata al 1961, Dis. G. Pascolini" shows stairs in the transverse corridor closed by the Constantinian basilica wall just where the apse begins, this being the corridor to the presumed caretaker's quarters; these stairs are later and do not concern us here. Miss Blake's notes include two color-coded plans, one of which shows the basilica and the stairs in that blocked corridor. The other shows only the Antonine layout with no stairs in the corridor; instead, outside stairs in the northwest corner of the shop just east of the corridor. There is an entry from the shop interior to the area under these outside stairs (a latrine?). These stairs also were blocked by the wall of the basilica. See above, p. vii.—J.D.B.

55 Gismondi, *Sc. di O.* I, p. 208, n. 7.

56 Becatti, *Sc. di O.* I, p. 127.

57 The last section on the left faced the area where the Schola del Traiano was built but had a means of access from the *angiportus*.

58 Gismondi, *op. cit.*, p. 208, n. 7.

59 *Ibid.*, p. 200.

of brick and reticulate interlocked. The rear wall of the next long narrow area (III, 2, 1) and the part of the east wall adjacent to it are apparently Trajanic; the west wall bounded a mercantile establishment (III, 2, 4). Here a Trajanic stamp was found. Remains of the Trajanic shops in front can be seen under those of a higher level. These had walls of reticulate work framed in fine-grained red bricks made from broken tiles. Walls almost certainly Trajanic under the Tempio dei Fabri Navales (III, 2, 2) show a mixture of broken tiles and bricks in the facing.[55] In both these areas, the Trajanic buildings at a lower level were covered by later structures. The shop house with the porticus in front is later (III, 2, 3).

Outside the Porta Marina on the northwest side of the Decumanus, walls faced with reticulate and brick (III, 7, 6 and 7) are clearly earlier than what appears to be a Hadrianic modification. The construction apparently continued into the unexcavated section at the west. Until the whole site is uncovered, this brief notice must suffice.

In addition to the Terme delle Sei Colonne (IV, 5, 10–11) there is only one important Trajanic structure (IV, 5, 18) on the southeast side of the Decumanus. Buildings of the first half of the first century before Christ were razed to make room for a shopping center with an *angiportus*.[56] The three shops facing the Decumanus with their rear rooms followed a familiar pattern. Substantial travertine insets made provision for a beam which secured the alley at night. Space was taken from the rear shop nearest to the alley for a staircase carried on a barrel vault between side walls to give access to apartments above the frontal shops. The *angiportus* was widened somewhat at the center to form a sort of court for a number of shops.[57] Arches of fine yellow *bipedales* marked the entrance and exit from this central section. The shops facing inward were each supplied with a window at the side of the doorway, hence the modern name Caseggiato delle Taberne Finestrate (pl. 19, fig. 1). Many of the windows were blocked with reticulate work later. There is no uniformity in the method of covering the apertures. Beams were used over the wider openings; low segmental arches were preferred for the others, but full voussoir arches and lintel arches of tile occur. In three or four instances, a segmental relieving arch apparently drew together a doorway with a wooden lintel and a side window extending to the end of the arch. The effect was not pleasing and the arrangement was seldom, if ever, repeated. Small windows with slightly curved lintel arches gave light to the mezzanines. A side door from Vico Cieco led into the central area, to a latrine under the stairs, and the stairs serving apartments above the southern part of the structure. South of the central court on the east side of the alley, four shops faced eastward. Only one had direct communication with the *angiportus*. A many-windowed hall, which was modified later, occupied the space opposite them. The walls were faced with the usual Trajanic mixture of broken tiles and triangles,[58] varying in color from yellow to light red. There were practically no bonding courses[59] and no relieving arches except over apertures. This structure possesses the only Trajanic vaults extant in Ostia. Pieces of tufa about double the size of a fist were laid in horizontal rows on a wooden centering, and mortar was poured over them to make either barrel or cross vaults. Holes in the walls indicate that the mezzanine floor under the vaulting was supported by beams. This complex furnishes another indication that experimentation was still the order of the day at Ostia.

As we have seen, the beginning of the lower section of the Cardo Maximus was masked by an ornamental fountain probably in the time of Trajan, but except for the Terme del Faro (IV, 2, 1), which was greatly modified in later times, no Trajanic masonry is found along the west side of the street. The excavated part of the area between the Decumanus and the Cardo has, however, yielded one group of buildings (IV, 2, 9–10–11) adjudged Trajanic in the official report.[60] They form the southwestern boundary of a large inner court which could be approached through a long wide passage from the Cardo or a shorter and narrower one from Via della Caupona. An earlier wall faced with reticulate defined the area on the southwest and served as a sustaining wall for a higher level within. In all three edifices, traces can be found of the wide bricks which were in use in the time of Trajan; but only a minute analysis, too detailed for a study of this kind, could separate the Trajanic masonry from the many modifications. The southernmost was utilized for the Mitreo degli Animali at a later period.[61]

A little Trajanic work is visible on the east side of the Cardo Maximus. Some shops of the first century of the Christian era fronted by *opus quadratum* (I, 13, 3) were rebuilt at a higher level in masonry displaying insets of reticulate framed in bricks made from broken tiles. The structure was converted into a *fullonica* later. South of the *fullonica*, a row of travertine columns was incorporated in a large milling establishment (I, 13, 4) which extended straight across the block with shops fronting on Semità dei Cippi as well as the Cardo. Piers probably supported a wooden roof over the central section. The main walls were, for the most part, faced with reticulate combined with fine-grained red bricks made from broken tiles. There was interlocking at the corners; but in some walls a single course of *sesquipedales* broke the long panels of reticulate; in others, three rows served the same purpose. The piers, on the other hand, exhibit a facing of lighter colored bricks made from *besales*, some triangular and some rectangular to breakjoint at the corners besides the *bipedales* used as bonders. Block-and-brick work betrays a later modification.

The increasing importance of Semità dei Cippi led to the almost complete reconstruction at a higher level of the edifice between Via della Fortuna Annonaria and the passage north of the great Claudian *horrea* (V, 1, 2). The official report ascribes this rebuilding to the time of Trajan, largely no doubt from the traces of construction faced with yellow triangles or reticulate interlocked with the same which appear throughout the area. This is not the place to enter into a detailed analysis of walls which show modifications of many periods. A narrow shop-house (V, 2, 6) had a porticus in front showing a few rows of yellow brick under the different type of masonry of a later renovation. A shop with a rear room stood on each side of a passage to the area behind. Stairs were later inserted in the passage. The interdependence of the next four units to the south gives a relative chronology within the period. The first (V, 2, 4) was earlier than the next two (V, 2, 2 and 3), which have common walls and appear to be contemporaneous. The

[60] *Sc. di O.* I, fig. 31.

[61] Becatti, *Sc. di O.* II, p. 92.

rear wall of the row of shops (V, 2, 1) facing the Claudian *horrea* blocked doorways of V, 2, 2 and formed the south wall of V, 2, 14, proving that these two units were later still. So much for the chronology. V, 2, 4, which later housed the Domus del Protiro, was probably a block of some pretention with shops in front, living quarters behind, and apartments above; V, 2, 3, a narrow-fronted house with three shops, one behind the other, having apartments above and a long narrow corridor to a court with two rooms opening on to it; V, 2, 2, a long comparatively narrow hall probably open to the sky with a small covered portion at the rear; V, 2, 1, a row of ground-floor shops; V, 2, 14, a smaller hall divided by piers into three parts. Blocks faced the buttress to the rear wall of the last named.

Near the Porta Romana, a Republican edifice with a porticus supported by tufa piers was converted into a shop house, the Caseggiato del Cane Monnus (II, 1, 1), so named from a mosaic picture, of which little has been excavated. Its earliest phase can be ascribed to the Trajanic period on the evidence of seven fragmentary stamps found *in situ* and identified by Bloch as part of *CIL*, vol. 15 (1), 437a. The bricks are mostly yellow triangles. The edifice shows many modifications. Outside the Porta Romana, there is another building faced in part with the same type of yellow triangles, in part with unrelieved reticulate. This too is listed in the official report as Trajanic.

HADRIAN (A.D. 117–138)

Hadrian apparently decided that the only way effectively to prevent frequent interruptions of the work of the busy port from inundations was to raise the entire central part of the city a meter or more. To this end, his engineers did not hesitate to do away with the old. Romanelli has delved under the streets of the imperial city for evidence of the earlier Ostia; and he wisely left one street, Via del Larario, open to show the ancient procedure. First a great sewer was constructed in the middle of the street to canalize the water which had caused the flooding. When the old buildings had been sheared off at the required height, new sidewalks were laid; and the streets filled in. The adjoining space was then ready for new structures. Some areas had already been raised by Trajan, but he was intent on satisfying the requirements of the growing community rather than in remodeling the town. With Hadrian the emphasis was different. The need for more shops, warehouses, apartment houses, and Baths had to be met, but the new construction was so planned as to make the port of Rome reflect the beauty and dignity of the city itself. It is, of course, impossible to tell to what extent Hadrian gave his personal attention to the development of the city, though inscriptions prove that it was not negligible. Two large sections of five or six blocks reveal the work of a single planner. Others, proved by their brick stamps to belong to the same period, show how a block was filled, edifice by edifice, by different builders, whereas yet others were clearly the work of contractors who built for speculation. The prevalence of the use of datable brick stamps permits us to trace the development of the Hadrianic city almost year by year.

Tiberius had given Ostia a new civic center by systematizing the space south of the Decumanus;[1] Hadrian turned his attention to the area at the

[1] See Blake, *RC* II, p. 63; Becatti, *Sc. di O.* I, pp. 115–116.

north of it, destroying the old Cardo, the Old Capitolium, and at least one other temple, and utilizing the space for a new Capitolium on a high podium.[2] Although it was built of brick-faced concrete, it was covered with glistening white marble and dominated the Forum, toward which it presented a façade of six columns of pavonazzetto across the front and two at the sides with a conventional entablature. It was flanked by a porticus on each side. Behind the twenty-one steps that led to the temple proper, the podium contained three barrel-vaulted rooms one behind the other, to which access was given through a relatively narrow doorway at the rear. An enormous relieving arch on the outside (pl. 20, fig. 2) marks the line of the vault of the first chamber. The pavement was of brick in the herringbone pattern. Three series of three slit windows on each side (pl. 21, fig. 2) lighted the three basement rooms. Travertine from earlier buildings supplied the lintels and sills. A tenth window gave light to the space under the stairs. A setback marks the beginning of the cellar walls and once furnished the foundation for marble revetment. In the facing of the podium triangular yellow bricks speckled with red pozzolana predominate over those of light yellowish red bricks and some of a dark red of better quality. They range from 3.5 to 4 cm. in thickness and are joined by layers of mortar 1 to 1.5 cm. wide, which show large inclusions of dark gray volcanic material. The cella walls, on the other hand, were faced with fine-grained red bricks made from tiles.[3] A few show traces of the original flanges of roof tiles. Most are 3.3 to 3.5 cm. in thickness laid with mortar joints about 1 cm. wide. Bonding courses of slightly thicker yellow *bipedales* appear in the podium but do not show up so conspicuously as they do against the red brickwork of the cella walls. Two large relieving arches with a smaller one higher up between them helped to distribute the weight in the lofty back wall at least while the concrete was setting. In the side walls, a small relieving arch at a lower level between two lintel arches topped by relieving arches mark the position of niches within. All relieving arches are of the same yellow *bipedales* as the bonding courses. The polychrome effect is rather striking, but it was entirely concealed by the marble revetment. The holes by which the panels were affixed are clearly visible in the brickwork. Marble pilasters once broke the monotony of the external facing. The wall was terminated by a series of rectangular niches. Opposite the entrance, an alcove was prepared for the statues of the three Capitoline divinities. The original platform seems to have disappeared in later reorganizations. A huge threshold of affricano remains, but little is left of the marble revetment which covered pavement, pedestal, and walls. Marble statues further embellished the niches. Brick stamps prove that the Capitolium was erected about A.D. 120.[4]

No brick stamps have been reported to indicate just when the porticoes flanking the temple were actually built, but there is no doubt that they formed part of the original plan. They were three steps above the Forum area and presented to it a long row of gray granite columns. The pavement was of marble. The west porticus had a straight back wall of brick-faced concrete, whereas the east porticus had three large rooms and a staircase opening off from it. The brickwork of all these walls resembles that facing the podium of the temple, but it was less carefully made. Breaks in the

[2] Becatti, *op. cit.*, pp. 129–130; Meiggs, *Ostia*, pp. 74, 136, 380–381, pl. 39c-d; Crema, p. 382, fig. 300.

[3] Gismondi, *Sc. di O.* I, p. 208, n. 9 (refers to broken tiles in the cella of the Capitolium).

[4] Bloch, *Bolli*, pp. 214–215; *idem*, *Sc. di O.* I, p. 215.

masonry show that the west wall was built in sections one at a time. There were no bonding courses and none of the great relieving arches which are conspicuous on the other side. These are practically contiguous, appearing two to a chamber, but not always in alignment. Although yellow *bipedales* predominate in these they were not used exclusively, as in the temple. These walls have been so much restored that it is difficult to gain a clear impression of the original masonry.

The northern limit of Hadrian's new Forum was fixed by the line of the old Castrum wall. Four piers *in antis* between the end walls of the porticoes rested upon it and probably supported an arcade along Via del Capitolium. Across the street a propylaeum of five arches with two rows of stout piers marked the beginning of the new Cardo Maximus. Only the central opening was a true passageway, though pedestrians could have used the side entrances to reach the porticoes which lined the Cardo. A room at the northwest corner with angle pieces for cross vaulting suggests that the two pillared halls also served some other purpose at times. The new Cardo was a broad avenue between porticoes leading to the Tiber. The Portici di Pio IX, as they are called (I, 5, 2, and I, 6, 1), presented to the street piers with pilasters attached, resting on molded terra-cotta bases and supporting no doubt an arcade long since vanished. No pilaster is preserved high enough to show the type of capital, if any. The facing was of red bricks made from broken tiles reinforced by at least two bonding courses of yellow *bipedales*. Lateral reinforcements here and there in similar masonry prove that the piers were too slender for the burden entrusted to them. Each porticus fronted a row of commodious shops with brick façades of less careful workmanship broken by broad openings with travertine sills and slightly curved lintel arches of *bipedales*. Over each doorway, a rather large window under a relieving arch supplied light to a mezzanine, the wooden floors of which were supported on a cornice composed of projecting tiles. The mortar joints were slightly wider, but there were no bonding courses. Rear and side walls were faced with reticulate work neatly interlocked into a brick frame (pl. 22, fig. 2). The bricks used throughout the shops were lighter in color than those in the piers but were equally fine-grained and broken from tiles, though often to triangular shape. Where the walls were broken it is possible to see that the aggregate consisted of small pieces of tufa in a white mortar speckled with unsifted dark pozzolana. Slightly curved lintels of *bipedales* covered doorways. Ample stairways attest a multiplicity of apartments above. The treatment of stairways had not yet become standardized. The one at the south end of each porticus became the norm. A broad passageway with a slightly curved lintel of *bipedales* was bisected by a wall. In its masonry was imbedded an oblique lintel of *bipedales* to help carry the stairs on one side, whereas a narrow passage remained under the second ramp which ascended in the opposite direction. A second staircase at the center of the West Porticus shows an even greater use of lintel arches. There was no intermediate wall originally, but an oblique lintel under the first ramp, a slightly curved lintel for the long corridor over the passageway below, and a second oblique lintel under a second ramp ascending in the same direction as the one below. Arches over the Via Tecta, springing from piers against the walls of adjacent buildings, served as buttressing agents for the long west wall. Against the long east wall of the East Porticus, partition walls of brick and reticulate work identical with those on the other side formed a row of smaller shops with mezzanines (I, 5, 1). Three of these had doorways to the shops along the Cardo. Three stairways prove that these also had independent apartments above. Two of the stairways followed the type first described; the one at the south effected the ascent by three ramps about a stairwell with a bewildering array of lintel arches. Strangely enough, lintels throughout the complex wherever the under surface is exposed show that the face was made up entirely of broken *bipedales* tapering sharply to make a good bond with the concrete core. They cannot therefore have had much structural value. All the shops were barrel-vaulted, and broken vaulting displays a dense aggregate of somewhat larger and more irregular pieces of tufa than that in the core of the walls, cemented together with the same kind of mortar. A detailed analysis of these structures seemed to be a necessary introduction to the rest of this unified Hadrianic development.

West of the Cardo and its dependencies and separated from them by a narrow passageway, a model granary (I, 8, 1), erroneously named "Piccolo Mercato," formed a part of the same development. A Republican building with a massive wall of squared-stone masonry determined its western limit, and the old Castrum wall was its southern boundary. The long side walls of brick-faced concrete were buttressed on the outside. It presented to Via dei Misuratori del Grano, which follows the oblique line of an earlier orientation, an arcade supported by slender piers faced with fine-grained red bricks. Each pier shows two travertine insets and a bonding course of yellow *bipedales* halfway between them. There were no capitals, but a rounded molding projected six courses below the impost molding which was composed of three projecting layers of tile. The arches were faced with *sesquipedales*. As in the porticoes flanking the Cardo, the piers were too slender and had to be reinforced almost immediately. A row of irregularly shaped shops masked the difference in alignment between the porticus and the main orientation. An unusually wide opening marked the entrance corridor to the open court inside. A part of the pilasters and the slightly curved lintel arch of yellow *sesquipedales* are all that remain of the ornamental doorway. A little more is preserved of the smaller gateway in the southeast corner. A rounded molding decorated with the effect of roping marked the place where a capital would normally begin, and dentil moldings followed the line of the pediment. West of the great northern gateway, an outside staircase ascended in two opposed ramps to apartments above the frontal groups. Over the slightly curved lintels, there were windows to light the mezzanine; and beam holes held the supports for its wooden floors. The steps were of travertine, the rampant arch of *sesquipedales*, the arch under the landing of *bipedales*, and the pavement of the landing of herringbone brick. The wall end between the ramps was rounded. East of the entrance, four shops with apartments over them completed this unit. Another unit farther east consisted of one large or two small shops with a two-ramp staircase of normal form to apartments above them. The central court was large enough for maneuvering the hand carts bringing grain from the Tiber or carrying it thence for shipment to Rome. A quadriporticus protected both the grain and those who handled it while it was being stored away in lofty barrel-vaulted chambers along the sides. The piers resembled those in front and once supported an arcade. Herringbone brick paved the quadriporticus. At the northwest and southeast corners ramps of easy gradient starting with travertine steps and paved with herringbone brick above them facilitated the carrying of sacks of grain for storage in upper chambers. Two heavy brick-faced piers supported low arches of *bipedales* (pl. 28, fig. 4), presumably for a passage from one side to the other across the center of the court. The span is too long to be bridged without intermediate supports, but there is no trace of any such (pl. 20, fig. 1). In the arches, every fifth *bipedalis* was whole to make a bond. The chambers at the west are only partly excavated. At the back of the court there were six more lofty storerooms, now used in part as an antiquarium. Small windows once stood over the slightly curved lintels of the openings, but there is no trace of a mezzanine, nor indeed of an upper story though one may have been added when I, 8, 10 was built. All the chambers were barrel-vaulted; and fallen vaulting shows concrete of the same composition as that used in the structures bordering the Cardo. The original brickwork throughout is analogous in every way to that found in the latter. The contractor had at hand three grades of brick: very fine-grained red made from tiles, perhaps exclusively from roof tiles, used in all piers and some façades; lighter red bricks also from tiles in most other secondary walls; speckled yellow triangles in less important parts particularly in the northeast unit. One pier in the northeast unit shows a red façade neatly interlocked with the yellow facing of the other three sides. Similar interlocking appears at the east of the doorway. The long east wall seems to have been rebuilt or refaced in the thin red bricks of the Severan epoch. Reticulate neatly interlocked with brick faced most inner walls and all partition walls. An enormous block of travertine was the cornerstone for a small unit of five shops and an outside staircase of one ramp at the southeast corner. It had a narrow doorway to one of the south chambers of the "Piccolo Mercato," with which it was contemporaneous.[5] A side doorway between the two shops facing Via delle Casette Repubblicane shows a relieving arch set on the brick band between reticulate panels at an appreciable distance over the slightly curved lintel of the doorway. Beam holes give evidence of a mezzanine floor over this unit. A well, lined with reticulate, stands in one of the shops. There seems to have been another self-contained unit near the southeast entrance—a doorkeeper's station, a small office perhaps, a small shop, a staircase of two ramps in this instance arranged at right angles to each other.

Brick stamps prove that a self-contained unit on the west (I, 8, 10), comprising three large shops, an outside stairway, and an entrance corridor to a medium-sized room behind two smaller shops, was contemporaneous with the rest. Since all walls were independent of the adjoining structures, it was probably the work of a different contractor. He made use of a part of the old Castrum wall as a foundation for his back wall of brick-faced concrete, but he apparently did not trust its stability. In any case, he commenced his brickwork in one instance with a slightly curved relieving arch and placed

[5] One of the shops has a pavement of *bipedales* several of which bear brick stamps of a later period. The south wall of this shop is faced with brick instead of the usual reticulate and brick. Consequently, it is conceivable that this pavement is part of a reorganization.

enormous relieving arches under the barrel vaulting of the rooms (pl. 22, fig. 4). Low lintels also appear under one of the partition walls. The stairs were carried on 40 cm. tiles, some of which were bonded through. The bricks used throughout were like those in the less important parts of the complex. The doorway and part of the masonry in the southwest corner were restored at a later time.

The eastern pomerial strip south of Via delle Casette Repubblicane has been included in this block. Two edifices in it, though they cannot be dated precisely, show construction which was probably Hadrianic. They were not, however, part of the development under consideration. Two shops (I, 8, 6) occupied the width of the early Porta Occidentale. Stairs from Via del Larario indicate that there were upper floors to what must have been the smallest shop-house of the period in all Ostia. Only brick was used to face its walls. Behind it there was a second independent unit (I, 8, 7) with a ground floor of three intercommunicating shops deep enough to make pilasters seem desirable in its partition walls. Outside stairs presuppose an upper story, but the walls are too thin to have supported more than one. Possibly three rooms were recessed behind a balcony. The usual combination of brick and reticulate was employed for this edifice. The rest of the space along Via del Larario was filled with what was probably Antonine construction. The western strip had already been built up with Trajanic shops (I, 8, 5).

According to the brick stamps[6] the smaller *horrea* to the west (I, 8, 2) of the "Piccolo Mercato" were built at approximately the same time,[7] though probably by a different contractor for private enterprise. He had at his disposal the same kind of bricks but employed them with less finesse; he used insets of reticulate in the front walls of the inner chambers as well as on all inside walls. Possibly he was availing himself of tesserae from the earlier warehouse which had occupied the site. In any case, he used as much as he could of its stone wall in his long east wall and kept its orientation throughout in complete disregard of Via dei Misuratori del Grano which stood at a higher level. It had the usual row of shops on each side of the entrance corridor, which was marked by two columns faced with rather wide (4 cm.) yellow bricks. These rested on carved travertine bases of unusual form. Although they probably belong to the original building period, they have no integral connection with it and could have been added at any time. A break in the masonry shows where the side walls of the corridor were prolonged inward. This probably represents a change in plan rather than a difference in date. The addition on each side of the corridor was furnished with two splayed windows to light a staircase[8] which consisted of two steps to a landing with the main ascent at right angles to them. The central court, which was paved with herringbone brick, was too narrow for the conventional granary. Some of the thresholds show openings for a suspended floor. Apparently it was essential to keep dry whatever was stored therein. Three chambers at the rear yielded more storage space; and a two-ramp staircase may have led to administrative offices above them. This tentative analysis must suffice until the whole site is laid bare.

Partition walls projecting from the west wall converted the long irregular

[6] Bloch, *Sc. di O.* I, p. 217.

[7] Ornamental pilasters on the west wall of the "Piccolo Mercato" would seem to indicate that it was constructed first.

[8] There is no trace of the stairs on the east side.

space between these *horrea* and Via Epagathiana into a row of shops (I, 8, 4). The three southernmost were reorganized by the builder of the Horrea Epagathiana in the Antonine era. Comparatively little has been excavated, but the usual speckled yellow bricks seem to have been used for the façade and combined with reticulate in the rear and partition walls. There was a complete reorganization in rather crude masonry at a later period.

Two edifices north of Via dei Misuratori del Grano were doubtless part of the same development, probably entrusted to a different contractor. At any rate, one of these, the Caseggiato del Balcone a Mensole (I, 6, 2) has its own wall abutting that of the west porticus along the Cardo. There was space for only a single row of shops along the street. No brick stamps have been reported, but the masonry is typically Hadrianic. The façade (pl. 24, fig. 4), much restored in modern times, had good, though not the best, Hadrianic brickwork; the inner walls, the usual combination of reticulate and brick. There were no bonding courses. The wide openings had travertine sills and slightly curved lintels of *bipedales* with masonry between them and the wooden doorframe. Above them rather large windows lighted the mezzanines beneath enormous relieving arches which marked the line of the barrel vaults under the main floor. What is new for Ostia is the balcony supported on great arches resting on huge travertine corbels, which graced both the sides which remain. The arches were faced with *sesquipedales* and outlined in a simple tile molding. There were probably three shops on each side of a space housing a two-ramp staircase and a latrine accessible from the street under the landing and the upper ramp. The stairs were carried on the usual rampant lintel of 40 cm. tiles. A door at the right of the landing led to the mezzanine, which must have had a wooden floor supported on beams. The evidence of the beam holes has been obscured by modern restoration.

Across Via della Fortuna, the Caseggiato dei Misuratori del Grano (I, 7, 1) has been half undermined by the Tiber and excavated only in part, but shows similar shops and mezzanines along the two sides that remain visible. The same type of balcony supported on travertine corbels ran across the main façade along the street of the same name. In the center, the main doorway, by all odds the finest preserved in Ostia (pl. 25, fig. 3), probably more or less duplicated the one of the more important "Piccolo Mercato" across the street. The frame consisted of pilasters faced with fine brickwork having a projecting tile molding, a yellow "frieze" and an impost where the capital would normally be; an entablature in which the architrave was reduced to two moldings with a plain yellow frieze between it and the capping cornice; and a low pediment outlined in simple cornices in which a dentil molding is conspicuous. The representation of a grain measure in the pediment[9] has given the monument its modern name. A slightly curved lintel of very fine-grained yellow *bipedales* topped the actual doorway. The representation of a measuring stick took the place of the keystone. The edifice presented to Via della Fortuna a totally different type of balcony supported on slender piers in every way analogous to those of the arcade in front of the "Piccolo Mercato." The yellow of the bonding courses is repeated in the "frieze" at the top of the piers. The elongated angle pier carried the framed plaque

[9] J. Carcopino, *Mél.*, vol. 30, 1910, p. 428; *idem*, *Ostie*, Paris 1929, p. 16.

of "*intarsio*" depicting Fortuna which gave the street its name. It has been conjectured that the inside housed another granary.

Early in his reign,[10] Hadrian also systematized the open space outside the sea gate of the Sullan Wall in a fashion reminiscent of the Greek agora. There was nothing in the area to interfere with the plan of this Foro di Porta Marina (IV, 8, 1), which was orientated with the wall and set back from the Decumanus to avoid the Precinct of Bona Dea.[11] Two columns of gray marble marked the main gateway which was supplemented by two side entrances. An inner porticus of gray columns with archaizing white capitals around the sides, a rectangular alcove in each side wall, and a small apsed hall at the head are the only architectural features. The enclosing wall on the side toward the Decumanus is faced with bricks made from fine-grained red tiles; on the inside, with insets of reticulate in rather indifferent brickwork, which was plastered over and stuccoed. The brickwork which faces the lower part of the apse for about a meter is generally of a better quality than the rest. Most of the brick used were triangular. This hall was paved with marble in a geometric design of pavonazzetto, giallo, and serpentino identical with one in the Atrium Vestae in Rome, and had at least a marble dado. Angle piers prove that the room was given a cross vault at a later period. The pavement of the portico was of white marble. Instead of the shops typical of a Roman forum, a long, narrow, arcaded warehouse (IV, 8, 5) was built along Via di Cartilio Poplicola. It resembles rows of Hadrianic shops elsewhere, but whether stairs led to upper apartments or upper storage space it is impossible to tell. Most of the rooms are intercommunicating. Some have doors onto the alley between them and the forum or the open space behind the forum; some have windows in addition to the doors, others windows alone, and one, two splayed windows. Somewhat later, an extraordinarily interesting cistern (IV, 8, 2) was built at the east corner of the forum. Exterior buttresses near together on three sides and an exceptionally heavy wall on the fourth should have been adequate to withstand the pressure of the water, but the spur walls on two sides abutted the enclosing wall of the forum,[12] and the diagonal buttress at the opposite corner was prolonged to the Sullan Wall. Stairs give access to the upper level of the cistern (the lower part is still enclosed), and a row of piers proves that this was covered. The concrete walls were faced with yellow triangles of a finer grain than that of the bricks in the adjacent walls. A layer of yellow *bipedales* stood at the beginning of the wall of the upper story. The masonry looks Hadrianic.

It is possible that Hadrian was responsible for completing the Terme di Porta Marina (IV, 10, 1) begun by Trajan,[13] but the official publication attributes a second phase to Antoninus Pius.[14]

Hadrian was probably responsible for starting the reorganization of the open triangular space near Porta Laurentina into the Campo della Magna Mater.[15] A temple of Magna Mater at the west corner and a sanctuary of Attis at the southeast one had already imparted a sacred character to the area. The Sullan Wall along the south side was given a reticulate facing with bands of brick between brick-faced pilasters which appears Hadrianic.

[10] No brick stamps have been reported.

[11] See Blake, *RC* II, p. 63; Crema, p. 367.

[12] They are not faced at the ends, a sure proof that they were later than the wall they abutted.

[13] See above, p. 149.

[14] See below, p. 204.

[15] G. Calza, *Acc. P. Mem.*, ser. 3, vol. 6 (2), 1947, pp. 184–205; Becatti, *Sc. di O.* I, p. 134; Meiggs, *Ostia*, pp. 140, 356–360.

The brick-faced columns of the porticus (IV, 1, 2) do not correspond to the pilasters, and Becatti suggests that the portico may have been an addition of Antoninus Pius. It has mostly been restored. No capitals were found. On the southeast side of the triangular area a sustaining wall was first built for the Cardo Maximus which stood at a higher level than the Campus. It was faced with reticulate and brick and strengthened with buttresses. There is a definite break between them and a continuation which with a back wall made a row of shops along the street (IV, 1, 9). The brick-faced façade with the pedimented gateway into the open area is almost certainly Hadrianic. The rest of the masonry making the shops is decidedly inferior. The back wall on the side toward the Campus was originally faced entirely with reticulate and brick though the northern part has now been refaced. The inner walls show a rough *incertum* which would of course have been concealed by plaster. The ramp leading down from the ornamental doorway to the Campus is paved with herringbone brick, and benches were built along its sides. There was apparently no upper story over these shops. The north-west boundary had already been determined by two sustaining walls for construction at a higher level. The two were not in alignment and were joined by a short cross wall. Some structures built against them of no great importance (IV, 1, 10) are classified as Hadrianic in the official chronology. It is possible that the cella at least of the Temple of Magna Mater at the west corner (IV, 1, 1) was rebuilt at this time. The spur walls of an earlier podium were arched over with red Hadrianic bricks to make ornamental niches along the sides. A brick cornice capped the podium wall. Marble steps led to the pronaos which must have been tetrastyle prostyle. Calza conjectures that two trenchlike openings in the landing at the third step may have held greenery of some sort. There was a travertine threshold and a base at the rear of the cella for a statue. The cella walls were of brick-faced concrete with a semicircular projection in the north wall for which the purpose is not clear. An altar stood in front. At the west corner of the precinct there seems to have been a gateway to an area as yet unexplored. The chronology of the edifices in the southeast corner is controversial. Some may be Hadrianic. To avoid needless repetition, it has seemed wise to treat the group as a whole in a later section.[16]

    The discovery of brick stamps of the early Hadrianic period in drains under the precinct of the four tempietti (II, 8, 2) indicates the start of a reorganization of the block. There was room in front of the precinct for a porticus along the Decumanus (II, 8, 1) with shops opening onto it. One seems to have yielded a *bipedalis* with a Hadrianic stamp.[17] What little remains of the original masonry shows the usual combination of reticulate and brick. This is no evidence for stairs either to a mezzanine or to upper stories. Nothing is left but the bottom of the piers of what must have been an impressive arcade behind the shop facing the tempietti. The presence of the Augustan shrine to Jupiter (II, 8, 4) in the eastern part of the precinct left room on the east merely for an *L*-shaped vestibule and a passageway approached by steps from the north of the precinct and leading to the porticus along the Decumanus. None of its brickwork is up to the usual Hadrianic standard. There is a huge relieving arch behind the shrine. Within the central court,

16 See below, pp. 209–210.

17 *CIL*, vol. 15 (1), no. 2197.

a nymphaeum (II, 8, 3) was probably a private dedication for which there is no independent chronological evidence. Its presence may have interfered with a more extensive use of the east side of the old precinct, in which case it may be early Hadrianic.[18] It is not aligned exactly with any other structure in the vicinity. The plan is conventional, comprising a vestibule and a nearly square chamber with a semicircular niche opposite the entrance and in each of the side walls. The walls are faced with reticulate reinforced by tufa quoins and brick bands. A few walls with insets of reticulate and several mosaics attest a Hadrianic renovation of the Domus di Apuleio (II, 8, 5). We are not concerned at the moment with the mithraeum (II, 8, 6) which was inserted at a later time in a room to the west of it. The official publication ascribes a Hadrianic phase to the edifice or edifices in the northwest corner of the old precinct (II, 8, 7). In what little is still visible, I saw little that appeared Hadrianic. The edifice at the west of the reduced precinct (II, 8, 8) had a strange plan consisting of five rooms enclosed on three sides with a corridor. They were divided into two units, one approached by a door on the west side, the other by a door on the east. A door in the east corridor could have shut off communication between the two. There is no indication of stairs to upper floors or terrace. The use of brick in partition walls when the outer ones were faced with reticulate suggests two building periods, both of which, however, may be Hadrianic. There has been considerable modern restoration throughout the block. The structure along Via dei Grandi Horrea (II, 8, 9) is later.

When the level was raised along the Decumanus west of the "Magazzini Repubblicani," a porticus with a lean-to roof (II, 2, 6)[19] was built replacing an earlier one at the lower level. The piers of the porticus rested on the brick-faced sustaining wall for the new Decumanus. Barely enough of them remains to show that they were faced with a red brick made from tiles. Practically all is a modern restoration. Fifteen shops and four staircases to upper apartments opened off from the porticus. Excavation has revealed how the new level was prepared for the shop fronts. Foundations for the walls were faced with bricks interlaced with a masonry of small stones laid in roughly regular rows beneath the travertine sills. Only five of the shops at the east end have been completely excavated. They show narrow doorways and small windows, some of them splayed, on to a wide passage (5.5 m.) paved in herringbone brick. Side and rear walls were faced with the usual combination of reticulate and brick. The bricks were largely yellow triangles. In the official publication, the Portico del Tetto Spiovente is ascribed to the early years of the reign of Hadrian.[20] The fact that no brick stamps have been found may be an indication that it was built before the reorganization of the industry in A.D. 123. With raising of the level, the street west of the "Magazzini Repubblicani" could no longer be entered from the Decumanus. At some time in the Hadrianic period, in all probability, the southern part of the space was utilized for a shrine facing the main street (II, 2, 4) and a long narrow hall connected with it by a doorway (II, 2, 5). The façade displayed pilasters of fine yellow brickwork against a red wall. The bricks used for it are about 3 cm. thick. The cross walls were faced with reticulate insets in a brick frame. Only the east wall of good brickwork

[18] Neuerburg, *Fontane*, pp. 47, 83, 183–184, no. 117.

[19] R. Paribeni, *Not. sc.*, 1920, p. 156; Calza, *Guida*, pp. 92–93.

[20] Becatti, *Sc. di O.* I, p. 133.

[21] Becatti, *Sc. di O.* II, p. 45.

[22] Bloch, *Sc. di O.* I, p. 219.

[23] Calza, *Sc. di O.* I, pp. 180–182; P. Harsh, *MAAR*, vol. 12, 1935, pp. 58–59. The name "caseggiato a navate" used by Calza in the old guide (p. 150) is a misnomer.

[24] Gismondi, *Sc. di O.* I, p. 208, n. 9.
[25] Calza, *Sc. di O.* I, pp. 183–185.

[26] Bloch, *Sc. di O.* I, p. 217. The stamps found in the three structures range in date from A.D. 114 to 117 in Casa Basilicale; I, 9, 2 has yielded only stamps of A.D. 114, but it appears coeval with Casa Basilicale. Caseggiato del Larario yielded those of A.D. 114 and 115.

[27] Calza, *Bull. Com.*, vol. 66, 1938, pp. 306–307; *idem, Nuovi Scavi*, pp. 8–10. The temples, strictly speaking, are in Regio I, Insula 15.

(bricks 3 cm. thick) is Hadrianic; the west wall was reinforced in a much poorer masonry obviously at the time of the Commodan organization of the area behind the Portico del Tetto Spiovente. The shrine had a niche colored red for a statue and a black-and-white mosaic floor of interlaced circles; the hall behind was later converted into a mithraeum.[21] A couple of brick stamps have been used as an indication of an early Hadrianic modification of what became the Terme dei Cisiarii (II, 2, 3).[22]

While all this more or less official construction was going on in the Forum area, individual peculiarities show that other builders were filling the blocks flanking the new section of the Forum on both the east and the west with private edifices. The block on the west already had the Curia (?) on the southeast corner at the higher level. Earlier buildings imposed a certain irregularity of plan except on the Casa Basilicale (I, 9, 1)[23] at the north of the Curia, which took the place of three small Republican houses. As the name implies, a court divided the ground plan into two parts. Six shops, three on each side of an entrance unit consisting of a corridor and an outside staircase, fronted Via delle Casette Repubblicane; three well-lighted rooms faced the court on the opposite side. Such an arrangement suggests a manufactory of some sort. The central court was bridged over so that those in the upper apartment over the shops could avail themselves of the space over the work rooms. It differs from the rest in having a façade faced with yellow triangles and a framed square for a terra-cotta plaque at each side of the entrance unit. The edifice to the west (I, 9, 2) must also have housed an industry. Originally it had barely enough masonry to carry cross vaults under the floor of the upper story, to which there was a flight of steps from Via del Larario. Although it had a common wall with the Casa Basilicale, its masonry was of a different type, more like that found in the official building of the period.[24] The Caseggiato del Larario (I, 9, 3)[25] may have been erected by the same contractor as built the Caseggiato del Balcone a Mensole (I, 6, 2). The façade of bricks from broken tiles is comparable. It had the same great travertine corbels to support a balcony across the front, the same large relieving arches over mezzanine level windows, and the same tile molding over the prominent arches. A greater use of travertine is present here (pl. 23, fig. 1). It appears as insets in door jambs as well as in the thresholds, as springers for straight lintel arches of tile over doorways, and as corbels to uphold mezzanines. The edifice was apparently an elegant little bazaar with some shops opening out into the street and others onto a court with a fountain. A charming little lararium in decorative terra cotta has given the edifice its modern name. Only one inside staircase suggests a limited use of upper stories. Brick stamps in all three structures (I, 9, 1–2–3) indicate that they were erected about A.D. 120.[26]

Via Epagathiana, Via della Foce, Via del Tempio d'Ercole, and a section of unexplored land bound an irregular space which could be used for a structural history of Ostia from the three Republican temples to the Domus di Amore e Psiche of the early fourth century after Christ.[27] Much of it had already been built over by Trajan at a new level. South of the Trajanic Baths of Buticosus, an apartment house (I, 14, 9) was erected which seems from its construction to be somewhat later. No brick stamps confirm the date. The ornamental entrance framed a flight of travertine steps and a passage under a second flight. The pilasters had a decorative terra-cotta base of six courses. The bricks facing the pilasters were slightly thinner than those in the rest of the façade (3 cm. as opposed to 3.2 cm.) and were laid with narrower joints. The stairs were carried on a concrete barrel vault within walls. The wall which served both staircase and passage was faced with brick, whereas the rest of the inner walls show reticulate insets in brick frames. A wall of the entrance corridor contained a curved niche of brick with an arch of *bipedales*. The bricks in these walls are 3.5 to 4 cm. thick. The slightly curved lintels over apertures were supported by wooden beams. There were three shops to the left and two to the right of the entrance unit. The rear of the house took a form which was to become familiar later—a corridor against an outside wall between two large rooms having three smaller rooms opening off from it. The lack of windows in the preserved part of the outside wall poses the problem of lighting. The edifice at the northwest corner (I, 14, 6) had a façade on Via del Tempio d'Ercole faced with bricks broken from tiles of a warm rich brick red seldom seen. Two stamps, one with a consular date of A.D. 127[28] and the other a few years later,[29] suggest a date near A.D. 130, the year ascribed to it in the official list. Partition walls between the three shops on the west were faced with a poor reticulate in a brick frame. Shops probably lined the north side also. Long narrow rooms stood behind them. The partition walls were faced with yellow bricks probably combined with reticulate, though only the outer walls are preserved high enough to show it. The whole house is poorly preserved, hence the uncertainty as to its plan. An outside staircase at the south may have led to upper apartments at least above the shops along Via del Tempio d'Ercole. I am convinced that the shops of I, 14, 7 along Via Epagathiana are Trajanic, but I am inclined to think that the northern row was Hadrianic, built after I, 14, 6 against which they abut. A part of the south wall of the latter became the north wall of the reception room of the Domus di Amore e Psiche which extended farther north than the northern wall of the late Hadrianic apartment house at the corner of Via del Tempio d'Ercole and Vicolo delle Terme di Buticosus (I, 14, 5) in which the Domus was later installed. Barely enough remains of this house to show that it was constructed of fairly good brickwork.

In the corresponding block at the east side of the Forum, we can trace the progress of the work from the northwest corner all around the block, the structural history of which becomes, as it were, an epitome of the intense building activity at the beginning of the Hadrianic period. These buildings were certainly the result of private enterprise. A blocked doorway proves that the first construction[30] to be erected at the new level (I, 2, 5) was earlier than the Forum porticus to the west of it. What little is left of the original building invites speculation as to its purpose. It was apparently erected for the revenue from the rental of its many shops. Only much later was it converted into a *thermopolium*. Of special interest is the balcony upheld by huge travertine corbels along Via di Diana (pl. 23, fig. 2; foreground). The corbels supported segmental arches of *sesquipedales*, and the resultant barrel vaults had *besales* set in the soffit. A long lintel of *bipedales* covered the

[28] A variant of *CIL*, vol. 15 (1), no. 1431, found *in situ* by Marion E. Blake in the top of the wall.

[29] Bloch, *Suppl.*, no. *20, found *in situ* by Doris Taylor Bishop in the top of a wall.

[30] R. Paribeni, *Not. sc.*, 1916, pp. 401–405, 427–428.

[31] Gismondi, *Sc. di O. I*, p. 208, n. 9.

[32] Paribeni, *Not. sc.*, 1916, pp. 411–413.

[33] The porticus was largely destroyed by the insertion of a late nymphaeum on the corner.

[34] Paribeni, *Not. sc.*, 1916, pp. 419–422.

doorway of each shop behind the balcony. A single row of tiles topped the lintel, and the window for the mezzanine stood between it and the segmental archway. Of no less interest is the entrance hall and row of intercommunicating shops along the Decumanus, all but one of which have doorways onto the central area. The wall-ends toward the street were finished with pilasters of the finest red brickwork.[31] They rose from bases of cut tile, which stood on ample travertine foundations. Unfortunately none of the entablature is preserved. This could be a slightly later addition. The row of shops just described interfered with the symmetrical plan of the next building (I, 2, 3), which was therefore presumably later; blocked side entrances prove that it was earlier than the structure on the east. The building consisted of an apsed hall with a side aisle on the east and only a narrow passage on the west leading to some rooms and a staircase at the rear. All was in good brickwork except the apse which was lined with reticulate reinforced by tufa quoins. The date of the next edifice, the Caseggiato del Pantomimo Apolausto (I, 2, 2),[32] is not attested by brick stamps, but it cannot be much later than the rest. To build it, someone gained possession of the southern part of Piazza dei Lari and thereby enlarged the area at his disposal for a business establishment of some sort at the level of the piazza, bringing it into correspondence with the somewhat lower Decumanus by an arcaded portico.[33] There were seven shops (?) and a long entrance corridor to a court which was apparently shared with the building to the north. Many of the rooms retain the selce paving of the piazza. Since there were no original stairs, this was not built as an apartment house. The brickwork was rather mediocre. At about the same time, in all probability, the northwest section of the piazza was expropriated for another business establishment or the ground floor of an apartment house. It consisted of seven rooms, and an entrance corridor and an outside staircase from the piazza (I, 2, 6).[34] Here also the selce paving appears in most of the rooms. Yellow bricks were largely used, and brick stamps bring it within the early Hadrianic orbit. The four large shops facing Via di Diana and what was left of the piazza had wide openings with straight lintel arches too long for stability. This is a defect that one meets again and again in Hadrianic work in Ostia. Enough is preserved of the stairs to show that they ascended in a straight line at least to the *piano nobile*, and Paribeni has demonstrated how they may have continued to another floor in the same line. Beam holes give evidence of a wooden balcony across the entire front above the mezzanine floor, a part of which has recently been restored (pl. 23, fig. 2, in background). From it comes the modern name Caseggiato del Balcone Ligneo. Fairly early in the Hadrianic period, the owner of the house at the northwest corner, the one with which we started (I, 2, 5), either remodeled or sold a part of it. The new construction shows a flight of steps from Via di Diana, a large room with three cross vaults in front, and a second staircase to apartments over the rebuilt shops at the east of the inner passage. The contractor who did the remodeling employed only brickwork strengthened by bonding courses and relieving arches, some of them enormous.

After these encroachments, the Piazza dei Lari had to be reorganized. An open shrine was erected at its head and an altar built in front of it. The angle piers, of which the one in the southeast corner seems to have been restored in antiquity, were faced with light reddish brown bricks made from tiles. Some came from roof tiles, but all maintained approximately the same range (3–3.5 cm.) in thickness. The intermediate piers along the sides were faced with somewhat thicker (3.5–4 cm.) yellow bricks, some of which at any rate were triangles. The shrine shows remains of at least two later transformations.

The block east of Piazza dei Lari was divided into two parts by the old Castrum wall. Although no brick stamps have been found to establish the date, the three edifices facing the Via dei Lari were or at least could have been Hadrianic. It is possible to trace the progression of the building program. The earliest (I, 1, 3), with two shops toward the Decumanus and two larger ones toward the side street with stairs to upper floors, was faced entirely with light reddish brown bricks. The brickwork of the façade was better than elsewhere. There were bonding courses but not of the yellow *bipedales* employed in official Hadrianic work. The stairs were carried in part on an oblique lintel of *bipedales*. Too little is preserved to show how the openings were covered. Only the façade with three doorways to a large hall (I, 1, 2) would seem to belong to the period under consideration, and very little of it remains. It was, however, later than the building to the south of it. The latest structure (I, 1, 1) was probably not finished until the Antonine era, but the façade of fine yellow brickwork, with openings too wide for the slightly curved lintels which covered them even though they were protected by enormous relieving arches, appears to me Hadrianic, though all provisions for the vaulting seem Antonine. Possibly building was suspended for a time until the defects could be rectified. The stairs behind the corner shop were carried on the usual oblique lintel. On the east side of the Castrum wall early shops had already filled the pomerial strip, but the area was reorganized at the Hadrianic level (I, 1, 4) with two shops toward the Decumanus and a porticus with shops toward Via dei Molini.[35] What little is preserved of this phase is not significant for the history of construction. No brick stamps are reported from this block.

Immediately to the east of the Hadrianic development known as the "Quartier des Docks," a long narrow block was also filled with Hadrianic construction, albeit private rather than public.

Numerous brick stamps from fallen walls and arches prove conclusively that the row of fifteen and more shops along Via dei Balconi (I, 4, 1)[36] was erected about A.D. 127, earlier than the other Hadrianic structures which filled the block. There was space for one shop in addition to the corner one along Via di Diana. The masonry is typically Hadrianic. Yellow bricks predominate in the façade; and one bonding course of the same color appears in each of the front walls. As often, the openings proved too wide for the slightly curved lintels of *bipedales* which covered them and had to be narrowed subsequently. Even so, only two remain. The inner walls were faced with reticulate insets in a brick frame. Occasionally two smaller ones were preferred to one large one. The most unusual feature is an enormous relieving arch as wide as the shop which breaks through the insets in each back wall (pl. 21, fig. 1). These appear almost as a decoration of the blank

[35] A. Boethius, *Skrifter*, vol. 4, 1934, pp. 164–195; Gismondi, *Sc. di O.* I, p. 208, n. 10.

[36] G. Calza, *Mon. ant.*, vol. 26, 1920, cols. 333–337. My description is, however, from personal observation.

[37] Bloch, *Sc. di O.* I, p. 216; see also G. Calza, *Mon. ant.*, vol. 26, 1920, cols. 332–410; Meiggs, *Ostia*, 246–247, 544.

wall presented to the garden behind it. Where the walls are preserved high enough, beam holes appear to support the wooden floor of a mezzanine. Space was left for three stairways. One shows five masonry steps up to a cross wall, but no further indication of steps there or elsewhere. Possibly wooden steps in a wooden frame are the answer. Slightly curved lintels of *bipedales* appear over doorways in partition walls. None of the vaulting remains.

Unfortunately, brick stamps do not permit a dating closer than the decade A.D. 128–138[37] for the apartment house comprising Insula di Giove e Ganimede, Insula di Bacco Fanciullo, Insula dei Dipinti (I, 4, 2–4). The southern unit, the Insula di Giove e Ganimede (I, 4, 2), had an independent east wall abutting the rear wall of the Caseggiato con Taberne (I, 4, 1); shops, outside stairs, and a secondary entrance on the south; a main entrance between two rooms on the west. The brick-faced south façade, preserved in part to the second story, shows no attempt at regularity. A high sidewalk gave access to four shops. The openings differ in both width and height; one had a window beside the door. Over the doorway leading to the entrance corridor there was a small window to light the passage when the door was closed. Next to it a square window lighted the landing to the stairs. Those of the next floor are set at the same level but vary in width and height. The larger ones are protected by relieving arches under the vaulting of a concrete balcony (?). *Bipedales* were used at the start of the wall and sometimes at the window sills. A rampant relieving arch seems to support the barrel vault under the travertine steps which served the mezzanines for both the shops and the house behind them as well as upper apartments. The mezzanine floors were supported on an impost of projecting tile. Rounded bricks appear in the wall of the upper level and a fine herringbone brick pavement in the upper corridor. A two-step landing led to the next flight of steps. The ramps were laid one over the other with two steps making the transition. The secondary entrance corridor was cross-vaulted; and a door led to the space under the stairs.

The original plan of this corner apartment is somewhat obscured by later modifications. The main doorway led through a wide corridor to a small court with a wide doorway onto the central garden. A richly decorated room, two stories high, opened off from it on one side. On the opposite side two rooms, one behind the other, received light from it through wide windows. It was also a source of light for yet another room at the south. Service rooms were located at the right of the main entrance corridor. We have already mentioned the secondary entrance from Via di Diana. Elaborate black-and-white mosaics of geometric design belong to the original building period[38] and may be an indication that the owner reserved this apartment for himself while renting the other two. The rather spectacular wall paintings belong to a later period. There was a mezzanine over the parts that were not two stories high. Travertine corbels shared with tile cornices the task of supporting the floor. No shops stood along Via dei Dipinti except for the side opening to the large corner one which faced Via di Diana. The foundations, once concealed by a high sidewalk, show rather small irregular tufa *caementa* laid in regular rows. The façade for this entire side was faced with yellow

[38] Becatti, *Sc. di O.* IV, pp. 14–16.

triangular bricks, with pedimented doorways having pilasters of red bricks of a slightly finer texture. The two apartments along Via dei Dipinti, Insula di Bacco Fanciullo and Insula dei Dipinti (I, 4, 3 and 4),[39] are self-contained units of identical plan lying between more or less public passages to the central garden and the outside stairs. The pedimented doorway to each is flanked by two high windows—a break with the tradition that all light should come from inside. The windows on the opposite side are low enough to give a view of the garden and large to furnish ample light to the large room at one end (three windows), the corridor with a window for each of the two rooms opening out of it, and the two rooms, one behind the other, separated by a large window (one window). There was a small window over the door to the garden. In each apartment the rooms of the two ends of the corridor reached to the first story. In the Insula di Bacco Fanciullo a false impost appears in the lofty southeast room probably to break the monotony of such a large surface for wall painting. There was a mezzanine over the rest. The black-and-white mosaic floors were of very simple pattern.

Except for the yellow bricks of rather coarse texture in the façade, light red bricks, also triangles, were used elsewhere. Inner walls were faced with the usual combination of brick and reticulate except that bricks alone are employed to at least shoulder height. Slightly curved lintels rested on the masonry above the wooden frame for all apertures except the narrow doorways to the garden, which show straight lintels. Inside windows are something of a novelty. In two cases a long lintel, upheld in the center by a partition wall, covered two narrow doorways. This arrangement is unusual in the interior of a house. Tile cornices on inner walls and large travertine corbels on outer ones supported the wooden floors above the parts which were not two stories high. There are no inner staircases and so access to them must have been from the outside staircases which served upper apartments. The one at the north ascending from the garden in its present state reveals the method of construction probably used in all three. The oblique lintel which appeared to carry the steps actually consisted of five or six broken *bipedales* between whole ones to make a bond. Some of the *besales* which covered the wooden centering still cling to the under side of the barrel vault. Beam holes on the inner façade prove that there was at least one balcony toward the garden at the first floor level.

Only the Caseggiato dei Dolii (I, 4, 5) is left to describe. Since its outside staircase was built against the oblique north wall of the Insula dei Dipinti, it must be somewhat later, but its construction is essentially the same. Its façade was faced for the most part with characteristic yellow bricks; the inner walls, in the older fashion of reticulate panels rather than insets interlocked with the brick frame. The stairs were carried in part of an oblique lintel arch, and slightly curved lintel arches remain over one or two doorways inside. The core of the walls consisted of small pieces of tufa laid in regular rows with a good mortar. One room shows angle piers to support cross vaulting which seem to be of the same masonry as the rest of the house. Too little has been excavated to reveal either its plan or purpose. Its modern name comes from a late deposit of storage jars.

At about the same time that the row of shops along Via dei Balconi (I, 4,

[39] Calza, *Mon. ant.*, vol. 26, 1920, cols. 332–410; P. Harsh, *MAAR*, vol. 12, 1935, pp. 27–29. My description is mostly from personal observation. See also Meiggs, *Ostia*, pp. 246, 248 fig. 14, 249; Crema, p. 458, fig. 584.

[40] Bloch, *Sc. di O.* I, p. 216.

[41] G. Calza, *Not. sc.*, 1915, p. 243, fig. 1; *idem, Guida*, pp. 130–132.

[42] The great arches are later.

1) was constructed, the block to the east was laid out, in all probability, although the Caseggiato di Diana (I, 3, 3) and the apartment house to the side of it (I, 3, 4) in the southwest corner were not built until the days of Antoninus Pius. The south wall of the Caseggiato del Mitreo di Lucrezio Menandro (I, 3, 5), which was at a lower level, was razed when the Caseggiato di Diana was erected. Unfortunately this house has not been completely excavated. Consequently, one can only speculate as to what purpose lay back of its unusual plan. Along Via dei Balconi, a row of shops, three on each side of an ample entrance corridor with a staircase at the side, is commonplace enough. The southernmost shop has its own rear room entirely independent of the rest of the house. But the entrance leads to a vestibule which had two high windows and a door in each side wall. A hall to the south received further light from four high windows in the east wall; doorways led to two of the frontal shops. The northern part stood at a higher level and had two windows and a door toward a wide passage at the east which stood at the same level. It was paved with herringbone brick. The northern limit was probably an oblique wall in alignment with the north wall of the edifice to the east. The façade with its wide openings was faced with brick. Usually fine-grained magenta bricks from tiles were employed at the base of the wall, but yellow bricks occupied the same place on each side of the entrance and were used on the wall limiting the staircase. Secondary walls were faced with the usual combination of reticulate and brick. The masonry presents no peculiarities. Brick stamps[40] indicate a date of about A.D. 127 for this house.

The interest in the discovery of a complete baking establishment in the eastern part of the block[41] has overshadowed the fact that the bakery was installed in a Hadrianic edifice, the Caseggiato dei Molini (I, 3, 1), of no less interest. It presented eight ample shops to Via dei Molini and two smaller ones to Via di Diana. There was nothing unusual about this arrangement, but behind the row of shops a large hall took the space of two shops and a larger one of three shops, leaving space for two smaller rooms at the north. Pilasters[42] divided the larger rooms in two and three sections respectively. All these rooms opened on to a private alley, the Angiporto di Silvano (I, 3, 2), which could be barred to the public by closing the door on Via di Diana. Beam holes suggest that a mezzanine existed over the smaller shops to the right of it, but if so, they must have been approached by temporary wooden steps or a ladder. Outer walls were of brick-faced concrete, whereas insets of reticulate marked the inner ones. The back walls show larger insets on the outside than on the inside. Two types of bricks were used. Fine-grained hard red bricks made from broken tiles faced the façade toward Via dei Molini and part of the one toward Via di Diana. They vary in thickness from 3.4 cm. to 3.9 cm. The rest exhibits for the most part speckled yellow bricks, about 3.5 cm. thick, also made from tiles. A few are light red. Horizontal joints are about 1.5 cm. wide, vertical ones 0.5 cm. There are no bonding courses or relieving arches. Apertures are covered with slightly curved lintel arches of *bipedales*. No vaulting is preserved. Terra-cotta plaques decorated the short walls between the openings of the shops along Via dei Molini. One depicting a deity with a snake is still *in situ;* one showing a draftsman's equipment was reused in a later pilaster, and frames indicate the position of two more, now gone.

Little remains of the edifice in the northeast corner (I, 3, 6). The building to the south supplied its south wall. Its west wall opened on to the same passage as the east wall of the Caseggiato del Mitreo di Lucrezio Menandro, with which it was probably contemporary. Barely enough is preserved to show that there were shops along the east and north sides. The north wall was oblique in correspondence to some earlier orientation. The masonry was concrete faced with the usual combination of reticulate and brick. There were bonding courses under the reticulate insets.

Across the Decumanus, the Caseggiato dei Triclini (I, 12, 1), which was certainly the Schola of the Fabri Tignuarii by the time of the Severi,[43] may very well have been built for them in the early Hadrianic period. Brick stamps leave no doubt as to the time when it was erected.[44] The ground plan consisted of an arcaded court with columns substituted for piers on the short sides; the customary tablinum (Caesareum) between alae at its head; three ample rooms furnished with triclinia, a kitchen and latrine under a stairway on its left side; five smaller rooms, purpose unknown, on the right; and independent shops and the necessary entrance corridors facing the streets at both the north and the south. An outer staircase from each street and a staircase at opposite corners of the court prove that there were independent apartments over each of the four sides, though there is no way of telling how many floors they served. Rather rough masonry resting on the mosaic of an earlier building raised the foundations of the piers to the new level. The wall construction is contemporaneous except for modifications which are obviously later. The façades and piers are faced with yellow triangles, 3.5–4 cm. thick, with the majority 3.7 cm. The bricks are fairly fine-grained with specks of red pozzolana in their composition. Mortar joints range from 0.5 to 1.3 cm. in width. The mortar is light gray with infrequent particles of black pozzolana and rather friable. Some bonding courses are visible in the piers. Inner walls display neat insets of reticulate in good brickwork (pl. 22, fig. 3). Two small insets are often preferred to one large one. The tufa tesserae are rather small (6–7 cm.) and fairly regular with joints averaging about 1 cm. Rectangular grooves in inner walls show where drainage pipes were located. All apertures were covered with slightly curved lintel arches of *sesquipedales* or *bipedales* with masonry beneath them. In one instance it is possible to see the position of the beam supporting the masonry. A high window in addition to the doorway assured light without interference with privacy to each of the five rooms on the west. A splayed window in a solid wall at the right of the secondary entrance on the south probably lighted the station of the doorkeeper. Two low relieving arches imparted stability to the steps at the southeast corner. Where it is possible to see, the stairs are carried in part on rampant lintels of *sesquipedales* with a full arch under the landing which in one case at least was paved with *bipedales*. One staircase is preserved high enough to show the same type of rounded wall end as appeared in the "Piccolo Mercato." The steps, like the door sills, were of travertine. There are traces of holes for the beams supporting the wooden floors of mezzanines over the rooms on the east and also of the

[43] P. Harsh, *MAAR*, vol. 12, 1935, pp. 23–25; G. Calza, *Palladio*, vol. 5, 1941, pp. 3–6; see also Crema, p. 458, figs. 586–587; Meiggs, *Ostia*, pp. 243–244, 543.

[44] Bloch, *Bolli*, pp. 96–98.

[45] Gismondi, *Sc. di O.* I, p. 208, n. 9.

windows which lighted them. The corridor leading to Via della Forica had a wooden ceiling supported by travertine corbels. The Caesareum was undoubtedly higher than the rest and vaulted. Vaulting probably supported the *piano nobile*. The Caesareum undoubtedly had a marble pavement, the court was paved with a coarse white mosaic, and the rest with herring-bone brick.

By the end of the reign of Hadrian, most of the rest of the block was filled by a large and rather elegant Bath. For these Baths, the builder appropriated the major part of an earlier Hadrianic house. The Caseggiato della Cisterna (I, 12, 4) had an arcaded court with rooms on three sides. Those on the east facing the Semità dei Cippi served as shops. An outside staircase carried on a rampant barrel vault between brick walls led to apartments above the shops. The entrance corridor was also barrel-vaulted. Primary walls were faced with bricks made from broken *bipedales*,[45] secondary ones with brick and reticulate. Lintel arches of *sesquipedales* topped the doorways. There were no brick stamps, but the masonry is typically Hadrianic. The interior was profoundly altered when a cistern was installed in the center of the cortile. Nothing remains to show what the northern part of the edifice was like. A modest establishment (I, 12, 5) was awkwardly fitted into the southeast corner of the block, possibly on what was originally an open square. It had its own north wall abutting the wall of the Caseggiato della Cisterna, and was somewhat later. It had been adjudged Hadrianic from the character of its masonry in the usual combination of reticulate and brick. Nothing about it requires special comment. It also was much modified at a later period.

The triangular area between the Cardo Maximus and the Semità dei Cippi has yielded some Hadrianic work, most of it of no particular importance; but just below the Forum Baths on the Semità there is an elegant little bazaar (I, 13, 1) which resembles closely the one near the great *horrea* by the Tiber, and like it should be ascribed to the time of Trajan or the early years of the reign of Hadrian. Five rather large shops, as regular as the irregular space permitted, opened off from a relatively narrow central court, whereas a single chamber stood at its head. The bazaar faced the Semità dei Cippi, but had a secondary opening on the south which was soon blocked up. The court was paved with herringbone brick; and travertine thresholds led to the shops. The external walls were faced with a very neat reticulate work set in a frame of red bricks (pl. 22, fig. 1). The reticulate tesserae, 7.5 cm. in the surface dimensions, were laid with narrow joints. The bricks were made from broken roof tiles, 3.5–4.2 cm. thick, which were extremely fine-grained. The careful masonry of the outer walls displays bands with six rows of bricks, reduced to five in the inner facing of the west wall; the less careful work of the partitions has bands of three. Plaster concealed the difference between rear and partition walls within the shops. Wooden lintels covered the doorways. Pivot marks in the travertine sills prove that the rooms were closed by doors rather than shutters. There is no indication of mezzanine floors. In the two shops where the walls are preserved high enough, there are splayed windows for light and air. Nothing remains to show how the chambers were roofed. There was no upper story. The edifice to the south of it (I, 13, 2) seems to be a little later. It shows a slightly different orientation and a masonry identical with that closing a doorway in the south wall of the bazaar. It was not an important structure, but it had an interesting façade toward the alley to the south, in that reticulate insets face the wall between each set of two windows. The walls are too narrow to have supported an upper story. The edifice in which a *fullonica* was inserted at a later time (I, 13, 3) exhibits some walls faced with bricks 3.5 cm. thick and mortar joints 2.5 cm. wide which may be Hadrianic, and the north wall of what became the Domus delle Gorgoni (I, 13, 6) is faced with the usual Hadrianic combination of brick and reticulate.

Hadrianic contractors soon turned their attention to the spaces left by Trajanic builders on both sides of Via della Foce. All construction that can be securely dated by brick stamps falls between A.D. 125 and 127.[46] On the northeast side, the southern part of the irregular area between Via delle Terme del Mithra and Via del Tempio d'Ercole contained an edifice (I, 16, 1), more likely private than public, which yielded one stamp of A.D. 123 *in situ*. Its ground plan exhibits two rows of intercommunicating shops with a common back wall between two irregularly shaped shops on Via della Foce and four chambers of uncertain purpose facing north. A flight of steps on each side is an indication of upper floors. There is nothing noteworthy about the construction.

At a slightly later date, a large apartment house with shops on the ground floor (I, 16, 2) was erected to the north of this, which has not been completely excavated. It was divided by a narrow passageway and a flight of steps into two units. The size and shape of the rooms was more or less determined by the irregularity of space available. The position of the doorways in the cross walls suggests a use of temporary partitions. The wall construction was the usual combination of brickwork for main walls and of brick and reticulate elsewhere. The bricks used with the reticulate (tesserae 7 cm.) were a magenta red (3–3.5 cm. thick) with mortar joints 1.5–2 cm. wide. There are no bonding courses except in the northwest corner where there is considerable restoration. One or two straight relieving arches appear at a low level; and a rampant lintel of *bipedales* seemingly carried the stairs. Slightly curved lintels of *sesquipedales* topped the doors and windows. The rooms in the northern unit were cross-vaulted with traces of the *besales* which once covered the *bipedales* laid on the wooden centering still visible. A pier in the center of the northernmost room made possible some interesting vaulting, but I am inclined to think that this was a later development.[47] Brick stamps for the most part found loose in the excavation belong overwhelmingly to the year A.D. 134,[48] which was, to be sure, the year of the reorganization of the brick industry, but the almost complete absence of later stamps would seem to relegate the edifice to the final years of the reign of Hadrian. There are traces of many different modifications throughout, but those in the northwest corner exhibit little difference in the type of masonry and seem directed to an attempt to counteract certain miscalculations of stresses on the part of the original contractor.

The next narrow slightly irregular block yields a small apartment house (I, 17, 1) with a ground floor almost entirely of shops and the Terme del

[46] See Bloch, *Sc. di O.* I, p. 219.

[47] Entirely personal observation.

[48] Bloch, *Sc. di O.* I, p. 219. He dates the edifice a little later (A.D. 138–140).

[49] Calza, *Nuovi Scavi*, p. 10.

Mithra (I, 17, 2), both apparently belonging to the same building period. Numerous brick stamps prove that the Baths at any rate were Hadrianic and not Trajanic as originally published.[49] An arcade of eleven arches originally formed the east façade (pl. 24, fig. 3). The piers rested on travertine foundations and culminated in a capping cornice of two rows of tile; the arches of *bipedales* were crowned with a continuous capping molding also of tile. The bricks, ranging from 3 to 3.7 cm. in thickness and from 16 to 37 cm. in length, were made from fine-grained tiles, some light in color, but most a magenta red. The vertical joints were very fine, the horizontal ones about 1 cm. Stairs near the south end led down to the service corridors. The eastern part of the basement was lighted by a series of recessed splayed windows which are a novelty; a long corridor on the west was lighted by overhead windows from a passageway at the west of the Baths. Water was raised by a water wheel from a great underground reservoir to a canal leading to the pools. Heating arrangements are less clear and require the analysis of an expert. Behind the façade, the masonry was of more ordinary brickwork or reticulate combined with brick in the usual fashion. The bricks are a trifle thicker than normal for the period. Some bonding courses were used, but no relieving arches in the part preserved. Apertures were covered with slightly curved lintels of *bipedales*. Later modifications have somewhat obscured the arrangement of rooms. The Baths themselves consisted of five or six large halls one behind the other. Two shallow pools were installed in the southernmost at a later period. The Baths were remade about A.D. 200 and given a new façade (pl. 24, fig. 3). Slightly later a mithraeum was inserted in an underground corridor; and in the fourth century or a little later wall tubes were removed from all the halls, an apse added, and the whole converted into a Christian church. Presumably the great porta santa columns belonged to the first phase, though the capitals are later.

North of this block an apartment house (I, 18, 1), only partly excavated, seems to belong to this same period.

Beyond the great Trajanic *horrea* (I, 19, 4), long side walls defined a block (I, 20, 1) which contained three units: four shops, opening off from an arcade oriented with Via della Foce rather than the rest of the edifice; five great halls which seem to have been modified in the course of construction and more drastically later; the warehouse which was not a granary. The complex is now inaccessible, and so I can give only a cursory description based on notes taken in 1949. It was originally called "Horrea Traiani" from a superficial resemblance to the Mercato di Traiano in Rome and the presence of a few Trajanic stamps in essential parts of the building. The majority of the stamps, however, prove that it was erected A.D. 125–126 or thereabouts.[50] A long barrel-vaulted hall is the most interesting feature. Wide doorways with lintel arches of upright *bipedales* under great relieving arches open off from it on both sides. A molding of tile outlines the arches. Pilasters, showing a rounded tile cornice where the capital would begin if there were one, and a two-tile cornice to act as capping member decorate the side walls. The decorative members are painted red. The bricks used at least in the façades are fine-grained, light reddish brown, and vary in thickness from 3 to 3.5 cm. or a little over. There are bonding courses of *bipedales*;

[50] See Bloch, *Sc. di O.* I, p. 219.

and in the arches every fifth or sixth tile of the facing is whole to act as a bonding member. The fallen vaulting exhibits medium-sized tufa *caementa* closely laid but not in definite rows. Amphorae were used sparingly to lighten the load, but not I think in the earliest phase since they appear in haunches of cross vaulting in another part of the complex which is manifestly later. A terrace paved with coarse mosaic rested on the barrel vault. Ample stairways could have led to storage places above. The majority of storerooms downstairs were supplied with a splayed window, probably for ventilation rather than light. North of these *horrea*, an apartment house with what appears to be Hadrianic brickwork has not yet been excavated.

Before turning to the extremely interesting development in the northern part of the area which stretched from Via della Foce to the Cardo degli Aurighi, we may pause for a moment to consider the Hadrianic work in the southern part of the region. Along the Decumanus a small shop house (III, 2, 1) was probably Hadrianic; and about A.D. 127 the Domus di Marte (III, 2, 5) replaced an earlier one at the corner. There is no external evidence for dating the former, but significant brick stamps were found in the latter. Presumably the Cardo remained at the old level, as the house was approached by a high sidewalk on that side. It was a small dwelling with shops toward each street and no sign of stairs to an upper floor. The façade of fine yellow brickwork toward the Decumanus was a later addition though it may still be Hadrianic; the one of moderately fine red brickwork toward the Cardo is coeval with the rather slipshod masonry inside. The reticulate is not always neatly interlocked with the brick as in good Hadrianic work. The house shows signs of many ancient modifications and considerable modern restoration. Beyond the Trajanic *horrea* of the Cardo degli Aurighi, a shop-row (III, 2, 7) terminating in a rather pretentious hall at the northwest was erected A.D. 126–127. The independent southeast wall blocked the side entrance to the Trajanic *horrea*, and brick stamps give the date. Too little is preserved to be of much use to this study. The inner facing of the hall shows some fine reticulate work with brick bands. Behind the shops, the ground stood at a higher level. A second row of shops facing a porticus (III, 2, 10) was built at the rear of the area. The position of its back wall proves that it was constructed later than the Trajanic development behind the Hadrianic shops of Via della Foce, but it shows the same formless facing with brick bands as appears in some of the Trajanic masonry. A third structure of uncertain purpose (III, 2, 9) bounded the area on the northwest and was probably contemporaneous. It had a varied masonry which is far from typical of any period. The short façade toward the Cardo of fine red brickwork displays the use of a recessed pilaster which is a new decorative effect. The rest of the exterior is faced with reticulate strengthened by brick bands and block reinforcements at the start of the partition walls and at the corners; the interior has the same crude masonry as the nearby shops. Block-work was used for the upper part of the northwest wall where high windows faced the side porticus of the Caseggiato degli Aurighi. Another edifice in the center (III, 2, 8), of which little remains, shows blocks reinforcing the reticulate facing on the outside. It is adjudged Hadrianic in the official publication and seems to reflect the same lack of finesse as the three others.

51 *Sc. di O.* I, pl. 10, fig. 1.

52 Bloch, *Bolli*, pp. 193–203, where it is called "La Casa della Caccia"; idem, *Sc. di O.* I, pp. 223–234.

53 *Sc. di O.* I, pl. 4, fig. 4.

54 G. Calza, *Palladio*, vol. 5, 1941, pp. 8–11.

Most of the space at the lower end of Via della Foce was already filled with Trajanic edifices when Hadrianic contractors took over. A narrow passage having Hadrianic construction on each side (III, 1, 8) once connected the road by the Christian Basilica with Via della Foce. It consisted of a complex of shops and a couple of rooms which may have been devoted to some business enterprise. A brick stamp of A.D. 123 found *in situ* suggests a date of about A.D. 125 for the edifice or edifices. The plan has been somewhat obscured by later modifications. The bricks used with the reticulate work were rather thick (4.2 cm.) and magenta. An oblique arch of *sesquipedales* upheld the outer stairs, and enormous relieving arches of the same strengthened the walls. Fallen vaulting reveals the use of huge ollae in the haunches. Few instances of this usage have been found in Ostia; on the other hand, few remains of vaulting have been preserved. At about the same time according to the brick stamps, a row of shops (III, 1, 14) was built in front of the area given over to Trajanic building. Why such an important strip was still free is a mystery. The fronts were apparently open, and most had back doors onto the area behind. The four at the southeast originally opened onto an inner corridor at the rear. Apartments over them were served by a staircase from Via della Foce; over the others, a staircase from Via della Calcara. The masonry of the usual combination of brick and reticulate is decidedly mediocre.

The ruinous condition in which the Caseggiato del Serapide (III, 10, 3)[51] was found made possible the collection of a vast number of stamps[52] that prove that the vast building complex which stretched from Via della Foce to the Cardo degli Aurighi was started in the mid-Hadrianic period. Other stamps prove no less conclusively that the Caseggiato degli Aurighi (III, 10, 1) at the other end was finished or profoundly modified during the reign of the Antonines. One has only to glance at a photograph of the Caseggiato del Serapide as it appeared on excavation[53] to realize how much of the following analysis is due to the acumen of Gismondi who was able to make an accurate restoration from the confusion of fallen members. The ground plan was simple with rooms and shops opening off from the cortile in the traditional fashion.[54] The cortile, on the other hand, is an early example of a lofty inner arcade. One of the slender piers of brick-faced concrete was still standing. It terminated in a tile cornice of three courses upon which rested great arches of *sesquipedales* set too far back to give the appearance of stability. Above the crowns of the arches a string cornice of three courses marked the presence of the pavement of the corridor at the first-floor level. The shops facing Via della Foce were intimately connected with the cortile. Here bonding courses appear at the beginning of the masonry under slightly curved relieving arches of upright tiles. Projecting tiles made an impost molding for a mezzanine floor of wood. Two rows of tiles roughly follow the curve upon which rested the barrel vaults. Rows of *besales* which were laid on the wooden centering remain imbedded in the concrete. The aggregate consists of rather small pieces of tufa laid with a minimum amount of mortar. Some pieces of tile serve as bonding members, but there is no real ribbing. The one shop restored to its original state along Via della Calcara has a cross vault, whereas the secondary entrance corridor from the street is barrel-vaulted. Windows both inside and out lighted the mezzanine chambers. Relieving arches over the inside windows helped to carry the cross vaulting of the arcade. Flights of stairs ascended in two ramps from the northwest and southeast corners[55] of the cortile. The one at the northwest at any rate had a rampant arch of *bipedales*. A door at the landing led to the mezzanine. The rooms on the northwest side, which were backed against a blank wall, have not been restored. In front of the entrance, there was originally a "tablinum" between a narrow room on the left caused by earlier construction[56] and a large one on the right. This southwest side was modified later by the insertion of the shrine to Serapis from which the house has received its modern name; and the "tablinum" became a passage to the Baths behind. Piers and façades were faced with yellow bricks, whereas both yellow and light red ones were used in the other walls. All the bricks were triangles made from *besales*.[57]

The Terme dei Sette Sapienti (III, 10, 2), named from the painting of the seven philosophers with their indecorous captions which were considered appropriate for the inn located there at an earlier time, incorporated a number of earlier walls mostly faced with brick and reticulate work that would seem to be Trajanic, but they also show enough construction practically identical with the two adjacent houses to justify Calza's conviction that they were part of the Hadrianic building complex. Some of this is discernible in the circular hall, which was probably merely a pretentious entrance. It was apparently originally two segments of a circle with a broad passage between them. Each had its own dome. Later, perhaps in the Antonine era,[58] the two parts were joined by three archways on each side, and the half domes were incorporated in a cupola. This hall needs a more detailed study than is feasible at the present time. The spectacular mosaic with the hunting scenes is probably Antonine. Against the usual Severan dating of the mosaic, Meiggs advocates a Hadrianic date.[59] It would seem to me more likely that the mosaic was laid when the monumental entrance between the apses was converted into the circular room with the cupola. Besides, the combination of acanthus scrolls with figures of men and beasts is not found to my knowledge before the middle of the century.[60] There is, moreover, a liveliness about the whole composition that makes a Severan date seem even less likely. Becatti[61] favors a Hadrianic date. Little else remains of this first phase except a large room in the southeast corner, which was evidently abandoned at the time of the Severan restoration, perhaps because it was too vast for adequate heating. Yellow triangles predominate in all the brickwork.

The Caseggiato degli Aurighi (III, 10, 1)[62] was certainly entrusted to the same contractor as the Caseggiato del Serapide. Identical slender piers supported a similar arcade (pl. 24, fig. 1) about a somewhat larger central court as well as an arcade with eight piers along the south side. The tile impost and the capping molding above the arches were the same, though the latter was protected with cover tiles. One difference, however, is noted at once and may indicate an improvement at a slightly later date. The arches rest firmly on the piers, imparting a sense of stability which is lacking in the other. The piers were stuccoed. A species of loggia stood between the

[55] This edifice stands at just about forty-five degrees from the points of the compass.

[56] The very red brickwork and reticulate appearing between the stairs and the Sala dei Sette Filosofi and in the niches of the circular room were probably Trajanic. Trajanic stamps (*CIL*, vol. 15 (1), nos. 1149, 1152) were found in the arches of thick (6 cm.) tiles in the west wall of the stairs. Others (nos. 29b, 63, 97b, 440, 822, 1348) were found loose. See Bloch, *Bolli*, pp. 70, 202.

[57] Gismondi, *Sc. di O.* I, p. 208, n. 10.

[58] Becatti, *Sc. di O.* I, p. 147.

[59] Meiggs, *Ostia*, p. 450.

[60] M. E. Blake, *MAAR*, vol. 13, 1936, p. 87.

[61] Becatti, *Sc. di O.* IV, pp. 133–136.

[62] G. Calza, *Palladio*, vol. 5, 1941, pp. 11–18; Crema, pp. 458–459, fig. 590.

[63] This became Via Tecta.

[64] The same type of balcony is found in the Caseggiato di Annio which is Hadrianic. See below, p. 185.

[65] The present partitions are later.

[66] See Meiggs, Ostia, pp. 311–336. Calza suggests (Palladio, vol. 5, 1941, p. 17) that the whole complex was built for the convenience and enrichment of some guild.

[67] See below, pp. 213–214.

court and the Cardo degli Aurighi and masked a change in orientation. To the Cardo it presented three arches between the arched doorways of the two entrance corridors. The four tall piers had travertine insets at two different heights and terminated in the impost moldings for the arches of which traces remain. Two narrow entrance corridors from the alley[63] at the west divided the western part into three units. The first to the left of the loggia consisted of two ample shops facing the Cardo, a large back room accessible from the west shop alone, a staircase rising from the loggia to apartments above, and a small room behind the stairs suitable for a door-keeper. This southwest corner has been restored, as much as possible from fallen parts, up to the third floor (pl. 30, fig. 1). The shops had the usual travertine threshold and a great beam as a lintel under a segmental relieving arch of tiles. A small window between beam and arch may have admitted a little light when the doors were closed; unusually large windows under enor-mous relieving arches lighted the mezzanine apartment. Over the relieving arches a continuous capping molding of tile marked the transition to a lunetted half-barrel vault of concrete which supported the balcony of the *piano nobile*. The chances are that this balcony did not extend all the way across the front.[64] The shops were cross-vaulted and two cross vaults covered the room behind them. A beginning of the cross vaulting for the second floor is still discernible. Fallen vaulting contains medium-sized irregular pieces of tufa laid in a minimum amount of hard mortar. The middle unit consisted of an apartment of three rooms, a shop facing the court, and a large latrine in the northwest corner. The three rooms, lighted from the alley as well as from the court, had doors in their partitions so arranged that they could have been subdivided into six rooms by temporary partitions.[65] They had wooden ceilings and had no connection with the mezzanine floor. The third unit was a part of the Baths. The southwest corner is less well preserved. Three shops facing the Cardo may have formed the ground floor for a superstructure with a balcony similar to the one on the west. A passage separated the shops from twin staircases, one ascending from the court, the other from the south arcade. Behind the stairs, a large hall par-tially divided into two parts by a partition, accessible from all four sides, would have been a suitable place for some one of the many guilds which formed such a part of the life of the ancient city.[66] Such was the Caseggiato degli Aurighi as originally planned. Whether the actual building extended into the Antonine period is still an open question. Certainly Antonine stamps were found there, but they may have come from a slightly later modification.[67]

The west wall of the last Trajanic structure on Via della Foce (III, 16, 5) established the alignment of the back walls of three edifices (III, 16, 4, 2, and 1) between it and the Cardo degli Aurighi. Such brick stamps as have been found confirm the evidence of the structural environment that these relatively unimportant buildings should be dated in the early Hadrianic era. In the time of Trajan, a passage undoubtedly connected Via di Annio with Via della Foce; in the time of Hadrian, this thoroughfare became the central passage for a market of conventional form (III, 16, 4) with stalls separated by wooden partitions. There was a staircase from the central passage on each side, but whether it led to lofts or terraces is incapable of proof. The walls seem too thin to have had apartments at an upper level. The walls were faced with the usual combination of reticulate and brick. The bricks were a mixture of broken roof tiles, tiles, and triangles. Two separate brick stamps confirm the Hadrianic date.[68] The pavements were of herringbone brick. The next edifice (III, 16, 2) had a ground plan consisting of two equal areas separated by a staircase. These areas were probably subdivided at a later time, and the upper floors were doubtless continuous. The façade is one of the few in Ostia displaying reticulate insets in a brick frame. The bricks were rather thick (4 cm. +). Two relieving arches with voussoirs of the same thickness appear in the back wall of the northern unit. They were outlined both inside and out by reticulate tesserae such as were used in the wall facings. Traces of black-and-white mosaics and red and yellow paintings with miniatures indicate that this was not an ordinary mercantile establishment. Masonry, mosaics, and wall paintings are in accord with the one early Hadrianic stamp. The end building facing the Cardo degli Aurighi (III, 16, 1) was probably contemporaneous. A buttress at what was probably its northwest corner yielded two Hadrianic stamps. The ground floor was given over to shops of various shapes and sizes. There may have been wooden steps to a terrace where masonry steps were inserted later, but there is no positive evidence of an upper story, and the walls are scarcely thick enough to have supported its weight. The walls are faced with a mediocre reticulate carelessly interlocked with brick, but there is one buttress entirely of blockwork. The edifice shows considerable remodeling.

Brick stamps indicate that the Insula delle Volte Dipinte (III, 5, 1) was an early Hadrianic structure. To the northeast of it, there was probably originally an open square, but it faced the street named for it on the northwest and took its orientation from the building preceding the Antonine Caseggiato delle Trifore along the Decumanus. There were no external shops to interfere with the direct lighting of the rooms, although a space equal in size to a room was cut off from the rest at the end and left open to the street on each side for a *thermopolium*. It had a door bringing it into communication with the rest of the house. The entire ground plan is most unusual. A narrow corridor bisected the house from northeast to southwest with the equivalent of four rooms on each side. The main façade is unique (pl. 23, fig. 3). It has an ornamental doorway with three high windows on each side in addition to the arched opening for the refreshment stand at the left corner. Even the ornamental doorway is unusual with its "pedimented" top practically resting on the low segmental arch of *bipedales* which covered the opening. A small window above the pediment lighted the entrance corridor. The windows were covered with very slightly curved lintel arches. A capping molding of projecting tiles marked the transition to the next story. The end façade toward the northeast is not without interest. A wooden doorframe apparently took the place of a lintel, but there was a segmental relieving arch with a simple terra-cotta plaque framed in tile set in the lunette of masonry beneath it. Three rooms well lighted by high windows occupied the front. The one at the right of the entrance was accessible from both corridors; the two on the left each had an additional window in the back to give some light to the cross corridor behind. Black-and-white mosaics of

[68] One had a donkey in the center of a form not used after the early years of the reign of Hadrian and also the letters *RIHA*. The *HA* might stand for Halotus of *CIL*, vol. 15 (1), no. 543, who was making bricks in A.D. 123. The other had *EX FIG CAE*. (No stamps for III, 16, 4 are listed in *Sc. di O.* I, p. 225.—J.D.B.)

[69] Becatti, *Sc. di O.* IV, pp. 101–102.

geometric design adorned the floor,[69] but the fine wall paintings and ceiling frescoes are the glory of the house. The ceilings were cross-vaulted. Two small windows over the doors at the ends were the main source of light for the long narrow cross-vaulted corridor, which was paved with coarse mosaic at the west but herringbone brick for the rest of the way. Four less richly decorated and much darker rooms stood on the other side of the corridor. The high windows were insufficient to dispel the darkness, and so the walls were given a white ground. The floors had black-and-white mosaics in three rooms, herringbone brick in the kitchen. The ceilings were depressed barrel vaults. The kitchen has a narrow cross vault at right angles to the door, an arch, and then a regular barrel vault. The space corresponding to the *thermopolium* contained a stair well with two ramps at right angles to each other. The stairs were carried in part on a rampant arch of *sesquipedales* (pl. 26, fig. 1), and the wall ends are rounded. The stair well was more than adequately lighted by three windows in addition to the wide doorway. A small pedestal stood at the landing. At the top of the stairs the lower part of the partition walls gives the floor plan of an upper apartment, and the beginning of a stairway proves that there was at least one more story. There was no mezzanine. The plan more or less duplicated the one below with four rooms on one side of a narrow corridor and three rooms, a kitchen, and a latrine on the other. Traces of wall paintings remain. The brickwork is none too good. Enough plaster remains on the rear wall to show that it was not supposed to be seen. The bricks are light yellowish red, 3–4 cm. thick, and very uneven in length. There are no bonding courses or relieving arches. The architect who planned this house was certainly experimenting with the use of cross vaults. Not only has he used depressed cross vaults in the more elegant rooms, but he has covered the long narrow corridor with a series of cross vaults where a long narrow corridor barrel vault would have been much simpler. The vaulting in the rooms was supported by angle piers in part at least.

Via di Annio was not a through street. Only two edifices with a space between them, which was later used as deposit for storage jars, were erected on its southeast side at about the time with which we are concerned. The small building at the north corner (III, 14, 2) retains little more than the end walls and traces of a staircase of its Hadrianic phase. The ground floor was probably broken up into shops with temporary walls.[70] The masonry preserved is entirely of brickwork but offers nothing of special interest. The building was certainly earlier than the double porticus behind it which closes its southern doorways. This building is adjudged Antonine in the official report.[71] The other, the Caseggiato di Annio (III, 14, 4) can be dated by its brick stamps A.D. 128–129.[72] It had wide shops along the two streets. Later modifications have somewhat obscured the inner arrangements, but there seems to have been a wall with high windows on the southeast side. An outside staircase at the north led to upper apartments. The travertine steps were set well back in the space reserved for them, but tile was substituted for travertine where, after a turn, the steps were no longer visible from the street. The shops (pl. 24, fig. 2) had the usual travertine thresholds and slightly curved lintel arches of upright *sesquipedales* with the masonry under

[70] The present dividing walls in blockwork are almost certainly later.

[71] See below, p. 215.

[72] Bloch, *Sc. di O.* I, p. 225.

them resting on a wooden beam. A window over the lintel was protected by a relieving arch. A continuous string cornice marks the rise and fall of these relieving arches. At least three framed terra-cotta plaques adorned the walls between the shop openings. A semicircular niche for a statuette occupied the corresponding position on the Cardo near the corner. The continuous string molding also marked the line of the concrete vaulting supporting the balcony, which was lunetted over the windows and had to be adapted to a narrower space at the staircase. This may very likely be the earliest example of this type of balcony. Set into the concrete, three *tabulae ansatae* of terra cotta bear the inscriptions: OMNIA, FELICIA (?), ANNI. A series of lintel arches of upright *besales* with triangular pieces to serve as springers outlines the top of this vaulting under a capping cornice of projecting tiles. The façades were entirely of brickwork except for a huge travertine block set in near the north end for no discernible reason. Lintel relieving arches at the floor level strengthened the inner wall enclosing the stair well. An oblique lintel arch developing into a full arch at the top helped to carry the second ramp. It was composed of rather short pieces of broken tiles. The partition walls were faced with the usual combination of brick and reticulate. The visitor is immediately impressed with the airiness of the interior in its original state.[73] The walls were little more than piers to support cross vaulting. Beam holes for a mezzanine appear only in the frontal shops and in the northernmost shop on the side street. If there were any in the rest as the arrangement of windows suggests, they were torn out before the walls received the final wall paintings. The contractor does not seem to be quite sure of the technique involved in making a cross vault. One frontal shop exhibits an angle pier in only one corner to help hold the vaulting; the other has a travertine block across the opposite corner for the same purpose. And when he divided the northern shop to make two cross vaults, he inserted a pilaster in only one wall. He made use of both *bipedales* and broken pieces on the centering at the angles, and broken pieces and *besales* elsewhere. Apparently, the making of cross vaults had not yet become standardized.

Between the great Trajanic *horrea* near the Tiber which are as yet unexplored and the strip of early Hadrianic edifices just described, there is a wedge-shaped area which was more or less filled with Republican and slightly later buildings, among them an extensive granary. The proximity to the Tiber made a drastic raise in level desirable. Once this was accomplished, Hadrianic contractors had the space to use for an extraordinarily interesting group of buildings.[74] First to be built was a trapezoidal warehouse (III, 17, 1) having its main entrance from the Cardo degli Aurighi. There is nothing distinctive in its plan of storerooms on each side of a passage, but its masonry is one of the finest examples of reticulate insets neatly interlocked with brick to be found in all Ostia. Fine-grained red bricks from tiles predominate, especially in the lower part of the walls. They are 3–4 cm. thick. The combination of brick and reticulate also appears in the external face on each side of an ornamental gateway of which only part of the pilasters remain. Traces of herringbone pavements are discernible in some of the storerooms. The absence of brick stamps indicates a date before the reorganization of

[73] Many of the openings were walled up later perhaps to give stability; and what is preserved of the wall paintings is later than these modifications.

[74] Bloch, *AJA*, vol. 63, 1959, pp. 225–240.

[75] Becatti, *Sc. di O.* IV, pp. 153–159.

the brick industry in A.D. 123 had made itself felt. The rest of the area was bisected by Via del Serapide, which terminated in an open square behind the *horrea*. Twin arcades with the street between them made a decorous front on Via della Foce. Intercommunicating shops opened off from each arcade and were in communication with large rooms behind. Each probably had stairs from the arcade to apartments over the shops, though the place where such a staircase would have been on the west has not yet been excavated. Both were erected at about the same time as the *horrea*, and both show virtually the same lack of brick stamps. Though they may have been planned by the same architect, they were apparently constructed by different contractors, as the masonry is not identical. The one at the west which developed into the Caseggiato di Bacco e Arianna (III, 17, 5) was constructed with more care than the other. A well-squared travertine block stood under the corner pier of the arcade, and travertine insets protected the edges. The piers were faced with good magenta bricks made from tiles, as were the front walls of the shops opening onto the arcade. Partition and rear walls were faced with panels of reticulate neatly set in a brick frame without interlocking; doors were covered with slightly curved lintels of *bipedales* outlined in a row of reticulate tesserae; the spaces for beams to support the mezzanines were carefully framed in tile. The arch facings, on the other hand, were made entirely of broken tile with no whole ones to make a bond. Large rooms with elaborate black-and-white mosaic pavements[75] opened into a colonnade which faced an open area with a small oblong pool. One of the mosaics has given the house its modern name. A stairway from Via del Serapide led to upper apartments possibly only over these large rooms. Pieces of fallen vaulting show that it was a compact mass of rather large tufa *caementa* held together by a minimum amount of firm mortar. The apartment house on the east side of Via del Serapide (III, 16, 6) exhibits a brickwork of magenta tiles which is not up to the usual Hadrianic standard. Rectangular panels of reticulate were used in the same way as in the other house, but tile cornices upheld the mezzanines. The corner pier of the arcade rested on a less carefully prepared block of travertine, and travertine insets protected the corners. The same type of masonry was used for the four large rooms in the rear. The side toward Via del Serapide was faced with brick and contained a stairway to apartments above. Brick stamps suggest that the arcade was soon sacrificed to the need of enlarging the commercial area possibly as a result of increased business due to the presence of the Baths. A crooked passage at the left led from the street to the Baths.

It is an indication of the growth of luxury in the second century that another Bath, the Terme della Trinacria (III, 16, 7), was erected in the same neighborhood almost immediately after the Terme del Mithra was completed. Possibly it was intended primarily for those connected with the cult of Serapis. These Baths show at least three distinct building periods. Our concern at present is simply with the earliest, which brick stamps prove is to be dated about A.D. 127. The raising of the general level made the Republican level available for all the underground passages necessary for the functioning of an ancient Bath. A detailed analysis of these requires the attention of a heating expert. They proved to be inadequate, for soon

after the Baths were completed, the engineers sacrificed one of the cisterns
to make a passage to the furnaces and built a larger one on the South. A
water wheel was used to lift the water from the underground reservoirs. The
plan is that common to most Ostian Baths—an open space for exercise, later
provided with an apsed pool, followed by a succession of heated rooms. In
the first phase, these rooms were provided with wide windows where they
would admit the afternoon sunshine. The windows were not on one line
but show a decreasing projection as they approach the room with the three
pools. Bloch has proved conclusively that although the *bipedales* of the
original *suspensurae* were re-used, the hypocausts were completely remade
in the time of Commodus. The arrangement of wall tubes also belongs to
this late phase. Important walls were faced with brick; secondary ones, with
a combination of brick and reticulate. The bricks came mostly from broken
tiles but vary considerably in thickness and texture. Although the back wall
of the earlier Hadrianic market against which they were built has the usual
arrangement of reticulate interlocked with brick, the Baths display in the
original parts the rectangular panels of reticulate like those found throughout
the development. The workmanship is mediocre. There were some large
arches over openings and an occasional poorly constructed relieving arch in
the body of the masonry.

Between III, 17, 1 and III, 17, 5 there were three practically contemporary
structures closely connected. An inscribed pediment proves that III, 17, 4
was a Serapeum; the Fasti Ostienses show that a temple of Serapis was dedicated by a certain Caltilius on January 24, 127; and brick stamps found in all
three structures range from A.D. 123 to 126.[76] The chronological correlation
between the brick stamps and the inscription is of the utmost importance
to a specialized study of the stamps. The Temple of Serapis (III, 17, 4) was
lifted up on a high podium at the head of a colonnaded court. The small
cella was enlarged by what appears to be an open forecourt so that it might
have a wider base for statuary at the back. The podium walls were faced
with rectangular panels of reticulate not interlocked with the brick frame.
What little masonry was necessary for the forecourt, except for the frontal
piers faced with yellow bricks, was in block-and-brick work. This may represent a change of plan in the course of construction, as Professor Bloch
suggests. Buttresses of the same masonry were added to the left side of the
podium wall at the same time. When the façade of the precinct along Via
del Serapide was built, piers were affixed to the buildings in front for four
arches over the street to furnish an impressive approach to the complex.
They, like the façade, were faced with yellow brick. A silhouette mosaic of
a bull stood in front of the ornamental doorway to the precinct, of which
only the start of recessed pilasters remains. A poor grade of reticulate, in
rectangular panels surrounded by brick without any interlocking, faced the
side and rear walls of the precinct. A course of *bipedales* stood under the
reticulate, and there was at least one large relieving arch. Some block-and-
brick work in these walls seems to be original. The court was paved with
a black-and-white mosaic depicting a Nile scene. The forecourt of the
temple also had a black-and-white mosaic.[77] An altar stood in front of the
temple. A wide doorway led originally from the sanctuary through a sort

[76] Bloch, *Bolli*, p. 225.

[77] Becatti, *Sc. di O.* IV, pp. 150–153.

[78] Becatti, *op. cit.*, pp. 143–148.

[79] *Ibid.*, pp. 143, 149–150.

of antechamber to a large edifice (III, 17, 3) at the south. The main feature was a large hall with many doorways. Although a through passage intervened, the formal entrance from the antechamber was marked by two brick-faced piers adorned with semicolumns and covered with marble. At present, its restored mosaic is its chief glory, the date of which is somewhat of an enigma. The pictures look Hadrianic, the arrangement seems Antonine as does the border with rectangles in isometric perspective. The careful workmanship is more in accord with the period of Hadrian.[78] The black-and-white mosaics in the rooms at the east and west are undoubtedly original.[79] The fundamental masonry throughout is identical with that in the Serapeum. Little can be said of the contemporary structure to the south of it (III, 17, 2), in which was inserted at a later time the Mitreo della Planta Pedis. It had no independent side walls. The façade along Via del Serapide and the broken wall in front of the great buttressed wall of the Trajanic *horrea* by the Tiber converted the space into a loggia and an area, the function of which is not clear. As in other parts of the complex, blocks are found here also particularly in the lower part of the piers. It is my conviction that the blocks came from early buildings demolished in the region.

The line of Trajanic shops along the Cardo degli Aurighi continued southward to Via delle Volte Dipinte with similar shops (III, 9, 23 and 24) having apartments above them. Connected with it was a row along Via delle Volte Dipinte, which obviously belong in date to the Insula delle Muse (III, 9, 22), the dwelling behind it. A stringcourse consisting of a plain terra-cotta molding passes over the slightly curved lintel arches of the shop openings along Via delle Volte Dipinte without interruption except for the doorway to the house and the gateway to the open space and then descends in a vertical line to cover a shop at a lower level and so continues over all the openings still preserved along the Cardo degli Aurighi. These are typical Hadrianic shops with travertine thresholds. Each had a doorway at a somewhat higher level into the strip of land at the rear. *Bipedales* mark the start of the brick facing of the walls and appear as bonding courses at wall ends. A cornice of projecting tiles supported a wooden floor for a mezzanine in these as well as in those in front of the Insula delle Muse.

[80] G. Calza, *BMIR*, vol. 12, 1941, p. 81; *idem*, *Palladio*, vol. 5, 1941, pp. 6–8; *idem*, *Nuovi Scavi*, p. 14. See also Becatti, *Sc. di O.* I, p. 136.

In the Insula delle Muse (III, 9, 22),[80] the architect did not hesitate to break away from the standard pattern for houses centered in an arcaded court. The entrance is not in the center of the side, and the tablinum is not opposite it. Unfortunately, nothing remains of the entablature above the pilasters of slightly finer brickwork which marked the entrance. The actual doorway was covered with a segmental arch having its own capping molding of tiles. An opening at the left of the long entrance corridor led to a landing for a flight of steps carried in part on an oblique arch of *sesquipedales*. There was a window at the landing. As in the shops, a tiled cornice held the wooden ceiling of the corridor. In the central court, the relatively low piers which supported the segmental arches of the quadriporticus were stout enough to have carried other arcades or the fenestrated walls of upper stories. The quadriporticus had a wooden ceiling supported in the same way as that of the corridor. The three rooms on the east had large windows toward the open area, doors to the court. The tablinum opposite them was marked by two piers *in antis*. Originally, it probably had a wooden ceiling also like all the rest of the rooms, but angle piers prove that it was later given a cross vault. In the northeast corner two rooms were recessed behind a secondary corridor with an outside door. The outer one had a large outside window, the inner one only indirect lighting, but the wall paintings had a white background to enhance this feeble illumination. An outside staircase from the great court at the northwest led to apartments above. Exterior walls, including those facing the central cortile, were faced with brick made from broken tiles; inner ones, with brick and reticulate. There is an occasional relieving arch of tile. All floors were paved with black-and-white mosaics of geometric design[81] and recall those of Hadrian's villa near Tivoli. All the walls were frescoed. Brick stamps prove that this unit was constructed about A.D. 130.[82]

This house formed the southeast corner of an extraordinary housing development (III, 9, 1–20). The contractors of the Hadrianic period[83] apparently had an area practically devoid of earlier buildings to exploit straight to the Sullan wall.[84] An enormous oblong court was laid out and enclosed on all four sides by masonry containing ample shops and well-lighted apartments. A strip of green separated it from the shoprow along the Cardo degli Aurighi. The main entrance to the development from Via delle Volte Dipinte was recessed between two apartment units. It consisted originally of three passageways, with the central one at any rate adorned by an ornamental doorway. Three-quarter columns of fine brickwork supported an entablature, now completely gone. The broad central entrance toward the Cardo degli Aurighi has been rebuilt in modern times, no doubt along the original lines. Pilasters of fine brickwork with the usual base of terra-cotta moldings have insets of large travertine blocks shaped to serve as springers for a long lintel of upright *bipedales* with a carved tile as a keystone.[85] A small window stands over the lintel under a segmental relieving arch which has its own molding of tile. The molding is continued along the sides to break the monotony of a smooth brick façade. The pilasters supported a normal type of entablature probably with a pediment. There were narrower entrances at each end of this side and probably three similarly placed on each side of the other two sides. All the entrances once had the travertine insets, but none are preserved above that point. The corridors were barrel-vaulted and show *besales* adhering to their soffits and traces of the *bipedales* which were laid on the temporary wooden centering.

Within the central court, two independent units were built with a strip of greensward between them. Three fountains in the open spaces at the northwest and southeast supplied the tenants with water. Circular depressions in the curbing of the pools show where the jars stood while they were being filled and the slave girls gossiped. There is nothing to show how the water was distributed. Environmental conditions placed no restriction on the architect when he came to planning these inner units. Each was divided into two independent parts by a cross passage with a formal doorway at each end. Each half was subdivided in such a way that it could easily be separated into two identical apartments. The main entrance to each was from the passage by a right-angled corridor which led into the heart of the house, but there was a secondary entrance at the side. No shops cut off the

[81] Becatti, *Sc. di O.* IV, pp. 128–133.

[82] Bloch, *Sc. di O.* I, p. 223.

[83] Hadrianic brick stamps can be seen in every part of the vast building project.

[84] A row of shops at the level of the Augustan colonnade in front of the Caseggiato degli Aurighi preceded, and it is possible that work began here at the higher level in the Trajanic period. For the planning see also Meiggs, *Ostia*, pp. 137, 139.

[85] The only other instance of this to my knowledge is in the Hadrianic Caseggiato dei Misuratori del Grano.

sunshine. Six windows lighted each corner room, five the broad corridor which furnished light to three inner rooms, and one to the room at the other end. The windows were large but placed high to insure privacy. The walling is not preserved high enough to show whether the corner rooms were actually higher than the rest, but inside stairs prove that there was a mezzanine floor over at least a part. One defect would appear to be the absence of any logical place for the kitchen. The latrine could be under the inner staircase. One broad outside staircase on each side was considered sufficient for all the upper apartments in each unit.

It is interesting to note the variations in the plan of the apartments in the enclosing sections. The many-windowed corridor was a fixture, but the room at each end was smaller and had a single window, whereas the rooms opening off from the corridor were not dependent on it for light, but had outside windows in the backwall. In one (III, 9, 6) a large reception room with columns *in antis* seems to have replaced two rooms facing the corridor. Not enough has been excavated of the corresponding unit (III, 9, 8) to reveal whether it had a similar arrangement. In the Insula delle Parieti Gialle (III, 9, 12), the corridor is more like a great hall, though the ground plan is fundamentally the same. This house and the Insula del Graffito (III, 9, 21) behind it could be entered only from outside the great central court. They shared a common façade at the southeast consisting of two small windows lighting parallel inner staircases between the two doorways. There were no outer staircases for apartments over these two units. This second house had no connection whatsoever with the inner court. It is a good example of the corridor apartment in its simplest form—stairs and entrance corridor, small room with one window, passage and corridor with five, large rooms with three, and two small rooms facing the corridor. It looks as if the apartment preceding the Domus dei Dioscuri (III, 9, 1) also had a hall in place of the corridor. Like the Insula delle Muse, it had shops and an outside staircase facing the irregular space that formed the continuation of Via delle Volte Dipinte, but it had none for the exclusive use of upper stories toward the court.

Because the Cardo degli Aurighi has a bend, the contractors had to reckon with an odd-shaped space on the southeast side. In the southern part, they erected a unit (III, 9, 11), of which the ground floor was entirely of shops, three facing the court, three in the opposite direction. Outside stairs from the court attest upper stories. The corridor house between it and the entrance corridor (III, 9, 10) had one shop and four rooms at the back, and inside stairs for a mezzanine. The narrowing northern part (III, 9, 9) was used for shops facing the court, but accessible through a door in the rear which was flanked by a window. There were two shops on each side of the entrance unit of passage and stairs (III, 9, 7) between two corridor apartments (III, 9, 6 and 8) on the northwest side. Arrangements on the southeast side are not entirely clear, but there was a unit of shops (III, 9, 2) corresponding to that on the opposite side.

The construction is homogeneous throughout this whole vast development though the actual building probably covered a number of years. Brick stamps observed in every section would all seem to be Hadrianic.[86] The

[86] Becatti, *Sc. di O.* I, pp. 136–137; Bloch, *Sc. di O.* I, p. 223.

majority are of A.D. 123, but presumably enough have been found of a slightly later date to suggest the official estimate of ca. A.D. 128. All outer walls as well as most enclosing stairs were of brick-faced concrete, whereas all inner walls were faced with reticulate in brick frames. The bricks were made from broken tiles about 3.6–4 cm. thick, prevailingly light to medium red. In general, bonding courses were not used,[87] and the number of relieving arches has been reduced to a minimum. Gates, as we have seen, were topped with lintels between travertine springers; such other apertures as retain their covering exhibit slightly curved lintels of *sesquipedales*. Little vaulting is preserved except over passages and under stairs.[88] The oblique barrel-vaulting carrying the stairs shows traces of the covering of *bipedales* laid on the centering and of oblong pieces of tile as well as *besales* laid on the joints. Occasionally pieces were set vertically to strengthen the bond. This became the usual method of constructing vaults, but the practice had not yet become standardized. It is quite possible that beams supported wooden floors, and there was no other vaulting. While the ceiling of some rooms reached to the first-floor level, inside stairs gave access to mezzanine floors over the rest. These were supported on tile cornices. The whole complex had an abundance of outside stairs. Practically all are single ramps. Two or three times those from the court and those from outside may have met at a common landing. One starts from a landing reached by two steps; another has a ramp to a landing and a second ramp at right angles. The walls are not preserved high enough to reveal what use may have been made of balconies.

Little remains of a small shop house at the southeast end of the next block (III, 3, 2). It consisted of two shops, opening back upon the Decumanus and the area to the rear, and a staircase to upper floors. The construction appears Hadrianic; and it would seem to have been erected at the same time as the two apartment houses to the southeast.

Possibly while the great Hadrianic development including the Case a Giardino was still in process of construction, an open space at the side of the Insula delle Volte Dipinte was filled with the Insula Trapezoidale (III, 4, 1) of which the purpose is unknown. A travertine threshold marks the entrance from the Cardo degli Aurighi to a small court. A shop at the left appears to be later. It is entirely of brickwork, whereas the façade at the right has reticulate insets in a brick frame. A stairway has been added at the back with walls faced with a reticulate reinforced with bands and quoins of brick which appear inferior to that in the rest. The side walls have an unusually long stretch of reticulate between bands of brick. The wall facing Via delle Trifore is pierced by three slit windows, and a fourth appears in the addition. Each is topped by a tile and a simple terra-cotta molding. Inside piers divide the space into three longitudinal sections. Twin doors under a large slightly curved lintel with the usual masonry between it and a wooden beam must have communicated with the back street before the stair well was added. Brick stamps give the approximate date as A.D. 128–130.[89]

The last block on the Decumanus before Porta Marina would seem to me to have been the work of the contractor who built the Hadrianic development including the Case a Giardino. It contained two units (III, 6, 2 and 3)

[87] Some are visible in the western part.

[88] One or two rooms along the south-east side show traces of barrel vaults.

[89] Bloch, *Sc. di O.* I, p. 222.

separated originally by a passage and stairways from both the street and the open space behind; these stairs may have met in a common landing. Each consisted of a row of shops on the Decumanus and a well-lighted space behind, suitable for living quarters. The conversion of the northeastern unit into the Domus del Ninfeo (III, 6, 1) has obscured the inner plan. The southwestern unit was a small edition of the corridor apartment. Its façade exhibits rather thick red bricks, whereas the other shows a great number of yellow ones and seems on the whole to be less carefully made. A course of *bipedales* separated the wall proper from the foundations. The masonry is typically Hadrianic with reticulate insets in inner walls, oblique lintels under stairs, slightly curved lintels over apertures, and tile cornices to support mezzanines. No vaulting remains. In the space behind, a two-chamber cistern (III, 6, 4) with a nymphaeum in front furnished water to these two units.[90] It was entirely of brickwork with rather thin bricks (3 cm.) united by mortar joints 1.5–2.5 cm. wide without, however, any admixture of terra cotta in the tufa *caementa* of the concrete core. Brick stamps have been reported for the Domus del Ninfeo (III, 6, 1), dating to A.D. 123; and for the cistern (III, 6, 4), of the same date;[91] but as yet none from the two other units (III, 6, 2 and 3).

Hadrianic builders seem to have tried to systematize the rest of the northwest side of the Decumanus almost to the sea. A Republican sepulchral monument at a low level imposed an obstruction. They solved that difficulty by surrounding it with a structure of small rooms (III, 7, 1), of which the purpose is not clear; they rebuilt the shops in front of the Domus Fulminata (III, 7, 3); and beyond a Trajanic edifice, they constructed an impressive arched vestibule to an area as yet unexcavated. Only the stout piers of the arches remain. No stamps have been reported from this construction either.

Late in his reign, possibly when he had finished embellishing the southern part of the Forum, Hadrian bestowed another Bath on Ostia in a space east of the Caseggiato dei Triclini, which was destroyed when the Foro della Statua Eroica (I, 12, 2) and the adjacent exedra (I, 12, 3) were built. What little remains shows a hall with a semicircular niche or pool projecting from each corner, showing the same love of curved lines that is so apparent in the Villa Adriana near Tivoli. The walls were faced with brick, and the Baths were lavishly decorated with marble.

Hadrian is commemorated in an inscription of A.D. 133[92] by the grateful citizens of Ostia for their city CONSERVATA ET AUCTA OMNI INDULGENTIA ET LIBERTATE at about the time that the foundations were finished for a completely new development on the north side of the Decumanus beyond the theater and the Foro delle Corporazioni.[93] Since this was part of the public land set aside in the Republican era, Hadrian's contractors did not have to reckon with earlier structures except for the Baths of Claudius, a large cistern which could be kept intact, and a Flavian beginning of new Baths at the higher level. A second inscription of A.D. 139[94] gives the information that, since the funds granted by Hadrian for Baths (certainly those in this development) were exhausted, Antoninus Pius had given as much as was needed to complete the work and adorn it with marble in fitting fashion. Brick stamps date the whole development (II,

[90] Neuerburg, *Fontane*, p. 187, no. 123.

[91] Bloch, *Sc. di O.* I, p. 222. (Miss Blake's note card states that she found a brick stamp in the nymphaeum—the card does not distinguish between cistern and nymphaeum. Without noting the form, she read the stamp thus:

PA
EX PRAER

And she hesitantly suggested an Antonine date. Professor Bloch wrote me that he believes this stamp is his *Suppl.* no. 32, 4 examples of which he found in the original construction in part of the west and the north walls of the cistern. They are recorded by him in *Sc. di O.* I, p. 222, under Is. VI, 1 in the paragraph beginning "Nella cortina della cisterna . . . ," where, as he writes, he should have referred to III, 6, 4.—J.D.B.)

[92] *CIL*, vol. 14, no. 95.

[93] For another belonging to the early years of his reign, see above pp. 158–165.

[94] *CIL*, vol. 14, no. 98.

3–6) in the late Hadrianic period.[95] A porticus of thirty-three brick-faced piers with inner pilasters, the Portico di Nettuno (II, 3, 1, and 4, 1) along the Decumanus, shaded a continuous row of shops broken only by entrances to buildings and to two streets within the development. Outside stairs gave access to upper apartments. The piers had bases and capitals of travertine and are stout enough to have carried a second order, but no trace remains of the superstructure. The shops present no unusual features.

Amid the shops facing the Portico di Nettuno with their overhead apartments reached by outside stairs, an entrance corridor led to a large edifice (II, 3, 2) which has been only partly excavated. It was probably a warehouse of some kind. At any rate, it consisted of a large arcaded court with two good-sized rooms on the north amply provided with splayed windows adapted to the storage of perishable goods. This side was equipped with both inside stairs for more storage space (?) and outside stairs for apartments. The arrangement of the rooms on the sides is not quite so clear. The edifice was flanked on the east by a narrow shop house, which must have bridged the secondary entrance corridor as there is only one outside staircase, and on the west by two apartment units of the newer style set directly on the street without an intervening row of shops. An ornamental doorway encasing stairs and entrance corridor served both units. Unfortunately, only the low pedestal, the molded base of lighter tile, and a part of the pilasters of fine brickwork with narrow joints are all that are left of this doorway. The street façade shows the high windows typical of the corridor houses. Only the northernmost room had windows on the side as well. A slight divergence from the usual plan gave each of these apartments two rooms at the outer end of the corridor. The area between them had a door and two windows on the south, where there was no possibility of an outside window, and a door and one window on the north where there was. The interior has not been fully excavated, but inner stairs on each side of the entrance corridor gave access to upper floors. This analysis, based mostly on the official plan, must suffice until the whole edifice is laid bare.

Another huge edifice with an arcaded central court (II, 12, 1) occupied the northeast corner of the development. It has not yet been entirely excavated. A "tablinum" with two columns *in antis* stood at the west end of the court, and a staircase took the place of the customary *ala* on each side of it. The entrances were, however, from the north and south. They were flanked by rooms opening outward but with the exception of two or three near the corners, no other rooms faced the streets. The rest opened onto the court or the corridor behind the "tablinum." Staircases with two ramps occupied the northeast and southeast corners. Again detailed analysis must await complete excavation.

On the west, the Portico di Nettuno brought a narrow strip of land between Via delle Corporazioni and Via della Fontana into the same complex. It was utilized for three main units separated by cross passages. The southernmost was divided longitudinally in such a way that there were five shops (II, 6, 4) facing east and a shop and a corridor apartment (II, 6, 3) facing west. This is called Insula dell'Ercole Bambino from one of the paintings. A narrow passage separated two shops back to back from the main part of the second

[95] For this chronological evidence, I am indebted to Bloch, *Bolli*, pp. 244–250. See also, *idem, AJA*, vol. 63, 1959, pp. 239–240.

unit, which practically duplicated the first but in the reverse arrangement—five shops (II, 6, 5) on Via delle Corporazioni and a corridor apartment (II, 6, 6) on Via della Fontana. The ceiling of one room, restored with the small pieces of painted stucco in place, has given the name, Insula del Soffitto Dipinto, to this apartment. The black-and-white mosaic of geometric pattern in this room is worthy of note.[96] Inner staircases led to mezzanines over the apartments, whereas each shop had its own mezzanine; but one outside staircase from each street was apparently considered ·sufficient for the upper floors of both these units. The third unit (II, 6, 7) the Caseggiato delle Fornaci, shows the same longitudinal division, but the partition wall is pierced by a doorway at each room. It was probably a manufactory of some sort with windows toward Via della Fontana and broad doorways toward Via delle Corporazioni. Here one inside staircase served the entire mezzanine floor, and an outside staircase from each street, the upper floors. Upstairs apartments were doubtless similar to those in the other two units. On Via della Fontana, a continuous tile cornice topped the slightly curved openings of the shops and the succession of straight lintels over the high windows of the apartment of the first two units, but was broken by the twin openings for the shop and corridor between them. These have their own slightly curved lintels with a capping molding, a window, and a low relieving arch over it. The third unit shows no such decorative element, nor does the façade toward Via delle Corporazioni.

The space behind the Portico di Nettuno and between Via della Fontana and Via dei Vigili was divided into two unequal parts by Via della Palestra. The more southernmost contained the Terme di Nettuno and its dependencies; the more northern the Caserma dei Vigili. For some reason the east wall of the Baths is not on the same line as that of the Caserma. The Terme di Nettuno (II, 4, 2) took the place of the Claudian Baths[97] which had to be sacrificed to the reorganization of the area at a higher level. A start had been made under the Flavians, but had not progressed far enough to interfere with the plans made by Hadrian. He was unable to finish them, and so Antoninus Pius and Commodus brought them to completion. Later they were extensively restored by Constantine. A site which shows evidence of so many different periods needs a more detailed analysis than is feasible at this time. The two great halls·leading to the Baths proper are paved with superb black-and-white mosaics depicting the marriage of Neptune and Amphitrite.[98] These have long been taken as the norm for Antonine mosaics of sea scenes, but they are undoubtedly Hadrianic. The Baths proper consist of a succession of rooms furnished with the necessary pools, hypocausts, and wall tubes for both cold and warm baths. The heating arrangements for both water and air are outside the limits of this study. At the northeast corner, there was a tank with exceptionally thick walls. Small travertine corbels support depressed arches under a ramp along each street which is just wide enough for a large water pipe (pl. 26, fig. 2). Whether they were provided simply to take care of the overflow or to fill the tank under some sort of pressure awaits solution. Adjacent to the tank, there were two shops with a two-ramp staircase to rooms above them. These were undoubtedly connected with the Baths in some way. The western part was devoted pri-

[96] Becatti, *Sc. di O.* IV, p. 64. For the building, see Meiggs, *Ostia*, pp. 246–247, and Crema, p. 458; for the painted ceiling, Meiggs, *op. cit.*, pp. 441, 444.

[97] Blake, *RC* II, p. 63. See also Meiggs, *Ostia*, pp. 75, 409–411, plan p. 412, pl. 3 B.

[98] Becatti, *Sc. di O.* IV, pp. 47–48.

marily to a large palestra enclosed on the north, west, and south by a porticus. The east wall was pierced by splayed windows to light a cryptoporticus for part of its length. Apparently, rooms connected with the Baths encroached on the southeast corner. A row of shops with partition walls not quite in alignment with those along the Portico di Nettuno occupied the south side. A latrine was placed in the northwest corner. An exedra having two columns *in antis* stood at the center of the remaining space on the west. On each side of it, rooms accessible from both the Palestra and Via della Fontana formed the ground floor for upper apartments. The actual construction of this phase is typical of all the Hadrianic work in this development. The entrances were given simple decorative treatment. The one on Via della Palestra had a high travertine base with a transitional molding carved on it.

The Caserma dei Vigili (II, 5, 1)[99] had a symmetrical plan resembling that of dwellings with a central court, but on a larger scale. The central part consisted of a large arcaded court, an Augusteum with an *ala* on each side and behind it, on the west, a row of intercommunicating rooms facing in the opposite direction onto an open corridor.[100] A single row of rooms opened off from the court on north, east, and south. A similar row on the west toward Via della Fortuna was a slightly later addition[101] and had its own outside stairs to upper apartments. The entrances on the north, east, and south were symmetrically placed with regard to the court and adorned with ornamental doorways. Stairways at the corners of the arcade led to the sleeping quarters of the *vigiles*, and an outside stairway near each end of the original structure gave access to upper floors from Via della Fullonica. Commodious latrines were placed in the southeast and northwest corners. The main façade faced Via dei Vigili (pl. 25, fig. 1). To judge from the stamps found, the kilns of Arria Fadilla furnished all the bricks for this façade.[102] Only the pilasters of fine red brickwork with their yellow base moldings remain of the ornamental doorway, but enough of the pedimented entablature was found in the street in front of it for a restoration.[103] Upon the pilaster and the nearby walls many names of ancient soldiers who once dwelt in these barracks can still be read. An upright travertine block framed the beginning of the doorjambs which terminated in a simple terra-cotta molding that served as impost for a segmental arch of *bipedales* outlined in a brick molding. The first two rooms on either side of the entrance each presents to the street three small slit windows under a slightly curved lintel of *sesquipedales* (pl. 25, fig. 2). The third, which was the corner room, on the other hand, originally had a lunette topped by a relieving arch of *bipedales* and divided by four piers into three windows. Other rooms with splayed windows are found on the south side.

The most significant fact for this whole building complex is the complete absence of any use of reticulate work. Brick stamps found throughout[104] prove that all the essential walls were erected during the last ten years of the reign of Hadrian. The brickwork is virtually the same everywhere. The bricks vary in color from yellow to red, though the majority are yellowish red. All seem to have been made from broken tiles but show a decided preference for the triangular shape. In thickness, they range from 3 cm. to 4 cm. with few reaching either the upper

[99] D. Vaglieri, *Not. sc.*, 1911, p. 404; *idem, ibid.*, pp. 165–166; Calza, *Guida*, pp. 98–102; *idem, Palladio*, vol. 5, 1941, pp. 2–3. See also Meiggs, *Ostia*, pp. 75, 305–308, pl. 3 C; Crema, p. 458, figs. 588–589.

[100] Hence, Reynolds (*Vigiles*, p. 109) suggests that they may have been officers' quarters.

[101] See Bloch, *Bolli*, p. 250. Hence, Reynolds (*op. cit.*, p. 108) considers that an independent row of shops was incorporated in the Barracks at a later date. He also mentions only to reject a conjecture that the room north of the Augusteum was used to house some piece of fire-fighting apparatus.

[102] Bloch, *Bolli*, p. 230.

[103] See R. Lanciani, *Not. sc.*, 1889, p. 37.

[104] Lanciani's conjecture (*Not. sc.*, 1888, p. 741; 1889, p. 19) that this was a noble house later adapted for use as a barracks, though almost universally accepted, has been disproved by the evidence of the brick stamps. See Bloch, *Bolli*, pp. 243–250. A. P. Torri (*Urbe*, vol. 5, 1940 (10), p. 16) clings to the old theory.

or lower limit. The mortar joints are rather wide (1.5 cm. to 2.5 cm.). The mortar is usually composed of lime and both red and black pozzolana. Bonding courses are on the way out. They occur, for the most part, only in the façades where the yellow color of the *bipedales* may have been considered a decorative element. In this complex they appear somewhat more frequently in the Caserma and in the northeast corner of the Baths than elsewhere, and are found in through passageways and stair walls. Relieving arches are also used with much less abandon. They appear low down on walls under which there are drains and in stair walls; they are employed over doors and windows; a few occur in walls for no discernible reason. Slightly curved lintels of upright tiles with masonry underneath resting on horizontal tiles are the favored coverings for doors and windows, though straight lintels are also found. In the Caserma, we have noted a new type of window with piers dividing a lunette into windows. Windows along the streets are comparatively high. An increase in the use of splayed windows is also discernible. We have already called attention to the many ornamental doorways. The decorative use of string cornice of tile continues to be popular. In one unit (II, 3), stairs are still carried on rampant arches of *sesquipedales* slightly curved at the top, but elsewhere the contractor apparently trusted the strength of his oblique barrel vault. Impost moldings of tile appear in several rooms with the holes for beams to support mezzanine floors above them. In the façade of the Insula del Soffitto specially shaped pieces of terra cotta cover the holes for the insertion of beams for a small balcony. There may have been other balconies for which there is no evidence. Most of the rooms probably had barrel vaults under the first floor. In the latrine in the southeast corner of the Caserma a cross vault starts from a barrel vault at the north and south and ends awkwardly without further support. Later modifications consist, for the most part except in the Baths, in blocking windows and doors.

Behind the Caserma, a Fullonica (cleaning establishment) (II, 11, 1) although not part of the same urban development, shows typical Hadrianic masonry in brick and reticulate work.

Along the Decumanus in front of the Grandi Horrea, a space still remained to be systematized by the city planners of the late Hadrianic period. Since there was to be no porticus in front, the dozen or so shops (II, 9, 2) were doubtless given a decorous façade along the main street. The walls are not preserved high enough for a restoration, and there is no trace of stairways to upper floors. The ground plan was unusual, with the shops falling into three units: two facing east and four with back rooms facing south were all in communication with a narrow corridor at the north; a western group of four larger shops opened onto a wider corridor also at the north; four shops in the center stood in front of a wide hall.

A little reconstruction outside the Porta Romana on the north side is in Hadrianic brickwork. With this, we come to the end of the Hadrianic work on the north side of the Decumanus, east of the Forum.

It is not unlikely that Hadrian had in mind from the first a plan to bring the southern part of the Forum with its Temple of Roma and Augustus into closer harmony with the northern part which he had rebuilt entirely. There is no way of telling when the space between the Basilica and Via del Tempio

Rotondo was utilized for a porticus (I, 11, 4) with five shops opening off from it. Only brick was employed for facing the walls, and the columns were also of brick with Doric capitals strongly reminiscent of those in the Foro di Porta Marina. The brickwork lacks the perfection of that intended to be exposed, and it is unthinkable that it should not have been covered with stucco simulating marble. A long porticus (I, 12, 11) with gray granite columns enclosed this part of the Forum on the east. An elaborate niche for a statue was built out from its back wall which was faced with quite ordinary brickwork obviously designed to be concealed from view. A stamp on one of the *bipedales* in a threshold occurs also in the Terme di Nettuno. Finally, on each side of the southern extremity of the Temple of Roma and Augustus, the brick-faced pylons remain of the monumental arches which were intended further to shut off the Forum area from the busy traffic already diverted from the Cardo Maximus through Via del Tempio Rotondo to Via del Pomerio.

On the south side of the Decumanus the gradual substitution of new edifices for those at the lower level continued under Hadrian. Private enterprise was responsible for most of these, but since brick stamps allow a more or less precise dating for only two or three of them, it has seemed best to present briefly the rest of the Hadrianic work topographically rather than chronologically, beginning with Regio IV.

There was considerable Trajanic construction north of the Campo della Magna Mater along the west and south sides of Regio IV, Insula 2; and structural activity continued without interruption into the Hadrianic period. A sizable edifice facing Via della Caupona (IV, 2, 7) had a narrow entrance court with a flight of steps to the right of it flanked by three shops on each side and a large oblong cortile with rooms on three sides. The walls were faced with the combination of brick and reticulate in common use in the early years of the reign of Hadrian. The building would appear to be a little later than the Trajanic edifice behind it. The front part was largely rebuilt at a later time. A small apartment house to the west (IV, 2, 8) shares a wall with it and was certainly built at the same time. It contained only four rooms in addition to the two frontal shops with a staircase between them. The usual combination of brick and reticulate was employed for its masonry also. Across an alley to the south of this, three rooms and an entrance corridor leading to the unexplored space beyond would seem to belong to the same building period. In the center of the block, two other Hadrianic structures survived the Antonine reorganization. Of one (IV, 2, 14) behind the later Caupona del Pavone only three rooms and a staircase were left when the eastern part was completely rebuilt. There were three small windows in the north wall and one window and a door in the alley to the south, and so only the central room was dependent entirely on the front opening for light, unless there was a window above the door. The walls are not preserved to the mezzanine level. They are faced with neat insets of reticulate in a brick frame and show the long strips of reticulate without intermediate brickwork which is to be associated with Trajanic or the earlier Hadrianic work. The bricks were mostly red and made from broken roof tiles, 4–5 cm. thick. Across the passage to the south two rooms and a staircase (IV, 2, 12) remain. The thick red bricks made from *bipedales* in the north wall of the stairs, the reticulate and brick in the back wall, and the yellow bricks, 3–5 cm. thick, from *besales* in the northeast corner were probably in use at the same time; the narrower bricks in the western part of the south wall belong to a later modification. The evidence for dating is poor; the official report ascribes it to Hadrian. No brick stamps have been reported for any of these structures.

Farther north facing an alley at its junction with the Cardo, a row of four shops (IV, 3, 2) has walls faced with reticulate and brick which appear Hadrianic. In the block north of this any Hadrianic work there may have been was eclipsed by the insertion of late Baths.

By the second century, Insula 5 of Regio IV was divided into five irregular strips, owing largely to the earlier houses at a lower level. Only the three toward the east show any Hadrianic work; and not any of it is particularly important from the standpoint of methods of construction. Most of the strip along Via del Pomerio was built over again at a later date. A wall of Hadrianic masonry seems to have closed the south colonnade of the Macellum (IV, 5, 2) and formed the north wall of a hall at the southwest corner. Pilasters along the sides could have supported transverse arches imbedded in a barrel vault. The walls were faced with the usual combination of brick and reticulate. The Insula del Sacello (IV, 5, 4) was inserted in an earlier structure[105] of brickwork ascribed on the official map to the time of Hadrian. It had a door between two windows opening toward the Cortile del Dionisio. Only this wall and the one toward the south would seem to me Hadrianic. South of it was an apartment house (IV, 5, 5) with the ground floor given over entirely to business, but with two flights of steps leading to apartments above. The fourth room from the north is marked by half columns of yellow brickwork in a façade of red, an indication that it served as a vestibule to the space behind. The rear and partition walls were faced with reticulate insets in brick frame. The next strip to the west has yielded clear evidence of a Republican and Augustan phase antedating the Hadrianic rebuilding of the entire northern part. This Hadrianic development (IV, 5, 7) was divided into two parts by a paved dead-end street. Shops faced the Decumanus and the east side of the street. Behind the shops on the west there was a business establishment of some sort, the plan of which is not quite clear. There is no evidence that there were stairs in the earliest phase of the edifice. Brickwork was used exclusively for the front part along the Decumanus and for the façades along the street, brick and reticulate interlaced for the rest. There is Hadrianic work in the area behind the Cortile del Dionisio which has not been fully excavated. A fine brick-faced archway led from the early *horrea* toward the rear of the central strip to another Hadrianic development (IV, 5, 14) which also has been partially excavated. A central passageway divided some rooms of uncertain purpose from a long narrow building consisting of two identical halls with a staircase of two ramps between them. The hall to the north, which alone has been fully laid bare, presented three doorways and eight high windows to the passageway at the east and three doorways to the west, which were blocked when the Schola del Traiano was built in the Antonine period. A central row of five piers supported a ceiling. The many

[105] Boethius, *Studies DMR* I, p. 448.

windows and doors suggest that this edifice was devoted to some industry or other where light was essential to the work. There was a second room at the north. The southern hall apparently had the same ground plan. The rooms in the northeast corner were faced with brick; the rest of the masonry shows the usual combination of brickwork in primary walls and brick and reticulate in secondary ones.

The next Insula (IV, 6, 1) contained a single complex with a broad passageway dividing it into two halves. An ornamental gateway at the south, of which only the beginning of the brick pilasters remains, shows that the passage was primarily an entrance corridor to an open space behind. On each side of it, a single shop faced the Decumanus, and at the south a large shop on the west side corresponded to the last two-room unit on the east. Between this unit and the shop facing the Decumanus, there are two units of three rooms each with a staircase between them. In each unit the rooms are intercommunicating, but none are furnished with the wide openings normal to shops. Perhaps they were a couple of small bazaars. There was only one entrance from Vico Cieco on the east, and that was through a corridor under the stairs. On the west side provision was made for a two-ramp staircase behind the north shop. Between this and a corridor behind the south shop, there was a large hall. The construction with the brick façades and partition walls faced with brick and reticulate is in accord with the date A.D. 126 ascribed to it in the official chronology.[106] One fact invites speculation: why the north shop and stairwell had an independent west wall when the east wall of the Caseggiato della Fontana a Lucerna (A.D. 120) was considered adequate for the large room of the southern end.

It is conceivable that the Portico della Fontana a Lucerna (IV, 7, 1), which lent dignity to a relatively long stretch of the south side of the Decumanus, was a public edifice, but there is no proof. It is one of the few buildings of the region that can be dated at about A.D. 120 on the evidence of the stamps[107] discovered in the walls of the shops opening onto it (IV, 7, 2). The slender piers for the long arcade had to be bolstered up on both sides with a similar masonry. What is left of the original work at the east end displays hard red bricks facing the foundations of the piers and good yellow ones facing the shafts. The west end was rebuilt probably in the third century. The Caseggiato della Fontana a Lucerna (IV, 7, 2) has its front part at the imperial level. The back wall of this long row of shops marks the raise in level from a row of rooms facing in the opposite direction. The façade is one of the few in Ostia having insets of reticulate in what is left of its original phase. Door originally alternated with window along the whole front. Slightly curved lintel arches of *bipedales* were the usual covering of apertures. A wooden beam formed a sill for a window to light the stairs. The porticus also fronted a second apartment house (IV, 7, 3) of which only the four shops, entrance corridor, and outside stairs along the Decumanus have been excavated. Its façade also displays the reticulate insets in a brick frame and its partition walls the usual combination of brick and reticulate. A dead-end street, Via della Caupona di Alexander Helix, passed through the porticus. On the other side of the street, an apartment house (IV, 7, 5) was erected between it and the Sullan wall. The Caupona di

[106] Sc. di O. I, p. 236.

[107] Bloch, Sc. di O. I, p. 227.

[108] Becatti, *Sc. di O.* I, pp. 135–136.

[109] Bloch, *Sc. di O.* I, p. 227.

[110] The street which the tomb faced was sacrificed for the Loggia which was at a much higher level.

[111] Bloch, *loc. cit.*

[112] The interior ramp belongs to a later modification.

Alexander Helix (IV, 7, 4) was later inserted in part of this house. All these structures were probably roughly contemporaneous and almost certainly Hadrianic. A more detailed analysis must wait until the whole area is excavated.

The Hadrianic work in Insula 8 is public in character and has been described above.

On the southwest side of Via di Cartilio Poplicola most of the construction in Insula 9 thus far unearthed seems to be Hadrianic or possibly a little later, but was not part of a single building project.[108] The Loggia at the corner (IV, 9, 1) can be dated about A.D. 130 on the evidence of the brick stamps.[109] A tomb of 25 B.C. interfered with any regular plan for the region.[110] Brick stamps indicate that a grandiose edifice of some sort (IV, 9, 3) was built on both sides of it with façades on both the Decumanus and Via di Cartilio Poplicola in the late Hadrianic or early Antonine period (A.D. 135–140).[111] Farther along the Via a second edifice (IV, 9, 4) was erected at about the same time. The rest of the block has not been excavated. The Loggia di Cartilio (IV, 9, 1) was an elegant commercial establishment consisting of an oblong space covered with a roof supported by piers, a small cortile, and a ramp at the east of it leading to a higher level at the rear. The outer piers rested on bases of yellow tile, were faced with red bricks and embellished with pilasters, and probably supported a decorative entablature of some sort. The bricks, ca. 3 cm. thick, were laid with very fine joints. The inner piers were faced with slightly thicker (3–3.5 cm.) yellow bricks of the same kind as those used for the rear wall. The bricks, though fairly uniform in size, were a mixed lot of triangles and tiles roughly broken to triangular shape. There were tufa insets in the piers but no bonding courses. The west wall shows a reinforcement of two long segmental arches.[112] Any detailed analysis of the edifice encompassing it (IV, 9, 3) must await further excavation. The brickwork consisted of bricks 3–3.5 cm. thick and mortar joints 1 cm. wide. The walls were reinforced with angle piers for cross vaulting. The irregular shape of the large room facing the Via must have added to the difficulty of laying the vault. *Bipedales* were used on the centering with *besales* on top of them. To the west of the Loggia two ramps led to a common landing. The purpose of the building beyond this (IV, 9, 4) is not clear. It had a row of four intercommunicating shops facing Via della Marciana with a staircase beyond them which presumably led to apartments over this part at least. There were three small rooms and a wide entrance on Via di Cartilio Poplicola, a large central court, and four small rooms on the side opposite the entrance. The masonry shows more care than most of that found in this part of the city. The *caementa* in the walls are mostly small pieces of the same kind of bricks as were used to face the walls and were laid in regular rows. Fine-grained magenta red bricks about 3.5 cm. thick, joined by fairly narrow layers of mortar, made a neat façade. Inside, speckled yellow bricks are noticeable among those of other colors. The bricks vary more in thickness (3.2–4.5 cm.), and the mortar joints are wider (1.5–2.5 cm.). Some triangles appear among the bricks made from broken tiles. There are many enormous relieving arches of *bipedales* but no bonding courses. Some of the arches were laid on a permanent centering of *bipedales*. Especially heavy tile cornices supported the mezzanines. In general the construction seems homogeneous. The few modifications are obvious.

Hadrianic building activities of lesser importance extended into Regio V, in the area between the Decumanus, Via degli Augustali, Via della Fortuna Annonaria, and Semità dei Cippi. This section of Ostia is a confused mass of walls of many periods which needs a more detailed analysis than is feasible for a study of this sort. A brief commentary follows. What little remains of the first shop house on the west along the Decumanus (V, 5, 4) apparently had the usual ground plan of shops and rear rooms with an outside staircase at the side. There is no doubt in my mind that a pretentious edifice in the southern part of the block (V, 5, 2) was built during the Hadrianic period over the remains of earlier structures. The same kind of yellow bricks were used as in the Caseggiato dei Triclini. Bonding courses, relieving arches, lintel arches both straight and slightly curved over apertures, and rampant lintels under stairs were all composed of speckled yellow *bipedales*. Neat insets of tufa reticulate (tesserae 5–6 cm. per side) appear in the outside wall at the southeast corner. The Terme dell'Invidioso did not take form here until later. A second shop house along the Decumanus (V, 6, 7)[113] had three shops and an outside staircase in front with a large hall behind them. Back of this unit, there was apparently a row of Hadrianic shops on Via del Mitreo dei Serpenti with living quarters at the rear. In the early years of the third century the structure was considerably modified; and before the century was over, it came to house the Mitreo dei Serpenti. In Insula 4, four shops (V, 4, 2), each with a central pier, faced Via della Fortuna Annonaria, and two halls with a central pier each and a space for a staircase (V, 4, 3) faced Via dell'Invidioso. The present staircase is, however, late. The masonry contains one relieving arch of *sesquipedales* sharply wedge-shaped with reticulate tesserae following the curve of the arch and high windows in the east wall with slightly curved lintel arches also of *sesquipedales*. No brick stamps have been reported from any of these structures. The masonry is none too good, but shows much of the combination of brick and reticulate usual in Hadrianic work.

South of Via della Fortuna Annonaria, half a dozen or so structures would seem to be Hadrianic or at least have a Hadrianic phase, as for example the walls or parts of walls in rather thick bricks (3.8–4 cm.) with fairly narrow mortar joints (1.5–2.2 cm.) in the edifice at the corner of Via della Casa del Pozzo (V, 2, 9). The next block to the east was almost entirely built over in the Hadrianic period. The northern structure (V, 3, 1) shows a curious adaptation of the usual plan for a Republican *domus* to the new fashion of introducing light from outside. A shop flanked each side of an entrance corridor leading into an "atrium" with an impluvium, but instead of side rooms a many-windowed wall on each side flooded the entire interior with light. Opposite the entrance a "tablinum" with two wide openings in each side wall was inserted in such a way that there was room for the customary "alae." No provision was made for sleeping quarters on the ground floor at this time, and no stairs belong to the original building period. The back wall shut off two openings of the Trajanic house behind, a clear indication that the edifice under discussion was later. The façade was of fine yellow

[113] Becatti, *Sc. di O.* II, pp. 101–104.

brickwork (mortar joints only 0.3 to 0.5 cm. wide) with a red base molding. The other walls exhibit light red bricks with a slight admixture of yellow ones. They were 3.5 to 4 cm. thick and joined with mortar 1–2 cm. wide. There was one small relieving arch. Beyond a Trajanic building, the southern part of the area was probably filled with construction at about the same time that the edifice along Via della Fortuna Annonaria was built. Six intercommunicating shops faced Via delle Ermette (V, 3, 5) having an outside staircase to the south of them. Only two of the shops were well enough preserved for study. The construction is similar to that in the rest of the block. A long narrow house (V, 3, 3) faced Via della Casa del Pozzo which had nearly as many windows as the edifice described above. Its entrance was marked on each side by a recessed three-quarters column. These columns rested on travertine blocks and had base moldings of yellow tile. The entablature is not preserved. Travertine thresholds and travertine insets in the side walls formed a sharp contrast to the red brickwork of the doorway. The ground plan is that of a modified corridor house. The two rooms north of the short longitudinal corridor may have been semi-public to give access to a cistern approached by steps at the east. In any case, the doorway had a travertine sill and insets like the outside entrance. The inner room was later transformed into the "tablinum" characteristic of the *domus* of the late Empire. A smaller room at the south, lighted by two good-sized windows, has angle piers for a cross vault. Two rooms on the east received light only from the corridor; and one of them was reduced in size for a narrow passageway leading by two right-angled turns to a latrine with a splayed window. A narrow doorway, later blocked, once opened onto what seems to have been a small separate apartment (V, 3, 4) with its main entrance on a back street. This rear façade exhibits fine yellow brickwork with pilasters indicating the presence of an ornamental doorway. A large room stood at the left of the main entrance, a smaller one to the right of it with a secondary entrance from Via delle Ermette. A room in the center with angle piers was isolated by passageways—one leading to a latrine identical with the one at the north, the other to an otherwise inaccessible room at the northeast corner. The wall construction throughout the area was essentially the same—fine façades of bricks from broken tiles with narrow mortar joints, having ornamental doorways and high windows carefully aligned, brick-faced exterior walls of the usual Hadrianic type, interior walls of brickwork with reticulate insets. There is one relieving arch of *sesquipedales* along Via della Casa del Pozzo and infrequent bonding courses of light *bipedales*.

Across Via delle Ermette, a partly excavated row of shops of the usual Hadrianic combination of brick and reticulate work (V, 8, 4) stands in front of an unexcavated area. The excavators call attention to a little Hadrianic masonry on the east side of a house built in the time of Antoninus Pius.

The space between Via degli Augustali and the Trajanic Horrea dell' Artemide was probably filled at one time with Hadrianic construction. A long wall divided the region in two. The eastern part was entirely rebuilt along the Decumanus during the reign of Commodus. Behind this, a wedge-shaped area (V, 11, 5) was left, which was subdivided into three parts by two cross walls—one Hadrianic, one later. The first contained a loggia with a double row of columns faced with yellow bricks to support a roof; the second was an open space filled with storage jars; the third a structure of uncertain purpose not fully excavated, showing two piers and a stairwell. A narrow corridor at the east formed a secondary entrance to the Magazzino Annonario. All seem to have belonged to the same building complex.

To the west, only a small shop house of six rooms including the shops (V, 11, 3) remains of the Hadrianic construction along the Decumanus. There were stairs for upper apartments. Behind this house but sadly truncated by a later collegiate temple, is what is left of the Caseggiato del Temistocle (V, 11, 2) with a curious ground plan divided into three main strips. The easternmost of these was subdivided into four units. These opened into a long narrow corridor, which in its turn had two doorways into a second corridor giving access direct or indirect to a row of small rooms. Partition walls throughout these two parts were very narrow. The western strip consisted of a row of normal intercommunicating shops and a long narrow hall, irregular because of the presence of earlier buildings. The walls were faced with the brick and reticulate characteristic of the period. The bricks were made for the most part from fine-grained red tiles about 4 cm. thick. The tufa tesserae ranged from 6 to 7 cm. per side and were well laid. The doorways in the long dividing wall had slightly curved lintels of thick (5 cm.) *bipedales*. I should very much like to know for what industry this strange edifice was intended.

A Hadrianic apartment house (V, 10, 1) was fitted into the awkward space between the Caseggiato del Temistocle and Via degli Augustali. The lower floor was given over entirely to shops; a stairway in their midst led to upper apartments. The walls show the usual combination of reticulate and brick. A part of the house was later enlarged to make a *domus* of the late Empire.

Farther south in this oddly distorted area, another edifice (V, 9, 2)[114] of uncertain purpose shows the same typically Hadrianic construction of brick and reticulate in the relatively little that is left of the original construction. The only unusual aspect of the construction is the lavish use of pilasters along the alley at the back. Pilasters on the west side are part of a rather far-reaching restoration in the poorer brickwork of the third century. The Mitreo di Felicissimo[115] was inserted in one of the rooms a little later. The relatively minor changes necessary were in block-and-brick work.

East of the Horrea di Hortensius, another large *horrea* complex (V, 12, 2) was erected in the early Hadrianic period (A.D. 120–125). It is dated by its brick stamps.[116] The only difficulty in the identification is the narrowness of the entrance corridor. It was flanked on each side by three shops, each with its own back shop and all but one with a door toward a long narrow room behind. The south wall of the only one of these excavated was wider than the others and heavily buttressed as though it was intended to carry a heavy load. There was a flight of stairs behind it, but whether to upper floors above the shops or upper storage chambers of the *horrea* is incapable of proof. Exterior walls were faced with red bricks, 3.5–4 cm. thick, laid with mortar joints about 1 cm. wide; the partition walls, with less homogeneous bricks more carelessly laid; the walls between the front and back shops, with reticu-

114 Becatti, *Sc. di O.* II, pp. 105-112.

115 It is named for the votive inscription in the mosaic floor.

116 Bloch, *Sc. di O.* I, p. 227.

117 Becatti, *Sc. di O.* II, pp. 113–117, where the question of the identification is ably presented. The association with Sabazius is based on one inscription (*CIL*, vol. 14, no. 4296).

1 *CIL*, vol. 14, no. 98. For an account of the inscription, see Bloch, *Bolli*, p. 245, n. 183. It is impossible to tell how much of the Quartiere dei Vigili (see above, pp. 192–196) was left to be finished by Antoninus Pius; and indeed the question is an academic one so far as this study is concerned, for there would be no change in technique so long as the same contractors were in charge of the work.

2 Julius Capitolinus, *SHA*, *Antoninus Pius*, 8, 3.

3 Bloch, *Bolli*, p. 279.

4 See above, pp. 149, 165.

5 A single Hadrianic stamp found loose is inadequate evidence. See Bloch, *Sc. di O.* I, p. 227.

6 Becatti (*Sc. di O.* I, pp. 146–147) believes it to be a new Antonine monument and cites Antonine stamps in proof of the date of what seems to me the second phase.

7 See just below.

8 Becatti, *op. cit.*, p. 147.

9 For the house, see above, pp. 198–199.

10 Bloch, *Studies DMR* II, 1953, pp. 412–418.

11 Becatti, *Sc. di O.* I, p. 142; Meiggs, *Ostia*, pp. 411–415; Crema, p. 406, figs. 497, 499. See also B. Kenneth Johnson, *MAAR*, vol. 10, 1932, pp. 143–144, pls. 42–47, for a suggestive though not entirely accurate reconstruction.

12 Bloch, *Sc. di O.* I, pp. 217–218. Such few earlier stamps as came to light can be easily accounted for as a casual use of material from buildings destroyed to make room for the Baths.

late insets in a brick frame. Brick-faced steps started the ascents to mezzanines, but travertine steps were used for the main flight. Doorways were covered with lintels of unusually short upright tiles. Behind this structure, the *horrea* still await excavation. The west wall was separated from the Horrea di Hortensius by an intercalary space with occasional buttressing cross walls. Only two doorways broke the long east wall facing Via del Sabazeo, which was faced with reticulate broken by wide bands of brick. The partition walls for a series of rooms along this wall were faced with a rough *incertum*. Only the one containing the so-called Sabazeo[117] has been completely unearthed; and it shows jambs of tufa blocks.

ANTONINES

ANTONINUS PIUS (A.D. 138–161)

At Ostia as in Rome, Antoninus Pius was called upon to finish work started by his predecessor. An inscription of A.D. 139,[1] of which unfortunately the provenience is unknown, states that the money appropriated by Hadrian for some Baths was not sufficient and that Antoninus Pius had given the necessary sum for their completion and for marble for their embellishment. The inscription almost certainly refers to the Terme di Nettuno (II, 4, 2). A Lavacrum Ostiense is the only public monument in Ostia attributed to Antoninus Pius in literary sources.[2] Bloch believes also that Julius Capitolinus had in mind the Terme di Nettuno.[3] The question arises as to whether there is any other possibility. The Terme di Porta Marina (IV, 10, 1), though begun by Trajan,[4] had a second phase in walls faced with speckled yellow bricks, ranging from 3 to 4 cm. in thickness. It is possible that Hadrian completed the Baths,[5] but more probable that the work was suspended for a time and resumed by Antoninus Pius.[6] The brickwork appears more Antonine than Hadrianic. Only complete excavation can settle the date of this second phase. At least, the Terme di Porta Marina has no better claim to be the Lavacrum Ostiense than the Terme di Nettuno. A more obvious identification would be the Terme del Foro (I, 12, 6), which, however, was a benefaction of M. Gavius Maximus rather than the emperor.[7] A small Bath (IV, 5, 6)[8] was probably built in the Antonine period at the rear of an earlier Trajanic or Hadrianic house.[9] Its walls were faced with light-colored bricks, mostly yellow, about 3 cm. thick. The rooms were small, but at least three of them were apsed. It was modified in a brickwork not essentially different from the original. Such a humble establishment would certainly not have been the gift of the emperor. Unless confirmatory evidence comes to light from some other source as yet unknown, we must apparently reject the evidence of Julius Capitolinus that Antoninus Pius personally presented Ostia with new Baths. After all, he was removed by five or six generations from the events he was narrating.

The Terme del Foro (I, 12, 6) though probably a benefaction of M. Gavius Maximus[10] rather than of the emperor himself, were the most sumptuous that the city was ever to receive.[11] Brick stamps, primarily from hypocausts, drains, and pavements,[12] suggest a date of about A.D. 158 for the start of the work. It cannot have been easy to find or make room for so extensive a monument in the center of the town. Although it was located behind the Caseggiato dei Triclini and the Hadrianic Baths along the Decumanus, it could be entered from the Forum through an earlier room converted into a sort of vestibule.[13] Apparently the pomerial strip on each side of the old Castrum wall was chosen for the rectangular part of the structure, whereas south of it space was created between the Cardo Maximus and Semità dei Cippi for the rest of the Baths, the *palaestra*, and three supernumerary buildings, and given monumentality by impressive arcades along the two streets. A Trajanic or early Hadrianic bazaar[14] was allowed to remain at its southeast corner; an earlier Antonine (?) building was partially appropriated at the southwest corner. This edifice (I, 12, 9) is somewhat of an enigma. It has an entrance from the Cardo marked by pilasters of fine yellow brickwork[15] and a long entrance corridor to a space behind, which later became part of the South Building of the Baths. The long room at the north of the corridor evidently housed a business that needed plenty of light, for there were three windows in addition to a door on the north and two on the east. The shop on the south of the entrance had a door to the space behind, and an east window lighted the room under the outside staircase. The brickwork is less uniform than in the best Antonine work. The apertures were covered with a beam under a slightly curved lintel of upright *bipedales*. It is probably either poor Hadrianic or Antonine masonry.

The main entrance to the northern section must always have been by a door between the two windows toward the western end of Via della Forica, though the present arrangement is late. This led to a large hall, which also had a doorway to the *palaestra* at the south. At the eastern end of the same street a secondary entrance gave admittance through a vestibule to a hall corresponding to the one at the other end.[16] This hall could be reached also from the *palaestra* through a corridor, which had in addition a wide doorway to a street at the east. Symmetry reigned between these two halls. The *frigidarium* in the center was equipped with a rectangular pool furnished with niches for statues at the center of both the north[17] and south walls, and these pools were flanked on each side by a small room which was slightly heated. The two on the north had large windows which would certainly keep them from being very warm,[18] but those on the south had doorways to heated rooms, the hypocausts of which supplied the warm air beneath their floors. One wall still shows remnants of the roof tiles arranged to provide space for the circulation of the hot air upwards, and it is quite possible that the traces of hollow wall tiles in the others represent a substitution at a later time. These rooms were cross-vaulted. Four great columns of cipollino stood on each side of the central hall of the *frigidarium*, presumably to support the vaulting. Two columns also of cipollino *in antis* separated this hall from a hall on each side, itself divided into three parts by two sets of cipollino columns *in antis*. The hall west of the *frigidarium*, and probably the one to the east as well, presented a tripartite lunetted window to Via della Forica. Little has survived of the marble which must once have embellished these stately halls.

With the northern series of rooms all symmetry comes to an end. Five rooms, different in shape, jut out to a varying degree into the central court of

[13] The bricks in the north wall are decidedly thicker and redder. There was also an early room to the north of it connected with the Hadrianic Porticus at the east of the Forum and an outside stairway to the east of it which had nothing to do with the Baths.

[14] See above, pp. 176–177.

[15] In its present state, it is practically all modern.

[16] Traces of earlier constructions are evident at this entrance; and the eastern wall of the hall is built against the west wall of a Hadrianic structure (I, 12, 5).

[17] The apse was a later modification.

[18] There may have been glass in these windows.

[19] Thatcher's analysis of the functioning of these rooms in the fourth century (*MAAR*, vol. 24, 1956, pp. 169–264) is the basis for the following account. I have, however, checked his findings to the best of my ability and endeavored to evaluate them for the second century. See also, E. D. Thatcher, *Jour. Amer. Inst. Architects*, vol. 29, 1958, pp. 116–129.

[20] One *praefurnium* (furnace) at the end of the service corridor was considered adequate for this room.

[21] This room was probably domed.

[22] Three *praefurnia* furnished the heat.

[23] Bloch, *Bolli*, p. 274.

[24] The present hypocaust is probably a third- or fourth-century renovation.

[25] It had two *praefurnia*, the western one of which supplied heat to the slightly warmed rooms at the west of each pool in the *frigidarium*.

[26] The present hypocaust is a substitution for the original one.

[27] A *testudo* consisted of a large semicylindrical conduit of lead so set that the water would flow down through its open end from the pool to its base which was slightly lower than the bottom of the pool. Here reheated by the *praefurnium*, it would rise and flow back again into the pool, thereby assuring a continuous circulation so long as the fire was stoked. Traces of the metal of the *testudo* remain in the masonry of the north pool.

[28] Two of the pools yielded Antonine stamps in the pavement of the hypocaust (Bloch, *Sc. di O.* I, pp. 217–218).

the gymnasium. Enough Antonine work remains in the walls of the southern part[19] to prove that its essential functioning was the same from the beginning. The octagonal room which was farthest to the west was only slightly heated artificially by a hypocaust,[20] but received the maximum benefit from the sunshine pouring in through its four great windows. They were placed high enough to protect the sunbather from drafts.[21] The hollow tiles necessary for the circulation of the hot air from the hypocaust warmed the passage to the oval room toward the east. Although this room jutted out far enough to receive its full quota of sunshine, it was equipped not only with a hypocaust[22] and wall tubes but also, in all probability, with vault tubes as well. Brick stamps[23] prove that the present hypocaust was a renewal. The low windows are a late restoration, but there is no reason to doubt that the original ones, though probably somewhat smaller, were planned to take advantage of as much sunshine as possible. It would have been the hottest room in the Baths and therefore probably the *sudatio* or sweat bath. It had an ellipsoidal vault of which a little remains. The next room to the east was considerably modified at a later period in order to change its function. Originally it was warmed artificially only by a hypocaust[24] with vents in the adjoining rooms.[25] Even the huge windows of the late restoration in the curved south wall would not have admitted much sunshine to raise the temperature, and doorways to four different rooms would have made it more or less of a passageway. It was undoubtedly a *tepidarium* from which one could pass either to the *sudatio* on the west or the warmer rooms on the east. It was probably barrel-vaulted. Although the next room, rectangular in shape, jutted yet farther into the exercise place behind, it was dependent not so much on sunshine coming through its south windows as on a hypocaust and hollow tiles in each of its inner walls, fed by no less than three *praefurnia* in its southwest corner. It had no need for a heated vault to make it a warm vestibule to the *caldarium* at the east and possibly a second *sudatio* on the north. Much of its walls have been refaced so the wall tiles as well as the hypocaust surely belong to a restoration. It was probably barrel-vaulted. It should be classified as a warmer *tepidarium* than the one on the west. Rather scanty remains of Antonine work indicate that in the next room, surely the *caldarium*, the three pools were part of the original plan, though they were deepened somewhat at a late period by raising the front wall. The apse on the south pool was a later addition, but a window in its west wall was apparently intended to admit as much sunshine as possible to the original rectangular pool. The room was warmed in the usual fashion by hypocaust,[26] wall tubes, and probably a heated vault, but the pools presented a new problem in heating which was admirably met by the ancient engineers. The water was heated by fires under boilers in the service area at the east, piped to the pools, and kept warm by a *testudo*[27] connected with the main *praefurnium*, at the center of the rear wall of each pool. A second *praefurnium* in each probably served merely to heat the air for the hypocaust,[28] which was apparently entirely independent of the hypocaust under the floor of the room. The wall tiles essential to its functioning were insulated by the lining of the pool and could have merely warmed the air above the pool. This was a refinement in the luxury of bathing occurring for the first time in Ostia.[29] A barrel vault probably covered the room and smaller ones the pools. Yet another warm room, completely insulated behind the second *tepidarium*, served, among other purposes, as a passage between *frigidarium* and *caldarium*. Through hypocaust and wall tubes it could be given a temperature high enough to induce sweating. It was, therefore, probably the second *sudatio*. In fact, three panels of tubes (pl. 27, fig. 1) were considered sufficient for the south wall; and the hypocaust heated by two *praefurnia* in the service area had heat enough to spare for neighboring rooms and some left over to be channeled across the *frigidarium* to the little room to the east of the cold pool at the north. The room was probably barrel-vaulted. Thatcher's research brings conviction that all these rooms with the southern exposure would have functioned admirably most of the year with the great windows of the Constantinian renovation unglazed. The whole layout would seem to indicate that this was the scheme from the first.

The architects who were responsible for the complex must have expended much time and thought on the best use of the space behind. Having once decided on the form of the supernumerary edifices, they had only to enclose the irregular central area in a colonnade on each of the straight sides to give the *palaestra* a dignity commensurate with the rest. For this they chose columns of a variety of marbles and granites, some of which have been re-erected. The shops of the adjacent buildings opened off from the colonnade. Two shrines in the southwest corner were probably later.

Barely enough remains of the arcades along the streets to show that they were nearly identical.[30] The lofty piers rested on two courses of re-used travertine blocks and had two sets of travertine insets on each side. Red bricks were chosen for the facing of the piers which terminated in a tile cornice six or seven courses before the springing of the arch of rather thin *sesquipedales* with narrow joints. At the northern end of the western arcade there are remains of an arch of fine yellow tiles, but the tiles employed at the other end were red. Behind the arcades, the two edifices and the one at the south show a fundamentally open structure of *T*-shaped and cruciform piers to carry the weight of at least one upper story. The thin partitions converting the space into shops were not bonded into the piers.[31] The doors from one shop to the next exhibit slightly curved tile lintels. Flights of steps in all three prove that there was at least one upper story or, less likely, a terrace; but, as Thatcher points out, the artificially heated rooms of the Baths would have lost the added advantage of the sunshine if the three buildings, particularly the one on the west, had been higher than one story above the ground floor. The West Building (I, 12, 10) was more closely associated with the Baths than the other two. The awkward space between the straight side of the *palaestra* and the curve of the Cardo was used to good advantage. As the space narrowed, the double row of shops gave way to a passage, a staircase, a large room opening in both directions, and a large triangular *forica* which could be entered directly from arcade and *palaestra*. This was lighted on both sides by a large lunetted window divided into three parts such as appear in the north façade of the Baths proper. The stairway could also be approached by a doorway in each side wall. The East Building (I, 12, 7) more or less incorporated the great cisterns which were

[29] Where they occur in others, they are part of a renovation.

[30] Much that appears now is a modern restoration.

[31] This was a wise precaution in case the piers settled, because of the weight they were carrying. See Thatcher, *MAAR*, vol. 24, 1956, p. 179.

vital to the functioning of the Baths. They must have risen to a respectable height and were provided with a water wheel to facilitate filling. Behind the arcade fronting Semità dei Cippi, there was a single row of seven shops, whereas facing the *palaestra* there was room for only four and a staircase. A court between the two rows took care of the divergence in orientation. The arch facing the barrel vault over the end of the court is a restoration, but unless I am mistaken there are traces of an arch of yellow *bipedales* which may have been original. The Southern Building (I, 12, 8) had to be adapted to three different orientations. A wedge-shaped space made the transition from that of the bazaar to that of the *palaestra* and was utilized for a shop and a rear room with an independent entrance from the passage. The shop was covered with two cross vaults. At the other end, a masking wall concealed the north wall of an earlier building, but the earlier orientation was kept for a room of the new edifice which was appropriated from it. From the *palaestra* all would have appeared regular—shop, passage, outside stairs, and four shops. Behind the shops this building was even more open than the others in that piers *in antis* took the place of partitions and divided the space in back into three sections, the eastern one of which had two large windows. For some reason not now apparent the western window was wider and higher than the other. The passage was barrel-vaulted, and a slightly curved lintel of *bipedales* over an opening in the side wall was sheared over at the top in accommodation to the impost. The staircase contained two ramps, one from the *palaestra*, the other from the open area behind. As in the West Building, these stairs could be entered from the sides as well as from the front. Every effort was made to render accessible the space above, which must have had a public or semi-public character.[32] The original brick-work is much less homogeneous than elsewhere in the complex and would appear to me more in accord with the masonry of the time of Marcus Aurelius. The presence of an Antonine (?) house at the west may have interposed a delay in the construction of this Southern Building.

The Baths were renovated so many times in antiquity, not to mention the modern restoration, no doubt in both cases with some re-use of such Antonine bricks as were lying about, that it is difficult to gain an impression of the original masonry. With an eye adjusted to the appearance of the brickwork of the shops fronting Semità dei Cippi, the student can detect Antonine construction here and there throughout the entire complex. The bricks are preponderately yellow, 3–3.2 cm. thick, and laid with mortar joints 1.5–2 cm. wide. There are no bonding courses in this section, though they do occur in the Baths proper, but not with the regularity found in earlier monuments. In general, relieving arches were employed sparingly and only where they were considered absolutely necessary. The covering of apertures, more than any other part of the wall, was subject to collapse and replacement. Comparatively few remain. There is at least one straight lintel of upright *bipedales* and a few slightly curved lintels in which it is possible to see traces of the original masonry in the midst of restoration. In the Baths themselves, the latter were sometimes protected by relieving arches (pl. 27, fig. 2). There were no stairways in the Baths. A low cross arch helped to support the barrel vault under the steps of the West Building. The *caementa*

[32] Becatti suggests (*Sc. di O.* I, p. 146) that it may have been a guild hall.

were laid crosswise in the lower part and lengthwise in the upper. They are mostly of tufa; and some of them are very large. A few pieces of tile were inserted to give a sort of bond. Even less of the room-vaulting remains. The passage from the hexagonal to the oval room was covered with a semi-circular vault in which bands of concrete with rather small tufa *caementa* were separated by single rows of tile. The oval room had an ellipsoidal dome of concrete having an aggregate of tufa with a slight admixture of tile (pl. 27, fig. 2). Traces of cross vaulting remain in one of the small rooms flanking the pools in the *frigidarium*. A tile aggregate was employed near the base and tufa *caementa* in small pieces above. A double cross vault covered one of the rooms in the South Building; and we have already mentioned the shearing off of the top of a slightly curved lintel at the impost of the barrel vault in the passage next to it. It is difficult to tell. how much of the little vaulting that remains is original.

During the reign of Antoninus Pius, those who were responsible for the public utilities saw to it that the Baths already in existence were functioning properly. An early Bath which had apparently outlived its usefulness was transformed into the Terme dell'Invidioso (V, 5, 2).[33] Hypocausts were remade in the Terme di Buticosus (I, 14, 8) with the same combination of stamped bricks as were used in the third phase of the villa at Sette Bassi, together with some re-use of Trajanic *bipedales*.[34] Brick stamps also prove that the Terme delle Sei Colonne (IV, 5, 11)[35] had an Antonine restoration. Until the Terme del Faro can be submitted to a more searching analysis than is feasible at present, it is impossible to tell whether the undeniably second-century brickwork is part of the installation of the Baths in a Trajanic building or merely a renovation of earlier Trajanic Baths.[36] The edifice was modified twice in the course of the century—once in very red bricks (3.5–4 cm. thick), once in somewhat thinner (3–3.5 cm.) lighter bricks—before it was given its present form in the thin bricks characteristic of the time of Commodus or Septimius Severus.[37] The room with the two pools almost certainly belongs to the second renovation. A water pipe impressed with the name of Cornificia, the sister of Marcus Aurelius, may give a clue to the date.

Calza believed that the reorganization of the Campus of the Magna Mater occurred in the reign of Antoninus Pius and probably through his instrumentality.[38] We have seen reason for attributing it to Hadrian.[39] Three shrines and a guild hall in the southeast corner are definitely later than the initial systematization, but whether late Hadrianic or earlier Antonine,[40] it is impossible to tell. Inscriptional evidence proves that the Temple of Bellona (IV, 1, 4), at any rate, was a benefaction.[41] If we could know which Gamala dedicated it,[42] we should have its date. The west wall of the cella was faced with the same type of reticulate and brick as the Hadrianic facing of the Sullan wall and is not well integrated with the contiguous walls of the temple. It may have been built originally to define the area. The temple was of conventional form with steps between two brick columns *in antis* leading to a pronaos. The brickwork does not meet the best Hadrianic standards. The bricks are a mixed lot, averaging 3.4 cm. in thickness, but showing none of the thinner bricks which sometimes appear in mixtures of

[33] See below, p. 220.

[34] Bloch, *Sc. di O.* I, p. 218. The seamonster mosaics probably belong to this renovation; see Becatti, *Sc. di O.* IV, pp. 29–30.

[35] Bloch, *op. cit.*, p. 226.

[36] *Ibid.*; Meiggs, *Ostia*, p. 419. See also above, pp. 147, 157.

[37] Meiggs, *op. cit.*, p. 443.

[38] G. Calza, "Il Santuario della Magna Mater," in *Acc. P. Mem.*, vol. 6 (2), 1947, pp. 184–205.

[39] See above, pp. 165–166.

[40] Becatti (*Sc. di O.* I, p. 145) favors the Antonine date.

[41] Bellona was built at the expense of the lictors and public slaves. See Meiggs, *Ostia*, pl. 38a.

[42] Meiggs, *op. cit.*, p. 201.

[43] Meiggs, *Ostia*, p. 360.

[44] The official report (*Sc. di O.* I, p. 236) seems to have identified a Hadrianic phase within the Severan.

[45] See above, pp. 160–165.

[46] G. Becatti, *Not. sc.*, 1940, pp. 36–50; G. Calza, *Palladio*, vol. 5, 1941, pp. 19–20. See also Crema, p. 458, fig. 583.

[47] See Meiggs, *Ostia*, p. 277.

[48] *CIL*, vol. 14, Suppl. no. 4709.

[49] Bloch, *Sc. di O.* I, p. 217.

the second half of the second century. The mortar joints are rather wide for Hadrianic work, but have been carefully raked. Of the porticus along the substructure of the Cardo only the lower part of the piers and a staircase remain, but it was probably contemporaneous with the temple. The Schola degli Hastiferi (IV, 1, 5) exhibits walls with good reticulate work outside and *incertum* inside reminiscent of the Hadrianic shops along the Cardo. The edifice would seem to be a little later than the shops but to have good claims to be Hadrianic. It was almost completely remade at a later time.[43] Piers along the east wall of a shrine to an unknown divinity (IV, 1, 8) show it was built later than the Schola degli Hastiferi with which it shared a wall. The brickwork in the other walls is not homogeneous though probably all contemporary. It shows some characteristics of the Severan age, to which it is ascribed in the official report.[44] Only the lower part of the brickwork of the third shrine (IV, 1, 7) remains. Its bricks would appear to me more like those used in the Hadrianic than in the Antonine era. Its orientation would seem more natural if it were earlier than the buildings to the east of it. These four small edifices illustrate the difficulty of dating private benefactions from the character of the masonry, especially when it was designed to be concealed by a marble revetment or stucco.

No public granaries erected in the Antonine era have come to light, but we have private enterprise to thank for an elegant warehouse designed for the storage of some commodity or commodities more precious than grain. The Hadrianic development known as the "Quartier des Docks"[45] left free an area at the southwest corner. Shortly after the death of Hadrian, two wealthy freedmen or at least men of freedman stock utilized it for a private storehouse (I, 8, 3)[46] possibly with space to rent.[47] A *tabella ansata*[48] of white marble discovered in the debris in front of the entrance, now restored to its place on the architrave, identifies it as the Horrea Epagathiana et Epaphroditiana (pl. 29, fig. 4). The relatively few brick stamps found bore a date equivalent to A.D. 137,[49] which accords well with the lettering of the inscription. The shape of the building was determined by its environment. The north wall abuts but is independent of the south wall of Horrea I, 8, 2; the east wall continues the line of the *horrea* in such a way as to leave the same intercalary space between it and the "Piccolo Mercato"; and the south wall rested on remnants of the Castrum wall. Because of the presence of earlier shops, the façade, on the west, is architecturally independent. The main entrance, well to the north of the center, led by a slight distortion to the center of the inner court so that merely a two-ramp stair well stood to the north of it, whereas four ample shops filled the space at the south. A pedimented entrance was the focal point of the façade (pl. 29, fig. 4). Its three-quarter columns of brick-faced concrete, with base moldings and bastard composite capitals in a lighter colored terra cotta, supported a narrow architrave, also light in color, a plain frieze into which the inscription was set, and a pediment in which both the horizontal and raking cornices were outlined in the same decorative fashion. Among the simpler moldings, a new one appears which is more characteristic of the age: small brick consoles support tiles hollowed out into miniature arches. The actual doorway was covered with an arch of the same fine brickwork as the columns and also light in color, which rested on a tile impost molding. At the right of the entrance, five Doric pilasters of more ordinary brickwork supported a narrow string cornice which in turn upheld the square windows of the mezzanine under segmental relieving arches of *sesquipedales*. The wide openings of the shops below with their travertine sills were covered with beams and then masonry under slightly curved lintels also of *sesquipedales*. The façade of the stair well was treated in exactly the same fashion except for the dividing wall and the two windows at the mezzanine level. A second string molding topped the segmental relieving arches throughout and outlined the small concrete arches of the lunetted half-barrel vault of the balcony across the front,[50] which probably served more for ornamentation and the protection of the passerby than for circulation. Upright tiles cut into an S-molding marked the top of the concrete vaulting under the usual projecting *bipedales* which formed the capping member. The balcony extended around the south corner, where a travertine block marked the angle. Travertine consoles supported the wooden floors of the mezzanine chambers. Similar corbels appear in the entrance corridor, which was covered with two cross vaults. In it, a secondary doorway with a travertine threshold, jambs, and lintel of enormous shaped pieces led to a vestibule.[51] The jambs still show cuttings for the insertion of a barrier of some sort. A fine pedimented niche of ornamental brickwork appears in each side wall of the vestibule,[52] which seems to have been covered with two cross vaults at the mezzanine level. The southernmost shop gave admittance to a long vaulted room[53] which could also be approached through a "shop" from Via delle Casette Repubblicane.

The vestibule led into a spacious court with a mosaic floor[54] and an arcaded quadriporticus of two orders. Opposite the entrance (pl. 29, fig. 2) a slightly curved lintel arch of *sesquipedales* broke the monotony of the arches of the arcade and marked the entrance to the "tablinum," which is further accentuated by a niche on each side practically identical with those in the vestibule. Travertine insets also distinguished this doorway from the arched openings of the porticus. Two cross vaults, one wider than the other, formed the ceiling. Doors were, however, so placed in the side walls that they did not impede circulation. The piers of the arcade terminated in impost moldings and had pilasters on the inner faces to help support the series of cross vaults of the porticus. A small square opening defined by lintel arches of tile pierced this vaulting at the two front corners, perhaps to give additional light to the stairs. A series of cross-vaulted rooms opened off from the quadriporticus. The doorways covered with slightly curved lintels were fortified with the travertine insets for barriers. The rooms were paved with herringbone brick and given fine stucco ceilings. Beam holes mark the level of the mezzanine chambers, which were lighted merely by small windows above the lintel arches.[55] The wide inner stairways at the front corners show rampant lintels of small *sesquipedales*, whereas large *bipedales* were employed in the same position in the outside staircase. The stairs led to an upper quadriporticus which presented to the court three arched windows on each side. From the court the transition was marked by a tile cornice protected by cover tiles. Upper rooms opened off from this arcade, the one over the "tablinum" projecting out beyond the others. They also seem to have been

[50] Such a balcony already appears in the Caseggiato di Annio (III, 14, 4). For the house, see above, pp. 184–185. It was also used in the Caseggiato degli Aurighi (III, 10, 1), the date of which is somewhat controversial. See below, p. 213 and n. 68.

[51] A small side doorway on the right could also be securely fastened on the inside.

[52] These are similar to those in the Caseggiato del Larario (I, 9, 3). For the house, see above, p. 168.

[53] It was barrel-vaulted to the line of the west rooms facing the court, then given a cross vault.

[54] Blake, MAAR, vol. 13, 1936, pp. 91–96, when I erroneously considered the building Hadrianic; Becatti, Sc. di O. IV, pp. 17–18.

[55] Those in the back had in addition slit windows opening out onto an intercalary space where they cannot have admitted much light.

56 This was later broken up into an apartment of small rooms.

57 Photographs in Becatti's article cited above show how complete the collapse of the edifice was, and arouse wonder at the extent of its restoration.

58 This is the date in the official publication.

59 The present arch is largely restoration.

60 It has no number, as Gismondi considered it part of the edifice across the street, a connection which Boethius (*Studies DMR* I, p. 444) considers most unlikely.

61 This building is difficult of access and somewhat overgrown.

furnished with insets for barriers and mezzanines. A long narrow hall at the south had no connection with these rooms.[56] The beginning of an inner staircase to a second story is preserved; the outside staircase indicates that part of the edifice at any rate was used for apartments.

Where so much has been restored with old material in modern times, it is difficult to obtain a clear impression of the original masonry.[57] In general, the bricks employed in the façade were a fine-grained brick red with yellow bricks used in parts for decorative effect, whereas those facing the rest were a miscellaneous lot of bricks of substantially the same thickness. Bonding courses occur. Most of the vaulting now visible is modern. Ancient vaulting appears only on the east side and on part of the north. Enough traces remain elsewhere to show that the contractor had no fear for the stability of the cross vault, which he uses everywhere except in one long hall. The vaulting in this hall has a cross vault corresponding to those in the rooms along the west side of the court. The vaulting in the "tablinum" also shows that he planned the cross vaults with reference to the whole rather than to the individual rooms.

South of them, another edifice (I, 8, 9), though virtually independent, must have been built at about the same time.[58] A passageway from Via delle Casette Repubblicane, separated from it by an outside staircase, led directly to the room running across the whole south side of the *horrea*. West of the staircase there were three shops of normal form, the two at the west facing a portico with an arcade of two arches, which flanked a passage from the street mentioned just above to Via Epagathiana. The masonry still corresponds closely to Hadrianic standards. The bricks range in thickness from 3.5 to 4 cm. and are a mixed lot with only a slight preponderance of yellow. Bonding courses occur with a certain regularity, and corresponding relieving arches in the partitions probably mark some weakness in the foundations at the base of the old Castrum wall. A slightly curved lintel of *bipedales* covers one doorway, and another not too securely set[59] spans the wide opening of one of the shops. The shops were barrel-vaulted, and one still shows *besales* adhering to its soffit where four *bipedales* laid on the wooden centering would have touched. Beam holes mark the level of the wooden floor of the mezzanine. South of the passage, two small shops with an outside staircase formed the ground floor of what must have been about the smallest apartment house in Ostia.[60] The masonry differs appreciably from the other. The average thickness of the bricks is greater. The first shop, though curtailed by the insertion of the stairs, still has provision made for a small wooden door at each end of its travertine threshold, as though it might have been subdivided by a wooden partition. The rampant barrel vault of the stairs was supported on a stout cross wall near the beginning and faced on the inside by broken *sesquipedales* in the usual fashion. There are, however, traces of a similar facing on the opposite side which would have appeared as a relieving arch in the body of the wall. In that case the house in question must have been earlier than the building to the south (I, 8, 8),[61] which is ascribed to the Antonine period in the official report. Some of the walls certainly appear Antonine from a distance.

During the reign of Antoninus Pius, headquarters were built for at least one important guild, the Schola del Traiano (IV, 5, 15).[62] The last of the fine Republican and Augustan houses along the West Decumanus was sacrificed to make room for it. The date (A.D. 145–155) is attested by brick stamps found in the masonry,[63] but the statue of Trajan from which it takes its modern name suggests that the guild was flourishing long before the erection of these headquarters. There is no inscription to indicate what corporation they served, and no evidence to show that they were a public benefaction. The original edifice consisted of a group of rooms in front of an enormous peristyle. It presented to the Decumanus an elaborate entrance flanked on one side by a shop and a flight of travertine steps and on the other by two shops.[64] Behind a porch having great columns of porta santa marble, the main entrance occupied the center of a curved wall with a curved niche on each side of it. Narrow entrance corridors isolated this central unit. The inner façade was concave. Travertine steps were cleverly fitted into the space behind the curve. Beyond each of these staircases there was a flight of tile steps descending to a basement. An apsed chamber with a rectangular arched niche preceded by two columns of bigio formed the focal part of each side unit. The brickwork is characteristic of the period. The bricks were a miscellaneous lot of different colors and textures, with a coarse yellow predominating. There are slightly more triangles than bricks made from tile. The thickness is rather constant (3–3.5 cm.);[65] mortar joints show the same variation (2–2.5 cm.) (pl. 28, fig. 1). There are no bonding courses and no relieving arches in the body of the masonry. Apertures were covered with slightly curved lintels of upright sesquipedales. There is no sign of cross vaulting. The barrel vaults show traces of a soffit of bipedales beneath a layer of besales a few of which were placed vertically to make a bond. Caementa were mostly of tile set without order in mortar as closely as possible. Marble thresholds belong to a later renovation; whether the marble revetments, of which traces remain, were original or not is incapable of proof. The colonnade of brick columns, stuccoed to look like marble, in the peristyle was curved at the ends. A long narrow nymphaeum with curved niches all around occupied the center of the peristyle. It was probably original, but it could have been added at any time before the row of rooms at the back was built. It has been largely restored in modern times. Such little of the ancient construction as remains exhibits rather short yellow bricks.

The two edifices east of the Loggia di Cartilio (IV, 9, 3 and 4), I have already treated as late Hadrianic or early Antonine buildings.[66] Meiggs has listed the second among the Antonine structures dated by brick stamps.[67] Presumably, he found some not included in Bloch's list. In any case, it seems wise to deal with such of the block as has been excavated as a whole, since the difference in date would be short at most.

Housing apparently continued to be a crying need which led to the construction of a few large edifices for speculation and a few incredibly small ones in odd bits of territory. Although the Caseggiato degli Aurighi (III, 10, 1)[68] may have been built in the Antonine period, it was an integral part of the complex comprising the Caseggiato del Serapide and the Terme dei Sette Sapienti and was certainly planned by the same architect. A few brick stamps found in situ and many found loose, forming an almost con-

[62] Becatti, Sc. di O. I, p. 146. Becatti believes it to be the guild hall of the Fabri Navales.

[63] Bloch, Sc. di O. I, p. 226.

[64] An inner staircase apparently supported on an oblique lintel arch served the upper rooms on this side.

[65] Bricks as thick as 4 cm. can be found.

[66] See pp. 200–201 above.

[67] Meiggs, Ostia, p. 549.

[68] See above, pp. 180, 181–182.

[69] Bloch, *Sc. di O.* I, p. 224.

[70] It is listed among the Antonine edifices in *Sc. di O.* I, p. 237. See also Becatti, *ibid.*, p. 147. Meiggs, *Ostia*, p. 138 n. 4, is doubtful.

[71] Becatti, *Sc. di O.* II, p. 69, speaks of the east façade as Hadrianic.

[72] *Idem, Sc. di O.* I, p. 147.

[73] Becatti, *Sc. di O.* II, pp. 69–75. A stamp (*CIL*, vol. 15 (1), no. 733a) of A.D. 148, found in a drain, gives a clue to the dating.

[74] The date is conjectural but reasonably certain.

[75] The east wall shows the mark of an ordinary gable roof; and holes for the necessary beams are still visible.

[76] This is Becatti's interpretation and fits his plausible conjecture that the so-called shrine was a banqueting hall for a social rather than a religious group.

[77] The threshold yielded a stamp (*CIL*, vol. 15 (1), no. 533) which is probably of the period of Marcus Aurelius or Commodus.

tinuous series from A.D. 126–141, give support to the Antonine date.[69] A *graffito* with the consular date A.D. 150 discovered under the stairs gives the *terminus ante quem* of the construction but does not settle the question of the date.[70] Repeated visits to the site have left the impression that there is no fundamental difference between the original masonry in the two apartment houses and the conviction that the slender piers at any rate were all constructed at about the same time. There was one important modification in a similar but slightly poorer masonry in the arcade about the court. The slender piers were widened to support inner arches for a mezzanine floor. Other piers were also widened in a similar fashion. This masonry could represent a change of plan in the course of building, possibly after the work had been suspended for a time.[71] It at any rate is Antonine and may account for the Antonine stamps. In any case, there is little difference between Hadrianic and early Antonine brickwork. The house has been described in the earlier section. A slight modification is discernible in the Terme, notably the conversion of the two hemicycles of the entrance into a casino.[72]

About the middle of the century, a narrow space between the Caseggiato degli Aurighi and a Hadrianic structure on the southeast was utilized for the worship of some unidentified cult, the Sacello delle Tre Navate (III, 2, 12).[73] To this end, the piers of the east arcade of the Caseggiato were encased in masonry on the exposed side and joined by partition walls about two meters high, a wall similar to the partitions was erected to the same height against the Hadrianic building, and a Hadrianic apse at the head was prolonged to make a shrine[74] and furnished with a black-and-white mosaic of geometric design. The earlier wall paintings prove that there were no masonry couches with brick columns at this time, but there may have been wooden columns to support a wooden roof.[75] A vestibule and a kitchen[76] were added at an oblique angle at the southeast corner. The walls exhibit facings of reticulate, brick, block-and-brick, and miscellaneous debris. The chief value of this edifice to the history of construction is the proof that a builder did not necessarily confine himself to one method but could use the material available with discretion. The difference in facing was concealed by stucco on the interior. Slightly later,[77] concrete podia were added, giving the hall the appearance of a mithraeum. Columns of brick-faced concrete were substituted for the hypothetical wooden columns. The walls were redecorated in a very similar style of fresco, and a mosaic was laid between the podia with a picture of a goblet, an altar, and a pig in front of the shrine.

Nearby, space was found for a small shrine (III, 2, 11) at the row of the Hadrianic shops with the porticus in front. Its rear and right wall were of the same type of "*opus incertissimum*" as the shops; its left wall and façade were of poor brickwork in rather wide bricks. The façade was given decorative treatment with brick-faced pilasters supporting a plain frieze over the lintel arch of the doorway, which terminated in a pediment outlined in three rows of tile without architectural carving. A wooden beam supported the lintel. Both lintel and frieze were composed of "upright" *bipedales*. The ceiling was barrel-vaulted with the remains of the broken tiles laid on its centering and a *besalis* or two clinging to its soffit. The poor masonry was concealed by stucco, but in itself is difficult to date. It is surely later

than the shops. The official publication ascribes it to the Antonine period.[78]
It may be even later.

On the opposite side of the Caseggiato degli Aurighi, there was a double
porticus (III, 14, 1). It is of particular interest because the piers supported
cross vaulting throughout. Later, partition walls were led from pier to pier.
The bricks used were a mixed lot, slightly thicker on the outside (3.5–4 cm.)
than was normal for the Antonine era, to which it is ascribed in the official
publication.[79] Somewhat narrower bricks were employed for the inner facing.
In any case, the back wall is later than the Hadrianic wall against which it
was built.

A long narrow edifice on Via Ovest delle Casette Tipo (III, 16, 3) was
later than the Hadrianic market at its rear.[80] It consisted of a long hall between
two projections. The hall would have presented to the street a broad opening
divided by two piers into three passages between two other doorways and was
subdivided crosswise into three parts. Originally it was connected with the
wings by wide doorways. Each wing contained two rooms, the one at the
southwest having a flight of stairs. It is difficult to say how much of an
upper story a structure of this sort would have. The facing consisted of
rather poor yellow bricks made from broken tiles (3.2–3.5 cm. thick). The
walls rested on a layer of *bipedales* but there were no bonding courses.

It is interesting to note how a contractor of the second century utilized
an irregular strip of land along the north side of the Western Decumanus
for a long narrow edifice, the Caseggiato delle Trifore (III, 3, 1). Although
he planned a practically uniform façade of shops along the Decumanus, he
divided the space into four units in accommodation to various changes in
environmental conditions. A raised platform brought the four together.
Between the Cardo degli Aurighi and the Decumanus, an irregular plot provided room for a shop with a rear room toward the former and one toward
the latter, in addition to a corner shop. At the opposite end, a room with
a flight of steps started the transition between two shops following the orientation of a Hadrianic building and the main row of shops along the Decumanus. There was space behind these three rooms for shallow rooms only.
Each of these had a door and one or two windows opening onto a species
of piazza behind. Beyond the stairs, a small unit consisting of a single shop
of the same dimensions as those at the left and a large rear room completed
the change, and with its projecting curved wall cut the rear façade into two
parts. Apertures in the wall were arranged in groups of three—a door between
two windows below, and three windows under an enormous relieving arch
above. The row of shops in the main section presents no peculiarities. They
are not intercommunicating. Cornices of tile show the position of their
mezzanines, and a flight of travertine steps in the center led to upper apartments. Behind the shops, two units of three intercommunicating rooms separated by an outside staircase faced Via delle Trifore. Each unit had an
outside door in the center and one or more rear exits through the shops to
the Decumanus. The rooms were well lighted by outside windows. There
was apparently no approach to the mezzanine from the rooms below. Access
was by way of the outside staircase through a corridor along the front wall.
Such an arrangement suggests that the ground floor was devoted to some

[78] Becatti, *Sc. di O.* I, pp. 147, 237.

[79] *Sc. di O.* I, p. 237.

[80] See above, pp. 182–183. (Doris Taylor Bishop noted Bloch's *Suppl.* no. 16 quite plainly located *in situ* in the ancient blockage of the doorway at the southwest corner of the northern wing, but there is no way of knowing the brick's original Hadrianic building site.—J.D.B.)

81 The wall paintings, of which there are considerable traces, may be used as an argument against this theory.

82 Boethius (*Studies DMR* I, p. 443 n. 14) lists this edifice among those having wooden floors between stories (*contignationes*). It would be interesting to know whether two large travertine corbels once supported balconies like those on Via di Diana.

83 Becatti, *Sc. di O.* I, p. 147, considers it from the period of Antoninus Pius, but the official map (*ibid.*, p. 140) shows it as from that of Marcus Aurelius.

84 C. L. Visconti, *Ann. d. Inst.*, vol. 19, 1857, pp. 334–338; Paschetto, *Ostia*, pp. 407–421.

85 Becatti, *Sc. di O.* I, p. 147; Meiggs, *Ostia*, p. 76; Becatti, *Sc. di O.* IV, pp. 159–172.

86 Bloch, *Bolli*, p. 278; idem, *Sc. di O.* I, pp. 225–226. A few earlier stamps probably indicate earlier construction at the site.

87 The range is 3.5–4 cm. in thickness.

industry,[81] whereas the mezzanine furnished an independent apartment. The edifice will doubtless be remembered best for its rear façade (pl. 30, fig. 3). As though wearied of the monotony of the row of shops along the Decumanus, the contractor has here arranged the apertures into six groups of three. At the ground floor, doorways give a certain variety. At the mezzanine level, on the other hand, windows alone, grouped under a large relieving arch, make the tripartite arrangement even more apparent. Nothing remains of the higher stories.[82] The foundations where they are exposed show a miscellaneous filling of large pieces of tufa. The walls throughout were of brick-faced concrete resting on a row of *bipedales*. The brickwork is not typical of the period of Antoninus Pius.[83] A mixed lot of bricks was used with discretion. Fine-grained red ones from broken tiles were chosen for the lower part of the façade along Via delle Trifore and for the bottom of some of the other walls. Yellow ones from *besales* predominate in some parts, and the usual mixture elsewhere. Although bricks can be found as wide as 3.8 cm., the majority tend to fall at the lower limit of a range of 3–3.5 cm. There were no bonding courses. Four depressed relieving arches were placed symmetrically low down in the body of the façade, and three of them correspond with similar ones in the lengthwise partition wall, in which, however, two or three others are visible. Apertures were covered with wooden beams under slightly curved lintels of *bipedales* in the façade and the lengthwise partition walls, but with straight lintels of the same in the crosswise partitions. The flight of steps in the western unit was carried in part by a rampant arch of *bipedales*. They were of tile. The vaulting shows a miscellaneous aggregate roughly laid. There as in all the vaulting, *bipedales* were placed on the wooden centering and then covered by *besales* before the *caementa* were laid. One novelty in these two flights was splayed windows in two of the risers to give light to the space under the stairs. Projecting tile cornices seem to have given support to the beams for the wooden floors of the mezzanines. Those in the apartment were barrel-vaulted, whereas the corridor in front of them was cross-vaulted. Such traces as are left show rather small *caementa* laid in more or less regular rows.

Many years ago, an edifice was partially unearthed near the Tiber[84] so magnificent that it was immediately named "Palazzo Imperiale" (Reg. III). It has since been uncovered more fully, though not completely, and lies quite apart from the rest of the excavations, more or less neglected, but by no means forgotten.[85] Most of its rich decoration of marble and mosaic has been carried elsewhere. Some day some scholar will give it the thorough study that it deserves and establish its chronology in more detail than is feasible at present. Although the type of masonry shows that the great south court and the rooms to the southwest of it were Commodan, a careful analysis of the brick stamps found proves that the main body of the complex was erected between A.D. 145 and 150.[86] Where brickwork alone is employed, notably in the eastern part of the southern section, it shows a miscellaneous facing composed of triangles, broken tiles, and broken roof tiles[87] laid with rather wide joints. The color is prevailingly yellow or light yellowish red. There are bonding courses and conspicuous relieving arches. Of more interest to our purpose, however, is the use of block-and-brick work in much of the central part. Although this is found occasionally in South Italy particularly in the region devastated by the earthquake of A.D. 62,[88] this is an early appearance of a more than casual use in the vicinity of Rome of a method of wall-facing that became common later.[89] It was carried out with great regularity in the columns and some of the half columns of the great peristyle as well as in most of the adjacent rooms and in the Baths, normally with either one or two rows of bricks to one of blocks. The bricks were made from broken tiles, the blocks from a stone resembling Monteverde tufa. The same fine masonry appears in one of the pretentious rooms in the less elegant northern section in which the majority of the rooms show insets of reticulate in frames of block-and-brick work. On the other hand, most of the masonry in the northwestern corner would appear from a distance[90] to be of Commodan brickwork, whereas brick occurs with reticulate in the northeastern corner. The Baths were beautifully appointed. The central hall, or palaestra, was embellished by a pavement of marble mosaic in a rich tapestry design,[91] a wall revetment of *alabastro fiorito* and *cipollino a mandorla*, and columns of polychrome marble. The pool at the center of the east side had a mosaic pavement and a marble facing for its walls adorned with niches alternatively curved and rectilinear. It was separated from the palaestra by columns *in antis*. The rooms to the left of it were fitted with hollow tiles connected with a hypocaust no longer apparent. All the rooms about the palaestra were paved with mosaics, most of them black-and-white, either geometric or figured with sea monsters or athletes.[92] In spite of all this elegance, the whole complex would seem to me more suited to the combined residence and business establishment of one of Ostia's wealthy merchants than to an imperial palace. The emperors may have been entertained there.

An analysis of the brick stamps led Bloch to the conclusion that the edifice was erected early in the reign of Antoninus Pius (A.D. 145–150).[93] Somewhat later a mithraeum was installed in a suitable place to the west of the great peristyle.[94] The palace was enlarged, probably in the reign of Commodus, by a second great peristyle to the south and a group of rooms connected with it.[95] As in all structures with a long history, there are plenty of indications of minor modifications and restorations, particularly in the section given over to the Baths.

The Caseggiato di Diana (I, 3, 3)[96] was the only private edifice of any importance to be erected in Regio I in the Antonine period. It took the place of an earlier edifice at a lower level.[97] One stamp[98] on a floor tile gives slight confirmation for the date at about the middle of the second century[99] suggested by the brickwork and the general arrangement. The ground plan is fundamentally that of an arcaded court[100] surrounded by rooms, but the court was little more than a light well; the rooms on the west were independent shops opening outwards; a reception room (?) stood between the shops in front and the court; a large hall faced the court on the opposite side; and rooms of indeterminate purpose, two of which were later made into a mithraeum,[101] lined the east wall. A cistern in the court supplied water for the tenants in upper apartments.[102] A brick cornice divided the north wall of the court into two registers, the upper one of which was diversified by a curved niche between rectangular ones. The edifice takes its modern name

[88] Blake, *RC* II, pp. 67, 75, 132, 139, 151, 153–157.

[89] Gismondi, *Sc. di O.* I, pp. 203–205. It occurs early in the Roccabruna of Hadrian's Villa. See below, pp. 252, 255.

[90] The section was too overgrown with brambles for study.

[91] Becatti, *Sc. di O.* IV, pp. 159–164; Nogara, *Mosaici*, pp. 34–35, pls. 69–70; M. E. Blake, *MAAR*, vol. 13, 1936, p. 125.

[92] Becatti, *op. cit.*, pp. 164–172; Blake, *op. cit.*, p. 92. The evidence precludes a first-century date.

[93] Bloch, *Sc. di O.* I, p. 226.

[94] See below, p. 228.

[95] See below, p. 234.

[96] G. Calza, *Not. sc.*, 1914, pp. 248–251; 1915, 324–327; idem, *Mon. ant.*, vol. 23 (2), cols. 602–603; idem, *Guida*, pp. 133–135; idem, *Palladio*, vol. 5, 1941, pp. 20–21; Müfid, *Stockwechbau*, p. 41; R. C. Carrington, *Antiquity*, vol. 7, 1933, pp. 144–146; P. Harsh, *MAAR*, vol. 12, 1935, pp. 25–27; Meiggs, *Ostia*, pp. 145, 240–244, pl. 8b.

[97] Calza, *Not. sc.*, 1914, p. 249.

[98] Bloch, *Sc. di O.* I, p. 216.

[99] Carrington (*op. cit.*) dates it in the latter part of the second.

[100] A line of doors takes the place of the corridor on the right.

[101] Becatti, *Sc. di O.* II, pp. 9–15.

[102] See Meiggs, *Ostia*, pp. 239–240.

from a terra-cotta plaque set in this court. The two shops facing Via di Diana alone were in communication with the main part of the edifice through their rear rooms. The one at the right had a small splayed window on each side of the broad opening. The corner shop belonged with the five independent shops fronting Via dei Balconi (pl. 30, fig. 2). All had travertine sills and beam holes for the wooden floors of mezzanines with windows under the usual barrel vaults supporting the first story. Wooden steps in each gave access to the chamber above it. Outside stairs (pl. 28, fig. 3), also of travertine, at the southeast corner led to apartments over the main body of the edifice; others on the west served apartments along Via dei Balconi.[103] The main entrance was through a long corridor next to the southeast stairs rather than in the center; a secondary entrance flanked the other staircase. Splayed windows brought light to this stair well from the cortile.[104] .The raised sidewalks on both streets seem to make a firm foundation for the massive structure, and a balcony supported by a half-barrel vault with lunettes over the mezzanine windows makes of the row of shops with their upper chambers an impressive base for the masonry above. The vaulting is terminated by a continuous row of lintel arches made of *besales* under a capping cornice of tile which faces the pavement of the balcony and its substruction. Although its floor was paved with tile and covered with *opus signinum* the balcony was probably decorative rather than functional, though it may have provided some protection from rain for the shops below. Between the horizontality of sidewalk and balcony, a continuous tile cornice, slightly curved over the lintel arches above the wide openings of the shops and straight elsewhere, forms a transition to the deeper relieving arches over the mezzanine windows and under the lunettes of the balcony. It is possible to walk through the rooms of the first-floor apartments; and the lower part of the stairs to a second is still preserved. One more story would be possible under the building regulations of Trajan for Rome, and a relieving arch found in the debris may have come from its walls. That makes five stories by English and American reckoning.[105] The brickwork follows the norm established by Gismondi (pl. 30, fig. 2). Yellow bricks sparsely sprinkled with red pozzolana predominate, though there is an admixture of other varieties. The mortar shows gray, white, and red pozzolana in its composition. There are still faint traces of the use of a curved tool on the joints, which Gismondi calls "*allisciatura.*" There are no bonding courses, but relieving arches of different sizes are found in the body of the masonry wherever the contractor felt them to be necessary.[106] Apertures were regularly covered with slightly curved lintel arches of *bipedales* over wooden beams firmly imbedded in the masonry; only full arches[107] appear over the openings toward the cortile under the influence of the arcaded courts which were becoming increasingly popular. *Besales* and *sesquipedales* were occasionally used for the lintels, and one or two were straight rather than curved. In other words, the contractor used whatever best served his purpose throughout the edifice. In like manner, barrel vaults and cross vaults were employed with discretion.[108] Everywhere *besales* adhere to the soffit with an occasional one placed vertically to make a bond. Most of them were stamped with small

[103] Two flights here equal three in the narrower staircase at the right.

[104] Another brought light from outside to a dark corridor, and another lighted a latrine.

[105] The number of stories is controversial. Part of the confusion comes from the difference between the continental and the English and American reckoning. Gismondi (*Palladio, loc. cit.,* p. 29, fig. 29) reconstructs it with only two upper floors.

[106] Note huge relieving arches under and over windows in the east wall of the cortile.

[107] Those on the east side were later reduced to square windows.

[108] The corridors from Via di Diana were barrel-vaulted, the west one with lunettes over the openings toward the court. The south hall had a flat ceiling; the ceiling of the north hall is not preserved. The rest of the rooms were covered with cross vaults, many of them depressed, two on the east having one arm elongated.

circles without lettering. Probably *bipedales* were used on the wooden centering.

Room was found for a narrow-fronted house of two shops and an outside staircase (I, 1, 1)[109] at the corner of Via di Diana and Via dei Lari. It presented to the streets a fine yellow façade of bricks about 3.2 cm. in thickness, laid without bonding courses. The overly wide openings of the shops were covered with slightly curved lintels of *sesquipedales* not securely based on the side walls, though they were protected by a segmental relieving arch over the small window at the mezzanine level, the floor of which was supported by a tile cornice. Mostly red tiles appear in the arches. The exposed face of the staircase at the back of the corner shop showed the usual rampant arch as a facing, this time of broken *sesquipedales*. The stairs could be ascended only from Via dei Lari. There are some traces of cross vaults. The house suffered considerable damage in antiquity and was much restored. Two other apartment houses crowded into restricted space have already been described.[110]

A vacant space in the center of a block was utilized for a small house of no importance (I, 14, 3). It seems to show two shops with an anteroom facing the court on the south, and on the north two rooms of different dimensions occupied the corners. There was a pool or fountain in the center. The walls were thin, and the brickwork too poor to repay analysis. It is listed among the Antonine structures in the official publication.[111]

So much for the Antonine masonry in Regio I.

Even less Antonine work has been uncovered in Regio II. There was a difference in level between the row of shops in front of the Grandi Horrea and the porticus with shops in front of the Sacred Area of the Quattro Tempietti, both part of a Hadrianic systematization of the north side of the East Decumanus. Even so, it seems strange that Via dei Grandi Horrea was cut off from access to the Decumanus. Whatever was planned for the intervening space, if anything, was never built. Later, probably in the Antonine period, a semicircular fountain[112] similar to those flanking the theater was installed. The basin was lined (II, 9, 1) with yellow bricks, 3.1–3.7 cm. thick. Behind the area in a narrow strip between the Hadrianic reorganization and the Sacred Area and Via dei Grandi Horrea, a long, narrow edifice (II, 8, 9) was erected, of a type made familiar in the Hadrianic period. It was divided into two or three units by staircases. The southernmost was a corridor apartment which consisted of a room at the south end large enough to require a central pier to support the vaulting, and an arched and probably barrel-vaulted corridor with three rooms opening off from it, two of which were intercommunicating. Only three large chambers have been excavated of the central unit, which must have been devoted to a manufactory of some sort. The rest remains to be excavated. The walls were thick enough to have carried several stories. No unusual features of construction are visible in this complex.

At the end of the reign of Hadrian there were no new public edifices south of the East Decumanus (Regio V), but private buildings were being erected whenever sites became available. This process continued into the Antonine

[109] Boethius, *Studies DMR* I, p. 444.

[110] Miss Blake's note was never written; but she seems to mean I, 8, 6 (Hadrianic; see above, p. 163) and the part of I, 8, 9 south of the passageway (Antonine; see above, p. 212 and also fn. 60 for Boethius's correction of Gismondi's analysis).—J.D.B.

[111] *Sc. di O.* I, p. 237.

[112] *Sc. di O.* I, p. 237; Neuerburg, *Fontane*, p. 184, no. 118.

113 For these, see Blake, *RC II*, p. 67.

114 See above, p. 176.

115 Becatti, *Sc. di O.* I, p. 144.

116 This was almost completely made over later.

117 G. Calza, *Not. sc.*, 1941, pp. 202–203. The stamps are *CIL*, vol. 15 (1), nos. 1146 and 1203.

118 Bloch, *Sc. di O.* I, p. 227.

119 The apse was a late addition where the re-use of old material is a distinct possibility. See Meiggs, *Ostia*, p. 549 n. 1.

120 For the Headquarters, see below, p. 227.

era until there was little space left for Severan structures. Few brick stamps have come to light to confirm the chronology after the time of Hadrian. This in itself militates against an ascription to Hadrian of buildings showing a masonry similar to his. It is difficult moreover to differentiate between work undertaken under Antoninus Pius and that of the time of Marcus Aurelius. Comparatively few buildings are preserved high enough to display how apertures were covered. With the possible exception of the Terme dell' Invidioso, all the edifices were the result of private enterprise. Consequently, they cannot be expected to show the precise masonry of public monuments. They are important, however, for showing structural trends.

It would be interesting to know why it was considered necessary to enlarge and reactivate early Baths[113] in the block next to the fine new Baths erected by Hadrian,[114] at only a slightly later date.[115] The northwest corner had already been used for a Hadrianic edifice (V, 5, 4) of no particular importance, but the Baths in the southeast corner were extended to the Decumanus and provided with no less than three main entrances—from the Decumanus, Via dell'Invidioso, and Semità dei Cippi—and secondary ones from Via del Sole. This is the Terme dell'Invidioso (V, 5, 2), named from a mosaic inscription. A small apartment house in the southwest corner (V, 5, 1)[116] shares a porticus with the western entrance of the Bath and was certainly planned at the same time, as was also a business establishment (V, 5, 3) to the north of it. In this complex the bricks used in the facings were a miscellaneous lot, in which yellow predominates. There are some bonding courses and relieving arches low in the body of the wall, not to mention one enormous relieving arch in the eastern perimetric wall, but they are not used with the precision of the Hadrianic masonry in Ostia. Both straight and slightly curved lintels of upright tiles, sometimes of *sesquipedales* and sometimes of *bipedales*, were employed over openings without the added protection of relieving arches. Though it is not apparent on the outside, broken tiles were used for the purpose. There is one fine splayed window in the east wall for which there is no apparent reason (pl. 29, fig. 1). One stair ramp faced with *sesquipedales* on the outside was laid on a straight centering contrary to the usual practice. No brick stamps have been reported, but such a combination of factors accords well with the period of Antoninus Pius. These Baths were renovated later and modified somewhat, but they remained fundamentally the same throughout the rest of their history.

The next block to the east along the Decumanus was provided with a row of shops beneath apartments (V, 7, 1) in front of the site used for the Headquarters of the Augustales at a later date. Calza,[117] relying on two brick stamps, considered them Hadrianic; but Bloch[118] reports these same two stamps from the apse of the Headquarters[119] and shows that one of the stamps at any rate could not have been impressed earlier than A.D. 150. Furthermore, the shops were almost certainly in use before the Headquarters were built,[120] since the north wall of the latter cuts off the rear doors and windows. The unit consisted of three independent shops, an entrance corridor to the space behind, and a staircase to the apartments above. The masonry in general follows the norm established by Gismondi for the Antonine period (pl. 26, fig. 3). The bricks are somewhat more mixed than usual. Yellow predominates, but, though most show the normal variation in thickness, some came from narrow tiles of about 2 cm. Among the rest, long pieces of *bipedales* and even of curved and dentil moldings can be seen. The mortar is about 1.5 cm. wide. Apertures were covered with beams under slightly curved lintels of *bipedales*. Low relieving arches in a corresponding position in each partition may mark the course of some drain.

Porticoes in front of shops on the south side of the Decumanus toward the Porta Romana have been ascribed to the Antonine period because of two different stamps: *CIL*, vol. 15 (1), no. 1057 of A.D. 137 and no. 2197,[121] extremely common in the Caseggiato degli Aurighi, the Antonine date of which is not proven without the shadow of a doubt. The two porticoes are quite independent of each other and belong to two edifices as yet unexcavated.[122] The one nearer to the center (V, 14, 1) exhibits a miscellaneous lot of bricks used with discretion. Fine-grained red ones from broken tiles, many of them under 3 cm. in thickness, appear in end walls; yellow ones ranging from 3 cm. to 3.5 cm. predominate in the partitions. The mortar joints with the former are 1.5–2, with the latter mostly 2 cm. wide. There are some yellow bonding courses. The frontal piers have been mostly relaid. In the other (V, 15, 1) large travertine blocks were re-used in the foundations of the piers. The bricks, averaging about 3.3 cm. throughout, are a brick red, those in the piers being darker than those in the rest. The mortar joints are 1.5 to 2.5 cm. Some yellow *bipedales* were used in the piers. One at any rate was only half of the square. Further information can come only through a complete excavation of the site.

At about the same time as the restoration of the Terme dell'Invidioso,[123] in all probability, a narrow strip of land to the east of them was utilized for a row of shops with a space behind them. This is the Caseggiato del Sole (V, 6, 1). The first unit occupied the area along the Decumanus left by a Hadrianic structure. It consisted of a shop with a rear room on the Decumanus, a corner shop, outside stairs, and a passage on Via del Sole. Seven shops lie between this and a passage and staircase at the opposite end. Passage and stairs, probably at both ends, were drawn together under a depressed arch. A low window appears over the passage and a higher one over the stairs. There is little out of the ordinary to report about the shops. Between the second and third and the fifth and sixth the partition walls were thicker, and each had an enormous relieving arch of *bipedales*.[124] They may have been called upon to carry the weight of walls in upper stories.[125] They alone had a door from one shop to the other, but all had doors to the space behind. The arrangement behind the row of shops is unique.[126] Four identical partition walls, each pierced by a door and two windows divided the area into five parts. A door in the south wall, later blocked, shows that there was a more or less public passage through the succession of doorways. The coarse wall covering on the west wall confirms the conjecture. Such a corridor would supply a current of air which would have been most grateful in summer. The first and fourth of these rooms were apparently courts open to the sky; the rest display the remainder of the holes for beams which supported a wooden ceiling. Each of the rooms between the two courts had doorways to two of the shops. In the first, a break in the wall painting

[121] Bloch, *Sc. di O.* I, p. 227.

[122] Miss Blake left no indication of her thought for this note, though it seems to be the progress of the excavation; but because of the notice of the Caseggiato degli Aurighi, see above, pp. 180, 181–182.—J.D.B.

[123] See above, pp. 209, 220.

[124] Only the beginning of one remains.

[125] There is no way of telling how many stories there were in the apartments fronting Via del Sole. They probably had wooden floors like the mezzanines. See Boethius, *Studies DMR* I, p. 443 n. 14.

[126] Becatti, *Sc. di O.* II, pp. 125–126.

127 Becatti, *Sc. di O.* I, pp. 144–145.

reveals where a light partition wall bisected the space to provide room for the proprietor of each shop. Presumably the same arrangement obtained in the second room. The room south of the second court could be approached directly from the alley to the south and from the entrance corridor at the west, but only indirectly through the court from the southernmost shop. Again the remains of wall paintings show that the space was split up into at least three rooms by light partitions, presumably for the accommodation of the proprietor of the shop. Accounts scratched on the walls leave no doubt as to the connection of the rooms with the shop. They must have made rather dim living quarters, but such would seem to have been their purpose. There are no criteria for an exact dating. Becatti[127] sees a similarity in masonry between this and the Terme dell'Invidioso, which is not, however, very marked. The edifice is later than the building to the east. The bricks used in the façade along Via del Sole were for the most part a very fine-grained yellow, 3.2 to 3.5 cm. thick, elsewhere a mixed lot of about the same thickness employed without discrimination. In one part of the east wall very red bricks appear. There are bonding courses and occasional relieving arches in the body of the wall in addition to the enormous ones mentioned above. *Sesquipedales* were used in the slightly curved lintels over apertures and were not reinforced by relieving arches. No shop front is preserved. The Antonine date given to the edifice in the official report is reasonable.[128]

128 *Sc. di O.* I, p. 237.

Via della Fortuna Annonaria must also have been an important thoroughfare. A small compact apartment house (V, 4, 1) was erected on the north side at the corner of Semità dei Cippi.[129] It had four shops fronting the Semità, two additional ones on Via dell'Invidioso, and one large one on Via della Fortuna Annonaria. Although apparently space was left for a two-ramp staircase at the back, no trace of steps remains, but there are marks of outside stairs from the alley at the rear. A mixed lot of bricks was used for the facings (3.4 cm. thick) with yellow predominating. A row of *bipedales* stood at the foot of each wall, but there were no bonding courses or relieving arches. A slightly curved lintel of *besales* over one doorway is the only covering for an aperture still extant.[130] The masonry looks Antonine.

129 Becatti, *Sc. di O.* I, p. 145.

Opposite it stood the Domus della Fortuna Annonaria (V, 2, 8) which gave its modern name to the street. It is practically the only dwelling designed for a single family to come from the Antonine period in Ostia. Comparatively few changes were made to transform it into a noble habitation of the fourth century.[131] It was necessary to descend from Via della Fortuna Annonaria to reach the central court. Rooms were grouped about three sides of a peristyle. A large room in the southeast corner was suitable for either a tablinum or a triclinium. A smaller room opened out of it, the mosaic pavement of which provides for a bed along the east wall and has a border that would seem to indicate that the chamber was originally open to the court. The doorway may, however, have been early converted into a window to make more effective the heating by hypocaust and hollow tiles in the north wall. The hot air came from a furnace at a lower level on the east. It is the first example of a heated room in a private house to come to light in Ostia. As it was customary to have a second room which could be used for

130 For V, 6, 3, inadvertently entered under both Antoninus Pius and Marcus Aurelius in the official chronology (*Sc. di O.* I, p. 237), see below, p. 228.

131 Becatti, *Case*, pp. 23–25. See also Meiggs, *Ostia*, pp. 90, 145, 254, 433–434; pl. 14a; Crema, pp. 453, 604.

either a reception or banquet hall, it is possible that one such opened off from the court on the west side but was destroyed when the apsed hall and nymphaeum were constructed.[132] Two shops facing Semità dei Cippi were also sacrificed. They may have antedated the house since the remains of the rear wall show insets of reticulate like that in the house to the south. In a second phase, perhaps when the house was built, spur walls were extended outward presumably to support the arches of a balcony over the shops. Between a large shop at the northeast corner and two large ones at the northwest, a row of comparatively small rooms opened alternatively toward Via della Fortuna Annonaria and toward the court. Those facing the street were undoubtedly shops, the others may have served the needs of the family. Outside stairs led to an apartment or apartments across the front; an inside staircase at the southwest corner of the court may have led to living quarters over the shops along the Semità. Whatever the arrangement, the proprietor had sufficient spaces to rent to assure himself a good income. The edifice is manifestly later than the building to the south, but no brick stamps have been found to confirm its date. The bricks used for the facings are a mixed lot, often wider than normal for the Antonine period. It is not impossible, however, that an Antonine contractor had on hand a residue of Hadrianic bricks, which might yield stamps if they could be examined. The bricks are not used with the precision found in the best Antonine work. Bonding courses are less conspicuous than in Hadrianic work. One or two small relieving arches appear in the body of the wall, but they are not used over the slightly curved lintel arches that cover the apertures. *Sesquipedales* are regularly used for these rather than *bipedales*. The mosaic pavement in the cubiculum is almost certainly Antonine. Such is the vague and almost intangible evidence upon which the investigator must rely. To Becatti,[133] Meiggs,[134] and the present writer, the house feels Antonine.

Unfortunately, such unanimity does not hold for the building to the east of it (V, 2, 9). The official chronology ascribes it to Hadrian,[135] but Meiggs[136] and the present writer to Antoninus Pius. The two structures have a common wall; and there is no indication, so far as I can see, that either backed against a pre-existing wall. Furthermore, as in the other, the contractor employed bricks showing a wider range in thickness than normal for the period. He did not, however, employ them indiscriminately but in each section used the ones of approximately the same thickness. There were no bonding courses or relieving arches, and the walls are not preserved high enough to show how apertures were treated. A row of splayed windows on the southern part of the west wall below the Domus della Fortuna Annonaria gave added light from what must have been an open space at that time.

Farther along the street, a fine house of about the middle of the first century was destroyed a hundred or so years later to make room for three units (V, 8, 1 and 2 and 3).[137] Shops along the streets on the north and west, with outside stairs to apartments above and more apartments over the living quarters on the east served by stairs from Via di Felicissimo, must have furnished a good income to the proprietor, who presumably occupied the rooms opening directly onto the court, which still shows some brick-faced piers for an arcade. Pilasters of fine brickwork are mute testimony of an

[132] Neuerburg, *Fontane*, pp. 194f, no. 135.

[133] Becatti, *Sc. di O.* I, p. 145.

[134] Meiggs, *Ostia*, p. 548.

[135] *Sc. di O.* I, p. 237.

[136] Meiggs, *Ostia*, p. 548, who includes with it V, 2, 10, of which little is preserved.

[137] Becatti, *Sc. di O.* I, p. 144.

ornamental doorway from Via della Fortuna Annonaria. A spacious vestibule led through a large hall with a room to the left of it, to the court. A room to the right of the hall faced the court, as did others on the east and south. Two small rooms on the south, approached from a secondary entrance, were entirely independent. The south façade was of fine yellow brickwork and had a broad entrance to the court. The house needs a more detailed analysis than is feasible at this time. There are remains of walls at a lower level; and some may have been incorporated in the Antonine house. There are traces of modifications in a similar masonry, besides those which are manifestly much later. The body of the masonry accords well with the Antonine date ascribed to it in the official publication. *Bipedales* appear at the base of the wall, but there are no bonding courses. One large relieving arch and two smaller ones occur in the body of the wall. The masonry is not preserved high enough to show how apertures were covered. Angle piers in the vestibule probably indicate that it was covered with a cross vault at some time.

At the corner where Via della Fortuna Annonaria meets Via degli Augustali, until recently an oblong space enclosed in a quadriporticus with brick-faced piers to support an arcade (V, 7, 3) stood alone and aroused speculation as to its purpose. The masonry appeared Antonine, but nothing more could be said about it. Further excavation has now revealed it to be one of the most completely equipped cleaning establishments (*fullonica*) to come out of the ancient world. One awaits with impatience the official publication of this important find.

MARCUS AURELIUS (A.D. 161–180)

There is little evidence that Marcus Aurelius was personally responsible for any construction in Ostia. No public buildings were erected there during his reign. The Headquarters of the Augustales, though built for the convenience of the city officials, was probably a local dedication. By this time basic needs had been met for the time being at least. A normal amount of private building continued. Two rather elegant apartment houses can be dated in his reign by the brick stamps; three others would seem to belong to it from the character of their construction. A modest cleaning establishment (*fullonica*) has been ascribed to this period in the official report, but the masonry seems to me to be Antonine. Too little is preserved of an edifice near the Porta Romana, also included in the official list, to tell its purpose. Meanwhile, the followers of Mithras were seeking available spaces in which to install the sanctuaries required by their cult. A description of the various edifices follows.

Space was found for the Fullonica (IV, 5, 3) south of a Hadrianic structure connected with the Macellum. Only one room was devoted to the actual cleansing process. How the rest of the edifice was employed is a matter of conjecture. There were two "shops" facing Via del Pomerio and two rooms at the south of an open court.

The corner between the Decumanus and Via della Foce was an impressive site for the substantial apartment house (III, 1, 1) which was erected there in the time of Marcus Aurelius. Brick stamps give the date.[138] It was divided

138 Gismondi, *Sc. di O.* I, p. 204. The stamps, not recorded by Bloch in *Sc. di O.* I, are *CIL*, vol. 15 (1), no. 401.

into two parts by a narrow passageway to an open space behind.[139] Four shops along the Decumanus have the angle piers for the support of cross vaults. Three had each its own rear shop with the beginning of steps to a loft and a latrine behind them. Part of the space behind the corner shop which was larger than the others was taken up by outside stairs from Via della Foce to apartments above. A narrow corridor at the west gave access to both the rear shops which, contrary to the usual practice, were intercommunicating. Beyond the stairs, a large shop facing Via della Foce had a secondary door on the passageway but no direct communication with any of the rest. The room behind it which completed the east unit, on the other hand, had a broad opening onto the open space, two doors (one of which was closed later) onto the passage, and one to a shop on the south. The western unit is of less interest—two shops to Via della Foce on the east, two rooms to the west, one with a wide opening to the area which was later closed, stairs and a corridor to a room behind in between the parts, a latrine with a splayed window beneath the stairs. Practically every wall had a door for easy communication between rooms and with the outside world. Large travertine blocks constituted the corner with a masonry of fine yellow bricks on the south side.[140] These are narrow (2.5 cm.) and broken to triangular or trapezoidal shape from *sesquipedales*. The rest of the façades are of finer brickwork than the other walls, which show a mixture of bricks of many sizes laid with considerable care. The doorways where preserved retain traces of the beam which stood under the slightly curved lintel of *bipedales*. A full arch appears in the northern unit where the landing for a second flight of stairs would have been.

The Porticus and Caseggiato dell'Ercole (IV, 2, 2–3)[141] is the most impressive of the apartment houses of the period, with its long portico extending from Via della Caupona almost to the entrance of the Terme del Faro and shading the whole length of the block along the Cardo Maximus. Both arcade and house take their name from the figure of Hercules carved on the tufa keystone of one of the eleven arches. The ascription of the monument to the time of Marcus Aurelius rests on comparatively few brick stamps,[142] but it is not at variance with the type of construction. Only the piers of the arcade remain, and these have been largely reconstructed. Travertine pieces hollowed out for the insertion of a barrier of some sort were set in rather higher than usual (1.5 m.). The apartment house facing the Porticus is a good illustration of Boethius's Type II,[143] in which the ground floor is composed of shops facing in opposite directions from a common back wall. It was divided into three units by passageways from the Porticus to a paved area behind it. In the two units toward the south, there were doorways between the front and back shops, but only one case of intercommunication within the row, though the majority had side doors to the passageways. Two flights of steps, one from the east and one from the west, were apparently considered sufficient for those dwelling in upper apartments facing the Cardo. The entrance to the paved area in the center from Via della Caupona was probably bridged over so that the two end shops belonged with one farther west as the ground floor of an apartment of five rooms along Via della Caupona, served by its own staircase.[144] So much for the ground

[139] This was an alley to the Palaestra behind. See Becatti, *Sc. di O.* I, p. 148.

[140] Gismondi, *Sc. di O.* I, p. 204.

[141] Becatti, *Sc. di O.* I, p. 145.

[142] Bloch, *Sc. di O.* I, p. 227.

[143] A. Boethius, *The Golden House of Nero*, Ann Arbor 1960, p. 159.

[144] Rooms were added to these on the west side of the court, but the masonry is different and probably bespeaks a later date.

145 A full archway to the passage distinguished the southwest shop of the southern unit from the rest.

146 The wall carrying the west stairs is gone.

147 Colored *bipedales* are found later, but there is no evidence of any such use of coloring matter elsewhere in this complex.

148 In some of the shops corner piers were added later to strengthen the vaulting.

149 *Sc. di O.* I, p. 237.

150 See above, p. 147.

151 See above, p. 198 (IV, 2, 12).

152 *CIL*, col. 15 (1), p. 273 gives A.D. 123–155 as the period of use of her stamps.

plan. Enough is preserved of the shops for a composite picture, though all the elements are not found in any one shop. They had the usual travertine sills and beams spanning the wide openings under the slightly curved lintel arches of *bipedales*.[145] There were almost certainly windows over the lintels, since they occur over the lintels of the doors in the common back walls, which incidentally are of *sesquipedales* rather than *bipedales* as in the rest. The walls show just one bonding course in the brickwork. The east stairway[146] was carried in part on an oblique lintel arch of *bipedales* and given additional support by both a small and a large relieving arch. The red coloring matter which emphasizes the enormous relieving arch was not applied, I think, until later.[147] The staircase from Via della Caupona rested on a rampant lintel of *bipedales*. Relieving arches were used sparingly in the rest of the masonry where a drain or some weakness in the foundation made them seem necessary, but the day of the lavish use of relieving arches was definitely past. The brickwork shows bricks that are somewhat thinner than those used in the preceding era, many of which are in short lengths. Herringbone brick paved the shops. Holes appear in the walls for the beams of mezzanine floors, but the ceilings were cross-vaulted,[148] whereas the passages were barrel-vaulted. A layer of *bipedales* was first laid on the wooden centering, then a layer of *besales*, and finally the aggregate of the vaulting itself.

A house in the center of the same block (IV, 2, 5) has been ascribed to the time of Marcus Aurelius in the official report.[149] It is obviously later than the Trajanic edifice to the south (Terme del Faro)[150] and the Hadrianic structure to the west.[151] A brick stamp *in situ* on a *bipedalis* with the name of Lucilla gives slight evidence for a somewhat earlier date.[152] The house had a chequered history, and each phase contributed to its brickwork, until it is difficult to judge of its original appearance. It has an interesting ground plan. Its only entrance was from the paved area behind the Caseggiato dell'Ercole. I would venture to guess that a simple outside staircase and vestibule preceded the elaborate stair well which occupies the space today. The southern part is reminiscent of the corridor house, with two small rooms receiving light only from the corridor between two large rooms, which in this case cannot have been very adequately lighted. The one at the east, if there ever was one, was destroyed completely when the space was appropriated for a large tank serving the Baths; the one at the west was curtailed by a broad ramp, but whether or not at the same time, it is impossible to tell. At some time the back wall of the two small rooms was rebuilt. Four rooms along the public passage on the north side completed the plan. Relieving arches at regular intervals at the bottom of the wall are a conspicuous feature in this north façade. Originally there were broad openings in the two western rooms. These were subsequently narrowed and finally walled up completely, so that there can have been little light in either room. Possibly when the ramp was built, this western part was devoted to storage space. The other two rooms had windows which seem low on the outside but are rather high on the inside, since the rooms were at a considerably lower level than the ground outside. A layer of *bipedales* stood two courses below the window sills; and other bonding courses occur inside. Slightly curved lintels of *bipedales* topped the windows.

Behind a shophouse of the Antonine period along the Decumanus,[153] space was cleared[154] for the Headquarters of the Augustales (V, 7, 2).[155] The building was identified by fragmentary inscriptions and some statues found in the course of excavation. It should probably be dated in the time of Marcus Aurelius.[156] Whether the Augustales owned and profited by the rentals from the earlier building or not, they certainly planned to derive income from that row of five shops fronting Via degli Augustali, which formed part of the same "blueprint" as their headquarters. These shops were entirely independent of the main edifice and were intercommunicating. The row stopped at a secondary entrance corridor to the inner court. What was planned for the space at the south is not clear, but a door connected it with the main building.[157] It terminated at a flight of outside steps probably serving apartments only along this east side, which would have added another source of income. Because of the earlier shops along the Decumanus, the main entrance, marked by columns of porta santa marble, led to a reception room cut off from the northeast corner of the central court. Calza believed that the enigmatic room at the southeast corner was a second reception room. Two granite columns *in antis* graced the entrance to the "tablinum" in the center of the south side, which probably rose above the roof of the quadri-porticus. Three rooms on each side of the "tablinum" were not symmetrically arranged. Doors alternated with windows along the west side of the court where six rooms, diminishing in size toward the north, filled the space left by the different orientation of the Decumanus and Via del Mitreo dei Serpenti. Cross walls divided these into a suite of three rooms, another of two, and two single rooms. There were no outside windows. The great piers of the arcade about the central court were brick-faced. In general, the masonry is homogeneous throughout. Slight modifications are easily discernible from the character of the wall construction. The original walls were faced with bricks varying in width from 2.5 to 4 cm. Many are short, some are slightly curved, and occasional ones are crumbly. Mortar joints average about 2 cm. in width. There are no bonding courses; and relieving arches appear only in that part of the south wall which was little more than a refacing of an earlier wall behind it. There was no second story over the main building. Stairs at the northwest corner were added later to give access to an apartment at the mezzanine level. The great apse was added to the "tablinum" at a much later date. Marble revetments for the walls and probably the mosaic floors were a part of the late transformation.

Three other edifices in Regio V can be ascribed to the time of Marcus Aurelius on the basis of their construction alone. Although the brickwork is still fairly good, it shows the miscellaneous use of bricks of various sizes characteristic of the period. An occasional brick has weathered badly. Since they add nothing to our knowledge of the building methods of the time, a brief mention must suffice. Space was made for a small house (V, 7, 5) at the southwest corner of the block which contained the Headquarters of the Augustales. Small as it was, it consisted of two parts on the ground floor, a

[153] See above, p. 220.

[154] A Hadrianic edifice was razed to the ground to make room for it.

[155] G. Calza, *Not. sc.*, 1941, pp. 196–209 with architectural drawings by Ziino, pp. 210–215. See also Meiggs, *Ostia*, pp. 220–221, 433, 549, pl. 12a.

[156] The only brick stamps found (Bloch, *Sc. di O.* I, p. 227), datable A.D. 130–150, represent a re-use of old material and should not be used to date the edifice. Calza (*Sc. di O.* I, p. 202) favors an Antonine date. Becatti (*Sc. di O.* I, p. 145) ascribes it roughly between A.D. 150 and 165. Gismondi (*Sc. di O.* I, p. 204) considers the masonry a product of the time of Marcus Aurelius as does Meiggs (*Ostia*, p. 549).

[157] The broad opening facing the street of the second room suggests that it was a shop at some time.

158 All are published exhaustively by Becatti, *Sc. di O.* II. See also Meiggs, *Ostia*, pp. 370–375.

159 Becatti, *Sc. di O.* II, pp. 87–92; *Sc. di O.* IV, pp. 177–179; Vermaseren, *CIMRM*, pp. 133–136.

160 Becatti, *Sc. di O.* II, pp. 53–57; *idem, Sc. di O.* IV, pp. 159–172; Vermaseren, *CIMRM*, pp. 124–128.

161 Becatti, *Sc. di O.* II, pp. 93–99; *idem, Sc. di O.* IV, pp. 197–199; Vermaseren, *CIMRM*, pp. 136–139.

162 Becatti, *Sc. di O.* II, pp. 47–51; *idem, Sc. di O.* IV, pp. 90–91; Vermaseren, *CIMRM*, pp. 121–123.

163 Becatti, *Sc. di O.* II, pp. 77–85; *idem, Sc. di O.* IV, pp. 142–143; Vermaseren, *CIMRM*, pp. 131–133.

164 Gismondi, *Sc. di O.* I, p. 204.

corner shop with a room suitable for some industry behind it, an outside staircase, and a shop and two rooms in the rear. Apartments of five rooms would have occupied the upper stories. Across Via del Mitreo dei Serpenti, another small apartment house (V, 6, 3) shows a similar masonry and is probably very nearly contemporaneous. The ground floor consisted of three shops facing Via della Fortuna Annonaria and an outside staircase between the second and third shops. Each shop had a rear room. Various openings in the back wall were closed at a later time until only three splayed windows remained. The stairs would have led to apartments of six rooms. Practically nothing is left of the third edifice (V, 18, 1) except the beginning of the perimetric walls.

By the time of Marcus Aurelius, the followers of Mithras were seeking available places which could be adapted to the ritual of their cult.[158] The earliest of these mithraea at Ostia, the Mitreo degli Animali (IV, 2, 11),[159] was established in a pillared hall of the time of Trajan. Few additional walls were needed, and these were brick-faced. Becatti ascribes a date about A.D. 160 to it because of the type of the mosaic floor and the style of the two statues found therein. The Mithraeum of the "Palazzo Imperiale"[160] contained two silver statuettes which can be dated by their dedicatory inscriptions at A.D. 162. The altar was dedicated by the same individual. If these belong to the period of the insertion of the shrine in an earlier porticus, we have another mithraeum at about the same time. The walls show masonry of three periods. The reticulate-and-brick of the west wall was left from an earlier use of the site; the thin red brickwork of the south wall apparently belongs to the Commodan enlargement. The poor slipshod masonry of the north wall and of the curtains between the brick piers indicate that the mithraeum was not an integral part of the palace architecture. Where a facing was needed brick was used. A room in a small Claudian warehouse supplied the site of the Mitreo delle Sette Porte (IV, 5, 13),[161] which has been ascribed to about A.D. 160–170 on the evidence of coins found in the concrete. What little masonry was needed for the transformation was faced with brick. At about the same time, the Mitreo delle Sette Sfere (II, 8, 6)[162] was installed in one of the shops of the Hadrian period in the original precinct of the Quattro Tempietti. The quality of the mosaics was the main consideration for the dating, but such brickwork as belonged to it is in keeping with the ascription, and piers of block-and-brick work do not nullify it. An inscription proves that the Mitreo della Planta Pedis (III, 17, 2)[163] was inserted in a Hadrianic loggia during the years in which Marcus Aurelius associated Commodus with himself in the reign (A.D. 176–180). The masonry used in the transformation was faced with block-and-brick work. The sanctuary was renovated (A.D. 255–259) but is in ruinous condition today. This brief survey shows the varieties of masonry employed by the humble denizens of Ostia for their places of worship. Plaster and mosaic concealed the different kinds of construction, both old and new, in each building; and statuary made it a fit sanctuary for the god in the eyes of the believer. The masonry is not important in itself.

In conclusion, the brickwork of the time of Marcus Aurelius differs little from that of Antoninus Pius.[164] Inner walls show a variety of bricks made from *besales*, *sesquipedales*, *bipedales*, and roof tiles. The bricks average 23–26 cm. $\times$ 3–3.5 cm., but many are thinner. The mortar joints range from 1.8–2.3 cm. Material was carefully chosen, on the other hand, for use in the façades. Bonding courses and relieving arches were employed sparingly, if at all. Beams under slightly curved lintels of *bipedales* were a favorite covering for apertures, though an occasional full arch is found. Cross vaulting was beginning to supplant barrel vaulting wherever practicable. These generalizations have only a tentative value, since only two of the edifices studied can be securely dated. Brick stamps were becoming very rare.

COMMODUS (A.D. 180–192)

By the time of Commodus, the increase in population had reached the point where the theater had to be enlarged, the central part of the Grandi Horrea rebuilt to give more room for storing grain, and a large new granary added to the many already in existence. During his reign, two more collegiate temples were erected and half a dozen new apartment houses. His contributions were all utilitarian. It is not always possible to distinguish his work from that of his successor.

Toward the end of the second century the theater (II, 7, 2) was entirely rebuilt at a higher level on a somewhat larger scale incorporating as much of the theater of Agrippa as could be of service.[165] A dedication in bronze letters proclaimed that it was inaugurated by Septimius Severus and Caracalla in A.D. 195.[166] Possibly they put on the finishing touches, but what is preserved is homogeneous and shown by brick stamps to belong to the time of Commodus.[167] It was still a theater of conventional form with an entrance in the center of the semicircle as well as at each extremity, and four stairways leading to the second and third tiers of seats. Surmounting the third order there was a colonnade of cipollino columns, which have been reerected behind the scaena. Of the outer porticus enough remains for a complete restoration, a part of which has been carried out. It, too, was conventional though rendered in brick (pl. 31, fig. 4), except that the lowest order was Ionic, the second Corinthian or composite, and the third Doric with slender pilasters between windows. Travertine blocks once supported the *velarium*. A two-course travertine foundation rested on the travertine plateau encircling the theater, which was in its turn enclosed by chains between posts. The Flavian semicircular fountains[168] beyond the circle were doubtless also restored at this time. All the decorative members except the capitals were effected by the use of three moldings—the *cyma recta* for transitions, a convex face to mark the fasciae, and quarter-circular faces to make the large torus of the column bases (pl. 31, fig. 2).[169] Three pieces of tile molded to shape formed the consoles supporting the capping cornice of the first order, and two small oblongs were united to make each dentil. Within the outer porticus, the wedge-shaped spaces between the supporting walls of the cavea were utilized for shops, each with a dark place behind it. The fronts of the shops rested on the foundations of the earlier porticus. The façade was of fine brickwork like that at each end of the semicircle of seats. The bricks were made from bright yellowish red tiles of very fine grain, ranging from

[165] Calza, *Il Teatro Romano di Ostia*, Rome and Milan 1927, pp. 5–32; see also Meiggs, *Ostia*, pp. 42–43, 80, 424–425, pl. 22.

[166] It has been largely restored in modern times.

[167] Bloch, *Sc. di O.* I, p. 221.

[168] See Blake, *RC* II, p. 133 for the earlier phase. One was later turned into a Christian oratorio. See Neuerburg, *Fontane*, pp. 182–183, nos. 115, 116.

[169] Fallen vaulting facilitates examination.

[170] For technical details, see also Gismondi, *Sc. di O.* I, p. 204; *idem, Anthema, studi in onore di Carlo Anti*, Padua 1953, pp. 293–308; Becatti, *Sc. di O.* I, p. 161.

[171] G. Calza, *Bull. Com.*, vol. 43, 1915, pp. 183–184.

[172] G. Calza, *Not. sc.*, 1921, p. 348; Gismondi, *Sc. di O.* I, fig. 33; Meiggs, *Ostia*, p. 549.

[173] Calza, *op. cit.*, p. 381.

[174] *Sc. di O.* I, pl. 54, 4.

2.4 to 3.2 cm. in thickness.[170] They were often broken to triangular shape. One bonding course occurs in each front. The same tiles (*bipedales*) made slightly wedge-shaped were used for an enormous relieving arch in each end wall. The joints are fine (not over 1 cm.). There is a similar relieving arch, less well made with more mortar between the tiles, in each radial wall. The rest of these walls is made of short pieces of *bipedales* of about the same thickness, but varying greatly in both color and texture. Some are full of large grains of pozzolana; others are fine-grained. There is one bonding course of thin red *bipedales*. Projecting brick cornices supported a wooden mezzanine in each shop for which brick steps were built in the corner. At the rear of the shops, an upper passage was upheld by a barrel vault with rough ribbing and an intrados of *besales*. Cross vaults covered the rest of the spaces. A place for a drain appears in the corner of some of the shops. There were travertine thresholds and pavements of *bipedales*. Some walls show traces of simple frescoes on thin plaster. The central passageway had a marble floor, a marble wall revetment, and a barrel vault richly decorated with stucco work, of which some traces remain. This whole decorative phase may belong to a late modification sustained when an arch was inserted in the middle of the passageway, the two shops on each side were converted into cisterns, and a basin was built in the orchestra itself for the performance of water spectacles. This change occurred in the second half of the fourth century and hence beyond the chronological limits set for this study.

Two offices from each side of the Piazzale delle Corporazioni (II, 7, 4) were appropriated in the enlargement of the theater.[171] Four great piers on each side, which formed the new entrance, exhibit the same fine red brickwork as the exterior of the theater. The level of the porticus was raised in correspondence to the new level of the theater, but there was no other masonry except perhaps that employed to close the entrances toward the Tiber so that the space might be used for new offices. Wooden partitions still separated the offices; masonry barriers were not substituted for these until later. Gradually the occupants of these offices came to announce graphically their reason for being there in black-and-white mosaics often with inscriptions in front of the space allotted to them. The mosaics were not part of the general reorganization.

The Grandi Horrea (II, 9, 7)[172] were completely reorganized in the second half of the second century. The ground plan was not changed, but the storage rooms were raised on suspended floors, and a second story was added. Stamps of the time of Marcus Aurelius and Commodus[173] indicate the period when the transformation started. The rooms facing the central area were rebuilt at a higher level on the east, south, and west, and probably on the north as well. More spacious rooms occupied the southern corners perhaps for the use of the administration. Ramps starting with travertine steps were added at the four corners. The walls are not preserved high enough to show how the apertures were covered; and no trace of vaulting remains. The wall facings show the discrimination in the choice of bricks from a large assortment characteristic of the age. On the south side toward the east end, the builder used fine-grained yellow bricks slightly wider than those employed elsewhere (3–3.5 cm.)[174] and decidedly shorter (12.3–16.5

cm.) and had them laid with narrow joints and red bonding courses. Those on the east side and probably those on the west are still predominately yellow, but coarser-grained, slightly thinner (2.2–3.5 cm.) and roughly broken to triangular shape, whereas the rear and partition walls were faced with the usual miscellaneous lot within a range of 2.9–3.5 cm. Red bonding courses, or rather pseudo-bonding courses since the *bipedales* are not whole to make a good bond, are still present. The northern part was wholly rebuilt at a slightly later period.[175]

The many warehouses already erected in Ostia apparently were not sufficient for the needs of the Capital and one of the Antonines, probably Commodus, had another enormous one built (II, 2, 7–8)[176] with its façade toward the Tiber, a blank wall buttressed by heavy pilasters separated by a passage from the back of the Hadrianic shops along the Portico dei Tetti Spioventi toward the Decumanus, and a double row of shops along the east side of a large porticoed court. The external walls were faced with broken tiles of reddish hue, and the inner ones with yellowish red triangles made from *besales*.[177] There are some of the red bonding courses which began to be used in the time of Commodus. Only a small part of the great warehouse has been excavated thus far.

When the level of the block in front of the theater was raised, a continuous flight of steps[178] led to a porticus with shops which constituted the ground floor of the Caseggiato degli Archi Trionfali (V, 11, 7).[179] Of the porticus, six piers remain more or less restored (pl. 28, fig. 2), but nothing of the entablature. The piers show the same fine red brickwork as the exterior of the theater, with which they are probably contemporaneous. Near the base, three rows of yellow bricks were used for decoration, which suggests a bichromy for the entablature. Two travertine insets appear in each of the outer corners of each pier. The fine brickwork of the face is interlocked with coarser brickwork used for the rest of the masonry, which like the inner walls of the theater showed a more variegated coloring. There were travertine sills between the piers. A row of six shops, broken by a passage to a warehouse in the rear and an outside staircase to apartments above, opens off from the porticus. There is nothing remarkable about the shops. They are rather large, and have the usual travertine sills and walls faced with light bricks ca. 3 cm. thick. There are red bonding courses or rather bonding courses reddened by coloring matter.[180]

The Portico degli Archi Trionfali stopped abruptly at a Republican monument, but west of it the Portico del Monumento Repubblicano (V, 11, 4) faced the Decumanus on a slightly different line though probably of the same building period. It fronted four shops, an entrance to the Hadrianic Magazzino Annonario and an awkward *L*-shaped space beyond it which partially encompassed the monument. A door from the corridor gave access to this space; and beyond it steps led to upper stories. The four shops each had a rear door to a rather large hall for transacting business, which could also be approached directly from the corridor. The south wall shows two building periods probably not very far apart. A splayed window toward the west end and an ordinary window at the east, having a carefully laid lintel arch of tiles, belong to the older part. Two large windows with wooden sills

[175] Becatti, *Sc. di O.* I, p. 153; Gismondi, *ibid.*, p. 206; Meiggs, *Ostia*, p. 549.

[176] Based on Becatti, *Sc. di O.* I, p. 143, supplemented by personal observation so far as possible.

[177] Gismondi, *Sc. di O.* I, p. 204.

[178] Later when three of the openings were included between the piers for arches over the Decumanus, the others were given individual flights of steps.

[179] What follows is from personal observation.

[180] Meiggs, *Ostia*, p. 549.

181 Becatti (*Sc. di O.* I, p. 148) suggests that it may have been the guild temple of the Augustales. See also Meiggs, *Ostia*, p. 328.

182 A curved niche was later inserted in the space below the northernmost.

183 This could be later in date.

184 The piers at the angles are later (bricks 2.4–4 cm. thick, mortar 2–3 cm.).

185 There are also traces of red coloring on the outside of the east side.

186 Meiggs, *Ostia*, p. 549.

187 D. E. Strong, *PBSR*, vol. 21, 1953, p. 140.

188 One would like to know why a narrow-fronted house was allowed to remain between it and the rest.

189 Becatti, *Sc. di O.* I, p. 148.

190 Gamala (?). See Meiggs, *Ostia*, pp. 499–500.

and architraves under cruder lintel arches pierced the later wall faced with miscellaneous bricks. There was a bonding course under the lintel. False bonding unites the two parts. A good relieving arch of red tiles appears in the west wall and a smaller one of yellow tiles in the east wall. The doors of the shops were covered with rather poor lintel arches of tiles under relieving arches of *sesquipedales*. Walls were of rather wide yellow bricks.

A collegiate temple[181] was erected at a level comparable to that of the Portico degli Archi Trionfali (V, 11, 1). The space for it was apparently obtained at the sacrifice of the northern part of the Caseggiato del Temistocle. Five or six steps gave access to a raised sidewalk which was continued far enough around the west side to serve a small dwelling—three or four shops and an outside staircase to upper apartments—which could also be entered from the temple precinct and was part of the same building period. The precinct wall was decorated on the inside by four high rectangular niches[182] on the west side and by three rectangular and one curved one on the east. Three travertine corbels in the last named indicate the presence of a shrine of some sort. The facing exhibits bricks of a fairly wide range in width (though most are 3 cm.) and length, but there is a certain homogeneity in the way in which they are laid. The joints are consistently about 2 cm. wide. There was one bonding course at the level of the niches and two enormous relieving arches of *bipedales*, 3 cm. wide in the southwest angle. Two piers *in antis* of the same type of masonry supported three arches to make an inner court for the altar which was faced with tufa blocks beneath a marble revetment.[183] The temple itself was approached by a high flight of steps.[184] The high podium is faced with the same type of brickwork as the precinct wall and capped with a tile molding. Since it housed two chambers, its walls were pierced with splayed windows three on each side and a door with a marble threshold on the west. The rear room had a large apse jutting out into the area behind. A bonding course in it shows traces of mostly red *bipedales*.[185] A depressed arch of *bipedales* led to an inner chamber. Each room was covered by intersecting barrel vaults of unequal length, but with the east-west axis prominent in one and the north-south axis in the other. *Bipedales* were first laid on the centering and then *besales*, some of which are marked with a small circle having a dot in the center, another indication of a late second-century date. The rather large tufa *caementa* were set without order in a mortar like that used for the joints of the brickwork. Meiggs[186] would ascribe the temple to the time of Marcus Aurelius and receives support from a piece of entablature possibly coming from it which is so dated by Strong.[187] It seems to me to belong to the same systematization of this section of the Decumanus as the buildings to the east of it.[188]

By the time of Commodus, the Macellum (IV, 5, 2)[189] was in need of renovation to bring it more into harmony with the other public buildings. Whoever was responsible[190] left the travertine colonnade along Via del Pomerio, but established a new colonnaded podium of gray marble columns opposite it. There were steps between the high travertine bases of the columns and two narrow openings topped by lintel arches of tile to the space beneath the podium. He paved the central area with marble, enclosing it partially with a gutter[191] on three sides, and built a pool in the center of it. Not content with changes limited to the central area, he added a long entrance corridor from the Decumanus and marked it by two lofty columns of gray granite,[192] had arcades built along both the Decumanus and Via del Pomerio (pl. 31, fig. 3), and filled the space between the arcades and the Macellum proper with shops[193] facing the streets or the market according to the dictates of convenience. Two flights of steps provided for upper apartments. Only the lower part of piers along the Decumanus remain. They show a half-hearted use of yellow bricks. Those along Via del Pomerio have been largely restored, but the original facing was predominately of thin red bricks (2.5–3 cm.) laid with narrow joints. They terminated in an impost of six tile courses, one of them dentilated; the arches of thin red *bipedales* were outlined by a single tile cornice. This is reminiscent of some of the fine Hadrianic façades. Small circular stamps having a dot in the center appear on the *besales* clinging to the soffit of the arches. They are an indication of a date late in the century. There were travertine sills between the piers. The arcades had a spectacular position where four streets converged into a trapezoidal *piazza*.[194]

Further west on the Decumanus on each side of the entrance to a space behind, a single room and an outside staircase at the east formed the ground floor for apartments of not more than three rooms above (III, 2, 1). The façade was faced with yellow bricks having pilasters of fine red brickwork. Behind this small apartment house was an arcaded court with a small temple at its head.[195] The side walls[196] and piers were faced with a miscellaneous lot of dark red bricks made from thin tiles, such as were commonly employed in buildings of the late second century. The temple (III, 2, 2)[197] rose on a high podium from a low level behind, but was approached by steps from the porticus at a much higher level in front. The walls of the podium were faced with the same kind of thin red bricks. There were no bonding courses. A door with a travertine sill and lintel led to a barrel-vaulted room under the steps which was lighted by a splayed window in the opposite wall. No means of access to the space under the cella is discernible. Block-and-brick work in the upper part of the walls inside and at the side of the steps probably come from a repair after some disaster in the late third or early fourth century.[198] Late cross walls of block-and-brick work partially block the entrance to the quadrangular area at the lower level in the rear, which is full of traces of earlier construction. This complex is the only work in Regio III ascribed to the period in the official report.[199] Earlier buildings were destroyed to make room for it.

On the north side of the *piazza* where Via della Foce, the Decumanus, and Via Epagathiana come together, a rather pretentious apartment house (I, 14, 2)[200] of strange form has the earmarks of the time of Commodus. Porticoes fronted the streets at the east and the west. The piers were set on "*bipedales*,"[201] and irregular pieces of travertine were inserted, two to a pier, at least in those at the west. Shops faced the porticoes, and a long narrow corridor between the two shops on the east made a connection with the shops on the west. Two flights of steps—one from the west portico, the other from the corridor—led to apartments above. Neither the quality nor

[191] There are abundant remains of another gutter nearer the periphery. It may be earlier.

[192] The official publication has a photograph of the raising of the great granite columns (*Sc. di O.* I, pl. 10, fig. 2).

[193] The shop walls were faced with the usual mixed lot of bricks displaying varied widths even within the row, some short lengths, and some badly weathered. There were bonding courses.

[194] Later the Taberne dei Pescevendoli (IV, 5, 1) were housed beneath the arcade along the Decumanus.

[195] Becatti, *Sc. di O.* I, p. 149; Meiggs, *Ostia*, pp. 327–328.

[196] Traces of early walls in *opus incertum* appear in the side walls at a low level.

[197] This is the Tempio di Fabri Navales.

[198] A Trajanic inscription found in the steps is an indication of a repair.

[199] *Sc. d O.* I, p. 237.

[200] Becatti, *Sc. di O.* I, p. 148; idem, *Sc. di O.* IV, pp. 25–27.

[201] They are actually half *bipedales*.

[202] The range is 2.5–3.5 cm. as opposed to 3–3.7 cm.

[203] Becatti, Sc. di O. I, p. 148.

[204] Paschetto, Ostia, pp. 411–412; Becatti, Sc. di O. I, p. 147; Meiggs, Ostia, p. 47. For the original period, see above, pp. 216–217; for the mithraeum, p. 228.

[205] Details of brick construction are from personal observation.

[206] Paschetto calls them storerooms rather than shops.

[207] J. Carcopino (Mél., vol. 31, 1911, pp. 219–220 n. 3) and Meiggs, (Ostia, pp. 47 and 76) tend to accept the traditional identification.

[208] Sc. di O. I, p. 237.

[209] Ibid., fig. 34.

the thickness of the bricks had been standardized at this time. The builder chose, for the most part, rather good yellow bricks for the two façades, though those used in the piers at the west were slightly narrower than those at the east.[202] Yellow bricks also predominate in the corridor, of the same range as those employed in the west façade but of inferior quality. The rest of the walls display the mixed lot characteristic of the period with varied widths, some short lengths, and an occasional brick that has weathered badly. Red bonding courses are present. Relieving arches carried the masonry over some weakness in the foundation. The travertine steps were upheld in part by rampant lintels of *sesquipedales* and were lighted by windows at the landings. Openings were covered with slightly curved lintel arches of *bipedales* with masonry underneath resting on wooden beams or boards. The large shops facing Via Epagathiana have angle piers for supporting cross vaulting now gone, and traces of three cross vaults covering one room are still extant. The house is called the Caseggiato del Mosaico del Porto from the main mosaic. Openings toward the south were cut off when a great nymphaeum was constructed on the north side of the *piazza* at a later period. Becatti[203] would also ascribe to the Commodan systematization of this section of the city some brick piers at the entrance to the Sacred Area of the Templi Repubblicani.

The "Palazzo Imperiale" was enlarged[204] by the addition of a south peristyle, and the rooms connected with it were faced in part with the thin red brickwork[205] which came to be used for the first time during the reign of Commodus. Columns of breccia corallina marked the entrance from the south; and pilasters show that there was an ornamental doorway as well. The fact that the new entrance was flanked by shops[206] would seem to me to indicate that it was not in reality an imperial villa, even though Ostia may have had one. The pilasters at the doorway and a few other walls exhibit an excellent facing of the thin red bricks (2.5 cm.) with fine joints between them. The same variety of brick was used for a reorganization of the rooms south of the mithraeum. The piers of the court and a few other walls had a similar facing of slightly wider bricks (3 cm.) diversified with yellow bonding courses. The rest of the walls were faced with more common bricks, but they are so bonded with the rest as to show contemporaneity.[207] Another structure ascribed to the same period seems to have been added to the same complex at the northwest corner; and another farther up the Tiber, though perhaps contemporaneous, probably had nothing to do with it. All conclusions must be tentative until this area has been fully excavated.

A shrine was inserted in the antechamber and three rooms on each side of a narrow corridor in a large hall of an earlier edifice on Via di Iside (IV, 5, 4) (pl. 29, fig. 3). The shrine shows a heavy unpleasing type of architecture with its decorative moldings emphasized by red coloring matter. The floors of the rooms have coarse black-and-white mosaics of geometric designs; and the walls in so far as they are preserved display a slipshod brickwork. It has been named officially the Insula del Sacello and listed among the edifices of the time of Commodus,[208] but there is no specific evidence on which to base the ascription. Gismondi favors a Severan date.[209]

In conclusion, although the mass of bricks which were being made in the time of Commodus show considerable variety in color, texture, and thickness, some kilns were putting out a thin red tile (2.4–3.2 cm.), which, wherever it is used, becomes an earmark of this or the succeeding period.[210] Some of the bricks made from these tiles bear stamps. Yellow bricks were usually chosen for the better masonry elsewhere. Red bonding courses, which were more apparent than real, were sometimes used in this predominately yellow masonry and, if the tiles were not red, they were often colored so for decorative effect. Secondary walls display a miscellaneous assortment of bricks. Even here a tendency toward the employment of slightly thinner bricks than in the preceding period is discernible. In one case at least, the fine red brickwork of the front of the piers is interlocked with the ordinary masonry of the back.

[210] See also Gismondi's résumé in *Sc. di O.* I, pp. 205–206.

IV. ITALY AWAY FROM ROME

IMPERIAL ESTATES

Civitavecchia

Trajan would also have fallen heir to all the great imperial estates throughout Italy. From Pliny the Younger[1] we learn that he had a sumptuous villa erected for himself at Centumcellae, from which he could watch the construction of the port as well as enjoy all the pleasures of a dwelling by the sea. Its site is known, but nothing remains visible above ground.[2] From it

[1] Pliny, *Epist.*, 6, 31.

[2] Bastianelli, *Centumcellae*, pp. 15–18, 60–61. For the port, see below, pp. 290–292.

probably came an *intarsio* of white marble, alabaster, broccatelli, lapis lazuli, and enamel used in wall decoration, which may be seen in the Museo Nazionale Romano.[3] Since Hadrian enlarged the villa and other emperors dwelt in it, the *intarsio* is not necessarily Trajanic.

Arcinazzo

Water pipes prove that Trajan either built a villa at Arcinazzo or modified an earlier one to suit the luxury of his time.[4] Excavations have been made on the left hand side of the road from Subiaco to Fiuggi at a site which may qualify as the imperial villa.[5] To be sure, the heavily buttressed sustaining wall of the terrace shows a masonry of a more primitive type than one would expect of the time of Trajan, but the fragments of cornices, columns, mosaics, and the like, lying about on the terrace are in keeping with an ascription to Trajan. Either the terrace was prepared for an earlier villa, or more likely the builders in this remote locality employed the methods to which they were accustomed. A crude reticulate of the intractable limestone of the region forms the major part of the facing. It is cut by rather wide bands of brickwork and protected by quoins of both blocks and bricks in alternate layers interlocked with the reticulate in the usual fashion (pl. 31, fig. 1). Tile bonding courses appear in the brickwork. The bricks seem to have been made from broken tiles.

Frascati

A somewhat similar situation occurs at Cappelletti[6] near Frascati, where water pipes show that Matidia, either the sister or niece of Trajan, possessed a villa. A substructure in the vicinity exhibits five great niches faced with reticulate broken by brick bands between pilasters of tufa blocks supporting brick arches. Such construction could be earlier than the time of Trajan.

Tivoli. Villa Adriana

After Hadrian became emperor, he was in Rome for not more than three years (A.D. 118–121) before he started on his first long voyage, which did not bring him back until the middle of A.D. 125. There is no way of telling how much time he spent in the Republican villa in the valley below Tivoli, which he had probably inherited.[7] In any case, he went often enough or stayed long enough to become enamored of the site and to plan how he might transform the villa into a residence suitable for an emperor and his court. Some of the work was probably started under his personal supervision, but most was doubtless left for contractors to build according to his specifications. Since a suitable tufa could be quarried in the vicinity, it was natural for them to use it for a reticulate facing[8] of the walls and sometimes for blocks as well. As there is no indication of a local brick industry, such bricks and tiles as were used had to be imported from Rome. Consequently, they seldom appear except in reinforcing bands at more or less regular intervals in the reticulate and as quoins along with tufa blocks. Brickwork was employed, however, when some special reason made it seem desirable. Tiles were the customary method of facing arches over openings and niches. The brick stamps[9] which have permitted students to follow the progress of the

[3] R. Mengarelli, *Not. sc.*, 1919, pp. 230–231.

[4] G. Gatti, *Bull. Com.*, 1887, p. 12; *Not. sc.*, 1892, pp. 117–118 (D. Marchetti).

[5] R. Bartoccini, *Fasti arch.*, vol. 10, 1955, no. 4293, supplemented by personal observation.

[6] T. Ashby, *PBSR*, vol. 1, 1900, p. 224; Grossi-Gondi, *Tuscolano*, pp. 188–189; Lugli, *Tecnica*, p. 524.

[7] For the earlier phase, see G. Lugli, *Bull. Com.*, vol. 55, 1927, pp. 139–183; Blake, *RC I*, p. 241. For the layout of the Villa, see Plan XVII at the back of this book.

[8] Hadrianic reticulate can be readily differentiated from that of the earlier periods by its regularity.

[9] Bloch, *Bolli*, pp. 117–183.

work come, for the most part, from pavement tiles and *bipedales* used to face arches. The masonry remained the same throughout the three phases which can be distinguished with the help of the stamps. If walls were the only consideration, this summary would perhaps be sufficient; but Hadrian and his contractors expended all their ingenuity on experiments in vaulting. To understand the vaulting, one must study the whole edifice; and to give a unified picture, one must trace briefly the development of the entire villa.[10] Hadrian's transformation naturally started with the original villa and was extended to include replicas or adaptations of edifices that interested him in his travels. Even now, visitors to the site of this great complex are impressed by its vastness. Yet they sometimes fail to realize that it extended far beyond the area which has been excavated.

The main entrance continued to be from the north. Hadrian left the "atrium" much as it was, but he converted the "tablinum" into a library with a semicircular niche for a statue and rectangular niches for the book-cases which he provided with concrete steps to give access to the higher shelves. Brickwork was used for most of this transformation. To the left of it, a "basilica" was built anew, and in the northeastern corner, a Bath was inserted in an earlier quadriporticus to serve until more adequate bathing facilities could be installed. This is completely overgrown at present. The nine small Republican rooms along the east side of the central court were left much as they were, probably to serve as sleeping quarters for the imperial party in the early days of Hadrian's occupancy. Of this group of rooms, to which the name North Palace is usually given, only the "basilica" yielded a series of brick stamps indicating that, though started early, it could not have been completed much before Hadrian's return from his first voyage, if indeed then[11] (pl. 32, fig. 2). In Republican times, the long central court was terminated by a semicircular exedra. To the west of this group of rooms, there was evidently originally a park with a series of apsed aediculae at the south end. A "winter triclinium" and a large hall of indeterminate purpose were laid out at the north end by Hadrian's contractors. Only the lower part of the walls remains. The semicircular nymphaeum[12] may have been added as a summer triclinium at the same time (pl. 33, fig. 1). At any rate, it was built before the south end of the area was systematized for the "Central Palace." A large curvilinear niche in the curved wall of the nymphaeum jutted out behind the curved back wall. There were three smaller niches, a curvilinear between rectangular ones, on each side. The semi-cupola shows the imprint of the *besales* which rested on the *bipedales* covering the wooden centering. It was the earliest of the semicircular nymphaea.

A Republican exedra which stood at the south end of the Central Court was enclosed in walls and converted into a nymphaeum[13] by inserting pipes in the concrete mass which would allow water to cascade into a pool at the bottom of the slope,[14] only to reappear again in two fountains with circular pools within an open space enclosed on the other three sides by a colonnade. The nymphaeum became part of the entrance to what has come to be called the Central Palace, where Hadrian was free to plan without regard to pre-existing structures. The transition was effected by a shallow hall with a deep apse, which presented to the Central Court merely a straight wall with

[10] A complete bibliography would be enormous. H. Winnefeld, *Die Villa des Hadrian bei Tivoli (Ergänzungsheft III, Jb. d. Inst.)*, Berlin 1895, is still fundamental. P. Gusman, *La villa impériale de Tibur*, Paris 1904, is still useful. Anderson-Spiers-Ashby (pp. 139–144), though out of date (1927), gives a clear overall picture. S. Aurigemma, *Villa Adriana*, Rome 1961, should also be considered; the photographs are informative. Aurigemma's *Lavori nel Canopo di Villa Adriana* (estratti dal *Bollettino d'Arte*, no. IV, Oct.-Dec. 1954, no. I, Jan.-Mar. 1955, and no. I, Jan.-Mar. 1956, bound as a book, Rome n. d.) is important for the recent excavations of that section. E. Hansen's study *La "Piazza d'Oro" e la sua Cupola (Analecta Romana Instituti Danici I, Supplementum*, Copenhagen 1960) is detailed and thorough. Kähler's work (*Villa*) is an exhaustive treatise covering most of the villa. The guide books by Paribeni, Mancini, Aurigemma, and Vighi, though brief, are scholarly. See also Crema, pp. 466–483; Frova, pp. 84–88, 408–410.

[11] There are seven pre-Hadrianic stamps, eight of A.D. 123, one of 125, and one later. See Bloch, *Bolli*, pp. 124–125.

[12] Neuerburg, *Fontane*, p. 236, no. 195; Aurigemma, *Villa Adriana*, pp. 164–166.

[13] Winnefeld, pp. 83–87; Paribeni, *La Villa*, pl. 35; G. Lugli, *Bull. Com.*, vol. 55, 1927, p. 198; Neuerburg, *Fontane*, p. 237, no. 197; Crema, p. 122.

[14] Aurigemma (*La Villa*, p. 52) believes that the concrete supported seats for an audience.

a door in the center[15] and a narrow passageway on each side.[16] The doorway was covered by a lintel arch of tile under a relieving arch of the same. No trace of the actual vaulting remains. The walls were of the usual reticulate work with brick bands which yielded no stamps; but stamps from the southern part[17] indicate that, though this may have been planned when Hadrian was in residence, it was probably not carried out until after he had started on his second voyage. The whole was lavishly adorned with marble. The corridor at the west led to a great oblong hall, known as the "Sala dei Pilastri Dorici" (pl. 34, fig. 2).[18] The outer walls were of the usual reticulate work with brick bands. The channeled Doric pillars, of which there are ample remains, must have upheld a second order of either pillars or columns to support a clerestory with a flat roof over the central hall.[19] They also supported the barrel vault over the quadriporticus. The corresponding tile impost is still clearly visible. The entablature furnishes a minor example of structural finesse which is not without interest. Great travertine double springers were prepared to rest on the pillars and extend over the ends of the thin slabs spanning the openings to hold them securely in place. Above these slabs, the oblique sides of the springers took the weight of the lintel arches off from them. The central part of the oblique side projected to provide for a more substantial lintel in the middle. In other words, there were three independent lintel arches between springers. At the southwest end of this area, a square hall flanked by two rather narrow barrel-vaulted corridors served as the antechamber to a hall with a shallow-curved wall forming the termination of a central court with a porticus around the other three sides, the "Sala del Trono."[20] The curved wall was niched. Though apparently the focal point for the "Sala dei Pilastri Dorici," it presents no structural innovations, except perhaps in the half dome,[21] which is faced to the top of the highest niche with reticulate work, but above that in the normal fashion with *besales* on top of *bipedales* as a more or less permanent centering for a concrete with an aggregate in regular rows. Both areas were richly decorated and contemporaneous. No brick stamps were found, so far as I know, to confirm the date, but the north wall abutted the protruding wall of the central niche of the nymphaeum (so-called Triclinio Estivo in the southeast corner of the Palace garden) in such a way as to show that it was later; and its west corner shut off the light from one of the windows of the "caserma," which was in fact the reason for the shallowness of the apse. It can therefore, like the nymphaeum at the other end, be ascribed with confidence to the second building period.

A Republican nymphaeum opposite the main entrance of the palace seems to indicate that the "Cortile delle Biblioteche"[22] was laid out before Hadrian enclosed it in a quadriporticus. The ground slopes down from its northeast side toward the Vale of Tempe so that the "Ospitale," or guest house, was erected at a lower level, though with the same orientation. This building with its five chambers on each side of a wide passage, each with alcoves for three beds, its "tablinum," commodious latrine, and necessary corridors, presents no peculiarities in wall construction.[23] Splayed windows high up in the back wall supplied additional air to the bedchambers. Winnefeld conjectures that there was an upper story, possibly because he envisaged it

[15] Mancini (*Adriana*, p. 12) mentions two corbels on the outside to support a loggia.

[16] Stairs, the remains of which are still visible at the north end of the west passage, indicate that there was a second story or terrace. What was true of the west passage was probably true of the east as well.

[17] The stamps are of A.D. 123 with one of 124. See Bloch, *Bolli*, pp. 125–127.

[18] Winnefeld, pp. 79–83; Paribeni, *op. cit.*, pl. 34; Aurigemma, *La Villa*, pp. 51–52; idem, *Villa Adriana*, pp. 167–169; Crema, p. 467.

[19] The nature of the marble pavement and the lack of stylobate and gutter are ample proof that the central part was covered.

[20] G. Lugli, *Bull. Com.*, vol. 60, 1932, pp. 130–132. Actually the purpose of the room is unknown.

[21] See E. Sjöqvist, *Skrifter*, vol. 12, 1946, p. 88 with figure 26, a fine photograph by J. Ward-Perkins.

[22] Winnefeld, pp. 35–38; Neuerburg, *Fontane*, pp. 234–235, no. 192. For the brick stamps found in the course of the excavation, see Bloch, *Bolli*, p. 159.

[23] The south wall belongs to an earlier phase of the villa; cf. Blake, RC I, p. 241.

[24] M. E. Blake, *MAAR*, vol. 13, 1936, pp. 79–81; see also Aurigemma, *Villa Adriana*, pp. 177–185.

[25] Lugli, *Bull. Com.*, vol. 60, 1932, pp. 118–120; Kähler, *Villa*, p. 38; Aurigemma, *Villa Adriana*, pp. 185–188.

[26] Lugli's interpretation of this as a vestibule seems not to have gained wide acceptance.

[27] Winnefeld, pp. 95–105; Kähler, *Villa*, pp. 31–44, 106–117; Aurigemma, *Villa Adriana*, pp. 172–175; Crema, p. 467.

[28] Between the "Greek Library" and the "Cortile," there were a barrel-vaulted room, a cross-vaulted room open to the Cortile, and a broad staircase which must have been at least in the "blueprint stage" when the "library" was planned. They were, however, later than a small room belonging to the same period as the "Latin Library." See Kähler, *op. cit.*, p. 43. These rooms have no connection with the structure behind them.

[29] Boethius (*The Golden House of Nero*, Ann Arbor 1960, p. 118) accepts the identification.

as barracks. But the rooms were embellished with such pleasing black-and-white mosaics[24] and graceful wall paintings that they would be suitable for members of the emperor's suite.

The presence of the guest house would seem to call for a dining room more or less connected with it; and lower down at the northeast a hall[25] was erected eminently suited for the purpose,[26] the open front of which looked out between two Corinthian columns *in antis* onto a park with a view of the mountains beyond. In its earliest phase, it was merely a large hall flanked by a barrel-vaulted corridor on each side and further isolated by a corridor at the back. These corridors would have facilitated service, and the three rooms opening off from them could have been used for the afternoon rest. This much was completed, in all probability, while Hadrian was in residence. At his return from his first voyage he apparently ordered the complex to be embellished by a porticus across the front with an independent approach through a broad corridor on the west. Although a careful study of the masonry reveals the two phases, there is no appreciable difference in the method of construction, which is of the sort usual in the earliest Hadrianic period. Somewhat later, a terrace was added in front of the porticus, and a wall with alternately curved and rectangular niches was extended obliquely from it to enclose the area in front of the two "libraries." This wall shows a masonry of flat irregular stones which was used in the Antonine period to substitute terraces for sloping ground. A later phase converting the west passage into four rooms and blocking doorways does not concern us here.

When Hadrian commenced to build on untouched land to the northwest of the "Cortile delle Biblioteche," he chose an orientation with the points of the compass in complete disregard of that of the Cortile. The two new edifices,[27] which have come to be called erroneously the Latin and Greek libraries, although contiguous or nearly contiguous[28] to the Cortile, face an open space to the north which could be reached by a narrow passage on each side of the Republican nymphaeum. Of the two, the one at the east ("Biblioteca Latina") was built first and manifestly became the model for the more elaborate plan of the larger one at the west ("Biblioteca Greca"). The main part of the earlier building consisted of two halls. A curved vestibule featuring two columns *in antis* led into a nearly square cross-vaulted room with a rectangular alcove on each of the other three sides. Nearly square passages flanking the south alcove gave access to a smaller barrel-vaulted room with an apse at the end, but with no alcoves. From another point of view, the two halls, the east and west alcoves excluded, could be regarded as a single long room with an apse at the end, the barrel vault of which was converted into a cross vault in the northern section. This arrangement, on the analogy of examples elsewhere, convinced Kähler[29] that the northern hall was a summer dining room. It was flooded with light from the open vestibule, whereas the rear hall received only indirect light from a large window in the back wall of the south alcove of the northern hall and a subdued light from a window over the apse. After the death of Antinous a relief of him as Bacchus was installed in the apse. A short porticus on the west was balanced on the east by three rooms—one rectangular, two with curved ends—deftly fitted into the triangular space between the main part of the edifice and the Cortile. A small triangular space with steps afforded a direct entrance from the latter. These rooms were lower than the rest but were brought up to the same level by a sort of vaulted mezzanine. There are traces of an upper story at least over the south hall, but no indication of the position of the stairs by which it could be reached. All construction farther to the south at the same level is later, though some of it no doubt still Hadrianic. Although the western edifice ("Biblioteca Greca") was certainly erected later, the time lag between the two was not long enough to exhibit any change in method of construction. A brick facing was employed almost exclusively for the lower part of the walls, but the bricks produced no stamps.[30] The rest of the walling was the usual combination of reticulate work with brick bands and either block or brick quoins. The north hall was provided with four rather than three alcoves, and staircases, one on each side of the north alcove, took the place of the open vestibule. But this alcove had a large window looking to the garden; and when the door on each side was open the whole hall must have been filled with light. This north hall was no doubt also a summer dining room and was certainly an entity in itself.[31] Stout corner piers were placed under the travertine corbels supporting the great cross vault, but further precautions were soon found to be necessary to insure its stability. To this end, the two northern corners were reinforced on the outside by substantial brick-faced piers and in correspondence to them stout walls running north and south, also brick-faced, were erected to meet a slight projection of the north wall of the east alcove. Since there are traces of a window in these north walls, probably arches rather than a barrel vault served to divert some of the weight to the stout outer walls. Three spur walls were built against the west foundation wall for further reinforcement. These were converted into two barrel-vaulted rooms which had no connection with the edifice under discussion. Artificial light seems to have been assured by candelabra on marble standards on each side of each alcove. The south hall (pl. 35, fig. 2) was smaller and lower. Unlike the edifice at the east, it was also supplied with three alcoves of its own, smaller than those in the north hall and each provided with a niche in its north and south walls. A smaller cross vault covered the central part. In contrast to the hall at the north, this chamber had only indirect light through the great window in the south alcove of the room in front and subdued light from a small window under the ceiling at the south end. Right-angled corridors on each side of the southern alcove of the north hall led on the west to a passageway and on the east to a single cross-vaulted chamber with curved ends. An irregular light well stood between this and a room belonging to an earlier phase of the site. During this second building period a colonnaded walk with an obtuse angle in accommodation to the structures to the south of it was connected with the short west porticus of the East Edifice to facilitate communication between the two. There are clear traces of a hall of much the same form above the south hall. Its floor was lower than the pavement of the room to the north of it. A small triangular space caused by the divergent orientation contained a small staircase. Both edifices were lavishly adorned with sectile floors and socles of polychrome marble, frescoes, and mosaic ceilings.

[30] Bloch, *Bolli*, p. 159.

[31] Kähler (*op. cit.*, p. 117, fig. 23), shows how the two rooms could actually be fitted into the same oblong with only the north, east, and west alcoves of the north hall protruding.

32 R. Paribeni, *Not. sc.*, 1922, pp. 239–246; Kähler, *Villa*, p. 22; Aurigemma, *Villa Adriana*, pp. 77–79; Crema, p. 406; Frova, p. 86.

33 Bloch, *Bolli*, pp. 130–131, 160.

34 Pliny the Younger had one in his Laurentine villa. See *Epist.* 2, 17, 20.

35 It is my conviction that these windows were not glazed.

36 I fail to see the point of a half-cupola here. The plastic model indeed does have a dome.

37 G. de Angelis d'Ossat, *III conv. st. archit.*, p. 246; *idem, Palladio*, vol. 5, 1941, p. 250 n. 13.

38 Winnefeld, pp. 59–61; Kähler, *Villa*, pp. 44–54, 117–122; Aurigemma, *Villa Adriana*, pp. 68–74; Crema, p. 481, fig. 604; Frova, p. 86, figs. 70c, 71. Brick stamps (Bloch, *Bolli*, pp. 121–122) confirm the date.

A site was prepared with a north-south orientation and steps leading up to it from the area later occupied by the "Teatro Marittimo."[32] It is quite possible that the *frigidarium* and the rooms immediately connected with it of the bathing establishment northeast of the "stadium-garden" were built at this time. Brick stamps were found only in the rooms in the southwest corner.[33] All of them were or could be of the year of the reorganization of the brick industry in A.D. 123. The most interesting part of these Baths, therefore, was probably in the process of construction at the same time as the Small Baths. The earlier part, if indeed it was earlier, needs no special comment. A vast open court with a large rectangular pool enclosed in a colonnade of granite columns supplied the outdoor swimming pool (*natatio*); a cross-vaulted hall with a small semicircular pool opening off from the fourth side was the *frigidarium*; and two rooms to the south were respectively a dressing room (*apodyterium*) and sweating room (*sudatio*). The former has not been completely excavated. The latter is conventional: semicircular niches in the four corners, a hypocaust, air vents flanking the niches, and an ovoidal cupola pierced by a window facing the north. It is intimately connected with the later rooms and must have received its final form when they were built. Opening out of it at the west was a circular room devoted to sun bathing, the earliest example of a *heliocaminus*[34] which has been preserved to us (pl. 32, fig. 3). No water was brought to its circular "pool," which Paribeni conjectures was filled with sand. Three furnaces behind a masking wall introduced heat into its hypocaust while five large windows with a southwest exposure were bringing in a maximum amount of warm sunshine.[35] A coffered half-cupola[36] still covers the hall. Amphorae were introduced into the mass of concrete to lighten the weight.[37] From this chamber the bather had the choice of passing into the hotter *sudatio* or into an apsed barrel-vaulted room, which was heated, though perhaps to a lesser degree, by hypocaust and sunshine through large windows in the south and west sides. A chamber to the east, jutting out yet farther to the south, had no hypocaust but would have been somewhat warmed by the rays of the sun. The room behind probably served as a dressing room. The many doors allowed each to take the Baths in his own way. As in all the Baths, bricks were used to face the lower part of the walls and some of the niches, at any rate. There were niches for statues; and some statuary was found, but in general these Baths were not decorated as lavishly as the other two.

Next in point of time, though part of the same early transformation of the villa, was the retreat,[38] which the emperor had prepared for his personal use. It was southwest of the "libraries" and at a lower level. The main approach was through a pillared vestibule at its north. The circular form of this miniature villa, which has come to be called quite inappropriately the "Teatro Marittimo," was admirably adapted to the space which it occupied between two levels. It was enclosed first by a heavy wall faced inside and out by the usual masonry, next by a porticus of Ionic columns, and finally by a moat. A single alcove in the outer wall afforded a vista through the whole complex to the park at the north. Double springers of travertine once supported lintel arches of tile behind the marble entablature of the porticus, which was covered with a half barrel vault. Approach to the central "island" was by means of a wooden bridge[39] which could be drawn aside by ropes when the emperor desired complete privacy. Inside, Hadrian allowed his penchant for curved lines to have full sway. A semicircular colonnade with a curved base and a curved passage on each side served as a vestibule to a colonnaded "atrium" with concave sides. Curved façades with two columns *in antis* masked the straight lines of the rooms on the other three sides, most of which had curved end walls. Opposite the vestibule, three rooms took the place of the tablinum between *alae* of the ordinary Roman house. A rectangular alcove in the central room probably contained the emperor's couch for dining or sleeping. Three little rooms at the west formed a small private Bath with both warm and cold pools. Three rooms on the east could have been devoted to reading and study with scrolls available in two small libraries. Brickwork faced what little masonry was used on the "island," but little of the original work is left. It was concealed by a marble revetment. The whole superstructure was so light that the vaulting would not have taxed the ingenuity of the ancient builder. Mere traces of it remain today.

Two openings on the west side of the circular enclosing wall of the "Teatro Marittimo" led down to a library of conventional shape, known as the "Sala dei Filosofi."[40] Seven niches in the apsed south wall provided the spaces for the bookcases, whereas a large opening with two columns *in antis* in the north wall supplied light and air. Its comparatively good state of preservation makes it an excellent place to accustom the eye to the Hadrianic masonry of reticulate work with brick bands and block and brick quoins. Doorways and niches were covered with slightly curved lintels and relieving arches of *bipedales*. The hall was probably covered by a timbered ceiling. A curved face was superimposed on its west side when the great north wall of the "Poikile" was erected.[41] This extraordinary wall, though belonging to the same general building period must, therefore, have been erected slightly later.[42] The masonry is identical. Foundations for columns and beam holes high up in the wall prove that it separated two promenades, one with a northern, the other with a southern exposure. For a time it stood alone. Later the land to the south of it was systematized, and it became the north wall of a great quadriporticus with slightly curved ends and a vast central pool. Because the hill was precipitous, four stories were needed on the west and three for part of the south side.[43] Fundamentally, these consisted of apsed chambers identical in size; actually, the construction was strengthened by a wall cutting off the apses and leaving rectangular chambers (4.7 m. × 6.1 m.), to which the name "Cento Camerelle" has been given. The only communication between the chambers was through outside balconies probably of wood,[44] and the only communication between floors was by three staircases strategically placed near the ends. There was no communication with the quadriporticus above. Latrines at the corners prove that the chambers were used for habitation, perhaps by soldiers, but more likely by the army of slaves which would be necessary in an establishment of this kind. Since it was a substructure, it displays more blocks than bricks in connection with its reticulate.[45] Consequently, few stamps were found, but the majority of them were of A.D. 123 or a little later.[46] Later still, the same type of substruction was built out obliquely from the center of the south wall to

[39] The grooves by which the temporary bridge was maneuvered are clearly visible in the floor of the moat when it is not filled with water. The present bridge was a late addition.

[40] Winnefeld, pp. 58–59; Aurigemma, *La Villa*, pp. 16–17; idem, *Villa Adriana*, pp. 64–67; Kähler, *Villa*, p. 44; Crema, fig. 388. Vighi (*Villa*, p. 84) doubts the ascription.

[41] A friend who is a contractor and builder on seeing this wall remarked that it could not stand without buttressing; but nevertheless it has stood for roughly two thousand years as a tribute to the strength of ancient concrete.

[42] One early stamp has been reported (Bloch, *Bolli*, p. 121).

[43] Winnefeld, pp. 57–58; Kähler, op. cit., pp. 22–23; Aurigemma, *Villa Adriana*, pp. 58–59, 64.

[44] Winnefeld believes that two of the balconies were of concrete.

[45] Personal observation.

[46] Bloch, *loc. cit.*

[47] Aurigemma (*La Villa*, pl. 5; *Villa Adriana*, fig. 26) reproduces a drawing of Piranesi showing a whole complex of rooms at the lower level to the northwest of the Poikile garden which are not now visible. These rooms appear also in a drawing of Rossini (Aurigemma, *Villa Adriana*, fig. 13).

[48] Winnefeld, pp. 57–58; Aurigemma, *Villa Adriana*, p. 166. Winnefeld (Taf. 7) gives the clearest plan. It is orientated with the points of the compass like most of the independent buildings of the first phase. For the chronology, see Lugli, *Bull. Com.*, vol. 60, 1932, p. 130. The walls have produced no stamps (Bloch, *Bolli*, p. 170). One stamp of A.D. 123 occurred on a *bipedalis* over a window which could have been inserted later (*ibid.*, p. 127).

[49] The rooms have not been excavated down to the pavement level. If the rooms were intended for grain, they should have been suspended.

[50] R. Paribeni, *Not. sc.*, 1922, pp. 235–238; J. Chillman, *MAAR*, vol. 4, 1924, pp. 103–120, pls. 50–56, Kähler, *Villa*, pp. 23–24, 55–60, 122–128, pls. 8–10; Vighi, *Villa*, pp. 20–24; Aurigemma, *Villa Adriana*, pp. 75–77; Crema, p. 471.

hold back the fill for widening the terrace upon which the Baths were built. A service passage was connected with it.[47]

Southwest of the palace as it existed in its first Hadrianic phase, a completely utilitarian structure[48] was erected, no doubt to store away the abundant provisions that would be needed for so vast an estate. The name "Caserma dei Vigili" is surely a misnomer. Three lofty cross-vaulted rooms opened off from each side of a broad central court, open to the sky and paved with herringbone brick. Travertine corbels supported an upper floor; and each outside wall was pierced with two splayed windows at each level. The splayed windows had travertine sills and lintels. The rooms were not intercommunicating. Travertine corbels on the front supported a concrete balcony with arch facings of tile to give independent access to each upper room. Since there is no indication of stairways, wooden steps or ladders must have been used to approach the balconies. Thus far the arrangement is obvious, but for some reason the southern end was cut off entirely from the rest and given its own doorway at the east end. It was divided into three bays, each with its own cross vault; and there was an analogous arrangement of splayed windows. The position of partition walls stretching outward is apparent on the outside of the south wall. There is also a small room jutting out from the northwest chamber, the purpose of which is not clear. There is nothing unusual about the masonry of reticulate with bands of brick.[49]

Contemporary with the long double porticus known as the "Poikile" but well to the south of it, a building was erected with the same orientation, which Kähler sees as a state dining room. It has been called the "Casino of the Semicircular Arcades."[50] In its earliest phase, however, a single semicircular arcade formed the termination of a basilica-like hall at the south, whereas at the north a rectangular colonnaded hall with a rectangular pool served as a sort of forecourt. A short passage on each side of it led to a nearly square vestibule, which had its counterpart at the two south corners of the central hall. This much was probably built before Hadrian started off on his first long voyage, but he apparently liked the effect so much that he left orders that semicircular arcades be added at the east and west, also to be furnished with fountains and greenery in the resultant lunettes. The many colonnades must have produced much the same light airy effect as those in the "Teatro Marittimo," the many doors and windows would have contributed to it, and the many fountains would have made it a delightful (summer dining) hall. As in the "Teatro," the outside walls follow the norm for the period, and brickwork was used for the inner walls. These bricks yielded no stamps. The walls were too thin to have supported functional vaulting, though hung vaulting adorned with glass mosaic may have given the same effect. It was doubtless protected by roofing supported by wooden beams. The eastern apse was extended to meet a space where a stadium-like garden was probably already being laid out. This extension consisted of a large hall with a rectangular alcove at the east end having a hall on each side nearly as long but narrower with a smaller room having a curved wall fitted into the space left by the curved wall of the apse at the west and a bastion-like projection on the east. The usual combination of brick bands with a reticulate facing prevails here also. These bricks yielded no stamps, but those of the *bipedales* used in the pavements confirm the chronology suggested above.[51] Pieces of concrete lying on the pavement show the marks of boards on the underside and the usual treatment for pavements on the other, that is, herringbone brick, concrete subpavement, and coarse mosaic. These appear to be parts of the actual roofing and indicate the presence of a terrace from which there would have been a superb view of the garden below. One slab displayed the beginning of a drain pipe. A suspended floor in some of the rooms in both parts is generally interpreted to mean that the rooms were heated, but it may have merely furnished the space for the conduits and drains necessary to the functioning of so many fountains and the watering of the gardens. Chillman has advanced the attractive conjecture that the rooms on the east were intended for the display of paintings and other works of art. A colonnade flanked them on both the north and the south sides. The whole complex was lavishly adorned with columns of pavonazzetto, cipollino, and granito, with sectile pavements of pleasing design showing almost every type of marble known to the Romans, and wall revetments in the lighter shades except in the great hall where affricano was used.

The orientation of the "hippodrome-garden" was more or less dictated by the configuration of the land. Recent excavations have shown that the southern part consisted of a colonnaded court with a rich sectile floor, having a semicircular nymphaeum at its south end.[52] Water seems to have splashed down three miniature staircases on each side into a semicircular pool. The hydraulic engineering apparently followed the same general lines as that later employed in the nymphaeum of the Canopus. More detailed information must await the official report.

The building in the center of the east side[53] would seem to have been intended for the recreation and refreshment of a limited number. A lofty central hall covered with a barrel vault was flanked on each side by two or three barrel-vaulted rooms, which were smaller and lower. A second barrel vault over each brought these rooms up to the same upper level. No use was apparently made of the intervening space. A corridor separated these rooms from the earth of the hillside behind them. At the upper level there was a court (palaestra?) with a row of rooms facing west and a miniature Bath at the southwest corner. There were three small heated rooms, each covered with a cross vault, for the most part open to the sky.[54] One of them retains a considerable part of its ceiling fresco. The brick stamps found in these rooms were all of A.D. 123.[55] Stairs led from the ground floor to an intermediate level. Lugli[56] conjectures that an enclosed space here was originally intended as a park or palaestra. However that may be, it was soon converted into a broad cryptoporticus amply lighted by sloping windows on the inner side of the barrel vaulting. These windows opened out in the intercolumniations of a wide quadriporticus about a great swimming pool. At a later period some makeshift heated rooms were added at the southwest corner of the quadriporticus.[57]

With the vicissitudes of the isolated Augustan structure which was apparently retained as a service villa in the time of Hadrian,[58] we are not concerned except for the fact that it separated the "Piazza d'Oro"[59] from the rest of

[51] Bloch, *Bolli*, pp. 129, 160–161.

[52] Vighi, *Villa*, p. 24; Aurigemma, *Villa Adriana*, pp. 79–81; Neuerburg, *Fontane*, pp. 236–237, no. 96.

[53] Mostly personal observation. See also Kähler, *op. cit.*, p. 24; Aurigemma, *Villa Adriana*, pp. 150–153.

[54] Obviously there must have been some arrangement for closing the opening.

[55] Bloch, *Bolli*, pp. 128–129.

[56] G. Lugli, *Bull. Com.*, vol. 60, 1932, pp. 134–136. This may represent merely a change of plan in the course of construction.

[57] One stamp of A.D. 126 was found there (Bloch, *op. cit.*, p. 129).

[58] G. Lugli, *Bull. Com.*, vol. 60, 1932, p. 133; Crema, p. 122.

[59] Winnefeld, pp. 63–79; Kähler, *Villa*, pp. 64–73, 132–137; Aurigemma, *Villa Adriana*, pp. 154–163; Crema, pp. 467, 471, 478–479, fig. 612; Frova, pp. 86–87; E. Hansen, La *"Piazza d'Oro"* (see n. 10 above); MacDonald, p. 135.

[60] Bloch, *Bolli*, pp. 127, 170.

[61] The plastic model shows a gable roof over the vaulting.

[62] The plastic model shows a flat passageway over the vaulting. The beam holes in the rear wall of the exedra on the east, which appear to him to be confirmatory evidence, would serve a passageway equally well.

[63] Kähler, op. cit., p. 165 n. 112.

[64] Winnefeld, pp. 73–74; Rivoira-Rushforth, pp. 132–134; Kähler, op. cit., p. 64; Aurigemma, *Villa Adriana*, figs. 162, 164; Crema, pp. 338–339, 478–479, fig. 615; Hansen, op. cit., pp. 36–37.

[65] Giovannoni, *Tecnica*, p. 34.

[66] Winnefeld, p. 75.

[67] Rivoira-Rushforth, p. 136 with fig. 161.

the East Palace. The infrequent brick stamps[60] from the Piazza indicate that this great peristyle (60 m. × 51 m.) with its adjoining edifices was planned by the emperor while he was home between voyages but executed after his departure. A long narrow area for a pool with fountains in the central area was surrounded by a double quadriporticus (pl. 34, fig. 3). The sloping roof[61] was upheld by columns, alternately granite and cipollino, down the center. The walls were faced with brick; and twice as many semicolumns of brick, as there were columns, corresponded with columns of brick in the outer arcade. All brickwork was concealed by fine stucco resembling marble, and the pavement was of polychrome marble. One structural peculiarity remains to be mentioned. The richly decorated corridors, often called cryptoportici, which flanked the east and west walls, were given cross vaulting rather than the more usual barrel vaults. Stout pilasters corresponding in position to the marble columns supported the cross vaults on the inside, but there is no evidence for similar pilasters on the outside. Kähler cites this as evidence for a second story.[62] The west corridor, which is in very ruinous condition, was merely a passage to the southern group of rooms; the east corridor may have duplicated it originally, but in its present state it opens out into a rather large cross-vaulted room at the south end.[63] There are traces of windows toward the east. Both had doorways near the ends to connect them with the central area.

The main approach[64] was from the north through a pavilion (pl. 33, fig. 2) made up of eight niches alternately rectangular and curved, with the rectangular recesses open at the north and south to make a passageway. The east and west ones were pierced with large windows in place of doors. All were round-headed. Re-entrant angles faced with brickwork on the inside gave space for shafts to support a lunetted pavilion dome,[65] of curved sections alternated with flat, having a small "eye" at the top. On the outside, buttresses were inserted at the points where the niches came together, and heavy corbels of travertine above them carried arches at the impost of the dome intended no doubt to strengthen as well as decorate it. The extrados begins at the top of these arches. This is said to be the first instance of blind arcading. The actual cupola, however, was made entirely of concrete without any ribbing. The inside of the niches and the outside of the wall were faced with the usual reticulate with brick bands. The brick was, however, more neatly interlocked with the reticulate than usual in the villa. Symmetrically placed to the east and west of the main entrance was a relatively small cross-vaulted pavilion with curved side niches and a rectangular alcove with a window facing north. This construction was also of reticulate with bands. All three pavilions were lavishly decorated. The one at the west has an exquisite polychrome mosaic of small tesserae.[66] A barrel-vaulted room, having no direct access from the Piazza, abutted the eastern pavilion on the north side. At the point of juncture are remains of what Rivoira calls "an undeveloped compound pendentive."[67] The south wall was formed by the wall enclosing the peristyle; the north wall had four great windows facing the park on the north. The entrance was from the east. It is difficult to say what was the specific purpose of such a room. The magnificent view of the mountains toward the east led to other supernumerary structures. Toward the north end of the corridor along the east side of the quadriporticus, a large semicircular apse of two stories, enclosed in straight walls, faced outward and was flanked on each side by a barrel-vaulted corridor and an apsed room divided into two parts by columns. Large beam holes would seem to indicate that there was a balcony on the back wall of the exedra to overlook the Piazza, which was perhaps connected with an open passage over the "crypto-porticus." The east passage, as we have seen, opened out into a rather large cross-vaulted room at the south end which may be later. A door in the north wall of this room led to a barrel-vaulted room with an apse. But from the Piazza the visitor would scarcely have been aware of these structures.

The most elegant rooms of the entire villa faced the "Piazza d'Oro" on the south.[68] The light airy effect of the "Teatro Marittimo" was achieved here on a grand scale. A sinuous octagon with alternately convex and concave sides, each consisting of two columns in antis, formed the focal point of the design. The concave side opposite the entrance opened into a semicircular nymphaeum with alternately curved and rectangular niches between miniature columns in its back wall; the concaves at the sides led into open courts, or light wells, with two curved and two straight sides, also consisting of two columns in antis. Each light well terminated in a chamber with an east-west barrel vault and was flanked by a room with a north-south barrel vault. Three of the corner rooms had east-west barrel vaults, whereas the one on the southeast corner (pl. 34, fig. 1) had a cross vault. The convex sides of the central room contained large curvilinear niches with apsed prolongations into the corners; these have been interpreted as mighty piers to support a dome. Since nothing remains of this vaulting,[69] the question of how the space was covered becomes an academic one so far as this study is concerned.[70] That it was vaulted seems a foregone conclusion from the vaulting in contiguous rooms.[71] The contractor apparently tried to do what he had already done successfully in the Small Baths,[72] but he failed, in the long run at least.[73] Possibly, the great light wells jeopardized its stability. Reticulate work with brick bands faced the greater part of these walls. The niches were covered with either a voussoir or a lintel arch of tile; apertures, with straight or nearly straight lintel arches of the same. The whole was, of course, richly decorated. It is now partially restored.

It is probable that the Small Baths,[74] which come next in the southward development of the villa, had already been started in the first building period.[75] Certain it is that the villa did not have at that time adequate bathing facilities for the number of persons frequenting it. These Baths were aligned with a road leading up the valley which was soon to be converted into the Canopus. The actual construction belongs almost entirely to the second building period, which was initiated by the emperor's return in A.D. 125 and completed for his return from his second voyage in A.D. 133. Rivoira has summed up the general impression with commendable brevity: "These Small Baths are remarkable for the singular design and shape of the rooms—square, rectangular, cruciform, circular, elliptical, polygonal; roofed by barrel-vaults, lunette barrel-vaults, cross-vaults, domes, semi-domes; their stability being in every case solely the result of the interpenetration and reciprocal thrusts of the rooms themselves."[76] He has, however, underestimated the importance

[68] Winnefeld, pp. 65–73; Paribeni, La Villa, pl. 31; Kähler, Villa, pp. 65–72. For the nymphaeum, see Neuerburg, Fontane, pp. 238–239, no. 199, and Hansen, La "Piazza d'Oro," pp. 20–25.

[69] An appreciable amount is left of the lesser vaulting.

[70] A tentative restoration is possible from a comparison with other cupolas constructed on a similar ground plan. See Kähler's restoration in plate 16 (op. cit. reproduced by Vighi, Villa, p. 69, and Frova, p. 85, fig. 70b), and the discussions with drawings of Hansen, op. cit., pp. 44–46; and F. Rakob, "Litus beatae Veneris aureum. Untersuchungen am Venustempel in Baiae" (Röm. Mitt., vol. 68, 1961, pp. 114–149).

[71] A. von Gerkan (Gnomon, vol. 8, 1932, p. 46) states his conviction that the hall was uncovered, which is also the belief of H. Glück, Der Ursprung des Römischen und Abendländischen Wölbungsbaues (Wien 1933), p. 126.

[72] There, however, the intermediate walls were straight, not concave.

[73] Aurigemma, La Villa, p. 48. There is no way of telling when it may have collapsed.

[74] Winnefeld, pp. 113–136; R. M. Kennedy, MAAR, vol. 3, 1919, pl. 77; Aurigemma, Villa Adriana, pp. 83–88; Crema, pp. 404–406, 478, 481, figs. 496, 611; Frova, pp. 87–88.

[75] Bloch, Bolli, pp. 131–133, 163–164.

[76] Rivoira-Rushforth, p. 135.

[77] It is my conviction that they were not glazed.

[78] Hypocaust piers and wall tubes have disappeared for the most part.

[79] This is the earliest instance known to me of this type of relaxing bath.

[80] Pliny, *Epist.* 2, 17, 12; 5, 6, 27.

[81] They must have received heat from the northwest furnace since there is no place for fires along the north wall.

[82] Rivoira (*loc. cit.*) lists this as one of the novelties. Blocks were largely used for the facing.

[83] Only one of the walls was actually straight.

of the monolithic quality of Roman concrete, which certainly contributed to the stability. Interest in the individual rooms has diverted attention from the general arrangement which was well thought out to meet every whim of the emperor and his guests. The main entrance was from the north, but there were a number of other entrances leading by corridors to various parts of the Baths. Large windows pierced walls facing west and south. Whether they were glazed or not is still an open question.[77] More rooms than usual were heated. The most impressive were aligned along the west side where they would receive the maximum benefit from the afternoon sun. Unfortunately, they are not well preserved.[78] The row consisted of a room with two pools,[79] a comparatively small *tepidarium* with a curved back wall, a large pool with curved ends, and a circular *caldarium*. A semicircular inner room, approached from the *caldarium*, probably served as the *sudatio*, or sweat bath. There were furnace rooms in the northwest and southwest corners and a low service corridor running between them, but it is not clear how the heat was canalized to the various warm rooms. Until the underground passage has been completely opened up, it will not be clear how many supernumerary fires there may have been. To the north of the *caldarium*, there was an unheated room which has been identified as the *sphaeristerium*, or game room, of which we have knowledge from literary sources.[80] South of an octagonal dressing room, three rooms—a large rectangular hall with a southern exposure, a barrel-vaulted corridor, and a passageway with curved ends—served to insulate these warm rooms from the *frigidarium* with its two apsed pools. East of the north entrance there were two small heated rooms;[81] and in the northeast corner a square room, the purpose of which is not clear, opened off from a vestibule leading from an open area on the east. This space, separated from the pools of the *frigidarium* by corridors, was probably the swimming bath, or *natatio*. Beam holes in a wall at the south of it must once have supported a balcony from which spectators could watch the swimmers. So much for the arrangement of the rooms. The north wall of the whole establishment has a singularly baroque façade; its gently curving walls connected three high pedimented niches flanked by columns supported by heavy travertine corbels. This north wall is not well integrated with the rest and belongs architecturally with the garden at the north.[82] In general, the inside walls of the warm rooms were faced with brick; the other walls, with the usual combination of reticulate with brick bands and block-and-brick quoins (pl. 32, fig. 1). Windows and doors were treated in the customary fashion, and corridors were furnished with overhead windows. A little more detailed information about the vaulting would seem to be in order at this point. The cupola of the *caldarium* was constructed over a hall with a circular interior and a more or less square exterior[83] which had the usual niches in the corners. The "eye" common to all *caldaria* of this form pierces the top. The ancient contractor, trusting no doubt to the buttressing value of the surrounding rooms, did not hesitate to place a dome on an inner room (*apodyterium*) of octagonal shape (pl. 36, fig. 2) with every other side convex. Having accommodated the wooden centering to the octagonal form, he felt no fear that his concrete, once solidified, would not stand firm. Large windows over the doors in the straight walls prove that he regarded them as mere curtains. A buttressing arch appears on the outside between the south pool of the *frigidarium* and the rectangular hall to the west of it. In general, corridors were barrel-vaulted, but a series of cross vaults covered the short passageways to the east of the *frigidarium*, which had triple windows toward the open area with the swimming pool. Cross vaulting was employed exclusively elsewhere. The *sphaeristerium* may have had a very low cross vault.

A complex of stately columned halls athwart the road leading up the Canopus valley and separating the Small from the Large Baths can be securely dated by the brick stamps in the period of the second voyage.[84] It has not yet been fully excavated. The ground plan, however, is clear.[85] Enough remains of the walls to show the usual reticulate work reinforced by brick bands and some blockwork, though columns and pilasters were of brick stuccoed over. The mention of heated rooms[86] comes as a surprise since the villa contains few if any rooms with suspended floors not connected with Baths.[87] Though it is called the "Vestibule,"[88] it was surely more than a mere vestibule, but rather a group of state reception rooms built perhaps in anticipation of the time when the emperor planned to transfer his court here more or less permanently. Though it is important to a study of Hadrianic architecture, it yields nothing to a knowledge of Hadrianic methods of building.

Hadrian took advantage of a natural valley between the eastern and western part of his vast estate to construct an artificial vale (195 m. × 75 m.) intended to call to mind the Canopus that he had admired in Egypt.[89] The configuration of the land determined the orientation of the various parts so that no two of them are in alignment with each other. The sustaining wall on the west was buttressed by two units of barrel-vaulted chambers—a latrine and ten rooms at a lower level and nine and a latrine at the upper level, which was apparently reached by outside stairs.[90] The rooms of the lower unit were lofty and divided vertically by wooden mezzanine floors supported by travertine corbels. The rooms were not intercommunicating, but beam holes attest the presence of a wooden balcony, probably approached directly from the upper level, across the front to give access to the mezzanine rooms. Both lines of doorways were covered by lintel arches of *bipedales*. Tile-faced concrete arches resting on heavy corbels supported an overhang at the first floor level, which was intended no doubt to protect the wooden balcony below, but incidentally formed a capping member for the unit. Small windows, each with its own lintel arch of *bipedales*, stood under the concrete arches to light the rooms when the door was closed. An upper story had rooms with a western exposure opening onto the upper level. The lower part now houses the museum, the upper part serves as a modern dwelling. Modern windows facing the Canopus valley in the latter very likely replaced ancient ones, but the whole wall has been too drastically restored through the years to give evidence. A similar plan was used for the upper unit, but the rooms were not so high. The level of the wooden balcony was approximately that of the first floor of the other, but the two façades were not brought into connection with each other. There is no evidence for an upper story. The same type of masonry was employed for both, but the upper

[84] Bloch, *Bolli*, pp. 133–135, 166–167. A hall to the west, serving as the forecourt of a small temple, may have been added later.

[85] W. L. Reichardt, *MAAR*, vol. 11, 1933, pp. 127–132, pls. 13–20; Vighi, *Villa*, plan following p. 40; Aurigemma, *Villa Adriana*, pp. 97–99.

[86] Vighi, *op. cit.*, p. 32.

[87] A service corridor connected it with the Cento Camerelle.

[88] Kähler, *Villa*, p. 25, sees in the edifice not a vestibule but a glorified gymnasium connected with the two Baths.

[89] Aurigemma, *La Villa*, pp. 27–34; *idem, Lavori* (see n. 10 above); *idem, Villa Adriana*, pp. 100–133; Crema, pp. 472, 477, figs. 606–608; Frova, pp. 86–87; see also F. Rakob, "Ein Grottentriclinium in Pompeji," *Röm. Mitt.*, vol. 71, 1964, pp. 182–194.

[90] Vighi, *Villa*, pp. 46–48. Mostly personal observation.

91 Bloch, *Bolli*, p. 169.

92 G. Lugli, *Bull. Com.*, vol. 60, 1932, p. 139.

93 These do not appear in the restoration.

94 Vighi (*op. cit.*, p. 36) suggests that this may have been a later development.

95 Neuerburg, *Fontane*, pp. 240–241, no. 201.

96 G. de Angelis d'Ossat, *Riv. Roma*, vol. 14, 1936, p. 339; idem, *III conv. st. archit.*, p. 238; idem, *Le cupole*, pp. 10, 13–14. Lugli (*Tecnica*, p. 690) lists it as a *volta con intercapedine e vuoti interni*.

97 Rivoira-Rushforth, p. 135; de Angelis d'Ossat, *III conv. st. archit.*, p. 227. Lugli (*Tecnica*, p. 689) lists it as a *volta a conchiglia* because of the shallowness of the curved sections.

unit showed a greater use of blocks, and the brick bands appear merely at the bottom and top of the reticulate. These were more ample service quarters than the Cento Camerelle could furnish. Though no brick stamps were found,[91] the masonry is undeniably Hadrianic. A few stamps *in situ* indicate that Hadrian built the sustaining wall on the east side, though the massive buttresses were probably Antonine.[92]

The canal, or *euripus*, for the Canopus was hollowed out of the tufa and supplied with steps[93] and landing places for light craft. The curved north end was treated like a pergola.[94] Its fantastic colonnade with the intercolumniations covered by an entablature alternately curved and straight has now been restored. Columns more widely spaced lined the basin on each side where they would be reflected in the water. Because of the distance between them, they doubtless upheld a wooden architrave. The eastern colonnade was double and probably an open pergola; the row of columns on the west was interrupted by six bases for caryatids, four maidens between Sileni. There were two bases for large statuary groups in the basin itself. At the south end beyond the *euripus* proper, there was a rectangular pool between wings broken up into small rooms with a varied vaulting of some interest. The light fantastic effect was maintained by a short colonnade at the rear of the pool with two columns *in antis* having an arched architrave in the center and apparently joining the outward curving walls also with two columns *in antis* of a room in each wing. Beyond this façade, a large semicircular nymphaeum (pl. 33, fig. 3)[95] with an elongated apse presents some very substantial masonry. On each side of the apse, apparently shallow curved niches with rounded tops for statues were alternated with deep rectangular recesses having slightly curved lintel arches of *bipedales* equipped with steps for cascades of water. Actually, the radial walls of these niches extended upward into a second story of barrel-vaulted rooms which served as buttresses for the weight of the semidome,[96] which was low on the outside and stepped at the bottom. The semidome was of the pavilion type and lofty on the inside. It is said to be the first example extant in which curved sections were alternated with flat.[97] The curved sections were wider, rising from the central apse and from brick-faced lunettes over the two central niches on each side; the straight, or veloidal, sections, from the wall proper. The thickness of the dome decreased as it approached the "eye" at the top. The concrete was faced with an enormous arch of *bipedales*. There are traces of a brick-faced curtain between the architrave of the colonnade at the rear of the pool and the arch facing the semidome, but not enough remains to show how it was treated. The elongated apse at the center was a common feature in temples of Serapis. The alternately curved and rectangular niches along the sides were furnished with jets of water; the barrel vault covered only the center with open spaces at the ends to admit shafts of light; the apse at the end was higher than the rest, and on it and several of the niches traces of rustic work remain. Water was brought down from a distributing reservoir on top, whence it issued from the "grotto" and cascaded down to a pool at the foot of the apse and thence flowed from pool to pool until it eventually reached the *euripus*. Two small aqueducts of three arches each, however, diverted some of the water to a channel along the top of the sides of the elongated apse and on to another at the base of the semidome from which pipes brought it to the fountains in the niches along the sides of the apse and to the stepped recesses in the great nymphaeum.[98] A wide corridor followed the line of the nymphaeum and its prolongation on the right. It was barrel-vaulted with square openings at regular intervals in the vaulting. On the left, a series of rooms took the place of the corridor; and beyond them there was a staircase leading to the top. On the right, a second stairway was almost entirely outside the nymphaeum. One stamp of A.D. 126 is more important than thirty or so of A.D. 123, the year of the reorganization of the brick industry. The Canopus belongs to the second building period.[99]

It is a foregone conclusion that Hadrian should have made some use of the higher land, sustained on the east of the Canopus by the retaining wall; this land had an even more extensive view than the elevation containing the "Small Palace."[100] Somebody, probably Augustus, had buttressed the north end of the hill with a row of lofty barrel-vaulted chambers. Since Hadrian's plan for the building he had in mind for the top called for a deeper substructure, he added another row of chambers, also barrel-vaulted, with an arcaded corridor in front of them which was covered with a series of cross vaults. The outside doorways of the earlier rooms still served as inner entrances except in a few cases where they were obscured by foundation walls for the edifice on top. This lofty substructure was three-storied. Travertine corbels within the chambers show where the wooden floors stood. Wooden balconies under the porticus must have given access to the upper stories, since the rooms were not intercommunicating. Steps near the ends, as in Cento Camerelle, reached only to the second floor level and not to the terrace on top, to which there was a broad stairway on the east. To whatever use this substructure was put,[101] it was built primarily to provide space for the halls on top. A fine tile cornice marks the transition to the superstructure. Its west wall shows a decorative use of brick pilasters on the outside,[102] which were doubtless stuccoed over to look like marble, as were the panels between them. It is not clear for what use these pillared halls were intended.[103] In any case they offer no structural information. In the substructure, brick stamps of A.D. 123 predominate; in the superstructure, those of A.D. 124.[104]

At the same time that Hadrian's contractors were building the elaborate reproduction in miniature of the Canopus of Egypt toward the south end of the estate, they were converting another valley toward the north into a reminiscence of the Vale of Tempe in Thessaly.[105] They may have cut away some of the tufa on the east side with this in view,[106] but from the nature of the terrain little masonry was needed beyond a sustaining wall on the west side.[107] But in order that his guests might enjoy the peace and quiet of nature in comfort, Hadrian had three structures erected on the west side. Near the foot of the valley,[108] a circular pavilion with twenty Doric columns stood within a semicircular colonnade having a shallow rectangular alcove between two deep semicircular ones, each fronted by four columns in antis.[109] East of the so-called summer triclinium, a three-story belvedere with enormous windows on three sides made a pleasant retreat for guests housed in the "Ospitale." Its architecture is straightforward and requires no comment. It is known as the "Padiglione de Tempe."[110]

[98] Vighi, Villa, p. 46, offers the attractive suggestion that the nymphaeum was also a cool summer dining room.

[99] Bloch, Bolli, pp. 142–144, 169, 183; Aurigemma, Villa Adriana, p. 127.

[100] Winnefeld, pp. 32–35 with pl. 2; G. Lugli, Bull. Com., vol. 60, 1932, pp. 136–140; Aurigemma, La Villa, pp. 26–27; idem, Villa Adriana, pp. 147–150; Crema, p. 472, fig. 603.

[101] Because of the resemblance to the quarters generally ascribed to the palace guard on the Palatine, this great substructure has come to be called the Praetorium, though it is much better adapted to storage space.

[102] Rivoira-Rushforth, p. 139.

[103] Comparatively little remains of them.

[104] Bloch, Bolli, pp. 140–141, 167–168.

[105] The brick stamps found in the two are the same. See Bloch, Bolli, pp. 169–170.

[106] The quarrying may have had the more practical purpose of supplying tufa blocks and reticulate tesserae.

[107] G. Lugli, Bull. Com., vol. 60, 1932, p. 116.

[108] The structures at the south end of the valley—the picturesque Teatro Greco, the Teatro Latino of which nothing is visible, and the "Palaestra" of which little remains—have no place in a study of this kind. See Aurigemma, La Villa, pp. 11–13; idem, Villa Adriana, pp. 39–50; Vighi, Villa, p. 96.

[109] Vighi, op. cit., p. 95; Neuerburg, Fontane, pp. 232–233, no. 189.

[110] Paribeni, La Villa, pls. 41, 42; Aurigemma, Villa Adriana, pp. 186–188.

[111] See above, p. 247.

[112] Bloch, *Bolli*, pp. 145–146. There are three of 124 and one of 125.

[113] Winnefeld, pp. 111–119. I have visited it briefly only once, but can recall nothing fundamentally different in construction from the rest of the villa. See also Aurigemma, *Villa Adriana*, pp. 136–142 (fig. 137 shows Piranesi's drawing of the plan); Crema, pp. 473, 478, 481, figs. 610, 618.

[114] It could be approached from the northwest through two pillared halls as well as from the large central court.

[115] De Angelis d'Ossat (*BMIR*, vol. 12, 1941, p. 127) presents this as the first example of the windowed drum.

[116] Winnefeld, pp. 115–118. It shows another experiment in placing a dome on an octagon with four concave sides.

[117] Winnefeld, pp. 123–125; Aurigemma, *op. cit.*, pp. 143–145; Crema, p. 473.

[118] G. Lugli, *Palladio*, vol. 4, 1940, p. 259; Winnefeld, pp. 119–121; Aurigemma, *Villa Adriana*, pp. 134–136; Crema, pp. 473, 482, figs. 389, 619; Frova, p. 86.

[119] Lugli, *op. cit.*, pp. 257–274 with plans by R. Bonelli.

[120] Bloch, *Bolli*, pp. 144–145, 172.

[121] The alcove opposite the door had its own curved niche for a statue.

We have already mentioned a large exedra facing the valley at the east of the Piazza d'Oro.[111] Various structures at a lower level beneath it have been excavated recently.

The land seems to have sloped up from the northwest to a fairly level space overlooking the Valle di Risicoli. Hadrian saw its possibilities and could not resist the temptation to lay out another villa which should be quite independent of the rest of the complex: the Piccolo Palazzo or Accademia. Since practically all the brick stamps found in the area belong to the year A.D. 123,[112] he apparently planned the villa during his brief sojourn in the City between the two voyages. So little of it is left—and it is on private property difficult of access—that we are dependent on old drawings for the general plan.[113] With two noteworthy exceptions, he seems to have relied on columns to give elegance to a rectilinear plan. It is not without interest that he repeated here on a smaller scale the double porticus of the north wall of the Poikile. A small vestibule at the southeast led to a large antechamber with a curved outer wall, which in turn led to a large circular hall, known as the Temple of Apollo (pl. 32, fig. 4).[114] Its inner face was divided into panels by brick-faced semicolumns supporting a series of lintels of upright tiles separated by travertine springers. Above a capping cornice supported by small brick mensoles there was an upper register of curved niches alternated with rectangular windows.[115] A tile cornice served as the impost for a mighty dome of which only a little remains. At the west corner of the great central court ("Accademia"), stood one of those fantastic structures with curved lines in which the emperor delighted.[116] Not enough remains for a completely satisfactory restoration. The apse of a hall seems to have formed its southeast niche. Still farther to the south are substantial remains of a small theater or odeum.[117]

At the northwestern end of this upper level, a cellular sustaining wall was built, which yielded Hadrianic stamps. This wall gave the opportunity for erecting a massive substructure at the lower level[118] for a belvedere at the upper. This monument is now known as Roccabruna[119] and is as remarkable for its construction as for its superb view out over the Campagna. It is quite obviously reminiscent of some monument that Hadrian saw on his travels. The nearly square substructure (16.5 m. $\times$ 16.75 m.) was faced with tufa blocks alternated for the most part with one or two rows of brick without any reticulate work whatsoever (pl. 36, fig. 3). This probably represents the earliest use of block-and-brick work in an important monument. It does not appear elsewhere in the villa. The bricks are mostly triangles, dark yellow in color and 3.2 cm. thick. The few brick stamps found bear the consular dates of A.D. 123 and 124.[120] On the west side, i.e., the front, an arched doorway between higher arched niches led into the inner chamber.[121] These niches started at the pavement; they were wide enough to be provided with a small rectangular recess topped with a lintel arch of *bipedales* reaching to the line of the impost of the half-cupola; and they were covered with a segmental arch of *bipedales* under a relieving arch of *sesquipedales*. At an appreciable height over the central doorway there was a relieving arch and above it a small window with a lintel arch, both of *bipedales*. The same sequence—arched opening (this time a window), relieving arch at a higher level, and a small window with a lintel arch—appeared at the center of each side with a secondary opening near the rear. A heavy balcony supported on concrete arches rising from travertine corbels formed the capping member of the lower story. The interior was octagonal in plan. Alcoves filling the entire space were alternated with walls, each having a small curvilinear niche. The alcoves were barrel-vaulted with faces of *bipedales*; and they show traces of the *besales* which were laid on the tiles resting on the wooden centering. The arches of the half-cupolas over the niches were faced with *sesquipedales*. The impost of the cupola rested on the arched top of the alcoves. The *caementa* in the concrete were of a light-weight tufa laid on the centering in even rows. The four windows high up in the sides were splayed down to slit windows in the dome which would be scarcely noticeable but served to air out the cupola. The dome was of the pavilion type. The concrete was unusually heavy at the corners.[122] The niches flanking the entrance were carved out of it in the front, but circular voids appear at the back, which remind one of the voids in the Pantheon. The one on the right seems to have been included in a passage lighted by an ordinary window and a slit window. There was no direct communication between floors. The hall had a fine marble pavement; wall and ceiling decoration were probably equally fine. So much for the original plan of the substructure. Very shortly, for the masonry is practically identical, a porch was added in front and relatively narrow passageways along the sides. Five arched doorways, the one at each end lower than the rest, pierced the new façade; and four transverse arches on projecting pilasters supported the nearly flat roof. These arches were double, the inner one of *sesquipedales*, the outer one of *bipedales*. The reason for the addition of the porch is not clear. Barely enough of the fundamental work of the upper story remains to show that it consisted of a square chamber with the angles cut off, enclosed in a circular colonnade of sixteen columns. A fragment of the vaulting lying on the ground at the upper level is a further aid in mental restoration. Unlike the lower part, the walls were brick-faced, though the brickwork was concealed by marble. It had a low pavilion dome reaching up to the "eye." Enough remained of the marble fragments for a satisfactory restoration.

The question of the dating of the Large Baths is too complicated for discussion here, but the chances are that they belong to the last phase of Hadrianic building activity (A.D. 133–138).[123] With exception of one circular hall and two semicircular pools, these Baths[124] were built along straight lines and contained none of the fantastic vaulting that distinguished the Small Baths. In general, the warm rooms lay along the west side where the sunshine streaming in through large windows would augment the artificial heat supplied from the *praefurnia* at the ends. They are, however, divided into two units by the great circular room, in which Mirick found no indication of the regular heating arrangements or of a water supply for the great round pool. He concluded, therefore, that it was a *heliocaminus* with a pool full of sand. The method of heating the three rooms south of the rotonda has been carefully worked out by Mirick. Service corridors from the *praefurnium* at the southwest corner hid the fires by which the rooms were heated. The room with the three pools nearest to the *praefurnium* was served by fires

[122] A different aggregate was used in this concrete.

[123] See Bloch, *Bolli*, pp. 135–138, 164–166, 168.

[124] Winnefeld, pp. 135–141; H. D. Mirick, MAAR, vol. 11, 1933, pp. 119–126, pls. 4–12; Paribeni, *La Villa*, pls. 22–24; Aurigemma, *La Villa*, pp. 25–27; idem, *Villa Adriana*, pp. 88–96; Crema, pp. 406, 477, figs. 495, 603; Frova, p. 87; Vighi, *Villa*, pp. 28–30.

[125] One looks in vain for any trace of the wall tubes necessary for the functioning of the hypocausts. Mirick (*op. cit.*, p. 124) uses clamp holes and vents to prove that the vaults also were provided with hollow tiles.

[126] E. Wadsworth (Mrs. H. F. Cleland), *MAAR*, vol. 4, 1924, pp. 62–63. A good illustration appears in Anderson-Spiers-Ashby, pl. 78.

[127] The slightly heated hall had only the lower part faced with brick.

under each of the pools. Because of the relatively small areas to be heated, piers along the walls of both the room and the pools were considered sufficient to support the suspended floor. The *caldarium* next, with its forest of hypocaust piers, was heated by fires at both its east and west sides; the *tepidarium* next, similarly equipped, by a fire at the west alone.[125] The great hall to the east of them had a hypocaust also, but Mirick contends that it was not heated. But the service corridor continues along its south side, and there is an opening in the south wall through which heat could have been introduced; and the "registers" in the east and west walls could have supplied the necessary draft. Such an arrangement, even with the help of the three large high windows in the south wall, could have done little more than temper the air. It was a large hall richly decorated by a fine ceiling of stucco work,[126] of which substantial traces remain (pl. 36, fig. 1). It would certainly be suitable as a general meeting place for those who frequented the Baths. North of the rotonda, three small rooms repeated in miniature those at the south. This unit had its own heating system starting from a *praefurnium* at the northwest corner and screened from view by a service corridor. A single fire produced the heat for *caldarium* and the *tepidarium* behind it. Two fires, one from the west and one from the north, warmed the room with the two small pools. In this room the same arrangement of piers outlined both the room and the pools, presumably to support a suspended floor. The fourth room with the apse was not heated. East of the row of heated rooms, the entire central part was taken up by the *frigidarium*, a large square hall with an open passage at the north and south sides. It was furnished with two pools—a semicircular one at the north, a rectangular one at the east. The semicircular pool had the usual alternation of curved and rectangular niches in its curved side, and both pools were viewed from the *frigidarium* through open fronts made by great cipollino columns *in antis*. A similar arrangement laid the rectangular pool open to the court behind, which could be reached by short corridors to the right and left of the pool. A comparatively small room at the northeast corner may have served as a dressing room for those approaching the Bath from the north. A larger dressing room (*apodyterium*) at the southeast corner completed the central part. The space farther to the east has not been fully excavated, but trial trenches have furnished the data for a fairly complete restoration. East of the rectangular pool was a court which would seem suitable for a *sphaeristerium*. It had a plain white mosaic floor and was probably covered with a wooden roof. A small central room between "*alae*" faced the court on the north and south. The east "*ala*" on the south was prolonged to give admittance to an isolated room which may have been a latrine. Still farther east, various entrances led to a great colonnaded court which was probably the *palaestra*. Its colonnade had a mosaic floor and the court a pavement of herringbone brick. Four columns *in antis* separated it from the "*sphaeristerium*." Wall construction presents no novelties. The general distinction between the use of brick in warm rooms and reticulate with brick bands elsewhere prevails here as in the Small Baths.[127] Apertures were covered with slightly curved lintel arches of *bipedales* under relieving arches of the same. The vaulting, however, needs further comment.

In the "*heliocaminus*," the heavy masonry between the outer square and the inner circle took much of the weight of the great cupola. The arched tops of the semicircular niches in the east corners helped to distribute the weight on the inside, whereas hood-shaped raccords[128] on the outside served to obviate a weakness caused by the angles between the curve and the straight wall. The cupola terminated in an "eye," faced with upright tiles laid on a preliminary row of horizontal *bipedales*.[129] Fourteen equidistant holes[130] running in parallel rows toward the top of the cupola may have been connected with some device for closing the "eye." The room with the warm pools at the south was cross-vaulted, undoubtedly with barrel vaults over the pools, and the two warm rooms between it and the "*heliocaminus*" were barrel-vaulted.[131] Two of the ceilings in the small rooms at the northwest— those beside the apse of the *frigidarium*—were cross-vaulted. The entrance corridor at the south end was barrel-vaulted, as was the short passage at right angles to it, but barreled in the opposite direction. The great southern hall—south of the *frigidarium*—had a cross vault supported on four heavy corbels carved to pulvinar shape. Such a use of corbels was an innovation.[132] The *frigidarium* imposed the greatest problem in vaulting (pl. 35, fig. 1). A lofty cross vault with *besales* still clinging to its soffit rested on heavy travertine corbels at the corners. Columns were placed below the corbels to appear to take the weight of the vaulting. The cross vault seems to have made a clerestory above the enormous tile-faced arches that spanned the void over the passageways at the ends of the hall. A half-cupola over the semicircular pool at the north was faced by a wall resting on the entablature of the two columns *in antis*, whereas cross vaults sprang from the columns of the rectangular pool which was east of the *frigidarium*. The corridor at the north of this pool, corresponding to the one at the south end of it, was cross-vaulted, as was also the room beyond it to the north. A tendency to alternate cross vaults with barrel vaults is still discernible, but cross vaults decidedly have the preference.

The Villa Adriana is too vast for a detailed description of each edifice. Some minor structures have been omitted entirely. An attempt has been made in the above pages merely to place the peculiarities of construction in their proper settings. The fundamental masonry shows complete confidence, perhaps even overconfidence, in the strength of the concrete. The builder used *caementa* of medium size in the core of the walls and of the same yellow-brown tufa as was employed for the reticulate facing. This was normally reinforced at the edges by either tufa blocks or a combination of tufa blocks and tiles and strengthened by bands of brick at more or less regular intervals. Examples of brick quoins interlocked with the reticulate, as in much of the Hadrianic work in Ostia, are rare. In the Roccabruna, alternate rows of blocks and bricks were used for the first time in an important edifice. The tesserae are normally 8 cm. per side; the bricks are triangles (24–28 cm. $\times$ 3.5–4 cm.); the mortar joints are 1.8–2.5 cm.[133] The mortar, though granular, is firm and white. The builder did not hesitate, however, to depart from the norm when it served his purpose. *Besales* were often laid flat on the wooden centering of the vaulting to make a more or less permanent centering; both *sesquipedales* and *bipedales* were used to face arches. The slightly curved lintel arch of *bipedales* was the preferred covering for

[128] Rivoira-Rushforth, pp. 135–136 with fig. 160.

[129] G. de Angelis d'Ossat, *III conv. st. archit.*, p. 233.

[130] *Ibid.*, p. 243 with n. 46. The closure of the "eye" would be as important to a *heliocaminus* as to a *caldarium*. I could not see the holes.

[131] One of these shows the gouges made by seekers after the metal clamps.

[132] Rivoira-Rushforth, p. 135 with fig. 159.

[133] G. Lugli, *Bull. Com.*, vol. 55, 1927, p. 149.

[134] The Domus Aurea and the Domus August(i)ana both have rudimentary pavilion arches.

openings. As usual, only every fourth or fifth *bipedalis* was whole to make a bond; the rest were broken pieces presenting a whole face. Relieving arches were used sparingly except to divert weight from lintel arches. Brickwork is found where conditions made it seem desirable. Hadrianic builders had sufficient confidence in the tenacity of their concrete to attempt anything in the nature of vaulting. They alternated barrel vaults with cross vaults wherever feasible and did not hesitate to rest cross vaults on corbels. To the simple hemispherical dome, they added the fullly developed pavilion cupola,[134] sometimes with spherical sections and sometimes with flat or veloidal sections alternated with spherical ones. They experimented—once successfully, once apparently unsuccessfully—with placing a cupola on an octagonal room with curvilinear sides, every other one of which was convex. At least once, they introduced amphorae into the mass to lighten the weight. As in the Pantheon, the extrados was shallower than the intrados. Once, at any rate, arches were used in the outside to strengthen the dome. They employed hood-shaped and niche-shaped raccords to distribute the weight. This is not the place to deal with the wealth of marble decoration in sectile floors and wall revetments, not to mention the columns, friezes, cornices, and statuary with which the villa was adorned.

[135] G. Lugli, *Bull. Com.*, vol. 60, 1932, pp. 111–150.

As Lugli has pointed out,[135] the Villa Adriana had an Antonine phase in which sustaining walls were substituted for natural slopes. The fundamental masonry had no true facing other than fairly regular rows of roughly shaped pieces of tufa of the same sort as constituted the aggregate of the concrete core. Where there were niches, as along the west side of the platform upon which stands the Casino Fede, the surface may have been covered with chunks of pumice to give a rustic effect; where semicolumns of masonry appear between niches alternately curved and rectangular under archivolts of *sesquipedales*, as in the wall along the north side of the terrace in front of the "libraries," it was probably plastered and stuccoed to look like marble; but where it sustained the high ground at the east of the Canopus with the help of mighty buttresses, it has stood the test of time without any apparent protection from the elements. There are a few other stretches of this type of Antonine walling. A certain amount of other reinforcement was needed and supplied. Here and there apertures were closed and other changes made as rooms were prepared for other uses. Lugli's careful analysis makes unnecessary a more detailed report. The villa still remained throughout the Antonine period essentially as Hadrian had left it.

Praeneste (Palestrina)

[136] Suetonius, *Augustus*, 72, 82.

[137] Aulus Gellius, N. A., 16, 13.

[138] Marucchi, *Palestrina*, pp. 120–124.

Augustus had a villa at Praeneste.[136] Tiberius recuperated from an illness presumably in this same villa, which is described as "*sub ipso oppido.*"[137] Below the modern town where the Campo Santo has been laid out, there are still the imposing substructions of a villa which was proved by brick stamps to be Hadrianic.[138] Since a fine statue of Antinous was unearthed there, we are doubtless justified in considering it the imperial villa as rebuilt by Hadrian. There were seven great halls, each divided into three rooms by transverse walls with arched openings. A corridor enclosed the block on the south and west at any rate, the external walls of which were fortified by spur walls. Nothing remains of the upper stories for comparison with the Villa Adriana near Tivoli, but certain similarities in the masonry are apparent in the substructures.[139] There are sections of reticulate work broken by bands of five rows of bricks.[140] The reticulate is composed of tesserae, 6–7 cm. per side, of a hard local tufa. The bricks seem to be of local manufacture, from a fine yellowish clay with a slight admixture of pozzolana. They were neither well mixed nor well fired, but they seem to have stood the test of time fairly well. Most of them are yellow though a few are a magenta red. The width varies from 3.4 to 4.5 cm. They were probably triangles from *besales*. The mortar joints were medium wide (1.25–1.75). For the barrel vaulting, tiles seem first to have been laid on the wooden centering, at least near the impost, and regular rows of fine *caementa* upon them. A second building showed reticulate with tufa blocks, as in places at the Tivoli estate. Two cisterns, one below the Barberini Gardens and the other below the road, probably belonged to the imperial estate, but whether they were Hadrianic or not is incapable of proof. The bricks were thinner (2.8–3.5), better mixed, and better fired. They show the same splotches of pozzolana grains and the same colors, though a larger proportion of them are magenta red. Even finer work appears about the doorways. There were some bonding courses. The reservoir below the road had some apses in front.

Antium (Anzio)

Hadrian also enlarged, and no doubt modified somewhat, Nero's villa at Anzio.[141] Walls and arches of fine brickwork, almost certainly his, lie prone in the sea where they fell at some indeterminate period.[142] On the other hand, considerable Hadrianic work was laid bare by the bombing during the last war. The greater part of it is now in a military preserve which is not open to study. When the time is ripe, a detailed analysis of this imperial villa would certainly repay the effort involved. Suffice it to say at this point that the Hadrianic brickwork, which Dr. Van Deman could examine in the main walls and combined with reticulate in the less important ones, seemed to her to be of local manufacture.[143] I have already dealt with the Hadrianic mosaics coming from there.[144]

Albanum (Castel Gandolfo)

The great Villa of Domitian at Albanum[145] was so complete in itself that it left little scope for Hadrian's enthusiasm for building. On the top terrace south of the theater, there are two rooms of typical Hadrianic masonry[146] which were probably appurtenances of the theater. They exhibit six rows of brick for every 89 cm. of reticulate. The bricks are triangles 3.5 cm. thick. Three stamps give the date. The need for a more abundant water supply led either Trajan or Hadrian to add the great cistern,[147] the remains of which are still visible in ruinous state in the Villa Torlonia. The hill was cut back to make room for it, and four heavy spur walls buttressed it on the side away from the hill. Piers and arches divided it into six barrel-vaulted chambers. The piers were faced with brick without bonding courses; the arches were faced with *bipedales*; and the walls, with reticulate reinforced at intervals of 90 cm. by five rows of brick. Corbels of peperino, inserted in the

[139] Magoffin, *Praeneste*, p. 50 n. 125.

[140] Details of construction are from Dr. Van Deman's unpublished notes, checked as far as possible by personal observation.

[141] Lugli (*RIA*, vol. 7, 1940, pp. 177–181) gives a general description. For the Neronian villa, see Blake, *RC* II, pp. 40–41; Crema, p. 324.

[142] Personal memory from visits before World War II.

[143] Dr. Van Deman's unpublished notes show with what care she examined the masonry that was then exposed. She reported bricks 4 cm. thick and tesserae 8–10 cm. per side.

[144] M. E. Blake, *MAAR*, vol. 13, 1936, pp. 77–78.

[145] Blake, *RC* II, pp. 134–135.

[146] G. Lugli, *Bull. Com.*, vol. 46, 1918, pp. 15–17.

[147] *Idem, Bull. Com.*, 47, 1919, pp. 153–195. Lugli favors Trajan. He does not, however, give the brick measures which might clinch the matter.

148 For the history of the villa see Lugli, *Bull. Com.*, vol. 42, 1914, pp. 281–291; *idem, Not. sc.*, 1946, pp. 60–83.

149 Julius Capitolinus, *SHA, Verus*, 8, 8.

150 Actually the Cassia, rather than the Clodia as stated by Capitolinus. See Martinori, *Via Cassia*, p. 13.

151 G. Lugli, *Bull. Com.*, vol. 51, 1923, pp. 47–62.

152 Julius Capitolinus, *SHA, Antoninus Pius*, 1, 8.

153 *Ibid.*, 12, 6.

154 *Ibid.*, 7, 10.

155 In a letter to Fronto (*Epistulae* 2, 6) 'written from Naples in A.D. 143, Marcus Aurelius mentions Laurentum, Lanuvium, Tusculum, Puteoli, and Tibur as though cataloguing family estates. Another letter (*Epist.*, 1, 4) was written from Baiae in the same year. Capitolinus (*op. cit.*, 7, 12) mentions estates in Campania.

156 M. Cornelius Fronto, *Epistulae*, 4, 4.

157 *CIL*, vol. 10 (1), no. 5909.

158 Capitolinus, *op. cit.*, 10, 4. See also *idem, Marcus* 6, 3 and *Verus* 2, 4.

piers to support the wooden centering, were left for decoration (?); and the whole was lined with *opus signinum*. The aqueduct of Malafitto Basso was restored to supply it with water. In the Villa of Pompey, which had long belonged to the imperial domain, there are some walls faced with reticulate, broken by bands of five or six rows of brick every 90 cm., which appear Hadrianic.[148] The date receives some confirmation from a brick stamp found in two different parts of the edifice. There does not, however, seem to have been a distinct Hadrianic phase.

Via Cassia. Acquatraversa

Of the luxurious villa that Lucius Verus had built for himself[149] five miles from Rome on the Via Cassia[150] at a locality now known as Acquatraversa,[151] little remains today except part of a niched sustaining wall of what was apparently an elaborate entrance at a lower level and some fallen masonry above where one would expect the residential quarters to be. The sustaining wall with its curvilinear niches was faced with a good brickwork. The bricks, about equally divided between red and yellow, were partly triangles (3.4–3.5 cm. $\times$ 18–22 cm.) and partly tiles broken to triangular shape (2.8–3.1 $\times$ 24–26 cm.). The joints varied from 1.8 to 2.5 cm. in width. In the concrete the *caementa*, of local red-brown tufa, were small and laid in regular rows. At a slightly later period this façade was masked by another also niched but faced with alternate bands of blocks and bricks. The bricks were identical with the yellow ones of the earlier façade, but the vaults were lower and the aggregate less regular. Evidently the earlier wall was not adequate to withstand the pressure of the mass of earth behind it. Two old engravings of Morillonio (1547) give an impression of the elegance of this approach, though it is difficult to tell at present how many details the engraver may have added from his imagination. Unfortunately, the collapsed remains of vaults on the top of the hill show a concrete with a poorer mortar than one would expect from an imperial residence; and the pieces of masonry from an upper floor are faced with bricks that are rather thin for the period (2.4–2.7 cm.). The villa site was early identified from the many fine busts of members of the Antonine period found in the vicinity.

Antoninus Pius was born at Lanuvium and educated at Lorium,[152] where he also died.[153] An account of what little is known of his villas is given below. He was a man of considerable property before he inherited all the holdings which came to him as emperor. Julius Capitolinus gives a picture of him living on his private estates, varying his residence with the season.[154] We do not even know exactly where most of them were situated.[155] A charming letter written by Marcus Aurelius to Fronto in A.D. 144/45,[156] describing a visit to Anagnia on the way to the family estate in Signia, is our only evidence for an Antonine villa in that locality. It has been identified with a place called Villa Magna, mentioned in a Severan inscription,[157] of which nothing now remains. As for the imperial estates inherited by him, it is unlikely that an emperor who preferred the relatively simpler Domus Tiberiana[158] to the Domus Flavia in Rome would make any unnecessary modifications in them. He would of course be under obligation to keep them in good repair. An elaborate retaining wall near the north entrance of the

Villa of Domitian at Albano[159] belongs in this category. Only two niches with traces of a second register and a series of arched recesses remain. The walls were faced with brick and the archivolts with *bipedales*. At Hadrian's Villa near Tivoli he had to finish the Great Baths,[160] but the other changes made by him, or possibly Marcus Aurelius,[161] were of much the same order as those at Albano. Terrace walls were substituted for natural slopes. This construction can be easily recognized because its concrete has no true facing, but merely fairly regular rows of roughly shaped pieces of tufa of the same sort as constituted the aggregate. When such a sustaining wall was decorated by niches along the west wall of the platform upon which stands the Casino Fede, the surface was probably covered with chunks of pumice to give a rustic effect. A similar wall north of the "libraries," showing semicolumns of masonry between alternately rectangular and curvilinear niches under archivolts of *sesquipedales*, was probably stuccoed over to look like marble. But the great sustaining wall east of the Canopus with its mighty buttresses has stood the test of time without any apparent protection from the elements. Another stretch of similar walling occurs in front of the Hadrianic colonnade at the northern entrance. A certain amount of reinforcement was needed and supplied in other places. Here and there apertures were walled up, and rooms prepared for other uses. Lugli's careful analysis makes unnecessary a detailed report. Since the seaside villa at Laurentum seems to show a more complete renovation, it has been given separate treatment below.

Lanuvium (Lanuvio)

A large concrete platform,[162] supported by an elaborate system of barrel vaults known as La Villa on the right side of the Via Appia shortly before the traveler from Rome reaches Lanuvio, has been identified with his birthplace because of the many statues of the Antonines found in the vicinity. There is, however, no evidence to show that he sought to transform it into a palatial imperial villa. Some walls faced with narrow salmon-colored bricks may belong to some modification instituted by him. Too little remains to be significant. Julius Capitolinus records his restoration of temples at Lanuvium.[163] Scattered remains there seem to belong to the Antonine period.[164]

Lorium and Alsium (Bottaccia; Palo)

From Julius Capitolinus we learn that Antoninus Pius was not only educated in his ancestral estate at Lorium, but constructed a palace there.[165] Since the ancient author implies that the palace was more or less ruined in his day (early fourth century), we cannot expect to find much of it extant today. Important statues which doubtless once adorned it have come to light near Bottaccia on the Via Aurelia.[166] One marble pavement with a rather intricate pattern of porphyry and serpentine against a white ground was unearthed in the same general region and ascribed by the excavator to Marcus Aurelius.[167] The correspondence between Marcus Aurelius and Fronto known as *De Feriis Alsiensibus*[168] proves conclusively that the Antonines had a seaside villa not far removed from their estate at Lorium. This was almost certainly the villa that was unearthed at Palo, ancient Alsium,[169]

[159] G. Lugli, *Bull. Com.*, vol. 46, 1918, pp. 26–29.

[160] Bloch, *Bolli*, pp. 135–138, 164–166.

[161] Lugli, *Bull. Com.*, vol. 60, 1932, pp. 111–150.

[162] G. B. Colburn, *AJA*, vol. 18, 1914, pp. 20–24. Walls faced with reticulate interrupted by bands of red brick were doubtless earlier.

[163] Capitolinus, *SHA*, *Antoninus Pius*, 8, 3. A fragmentary inscription proves that the temple on the Acropolis underwent some slight reorganization at this time. See A. Galieti, *Bull. Com.*, vol. 56, 1928, pp. 236–237.

[164] G. Bendinelli, *Mon. ant.*, vol. 27, 1921, cols. 359, 363.

[165] Julius Capitolinus, *SHA*, *Antoninus Pius*, 1, 8.

[166] G. Amati, *Giornale arcadico di scienze, lettere ed arti*, vol. 27, 1824, pp. 78–103; A. Coppi, *Acc. P. Diss.*, vol. 7, 1836, pp. 365–376; Tomassetti, *Campagna*, vol. 2, pp. 492–493; G. Schneider-Graziosi, *Bull. Com.*, vol. 41, 1913, pp. 57–61.

[167] Schneider-Graziosi, *loc. cit.*

[168] Letters written in A.D. 162.

[169] E. L. Tocca, *Bull. Inst.*, 1867, pp. 209–212.

170 L. Borsari, *Bull. Com.*, vol. 26, 1898, pp. 37–39. The report mentions porphyry, serpentine, alabaster, jasper, colognino, and Greek marble.

171 In fact, the mention of many brick stamps suggests an earlier Hadrianic phase, though the contractor may have bought up a Hadrianic deposit or bricks and tiles as elsewhere.

172 Nibby, *Dintorni*, vol. 2, pp. 202–206; R. Lanciani, *Mon. ant.*, vol. 13, 1903, cols. 142–151.

173 Herodianus, 1, 12.

174 A similar use of triangular bricks is found at Sette Bassi. See above, pp. 106–111.

175 Russell Meiggs recalls red bonding courses, which he believes to be an earmark of the Commodan era. I failed to notice them on a brief visit in 1952. For the raccord in the Great Baths at Tivoli, see above, p. 256, and Rivoira-Rushforth cited there.

176 G. Lugli, *Bull. Com.*, vol. 51, 1923, p. 30.

177 *Ibid.*, pp. 35–36, 40.

178 Not too safe a criterion. Brick stamps prove that there was an extensive Severan repair to which the mosaics may have belonged. See M. E. Blake, *MAAR*, vol. 17, 1940, pp. 94 and 96 for two of them.

1 Paribeni (*Optimus Princeps* II, p. 130) still favors a possible Trajanic date for the amphitheater at Verona. The great amphitheater at Pozzuoli, begun in the first century, may not have been completed until the early years of the reign of Trajan. An early second-century date has been suggested for the amphitheaters at Arezzo and Bene Vagienna; see Neppi Modona, *Edifici teatrali*, pp. 267–270, 278–279; Crema, figs. 334–336, 340. For the amphitheater at Lecce, see below, p. 262.

2 Pietrangeli, *Spoletium*, pp. 60–62; Neppi Modona, *op. cit.*, p. 275.

3 Moretti, *Ancona*, p. 41 n. 4, pp. 65–70; Neppi Modona, *op. cit.*, p. 274.

many years ago. The elaborate plan and the great variety of polychrome columns bespeak a sumptuous imperial villa,[170] but mere possession does not necessarily mean that Antoninus built it, though he may have done so.[171]

Laurentum (Tor Paterno)

Little more than a seventeenth-century plan[172] remains of an imperial villa at Tor Paterna, ancient Laurentum, in which construction of the period of the Antonines was added to a Neronian nucleus. The number of Antonine busts found in the excavation would suggest imperial ownership at least when the renovation was carried out, even if we did not have a record that Commodus took refuge there from a plague at Rome.[173] The old drawing shows a villa built for the most part along straight lines, but the front wall was diversified by three niches on each side of the broad entrance; and there was a small apsed room facing it on each side. At least one spacious hall was apsed. Thin, prevailingly yellow bricks and wide joints differentiated the Antonine masonry from the walls faced with the thick triangles and narrow joints of the Neronian phase. Many of the Antonine bricks were also triangles.[174] Amid the scanty remains still extant, there is at least one arch making a niche-like raccord such as is found in one place in Hadrian's villa near Tivoli.[175]

Prima Porta

Either Antoninus Pius or the members of his family succeeding him made some additions to the imperial estate at Prima Porta. On the basis of its construction, a rectangular reservoir at the foot of the hill has been deemed an addition of theirs.[176] Its exterior was faced with bands of reticulate, of brick, and of block in quite unorthodox fashion; its interior entirely with reticulate. The archivolts were of fine-grained red *sesquipedales*. On the opposite side of the Fosso di Monte di Oliverio, a thermal establishment of at least a dozen rooms[177] was added to the villa complex. When it was discovered in 1878, it was ascribed to this period because of the nature of its black-and-white silhouette mosaics of sea monsters and athletes.[178] No record was made of its wall construction.

PUBLIC MONUMENTS

AMPHITHEATERS AND THEATERS

None of the great amphitheaters of Italy can be attributed to Trajan with confidence.[1] The concrete amphitheater at Spoleto,[2] faced for the most part with small irregular blocks of stone, exhibits arches and low relieving arches of tile. The monument has been ascribed to the early years of the second century largely on the basis of the construction. Apparently the old amphitheater at Ancona became too small for the increase in population following the building of Trajan's port. Additional seating space was gained by adding another story, and this necessitated strengthening the walls.[3] The stone arch of the entrance, known as Arco Bonarelli, was supplemented by a double arch of tiles on the outside, and walls of rather rough reticulate with bands of brick served the same purpose in other parts of the structure. Such an enlargement was probably initiated at any rate in the time of Trajan.

The amphitheater at Santa Maria Capua Vetere[4] is the only monument of the kind displaying masonry comparable to that in other types of Hadrianic edifices[5] away from the Capital. It was obviously modeled after the Colosseum. Like the Colosseum, it had an exterior façade of travertine with great arches of shaped voussoirs under the usual entablature supported by Doric half columns in the lower order. Only a fragment of the second order remains. Each keystone was decorated with a bust or a head of a divinity in high relief. Since sculptured keystones of different proportions have come to light from time to time, it is assumed that the same type of decoration occurred in the upper orders. The entrances to the subterranean corridor were covered with great travertine arches made of rusticated voussoirs.[6] Some seem to rest on travertine pilasters, but others spring from the inner brick walls. There were windows in the vaulting. Even the main sewer had a ponderous top made of three specially shaped pieces. The interior was constructed of brick-faced concrete. The bricks were made from red-brown *besales*, 3.5–4.5 cm. in thickness, which were broken to triangular shape along definite lines. The bricks were 24 to 27.5 cm. in length. They were of local manufacture[7] and bore but one stamp, C.I.F.A.F., which has been interpreted to mean Colonia Iulia Felix Augusta Fecit. The foundations for the walls were carefully prepared. There was a layer of concrete 80 cm. thick, next a row of travertine blocks, and finally a course of larger triangular bricks (33–39 cm. × 4–4.5 cm.). An inscription[8] records that Hadrian embellished the monument with columns, and granite columns with travertine capitals have been found. Pesce conjectures that they formed a colonnade at the top. There were also sculptured reliefs of animals and a sculptured frieze of garlands swinging from Silenus heads, not to mention numerous statues which may also have been a part of the Hadrianic benefaction.

It may have been because of the presence of an imperial villa at Tusculum that Antoninus Pius bestowed an amphitheater on the town.[9] The lower part of the edifice was of squared-stone construction; the arched walls of the substructions and of the supports of the seats were of concrete faced with a reticulate of tufa and selce with bands of brick. The bricks (3.1–3.6 cm. × 17–27 cm.) were light red. Three examples of the same brick stamp,[10] found in one of the arches of the vaulting, are the evidence from which the date has been established.[11]

The small amphitheater of Lucus Feroniae, recently excavated,[12] was built near the middle of the second century. Brick stamps and coins confirm the date. Its walls were constructed in a coarse reticulate; its doorways had tufa blocks.

By the beginning of the second century concrete was the normal material used in the construction of theaters, but the matter of the facing was left to the individual contractor. Reticulate work with brick bands was chosen for a small theater built near the temple of Diana at Nemi[13] to replace an earlier one devoted to the service of the cult. Brick alone faced the platform of the stage and the *scaena*. An incrustation of "stalactites" gave to the niches on the front of the stage the appearance of sylvan grottoes. The vast amount of

[4] A. Maiuri, *Boll. d'Arte*, vol. 8, 1928–1929, pp. 555–557; G. Pesce, *I rilievi dell'anfiteatro campano*, in *Studi e materiali del Museo dell'Impero Romano*, vol. 2, Rome, 1941 (reviewed by Squarciapino, *BMIR*, vol. 13, 1942, pp. 52–53); Crema, p. 436; Neppi Modona, *op. cit.*, p. 270; Frova, p. 67.

[5] Pesce establishes the date by a careful comparison with other buildings.

[6] Lugli (*Tecnica*, p. 680) mentions a use of rough stones set radially behind the arches to strengthen the concrete, but I do not know whether the practice was universal throughout the monument.

[7] Lugli (*ibid.*, p. 622) also lists the bricks as regional.

[8] *CIL*, vol. 10, no. 3832.

[9] T. Ashby, *PBSR*, vol. 5, 1910, pp. 339–341; Neppi Modona, *op. cit.*, p. 271.

[10] *CIL*, vol. 15 (1), no. 622; no. 1370 was also found at the site.

[11] He is credited also with restoring the amphitheater in Capua (*CIL*, vol. 10, nos. 3831, 3832, 5963) and Firmum Picenum (*ibid.*, no. 5353). The amphitheater at Luni has been judged Antonine; see Neppi Modona, *op. cit.*, p. 276.

[12] R. Bartocini, *Acc. P. Rend.*, vol. 33, 1960–1961, pp. 173–184.

[13] L. Morpurgo, *Not. sc.*, 1931, pp. 237–305; Libertini, *Teatro*, pp. 178–179; Crema, pp. 84, 428; Neppi Modona, *op. cit.*, p. 108.

[14] Lugli, *RIA*, vol. 7, 1940, p. 174.

[15] Lugli, *Tecnica*, p. 511.

[16] G. Lugli, *VII cong. st. archit.*, 1950 (published 1956), pp. 101–103; Crema, p. 142; Neppi Modona, *op. cit.*, pp. 98–99.

[17] *BMIR*, vol. 10, 1939, p. 79 with fig. 5.

[18] R. Bartoccini, *BMIR*, vol. 9, 1938; idem, *Dioniso*, vol. 5, 1935–1936, pp. 103–108; (cf. the résumé in *BMIR*, vol. 13, 1942, 64–65); Crema, p. 440; Neppi Modona, *op. cit.*, pp. 103–104, 265.

[19] C. Drago, *BMIR*, vol. 13, 1942, pp. 60–62; Crema, p. 440.

[20] *CIL*, vol. 5, nos. 534, 535.

[21] V. Scrinari, *Tergeste*, Rome 1951, pp. 79–81; Lugli, *Tecnica*, p. 654 pl. 192, 2; Crema, p. 416; Neppi Modona, *op. cit.*, p. 120.

[22] G. Moretti, *Not. sc.*, 1914, pp. 127–129; G. Monaco, *Forma It.*, Reg. I, vol. 1 (1), cols. 7–11; C. Carducci, *Not. sc.*, 1938, pp. 317–324; Crema, p. 197; Neppi Modona, *op. cit.*, pp. 116–118.

[23] Meomartini, *Benevento*, p. 77 with photos on pp. 38–40; R. Pane, *Not. sc.*, 1924, pp. 516–521; A. Maiuri, *Boll. d'Arte*, vol. 7, 1928–1929, pp. 557–559; Lugli, *Tecnica*, p. 597; Neppi Modona, *op. cit.*, p. 109.

marble found in the course of excavation attested the sumptuousness of the finished monument. The theater has been ascribed to the first half of the second century largely on the type of lettering in an inscription. The brick stamps would suggest to me a somewhat earlier date. The excavation was conducted merely by trenches and the site has been returned to agricultural production. The more conventional insets of reticulate in a brick frame ("*opus mixtum*") appear in a theater, circus, or gymnasium which serves as the foundation of a modern edifice at Anzio. Lugli ascribes it to the early years of the second century.[14] To the same period, in his judgment, belongs a restoration of the theater at Sessa Aurunca, also in "*opus mixtum*."[15]

With the exception of a band of three rows of brick in the radial walls of the theater at Catania,[16] the entire masonry was of blockwork or concrete faced with blockwork (*opus vittatum*). The façade of limestone blocks is of special interest for the lintel arch of stone, four courses below the impost of the arches. The piers had the usual pilasters for the apparent support of the entablature. The façade was keyed into the radial walls of concrete which were faced with the same kind of blocks less carefully squared, having the band of brick mentioned above. The *caementa* of the vaulting were of local volcanic material laid with care on the wooden centering, radially at the arches and horizontally in the intrados. The theater can be ascribed to the first half of the second century. At Teramo,[17] remains of a theater have been considered Hadrianic in spite of the rather crude arches of squarish blocks rather than the fitted voussoirs which had long been in vogue. Its façade was in squared-stone masonry. Even cruder masonry of squared stone and *opus incertum* has been reported from a theater at Lecce, which was partially hewn out of the native rock. The same materials were employed in the amphitheater[18] at this site. An inscription indicates that the amphitheater, though promised and possibly started in honor of Trajan, was not completed until the time of Hadrian.[19]

An inscription[20] seems to prove that the theater at Trieste[21] was built and dedicated by a public-spirited individual of the time of Trajan. There, insets of sandstone blocks were used with brick. The blocks, though varying greatly in length, were well squared and carefully laid; the bricks, to judge from the photograph, were dark red.

A typically northern method of construction was used for the theater at Libarna (Serravalle Scrivia),[22] which should probably be ascribed to the early years of the colony sent out by either Nerva or Trajan. The walls were faced with split river stones and reinforced by brick quoins and either single or double rows of brick. Brick relieving arches protected an earlier drain. Apsed rooms seem to have been inserted under the seats on the south side to prevent collapse, and an outer porticus of two stories added to preserve the decor. Original brick pilasters adorned the external wall. Marble concealed the apparent crudeness of the work.

Brick-faced concrete appears in other monuments of this kind. The theater at Benevento[23] shows a nucleus of river stones and mortar faced on the inside with bricks reinforced by bonding courses. The exterior was of travertine. Beneventum enjoyed a new prosperity under Trajan which may have produced the theater. Dr. Van Deman could not decide between a Trajanic and a Hadrianic date on the basis of construction alone.[24] Helvia Recina (modern Macerata) also has a theater with this type of facing.[25] According to Dr. Van Deman, the brickwork resembles closely that of the building near by, which has been identified as the Balneum Traiani. Hence she considered the two contemporaneous and therefore Trajanic.[26] Lugli ascribes the theater to this date or a little later. The brick-faced theater at Urbisaglia must have been built at about the same time.[27]

Most elegant of all is the brick-faced theater at Taormina,[28] which in its present state is entirely Roman. It is quite possible that an Augustan phase can be detected in an almost complete rebuilding, but I am convinced that the major part of the brickwork was not Augustan as Dr. Van Deman thought.[29] There is no definite evidence for dating the restoration. The bricks used were of local origin, some of them even bearing Greek stamps. They show so many different sizes and shapes that they suggest a re-use of material from many earlier structures. Although they range in thickness from 4 to 11 cm., few are thinner than 5 cm. or thicker than 8 cm. Triangles or approximate triangles prevail, though rectangles and squares occur with considerable frequency. The lengths show that the triangles were made from both *besales* and *sesquipedales*. Both these tiles, rendered wedge-shaped, are used to face arches; *bipedales* never, though the effect is sometimes gained by the use of two or three pieces symmetrically arranged to breakjoint. The bricks vary in color from yellow to red; the mortar is white, fine-grained, and compact. The walls of the lower part of the *cavea* were laid on a foundation course of large rectangular bricks arranged as headers. Bonding courses and relieving arches are used with a complete understanding of their function. At the *summa cavea*, a podium with niches alternately pedimented and lunetted supported a colonnade behind which there was a cross-vaulted corridor. A second passageway behind this was covered by a barrel vault resting on cornices composed of three rows of brick. There is considerable modern restoration. The competence with which the material is handled suggests a date in the Trajanic or possibly early Hadrianic period.[30] This is not the place for a wall-by-wall analysis, but the above résumé shows to what extent Roman methods of building had been adopted by local contractors. The little theater, or odeum, was also brick-faced, but was probably somewhat earlier. Scanty remains of a theater uncovered at Santa Maria Capua Vetere[31] show a brickwork so similar to that of the amphitheater—triangles (4 cm. thick) laid with mortar joints 1–2 cm. wide resting on a foundation course of *bipedales*—that it is also probably Hadrianic. According to A. de Franciscis, this was a restoration of an Augustan theater.[32] Parts of the theater at Ventimiglia[33] have also been assigned to the early second century.

ARCHES

By the time of Trajan, Rome apparently desired to add no territory to her vast domain. Wars were still being fought, but honorary arches were conferred upon the emperor for public benefits rather than triumphs with arms. The earliest (A.D. 102), at Pozzuoli, commemorated the completion of the Via Antiniana, the continuation of the Via Domitiana from Puteoli

[24] Unpublished note.

[25] Lugli, *op. cit.*, with pl. 172, 3.

[26] Unpublished note.

[27] Lugli, *op. cit.*, p. 597; Neppi Modona, *op. cit.*, p. 111.

[28] M. Santangelo, *Taormina e dintorni*, Rome 1940, pp. 35–57; Lugli, *op. cit.*, pp. 628–630; Crema, pp. 84, 416; Frova, p. 791; Neppi Modona, *op. cit.*, p. 98.

[29] I followed her judgment in *RC* I, p. 283.

[30] Lugli, *op. cit.*, p. 630.

[31] G. F. Carettoni, *Not. sc.*, 1943, pp. 149–154; Neppi Modona, *op. cit.*, pp. 105, 270.

[32] A. de Franciscis, *Not. sc.*, 1952, pp. 307–308.

[33] N. Lamboglia, *Liguria Romana*, Roma 1939, pp. 249; idem, *Il teatro romano e gli scavi di Ventimiglia*, Bordighera 1949; Crema, p. 94; Neppi Modona, *op. cit.*, pp. 118–119.

[34] H. Kähler, *Studies DMR* I, pp. 430–439, pls. 27–30; *idem, RE, Triumphbogen*, no. 18 a, col. 410. For the road, see below, p. 282.

[35] See below, pp. 282–284.

[36] The victory motive is there but subordinated to the general concept.

[37] See below, pp. 293–294.

[38] For the sculpture, see Strong, *Sc. rom.*, pp. 205–206. No trace of the arch has ever come to light.

[39] *CIL*, vol. 9, no. 4063.

[40] T. Ashby, *JRS*, vol. 11, 1921, p. 173; Martinori, *Via Flaminia*, p. 155; Kähler, *RE, Triumphbogen*, no. 9, col. 407.

[41] With Kähler, *RE, Triumphbogen*, cols. 485–486, compare fig. 14 (Beneventum) with fig. 11 (Titus); Crema, p. 441, fig. 554; Frova, pp. 68, 77, 79.

[42] The ends bore no sculpture.

[43] E. Petersen, *Röm. Mitt.*, vol. 7, 1892, pp. 239–264; A. von Domaszewski, *Jh. ö. arch. Inst.*, vol. 2, 1899, pp. 173–192; Meomartini, *Benevento*, pp. 100–108; Strong, *Sc. rom.*, pp. 191–201; Paribeni, *Optimus Princeps* II, pp. 255–264; C. Pietrangeli, *L'Arco di Traiano a Benevento: Documentario fotografico "Athenaeum,"* Novara 1947; P. Veyne, *Mél.*, vol. 72, 1960, pp. 191–219; O. Vessberg, *Skrifter*, vol. 22, 1962, pp. 159–164; F. J. Hassel, *Der Trajansbogen in Benevent. Ein Bauwerk des römischer Senats*, Mainz 1966.

[44] Walton (*MAAR*, vol. 4, 1924, p. 175, n. 1) notes traces of the *anelli* between the dentils, which are usually considered exclusively Domitianic.

[45] G. A. Snijder, *Jb. d. Inst.*, vol. 41, 1926, pp. 94–128.

to Neapolis;[34] the second (A.D. 114), at Benevento, the laying of the Via Traiana[35] from Beneventum to Brundisium;[36] the third (A.D. 115), the building of the harbor at Ancona.[37] Since honorary arches had long since reached their final form from the point of view of construction, Trajan's architect could concentrate on the sculptural decoration at Pozzuoli[38] and Benevento and on the effectiveness of the proportions at Ancona. An inscription mentions an arch at Carsulae;[39] an arch is still extant there which has been attributed to Trajan on the doubtful evidence of some coins.[40] Only the outline of the span remains; and it appears more Augustan than Trajanic. It was probably the north gate of the city rather than an honorary arch. We turn now to the two arches which are preserved: at Benevento, and at Ancona.

In architectural plan and general proportions the arch at Benevento resembles closely the Arch of Titus at Rome,[41] but it has a wealth of carving covering every available surface of the main façades[42] except the foundations of the pylons, which alone present smooth faces and simple moldings. This is not the place to enter into a discussion of the artistic value of the sculpture.[43] Suffice it to say, that the reliefs facing Rome dealt with benefactions bestowed upon the Capital, those on the opposite side with provincial administration, those in the passageways with events taking place at Beneventum itself—the sacrifices preceding the departure of the troops and a largesse to the children—whereas the small frieze depicted the anticipated (?) triumphal procession. The coffered barrel vault enclosed at the center a small relief of Victory bestowing a crown on the emperor. The victory motive appears again in the small friezes between the panels of the pylons, where winged figures in the act of slaying a bull stand in apposition with a censor between them. Winged victories bearing trophies adorn the spandrels toward the city, and river gods appear in the corresponding position on the other side. One has only to recall the many bridges on Trajan's Column to appreciate the appropriateness of this piece of imagery. The passage of time is signified by tiny figures of the seasons standing on miniature pedestals at the bottom of the spandrels, one for each. The keystones are console-shaped and decorated with draped figures. The channeled semicolumns, four for each face, have ornate composite capitals. The lines of the fasciae of the architrave, the moldings above the friezes, and the capping cornice[44] with its supporting consoles are all carved, though the carving lacks the richness of that of the Flavian period. The fasciae of the simulated voussoirs of the arches, on the other hand, are plain, though the soffit is carved. The actual voussoirs are not only carefully cut for the position which they were to occupy, but bear the carving of the spandrels. The attic, which was almost certainly an addition of the time of Hadrian,[45] continues in the same allegorical strain. On the side toward Rome, two panels separated by the inscription show Jupiter, flanked by Minerva and Juno and accompanied by other divinities, extending his thunderbolt toward Trajan, who, accompanied by Hadrian and lictors, was being received by Roma, the Penates, and the consuls as he was about to pass under an arch near the Temple of Jupiter Custos. The opposite side depicts Mesopotamia and her rivers doing obeisance to Trajan accompanied by Hadrian, while the divinities, Liber, Libera, Diana, and Silvanus stand before the emperor (broken off) on the other side of the inscription. The mixture of divine and human figures would seem to have been carried to excess. It will be noted at once that Hadrian is definitely presented as the heir.[46]

The arch[47] commemorating the completion of the harbor at Ancona[48] was skillfully fitted into a difficult environment. Since the space at the disposal of the architect was narrow, he was forced to depend on height to gain impressiveness. He had a secondary object in creating a landmark which should be visible to the ships coming in from the sea. Furthermore, he added to the apparent height by emphasizing the vertical at the expense of the horizontal members. Each angle column had its own pedestal, entablature, and pedestal-like projections in the attic. The columns flanking the archway carried the projection of the entablature on which the main inscription rested and formed the pedestal for the statuary in the center. The graceful capitals of the channeled Corinthian columns and the console-shaped keystones with their sculptured heads are the only carved decoration except for simple cornices and moldings. It is probable that the holes between the columns on the face bore the bronze prows of ships.[49] A line of holes on the seaward side of the attic presupposes some other bronze decoration. The quadriga[50] on top and the statues of Plotina and Marciana, one on each side of it, were also probably of bronze. The landward side of the attic bore the dedicatory inscription in bronze letters.[51] Both arches may well be the work of Apollodorus. A brick-faced arch spans the Via Traiana shortly before it enters Canusium.[52] It was not the city gate but stood in front of it perhaps as a memorial to the emperor who built the road.[53] Its broad single arch was faced with *bipedales* and outlined by a tile molding; its barrel vault was strengthened by a laddered reinforcement. The tile impost molding became a stringcourse emphasizing the central part, which was flanked by twin pilasters on each side. These seemed to uphold the attic, of which mere traces remain. The brickwork appeared somewhat later than the time of Trajan to me, but I have not been able to confirm the impression by measurements. Tradition has it that the brickwork was entirely concealed by marble of which nothing is left.

No remains are extant, to the best of my knowledge, for the rest of the second century in Italy. Inscriptional evidence tells of one arch erected at Falerone in the time of Hadrian[54] and of another on the mole at Pozzuoli under Antoninus Pius.[55]

BATHS

New public Baths were built in the second century in Rome and Ostia and of course elsewhere as well. Throughout Italy, when earlier Baths proved inadequate, they were enlarged; and, since Baths more than any other type of edifice were subject to damage from fire and water, most have been repaired more than once. Often not enough remains to show whether they were part of the original Bath, an enlargement, or a repair. No remains have been included here for which there is no evidence of the date.

The Baths of Pisa have long had a place in every discussion of Roman dome construction. In 1942–1943, five more rooms of these Baths (popularly known as "Bagno di Nerone") were uncovered.[56] Although there may have

[46] Beneventum had a secondary honorary arch, now known as Arco del Sagramento. It had a travertine socle, central arch faced with a double row of bricks, apparently somewhat interlocked, and side windows with a single row. It is hazardous to suggest a date. See Meomartini, *op. cit.*, pp. 43 (photo), 82; Kähler, *op. cit.*, no. 4 b, cols. 406–407.

[47] Kähler, *RE, Triumphbogen*, no. 1, col. 403; Moretti, *Ancona*, pp. 52–57; Paribeni, *Optimus Princeps* II, p. 245; Crema, p. 441, fig. 555; Frova, pp. 77–78.

[48] See below, pp. 293–294.

[49] Kähler's suggestion of garlands is not tenable to Moretti nor to me.

[50] Marks on the top prove that the central figure was a quadriga.

[51] *CIL*, vol. 9, no. 5894.

[52] N. Jacobone, *Ricerche sulla storia e topografia di Canosa antica*, Canosa 1905, pp. 46–48; T. Ashby, *PBSR*, vol. 8, 1916, p. 155; Kähler, *RE, Triumphbogen*, no. 7, col. 407.

[53] A. Pagenstecker (*Apulien*, Leipzig 1914, pp. 74–75) is surely wrong in considering it earlier than the Via Traiana. One other possible time for its erection would be to commemorate the elevation of the town to the Colonia Aurelia Augusta Pia in the time of Antoninus Pius (P. Romanelli, *Enc. it.*, vol. 8, p. 763).

[54] *CIL*, vol. 9, no. 5438; *RE, Triumphbogen*, no. 10, col. 407.

[55] *CIL*, vol. 10, no. 1641; *RE, loc. cit.*, no. 18 b, cols. 410–411.

[56] A. Minto, *BMIR*, vol. 13, 1942, p. 78; S. Aussant, *Arti*, vol. 5, 1942–1943, pp. 225–226. C. Lupi, *Nuovi studi sulle antiche terme pisane*, Pisa 1885, is still fundamental. N. Toscanelli, *Pisa nell'antichità*, Pisa 1933, vol. 2, pp. 594–601, has been somewhat invalidated by the latest excavations; Crema, p. 406.

[57] This is based on inscriptional evidence; see Lupi, *op. cit.*, p. 121 with fig. on p. 122.

[58] G. de Angelis d'Ossat, *III conv. st. archit.*, p. 246.

[59] Somewhat similar masonry occurs in an aqueduct serving San Giuliano, which has been ascribed to the second century. See Toscanelli, *op. cit.*, pp. 641–648.

[60] C. Roccatelli, *I cong. st. archit.*, pp. 47–48. Lupi (*op. cit.*, p. 139) believes that the dome is much later than the time of Antoninus Pius; but it would seem to me to belong to the same general period as the cupolas of Hadrian's Villa. See Rakob, *Röm. Mitt.*, vol. 68, 1961, p. 140.

[61] C. Avvolta, *Bull. Inst.*, 1829, p. 176; Cav. Manzi and Fossati, *ibid.*, pp. 197–199. Paribeni (*Optimus Princeps* II, p. 130) lists it among the public works of the time of Trajan, along with another Bath at Corfinium, known only from inscriptions (*CIL*, vol. 9, nos. 3152 and 3153).

[62] *CIL*, vol. 11 (1), no. 3366.

[63] M. E. Blake, *MAAR*, vol. 13, 1936, p. 150.

[64] Bastianelli, *Centumcellae*, p. 66.

[65] T. Ashby, *JRS*, vol. 11, 1921, p. 164; Pietrangeli, *Ocriculum*, pp. 67–71; Crema, pp. 339, 477; F. Rakob, *Röm. Mitt.*, vol. 68, 1961, pp. 114–149.

[66] M. E. Blake, *MAAR*, vol. 13, 1936, pp. 149–150.

been an earlier bathing establishment at the site, the main construction was probably Hadrianic with an addition of the time of Antoninus Pius.[57] Three of the rooms stood in such intimate relation to the octagonal room, which has been an object of speculation for many years, as to show conclusively that it was a *sudatio*, or *laconicum*. All three had hypocausts; and the other two were certainly *caldarium* and *tepidarium*. A conduit suitable for conducting heat to the octagonal room was found in the course of the excavation in addition to many fragments of hollow wall tubes. The concrete throughout was composed of an aggregate of a spongy local stone (*panchina*) and a mortar made with imported pozzolana.[58] The lower part of the walls was faced with bricks many of which were triangles. *Bipedales* formed the bottom course and a bonding course about a meter higher up. The upper part was faced with bands of three courses of *panchina* cut to brick size alternated with two rows of brick.[59] The octagonal room was rectangular on the outside and had the usual curved niches in the sides corresponding to the corners which were a little wider than the others. The pavilion vault rose in eight sections on the inside to an octagonal "eye," about two meters across.[60] As often in Roman cupolas the extrados is shallower than the intrados, and the octagonal form becomes a circle. Each section had a splayed window (72 cm. × 96 cm.) set perpendicularly. These windows were framed in brick. The concrete of the vaulting was the same as that in the core of the walls except that the *caementa* were somewhat larger. They were laid in regular rows. The Baths were lavishly decorated with marble.

Remains of a public Bath at Tarquinia came to light many years ago[61] which was said to be reminiscent of Hadrian's Villa near Tivoli. An inscription showed that they were restored by a public-spirited citizen, who has been identified as P. Tullius Varro.[62] It is not possible to tell whether walls faced with bichrome reticulate work belonged to this restoration or to the original edifice. A brick facing appeared in walls enclosing a room with a hypocaust. The Baths were richly decorated with black-and-white figure mosaics,[63] painted stucco, marble, and glass mosaic. Another inscription attests a restoration by a V. Petronius in the Antonine period. A bathing establishment at Civitavecchia[64] displaying walls faced with reticulate reinforced by brick bands may well have been Trajanic, though there is no clear evidence for dating.

What is still visible of the Baths at Otricoli (ancient Ocriculum)[65] arouses the hope that the site may some day be completely laid bare. Enough remains of an octagonal room to show that it had a pavilion cupola of the type which the Italians aptly call "*ad ombrello*." From this room came the elaborate polychrome mosaic now in the Sala Rotonda of the Vatican.[66] The core of the walls was composed of small pieces of tufa with a minimum amount of mortar. The walls themselves were faced with bricks averaging 3 cm. in thickness and 17 cm. in length, partly triangles and partly roughly broken to shape; the mortar joints were 1.7 cm. in width. Doors alternated with niches in the eight sides. These were covered with arches of *bipedales* in which every fourth or fifth one was whole to make a bond. Triangular pendentives of concrete made the transition from the octagon to the circle beneath a tile cornice which formed the apparent impost. Lunettes faced with brick filled the spaces beneath the curved sections of the cupola. The dome is not preserved high enough to reveal whether it had any other interesting features. The side walls were prolonged to make rooms, the level of which was at the height of the niches, suggesting the presence of hypocausts. These were probably all barrel-vaulted. There was in addition a circular room less well preserved, which also had a pavilion cupola. The Baths were a benefaction of L. Julius Julianus, but unfortunately there is no clear evidence for his dates. Pietrangeli ascribes them to the second century; Rakob,[67] to the time of Hadrian; Ashby, to the end of the second or the beginning of the third; Rivoira,[68] to Caracalla or Heliogabalus; Crema, to the Antonines; I favor an Antonine date, or possibly Severan. Terra-cotta plaques and wall mosaics indicate that a large public Bath at Aquileia[69] was built in the early years of the second century. It apparently yielded one large heated pool, but until it can be fully excavated, it is impossible to describe its arrangements or give a clear account of its original wall construction.

Only a large black-and-white mosaic of sea creatures,[70] real and imaginary, remains of what must have been a large public Bath in Mevania (modern Bevagna). The walls had been razed to the ground, but the mosaic, from the simplicity of the arrangement combined with the effectiveness of the individual figures, suggests a Hadrianic date for these Baths. Some pieces of a marble wall revetment also came to light. A sea-monster mosaic from Sassaferrato, now in the National Museum in Ancona, has been ascribed on stylistic grounds to the Antonine period.[71] Presumably, it came from a public Bath but no information is available as to its provenience. Possibly to be ascribed to the late second century is a mosaic of sea creatures from Falerone,[72] also in the Ancona museum. The building from which it came is also unknown.

South Italy also supplies its quota. The two chief Baths at Terracina yield little of value to our knowledge of Baths as such; but they do show a succession of methods of wall facing which can be reduced to a relative chronology important to an analysis of the construction in the region in which they occur. The chronology is Lugli's. In the Maritime Baths[73] four phases are discernible: 1st, reticulate (early Empire); 2nd, reticulate with brick bands (Flavian); 3rd, yellow bricks, 3.5–4 cm. thick, with bonding courses (Trajan); 4th, limestone reticulate with quoins of brick and tufa (Hadrian). The Neptune Baths[74] show a wider range: 1st, variegated reticulate (mid-1st); 2nd, dark yellow triangles, 3.5–4.2 cm. thick, with arches of *bipedales* (Flavian-Trajan); 3rd, reticulate with bands of yellow brick apparently not triangles and a terminal row of limestone blocks (Trajan-Hadrian); 4th, crude reticulate with two rows of broken tile (Antonine); 5th, block-and-brick (third century).

Tantalizing remains of what may have been a public Bath facing what was probably the *cardo maximus* of ancient Capua (S. Maria Capua Vetere)[75] arouse hopes that the establishment may eventually be laid bare. Black-and-white mosaics[76] were found and bits of ceiling frescoes. De Franciscis who made the report would ascribe the edifice to the second century.

In the Baths at Sepino (Saepinum)[77] hollow tiles (42 cm. × 19 cm. × 13 cm.) were used along with more ordinary piers in a hypocaust which were larger than those employed in the walls. Possibly, they represent a re-use of

[67] Rakob, *op. cit.*, p. 141.

[68] Rivoira-Rushforth, p. 134.

[69] G. Brusin, *Not. sc.*, 1929, pp. 109–138.

[70] M. E. Blake, *MAAR*, vol. 13, 1936, pp. 150–151; C. Pietrangeli, *Mevania*, pp. 81–84.

[71] Buccolini, *Not. sc.*, 1890, p. 348; G. Moretti, *Not. sc.*, 1925, pp. 110–113; Blake, *op. cit.*, pp. 151–152.

[72] Moretti, *op. cit.*, pp. 127–129; Blake, *op. cit.*, p. 152.

[73] Lugli, *Forma It.*, Reg. I, vol. 1 (1), cols. 135–139, no. 82; Crema, p. 406.

[74] Lugli, *op. cit.*, cols. 107–112, no. 66.

[75] A. de Franciscis, *Not. sc.*, 1957, p. 362.

[76] Photos from the Museo Nazionale di Napoli, nos. 3916 and 3917.

[77] A. Fulvio, *Not. sc.*, 1878, pp. 374–377.

[78] P. Orsi, *Not. sc.*, 1922, pp. 156–161.

[79] It shows a hexagonal hall with a semicircular exedra on three sides and circular *laconica* on four with an entrance on the eighth.

[80] Orsi, *op. cit.*, pp. 161–166.

[81] *Ibid.*, p. 167.

[82] N. Putortì, *Not. sc.*, 1924, pp. 91–92; M. E. Blake, *MAAR*, vol. 13, 1936, p. 165.

[83] P. Orsi, *Not. sc.*, 1896, pp. 107–113.

[84] G. Rizza, *Not. sc.*, 1949, pp. 190–192.

[85] B. Pace, *Not. sc.*, 1946, pp. 162–174.

[86] I. Sgobbo, *I cong. st. rom.*, vol. 1, pp. 186–194.

[87] There has been no final official publication. This account is based on the following: Maiuri, *Campi Flegréi*, pp. 71–74; *idem*, *Boll. d'Arte*, vol. 36, 1951, pp. 359–362; I. Sgobbo, *III cong. st. rom.*, vol. 1, pp. 302–304; G. de Angelis d'Ossat, *BMIR*, vol. 12, 1941, pp. 121–132; Crema, pp. 339, 413, 478, figs. 613–614; F. Rakob, *Röm. Mitt.*, vol. 68, 1961, pp. 114–149.

[88] Another local name is the "Il Truglio."

earlier material. If so, it is possible that the Baths belong to the Antonine period when Saepinum became a municipium.

Rhegium (Reggio Calabria) was well supplied with Baths.[78] An inscription seems to indicate that Hadrian restored a Bath, the remains of which were uncovered when the Prefecture was built in 1922. A fantastic plan made in 1810[79] does not inspire confidence. In 1922 it was possible to determine that the Baths had sustained a radical restoration, possibly after an earthquake. This complicates the interpretation of the sketchy plan which could be made at that time. The mosaic patterns reported from a second Bath[80] brought to light under the Istituto Tecnico in 1913 look Hadrianic. They probably belong to a restoration, which may have been far-reaching. Possibly a part of the same Baths[81] was uncovered when the foundations of the Ufficio d'Igiene were laid. For these three Baths, information is not sufficient for our purpose. In 1924, a black-and-white athlete mosaic was uncovered between the Fata Morgana and Marina Alta, belonging to a Bath[82] for which there is no further information. The subject was popular in the late second century and the third century.

A passing reference must suffice for what must have been a rather elaborate Bath at Tarentum[83] erected or extensively restored in the second century, since even in 1896 the remains had already been sacrificed to the needs of the modern city.

It is interesting to note that at Centuripe (Sicily),[84] bricks 7–8 cm. thick were still being used in Baths of the second century, if the official dating is correct. Moreover, the bricks were either 30–40 cm. square or rectangles of the same length but half the width. At Comiso (Sicily),[85] sumptuous Baths were apparently erected in the second century only to be completely destroyed in the fifth and rebuilt. The walls belong to the restoration, but a black-and-white sea-monster mosaic at a lower level belonged to the earlier Baths. It was rather crudely executed by a local craftsman.

THERAPEUTIC BATHS

Undoubtedly, the earliest therapeutic Baths were erected on the hillsides about the Bay of Baiae and elsewhere in the vicinity where there were hot mineral springs and exhalations of vapor. Sgobbo[86] has shown to what lengths the Romans went to pipe these volcanic benefactions to a place where they could benefit ailing humanity. The bathing establishment, of which the "Tempio di Mercurio" was a part, shows how effectively a plan of several levels had been worked out in the Augustan era. An aqueduct and great cisterns at the top of the hill supplied the ordinary water necessary for the filling of open pools and the functioning of nymphaea and fountains, whereas conduits brought the mineral water or vapor to the chambers prepared to receive them. Our concern is, however, with the establishments which were added in the second century.

Recent excavations[87] have proved that the so-called Tempio di Venere[88] was part of a large bathing establishment. It is not quite clear whether it was merely a grand entrance or a nymphaeum with a pool of healing mineral water. It was not an isolated building, but not enough of the surrounding rooms is preserved to show whether the main part of the Baths was located here or at the next higher level, where an artificial terrace was built for a group of rooms against the hill. The terrace terminated at the north end in an apse. The focal point of the rooms on the west was an apsed hall given over entirely to a large pool. The apse was covered with a semi-cupola. On each side, there was a hall having alcoves to give it the form of a Greek cross. Two rooms to the north which were beautifully decorated with stucco work were later turned into cisterns. Some of the small rooms here and higher up would have been suitable for *laconica*. A combination ramp and stairway at the north gave access to various levels above. Large cisterns at the top supplied ordinary water for non-therapeutic uses. The walls in this upper part were faced with reticulate having brick reinforcements. There was nothing here to prepare the mind for the originality displayed in the "Tempio di Venere" below. The main entrance to the "Tempio" was in a deep apse flanked by a shallow apse on each side from a street along the shore, but there were secondary entrances through the niches and at the rear toward the hill. The lower part exhibited the common plan of a circle (dia. 6.3 m.) within a square with semicircular niches in the corners; the upper part, though retaining the circular interior, had an octagonal exterior with a large window in each face. This is said to be the earliest use of the windowed drum. A pilaster strengthened each corner, and these pilasters were slightly convex and had drain pipes embedded in them. The windows were topped by segmental arches of tile. There were corbels below the windows for the support of a balcony.[89] The hall was covered by a pavilion cupola in which curved sections were alternated with flat ones, sixteen in all. The curved sections rose from the window arches, the flat ones from a space lower down so that there was no continuous impost. Not enough of the cupola remains to show whether or not it had the usual "eye." The structure was of concrete throughout, composed of an aggregate of the local yellow tufa in a pozzolana mortar. The entire walling inside and for most of the outside was faced with brick. Above the window arches the outside facing changed to reticulate (tesserae 7.5–8 cm. per side) with brick edges and bonding bands of three or four rows of brick. The bricks, brick red in color, were made from *besales* cut diagonally. Whereas the length was fairly constant (23 cm.), the width varied from 2.5 to 3.5 cm., but the difference was accurately compensated for by the width of the mortar. There were no bonding courses as such, but a row of larger tiles marked the height of the impost of the inner arches on the side toward the sea, and unusually large tiles (80 cm. × 54 cm.) were used in relieving arches under the windows. The interior was faced with marble up to the windows but was covered with stucco for the rest of the way. Remains of stucco, cut by re-entrant bands for decoration, appear on the outside. There has been considerable controversy over the date of the structure.[90] Since it shows no damage from the earthquake of A.D. 62, it was presumably built after that time. Similar innovations appear in the Villa Adriana near Tivoli and in other Hadrianic buildings. Triangular bricks are not unknown though they are usually somewhat wider.[91] There are no brick stamps. A Hadrianic date for this structure and in fact for the whole establishment is plausible.

[89] Maiuri (*op. cit.*, p. 74) conjectures that there was an inner balcony at this point. For the windowed drum in the Temple of Apollo in the Accademia at Hadrian's Villa, also said to be the first example, see above, p. 252 and fn. 115.

[90] Sgobbo ascribed it to the middle of the first century; Maiuri first favored a Neronian date but was won over to the Hadrianic date proposed by de Angelis d'Ossat.

[91] There is no reason for believing that these bricks came from Roman yards and would adhere to Roman measurements.

[92] Sgobbo, *III cong. st. rom.*, vol. 1, pp. 301–302.

[93] Maiuri, *Campi Flegréi*, pp. 66–67; Sgobbo, *op. cit.*, p. 308; Crema, pp. 336, 413, figs. 391–392. Dr. Van Deman reported signs of an earlier period with tufa quoins and bonding courses reinforcing the reticulate.

[94] Maiuri, *op. cit.*, pp. 142–144; de Angelis d'Ossat, *BMIR*, vol. 12, 1941, p. 123; Crema, pp. 339, 413, fig. 393; Rakob, *Röm. Mitt.*, vol. 68, 1961, pp. 133–149.

[95] Maiuri considers it earlier in the above publication, but has since been won over to De Angelis's dating for the "tempio di Venere." Dr. Van Deman (unpublished notes) ascribes it to the late second century. Rakob considers it Antonine.

[96] V. Macchioro, *Mon. ant.*, vol. 21, 1912, cols. 225–284 (summarized in *AJA*, vol. 18, 1914, pp. 232–233); idem, *Vie d'Italia*, vol. 31, 1915, pp. 525–532; Crema, p. 406.

[97] E. Gábrici, *Not. sc.*, 1908, pp. 399–415.

North of the Terme di Venere there was a second bathing establishment[92] which goes by the name Acqua della Rogna. It was very tastefully adapted to three terraces: a theater nymphaeum at the top with a terrace for seats and a circular pool in the center of the orchestra, an ambulatory supported by stout vaults (34.8 × 28.6 m.) in the center, and a vast pool at the bottom. An aqueduct at the top brought water to large cisterns at the sides of the nymphaeum whence it could be distributed to pools and supernumerary fountains. There were apparently rooms enclosing the basin. Some of the walls, at any rate, were faced with reticulate.

At Baiae, another "*truglio*" known as "Tempio di Diana"[93] served the same purpose for a second bathing establishment as the "Tempio di Venere" did for the one just described. There are traces of five levels here also, though the top one did not reach the summit of the hill; but they have not been set free from later buildings. The great octagonal hall, of which merely a half is preserved, is a conspicuous landmark. The interior was circular (dia. 29.5 m.) with a niche alternately curved and rectangular corresponding to each of the eight sides under a large window. The walls were faced with block-and-brick work, in which two rows of brick alternate with one of blocks. Only half of the cupola remains to show that it was higher than normal and that the thickness decreased toward the top where there is no evidence of an "eye." This establishment may well have been Antonine.

Similar in construction and in general plan to the "Tempio di Venere" is the "Tempio di Apollo" on the shores of Lake Avernus.[94] It was also part of a large establishment of which only traces remain. Its entire plan consisted of a circle within an octagon, and like the "Tempio di Diana" had curvilinear niches alternating with rectangular ones under the arched windows of the second story. There seems to have been an inner and an outer balcony at the second-story level. The dome is mostly gone but presents no discernible peculiarities. The walls were brick-faced, but a semicircular corridor at the rear for the circulation of the hot vapor shows a facing of reticulate and brick. The "Tempio di Apollo" was nearly contemporaneous with the "Tempio di Venere."[95]

The extraordinary Baths at Agnano[96] should probably be ascribed to the time of Hadrian, at least in their original state. They consisted of a series of rooms of different shapes—circular, semicircular, apsed, hexagonal, and pentagonal—only one of which was connected with a furnace for artificial heating. The rest were warmed by the circulation of the exhalations of the volcanic region in which the Baths were situated. A rather elaborate water system proves that they were not merely vapor baths. The walls were of concrete faced with a regular reticulate of tufa reinforced with quoins of both tufa and tile and with brick pilasters and relieving arches. Some walls were brick-faced. The part containing the cold pools shows a rougher reticulate with a greater use of blocks, and appears somewhat later than the rest. Since these therapeutic Baths were active for many years in one form or another, there were of necessity many modifications.

Springs of mineral water in the vicinity led to the erection of an extensive bathing establishment at Teanum Sidicinum (modern Teano).[97] It was only partially excavated but has yielded a *frigidarium, tepidarium, sudatio* or *laconicum,* and a number of other rooms devoted to the amenities of the typical Roman Bath. The heated rooms had the usual hypocaust and double wall. The ground plan, in so far as revealed, shows only three or four apses to relieve the monotony of straight lines. The walls were made of irregular pieces of limestone held together by mortar and faced with small irregular blocks of the same limestone; the vaults were of solid concrete with no indication of any other form than the barrel vault. Pavements and wall revetments were of marble, but fewer varieties are reported than from the great imperial Baths; and the patterns in the sectile floors were simpler. Frescoed walls, stuccoed ceilings,[98] and the number of statues found attest the elegance that could be achieved in a prosperous provincial town. The original phase of the Baths was ascribed by the excavator to the second century.

Brick stamps found at the site and a lead pipe with the inscription AELIAE CRIS(pinae) prove that Baths were either erected at Aquae Albulae[99] in the time of Hadrian to take advantage of the sulphurous springs or extensively enlarged. The method of construction was also adjudged Hadrianic. Marble pavements, columns of verde antico, and numerous statues removed from them attest their elegance. Borsari speaks of conspicuous remains in his day.

An impressive *caldarium* was the first step in converting a small therapeutic Bath of the Republican period at Aquae Tauri[100] near Civitavecchia into an elaborate imperial bathing establishment.[101] It is possible that the work was started under Trajan, but, if so, it was apparently soon suspended as the walls yielded Hadrianic stamps. The Republican rooms were adapted to other uses, and very shortly other rooms were erected at the south. Niches on the outside of the south wall of the *caldarium* corresponding to those on the outside on the north prove that the *caldarium* was the only addition for a time. A deep pool lined with white marble practically filled the large hall[102] and made the healing water from warm springs available to a number of bathers at the same time. The floor of the pool was suspended, according to Bastianelli, more for insulation than the circulation of warm air, though the evidence of three furnaces and hollow wall-tubes proves that heat was needed to maintain the pool at an even temperature.[103] The walls show Hadrianic masonry at its best. The core, composed of a fine aggregate in a compact mortar of pozzolana and lime, was faced with triangles. There were bonding courses. The well-preserved lofty east wall was pierced with windows in two registers—the lower three were covered with depressed arches, the upper three, a tall one in the center, were fitted into the space beneath an enormous relieving arch. The side ones had slightly curved lintels. Large windows in the north and originally in the south wall brought additional light. Pieces of rather thick greenish glass[104] found in the course of the excavation show that all the windows were glazed to prevent the dispersal of heat. The ceiling was cross-vaulted. The hall was beautifully decorated. Curved niches provided places for statuary; rectangular niches were framed in columns of colored marble having Ionic capitals and no doubt supporting entablatures. The walls have marble socles, and the ceiling, beautiful coffered stucco work. The addition on the south furnished all the usual amenities of a well-appointed Bath, with the possible exception of the *sudatio,* or *laconi-*

[98] Some of the frescoes and stucco work seem to have come from a later renovation.

[99] L. Borsari, *Not. sc.,* 1902, pp. 111–113; T. Ashby, *PBSR,* vol. 3, 1906, pp. 117–119.

[100] R. Mengarelli, *Not. sc.,* 1923, pp. 321–348; S. Bastianelli, *Not. sc.,* 1933, pp. 398–421; idem, *Not. sc.,* 1942, pp. 325–352; idem, *Centum-cellae,* pp. 67–82.

[101] Mengarelli, *BMIR,* vol. 13, 1943, p. 181 n. 1.

[102] Dimensions: 23 m. × 10.7 m.

[103] At first, Bastianelli was loath to accept the idea that there was any artificial heating.

[104] The glass was set in wooden frames which were covered with lead foil at least in a late period.

[105] Dimensions: 11.1 m. × 10.22 m.

[106] This is deduced from the lack of incrustation elsewhere.

[107] Casale Castagnola near Centumcellae yielded a bathing establishment near some sulphurous springs; but there is no evidence for dating (Bastianelli, Centumcellae, pp. 61–62).

[108] C. Zei, Boll. d'Arte, vol. 11, 1917, pp. 155–170; A. Gargana, BMIR, vol. 4, 1935, pp. 3–10.

[109] Lugli, Tecnica, p. 604; F. Rakob (Röm. Mitt., vol. 68, 1961, p. 140) favors a Hadrianic date for a part of this structure.

[110] L. Borsari, Not. sc., 1893, pp. 330–331.

[111] One Hadrianic stamp was found in the cover of a drain.

[112] See above, p. 11.

[113] See above, p. 145.

[114] Pliny, Epist., 4, 1; 9, 39.

[115] Ibid., 10, 8.

[116] Pietrangeli, Mevania, p. 71; Crema, p. 382.

[117] CIL, vol. 14, no. 2795.

cum. The rooms were logically arranged but not according to any stereotyped plan. Stairs at the southeast corner led to a large upper room[105] with terraces on the east and south. Two rooms stood at the west of it at a lower level. Whether there were any more rooms in this unit is not clear. The columns of the Republican caldarium were encased in piers apparently to support a terrace at the northwest corner, but there is no evidence how access to it was accomplished. Heating arrangements were well thought out. As in Hadrian's Villa near Tivoli, they were concealed by barrel-vaulted service corridors at a lower level on the outside. One praefurnium penetrated within the body of the structure from the east corridor to give more direct heat to two of the rooms. In fact, conduits seem to have conducted the hot air to the center of each room for distribution. Dressing rooms on the west had their own service corridor. Only the furnace for the tepidarium has yet to be uncovered. Mineral water from hot springs was used only in the caldarium;[106] ordinary water from several sources was piped to a circular distributing reservoir on the east side. Conduits had brick walls and roofs made of bipedales set "a capanna." The south annex was as lavishly decorated with marble as the caldarium. Practically every colored marble known to the Roman was pressed into service for pavements and wall revetments.[107]

Of the dozen or so Baths erected at Viterbo[108] to take advantage of the mineral springs in the locality, one, at any rate, the Terme del Bacucco, has been ascribed to A.D. 113–115.[109] Not enough has been preserved of the others for an exact chronology. Like all Baths, they probably had several phases. Reticulate broken by brick bands was the favored facing. Some of them may have been erected in the second century.

Borsari implies rather than states that Baths found at Leprignano[110] were erected in the second century.[111] The walls, which were brick-faced, were nearly razed to the ground. The Baths were apparently built at this spot to take advantage of springs of ferruginous water.

TEMPLES AND SANCTUARIES

Trajan apparently did not bestow a new Capitolium on any community at all in Italy. He commemorated on coins the erection of only two temples in Rome.[112] At Ostia he caused a restoration of the Temple of Hercules when he had the level raised in its vicinity.[113] He was not responsible so far as I know for temples elsewhere on the Peninsula. Pliny the Younger had an ancient temple of Ceres at Tifernum Tiberinum rebuilt on a larger scale and lavishly decorated.[114] Whether he ever actually erected the temple in which he proposed to place the statues of the emperors[115] is open to question.

Hadrian, whose benefactions to Rome and Ostia have been described, may have given Mevania (Bevagnia) in Umbria a temple.[116] The walls of the cella, in block and brick, have been judged Hadrianic.

CURIA

In an inscription of A.D. 140 from Gabii[117] recording the dedication of a shrine to Comitia Augusta, mention is made of the Curia Aelia Augusta.

The name implies that Hadrian built or less probably restored the Curia at that site. Many years ago a whole area was uncovered, identified as the Forum with the Curia, the shrine, and various other rooms adjoining it, and completely covered over again so that our only knowledge of it comes from a brief account and plan given by Visconti.[118] It looks like a well-integrated plan of contemporary or nearly contemporary buildings. The Forum opened directly upon the Via Praenestina. On the other three sides, there was a colonnade of Doric columns on a low wall with a terrace above. Semicircular niches with pedestals for statues alternated with doors to adjacent rooms along the side. Five openings apparently originally[119] gave access on an equal number of chambers at the rear, the central one of which was the Curia. Though the Curia seems to have taken the conventional form of a temple, it faced outward, though it could be entered by a back door from the Forum. The shrine to Domitia was on the upper right-hand corner. The whole layout appeals to me as Hadrianic, though there is of course no proof.

Recent excavations at Alba Fucens[120] have revealed that in the period of Trajan the sanctuary of Hercules received attention. The portico of the sacred area was modified as a part of a reconstruction which affected the center of the town, including the basilica and its environs.[121] The temple of the god apparently was embellished with a group of statues in the period of Hadrian or soon thereafter. These changes, although important for the history of the sanctuary and the development of the town, are not significant for the present study.

Julius Capitolinus[122] attributes to Antoninus Pius *templa Lanuviana*. A fragmentary inscription, (traia)NI PAR(thici), found at Lanuvium, may allude to his gifts to the citizens. Walls of a temple area there are probably not Antonine, as Bendinelli thought,[123] but first century.[124]

PORTICOES

An extraordinarily fine entablature[125] has been recovered from a late fortification tower at Aquileia and remounted on columns so that its beauty can be fully appreciated. Since it is too long for the pronaos of a temple, it probably decorated an important porticus. Both sides were treated with equal care; and the underside of each block had its own carving between the supporting columns. Stylistic characteristics suggest a Trajanic date for the monument, of which nothing further is known. Possibly it was a porticus of this type that Calpurnius Fabatus, the grandfather-in-law of Pliny the Younger erected at Comum (Como) as a memorial to himself and his son.[126] Pliny himself had built at his expense a porticus at Tifernum Tiberinum to shelter those who came to take part in the great annual festival at the Temple of Ceres.[127] No remains of these are left for study.

ENGINEERING WORKS

Of the five emperors whose reigns spanned the second century, only Trajan contributed much to Italy in the way of engineering monuments. He brought a new aqueduct to Rome and added a new arterial highway to

[118] E. Q. Visconti, *Monumenti Gabini della Pinciana*, Milan 1835, pp. 18–19, with pl. 1, fig. C. See also T. Ashby, *PBSR*, vol. 1, 1902, pp. 185–186; G. Pinza, *Bull. Com.*, vol. 3, 1903, pp. 327–330.

[119] The plan seems to have been modified somewhat in the upper left hand corner.

[120] F. de Visscher, J. Mertens, and J. Ch. Balty, *Mon. ant.*, vol. 46, 1963, cols. 333–396.

[121] J. Mertens, *Acc. L. Mem.*, ser. 8, vol. 5, 1953, pp. 171–194.

[122] Julius Capitolinus, *SHA*, *Antoninus Pius*, 8, 3.

[123] G. Bendinelli, *Mon. ant.*, vol. 27, 1922, col. 296.

[124] M. Cagiano de Azevedo, *Acc. P. Mem.*, vol. 5, 1941, pp. 9–11.

[125] G. Brusin, *Gli scavi di A.*, pp. 99–100; idem, *Aquileia e Grado*, pp. 100–101.

[126] Pliny, *Epist.*, 5, 11.

[127] *Ibid.*, 9, 39.

[1] Julius Capitolinus, *SHA*, *Marcus Antoninus*, 11, 5.

[2] Van Deman, *Aqueducts*, pp. 15–17.

[3] *Ibid.*, pp. 274–275; 326–327.

[4] Tesserae, 7–8 cm. per side.

[5] Bricks, 3–4 cm. × 20–27 cm.

[6] Horizontal joints, 1.3–1.6 cm.; vertical, 1 cm.

[7] Frontinus, *De Aquis*, 2, 87.

[8] Van Deman, *op. cit.*, pp. 6–8, 143. Ashby (*Aqueducts*, p. 156) considers the reservoir Severan.

[9] Van Deman, *op. cit.*, pp. 184–186.

[10] Van Deman, *Aqueducts*, pp. 331–334; Ashby, *Aqueducts*, pp. 299–307; Nash I, pp. 52–54.

the Roman road system, besides modifying and extending some that were already in existence; but his main service was in building new ports at Portus and Centumcellae and reorganizing those of Terracina, Ancona, and perhaps Rimini. Like the emperors who followed him he was obligated to keep all existing facilities in good repair. Hadrian built one new road from Aquileia to Ponte di Isonzo; Antoninus Pius paid especial attention to the ports and seems to have converted the embankments of Trajan at Terracina into a true harbor; Marcus Aurelius according to Julius Capitolinus[1] maintained *vias urbis et itinera* with special care, but in general it was the maintenance of what had already been constructed by others that was the forte of Trajan's successors at least so far as Italy was concerned.

TRAJAN

AQUEDUCTS, RESERVOIRS, AND EMISSARIUM

Rome was already well furnished with water and so it is not strange that Trajan's interest in the aqueducts lay more in the administration of the water supply than in the construction.[2] He inherited from Nerva an able administrator in the person of Sextus Julius Frontinus whose work on the aqueducts is too well known to require comment. To him must be attributed certain changes to improve the supply from the existing aqueducts. Since the water of the Anio Novus was not up to the standard set by him, he had the intake moved from the forty-second milestone of the Via Sublacensis to the second of Nero's lakes near Subiaco,[3] which then served as a great clearing tank for the aqueduct. Some walls connected with the sluices clearly belong to this change. They consist of a coarse concrete core composed of small *caementa* of local limestone laid in rough rows in a good mortar of clean lime and dark gray pozzolana and a facing of coarse reticulate[4] made of the same limestone broken by rows of dark red triangular bricks of local manufacture.[5] The joints[6] are fairly close. Some rock-cut channels with rounded roofs belong to this period. Trajan's attention was apparently called to the fact that the Aventine had not been adequately provided with water, since the earlier branch of the Marcia leading to it was rendered unusable by Nero's changes.[7] There are no sure remains of this benefaction with the possible exception of a large reservoir of five vaulted chambers, the so-called Piscina Publica, and a few fragmentary walls and arches under the former Castello dei Cesari.[8] These have a facing of bricks made from roof tiles. The restoration of water to the Aventine was no doubt largely responsible for its transformation into an aristocratic residential section. A small reservoir[9] made of concrete lined with brick uncovered in 1720 in the slope above San Cosimato may have been added to the Alsietina to save the water from the Naumachia for the use of nearby gardens by Trajan at the time when the Aqua Traiana was being built. This was the one new aqueduct brought to Rome in the second century.

Aqua Traiana

The Aqua Traiana[10] was built primarily to supply the Trastevere region with wholesome water, though it also had a secondary purpose as we shall see. Its sources were above Lake Bracciano. The course, which was, for the most part, slightly below the level of the ground, presented a few difficulties. Not far from the beginning, there was a clearing tank of brick-faced concrete, which may have been original. It is no longer in existence. Only one stream, the Galera (modern Fosso di Cesano) had to be spanned. A line of low arches at either side led to one or two arches over the river proper. Only a few courses of cut stone with the remains of a pier of brick-faced concrete are left today. The bricks are broken roof tiles (3.5–4 cm. × 25–27 cm.). In general, the construction follows as closely the type prevalent in Rome as local conditions would permit. Dr. Van Deman describes the concrete as "of superior quality, of medium fine texture and homogeneous in composition." Local aggregate was used, either selce or tufa, which in the neighborhood of Rome came from the Monte Verde quarries. The *caementa* in the walls were of medium size and laid in regular rows, whereas those of the foundations and vaults were somewhat larger and laid without order; the mortar also doubtless differed in accordance with the kind of pozzolana employed, but near Rome was of the characteristic Trajanic type composed of well-screened, well-washed, red pozzolana in a white lime. The outer facing where visible is regularly of reticulate with bands of three to six rows of brick. The stones used in the tesserae correspond to those employed as aggregate. The size of the tesserae differed somewhat from section to section.[11] The bricks were made from broken roof tiles, which are dark red, even in texture, and well fired.[12] They present sawed fronts. In one case at least there is a cornice of two or three rows of tiles. The inner facing, wherever it can be seen, is of reticulate alone of somewhat less careful workmanship. The arch facings are of single semicircles of *bipedales* broken in half and reduced to wedge shape before being used, except that every fifth one was a whole tile to make a better bond. These *bipedales* are coarser in texture than the roof tiles and light red or reddish yellow instead of dark red. This aqueduct had its terminal basin where the Villa Spada stands today. Coins[13] struck in A.D. 109 at the command of the Senate doubtless give its general appearance, a "river god" reclining in a grotto. The legend gives the name Aqua Traiana. A terminal *cippus* of A.D. 108/9 confirms the date.[14] The Fasti Ostienses[15] in recording the events of A.D. 109 describe the aqueduct as supplying water to every part of the city. It is not without significance that its inauguration is here reported as two days after that of the Baths of Trajan, for a lead pipe supplying the Baths came to light in 1935 marked THERM(ae) TRAIAN(i) and AQ(ua) TR(aiana).[16] It is exceedingly unlikely that it was the only source of water for such enormous Baths.

Other Aqueducts

New sources of water had to be found for communities which had come into prominence during the reign of Trajan. The remains of piers faced with brick, walls with reticulate, and vents with brick and reticulate belonging to an aqueduct which brought water to Centumcellae (Civitavecchia)[17] have been uncovered from time to time. The water was collected in a reservoir and then piped to all parts of the city. In like manner, Trajan may have been responsible for planning and perhaps even starting the aqueduct

[11] The range is 6.5–8 cm. with the selce tesserae larger and more irregular than the others.

[12] The normal size 3.3–3.8 cm.; but thicker ones are found.

[13] Cohen, vol. 2, Trajan, nos. 20–22; *BMC, Emp.*, vol. 3, Trajan, nos. 873–876, pl. 33, fig. 3, 975–976, pl. 38, fig. 5, 1008, pl. 40, fig. 4; Strack, *Reichsprägung*, vol. 1, pp. 192–194, pl. 7, fig. 417.

[14] *CIL*, vol. 6 (1), no. 1260; cf. 31567, (vol. 11, no. 3793).

[15] G. Calza, *Not. sc.*, 1932, pp. 188–205; Degrassi, *Fasti O.*, no. 22, pp. 198–199, 200–201; H. Bloch, *AJA*, vol. 48, 1944, pp. 337–341.

[16] A. M. Colini, *Bull. Com.*, vol. 66, 1938, pp. 244–245.

[17] S. Bastianelli, *Not. sc.*, 1940, p. 196; idem, *Centumcellae*, p. 45. The date is furnished by an inscribed water pipe. See below, p. 292.

[18] For the aqueduct, see below, pp. 279–280.

[19] *CIL*, vol. 11 (1), no. 3003.

[20] G. Calza, *Not. sc.*, 1932, p. 192; Degrassi, *Fasti cons.*, p. 33. See also Paribeni, *Optimus Princeps* II, p. 130.

[21] See Blake, *RC* II, pp. 134–138.

[22] G. Lugli, *Bull. Com.*, vol. 42, 1914, p. 268; *idem, Bull. Com.*, vol. 47, 1919, pp. 187–195. Brick stamps (*CIL*, vol. 15 (1), nos. 637, 1097, 1356, 1449, 2273) prove the date to have been Trajanic or early Hadrianic.

[23] Al. Doboși, *Eph. daco.*, vol. 6, 1935, pp. 356–357.

[24] See Blake, *op. cit.*, pp. 84–85.

[25] Brissé and de Rotrou, *Lac Fucino*, pp. 44–45. See below, p. 279.

[26] *CIL*, vol. 9, no. 3915.

carrying water from Valle dell'Amasena to Terracina[18] which is attributed to Antoninus Pius by Julius Capitolinus. Inscriptional evidence[19] proves that a certain Mummius Niger Valerius Vegetus, probably the Q. Valerius Vegetus who was consul in A.D. 112,[20] built an aqueduct for Viterbo. These are the examples which have come to my attention. There may well be others.

Reservoirs

Clearing tanks and reservoirs were an essential part of aqueduct construction; they were equally necessary for Baths and the great villa complexes. Remains of cisterns scattered over the countryside in profusion are often all that is left of a sumptuous villa. They would merit a special study. Even the many cisterns built for the Alban estate of Domitian[21] had proved to be insufficient by the time of Trajan, and space for a huge additional reservoir was hollowed out of the slope below Castel Gandolfo in the Orti Torlonia.[22] The front and side walls where they emerged from the hill were heavily buttressed with two spur walls on the front and two on each side. The huge rectangle (43.38 m. $\times$ 31.8 m.) was divided into six chambers by arched partition walls. The piers were brick-faced without bonding courses. Two peperino corbels on the sides of each pier were doubtless intended to facilitate construction though they were inserted below the actual impost of the arch. The arches were faced on each side with half *bipedales*. Similar corbels in the walls above the arches supported the centering for the barrel vaults. The concrete contained a mixed aggregate of selce, peperino, travertine, and marble in an abundant reddish and rather earthy mortar. The walls were faced with a reticulate of peperino broken every ninety centimeters by five rows of brick. Broken tiles begin to appear among the triangles made from *besales*. These give a reddish hue to the whole which does not appear in the Domitianic work. The reservoir was lined with *opus signinum* to make it impervious to water. A flight of concrete steps faced with tile led to the bottom of the cistern. The water was supplied by the aqueduct known as Malafitto Basso, which, if built originally under Domitian, was restored and lengthened under Trajan or Hadrian.

A reservoir at Bovillae is popularly known as the *casa rossa*[23] because of the red color of the triangles which face its peperino concrete. Bricks of that color were used in the time of Trajan and the early years of Hadrian. The tile bonding course found at the bottom and near the top accords well with such a date. It is a pity that there is no sure way of dating this edifice; hence we can add it only tentatively to the examples of the use of triangular bricks in the period under consideration. There is nothing remarkable about the edifice itself. It is divided longitudinally into two chambers, each with its own barrel vault; and there is a single arch in the partition wall.

Emissarium at Lago Fucino

The Emissarium at Lago Fucino,[24] abandoned by the followers of Claudius, had fallen into complete disrepair when Trajan undertook to restore it to usefulness.[25] An inscription[26] discovered in the church at Avezzano in the seventeenth century, expressing the gratitude of those dwelling near the lake, is the only record of Trajan's interest in this engineering project. Since the inscription can be dated at A.D. 117 it was a late accomplishment and may never have been completed.

HADRIAN

By the time of Hadrian, four of the great aqueducts[27]—Anio Vetus, Marcia, Claudia, and Anio Novus—were in need of a general overhauling; and the job was ably performed by Hadrian's engineers. In the upper reaches, the work consisted of minor repairs to channels, the restoration of existing bridges, or the substitution of lofty bridges, often of two tiers, for low ones in deep valleys; in the lower reaches, the work of encasing or buttressing of walls and the reinforcement of high arches to forestall collapse. Concrete was used almost exclusively and was everywhere of much the same quality. It was compact in texture and homogeneous in composition. The aggregate varied in accordance with what was readily available, but not in the size of the *caementa* used in the walls. Heavier, larger pieces were occasionally employed in the foundations and larger ones in the roofs. Whereas those in the foundations and vaults were laid with little attention to order, those in the walls were arranged in more or less even rows. The pozzolana in the mortar also depended on what was at hand, but was apparently carefully washed and screened before being mixed with a good quality of lime. Reticulate with tufa quoins formed the facing at times, especially in the upper part of the course, but appeared more often with bands of brick or as insets in a brick frame. The combination of brick, reticulate insets, and tufa quoins is not unknown.[28] In one section quoins of triangular bricks supplemented tufa blocks.[29] The tesserae, though of local stone—tufa of various kinds, limestone, even selce at times—were fairly uniform in size within the limits of 6.5 to 7.5 cm. per side. Tesserae as small as 6 cm. in the surface dimensions occur in one section and those as large as 8 cm. in another.[30] A smooth surface was often obtained by sawing. Joints were fine. The bricks used in combination with the reticulate, like those in the brickwork, were of local manufacture up to the point where it became practicable to bring them from the Roman kilns. With the exception of a few districts which produced a dark red tile,[31] they were pinkish yellow or yellowish pink[32] and have a speckled appearance from the pozzolana in their composition. They are almost invariably[33] triangles made by cutting *besales* obliquely. The majority fall within the range of 3 to 4 cm. Near Rome, bricks made from broken tiles appear occasionally. Brick stamps can be found at times. The vertical joints tend to be narrower than the horizontal ones (roughly 0.1 cm. as opposed to 1.5 cm.). Horizontal joints show signs of raking. Bonding courses of *bipedales*, sometimes of local manufacture and sometimes from Rome, occur rather frequently in the brickwork. They tend to be thicker than the bricks, with the majority between 4 to 5 cm. The same *bipedales* are used to furnish cornices of from one to five rows at the springing of the arches, which are faced with the same, except where *sesquipedales* are used for one of two double curves. They are regularly reduced to wedge shape and sometimes bear stamps.[34] Near the city, traver-

[27] The following account is a summary of the material given by Dr. Van Deman, *Aqueducts*, especially pp. 63–64, 133–135, 259–261, 327.

[28] *Ibid.*, pp. 48–49.

[29] *Ibid.*, pp. 86–87.

[30] *Ibid.*, p. 231.

[31] *Ibid.*, pp. 47, 79, 292.

[32] Minor repairs to Acqua Celimontana, apparently not mentioned by Dr. Van Deman, show pale yellow bricks (3.8 cm. × 22.8 cm.) with brick stamps of A.D. 123. See A. M. Colini, *Acc. P. Mem.*, ser. 3, vol. 7, 1944, p. 95 with fig. 47d, p. 98, n. 44.

[33] See Van Deman, *op. cit.*, p. 210, for some roof-tile bricks.

[34] *Ibid.*, pp. 109, 242–243, 244, 247–248, 250.

[35] *Ibid.*, pp. 238–245.

[36] *Ibid.*, pp. 80–81, 293–294.

[37] *Ibid.*, p. 210.

[38] *Ibid.*, pp. 80–81, 198, 199, 210.

[39] *Ibid.*, p. 252.

[40] *Ibid.*, pp. 48–49.

[41] T. Ashby, *PBSR*, vol. 4, 1907, p. 77; Van Deman, *Aqueducts*, p. 109. For the villa, see above, p. 103.

[42] Van Deman, *op. cit.*, pp. 172–173.

[43] Lugli, *MAR, Suppl.*, pp. 33–37.

tine corbels which once held the centering are still in position.[35] A wall facing of alternate blocks and bricks can be seen in one or two places;[36] and once or twice the alternation is carried over into arch construction.[37] Cut-stone work was still preferred at times to face the piers of bridges below the water line[38] and once for the outside walls of a reservoir.[39] So much for facings. The typical channel was pointed with the concrete set against boards instead of tiles. Ponte Taulella of the Anio Vetus had an arch faced with a double curve of *bipedales* and transverse rows of small tiles set on edge in the soffit,[40] but without the whole tiles which give a ladder effect in later masonry. From this brief résumé, it is apparent that Hadrian's interest in the aqueducts consisted merely in keeping them in good repair. His contribution is to construction rather than to engineering in the narrower sense of the word.

Notable Reservoirs

The two-storied pentagonal reservoir collecting water from the Aqua Marcia for the Villa Vignacce is notable for the blockwork and the block-and-brick work which is combined with the reticulate of the facing of its concrete walls and for the amphorae used in the vaults of the second story to lighten the weight.[41] The use of block-and-brick work was extended to the voussoirs of the arches. Local tufas were employed for the blocks and for most of the aggregate. The mortar is typical of the period. Small niches decorated the north wall on the outside. From the standpoint of engineering rather than construction the method of circulation of the water is interesting. The water apparently entered at the bottom, gradually filled at least two of the chambers, then rose through an opening in the vault of the central chamber until it reached an aperture conducting it back into the aqueduct. A brick stamp confirms the date.

In Rome a clearing tank was added to the Virgo at the foot of the Horti Luculliani on the Pincian[42] after the time of Frontinus, probably during the reign of Hadrian. An engraving of Fabretti depicts two upper and two lower barrel-vaulted chambers. The water entered the upper left-hand chamber, descended through an opening to the chamber below it, passed through an opening into the lower right-hand chamber, and then, presumably having deposited all its sediment, rose to the chamber above and thence back into the aqueduct again. The inner part was apparently made impervious with *opus signinum*; but there is no indication of a facing of any kind for either inside or outside. The remains are not visible today.

Rome has one reservoir[43] which is quite as imposing as any visible elsewhere in Italy. It is located on the edge of the Quirinal under the Collegio Germanico-Ungarico on Via S. Nicola da Tolentino. A great rectangle (38.55 m. × 20 m. or thereabouts) was cut out of the hill for its foundation, which consisted of four vaulted chambers not communicating with each other in any way. They were not accessible in antiquity; and both walls and vaults were left unfaced. The reservoir proper consisted of four aisles, each 38.55 m. × 4.32 m. × 3.3 m. to the top of the lunetted barrel vault. Eight arches in the side walls allowed for the free circulation of the water. The entire interior was lined with *opus signinum* with the usual "quarter-columns" in the angles. Consequently, the facing of the concrete is not visible. Where the structure emerges from the ground, it exhibits a fine brickwork, which has been adjudged Hadrianic. It is not possible to tell how it was supplied with water.

Other Aqueducts

Hadrian was responsible for bringing water to Gabii[44] from the springs which later supplied the Aqua Alexandrina.[45] Four low arches faced with tile, resting on piers with a reticulate facing, seem to have belonged to it. It is impossible to tell whether Trajan or Hadrian planned the aqueduct of San Lorenzo dell'Amaseno to furnish water for some of their benefactions in Terracina and, indeed, whether any of the construction was carried out by their engineers. In the absence of proof, treatment of it has been deferred to the section on the Antonine aqueducts simply because Julius Capitolinus attributes it to him.[46]

Emissarium at Lago Fucino

In addition to the aqueducts, Hadrian turned his attention to the abortive attempt to drain the Fucine Lake.[47] There was nothing spectacular in what his engineers did there.[48] They constructed a collector out into the lake of stout oak planks fastened to poles tipped with iron and joined by cross beams; they made a curving inclined wall on one side of the canal to replace a vertical one which had collapsed; they constructed a preliminary basin with a safety sluice gate at the entrance of the canal. Thus they restored to partial effectiveness at any rate the work which had been planned so admirably by their Claudian predecessors and so poorly executed because of the graft of the contractors.[49]

THE ANTONINES

Little Antonine work has been reported from the great aqueducts supplying water to Rome. One section of Hadrian's restoration of the Aqua Claudia was left for him to finish; that was the lofty bridge with enormous piers and heavy abutments which carried the aqueduct over the Fossa della Mola.[50] Among the Hadrianic brick stamps two were found of Antonine date (A.D. 140 and 142 respectively).[51] The work does not differ essentially from that of the preceding period. The concrete core consisted of closely packed rows of small pieces of local tufa in a good clear white or dark gray mortar; the facing was of triangular bricks (3–3.5 cm. $\times$ 24–26 cm.) pinkish red to yellow and speckled with pozzolana, which were probably of local manufacture. The joints were medium fine, the vertical ones being narrower than the horizontal. There were bonding courses of pinkish red *bipedales* (3.8–4.2 cm. thick). They furnished the stamps of paramount importance to the dating. According to Dr. Van Deman, no other work of any of the Antonine emperors is found in the aqueduct system.

Other Aqueducts

Antoninus Pius almost certainly completed the aqueduct supplying Terracina with water, which is named from San Lorenzo dell'Amaseno.[52] It

---

[44] CIL, vol. 14, no. 2797.

[45] Nibby, *Dintorni*, vol. 2, p. 86; Tomassetti, *Campagna*, vol. 3, p. 504; T. Ashby, *PBSR*, vol. 1, 1902, p. 198.

[46] See below and the next page.

[47] Spartianus, *SHA*, Hadrian, 22, 12.

[48] Brissé and de Rotrou, *Lac Fucino*, pp. 45–49, 243–256.

[49] See Blake, *RC* 11, pp. 84–85.

[50] Van Deman, Aqueducts, pp. 220–223, 261–262.

[51] CIL, vol. 15 (1), nos. 223a, 1065.

[52] The dating and the description are based entirely on Lugli. See Lugli, *Forma It.*, Regio I, vol. 1 (1), cols. 45–54; *idem*, Tecnica, pp. 97, 525, 636, 637, 651, 653, pl. 86, 1–2.

53 Two bridges show that the apotropaic significance of the phallus had not been forgotten even in the second century after Christ.

54 Lugli, *op. cit.*, cols. 93–94.

55 G. Lugli, *VII cong. st. archit.*, 1950 (1956), p. 104, fig. 15; *idem*, *Tecnica*, pp. 636, 637, 651–652, 655, pl. 90, 4.

56 Livy, 43, 4.

57 F. Lombardi (*Anzio, Antico e Moderno*, Rome 1865, p. 232) found remains of an aqueduct which he attributed to Nero.

58 Julius Capitolinus, *SHA*, *Antoninus Pius*, 8, 3.

59 G. Lugli, *RIA*, vol. 7, 1940, pp. 176–177.

60 Paribeni, *Optimus Princeps* II, pp. 120–128.

61 *CIL*, vol. 10 (1), pp. 684–694, *passim*.

62 *Ibid.*, nos. 6813, 6818.

63 *Ibid.*, no. 6819.

traversed fifty-four kilometers and gave evidence of having been built in haste by a number of different gangs working simultaneously. Some of the masonry is very rough, but the bridges carrying the aqueduct over the stream beds are well built, though they display great variety in treatment. The piers were made of robust squared-stone masonry[53] carried up to the springing of the arch, or of concrete faced with blocks, or with a combination of blocks and bricks. The walls were regularly of fine reticulate work with bands of brick made from tiles. Brick cornices appear at times; and there are at least two instances of lintel arches of tile to strengthen the masonry. The tiles were reddish and varied in width from 2.4 to 3.5 cm. The intrados of roughly shaped pieces of local stone was fronted by arches of *bipedales*. In one instance at least a few limestone blocks appear among the tiles. Once a lintel arch of stone was necessary because of a slight incline. Within Terracina itself there are the remains of an interesting distributing reservoir.[54] It consisted of two concentric drums within a square. The water was conveyed to the central part from above, then passed through a series of small apertures into the outer ring, which was covered with an annular barrel vault, whence it was carried in different directions by five conduits. The walls were of brick-faced concrete, the bricks being made from a fine quality of red tile. A brick arch of the aqueduct is reported nearby; and part of one of the subsidiary arches also appears near the Terme Neptuniane, not to mention a reservoir faced with reticulate and brick. The Baths themselves show a slight modification in the same type of construction whereby a porticus was converted into a row of rooms. The walls were rough work but reinforced by two or three bands of brick at intervals. The vaults were low and the pavements were of oblong tesserae. The aqueduct supplying Terme Imerensi[55] has been ascribed to the second half of the second century on the basis of its construction. The piers were of well-squared blocks of limestone of different heights. The arches were of concrete faced with voussoirs of lava and tile in alternation. Pieces of limestone were laid radially on the centering behind the arches with much mortar in the interstices. Elsewhere the aggregate showed some brick and lava with the limestone. Water had been brought to Anzio in 170 B.C.[56] This[57] or another aqueduct was restored by Antoninus Pius.[58] An arch faced with what appeared to be Antonine masonry to Lugli is still visible in the garden in front of Villa Albani.[59]

NERVA AND TRAJAN
ROADS AND BRIDGES

Trajan's name can be added to the list of great roadbuilders of antiquity.[60]

Via Appia

When Trajan turned his attention to the Via Appia, he was certainly continuing a reorganization already far advanced by Nerva. The milestones give evidence of Nerva's work at intervals from Rome to beyond Terracina.[61] The two nearest to Rome report a restoration in A.D. 97 of a section paved by Vespasian in A.D. 76.[62] The milestones also indicate that Trajan's work commenced at the thirty-ninth (Roman) mile from the city in A.D. 100.[63]

For ten miles through the Pomptine marshes, he either completed work started by Nerva[64] or built anew[65] as occasion demanded. The fifty-third milestone bears a date equivalent to A.D. 110, indicating that ten years had passed since he started the restoration.[66] So much for the evidence of the milestones. Approximately two kilometers before the road reached the Porta Romana at Terracina, the selce paving of Nerva or Trajan can be seen over the earlier pavement of limestone blocks.[67] A kilometer nearer the gate two fine pieces of Trajanic paving give the width as 4.1–4.2 m. from curb to curb.[68] About three kilometers within the gate the older Via Appia ascended Monte Sant'Angelo[69] and maintained a course somewhat back from the sea until it reached the head of Lago di Fondi. Traces of it have come to light at intervals,[70] some of which resemble Trajanic work elsewhere; but Trajan's real contribution was a shore road which required the attention of his engineers.

Via Appia Traiana[71]

Between the bifurcation in the city and Pesco Montano, three tracts of typically Trajanic roadbuilding indicate clearly the course of the new shore road.[72] Pesco Montano presented the first obstacle to be overcome. The rock was cut away perpendicularly with numbers carved in carte ansate[73] every ten (Roman) feet beginning at the top to record the amount removed, a hundred and twenty-eight feet (36 m.) in all. At the foot, two steps formed a natural curb and bench for the accommodation of weary travelers. A niche cut on the east side of the rock is generally interpreted as a shrine to commemorate the completion of the cutting under Trajan. Between Pesco Montano and Torre Gregoriana, where another cutting was necessary, the road, though founded on rock, was paved, and in some places the pavement was covered with opus signinum. It was protected by a parapet partly cut in the native rock and partly built of irregular blocks of limestone. At Torre Gregoriana the rock did not present a continuous surface, and concrete faced with reticulate appears where the rock is lacking. Beyond a culvert, there was another cutting forty meters long and eight meters high accommodated to the curve of the coast line. Near Canneto, the road was carried on a substructure faced with pieces of limestone, large and crudely shaped at the bottom, but forming a reticulate at the top. A great exedra (total length 25 m.) marked the junction on this shore road with the earlier Via Appia.[74] In the center of the exedra a pedestal 3.65 m. wide was evidently intended for a statue of the emperor. There is no typically Trajanic work, to my knowledge, between Canneto and Benevento. At Benevento itself, Ponte Lebbroso,[75] which carries the Appia, is like the Trajanic bridges of the Via Traiana[76] in having piers of squared-stone masonry and arches faced with double curves of bipedales. There are triangular cutwaters of squared-stone masonry and spandrels with small flood arches in brickwork.[77] About ten (Roman) miles from Benevento, the Via Appia crossed the Calore on a bridge[78] of which enough remains to show that it had two piers with triangular projections and traces of at least two others. The concrete in them had an aggregate of river pebbles and was faced at the angles and in part elsewhere with bipedales. The arches were also faced with bipedales. Such

[64] Ibid., nos. 6823 (?), 6824, 6826, 6832.

[65] Ibid., nos. 6827, 6833, 6834, 6835, 6839.

[66] Ibid., no. 6839.

[67] Lugli, Forma It., vol. 1 (1), col. 11, no. 19.

[68] Ibid., col. 8, no. 7; col. 9, no. 10.

[69] Ibid., cols. 34–35, 153, 181–209.

[70] Ibid., cols. 185–209 passim. The remains are not dated and may be undatable.

[71] Ibid., cols. 209–218.

[72] Ibid., col. 97, no. 48; col. 105, no. 62; col. 113, no. 68. The name as usually applied starts at Pesco Montano.

[73] CIL, vol. 10 (1), no. 6849.

[74] Lugli, op. cit., cols. 215–216.

[75] Meomartini, Benevento, pp. 34 (photo), 75; Enc. it., vol. 6, pl. 158; M. Ballance, PBSR, vol. 19, 1951, p. 99; Gazzola, Ponti, p. 91, no. 108.

[76] See below, pp. 282–284.

[77] Lugli (Tecnica, pl. 81, 1 and 2) considers the Ponte Apollosa and the Ponte Tufaro not far from Benevento to belong respectively to the time of Trajan and a somewhat later period. In an earlier work (RC I, p. 211) I have relegated them to a much earlier date. They still look early to me. For the bridges, see Gazzola, pp. 86–88, nos. 102–103.

[78] S. Aurigemma, Not. sc., 1911, p. 356, n. 1 with fig. 2.

[79] See below, p. 285.

[80] *CIL*, vol. 10 (1), nos. 6926, 6927, 6928.

[81] *Ibid.*, no. 6931.

[82] Paribeni, *Optimus Princeps* II, p. 127.

[83] Beloch, *Campanien*, p. 128.

[84] H. Kähler, *Studies DMR* I, pp. 430–439.

[85] *CIL*, vol. 9, no. 5971.

[86] *CIL*, vol. 9, no. 6890.

[87] *CIL*, vol. 9, no. 5947.

[88] *CIL*, vol. 10 (1), nos. 6887–6888.

[89] *CIL*, vol. 11 (2), no. 6622; Dessau, vol. 1, no. 299.

[90] T. Ashby and R. Fell, *JRS*, vol. 11, 1921, p. 186–187; M. Ballance, *PBSR*, vol. 19, 1951, p. 112; Gazzola, *Ponti*, pp. 130–131, no. 178. This bridge was destroyed by the retreating German army (*Arti fig.*, vol. 1, 1945, p. 75). See also Paribeni, *op. cit.*, p. 126.

[91] Ballance considered the brickwork later, not realizing perhaps how common the combination was in Trajanic brickmaking.

[92] Ashby-Fell, *op. cit.*, pp. 174–175. See also Ballance, *op. cit.*, p. 102 and Gazzola, *Ponti*, pp. 59–60, no. 96 for the bridge.

[93] Paribeni, *op. cit.*, pp. 124–126.

[94] *CIL*, vol. 9, nos. 5999–6053 where all the milestones are recorded.

[95] Strabo, 6, 3, 7. In a report of recent excavations at Ordona, J. Mertens (*Not. sc.*, 1962, pp. 311–339) discovered sections of a road which he believed to be the Via Traiana.

[96] *BMC, Emp.*, vol. 3, Trajan, nos. 484–491, 986–989, 998–999, 1012–1013; Strack, *Reichsprägung*, part 1, pp. 211–212. Not all the coins were struck in A.D. 112. Some were issued in 114 or even later.

construction should be Trajanic. At a somewhat later period, a slight change in the course of the road necessitated building a new bridge.[79]

Via Antiniana (Puteolana)

Three milestones state that he completed work begun by Nerva on the extension of the Via Domitiana to Neapolis in A.D. 102;[80] a fourth of the same date[81] makes no mention of Nerva and may indicate some change in plan from the projected course.[82] Its whereabouts near Puteoli can be traced by substantial remains;[83] and Kähler[84] has brought an inscription and some sculptured panels forward as evidence that an arch was erected there to commemorate the benefaction.

Repairs to Roads from Rome and Their Branches

Trajan's road repairs were not confined to the Via Appia system, nor were they part of a general reorganization of the entire network of Roman arterial highways in any given year. The paving of the Via Sublacensis, a branch of the Via Valeria, itself a continuation of the Via Tiburtina, may have been motivated by the desire to make access to his villa at Altipiano di Arcinazzo easier. One milestone dates it A.D. 103–105.[85] Another (A.D. 105) records the restoration of a bridge over the Liris River near Fregellae on the Via Labicana.[86] The rebuilding of a bridge does not necessarily imply a general repair of the road, since a bridge may be swept away by a flood at any time of freshet. On the Via Salaria between Reate and Interocrium, the emperor was apparently forced to build a stout retaining wall to prevent landslides. This construction is recorded on a milestone on A.D. 111.[87] This masonry, like the bridge over the Liris, may have resulted from an actual collapse. Two milestones belonging to the Via Latina or a ramification of it between Anagni and Ferentino bear a date equivalent to A.D. 115.[88] Not far from Forum Semproni (Fossombrone) an inscription was found in the Metaurus River commemorating a construction also of A.D. 115.[89] Paribeni accepts its identification with a bridge of the Via Flaminia at Calmazzo,[90] which had piers and supporting walls faced with squared-stone masonry and one brick-faced arch.[91] The piers have triangular cutwaters upstream and rectangular buttresses downstream. The inscription probably came from one of the parapets of the bridge. Ponte Fonnaia, also of the Via Flaminia, has been tentatively attributed to Trajan without any real reason.[92]

Via Traiana[93]

Over thirty-six milestones,[94] identical except for the mile recorded, proclaim that Trajan made the road from Beneventum to Brundisium at his own expense, giving the date as A.D. 108/9. The road followed a secondary route slightly longer than the Appia by actual measurement but easier and therefore quicker in the time required to make the journey. It would seem to be practically identical with the mule track described by Strabo[95] as passing through Herdoniae, Canusium, Netium, Caelia, and Egnatia. That sections through towns were already paved goes without saying, but Trajan was certainly responsible for bringing the whole two hundred and five miles or thereabouts into an integrated road system. Coins struck in A.D. 112[96] probably commemorate its completion, which was no doubt planned for the transportation of the troops starting out on the Parthian campaign. Dr. Ashby and Dr. Robert Gardner followed its entire course without discovering anything remarkable in the actual road construction.[97] A cippus found along the course of the road adds the significant ET PONTES[98] to a wording identical with that of the milestones. There are many bridges in more or less ruinous condition from which one may gain a clear picture of Trajanic bridge-building. At Benevento a brick arch of the period rests on the Republican arch of cut-stone masonry.[99] In the first part of the course where mountain valleys required strong bridges, the banks were sometimes faced with limestone blocks[100] and stoutly buttressed, and the concrete piers were also faced with limestone at least in the lower part. These blocks (62–74 cm. high) were highly rusticated and fastened together by iron clamps. In Ponte dei Ladroni, shortly beyond Forum Novum, the central pier had a triangular cutwater as a further protection. A little beyond this point, the six-arched Ponte delle Chianche showed squared-stone masonry only at the base of the pier in the center. Ponte San Spirito slightly farther along, though in a ruinous state, displayed a projecting top course of limestone blocks to serve as the support for brick-faced arches. The next two bridges are entirely of brickwork. Two miles west of the Ofanto some re-used rusticated blocks of limestone (74 cm. high) in the piers of a bridge seem to indicate that a stone facing was used here also. All the rest of the bridge construction was probably originally of fine brickwork.[101] The bricks (21–26 cm. × 4–4.5 cm.) were dull red and laid with very fine joints.[102] One brick stamp has been reported.[103] Bonding courses occur in the piers; and in one case at least whole *bipedales* were used in the facing.[104] Where the bridges were entirely of brickwork, the embankments were also of brick-faced concrete strengthened by rather low buttresses sloped off at the top.[105] The arches were faced by double curves of *bipedales*, and the intrados was also tiled. The spans sometimes reached a width of fifteen meters. The bridges most important for the brickwork are Ponte delle Chianche, Ponte Rotto (Cervaro), and Ponte Rotto (Ordona).[106] In the last-named bridge where the facing has fallen off, it is possible to see that river-pebbles were used as aggregate. A viaduct at Apani had walls faced with reticulate and brick, with buttresses faced in the same manner. The bricks varied from 3 to 3.5 cm. in thickness; the mortar joints from 1–1.8 cm. in width. The bridge no longer exists.[107] All these remains may be seen above ground. Excavations to determine the nature of the foundations would undoubtedly add to the knowledge of Roman bridgemaking.[108] Wherever a new road has been built, it is logical to look for some new construction along its course. Recent excavations at Ordona have revealed walls identified as Trajanic. There are the remains of a tomb of very fine workmanship at Bagnoli[109] which may be Trajanic and a large cistern at Canusium faced with reticulate and fine brickwork[110] which may qualify. The bricks are magenta and the mortar pinkish white. Why the Romans chose Beneventum as the place for the erection of a most impressive monument in honor of the Optimus Princeps[111] is open to question, but there can be no doubt that it was connected somehow with the Via Traiana. Possibly, the departure of the troops from

[97] T. Ashby and R. Gardner, *PBSR*, vol. 8, 1916, pp. 104–171.

[98] *CIL*, vol. 9, no. 6005.

[99] Blake, *RC* I, p. 211.

[100] At Ponte Valentino, they were further strengthened by interlocking courses, and there was a second wall behind this with an earth fill in between. See Ashby-Gardner, *op. cit.*, p. 124, Gazzola, *Ponti*, pp. 103–104, no. 130.

[101] One assumes that they were the same everywhere, although all details are not presented in each case.

[102] Horizontal, 1 cm.; vertical, 0.5 cm. The mortar is described as pinkish. Unless the ingredients were imported from the vicinity of Rome, which seems unlikely, it has no significance for this study.

[103] *CIL*, vol. 9, no. 6011.

[104] Ashby-Gardner, *op. cit.*, p. 146.

[105] They vary in width from 1.2 to 1.75 m. and in projection from 2.28 to 2.8 m. and are spaced 2.7 m. apart.

[106] Ashby-Gardner, *op. cit.*, pp. 132, 142–144, 145–146.

[107] *Ibid.*, pp. 168–169.

[108] *Ibid.*, p. 117, n. 2.

[109] *Ibid.*, p. 154.

[110] *Ibid.*, p. 157.

[111] *CIL*, vol. 9, nos. 1558, 5998.

[112] *CIL* gives the date as A.D. 115, but Dessau (vol. 1, p. 78, no. 296) as 113/14.

[113] Ashby-Gardner, *op cit.*, p. 117; H. Kähler, *RE*, *Triumphbogen*, cols. 404–406.

[114] See above, pp. 263–264.

[115] Lugli, *Enc. it.*, vol. 34, p. 154.

[116] Martinori, *Via Cassia*, pp. 88–90, 101–107. He refers to Moretti, "Via Cassia e la Via Traiana Nova," Orvieto 1925, which I have not seen. *Cf.* also, Paribeni, *Optimus Princeps* II, pp. 127–128.

[117] A. Cozza, *Bull. Inst.*, 1882, pp. 241–242.

[118] *CIL*, vol. 9, no. 5833. A road bearing right from the Clodia at Cassacia has been suggested for another. See Martinori, *op. cit.*, p. 174.

[119] E. Brizio, *Not. sc.*, 1888, pp. 617–622.

[120] This is a mere conjecture; but the combination of squared-stone masonry with brickwork is a common practice in Trajanic bridge-building.

[121] *CIL*, vol. 11 (2), no. 6813.

[122] Paribeni, *Optimus Princeps* II, pp. 130–149.

[123] See above, p. 42.

[124] See above, pp. 53–55.

[125] See above, p. 38.

[126] G. Jacopi, *Mon. ant.*, vol. 39, 1943, cols. 13–26.

Beneventum over the new road was considered the real start of the Parthian campaign; and so it appeared the suitable place to welcome back the triumphing emperor by a new arch. The main body of the arch seems to have been erected in A.D. 114,[112] though many believe that the attic was added by Hadrian after the death of Trajan in A.D. 117 before he had had a chance to pass under it.[113] A description of the arch itself belongs in another section.[114] Lugli credits Trajan with continuing the Via Traiana from Brindisi through Lecce to Otranto and thence to Taranto.[115]

Via Traiana Nova

Two milestones of the Via Traiana Nova of A.D. 108 define its course as a *Volsinis* (Bolsena) *ad fines Clusinorum* (Chiusi).[116] It was apparently a substitute for a badly deteriorated section of the Cassia. Remains of paving here and there and scanty traces of ancient bridges serve to indicate its route. At its junction with the Cassia, there was a ponderous dam[117] (100 m. × 6 m. × 4.75 m.) across the valley of the Clanis (Chiana) which was evidently an ancient attempt at flood control of the Tiber by impounding some of the water of its tributaries. It had an opening 11.65 m. wide provided with sluice gates. The dam was of heavy concrete faced with brick; the arch of the main opening was faced with a double curve of tiles in the usual Trajanic fashion; the apertures of the sluice gates were lined with *pietra concia*. This was probably one of the three Trajanic roads mentioned in an inscription.[118]

Via Aemilia: Bridge

Extremely interesting remains of a Roman bridge have come to light at Castel San Pietro sul Sillaro,[119] which once carried the Via Aemilia over the stream. It was a treacherous spot; and Trajan apparently had to rebuild the original bridge almost completely.[120] The bank was protected by a wall of squared-stone masonry in which the blocks were held together by clamps leaded into place. Behind it an inclined brick-faced wall with an earth fill between it and the stone wall evidently represents an attempt at flood control. The foundations of the bridge proper were laid in accordance with the precepts of Vitruvius, having a palisade of iron-tipped piles fastened together by transverse slabs and a floor of *opus signinum* to form caissons for the concrete foundations of the piers. An inscription gives the date as A.D. 100.[121]

For Trajan's roadbuilding and other engineering works outside Italy, the reader is referred to Paribeni's account.[122]

HADRIAN

Hadrian was more interested in architecture than in engineering. In Rome, his engineers did what was required, notably raising the level about the Pantheon,[123] which necessitated a new system of streets and sewers. They built the Pons Aelius[124] as an approach to the Mausoleum of Hadrian and regulated the banks of the Tiber at that point. They seem to have modified the Trajanic embankment near the Marmorata.[125] Farther down the river on the right side, in a district known as Pietra Papa, more of the same type of embankment has come to light.[126] The slope was faced with coarse reticulate broken by two bands of six rows of brick. It was interrupted by a flight of travertine steps. Tufa quoins protected the junction with the steps. A drain connected with a building in the rear yielded stamps of A.D. 123 and 134,[127] a possible indication that this stretch of embankment was slightly later than the other. According to Dr. Van Deman's unpublished notes, there was a Hadrianic restoration of the Cloaca Maxima system near the beginning of the Arch of Titus.

Roads, like aqueducts, must be kept in repair if a country is to prosper. Hadrian did his part to maintain the road system in good repair, but did not indulge in any spectacular roadbuilding in Italy. It seems probable that he restored the Via Appia Antica[128] from Beneventum to Aeclanum when he raised the latter to a colony. If so, his engineers were responsible for Ponterotto and Ponte San Sassio. These resemble closely the Trajanic bridges in the vicinity.[129] Dr. Van Deman noted one difference in Ponterotto[130] which confirmed the Hadrianic date for her. The bricks in the facings were mostly triangles (3.2–3.6 cm. $\times$ 25.5–29 cm.) with sawed fronts and molded sides. They were light red to magenta with darker grains of sand, not pozzolana, in their composition and probably of local manufacture. Meomartini[131] considers the Ponte Fratto, which carried the Via Latina over the Calore, Hadrianic, but does not report its construction. The Via Salaria crossed Fosso di Malpasso and Fosso della Buffalotta on a single bridge known as Ponte di Malpasso near Castel Giubileo.[132] During the Hadrianic period an arch faced with a double curve of *bipedales* was substituted for an earlier one of stone. It was destroyed in 1852, but brick stamps attest the Hadrianic date. A column from Montepulciano, now in the Museo Archeologico in Florence,[133] records a repair of the Via Cassia from Clusium to Florentia in A.D. 123, but no evidence of the actual road has been reported to the best of my knowledge. Merckel[134] states that a double road was built by Hadrian from the harbor at Aquileia to Ponte di Isonzo to facilitate traffic. None of these bridges has been examined by me.

THE ANTONINES

Most of the roadbuilding for which Antoninus Pius was responsible was aimed at the consolidation of the Provinces.[135] He seems to have put the Via Aemilia in good condition in connection with a rather extensive program of road building for Southern France. He had several roads constructed in the Rhine valley. A bridge of the Via Latina near Fregellae is credited to him on a milestone.[136]

TRAJAN

HARBORS

With the continued growth of the City, an adequate port at the mouth of the Tiber became an ever more pressing need. Claudius, to be sure, had had a tremendous open harbor dug out and protected by moles, but its mouth was perhaps too open and the left mole, built on sand, too weak to withstand the forces of nature. Trajan's engineers decided that an inner basin was required where ships could ride at anchor undisturbed by the

[127] *CIL*, vol. 15 (1), nos. 1029c, 1073, 674. The bricks were 4 cm. thick.

[128] What follows on the Via Appia is based on Dr. Van Deman's unpublished notes.

[129] See also F. Colonna, *Not. sc.*, 1890, p. 394. Aurigemma (*Not. sc.*, 1911, p. 355 n. 1) considers it Trajanic.

[130] See above, p. 281.

[131] Meomartini, *Benevento*, p. 99.

[132] T. Ashby, *PBSR*, vol. 3, 1906, p. 23. See also Nibby, *Dintorni*, vol. 1, pp. 129–130.

[133] *CIL*, vol. 11 (2), no. 6668.

[134] Merckel, *Ingenieurtechnik*, p. 172.

[135] See Bryant, *Antoninus Pius*, pp. 53–55.

[136] *CIL*, vol. 10, no. 6891.

fury of the elements, and made plans to reorganize all the facilities of the earlier port. While they were grappling with this problem, Trajan apparently came to the conclusion that Rome needed another port not too far distant to care for her far-flung commerce, and Centumcellae was the result. He also had the harbors at Terracina and Ancona reorganized and probably at Rimini as well.

Portus (Porto)

To provide space for an inner harbor (plan XV) at the mouth of the Tiber, Trajan's engineers were forced to change the course of the southern canal of Claudius. The new canal, the Fossa Traiana,[137] took its orientation from the south wall of the proposed hexagonal basin until, released from the necessity of a special orientation, it could take its natural course to the Tiber. It was forty-five meters wide, had an artificial bed, and side walls of concrete faced with bricks. A new canal (no. 1)[138] connected the *fossa* with the basin. Its course is clear; but no trace of its construction remains. The contractors made free use of part of a Claudian canal (no. 3)[139] to join the basin to the sea. Trajanic remains are visible on the south side of this in two parallel walls of concrete faced with coarse reticulate, having a passageway of some sort between them. On the north, an isolated lighthouse (no. 8)[140] marked the entrance to the channel. The rectangular base can still be seen beneath the later construction. It was made of concrete with a uniform aggregate of tufa in a whitish mortar; and there are openings to break the force of the waves. Part way up, travertine corbels supported a balcony. The foundations were refaced later, and all the upper part restored. The wet dock, or *darsena* (?), (no. 4)[141] parallel to the entrance canal at the south seems to have retained its Claudian form.

One other task remained before the area was entirely ready for the hexagonal basin. A sustaining wall (no. 12)[142] had to be built north of the entrance canal and east of the Claudian port. It was faced with selce reticulate to withstand better the action of the waves, but was given ornamental treatment above. Travertine corbels inserted in the reticulate supported the tile-faced arches under an overhanging balcony. Behind, there was an arcade with a semicircular exedra in the center facing the sea. The balcony was paved with plain white, the exedra with black-and-white mosaic. There were rooms behind the arcade. At the lower level, the space behind the wall was utilized for a long service corridor with a cryptoporticus behind it, which received light from an open court at the upper level. The west wall of the corridor was faced with brick above an exposed foundation[143] and furnished with loop holes for light, which apparently sometimes admitted water as well, for there was a gutter to take care of it. The east wall was faced with reticulate insets in a brick frame. A barrel vault covered the corridor. The cryptoporticus displayed the same combination of brick and reticulate in both walls. Doorways leading into some half-subterranean rooms at the east and north were topped with segmental arches of *bipedales*. A series of cross vaults covered the cryptoporticus. A similar terrace (no. 13) extended eastward from the northern extremity.

Much commercial activity must have been centered from the first in the

[137] Lugli-Filibeck, p. 66.

[138] *Ibid.*, p. 73. The numbers throughout refer to Lugli's classification.

[139] *Ibid.*, pp. 73–74.

[140] *Ibid.*, pp. 81–83.

[141] *Ibid.*, pp. 74–75. The identification is almost certain.

[142] *Ibid.*, pp. 87–90.

[143] This indicates that the level was lowered at this point.

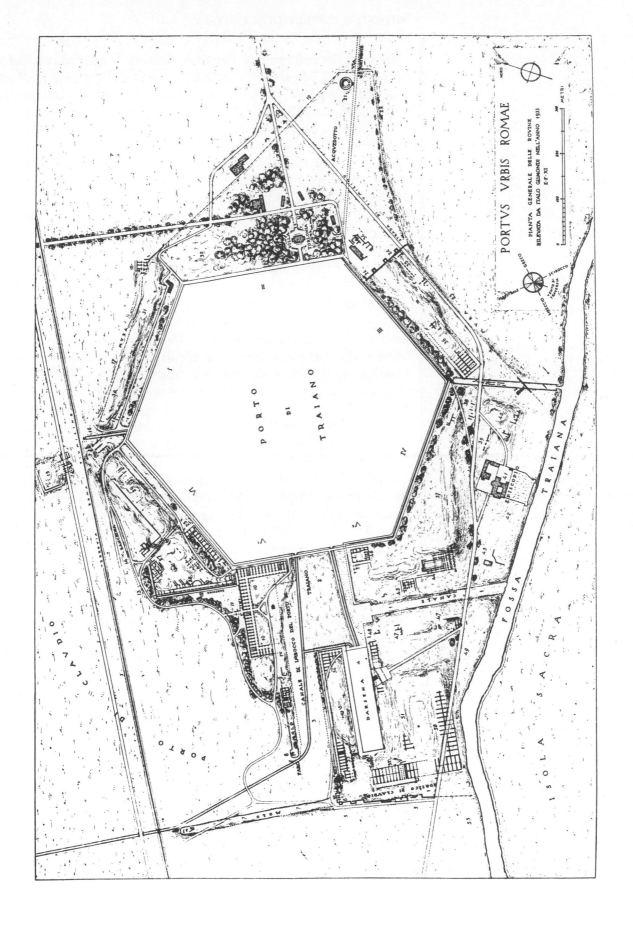

PORTVS VRBIS ROMAE

PIANTA GENERALE DELLE ROVINE
RILEVATA DA ITALO GISMONDI NELL'ANNO 1933
E.F. XI

PLAN XV. TRAJAN'S PORT

I. Gismondi

region to the southwest of the basin between the entrance canal and the Fossa Traiana, where the wet dock was located and the cross canal connected the two waterways. Trajanic warehouses were built at right angles to the extremities of the Porticus of Claudius, the ones on the north (nos. 53 and 54)[144] running parallel to the entrance canal and the one on the south (no. 50)[145] facing the Fossa Traiana. In this section, the builders evidently had to reckon with the sand dumped when the Claudian harbor was dug out. They solved the problem by laying thick foundation walls of concrete and facing them with a coarse reticulate (tesserae 10 cm. per side). Two of these (nos. 53 and 50) had this type of foundation, as did the "grande mercato" (no. 48)[146] along the south side of the *darsena*. The wall construction of the first two consisted of insets of tufa reticulate in a brick frame, the two methods of facing being neatly interlocked at the sides. The wall ends of Number 50 displayed exceptionally fine brickwork of red bricks made from tiles which Lugli thinks may even be Hadrianic. The two farther inland (nos. 54 and 48) showed only brickwork in the part preserved—the former in walls and buttresses, the latter, in piers. They were enlarged shortly after they were built. There may have been reticulate work in partition walls. Farther south along the transverse canal, the "mercato piccolo" (no. 47)[147] and the "grande magazzini" (no. 45)[148] on the opposite side had walls faced with the usual combination of reticulate and brick. There is obviously a great deal more Trajanic construction to be unearthed in this section.

The restoration of the hexagonal basin of Trajan's port by the late Prince Don Giovanni Torlonia made possible a reappraisal of the work of Trajan's engineers.[149] It consisted of a huge hexagon (357.77 m. per side) with an opening toward the sea in its southwest side. The pool was enclosed in a quay of concrete having a tufa aggregate which gave way to a stratum of selce *caementa*, twenty centimeters thick at the top. A single step, designed for the insertion of blocks of travertine with circles for holding mooring ropes, led to an inclined surface. The discovery of these travertine blocks proves that small posts formerly thought to have been used in mooring served some other purpose. A brick wall three meters high, following the line of the quay at a distance of six meters from the water, probably formed a customs barrier. It was pierced on each side by five doorways which were too narrow for carts. A wide street paved with selce ran along the other side of the wall. Opposite the mouth, where a temple was built at a later time, there was doubtless a Trajan monument of some sort. South of the mouth, scanty remains attest the presence of a Trajanic wharf; whatever stood north of it was destroyed when a large warehouse was located there in the Severan period. Of the other Trajanic structures which probably engirdled the basin, practically nothing has been uncovered except on the northwest and the north sides. Such of these remains as were visible in 1913 were carefully studied and analyzed by Dr. Van Deman.[150] The result of that study is given here for the first time. I have not been given the opportunity for an independent analysis.

A wall divided the northwestern section[151] into two unequal parts. The western section may have contained the civic center which would surely be necessary for the administration of the affairs of the busy harbor. Of the

144 *Ibid.*, pp. 118–119.

145 *Ibid.*, pp. 112–113.

146 *Ibid.*, pp. 110–111.

147 *Ibid.*, p. 110.

148 *Ibid.*, loc. cit.

149 *Ibid.*, pp. 66–72. See also G. Calza, *Not. sc.*, 1925, pp. 54–57.

150 Lugli (Lugli-Filibeck, p. 131) conjectures that the *portico-magazzino* no. 12 may have continued in a straight line to the canal, in which case there would probably have been a canal parallel to it to facilitate unloading.

151 Lugli-Filibeck, pp. 97–101.

rooms along the west side (no. 28), Dr. Van Deman saw and analyzed four fragmentary walls. Two wall ends, turned toward the Port of Claudius, were faced with reticulate work, one toward the center with brick, as was the curved wall connected with it. The bricks were practically all magenta and ranged from 3.5 to 4.3 cm. in thickness with mortar joints varying from 1.3 to 1.6 cm. in width. The nucleus had a tufa aggregate in a dark gray mortar. The pozzolana used in it was apparently washed and sifted medium fine. A porticus (no. 25)[152] faced the hexagonal basin with a row of storage rooms opening out of it. Probably another row faced inward from the common back wall in true *horrea* fashion. These walls showed the reticulate work typical of the period with bands of brick. The tesserae (6.5–7.1 cm. in the surface dimensions) of yellowish gray tufa were laid with joints (0.7 to 1.1 cm. wide) of a reddish mortar. Most of the bricks measured fell within the range of 3.5–4 cm. In this section an occasional brick was yellow. The joints were raked. The corridor was cross-vaulted. Along the north side, a two-story edifice (no. 27)[153] was erected, taking its orientation from the porticus in front rather than from the north terrace (no. 13). It was cut by a later wall, and only the lower floor is preserved to any extent. Within it, a three-sided cryptoporticus, receiving light and air from an open court above, is also covered with a series of cross vaults. On the northwest the edifice abutted an earlier one at a different orientation. In the center of the area, a number of rooms were uncovered between 1864 and 1867 which were so richly decorated that the name "Palazzo Imperiale" was arbitrarily given to the whole complex.[154] A reappraisal of the brick stamps reported by Lanciani convinced Bloch that the building was probably early Hadrianic.[155] In any case, there is no cogent reason for thinking that it was the dwelling of either emperor.

The eastern section, according to Lanciani's plan,[156] contained a large warehouse (no. 29) with three parallel lines of storerooms facing in both directions from a common back wall. For some reason, perhaps the presence of a Claudian edifice, these *horrea* were set well back from the usual building line. Barely enough remains visible today to show that it was a pretentious structure of two stories. Lugli[157] reports walls faced with fine *opus mixtum*, which in his terminology means the usual combination of reticulate and brick. The lower rooms were cross-vaulted. Dr. Van Deman's notes present the construction in more detail, though it is not possible today to tell just where she found her specimens.[158] At any rate, they attest Trajanic work in the area: the nucleus of the walls showed an aggregate of either brown to grayish brown tufa or broken tile laid on the flat side in irregular rows; the mortar was reddish to brownish gray in accordance with the color of the pozzolana used in its composition. The pozzolana was evidently washed and sifted medium fine; the lime was clean; and the proportions of the two well calculated to make a good mortar. The bricks were practically all made from fine-textured, well-baked magenta tiles, averaging about 4 cm. in thickness with a range of roughly 3.5 to 4.4 cm. Grains of red pozzolana appeared in occasional specimens. The joints were usually 1.8 to 1.9 cm. in width. At least one bonding course occurred in the walls seen. No doubt reticulate work was used, but none appeared in the parts uncovered. Other traces of

[152] *Ibid.*, p. 96.

[153] *Ibid.*, p. 100. This edifice was not analyzed by Dr. Van Deman.

[154] R. Lanciani, *Ann. d. Inst.*, 1868, pp. 170–175; Lugli-Filibeck, pp. 97–100.

[155] Bloch, *Bolli*, pp. 100–102.

[156] *Mon. ined.*, vol. 8, pl. 49.

[157] Lugli-Filibeck, pp. 100–101.

[158] Her sketch fits into Lanciani's plan (*loc. cit.*) better than into Gismondi's (Lugli-Filibeck, pl. 2).

159 Lugli-Filibeck, pp. 90–91 (not included in Dr. Van Deman's notes).

160 *Ibid.*, p. 101.

Trajanic work came to light at the northwest extremity of the port in a warehouse (no. 15)[159] later converted into Baths.

Somewhat similar *horrea* (nos. 30 and 31)[160] occupied the entire north side in Lanciani's plan; and clear traces of at least four parallel long walls and five cross walls were still visible in 1913 when Dr. Van Deman made the following observations regarding the construction. The core of the walls consisted of concrete with an aggregate of grayish brown, reddish brown, or hard gray tufa with an admixture of tile in parts, laid in rough rows in a dark gray mortar composed of sharp-angled gray to almost black pozzolana in a clean lime. The pozzolana was apparently washed, but only coarsely sifted. This nucleus was faced either with brickwork or the combination of brick and reticulate which is found throughout the Trajanic construction. The bricks were made of magenta or occasionally yellow roof tiles of fine texture. There were no triangles. The majority of bricks came within the range of 3.5 to 3.8 cm.; the majority of the joints were 1.4 to 1.8 cm. wide, though an occasional one exceeded the limit in each direction. The ingredients were well chosen to make a firm mortar. The reticulate tesserae were all of brownish gray tufa, with dimensions 6.7 to 7 cm. in the exposed surface. In one wall a bonding course was found part way up. No vaulting was preserved. Lugli reports one wall that he adjudged Trajanic in which dark yellow bricks averaging 3.2 cm. in thickness were combined with a reticulate of tesserae 9 cm. × 9 cm.

No Trajanic construction connected with the other three sides has been uncovered, to the best of my knowledge. It will be noted at once that no apartment houses like those at Ostia have been unearthed in the vicinity of the basin. Probably, except for those whose duty it was to guard the properties, all dwelt in Ostia proper. The Trajanic tombs in the cemetery at Isola Sacra are described elsewhere.

From this brief résumé it is clear that coarse reticulate, often of selce, was used to face exposed concrete foundations, and that brick facing with insets of reticulate was the preferred facing for walls, though there are walls faced with brick alone particularly in façades. The bricks, where the color is reported, were usually magenta but occasionally dark yellow, and all were made from roof tiles, or possibly their counterparts in unflanged tiles. The normal width ranged from 3.5 to 4 cm., though plenty of specimens exceeded the limits in each direction. An occasional bonding course appears in the brickwork. Comparatively few brick stamps have been reported. Not many vaults have been preserved, but the contractors apparently did not hesitate to use cross vaults where they best suited their purpose.

Centumcellae (Civitavecchia)

161 Pliny, *Epist.*, 6, 31, 15–17 (Loeb Library translation; Melmoth, rev. by Hutchinson).

Of the arbor of Trajan at Civitavecchia, we have the description of an eyewitness to the construction which is worthy of full quotation:[161] "Here is a villa, surrounded by the most verdant meadows, and overhanging a bay of the coast where they are at this moment constructing a harbour. The left-hand mole of this port is protected by immensely solid masonry; the right is now being completed. An island is rising in the mouth of the harbour, which will break the force of the waves when the wind blows shorewards, and afford passage to ships on either side. Its construction is highly worth seeing; huge stones are transported hither in a broad-bottomed vessel, and being sunk one upon the other, are fixed by their own weight, gradually accumulating in the manner, as it were, of a rampart. It already lifts its rocky back above the ocean, while the waves which beat upon it, being tossed to an immense height, roar prodigiously, and whiten all the sea round. To these stones are added wooden piles,[162] which in time will give it the appearance of a natural island. This port will be, and already is, named after its great author, and will prove of infinite benefit, by affording a haven to ships on a long stretch of harbourless coast." This letter is dated by Sherwin-White as probably mid-107.[163] The fifth-century description of Rutilius Namatianus gives a clearer picture of the whole harbor as it appeared in his day: "To Centumcellae we changed our tack before a strong South wind: our ships find mooring in the calm roadstead. An amphitheatre of water is there enclosed by piers, and an artificial island shelters the narrow entrances; it rears twin towers and extends in both directions so as to leave a double approach with narrow channels. Nor was it enough to construct docks of wide harbourage; to keep the vagrant breeze from rocking the craft even when safe in port, an inner basin has been coaxed into the very midst of the buildings, and so, with its surface at rest, it knows naught of the wayward wind—."[164] These descriptions contributed fully as much to the plans drafted by Fontana (1669)[165] and Canina (1832)[166] as what remained of the port after the destruction meted out to it by the Saracens in A.D. 828. A plaster model made by Cordelli for the Mostra Augustea (1937), now in the Museo della Civiltà Romana at Rome, gives a good general impression,[167] though details must be modified in the light of more recent finds. A coin labeled PORTUM TRAIANI, long thought to represent the harbor at Civitavecchia, is now ascribed to Porto.[168] Apollodorus was probably responsible for the plan. After the bombardment of World War II, a more precise analysis of the port became possible.[169] The wall of the breakwater was of squared-stone masonry. The round towers at its ends had long since been converted into the lighthouse of Pope Paul V and the fortress of Pope Gregory XVI respectively. The ancient lighthouse probably stood at the center. A square form would best suit the site. The roughly curved moles defining the open port also terminated in round towers which were utilized by the popes for fortifications. One of these, now destroyed, was faced with reticulate insets in a brick frame. The bombing revealed small rooms attached to the other, built for the ancient guardians. There was no symmetry in the arrangement of the buildings about the port. The remains of a dockyard on the south side disappeared in the construction of the modern wet dock. Next to it, a richly decorated edifice may have served as barracks for the sailors and their officers.[170] On the east side facing the entrance, a long porticus with columns of rose and black granite having Doric capitals of white marble gave access to a series of rooms (15 m. × 5.7 m. × 5 m. high) which were used as temporary warehouses. These *horrea* were probably three stories high, at least in the central part. The walls were faced with reticulate terminating in rows of brick at the impost. An opening in the north side led to the closed harbor, or *darsena*, of rather irregular shape,

162 Concrete blocks (*pilae*) used in underwater work as advocated by Vitruvius (5, 12, 4) would fit the context better than "wooden piles." See Ch. Dubois, *Mél*, vol. 22, 1902, pp. 442–447 for a discussion of the question. Pliny's letter gives the impression of a distant view which could scarcely take note of concrete pillars at points of stress as envisaged by Lehmann-Hartleben (*Klio, Beiheft*, no. 14, 1923, pp. 192–195).

163 A. N. Sherwin-White, *The Letters of Pliny*, Oxford 1966, p. 391. A brick stamp (*CIL*, vol. 15 (1), no. 261 a 8) proves that a naval cemetery had been established there before A.D. 108 when Nicomachus passed from the ownership of Domitius Tullus to that of Domitia Lucilla. See Bloch, *Bolli*, p. 46.

164 Rutilius Namatianus, *De Reditu Suo*, 1, 237–246 (Loeb Library translation). Sherwin-White, *op. cit.*, p. 396, suggests that Pliny's account, when compared with Namatianus and the plans of Collicola (*ca.* 1727), "is incomplete, doubtless because he saw the works at an early stage of construction."

165 C. Fontana, *Pianta antica del porto ed acquedotto di Civitavecchia*, Calcografia Camerale, 1699.

166 L. Canina, *Archit. rom.*, vol. 3, 1832, pl. 160.

167 A photograph of it appears in Bastianelli, *Centumcellae*, plate 3.

168 *BMC, Emp.*, vol. 3, Trajan, no. 770 A, pl. 28, fig. 2. *Cf.* Lugli-Filibeck, p. 32 with n. 67; Paribeni, *Optimus Princeps* II, p. 109; Strack, *Reichsprägung*, part I, pp. 212–213. Mattingly (*BMC, op. cit.*, p. civ) still thinks that it may represent the harbor at Civitavecchia.

169 Bastianelli, *Centumcellae*, pp. 36–44.

170 R. Mengarelli, *Not. sc.*, 1941, pp. 179–186; idem, *BMIR*, vol. 13, 1943, p. 78. The construction was Trajanic reticulate, but there were later modifications. It had to be covered over again.

171 *CIL*, vol. 11, no. 3548b. See also Lanciani, *Acque*, p. 464, n. 291; Paribeni, *Optimus Princeps* II, p. 116.

172 See above, p. 275.

173 S. Bastianelli, *Not. sc.*, 1940, p. 189; *idem*, *Centumcellae*, p. 45.

174 Bastianelli, *Centumcellae*, p. 49 note.

175 *Ibid.*, p. 45.

176 *Ibid.*, pp. 66–67.

177 *Ibid.*, pp. 64–75; see above, pp. 271–272.

178 M. de la Blanchère, *Mél.*, vol. 1, 1881, p. 327; Ch. Dubois, *Mél.*, vol. 22, 1902, p. 442; K. Lehmann-Hartleben, *Klio, Beiheft*, no. 14, 1923, p. 206; Lugli, *Forma It.*, Reg. I, vol. 1 (1), cols. 125–132, no. 73; Paribeni, *Optimus Princeps* II, pp. 116–117.

179 An inscription (*CIL*, vol. 10, no. 6310) gives evidence of some benefaction of Trajan early in his reign; a relief found in Terracina (Lugli, *op. cit.*, pl. 1), now in a private collection in Rome, shows an emperor, probably Trajan, superintending the erection of a building in squared-stone masonry, perhaps a lighthouse. The relief has additional value in showing how the Romans shaped the blocks at the site and swung them into place. *Cf.* Lugli, *op. cit.*, cols. 128, 147–150.

180 Lugli, *op. cit.*, col. 133, no. 74.

181 See above, p. 281.

182 *Cf.* Tacitus, *Hist.*, 3, 76–77.

which had been dug out of the land and fortified by a sustaining wall faced with reticulate before the water was admitted. The harbor was enclosed on three sides by a wall of sandstone blocks, which has almost totally disappeared. Three arched gates framed in travertine in the east wall led to warehouses of which enough remains to show rooms 4.7 m. $\times$ 6 m. faced with reticulate.

An inscription on a water pipe[171] proves almost without doubt that Trajan was responsible for bringing fresh water to the port by means of an aqueduct.[172] Many other public buildings would be required in a busy port. A substantial residue of a basilica of traditional form came to light northwest of the *darsena* only to be reburied to form a public square for the modern city.[173] More recently scanty remains of Baths and a public latrine[174] have been unearthed, but no trace of either theater or amphitheater has appeared as yet.[175] The construction of such a harbor would necessitate a commensurate amount of private building. Casual excavations have revealed walls faced with reticulate which once probably belonged to the dwellings in the original city. Of the villa of the emperor from which the Younger Pliny watched the construction going on in the harbor, we have no further knowledge.

The therapeutic value of the hot springs near Civitavecchia had been known for many years before the foundation of Trajan's port. Doubtless those who came to live in Centumcellae availed themselves of such bathing establishments as were already in operation. Poggio Ficoncella shows remains of concrete faced with reticulate reinforced by brick which may be Trajanic.[176] Brick stamps have been cited as evidence that Trajan commenced the transformation of the relatively simple Republican Baths, a little farther to the south, into the sumptuous bathing establishment known as Terme Taurine.[177] If so, his contribution was slight since Hadrianic stamps were found in the earliest additions to the Bath which first occupied the site. Possibly the brickyards were still supplying Trajanic bricks to Hadrianic projects.

Terracina

The problem at Terracina was somewhat different since it had had a harbor from early days. The remains of its mole of undressed stone were leveled off and covered with a layer of *opus signinum* to serve as the foundation for later Roman work.[178] The original harbor had to be dug out of the sand, and the sand thus removed was piled up until it formed the elevation known as Montone. There is no clear indication that Trajan restored this early port.[179] That such a restoration was contemplated is suggested by a branch of the Via Appia Traiana leading in that direction,[180] but the cutting away of Pesco Montano[181] would in itself necessitate a complete reorganization of the port, which was apparently not in good shape for ships of appreciable size at the time of the struggle between the followers of Vitellius and Vespasian.[182] Two new moles may perhaps be attributed to Trajan, in part at least. One was roughly parallel with the shore; the other, with Montano. The latter was built out into a curve by Antoninus Pius. The first is now entirely covered by the penitentiary erected by Pius II, but the second exhibits two building periods not very far apart, ascribable to Trajan and Antoninus Pius respectively. The facing of the earlier part is typically Trajanic—brick with insets of reticulate and bands of five rows of brick at intervals. The reticulate work is accurate. The bricks, cut from tiles, are dark yellow. On the inner side, alternate rows of tufa and limestone tesserae give to the reticulate a variegated effect. At one point, a bit of wall faced with reticulate without brick at a lower level undoubtedly belongs to some earlier construction. To Antoninus Pius, however, belongs the credit for the construction of a truly effective port at Terracina.[183]

Closely connected with the re-establishment of a usable port and the reorganization of the Via Appia near Pesco Montano was a series of rooms and a long porticus facing the Via Appia.[184] Behind the porticus there were other rooms, for the most part unexcavated, and traces of stairs leading to a second story. Brick with reticulate faced the walls, brick alone the piers. The bricks were a clear rose color, 3.6–4 cm. thick. The walls were stuccoed and decorated with a cornice of stucco work, and the vaults were also stuccoed. One vault retains traces of painting. It is impossible to state categorically whether this structure is Trajanic or Hadrianic. A restoration of the efficiency of the harbor would naturally bring with it a certain amount of building within the city. Two of the Baths—the so-called Neptunian and the Maritime—contain masonry which was or at any rate could be Trajanic. The former[185] exhibits some walls faced with dark yellow triangles (3.5–4.2 cm. thick) and others slightly later with reticulate, having bands of yellow brick made from tiles, which terminated in a row of limestone blocks; the latter[186] displays a facing of yellow brick made from *bipedales* (3.5–4 cm. thick) with bonding courses for a rectangular room with an oval interior.

Ancona

The inscription[187] on the commemorative arch at Ancona leaves no doubt that Trajan rebuilt the port.[188] Traces of Trajanic fortifications have come to light on the northern slope of Monte Guasco at two different levels.[189] In each case only a single room remains, having walls and barrel vault of concrete. It is probable that a natural mole, extending out from the mountain at the extreme east, which had been sufficient protection in the time of Augustus, had become so eroded as to endanger the safety of the ships at anchorage. At any rate, Trajan's engineers took advantage of another projection farther to the northwest to build another mole. Scholars have not yet come to an agreement as to its length. No one doubts that an inclined passage on top of it led from the shore to the Arch of Trajan, but whether it terminated in steps to the sea on the other side of the arch or continued for another hundred meters or so is not clear. It was eleven meters wide; and there is some indication that the mole was supported partially at least by arches.[190] In years past a wall of squared blocks was discovered in a part of its course, and many squared blocks were found in the vicinity. In fact, travertine blocks evidently from the Trajanic construction were employed in the fifteenth century for facing the pedestal of the arch. Although little remains of the mole as a whole something of its construction can be learned from a study of the foundations prepared for the arch.[191] The promontory consisted of a rocky core which protruded from the water in places.

[183] See below, p. 296.

[184] E. Ghislanzoni, *Not. sc.*, 1911, pp. 95–104; Lugli, *op. cit.*, cols. 113–114, no. 69.

[185] Lugli, *op. cit.*, cols. 107–112, no. 66. See below, pp. 294–295, and above, p. 267.

[186] *Ibid.*, cols. 135–139, no. 82. See below, pp. 294–295, and above, p. 267.

[187] *CIL*, vol. 9, no. 5894.

[188] K. Lehmann-Hartleben, *Klio, Beiheft*, no. 14, 1923, pp. 198–199; Paribeni, *Optimus Princeps* II, pp. 118–119; E. Galli, *Boll. d'arte*, vol. 30, 1937, pp. 321–336; N. Alfieri, *Riv. fil. cl.*, vol. 66, 1938, pp. 371–375; M. Moretti, *Ancona*, Rome 1945, pp. 44–50; P. Giangiacomi, *Traiano e Ancona*, Ancona 1936.

[189] Alfieri, *op. cit.*, p. 375; Moretti, *op. cit.*, pp. 50–51.

[190] Alfieri, *op. cit.*, p. 372.

[191] Galli, *op. cit.*

At the site of the arch this was leveled off with a bed of concrete, on which was built an elongated octagonal foundation faced with limestone blocks from Monte Conero, arranged in pseudo-isodomous rows. The blocks on the exposed sides are somewhat larger than those on the other. Pozzolana was used to even the beds between the courses. Even so, there was some slight interlocking. Four rows are preserved under the left pylon. They reveal an inclined batter which could, I think, reach the actual podium of the arch. The proportions of the arch were sadly thrown out of kilter by the fifteenth-century pedestal. The break between the octagonal foundation and the rectangular pylons was brought into sharp relief by the contrast between the soft yellow limestone and the bluish white Hymettian marble of the arch itself.[192] Attempts have been made to restore the port on paper from other types of evidence,[193] none of which is entirely satisfactory. Many have tried to fit the scene of departure for Dacia on the Column of Trajan in Rome to the ancient topography of this port, but recently Degrassi[194] has identified it with the harbor at Brindisi with more plausibility.

Ariminum (Rimini)

The ancient port of Ariminum was a veritable quarry for ancient marble up to its destruction in 1807. That it should be added to the ports reorganized by Trajan seems likely,[195] but nothing remains for study except possibly some foundations covered by the sea.

HADRIAN

The main engineering work had all been completed before the time of Hadrian, and so his contributions were to be the amenities of the life in the port. A pile of bricks, some of which have stamps, is all that remains of the Porticus of Claudius at Porto.[196] There are slight indications of Hadrianic work in some of the warehouses.[197] Barely enough is left of a complex known as "Palazzo Imperiale"[198] to show that the original building period was probably Hadrianic. The walls were faced with reticulate reinforced by brick bands or reticulate insets in brick frames. The estimate of the date comes from the late Trajanic and early Hadrianic brick stamps. Hadrian's contribution to Ostia was such as to require a separate section.[199] At Terracina, he seems to have been most concerned with increasing the available water supply for the Baths. To the "Terme Neptuniane"[200] he apparently added a barrel-vaulted cistern at the east with a porticus along its west side. The rear wall of the porticus exhibits a facing of reticulate and brick (1.2 m. of the former to 30 to 45 cm. of the latter). The bricks are a dark yellow. The wall terminates in a row of limestone blocks; and the same type of blocks was used for piers to support a sloping roof. The porticus ended in a room at the north. A castello d'acque[201] with two external niches was added to the Grande Terme alla Marina probably at about the same time. The facing was of limestone reticulate with quoins of brick and tufa blocks in alternation. To a long narrow cistern near the railroad, a shorter, wider reservoir (22.8 m. $\times$ 4.6 m.)[202] was added in the time of Hadrian or his immediate successor. The walls were faced with reticulate and brick. Heavy

[192] For the arch, see above, p. 265.

[193] Several were based on a coin (BMC, Emp., vol. 3, pl. 32, 1; 35, 2), now universally considered to represent the bridge over the Danube.

[194] A. Degrassi, Acc. P. Rend., ser. 3, vol. 22, 1946–1947, pp. 167–183, where the whole problem is discussed at length.

[195] Paribeni, Optimus Princeps II, pp. 119–120.

[196] Bloch, Bolli, pp. 99–100.

[197] Lugli-Filibeck, pp. 112, 119.

[198] Ibid., pp. 97–100; Bloch, op. cit., pp. 100–102; G. Calza, Not. sc., 1925, pp. 66–67.

[199] See above, pp. 158ff.

[200] Lugli, Forma It., vol. 1 (1), cols. 109–110.

[201] Ibid., cols. 136, 138.

[202] Ibid., col. 42.

buttresses appear on the side opposite the earlier cistern. He also no doubt started work on the Acquedotto di San Lorenzo dell'Amaseno.[203] He did not, to the best of my knowledge, leave his mark on the other important harbors.

THE ANTONINES

Portus (Porto)

It was essential that harbors should be kept in good condition to protect Roman shipping. A restoration of a *pharos*, presumably the lighthouse at Portus, is attributed to Antoninus Pius by Julius Capitolinus.[204] Antonine masonry has been found in the preparation of the site for the new international airport at Fiumicino[205] in such a position that it could be part of a harbor light, though I am inclined to doubt whether it is the site of the great lighthouse described by Pliny.[206] The masonry is block-and-brick work similar to that used in the "Palazzo Imperiale" at Ostia.[207] Porto itself has one important monument to add to the rather meagre list of those that can be ascribed to the time of Marcus Aurelius: a large and important granary (no. 10).[208] Brick stamps confirm the date suggested by the type of brickwork.[209] The facing of the walls was fine red brick broken roughly to trapezoidal shape from any kind of tile available: *besales, sesquipedales*, and *bipedales*. The concrete showed fragments of brick, selce, and marble in the midst of *caementa* of tufa. A granular brown tufa formed the aggregate of vaulting. The warehouse stood north of the entrance canal, facing it, on a tongue of land at the west side of the basin (plan XV, above p. 287). It was restricted in shape to a row of rooms (108 m.) on the east, another (185 m.) on the north, and the third (65 m.) on the west, thus defining three sides of a court open to the south. There was a quay on the east and south which facilitated loading and unloading whatever commodities were stored in the warehouses. A passageway in the center of the north side gave an exit in that direction. The rooms all opened inward onto a porticus; a few had a secondary opening on to the quay. The rooms were three deep on the side toward the basin, but two deep on the other two sides. Pilasters on the outside not only marked the position of each partition wall but also stood halfway between them. Pilasters in the partition walls carried the cross vaults with which the rooms were covered. Pilasters in the inner walls and on the piers, with the aid of brick arches corresponding to the partition walls, supported the succession of cross vaults over the porticus, which received its light from an occasional *lucernario* in the vault as well as from doors and windows on the porticus. Great arches of *bipedales* also helped distribute the weight of the vaulting so as not to press too heavily on the doorways. Two great blocks of travertine were inserted in each door jamb. Splayed windows between the pilasters gave light to the innermost rooms. Four barrel-vaulted ramps led to an upper floor which duplicated the chambers of the ground floor, except that it probably had a wooden roof instead of vaulting. Brick stamps also indicate that Antonine work in the "Palazzo Imperiale" should be ascribed to the same period.[210] Some Antonine work is reported on the mole which terminated in the Trajanic lighthouse (no. 8).[211] A few brick stamps found in a warehouse (no. 49) along the Fossa

[203] See above, pp. 275–276.

[204] Julius Capitolinus, *SHA, Antoninus Pius*, 8, 3.

[205] Personal observation.

[206] Pliny, *N.H.*, 16, 202. See also Blake, *RC II*, p. 83, and Meiggs, *Ostia*, pp. 154–158.

[207] See above, pp. 216–217.

[208] Bloch, *Bolli*, pp. 279–280. It was my privilege to visit the site briefly with Professor Bloch and to satisfy myself that the masonry was in accord with the stamps. Lugli (Lugli-Filibeck, pp. 83–86) attributed it to Septimius Severus.

[209] *CIL*, vol. 15 (1), nos. 186, 737, 758, 1145.

[210] Lugli-Filibeck, p. 98; Bloch, *op. cit.*, pp. 275 and 280. For the "Palazzo" see above, p. 289.

[211] Lugli-Filibeck, pp. 81–82.

[212] *Ibid.*, pp. 111–112.

[213] Lugli-Filibeck (p. 133), lists nos. 15, 27, 51 and (p. 101) mentions no. 29.

[214] *Ibid.*, p. 104.

[215] M. de la Blanchère, *Mél.*, vol. 1, 1881, pp. 322–348; Lugli, *Forma It.*, vol. 1 (1), cols. 126–132.

[216] See above, pp. 292–293.

[217] *CIL*, vol. 10 (1), nos. 1640 and 1641. Beloch, *Campanien*, pp. 132–133.

[1] See above, pp. 104, 107, 109, 111, 112, 113–115.

[2] D. Levi, *Not. sc.*, 1935, pp. 221–228. I regret that I had not discovered this article when I published this Bath in summary fashion (*RC* II, pp. 148–149). I was apparently deceived in thinking that *opus mixtum* in earlier reports meant reticulate and brick. There is no reticulate work. I have not visited the site.

Traiana give evidence of further building activity by either Antoninus Pius or Marcus Aurelius.[212] A few other warehouses show traces of Antonine restorations,[213] and a small isolated edifice (no. 39) of which little remains has also been ascribed to the second half of the second century.[214] Such is the evidence of Antonine masonry at Porto.

Gaeta and Terracina

The restoration of the harbors of Gaeta and Terracina is also accredited to him in the same source. To the best of my knowledge, no harbor work of his has been reported from Gaeta, but there is abundant evidence of a restoration at Terracina.[215] Trajan's work consisted of two embankment walls meeting in an obtuse angle.[216] Two rather similar methods of construction can be differentiated in the one stretching from the northeast to the south-west. Presumably, the upper part, which is faced with a less regular reticulate broken by bands of six rows of thinner and redder bricks all made from tiles, should be ascribed to the Antonine reconstruction. More masonry of the same kind is visible behind the junction of the two embankments. From the end of the Trajanic construction at the left of the new harbor, the engineers of the Antonine period built a curved mole probably with a lighthouse at its end. It apparently consisted of a series of vaulted chambers supporting a platform covered with *opus signinum*. Unfortunately, the cores of the walls, consisting of concrete made with a tufa aggregate, could not withstand weathering after the facing had been washed away. The vaults, on the other hand, had a limestone aggregate and survived. When the mole left the shore, its outer face was inclined at the top and, though the lower vertical part was faced with reticulate, showed a facing of large limestone blocks to repel the force of the waves; the inner face was provided with a platform to facilitate unloading, complete with mooring rings and in part at least with mooring posts of marble, which de la Blanchère took to be the columns for a porticus. An inscription[217] indicates that Antoninus Pius restored six piers of the mole of the harbor at Puteoli, which had collapsed in a storm toward the end of the reign of Hadrian.

PRIVATE EDIFICES (OF MORE THAN ORDINARY INTEREST)

Baths connected with villas in the vicinity of Rome have been presented in their proper environment.[1] The description of a few outstanding ones in the rest of Italy follows:

Excavations at Massaciuccoli in 1932[2] served to clarify somewhat the picture of the great country estate in which a luxurious Bath was combined with a large addition given over to agricultural pursuits. The excavation did not uncover the living quarters or give the entire plan of the more humble part, but it is the Bath that concerns us here. The arrangement of rooms was a little unusual in that the furnace with its *praefurnium* was at a lower level between heated rooms on the west side. The northernmost of these had a heated alcove with a suspended floor, which Levi considers a heated *cubiculum*. It would seem more natural to me to consider it a heated pool especially as there are traces of *opus signinum*. Levi mentions rectangular tiles (30 cm. × 14 cm.) laid upright against the brick facing for protection against dampness. This sounds to me like a method of procuring the draft necessary for the circulation of the hot air in the hypocaust. Farther north a large hall extending across the whole width of the edifice was also heated, but mere traces of it remain. On the west side, a square pool lined with marble opened off from a fairly large hall with a suspended pool, a black-and-white mosaic depicting sea monsters, and traces of a marble wall revetment. A corridor at the east of the pool led to a large hall. A vertical terra-cotta conduit in the corridor may have been connected with the heating arrangements. A square of marble paving in the northwest corner may indicate that the hall was subdivided in some way. An earlier wall was utilized for the northern part of the eastern perimetric wall. Bricks faced the greater part of the rooms devoted to the Bath. Only in the southern part was the masonry the same as that used in the rest of the villa, namely, roughly shaped blocks with pieces of bricks in the interstices. Judging largely from the style of the statues found in the course of the excavation, Levi ascribed the Bath to the time of Trajan. The fact that there is not a single curved wall in the entire plan supports his dating.[3]

The plan of the "Bagno d'Agrippa" on the Island of Pianosa[4] with its elaborate arrangement of rooms, including perhaps a special pool of sea water, appears too complicated for the time of Agrippa Postumus, to whom the villa may have belonged originally. It looks Hadrianic to me, but I have no more information with regard to it. I mention it here merely to draw attention to it for anyone who would make a special study of ancient Baths.

Suspended floors, double walls, and black-and-white mosaics of imaginary sea creatures identify a few rooms as part of the Bath of a villa in a rather remote spot in Umbria, known as Guardea today.[5] The walls were faced with irregular pieces of limestone combined with irregular courses of tile. These rooms have been ascribed to the second century.

That part of a suburban villa of the second century at Bologna[6] which it was possible to excavate yielded three suspended floors. The piers supporting the floor of the most important of these were round to allow a freer circulation of air.

There are doubtless many more Baths of the period than have come to my attention. They, and the project, are commended to whoever would undertake the special study of ancient *thermae*.

[3] Toscanelli (*Pisa nell'antichità dalle età preistoriche alla caduta dell'Impero Romano*, Pisa 1933–1934, vol. 2, pp. 649–650) connects the Baths with terraces on one of which rooms reminded him of Hadrian's villa, though on a smaller scale.

[4] N. Toscanelli, *op. cit.*, p. 678, fig. 80.

[5] P. Romanelli, *Not. sc.*, 1926, pp. 275–276. For the mosaic, see M. E. Blake, *MAAR*, vol. 13, 1936, p. 152.

[6] A. Negrioli, *Not. sc.*, 1932, pp. 51–88.

V. SUMMARY

[1] RC II, pp. 158–165.

The second century of the Roman empire saw for its first half the continuation of the intensive building activity of the first century. The stability created by the Augustan empire fostered an economic and social growth even though the Julio-Claudian dynasty ended in a catastrophe which could have opened up an era of revolution and destruction again. But the swift accession of Vespasian preserved the empire's stability; nor was it hindered by the reaction against Domitian. The growth therefore of Rome and its supporting areas continued. Hence building kept pace until in the middle of the century supply and demand for structures approached an equilibrium, as the empire entered its middle years and began to show signs of its decay. It seems not inappropriate to close Miss Blake's work with a few general statements on construction. One might like to see as thorough a summary as she provided for her previous volume.[1] But, first, it would be rash of me to attempt a synthesis merely from the text and without the expertise gained from on-site study which Miss Blake and Mrs. Bishop had; and, second, Mrs. Bishop often remarked that Miss Blake's running summaries in the text were so good that she felt no pressing need for a detailed synthesis; nevertheless Mrs. Bishop did leave an outline, although this actually amounts to little more than a list of the headings treated by Miss Blake in her second volume.

The development by the beginning of the first century of a nearly perfect concrete and the consequent recognition of the freedom to experiment is probably the principal contribution of the first century to construction. But many problems, especially doming and complex vaulting, were not solved until the second century. For example, in the Domus Flavia Rabirius's brilliant attempt to barrel-vault the basilica soon needed reinforcement; and so Hadrianic spur walls were added to bolster its stability. Contrast, on the other hand, the vaulting in Trajan's Market, the Pantheon dome, and the highly complex vaulting and doming in the Villa Adriana. The use of bricks for facing in the first century led to the use of bonding courses of *bipedales* as a means of protecting the triangular bricks of the facing. Bonding courses are a regular feature of second-century brickwork.

Squared-Stone Masonry

So useful and inexpensive, so strong, so easily handled, and so open to creative designing was concrete that squared-stone masonry was reserved for special effects in special buildings. As examples in Rome one might quote the so-called Arch of Drusus over the Via Appia, the bases for Trajan's Column and the Column of Marcus Aurelius where massive solidity was needed; also the base of the temple of Venus and Rome, the temple of Antoninus and Faustina, the Hadrianeum, the Commodan temple of Jupiter Heliopolitanus, the *ustrina* of Antoninus Pius and of Marcus Aurelius, and various specific parts of Hadrian's Tomb, all being places where religious feelings and a certain idealism and tradition would be controlling factors. Nero's attempt to promote Gabine stone and peperino as fire breaks seems to have borne fruit in the second century only for the fire walls of peperino on a travertine base which Apollodorus provided for the Forum of Trajan and the Basilica Ulpia. Peperino was used extensively in the Basilica Argentaria, partly on a travertine base. The use of cut stone for corbels, springers, and voussoirs continued, but regularly of travertine; yet even here concrete and brick or tile could become adequate substitutes. The relative strength and ease of working travertine made its use preferred where stress and wear were important factors. For example, in the Hadrianeum the masonry under the columns was travertine; elsewhere peperino. The podium of the temple of Antoninus and Faustina was peperino on a travertine foundation; but the few mason's marks on the peperino long after such marks were discontinued seem to show re-use of convenient blocks. In both this temple and the Hadrianeum the peperino had been covered by a marble revetment. Utilitarian uses of cut stone might be the proper title for Trajan's re-use of stone from Domitian's naumachia to repair the Circus Maximus and the use of Gabine stone and travertine to face the Pons Aelius. One should probably also note here as stone masonry the actual columns of Trajan and Marcus Aurelius.

Outside of Rome, the squared-stone masonry in the Villa dei Quintili along the Via Appia may well be the remains of an earlier structure. Elsewhere, so thoroughly did the Trajanic, Hadrianic, and Antonine builders trust their concrete that at Ostia and the Villa Adriana one finds no squared-stone masonry. No doubt for Ostia, economic factors and the lack of old traditions, such as at Rome, controlled the building there. But at the Villa it was imperial preference for the versatility of concrete and brick. Public works outside Rome still used stone, such as the amphitheaters at Santa Maria Capua Vetere (Hadrianic) and Tusculum (Antoninus Pius). But by the beginning of the second century concrete was the normal material for the construction of theaters.

Utilitarian uses of squared-stone masonry outside Rome seemed mandatory for the piers of aqueducts and bridges, for embankments to protect bridges from floodwater erosion of the banks, and for harbor moles as being the best protection against the pounding of the waves.

Marble of course was the decorative stone of choice, particularly in the imperial city, where, for example, Trajan's Forum was faced and paved with marbles and the Basilica Ulpia made extensive use of marbles. Elsewhere, since marble was expensive, it could be used only when wealth or civic pride or imperial power dictated it.

Concrete

The mastery of the manufacture of concrete by the Romans was extraordinary. Pozzolana was the normal admixture to make mortar. By the second century the builders had learned to choose and wash the pozzolana and mix the lime more carefully, apparently, than at times in the first century, unless repairs undertaken by the later emperors of earlier buildings and the re-use of earlier materials (e.g. early Hadrianic bricks) in later buildings (e.g. Antonine) indicate cut-rate building methods and consequent collapse rather than deliberate wrecking of a structure. Both the pozzolana for the mortar and its condition and the *caementa* for the concrete have been noted by Miss Blake at the appropriate times when it seemed important to do so.

One would think that only in a protected archaeological setting would poor mortar survive to our time. Such a thing occurred in the mithraeum under Santa Prisca on the Aventine. In wall K3 of Room Y, the excavator reports that the mortar was so poor that the facing came away from the core.[2] This wall is an original wall in House II of the Domus (Privata) Traiani and is therefore Trajanic in date. That apparently it was only one batch of mortar is proved by the fact that the rest of that construction does not show this failure. It may test Miss Blake's conclusion that facing and core must have risen together;[3] for if the mortar for the core and the facing was the same—i.e., the same batch—the core should also have disintegrated. But the report is not clear on this point; further, a glance at any photograph of brick arches is convincing; see for example pl. 20 fig. 1, pl. 28 fig. 4, both showing the broad arch of the Piccolo Mercato in Ostia. Miss Blake is surely right.

Trajan's Market yields a fine example of Trajanic brick-faced concrete.[4] For foundations one finds aggregate of selce with some travertine; for walls, broken bricks in close irregular rows; for vaults, yellowish gray tufa. Hadrianic practice in the city is summarized in connection with the Horti Sallustiani.[5] For foundations, the aggregate is selce, except for much travertine and marble on the Palatine. In the temple of Venus and Rome tufa replaces selce. For walls, generally bricks of various kinds in closely packed rows; but there is much marble and travertine in the walls of the porticus of the Domus August(i)ana. For vaults, tufa. Antonine concrete is briefly described in the repairs to the Colosseum.[6] The number of monuments of the period of Antoninus Pius to Commodus wholly or in part of concrete is very small. The type of construction in these is in general identical with that of Hadrian. But it is true that practice varied with the builder, the availability of materials, and the locale; compare the concrete used in Trajan's Market with that used for the quay lining Porto.[7]

Facings for Concrete

The first century saw the transition from reticulate to brick facing. Hence Trajan's Market used brick facing with bonding courses and relieving arches of various types; likewise Trajan's Baths. But the Trajanic embankment of the Tiber was faced with reticulate broken by a band of five rows of brick.

[2] Vermaseren and van Essen, fig. 5 (opposite p. 24), p. 40, fig. 23 on p. 81, pl. 27, 1 and 2.

[3] *RC II*, pp. 160–161.

[4] See above, pp. 19–28.

[5] See above, pp. 61–64; compare the base ring for the Pantheon, p. 42 above.

[6] See above, p. 70.

[7] See above, p. 288.

Farther downstream, Hadrianic facing is found: brick or a combination of reticulate and tufa blocks; yet the embankment built for the Pons Aelius was faced with a tufa reticulate; but that was much closer to the center of the city and may have been influenced by factors other than mere economics. The Pantheon and associated structures show Hadrianic work at its best.

Private construction in the city regularly was faced with brick. La Casa di Via Giulio Romano, at the foot of Ara Coeli, however, was faced with reticulate until it was free-standing; then brick. Isola Grande shows a little reticulate, but mainly brick. The construction under Santa Pudenziana shows one strange wall: herringbone panels between brick bands, the pattern being composed of alternate rows of bricks and small tufa blocks. In Ostia of course one can find the full range of facings for the period.

In general Trajanic facing for concrete consisted of broken roof tiles, often approaching triangular form; sometimes it was mixed with reticulate. Hadrianic facings were more generally brickwork, except at Villa Adriana where lack of local brick made reticulate imperative. The Hadrianic facings in the city were also of broken roof tiles, and not infrequently triangular bricks made from *besales*, as in the Domus August(i)ana, and also reticulate. Antoninus Pius continued Hadrianic practices so that at Ostia at times it is difficult to tell whether the work is late Hadrianic or early Antonine.

The use of blocks varies. In Le Vignacce the angles are formed of block and brick. In the Villa dei Quintili when the "hippodrome" was widened into a garden, the boundary wall and the adjacent nymphaeum were faced with block and brick. The north façade of Sette Bassi consisted of multiple rows of block and brick. In isolated villas along the Via Praenestina one finds tufa blocks used in various ways, even as if the blocks were substitutes for bricks.[8] In the imperial estates the usage varies a bit. Whereas at Arcinazzo the reticulate is rough because of the intractable limestone, there are bands of brick, and block-and-brick quoins. In the Villa Adriana, since the bricks had to be imported from Rome, the normal facing was tufa reticulate quarried locally: bricks were used for reinforcing bands and coupled with tufa blocks for quoins: thus the Biblioteca Greca and the Small Baths, for example. The Roccabruna is interesting because rows of block and brick alternate.

Vaulting

As one studies Trajan's Market, it soon becomes apparent that Trajan's builders felt completely at ease with the barrel vault. The impression of *besales* at regular intervals in the concrete of the vaults added at the Capitoline because of the *forica* marks a new development in vault construction. Further reinforcement came from frequent arches of *bipedales*. While the nature of the site of the Market doubtless helped Apollodorus solve the problem of stress in a way that Rabirius had not been helped, still the later generation had learned well from the earlier.

Vaulting depends on the imagination for its use. The usual type of vaulting is the barrel, laid horizontally. Raking barrel vaults are found, for example, under stairways; examples are best seen in Ostia. Cross vaulting is in effect two barrel vaults over the same space but laid at right angles to each

[8] For a summary of techniques in the villas, see above, pp. 116–117.

[9] See above, p. 247.

other and without intrusion into the other's vaulted space at the point of intersection. In Trajan's Market there is a good example of cross vaulting with its six bays supported by huge travertine corbels resting on stout brick-faced piers. In Trajan's Baths we have the first instance of cross vaulting on columns. In Ostia in the Terme dei Sei Colonne there is a cross vault; if it belongs to the original construction, then it is an early example of what became later a common technique. From then on, variety in vaulting; for example in the Terme di Severo e Commodo: cross vaults, barrel vaults strengthened by brick arches projecting from the soffit, ribbed barrel vaults, the dating being probably late Antonine. Hadrianic builders were ready to attempt any vault for which they could build the centering; indeed Hadrian and his builders expended much ingenuity on experiments in vaulting. Rivoira's summary of the construction of the Small Baths in the Villa, already quoted by Miss Blake,[9] remains the best concise tabulation of the kind of construction problems Hadrian posed for his builders. Several special vaulting problems created by Hadrian can be seen in the vestibule of the Piazza d'Oro, said to be the first example of blind arcading, in the great hall at the south of the Piazza with its sinuous curves, and in the Accademia. The sinuous octagon in the Piazza shows that in the long run at least here was one problem they did not solve, for the vaulting has disappeared, endangered perhaps by the great light wells which are a basic part of the design.

At Sette Bassi in the substructure of the main block the balancing of cross and barrel vaults reminds one of the Villa Adriana. A further interesting feature of this block is that it exhibits one of the first uses of laddered ribbing in cross vaulting. In general, Miss Blake's discussions of the vaulting of the various monuments is illuminating; so likewise of niches, cupolas, and domes; one is referred back to them through the Index.

One of the most elusive features of Miss Blake's book has been her tantalizing references to the rare *volta a vela*. An example occurs in the Sedia del Diavolo; another in the tomb in the ex-villa-Patrizi at the site of the Palazzo della Direzione Generale delle Ferrovie dello Stato. From the treatment in the text and the small handful of note cards, it is obvious that she intended to write a special discussion of the *volta a vela*. But the note cards are enigmatic reminders such as "volta a vela? Theater at Ferentino T? (sc. Trajanic)" or "volta a vela Capella Greca in catacombs of Santa Priscilla A.P. (sc. Antoninus Pius)." Nor did Mrs. Bishop leave any notes at all. At present there the matter must rest.

Bricks and Brickwork

Trajanic brickwork is of broken roof tiles. The tiles range 3.3–4.3 cm. in thickness, 20–33 cm. in length, and, when broken, tended to triangular form. In quality, they exhibit a fine texture, are well fired, and when struck have a metallic ring. In color they are generally ocher red to dragon's blood red, at times yellowish red or clear yellow. When laid up, the bricks were bedded in a clean, white and red mortar, which was very compact, hard as flint. The pozzolana was clean, red, sharp, finely sifted, free from earthy admixtures, but with a mixture of reddish brown and gray particles; the lime was abundant, clean, and excelled in whiteness only by that of Hadrian.

The horizontal joints were 0.7–1.75 cm., carefully raked; the vertical, 0.5–0.8 cm. Bonding courses of thick, light-colored *bipedales* occur in the Forum of Trajan, less often elsewhere. The period is marked by the abandonment of cut stone for points of pressure and external walls, by the finished technique in quality of mortar and beauty of facing, by the use of sawed tiles in facing and decorative parts. Trajanic concrete can be distinguished from its predecessors by the clean white and red color of the mortar, its fine composition and hardness, and the use of roof tile for bricks in the facing.

Hadrianic brick work is likewise of broken roof tiles, not infrequently of triangular bricks made from *besales*. The thickness of tile used for bricks is 3.3–4 cm.; of triangular bricks, 3.4–4.3 cm., with abundant brick stamps. In length, the tile bricks were 25–35 cm.; the triangular bricks, 20–30 cm. In shape the tile bricks tended to triangular form; the triangular bricks were, of course, triangular. In quality, the tile bricks retained the Trajanic fine texture but were much less carefully fired. The triangular bricks were more homogeneous than the later Julio-Claudian bricks, etc., and were well fired. The color of the tile bricks was the same as the Trajanic; of the triangular bricks, yellowish red to reddish yellow but without the Neronian mottling and streaking. The mortar was the same for the facing of tile and triangular bricks; it was clean, white and red, of fine composition, notable for its cohesiveness and hardness. The pozzolana was sharp-angled, fine, clean, carefully sifted and probably washed, red in color, at times reddish brown and gray. The lime was exceptionally fine and clear white. The horizontal joints were 1–1.6 cm., carefully raked; the vertical, 0.5–1.7 cm. Bonding courses were used more regularly in this period than before or after. Later Hadrianic monuments show some loss in perfection of form and technique, the resemblance to Trajanic work being greater in the earlier Hadrianic monuments. Triangular bricks appear in Hadrian's later monuments, for example the aqueducts.

The Antonine period followed Hadrianic practice; but the number of monuments is small. Private construction of all periods, however, could vary greatly from the imperial norm, whether in Rome or in the country or in Ostia.

Tiles

In general, tiles were used in the second century as in the first.[10] In addition they were used as imposts, for entablatures, capping cornices, stringcourses which were at times chipped to form molding. The cornices could be ornately molded; see for example the cornices in the temple of Faustina-Ceres in the Villa of Annia Regilla, the tomb of Annia Regilla, the Barberini tomb, the entablature of the Commodan theater at Ostia. And no doubt one should include here the ornamental plaques to be seen on some of the Isola Sacra tombs and elsewhere.

General Contributions to Architecture

Since by the time of Trajan the Roman mastery of concrete was complete, there remained only a few structural problems to solve, principally vaulting. This was done very quickly; for while Rabirius struggled with vaulting, Trajan

[10] RC II, p. 164.

[11] *RC* II, p. 164.

[12] See above, p. 29.

did not; and Hadrian seems to have set himself the intellectual problem of finding out just what vaulting could be done. While the Flavian age may have been responsible for the fundamental plan of all the great Baths,[11] certainly if not Rabirius, then it was the architect of Trajan's Baths.[12] While *horrea* had always been a necessity for urban Rome, the great need for more and better warehousing at Rome and Ostia produced not only newer structures but also forced remodeling of the old. The apartment house became such an extensive pile that it was necessary to regulate its height. Though the first century saw the colossal statue of Nero, it was the second which produced the columns of Trajan and Marcus Aurelius; for these there were perhaps precedents but not in size or style or decoration.

Closely allied to architecture is city planning. While Trajan planned brilliantly for his Forum and the Market, much planning is also shown in the Trajanic parts of Ostia. Here one might mention the nymphaeum (IV, 4, 5) which masked the awkward orientation caused by the acute angle between the Cardo Maximus and Via del Tempio Rotondo. The Pantheon area illustrates city planning as Hadrian liked to do it. No explicit comparison between Hadrianic Rome, the Villa Adriana, and Hadrianic Ostia has been drawn, particularly because the history, uses, and requirements differed so much; but it takes not much thought to see how Hadrianic methods and ideas combined to satisfy the requirements of use and need. One should add here also the evidences of more luxurious living in Ostia as shown by the porticoes and baths.

To parallel Miss Blake's tantalizing references to the *volta a vela*, I find Mrs. Bishop's frequent mention in conversation of the importance of relating construction to architecture and to the city area and its uses an equally tantalizing memory. Again no notes; but I am certain that specific ideas were in her mind, had she been the one to write this chapter.

Of architectural decoration little need be said, for in general it is of secondary importance. But one must admit that this causes some unfairness, particularly with respect to the Villa Adriana; yet Miss Blake did generally exclude it from her text.

—J.D.B.

INDEX

INDEX

Functional construction and structural history are so closely related that *RC III* frequently interweaves them. Yet Miss Blake generally viewed construction as a technique to be studied for itself. But often there have been good studies of the interrelation of use and construction, for a structure must conform to the use expected of it; for example, I cite the work of James E. Packer, *The Insulae of Imperial Ostia, MAAR* vol. 31, 1971, which should be read along with the chapter here on Ostia. This Index is constructed, I hope, for both the excavator and the student of function. In accordance with Mrs. Bishop's intentions and my own experience with the multiple indices of *RC* I and II, *RC* III has only one alphabet. Inevitably this simplification affects clarity here and there. But the text itself shows some lack of uniformity, e.g., the use of cupola and dome interchangeably. Some entries might be profitably subdivided, e.g., walls into front, side, back, shared, exterior, interior, supporting upper floors, bearing, and non-bearing But such lacks, I think, are balanced by ease of entry into the text itself. *Quod erat faciendum.*—J.D.B.

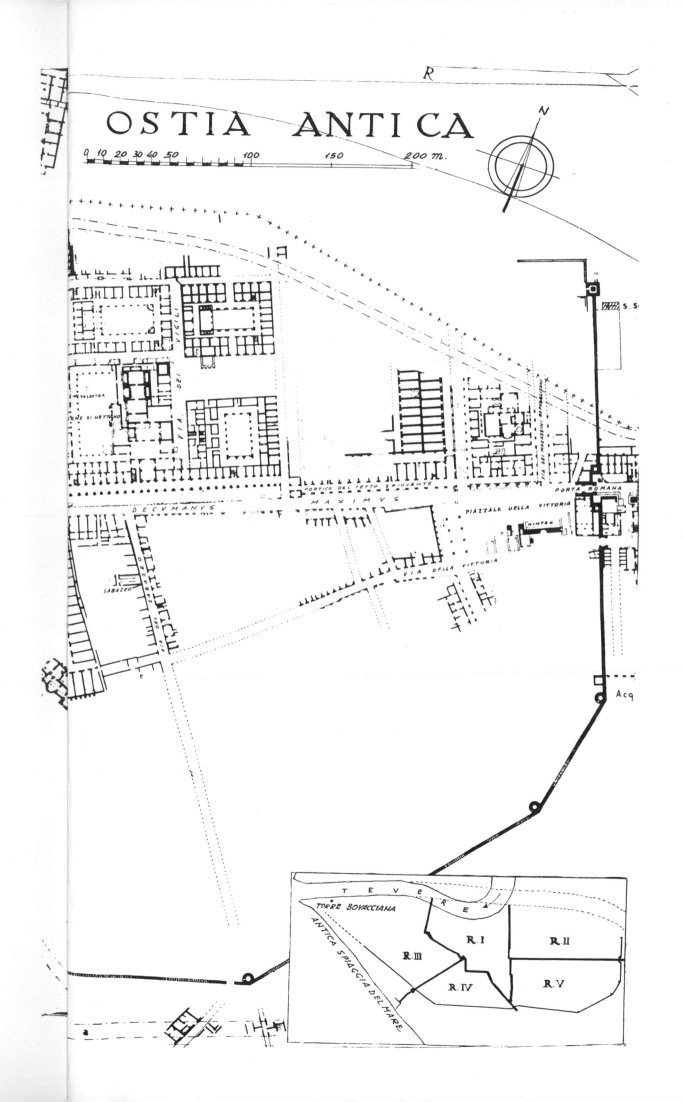

OSTIA ANTICA

0 10 20 30 40 50   100   150   200 m.

PLATE 1

Fototeca Unione

Fig. 1. Basilica Argentaria (see page 18)

Fototeca Unione

Fig. 2. Latrine above steps of Forum Iulium (see page 18)

Fototeca Unione

Fig. 3. Hemicycle of Trajan's Market (see page 21)

PLATE 2

Fototeca Unione

FIG. 1. Trajan's Markets: extrados of smaller hemicycle north of grand hemicycle (see page 22)

Fototeca Unione

FIG. 2. Trajan's Markets: double relieving arch in façade southeast of grand hemicycle (see page 22)

Fototeca Unione

FIG. 3. Trajan's Markets: northern branch of the Via Biberatica from the north (see page 23)

Fototeca Unione

FIG. 4. Trajan's Markets: southern branch of the Via Biberatica (see page 25)

PLATE 3

Fototeca Unione

FIG. 1. Trajan's Markets: doorway on east side of the "basilica" (see page 27)

Fototeca Unione

FIG. 2. Trajan's Markets: windows of small apse north of grand hemicycle (see pages 23, 28)

Fototeca Unione

FIG. 3. Trajan's Markets: Basilica Traiana (see page 26)

Fototeca Unione

FIG. 4. Trajan's Markets: rooms above the "basilica" (see page 27)

PLATE 4

Fototeca Unione

Fɪɢ. 1. Trajan's Baths: library (see page 31)

Fototeca Unione

Fɪɢ. 2. Trajan's Baths: northeast side (see page 31)

PLATE 5

FIG. 1. Ludus Magnus, below (see page 34)

FIG. 2. Ludus Magnus (see page 34)

FIG. 3. Trajan's Emporium: Tiber embankment (see page 38)

PLATE 6

Fototeca Unione

FIG. 1. Pantheon: interior, detail of soffit (see page 46)

Fototeca Unione

FIG. 2. Pantheon: exterior detail (see page 44)

Fototeca Unione

FIG. 3. Horti Sallustiani: south wing (see page 63)

Fototeca Unione

FIG. 4. Basilica Neptuni (see page 48)

PLATE 7

Fototeca Unione

Fɪɢ. 1. Pons Aelius: before the embankment built in 1892 (see page 55)

Fototeca Unione

Fɪɢ. 2. Pons Aelius: ramp on the left bank of the Tiber, discovered in 1892 (see page 55)

PLATE 8

FIG. 1. Pons Aelius: ancient ramp on the left bank of the Tiber, seen from above (see page 55)

PLATE 9

Fɪɢ. 1. Mausoleum Hadriani (see pages 56, 58)

PLATE 10

Fototeca Unione

FIG. 1. Templum Matidiae on a medallion of Hadrian
(see page 51)

Fototeca Unione

FIG. 2. Sacellum Bacchi on a medallion of Antoninus Pius
(see page 69)

Fototeca Unione

FIG. 3. Horti Sallustiani: the great cupola and central hall (Piranesi) (see page 61)

PLATE 11

Fototeca Unione

Fɪɢ. 1. Temple of Antoninus and Faustina (see page 67)

Anderson

Fɪɢ. 2. Hadrianeum (see page 68)

PLATE 12

Fototeca Unione

FIG. 1. Santa Pudenziana: Thermae Novatianae (see page 96)

Foto Comune di Roma

FIG. 2. Capitolium: Isola Grande (see page 83)

Fototeca Unione

FIG. 3. Sette Bassi: great front wall before its collapse in 1952 (see page 109)

PLATE 13

Metropolitan Mus. of Art

Fig. 1. Sette Bassi (Piranesi) (see page 110)

Fototeca Unione

Fig. 2. Sette Bassi: detail of construction (see page 109)

PLATE 14

Fototeca Unione

FIG. 1. Ostia: Isola Sacra: Tomb 97 (see pages 119, 122)

Fototeca Unione

FIG. 2. Ostia: Isola Sacra: Tomb 95 (see page 120 (*bis*))

Fototeca Unione

FIG. 3. Ostia: Isola Sacra: Tombs 29, 30
(see pages 120, 121 (*ter*))

Fototeca Unione

FIG. 4. Ostia: Isola Sacra: Tomb 19 (see pages 121, 122)

PLATE 15

Fototeca Unione

Fig. 1. Ostia Isola Sacra: Tomb 15 (see page 119)

Fototeca Unione

Fig. 2. Ostia: Isola Sacra: Tombs 41, 42 (see page 119)

Fototeca Unione

Fig. 3. Ostia: Isola Sacra: Tomb 11 (see page 120

Fototeca Unione

Fig. 4. Ostia: Isola Sacra: Tomb 16 (see pages 120, 121)

PLATE 16

Alinari

Fig. 1. Via della Caffarella: Tomb of Annia Regilla
(see page 129)

Fototeca Unione

Fig. 2. Ostia: Isola Sacra: Tombs 80, 79, 78, 76
(see page 120 (*bis*))

Fototeca Unione

Fig. 3. Via Nomentana: Sedia del Diavolo (see page 135)

Fototeca Unione

Fig. 4. Via Latina: Barberini Tomb (see page 132)

PLATE 17

Fototeca Unione

FIG. 1. Via Appia: Carceri Vecchie (see page 131)

Fototeca Unione

FIG. 2. Via Appia: Tomb of Veran(n)ius (see page 129)

Fototeca Unione

FIG. 3. Via Appia: La Conocchia (see page 130)

PLATE 18

Fototeca Unione

FIG. 1. Ostia: Terme di Buticosus (see page 147)

Fototeca Unione

FIG. 2. Ostia: Horrea on the Cardo degli Aurighi
(see page 151)

Fototeca Unione

FIG. 3. Via Latina: Barberini Tomb: detail of construction
(see page 132)

Fototeca Unione

FIG. 4. Via Appia: Carceri Vecchie: detail of construction
(see page 131)

PLATE 19

Fototeca Unione

Fig. 1. Ostia: Sette Finestrate, IV, 5, 18 (see page 156)

Fototeca Unione

Fig. 2. Ostia: Via del Calcara, Caseggiato del Serapide
(see page 154)

Fototeca Unione

Fig. 3. Ostia: Casette-tipo (see page 155)

Fototeca Unione

Fig. 4. Ostia: Via del Calcara, tufa reticulate, tufa blocks,
and brick (see page 154)

PLATE 22

Fototeca Unione

FIG. 1. Ostia: Bazaar: exterior shop wall (see page 176)

Fototeca Unione

FIG. 2. Ostia: Portici di Pio IX: Back wall of a shop
(see page 160)

Fototeca Unione

FIG. 3. Ostia: Caseggiato dei Triclini: reticulate insets
(see page 175)

Fototeca Unione

FIG. 4. Ostia: Via delle Casette Repubblicane: shop with
arches in Castrum wall (see page 163)

PLATE 23

Fototeca Unione

Fototeca Unione

FIG. 1. Ostia: Caseggato del Larario (see page 168)

FIG. 2. Ostia: Via di Diana: balconies (see pages 169, 170)

Fototeca Unione

FIG. 3. Ostia: Insula delle Volte Dipinte: façade on Via delle Volte Dipinti (see page 183)

PLATE 24

Fototeca Unione

FIG. 1. Ostia: Caseggiato degli Aurighi: court (see page 181)

Fototeca Unione

FIG. 2. Ostia: Caseggiato di Annio (see page 184)

Fototeca Unione

FIG. 3. Ostia: Terme di Mitra (see page 178 (bis))

Fototeca Unione

FIG. 4. Ostia: Via della Fortuna: Caseggiato del Balcone a Mensole (see page 164)

PLATE 25

Fototeca Unione

FIG. 1. Ostia: Caserma dei Vigili: main gate (see page 195)

Fototeca Unione

FIG. 2. Ostia: Caserma dei Vigili: façade with windows, to left of main gate (see page 195)

Alinari

FIG. 3. Ostia: Caseggiato dei Misuratori di Grano (see page 164)

PLATE 26

Fototeca Unione

Fɪɢ. 1. Ostia: Insula delle Volte Dipinti (Vico del Lupanare):
arch supporting stairway (see page 184)

Fototeca Unione

Fɪɢ. 2. Ostia: Terme di Nettuno: ramp and tank
(see page 194)

Fototeca Unione

Fɪɢ. 3. Ostia: Shop along the Decumanus (see page 220)

PLATE 27

FIG. 1. Ostia: Terme del Foro: panels of tubes (see page 207)

FIG. 2. Ostia: Terme del Foro: the oval room (see pages 208, 209)

PLATE 28

Fototeca Unione

Fɪɢ. 1. Ostia: Schola del Traiano: NE corner of inner curved façade (see page 213)

Fototeca Unione

Fɪɢ. 2. Ostia: pier of Porticus of Caseggiato degli Archi Trionfali (see page 231)

Fototeca Unione

Fɪɢ. 3. Ostia: Caseggiatto di Diana: outside stairway (see page 218)

Fototeca Unione

Fɪɢ. 4. Ostia: Piccolo Mercato: detail of pier supporting broad arch (see page 162)

PLATE 29

Fototeca Unione

Fig. 1. Ostia: Terme dell'Invidioso: window and east wall from inside (see page 220)

Fototeca Unione

Fig. 2. Ostia: Horrea Epagathiana: entrance from vestibule into the court (see page 211)

Fototeca Unione

Fig. 3. Ostia: Sacello di Iside (see page 234)

Fototeca Unione

Fig. 4. Ostia: Horrea Epagathiana: entrance (see page 210 (*bis*))

PLATE 30

Fototeca Unione

FIG. 1. Ostia: Caseggiato degli Aurighi: restored balcony
(see page 182)

Fototeca Unione

FIG. 2. Ostia: Caseggiato di Diana: façade and shop interior
(see page 218 (*bis*))

Fototeca Unione

FIG. 3. Ostia: Caseggiato delle Trifore: grouping of windows and doorways (see page 216)

PLATE 31

FIG. 1. Arcinazzo: wall of the villa (see page 237)

FIG. 2. Ostia: Theater: entablature of the second order
(see page 229)

FIG. 3. Ostia: Via del Pomerio: piers (see page 233)

FIG. 4. Ostia: Theater exterior: detail of pilaster (see page 229)

PLATE 32

FIG. 1. Hadrian's Villa: Small Baths: detail of construction (see page 248)

FIG. 2. Hadrian's Villa: Basilica (see page 238)

FIG. 3. Hadrian's Villa: Heliocaminus (see page 242)

FIG. 4. Hadrian's Villa: Accademia: Temple of Apollo (see page 252)

PLATE 33

Fig. 1. Hadrian's Villa: Triclinium and nymphaeum
(see page 238)

Fig. 2. Hadrian's Villa: Piazza d'Oro: vestibule
(see page 246)

Fig. 3. Hadrian's Villa: Canopus and Serapeum (see page 250)

PLATE 34

Fototeca Unione

Fig. 1. Hadrian's Villa: Piazza d'Oro: SE corner (see page 247)

Fototeca Unione

Fig. 2. Hadrian's Villa: Sala di Pilastri Dorici (see page 239)

Fototeca Unione

Fig. 3. Hadrian's Villa: Piazza d'Oro: NW side (see page 246)

PLATE 35

Fototeca Unione

Fig. 1. Hadrian's Villa: Great Baths: apsidal hall with cross vaulting (see page 255)

Fototeca Unione

Fig. 2. Hadrian's Villa: Greek Library (Rossini) (See page 241)

PLATE 36

Fototeca Unione

Fɪɢ. 1. Hadrian's Villa: Great Baths: stucco soffit of the great hall (see page 254)

Fototeca Unione

Fɪɢ. 2. Hadrian's Villa: Small Baths: octagonal room (apodyterium) with the spring of the cupola (see page 248)

Fototeca Unione

Fɪɢ. 3. Hadrian's Villa: Tower of Roccabruna (see page 252)